Stone Soup

THE COMIC STRIP

by
Jan Eliot

The Third Collection of the Syndicated Cartoon

FOUR PANEL PRESS
Eugene, Oregon

Published by Four Panel Press, P.O. Box 50032, Eugene, OR 97405.

Stone Soup is distributed by Universal Press Syndicate.

ISBN 0-9674102-1-5

Library of Congress Control Number: 2001131457

A portion of the profits from this book will go to alleviate hunger through our local food bank, Food for Lane County.

For my Dad, the
first Wally in my life.

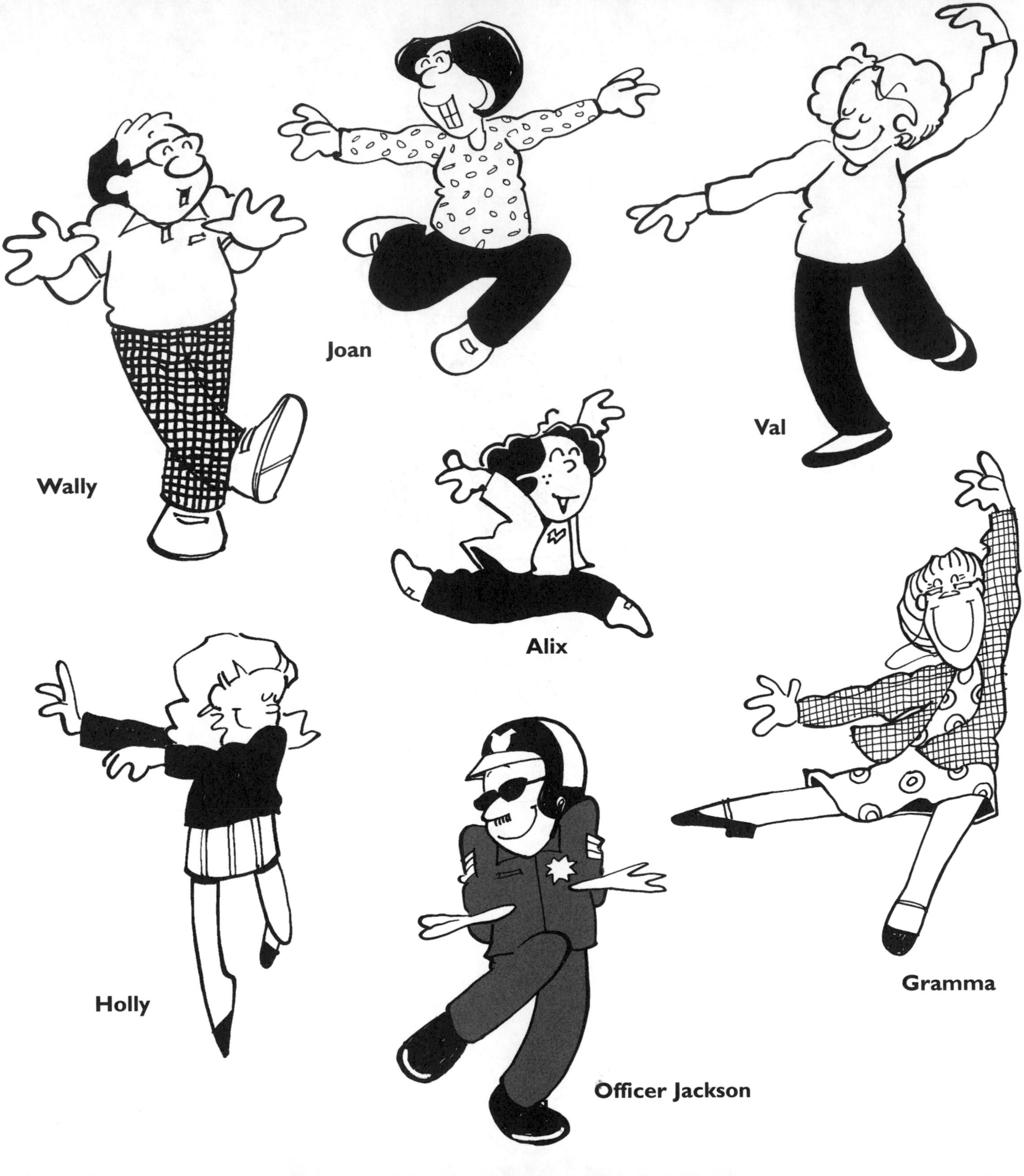
Joan
Val
Wally
Alix
Holly
Gramma
Officer Jackson

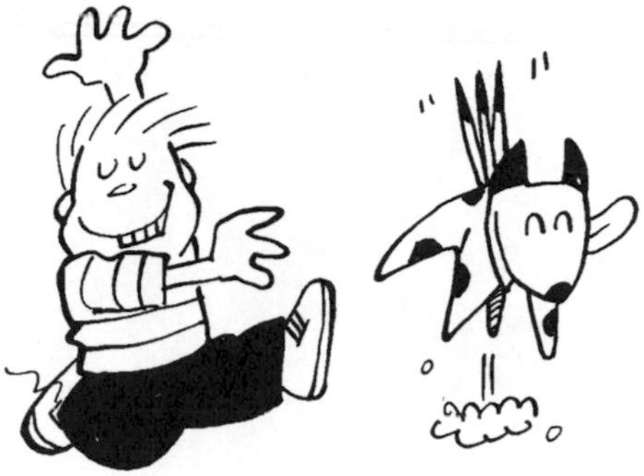

Who's Who in *Stone Soup*

Stone Soup is a comic strip based on my own experiences as a single mom. I create characters and situations out of what happens in the world around me, hoping for authenticity that will strike home with my readers.

Wally is the nice guy next door. He is in love with Joan, who has been living with her sister, Val, ever since Joan's husband went out for milk— and ended up in the Virgin Islands. Joan has an energetic 2-year-old named Max. Val is a widow who lost the love of her life and wasn't interested in a new one until a handsome motorcycle cop pulled her over for speeding. She has a happy 9-year-old named Alix and an angst-ridden middle-schooler named Holly. Gramma (with all of her opinions) lives upstairs, and Biscuit, politely referred to as an "active breed," is the family dog.

Thanks for reading *Stone Soup!*

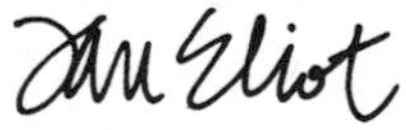

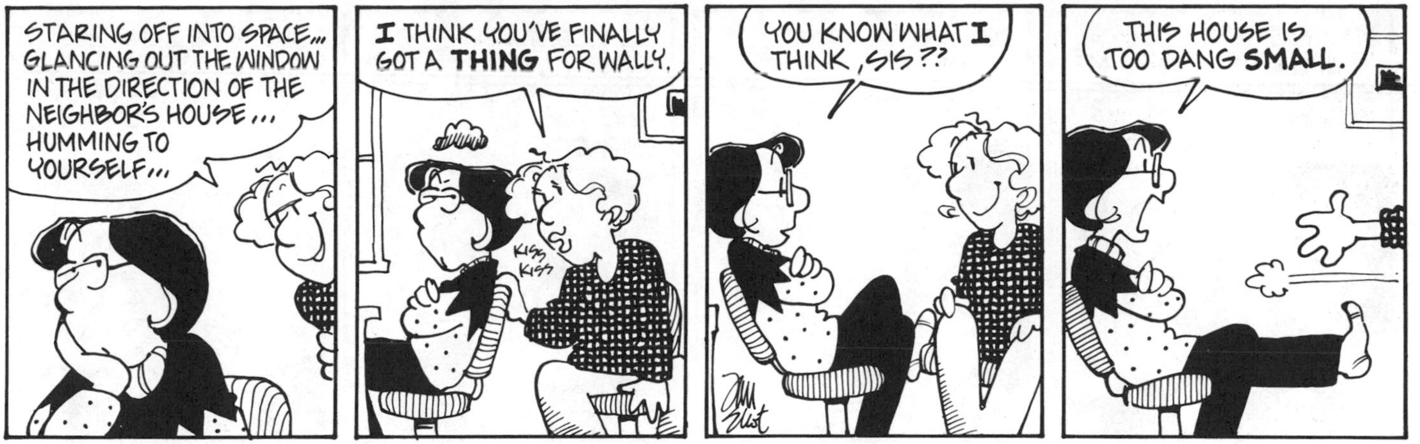
STARING OFF INTO SPACE,... GLANCING OUT THE WINDOW IN THE DIRECTION OF THE NEIGHBOR'S HOUSE... HUMMING TO YOURSELF...
I THINK YOU'VE FINALLY GOT A THING FOR WALLY.
KISS KISS
YOU KNOW WHAT I THINK, SIS??
THIS HOUSE IS TOO DANG SMALL.

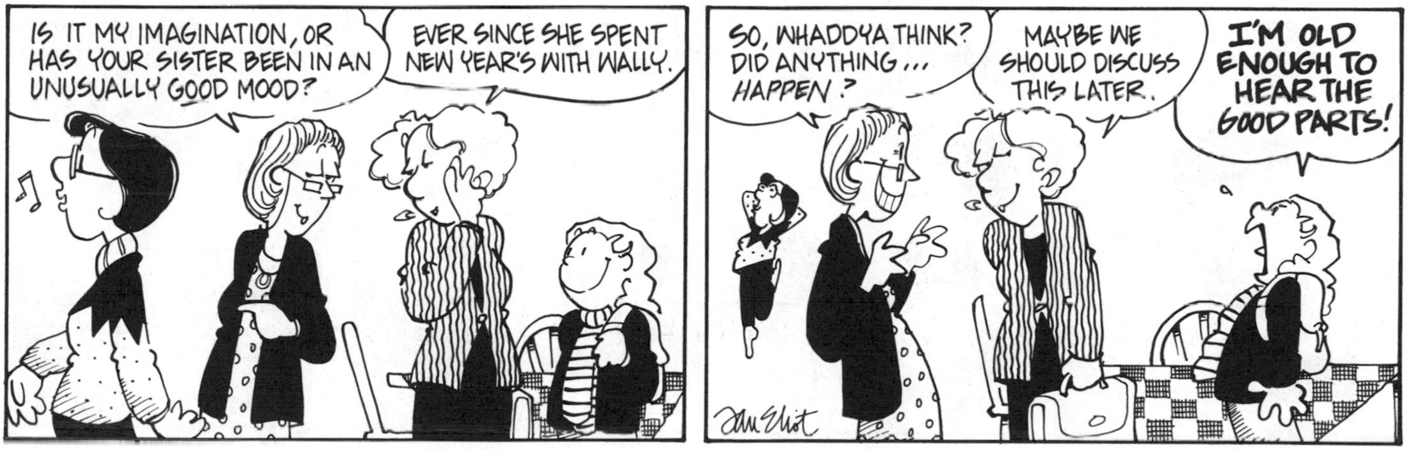
IS IT MY IMAGINATION, OR HAS YOUR SISTER BEEN IN AN UNUSUALLY GOOD MOOD?
EVER SINCE SHE SPENT NEW YEAR'S WITH WALLY.
SO, WHADDYA THINK? DID ANYTHING... HAPPEN?
MAYBE WE SHOULD DISCUSS THIS LATER.
I'M OLD ENOUGH TO HEAR THE GOOD PARTS!

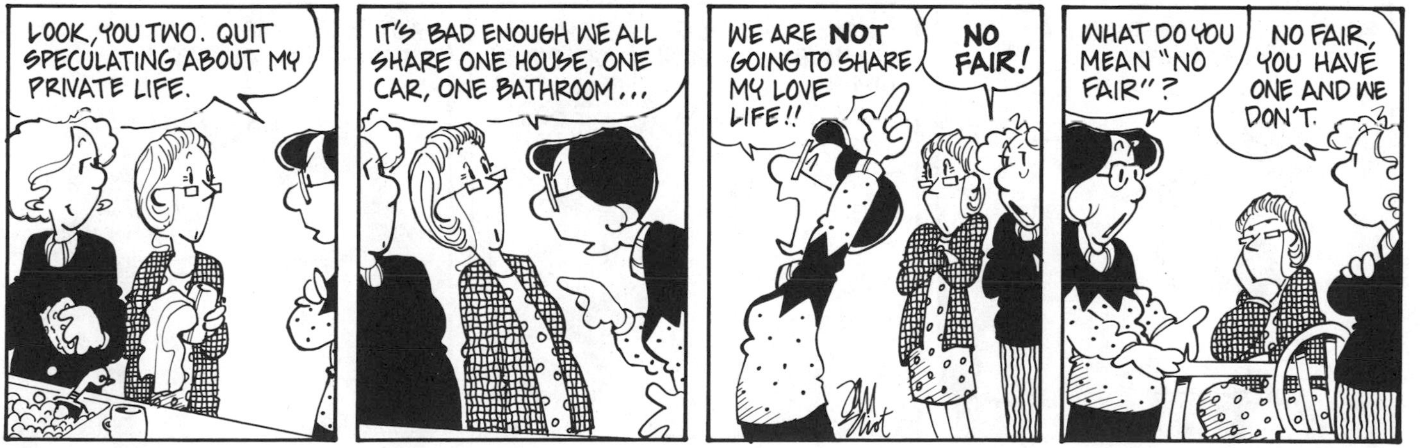
LOOK, YOU TWO. QUIT SPECULATING ABOUT MY PRIVATE LIFE.
IT'S BAD ENOUGH WE ALL SHARE ONE HOUSE, ONE CAR, ONE BATHROOM...
WE ARE NOT GOING TO SHARE MY LOVE LIFE!!
NO FAIR!
WHAT DO YOU MEAN "NO FAIR"?
NO FAIR, YOU HAVE ONE AND WE DON'T.

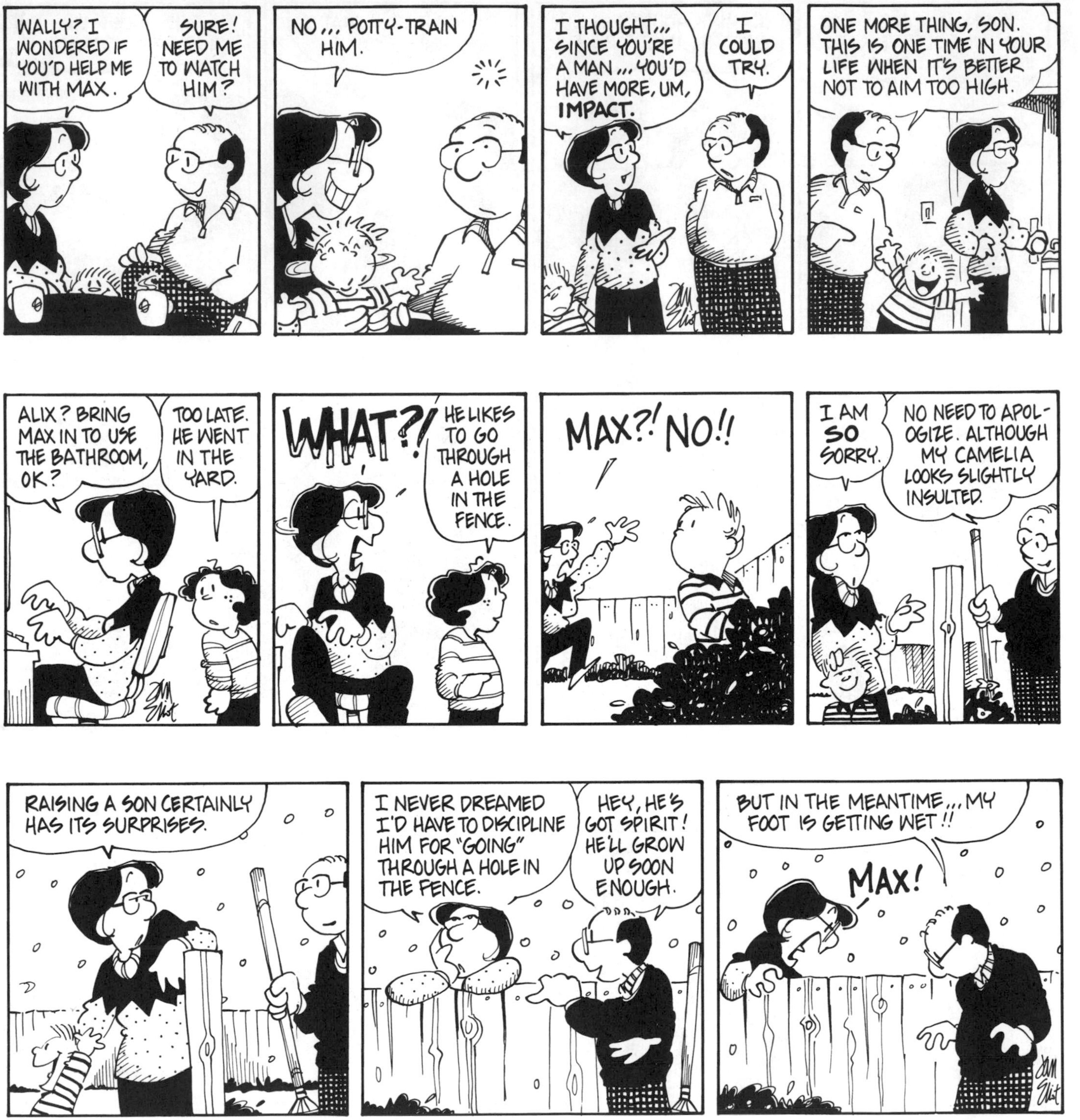
WALLY? I WONDERED IF YOU'D HELP ME WITH MAX.
SURE! NEED ME TO WATCH HIM?
NO ... POTTY-TRAIN HIM.
I THOUGHT ... SINCE YOU'RE A MAN ... YOU'D HAVE MORE, UM, **IMPACT.**
I COULD TRY.
ONE MORE THING, SON. THIS IS ONE TIME IN YOUR LIFE WHEN IT'S BETTER NOT TO AIM TOO HIGH.
ALIX? BRING MAX IN TO USE THE BATHROOM, OK?
TOO LATE. HE WENT IN THE YARD.
WHAT?!
HE LIKES TO GO THROUGH A HOLE IN THE FENCE.
MAX?!
NO!!
I AM **SO** SORRY.
NO NEED TO APOLOGIZE. ALTHOUGH MY CAMELIA LOOKS SLIGHTLY INSULTED.
RAISING A SON CERTAINLY HAS ITS SURPRISES.
I NEVER DREAMED I'D HAVE TO DISCIPLINE HIM FOR "GOING" THROUGH A HOLE IN THE FENCE.
HEY, HE'S GOT SPIRIT! HE'LL GROW UP SOON ENOUGH.
BUT IN THE MEANTIME ... MY FOOT IS GETTING WET!!
MAX!

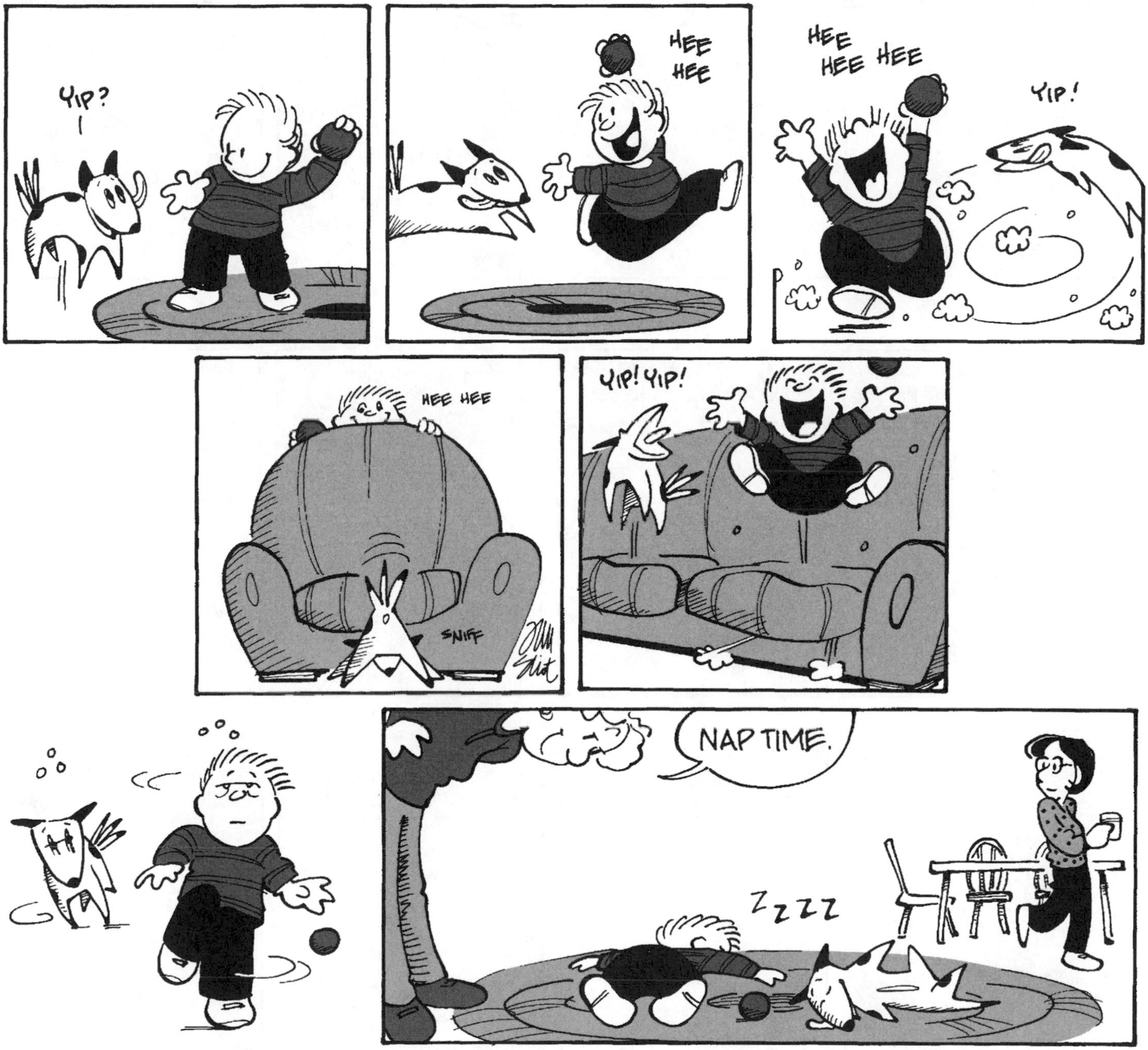
YIP?
HEE HEE
HEE HEE HEE HEE
YIP!
HEE HEE
SNIFF
YIP! YIP!
NAP TIME.
ZZZZ

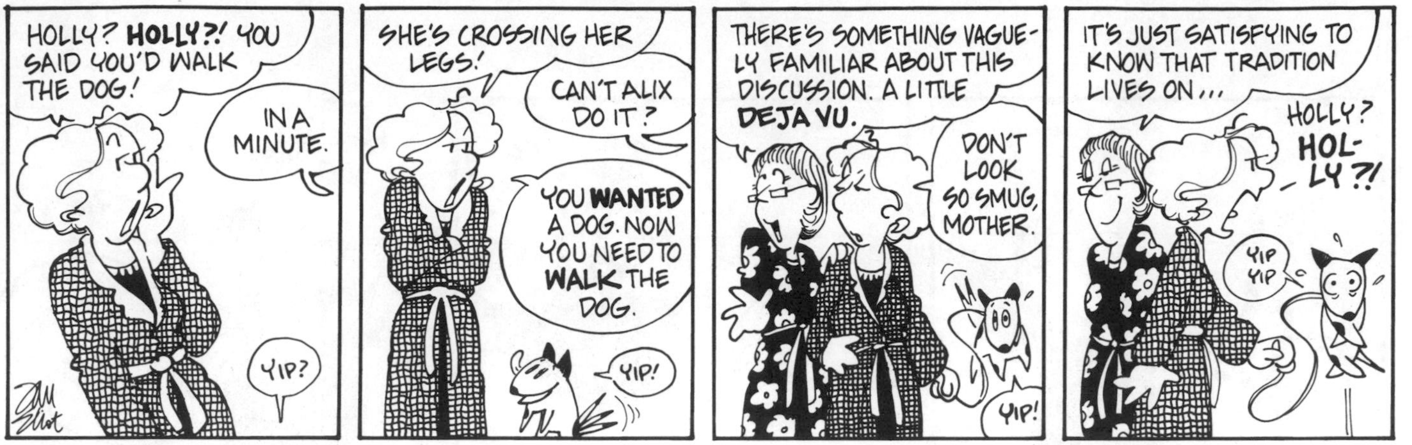
HOLLY? HOLLY?! YOU SAID YOU'D WALK THE DOG!
IN A MINUTE.
YIP?
SHE'S CROSSING HER LEGS!
CAN'T ALIX DO IT?
YOU WANTED A DOG. NOW YOU NEED TO WALK THE DOG.
YIP!
THERE'S SOMETHING VAGUELY FAMILIAR ABOUT THIS DISCUSSION. A LITTLE DEJA VU.
DON'T LOOK SO SMUG, MOTHER.
YIP!
IT'S JUST SATISFYING TO KNOW THAT TRADITION LIVES ON...
HOLLY? HOL-LY?!
YIP YIP

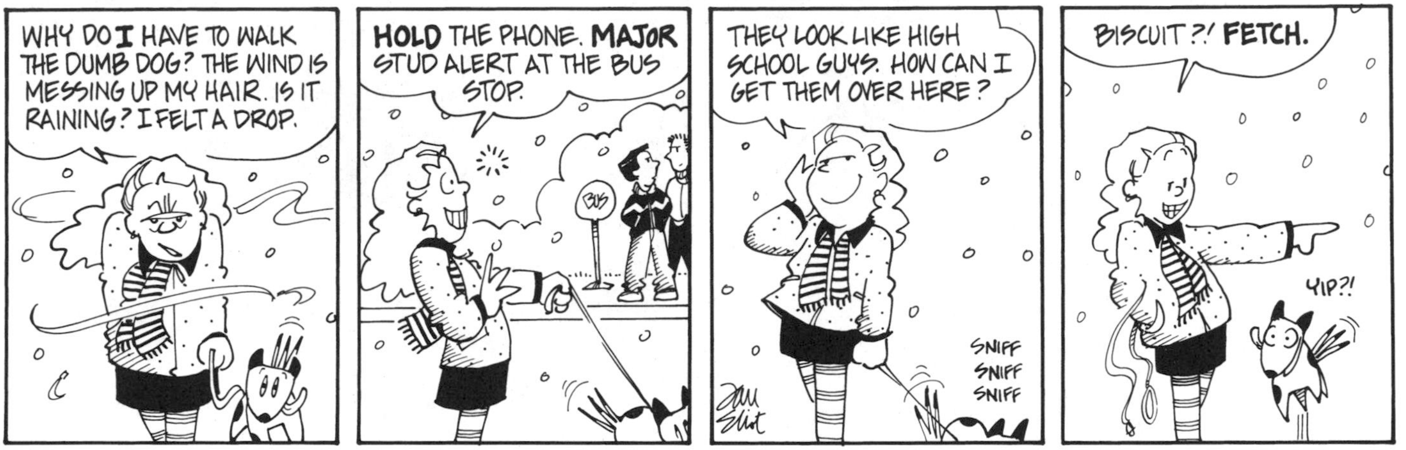
WHY DO I HAVE TO WALK THE DUMB DOG? THE WIND IS MESSING UP MY HAIR. IS IT RAINING? I FELT A DROP.
HOLD THE PHONE. MAJOR STUD ALERT AT THE BUS STOP.
BUS
THEY LOOK LIKE HIGH SCHOOL GUYS. HOW CAN I GET THEM OVER HERE?
SNIFF
SNIFF
SNIFF
BISCUIT?! FETCH.
YIP?!

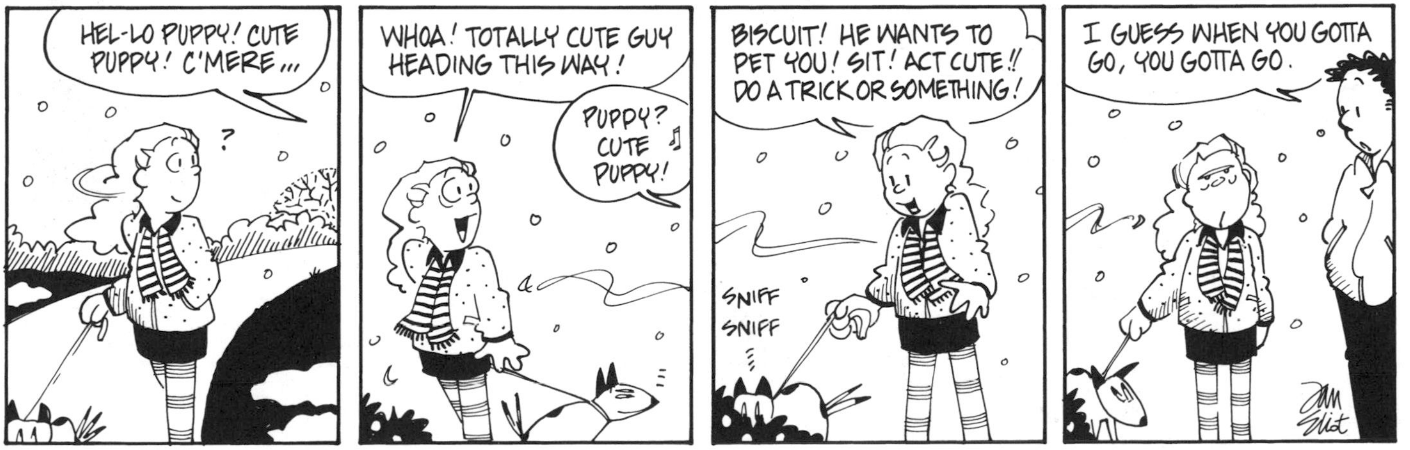
HEL-LO PUPPY! CUTE PUPPY! C'MERE...
WHOA! TOTALLY CUTE GUY HEADING THIS WAY!
PUPPY? CUTE PUPPY!
BISCUIT! HE WANTS TO PET YOU! SIT! ACT CUTE!! DO A TRICK OR SOMETHING!
SNIFF
SNIFF
I GUESS WHEN YOU GOTTA GO, YOU GOTTA GO.

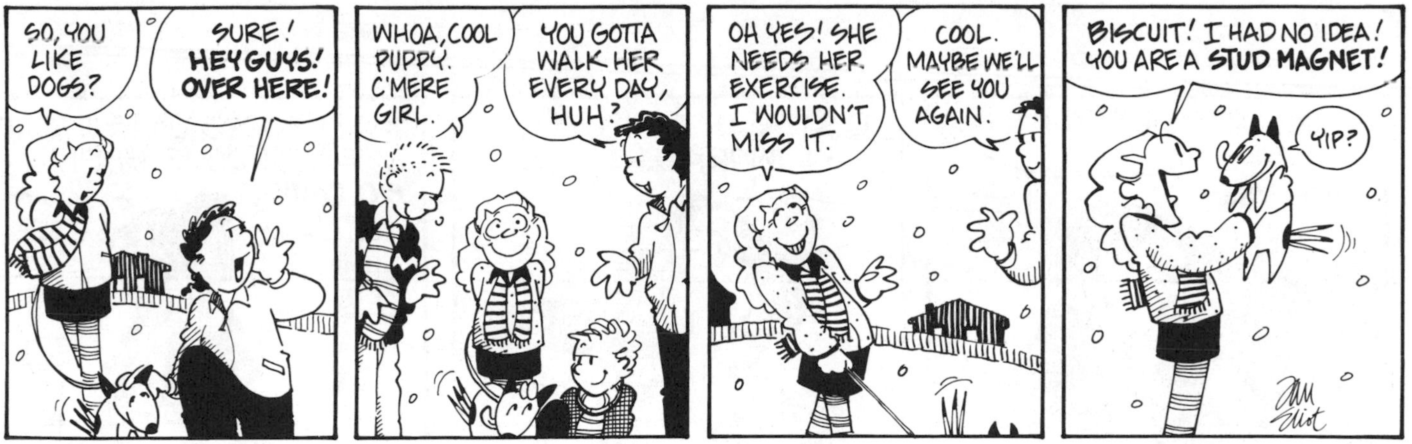
SO, YOU LIKE DOGS?
SURE! HEY GUYS! OVER HERE!
WHOA, COOL PUPPY. C'MERE GIRL.
YOU GOTTA WALK HER EVERY DAY, HUH?
OH YES! SHE NEEDS HER EXERCISE. I WOULDN'T MISS IT.
COOL. MAYBE WE'LL SEE YOU AGAIN.
BISCUIT! I HAD NO IDEA! YOU ARE A STUD MAGNET!
YIP?

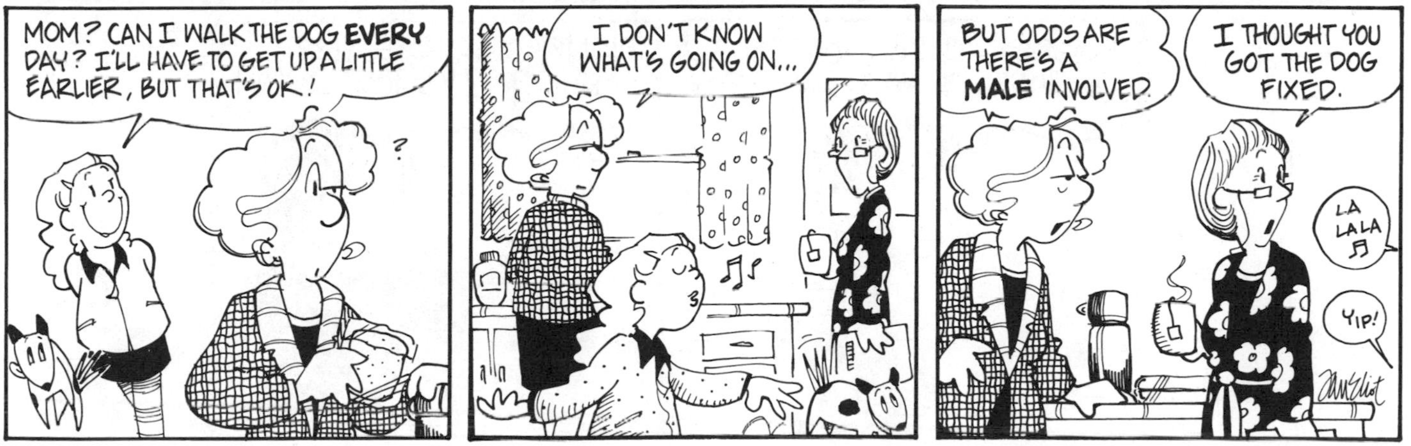
MOM? CAN I WALK THE DOG EVERY DAY? I'LL HAVE TO GET UP A LITTLE EARLIER, BUT THAT'S OK!
?
I DON'T KNOW WHAT'S GOING ON...
BUT ODDS ARE THERE'S A MALE INVOLVED.
I THOUGHT YOU GOT THE DOG FIXED.
LA LA LA
YIP!

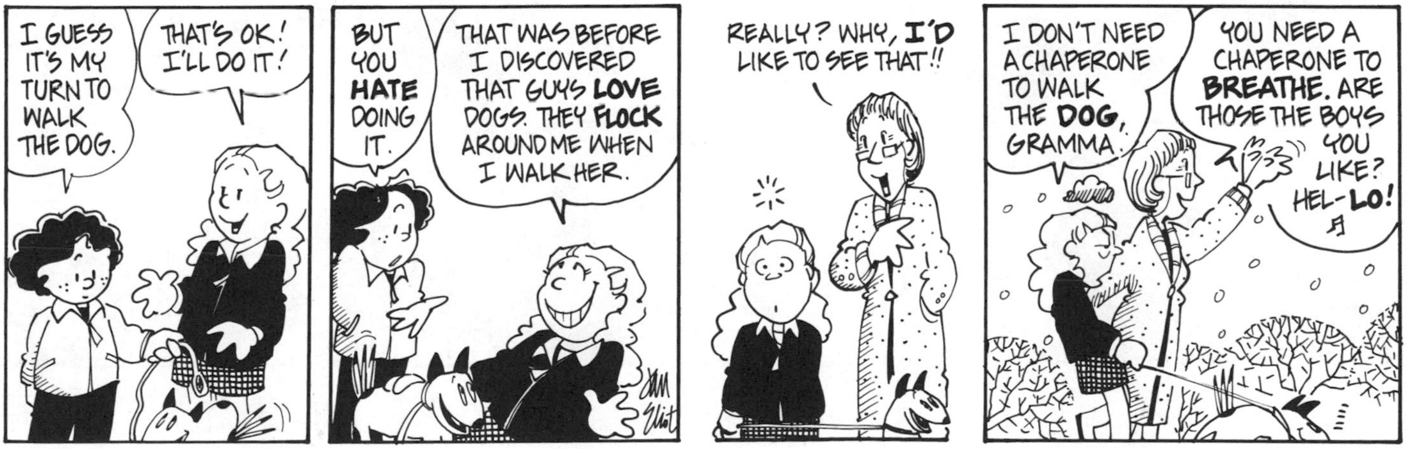
I GUESS IT'S MY TURN TO WALK THE DOG.
THAT'S OK! I'LL DO IT!
BUT YOU HATE DOING IT.
THAT WAS BEFORE I DISCOVERED THAT GUYS LOVE DOGS. THEY FLOCK AROUND ME WHEN I WALK HER.
REALLY? WHY, I'D LIKE TO SEE THAT!!
I DON'T NEED A CHAPERONE TO WALK THE DOG, GRAMMA.
YOU NEED A CHAPERONE TO BREATHE. ARE THOSE THE BOYS YOU LIKE? HEL-LO!

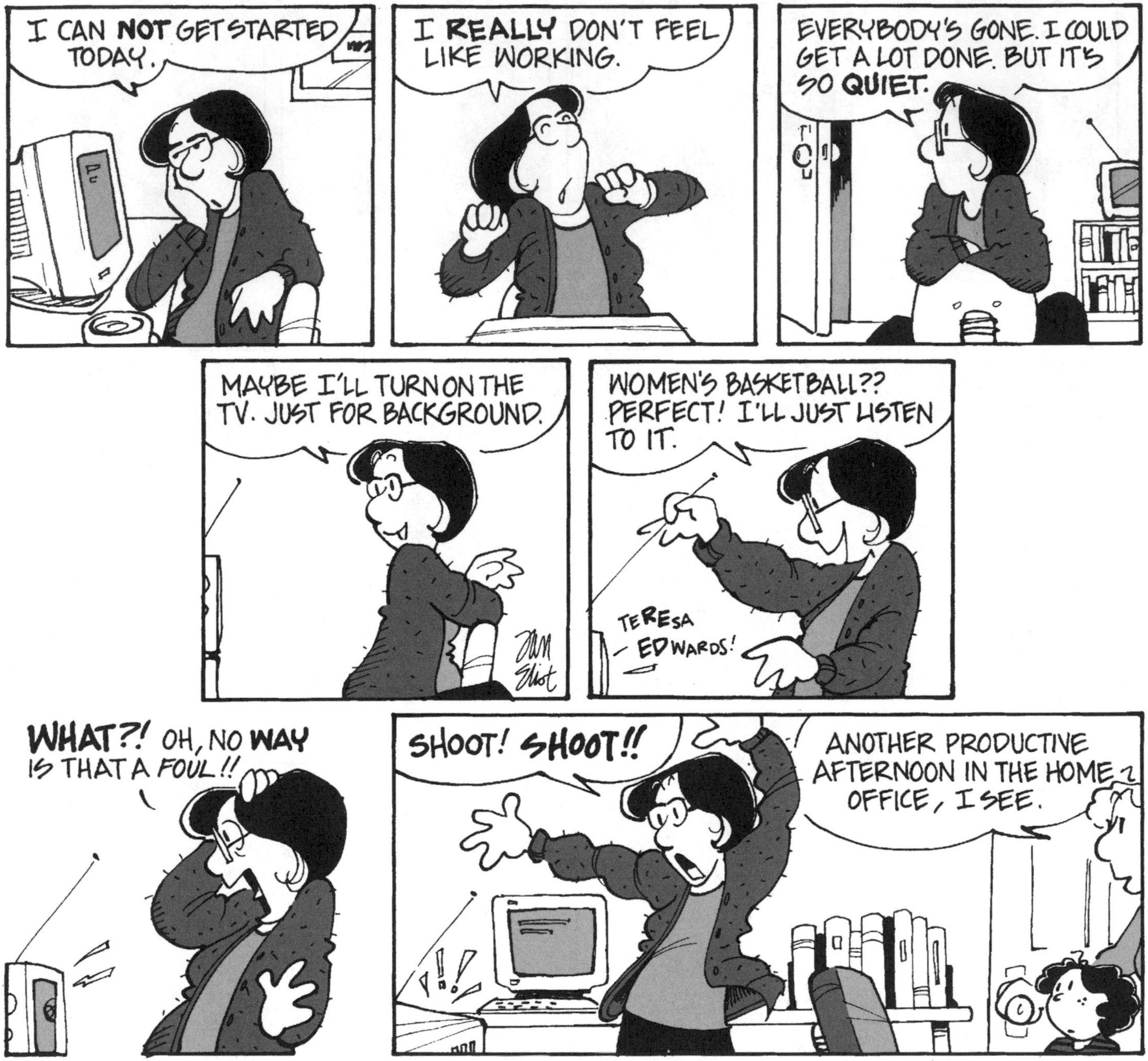
I CAN NOT GET STARTED TODAY.
I REALLY DON'T FEEL LIKE WORKING.
EVERYBODY'S GONE. I COULD GET A LOT DONE. BUT IT'S SO QUIET.
MAYBE I'LL TURN ON THE TV. JUST FOR BACKGROUND.
WOMEN'S BASKETBALL?? PERFECT! I'LL JUST LISTEN TO IT.
TERESA EDWARDS!
WHAT?! OH, NO WAY IS THAT A FOUL!!
SHOOT! SHOOT!!
ANOTHER PRODUCTIVE AFTERNOON IN THE HOME OFFICE, I SEE.

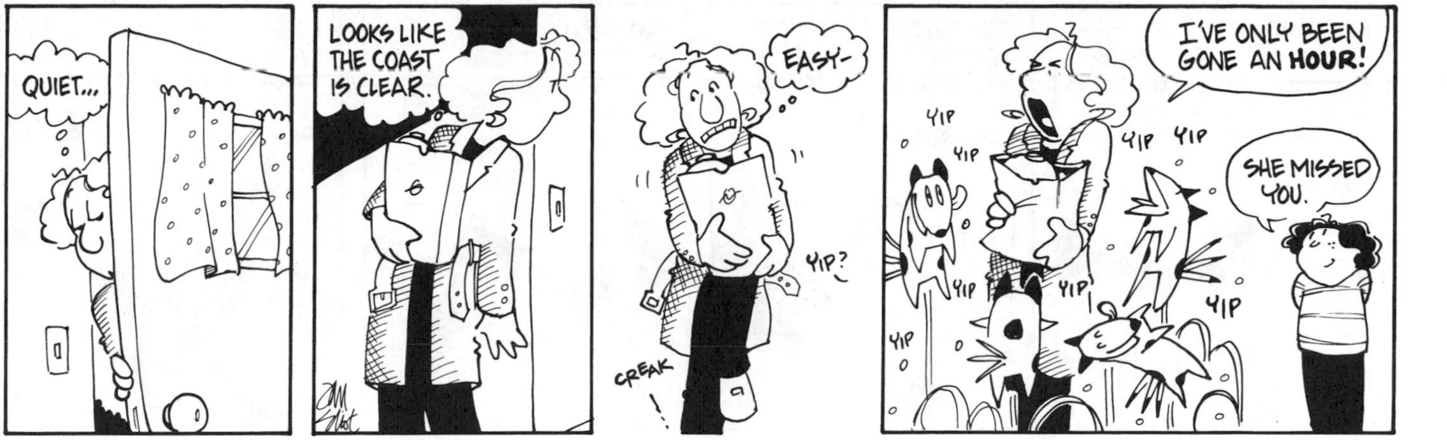
QUIET...
LOOKS LIKE THE COAST IS CLEAR.
EASY-
YIP?
CREAK
I'VE ONLY BEEN GONE AN HOUR!
YIP
YIP
YIP
YIP
YIP
YIP
YIP
YIP
SHE MISSED YOU.

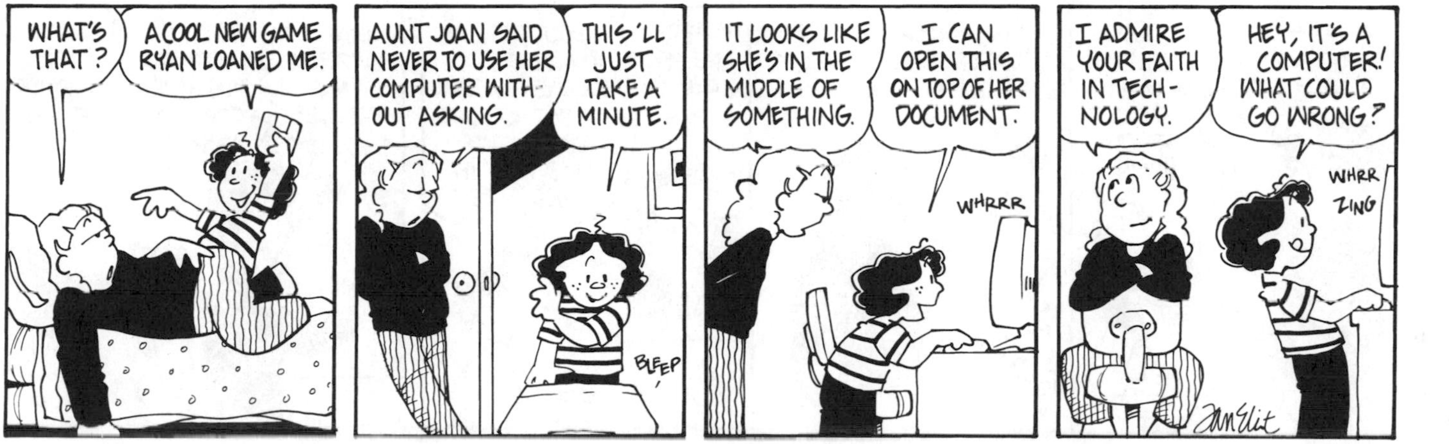
WHAT'S THAT?
A COOL NEW GAME RYAN LOANED ME.
AUNT JOAN SAID NEVER TO USE HER COMPUTER WITH-OUT ASKING.
THIS'LL JUST TAKE A MINUTE.
BLEEP
IT LOOKS LIKE SHE'S IN THE MIDDLE OF SOMETHING.
I CAN OPEN THIS ON TOP OF HER DOCUMENT.
WHRRR
I ADMIRE YOUR FAITH IN TECH-NOLOGY.
HEY, IT'S A COMPUTER! WHAT COULD GO WRONG?
WHRR
ZING

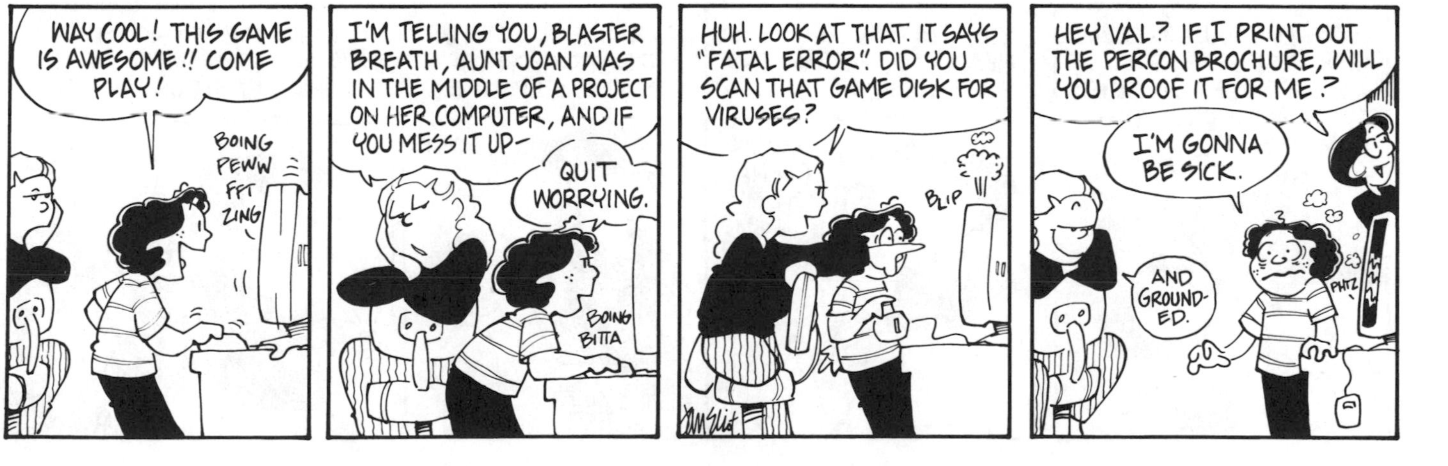
WAY COOL! THIS GAME IS AWESOME!! COME PLAY!
BOING
PEWW
FFT
ZING
I'M TELLING YOU, BLASTER BREATH, AUNT JOAN WAS IN THE MIDDLE OF A PROJECT ON HER COMPUTER, AND IF YOU MESS IT UP-
QUIT WORRYING.
BOING
BITTA
HUH. LOOK AT THAT. IT SAYS "FATAL ERROR". DID YOU SCAN THAT GAME DISK FOR VIRUSES?
BLIP
HEY VAL? IF I PRINT OUT THE PERCON BROCHURE, WILL YOU PROOF IT FOR ME?
I'M GONNA BE SICK.
AND GROUND-ED.
PHTZ

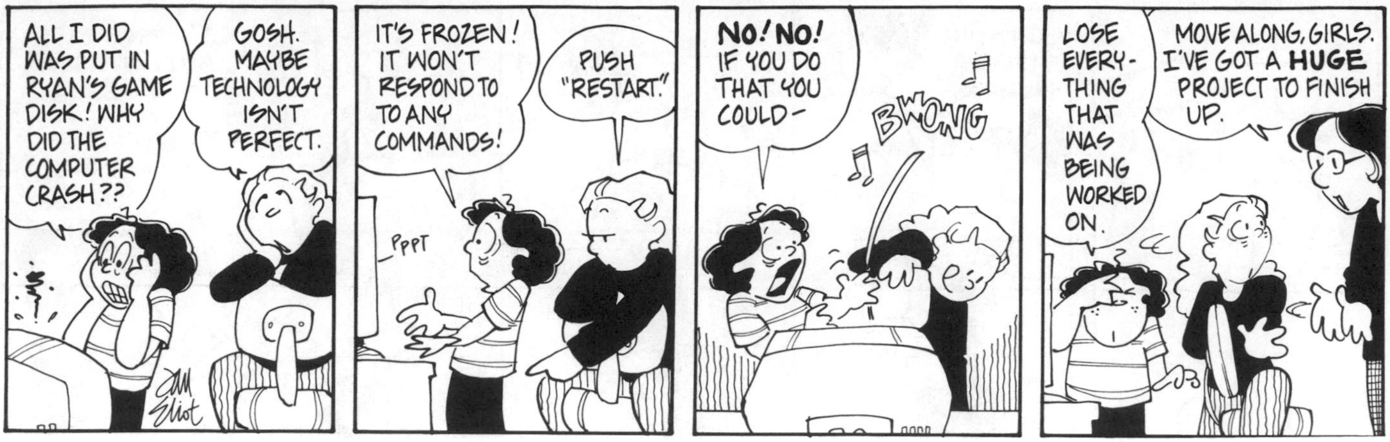
ALL I DID WAS PUT IN RYAN'S GAME DISK! WHY DID THE COMPUTER CRASH??
GOSH. MAYBE TECHNOLOGY ISN'T PERFECT.
IT'S FROZEN! IT WON'T RESPOND TO TO ANY COMMANDS!
PUSH "RESTART."
PPPT
NO! NO! IF YOU DO THAT YOU COULD—
BWONG
LOSE EVERY-THING THAT WAS BEING WORKED ON.
MOVE ALONG, GIRLS. I'VE GOT A HUGE PROJECT TO FINISH UP.

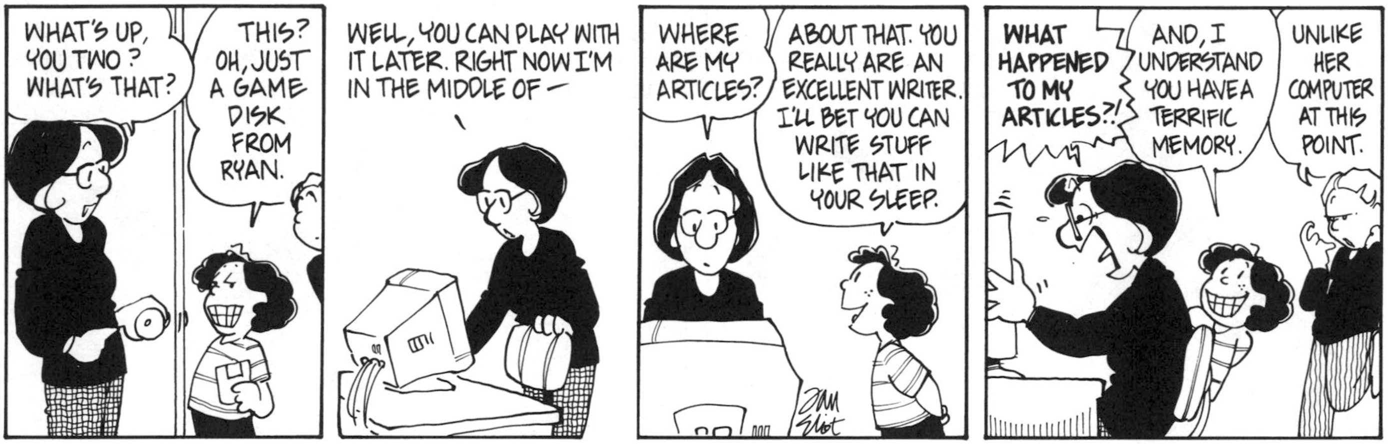
WHAT'S UP, YOU TWO? WHAT'S THAT?
THIS? OH, JUST A GAME DISK FROM RYAN.
WELL, YOU CAN PLAY WITH IT LATER. RIGHT NOW I'M IN THE MIDDLE OF—
WHERE ARE MY ARTICLES?
ABOUT THAT. YOU REALLY ARE AN EXCELLENT WRITER. I'LL BET YOU CAN WRITE STUFF LIKE THAT IN YOUR SLEEP.
WHAT HAPPENED TO MY ARTICLES?!
AND, I UNDERSTAND YOU HAVE A TERRIFIC MEMORY.
UNLIKE HER COMPUTER AT THIS POINT.

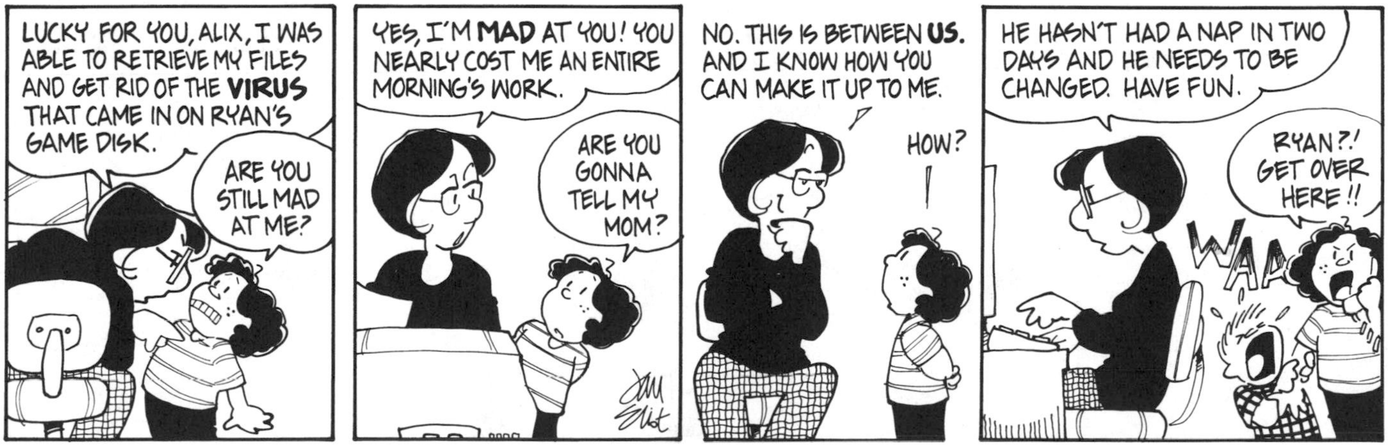
LUCKY FOR YOU, ALIX, I WAS ABLE TO RETRIEVE MY FILES AND GET RID OF THE VIRUS THAT CAME IN ON RYAN'S GAME DISK.
ARE YOU STILL MAD AT ME?
YES, I'M MAD AT YOU! YOU NEARLY COST ME AN ENTIRE MORNING'S WORK.
ARE YOU GONNA TELL MY MOM?
NO. THIS IS BETWEEN US. AND I KNOW HOW YOU CAN MAKE IT UP TO ME.
HOW?
HE HASN'T HAD A NAP IN TWO DAYS AND HE NEEDS TO BE CHANGED. HAVE FUN.
RYAN?! GET OVER HERE!!
WAA

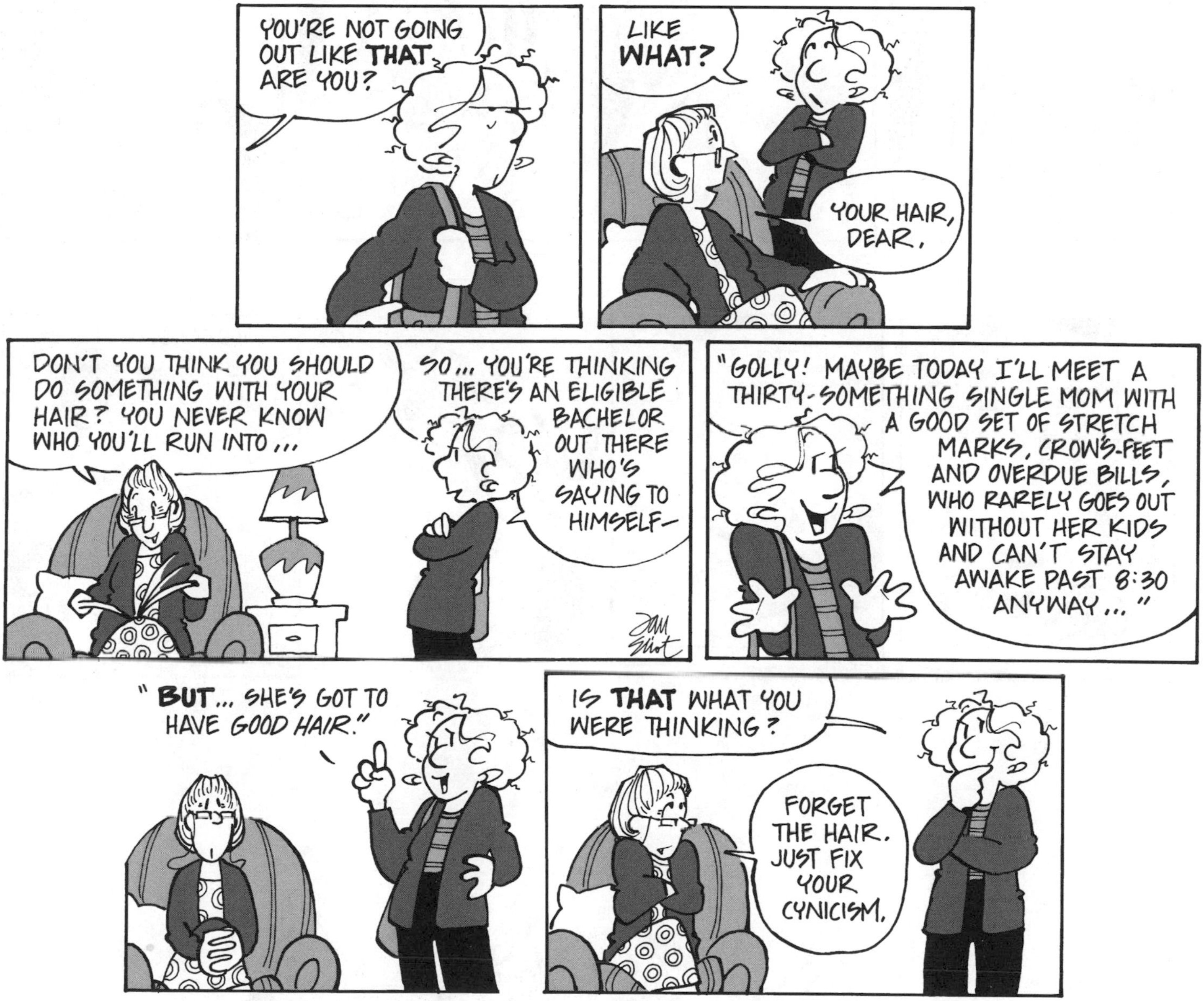
YOU'RE NOT GOING OUT LIKE **THAT**, ARE YOU?
LIKE **WHAT?**
YOUR HAIR, DEAR.
DON'T YOU THINK YOU SHOULD DO SOMETHING WITH YOUR HAIR? YOU NEVER KNOW WHO YOU'LL RUN INTO...
SO... YOU'RE THINKING THERE'S AN ELIGIBLE BACHELOR OUT THERE WHO'S SAYING TO HIMSELF–
"GOLLY! MAYBE TODAY I'LL MEET A THIRTY-SOMETHING SINGLE MOM WITH A GOOD SET OF STRETCH MARKS, CROW'S-FEET AND OVERDUE BILLS, WHO RARELY GOES OUT WITHOUT HER KIDS AND CAN'T STAY AWAKE PAST 8:30 ANYWAY..."
"**BUT**... SHE'S GOT TO HAVE *GOOD HAIR.*"
IS **THAT** WHAT YOU WERE THINKING?
FORGET THE HAIR. JUST FIX YOUR CYNICISM.

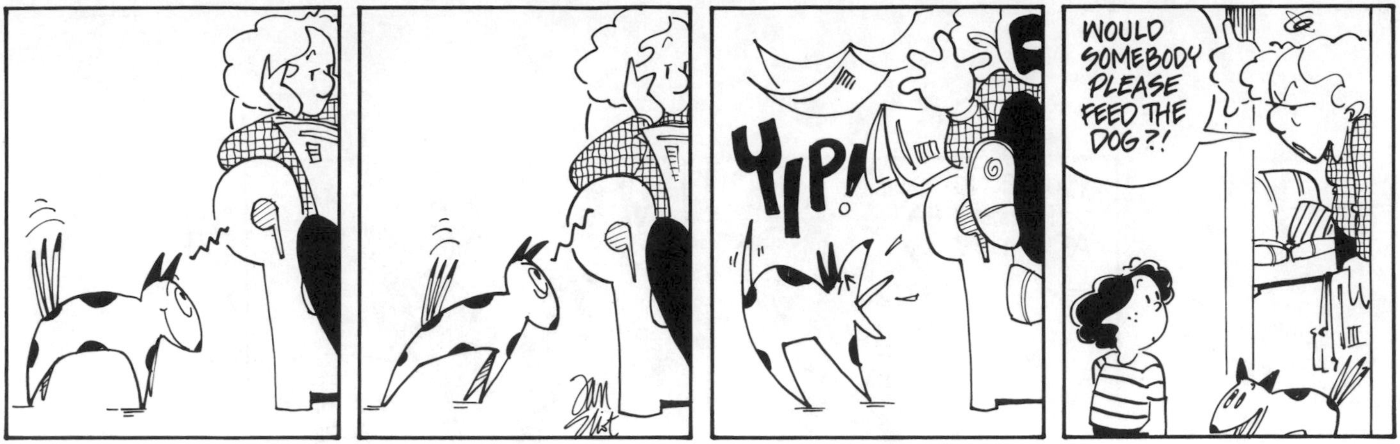
YIP!
WOULD SOMEBODY PLEASE FEED THE DOG?!

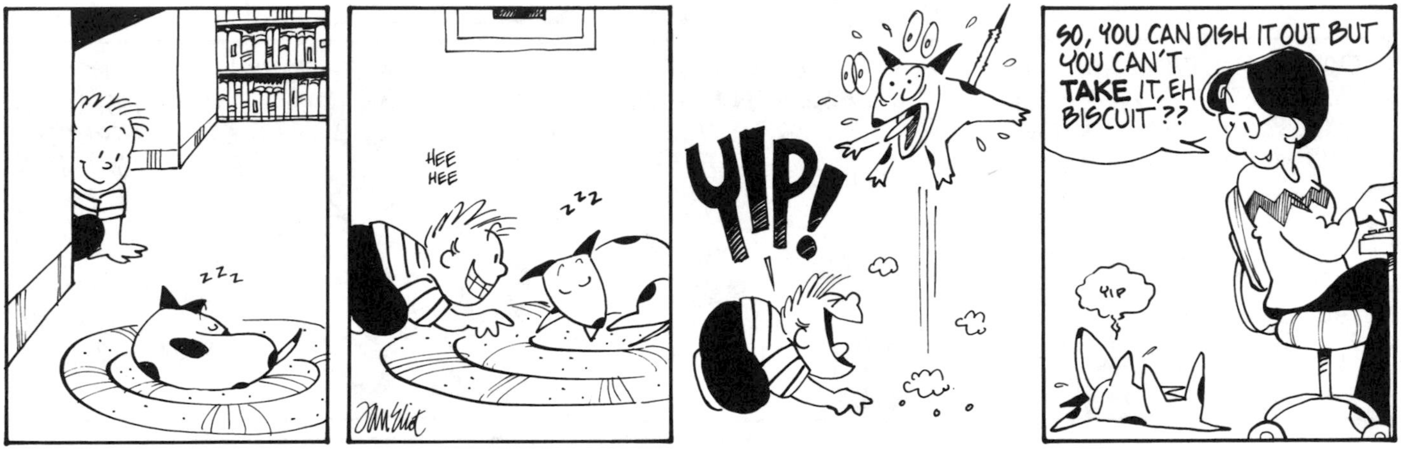
Z Z Z
HEE HEE
Z Z Z
YIP!
SO, YOU CAN DISH IT OUT BUT YOU CAN'T **TAKE** IT, EH BISCUIT??
YIP

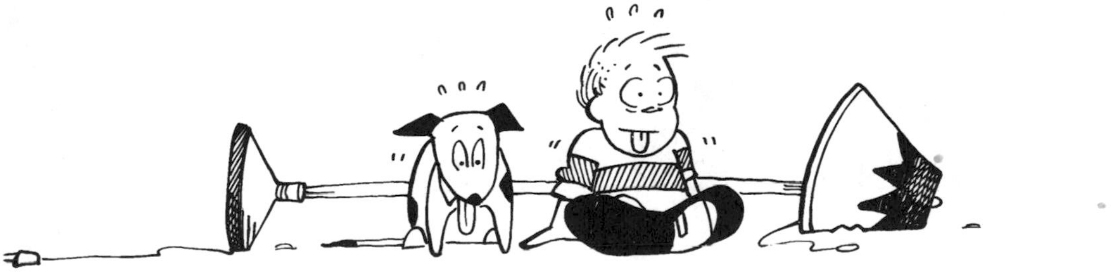

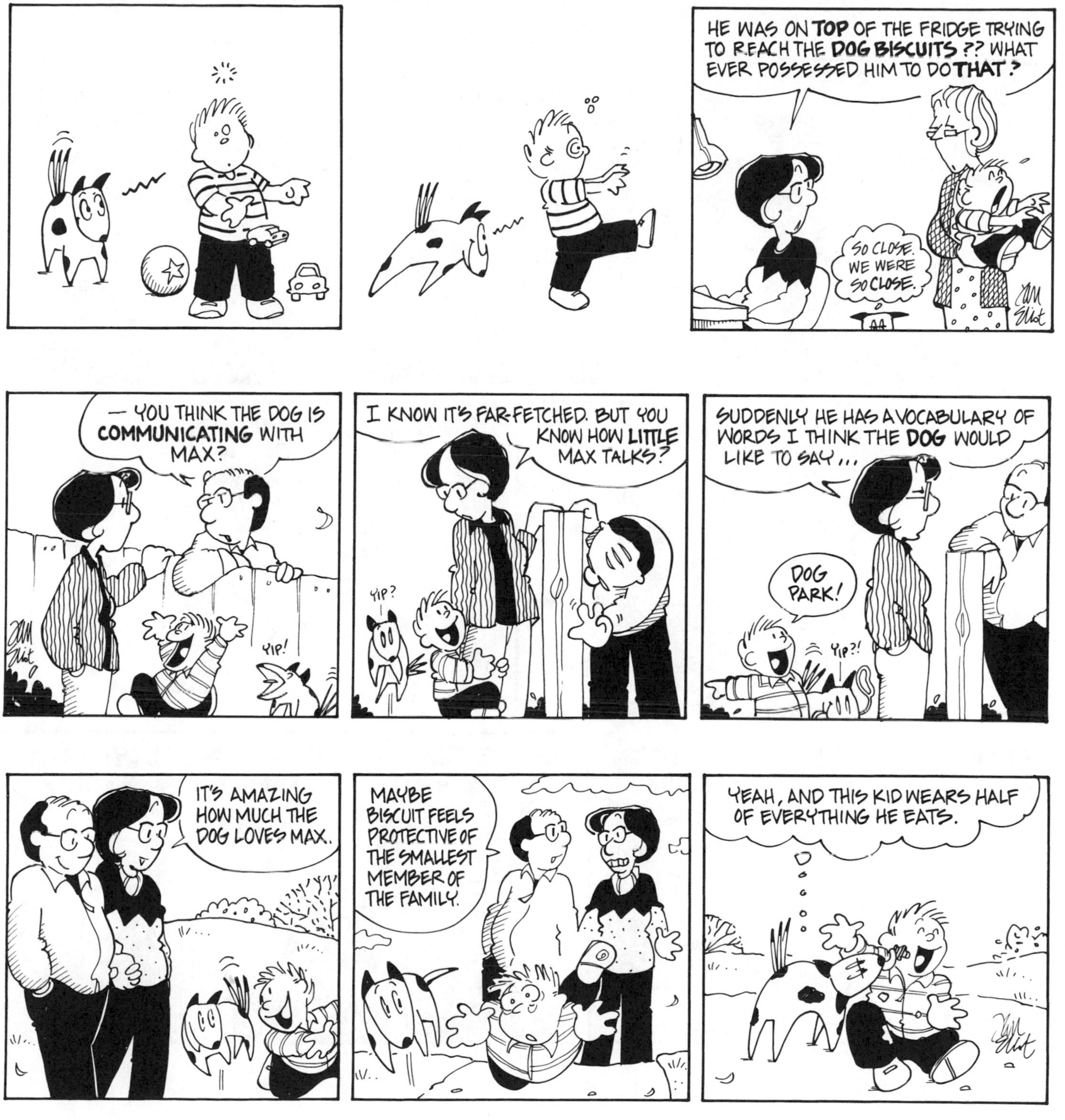
HE WAS ON TOP OF THE FRIDGE TRYING TO REACH THE DOG BISCUITS ?? WHAT EVER POSSESSED HIM TO DO THAT?
SO CLOSE. WE WERE SO CLOSE.
— YOU THINK THE DOG IS COMMUNICATING WITH MAX?
YIP!
I KNOW IT'S FAR-FETCHED. BUT YOU KNOW HOW LITTLE MAX TALKS?
YIP?
SUDDENLY HE HAS A VOCABULARY OF WORDS I THINK THE DOG WOULD LIKE TO SAY...
DOG PARK!
YIP?!
IT'S AMAZING HOW MUCH THE DOG LOVES MAX.
MAYBE BISCUIT FEELS PROTECTIVE OF THE SMALLEST MEMBER OF THE FAMILY.
YEAH, AND THIS KID WEARS HALF OF EVERYTHING HE EATS.

THEATER II

OK EVERYBODY, LISTEN UP.

ANYONE WHO CAN'T WATCH A MOVIE WITHOUT TALKING PLEASE LEAVE OR MOVE TO THE FRONT ROW.

IF YOU HAVE A PAGER OR A CELL PHONE, TURN IT OFF **NOW**.

SMALL CHILDREN SHOULD BE PACIFIED WITH SODA, CANDY OR POPCORN... WHATEVER IT TAKES. AND REMOVE ALL CELLOPHANE **BEFORE** THE MOVIE STARTS.

REMEMBER — IF I WANTED TO LISTEN TO **YOU** TALK, I WOULD HAVE RENTED A VIDEO AND COME TO YOUR LIVING ROOM.

GOING TO THE MOVIES WITH YOU IS QUITE AN EXPERIENCE.

MAY DAY! MAY DAY! REALLY TALL FAMILY HEADING THIS WAY!!

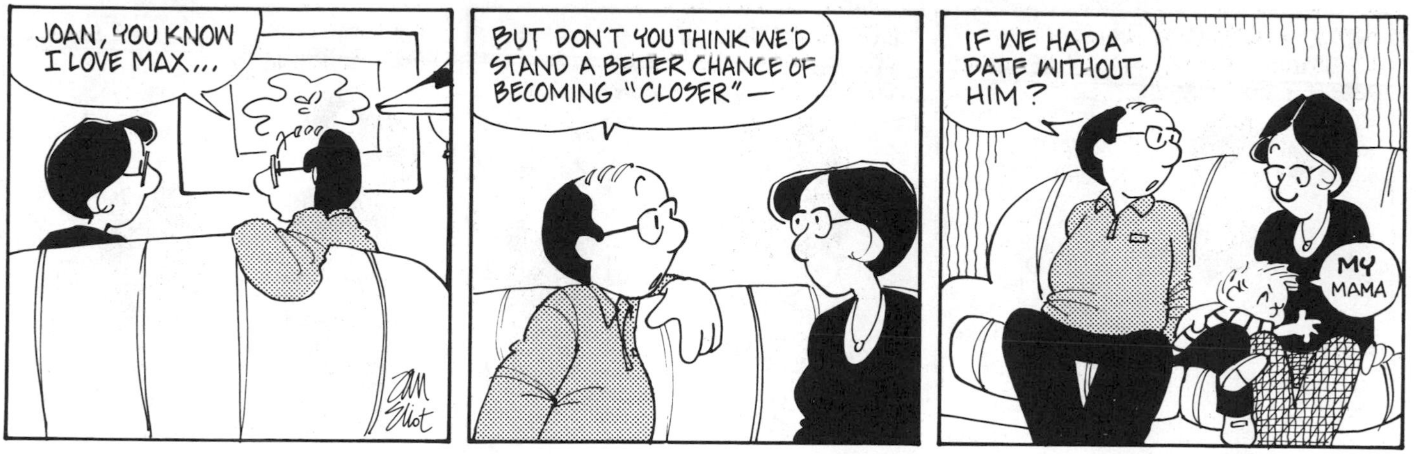
JOAN, YOU KNOW I LOVE MAX...
BUT DON'T YOU THINK WE'D STAND A BETTER CHANCE OF BECOMING "CLOSER"—
IF WE HAD A DATE WITHOUT HIM?
MY MAMA

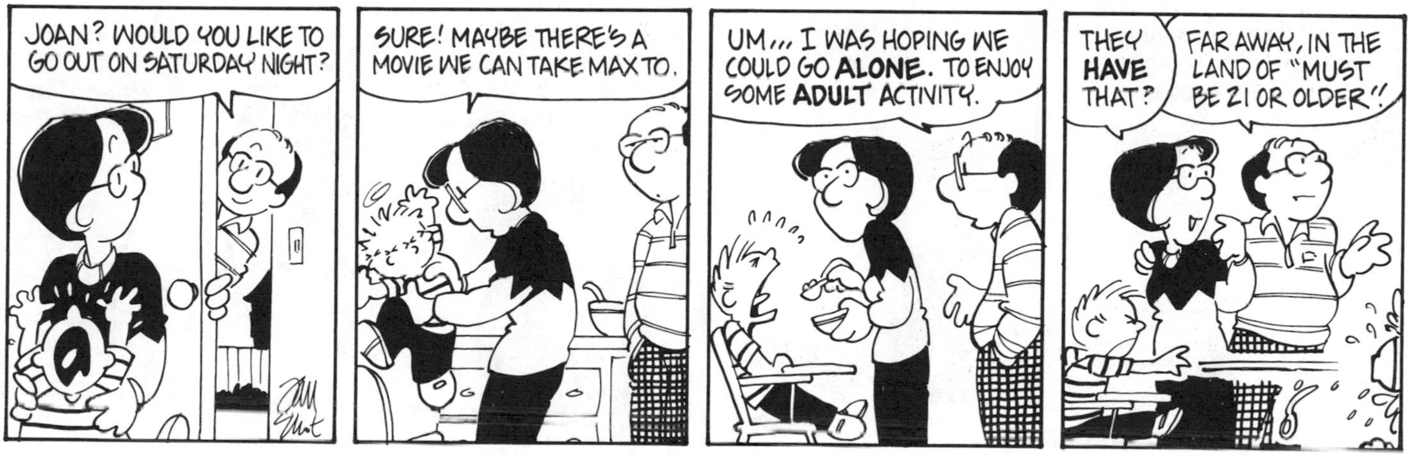
JOAN? WOULD YOU LIKE TO GO OUT ON SATURDAY NIGHT?
SURE! MAYBE THERE'S A MOVIE WE CAN TAKE MAX TO.
UM... I WAS HOPING WE COULD GO **ALONE**. TO ENJOY SOME **ADULT** ACTIVITY.
THEY **HAVE** THAT?
FAR AWAY, IN THE LAND OF "MUST BE 21 OR OLDER"!

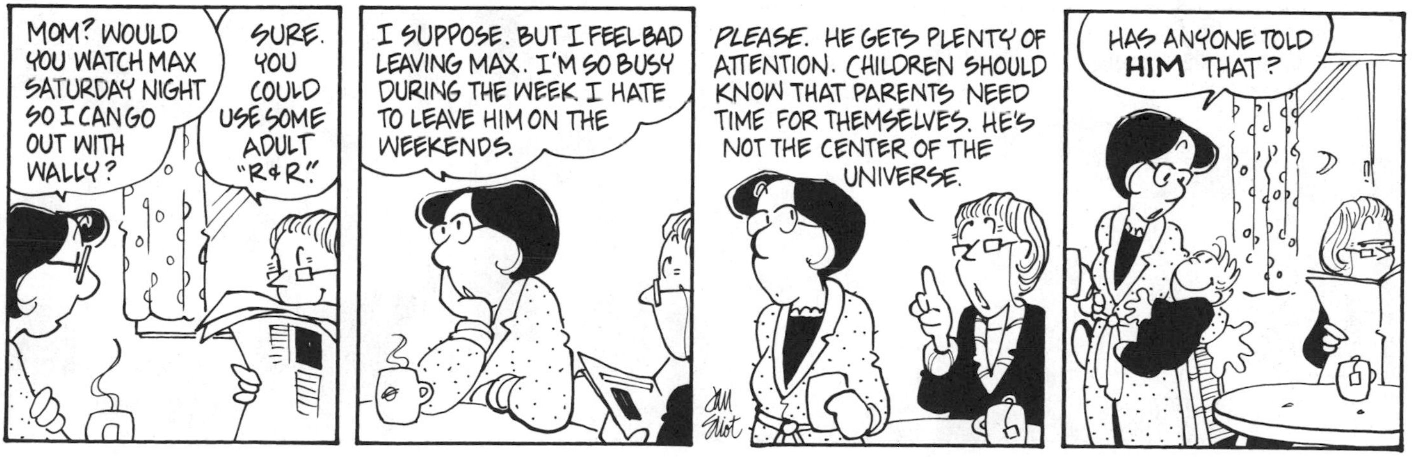
MOM? WOULD YOU WATCH MAX SATURDAY NIGHT SO I CAN GO OUT WITH WALLY?
SURE. YOU COULD USE SOME ADULT "R&R."
I SUPPOSE. BUT I FEEL BAD LEAVING MAX. I'M SO BUSY DURING THE WEEK I HATE TO LEAVE HIM ON THE WEEKENDS.
PLEASE. HE GETS PLENTY OF ATTENTION. CHILDREN SHOULD KNOW THAT PARENTS NEED TIME FOR THEMSELVES. HE'S NOT THE CENTER OF THE UNIVERSE.
HAS ANYONE TOLD **HIM** THAT?

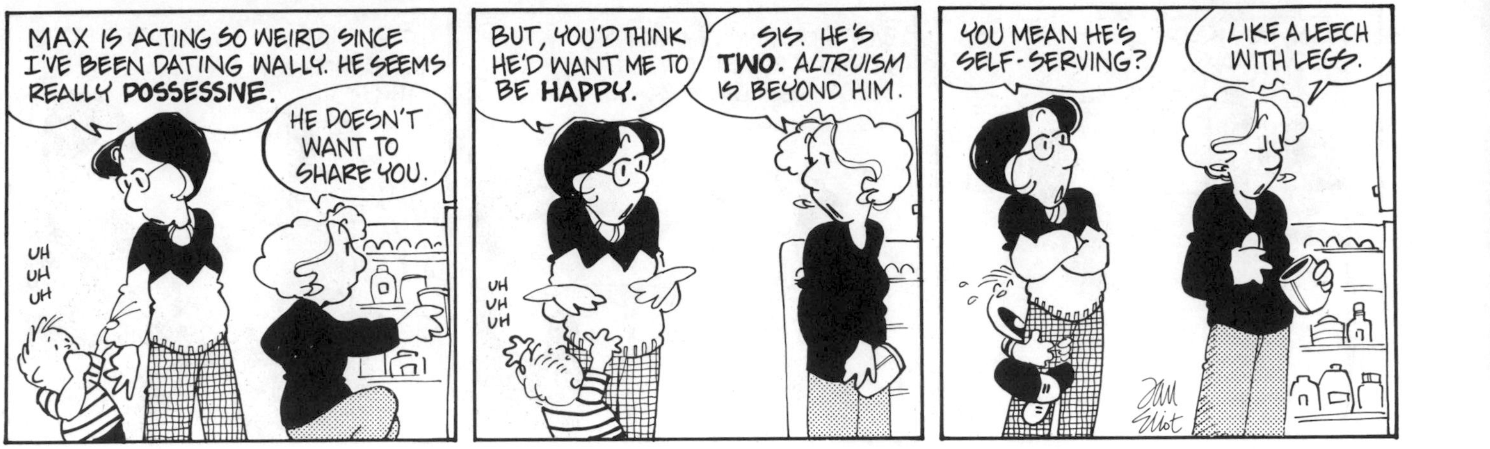
MAX IS ACTING SO WEIRD SINCE I'VE BEEN DATING WALLY. HE SEEMS REALLY **POSSESSIVE**.
HE DOESN'T WANT TO SHARE YOU.
UH UH UH
BUT, YOU'D THINK HE'D WANT ME TO BE **HAPPY**.
UH UH UH
SIS. HE'S **TWO.** *ALTRUISM* IS BEYOND HIM.
YOU MEAN HE'S SELF-SERVING?
LIKE A LEECH WITH LEGS.

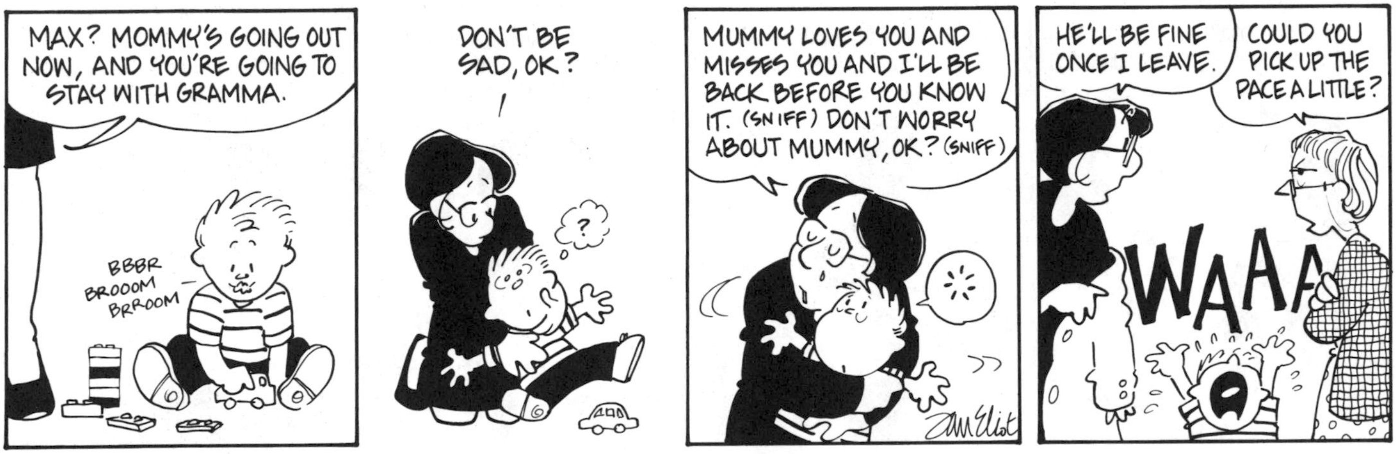
MAX? MOMMY'S GOING OUT NOW, AND YOU'RE GOING TO STAY WITH GRAMMA.
BBBR BROOOM BRROOM
DON'T BE SAD, OK?
?
MUMMY LOVES YOU AND MISSES YOU AND I'LL BE BACK BEFORE YOU KNOW IT. (SNIFF) DON'T WORRY ABOUT MUMMY, OK? (SNIFF)
HE'LL BE FINE ONCE I LEAVE.
COULD YOU PICK UP THE PACE A LITTLE?
WAAA

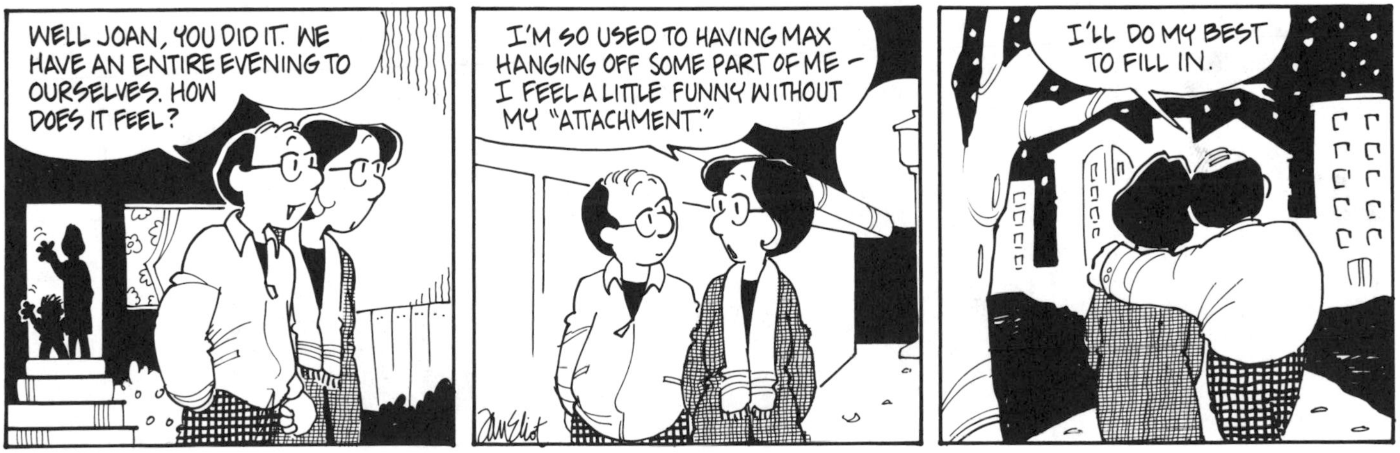
WELL JOAN, YOU DID IT. WE HAVE AN ENTIRE EVENING TO OURSELVES. HOW DOES IT FEEL?
I'M SO USED TO HAVING MAX HANGING OFF SOME PART OF ME - I FEEL A LITTLE FUNNY WITHOUT MY "ATTACHMENT."
I'LL DO MY BEST TO FILL IN.

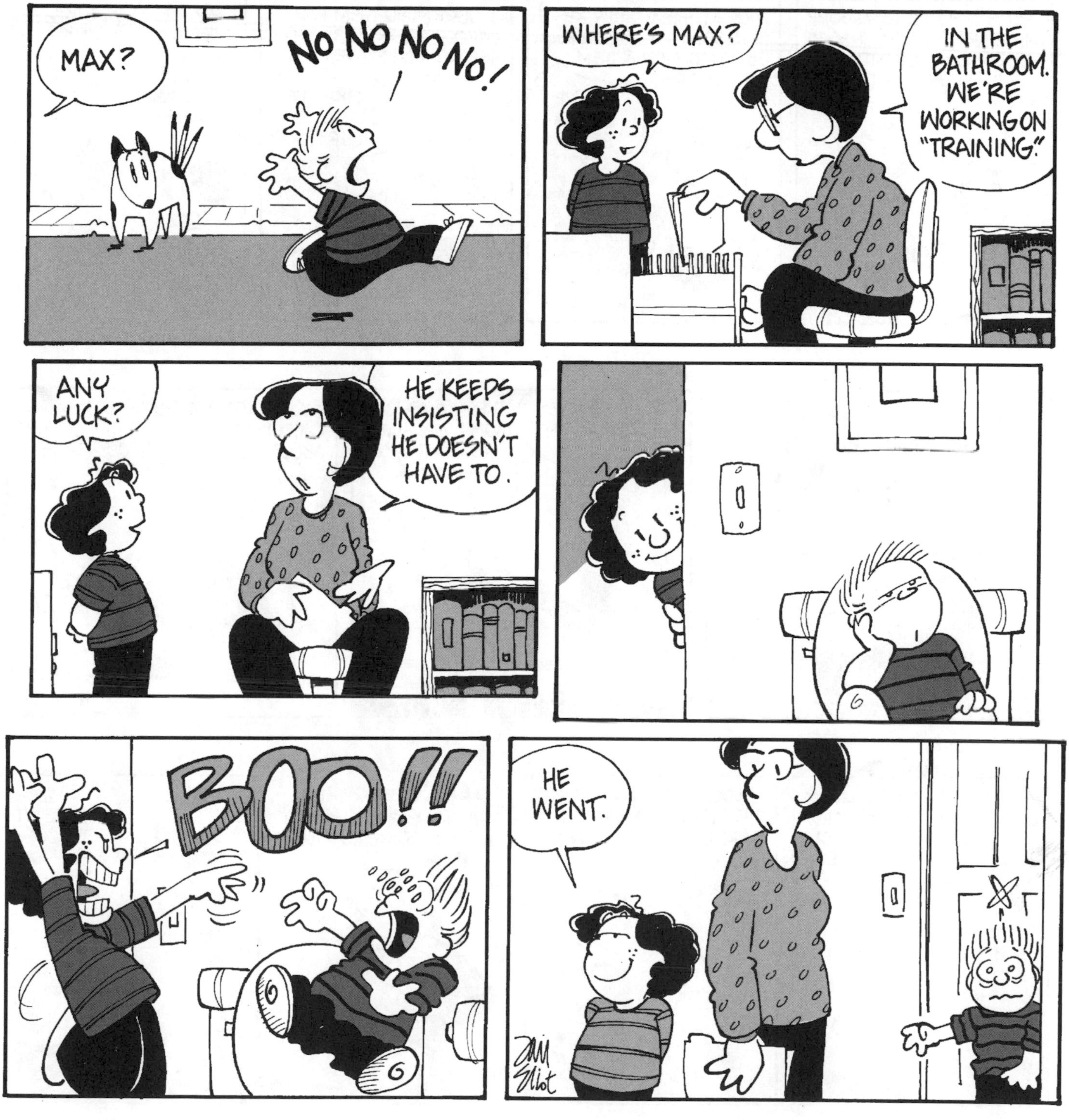
MAX?
NO NO NO NO!
WHERE'S MAX?
IN THE BATHROOM. WE'RE WORKING ON "TRAINING."
ANY LUCK?
HE KEEPS INSISTING HE DOESN'T HAVE TO.
BOO!!
HE WENT.

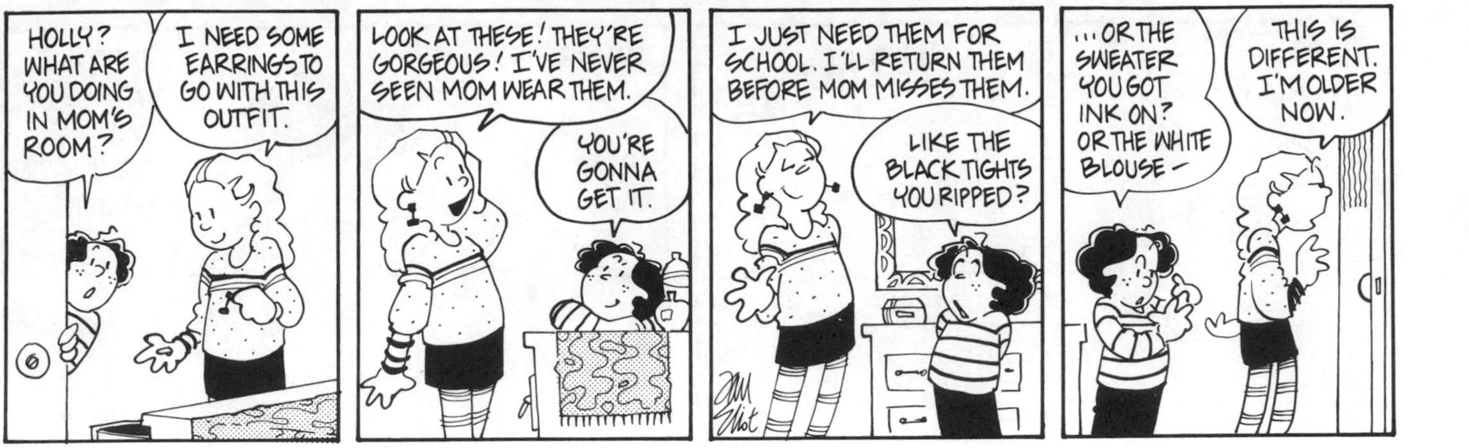
HOLLY? WHAT ARE YOU DOING IN MOM'S ROOM?
I NEED SOME EARRINGS TO GO WITH THIS OUTFIT.
LOOK AT THESE! THEY'RE GORGEOUS! I'VE NEVER SEEN MOM WEAR THEM.
YOU'RE GONNA GET IT.
I JUST NEED THEM FOR SCHOOL. I'LL RETURN THEM BEFORE MOM MISSES THEM.
LIKE THE BLACK TIGHTS YOU RIPPED?
...OR THE SWEATER YOU GOT INK ON? OR THE WHITE BLOUSE—
THIS IS DIFFERENT. I'M OLDER NOW.

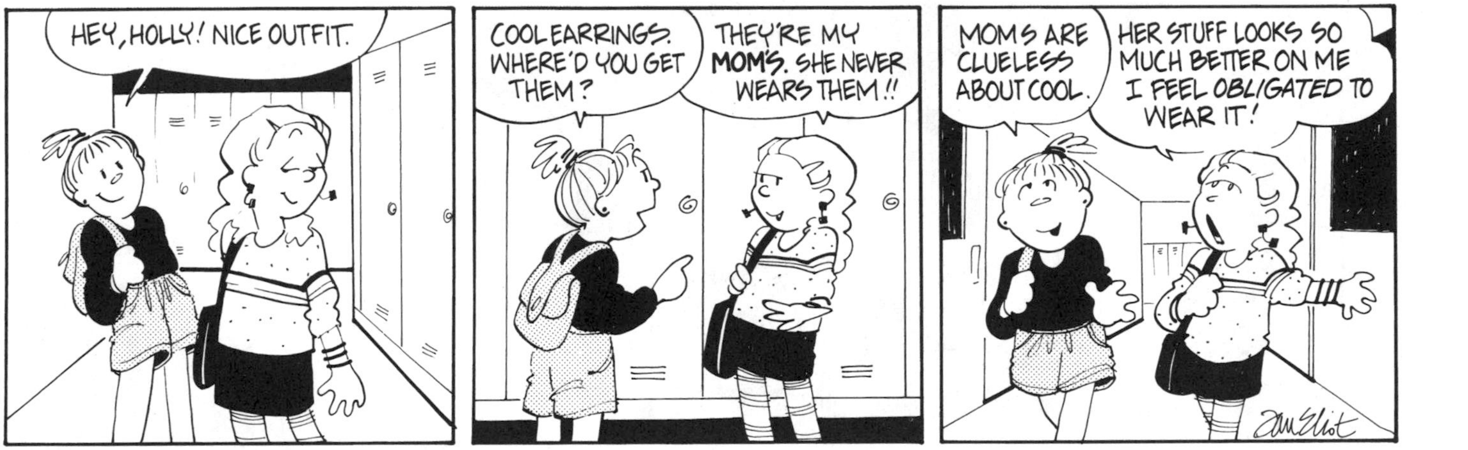
HEY, HOLLY! NICE OUTFIT.
COOL EARRINGS. WHERE'D YOU GET THEM?
THEY'RE MY **MOM'S**. SHE NEVER WEARS THEM!!
MOMS ARE CLUELESS ABOUT COOL.
HER STUFF LOOKS SO MUCH BETTER ON ME I FEEL *OBLIGATED* TO WEAR IT!

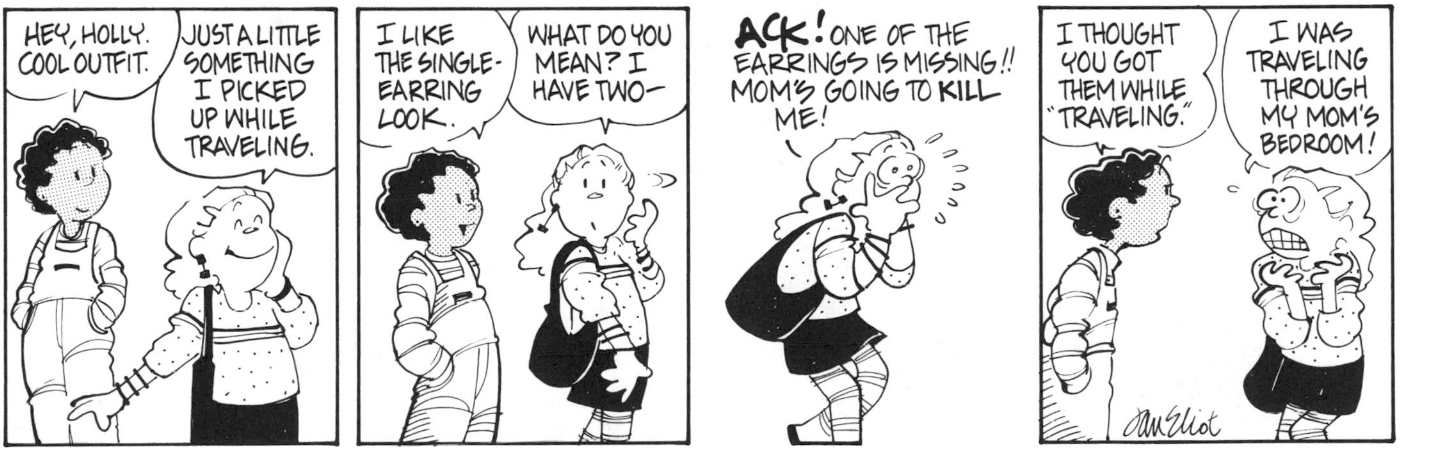
HEY, HOLLY. COOL OUTFIT.
JUST A LITTLE SOMETHING I PICKED UP WHILE TRAVELING.
I LIKE THE SINGLE-EARRING LOOK.
WHAT DO YOU MEAN? I HAVE TWO—
ACK! ONE OF THE EARRINGS IS MISSING!! MOM'S GOING TO **KILL** ME!
I THOUGHT YOU GOT THEM WHILE "TRAVELING."
I WAS TRAVELING THROUGH MY MOM'S BEDROOM!

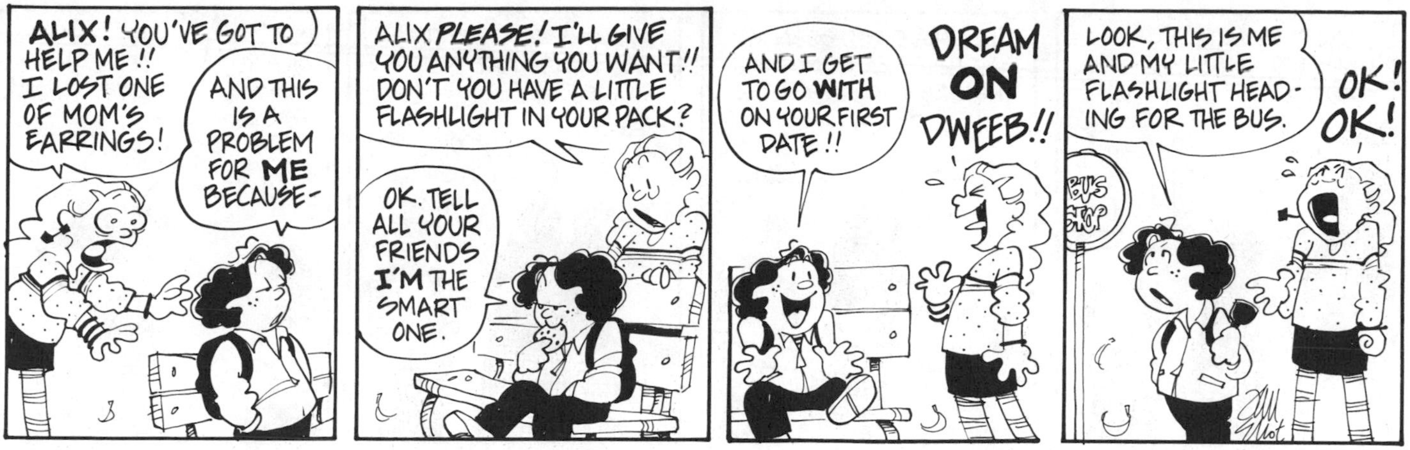
ALIX! YOU'VE GOT TO HELP ME!! I LOST ONE OF MOM'S EARRINGS!
AND THIS IS A PROBLEM FOR ME BECAUSE-
ALIX PLEASE! I'LL GIVE YOU ANYTHING YOU WANT!! DON'T YOU HAVE A LITTLE FLASHLIGHT IN YOUR PACK?
OK. TELL ALL YOUR FRIENDS I'M THE SMART ONE.
AND I GET TO GO WITH ON YOUR FIRST DATE!!
DREAM ON DWEEB!!
LOOK, THIS IS ME AND MY LITTLE FLASHLIGHT HEADING FOR THE BUS.
OK! OK!
BUS STOP

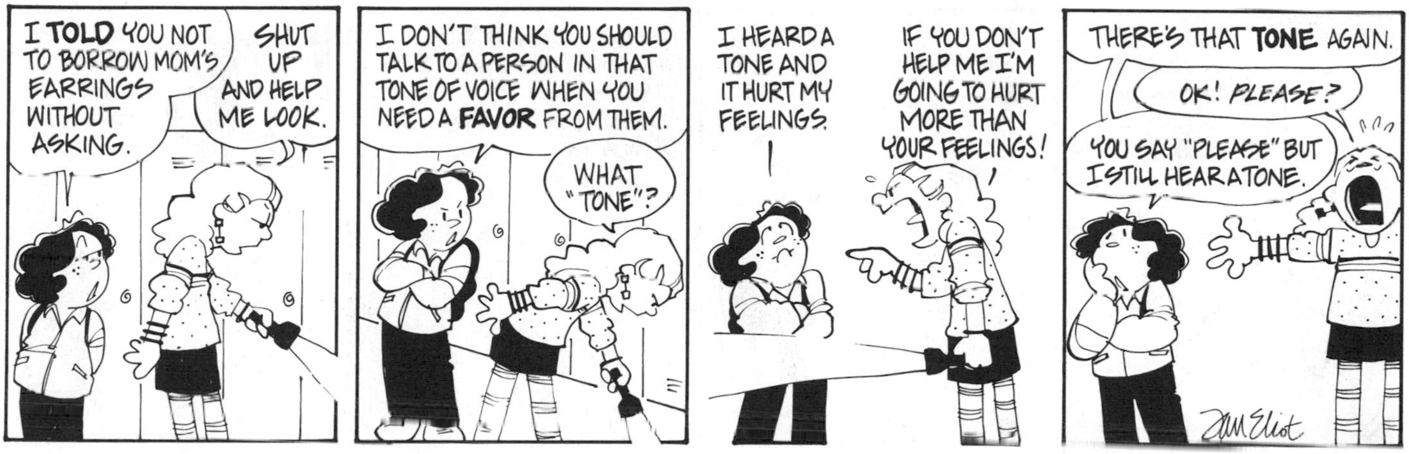
I TOLD YOU NOT TO BORROW MOM'S EARRINGS WITHOUT ASKING.
SHUT UP AND HELP ME LOOK.
I DON'T THINK YOU SHOULD TALK TO A PERSON IN THAT TONE OF VOICE WHEN YOU NEED A FAVOR FROM THEM.
WHAT "TONE"?
I HEARD A TONE AND IT HURT MY FEELINGS.
IF YOU DON'T HELP ME I'M GOING TO HURT MORE THAN YOUR FEELINGS!
THERE'S THAT TONE AGAIN.
OK! PLEASE?
YOU SAY "PLEASE" BUT I STILL HEAR A TONE.

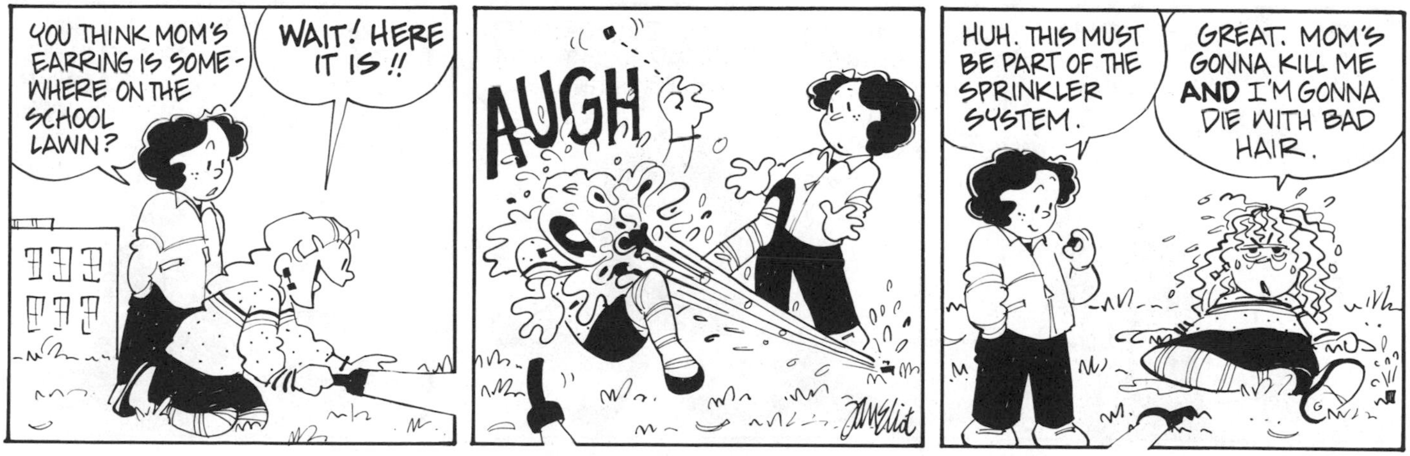
YOU THINK MOM'S EARRING IS SOMEWHERE ON THE SCHOOL LAWN?
WAIT! HERE IT IS!!
AUGH
HUH. THIS MUST BE PART OF THE SPRINKLER SYSTEM.
GREAT. MOM'S GONNA KILL ME AND I'M GONNA DIE WITH BAD HAIR.

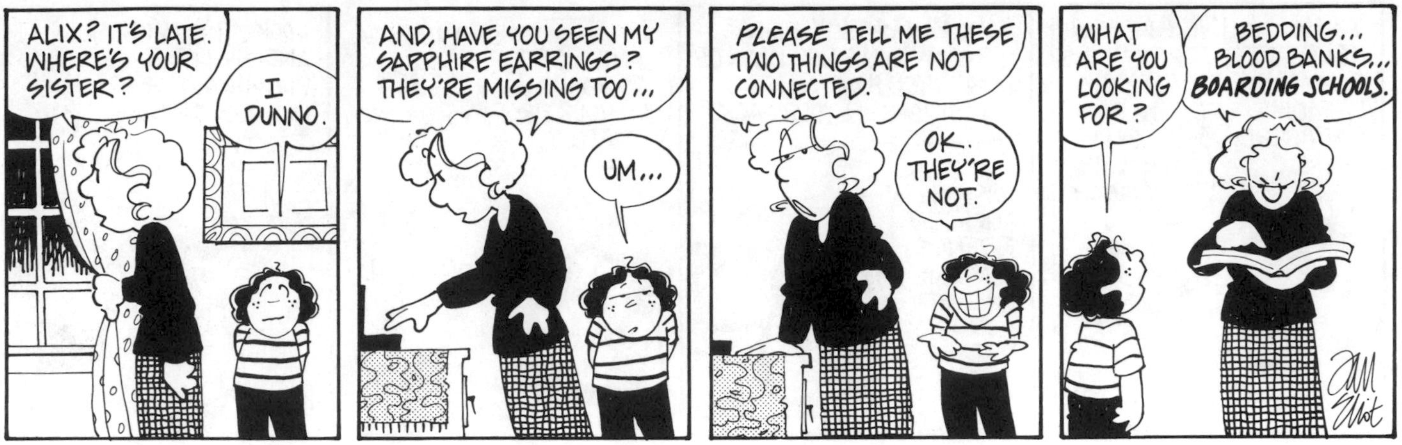
ALIX? IT'S LATE. WHERE'S YOUR SISTER?
I DUNNO.
AND, HAVE YOU SEEN MY SAPPHIRE EARRINGS? THEY'RE MISSING TOO...
UM...
PLEASE TELL ME THESE TWO THINGS ARE NOT CONNECTED.
OK. THEY'RE NOT.
WHAT ARE YOU LOOKING FOR?
BEDDING... BLOOD BANKS... BOARDING SCHOOLS.

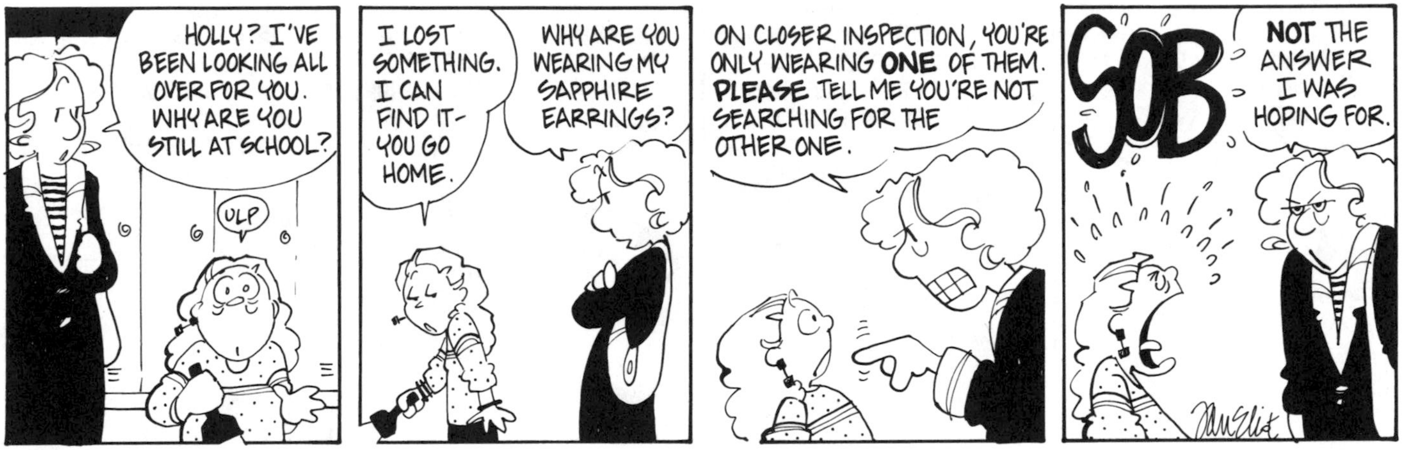
HOLLY? I'VE BEEN LOOKING ALL OVER FOR YOU. WHY ARE YOU STILL AT SCHOOL?
ULP
I LOST SOMETHING. I CAN FIND IT- YOU GO HOME.
WHY ARE YOU WEARING MY SAPPHIRE EARRINGS?
ON CLOSER INSPECTION, YOU'RE ONLY WEARING ONE OF THEM. PLEASE TELL ME YOU'RE NOT SEARCHING FOR THE OTHER ONE.
SOB
NOT THE ANSWER I WAS HOPING FOR.

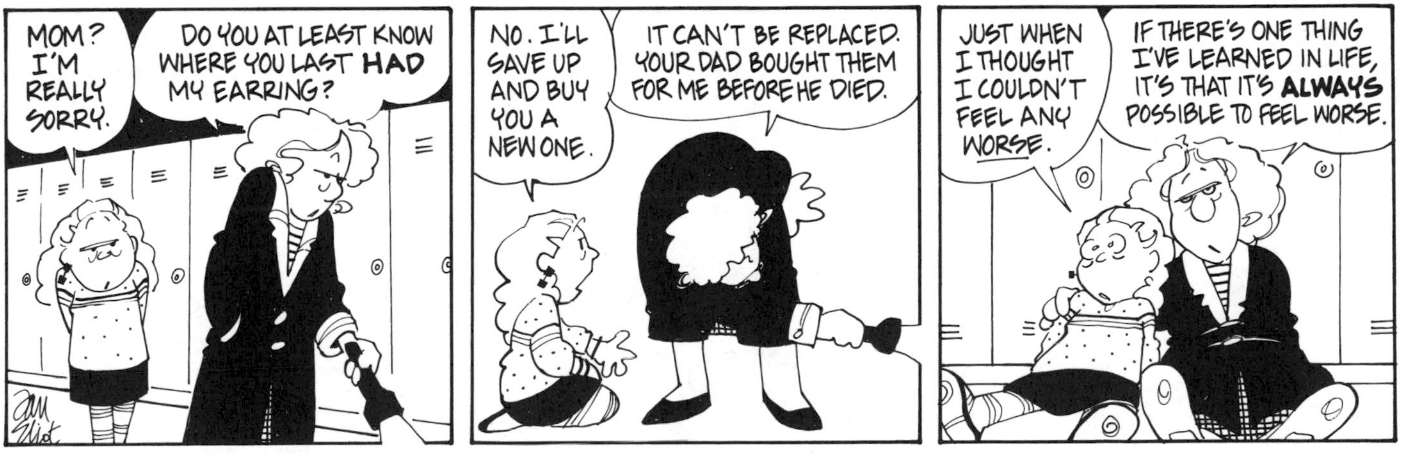
MOM? I'M REALLY SORRY.
DO YOU AT LEAST KNOW WHERE YOU LAST HAD MY EARRING?
NO. I'LL SAVE UP AND BUY YOU A NEW ONE.
IT CAN'T BE REPLACED. YOUR DAD BOUGHT THEM FOR ME BEFORE HE DIED.
JUST WHEN I THOUGHT I COULDN'T FEEL ANY WORSE.
IF THERE'S ONE THING I'VE LEARNED IN LIFE, IT'S THAT IT'S ALWAYS POSSIBLE TO FEEL WORSE.

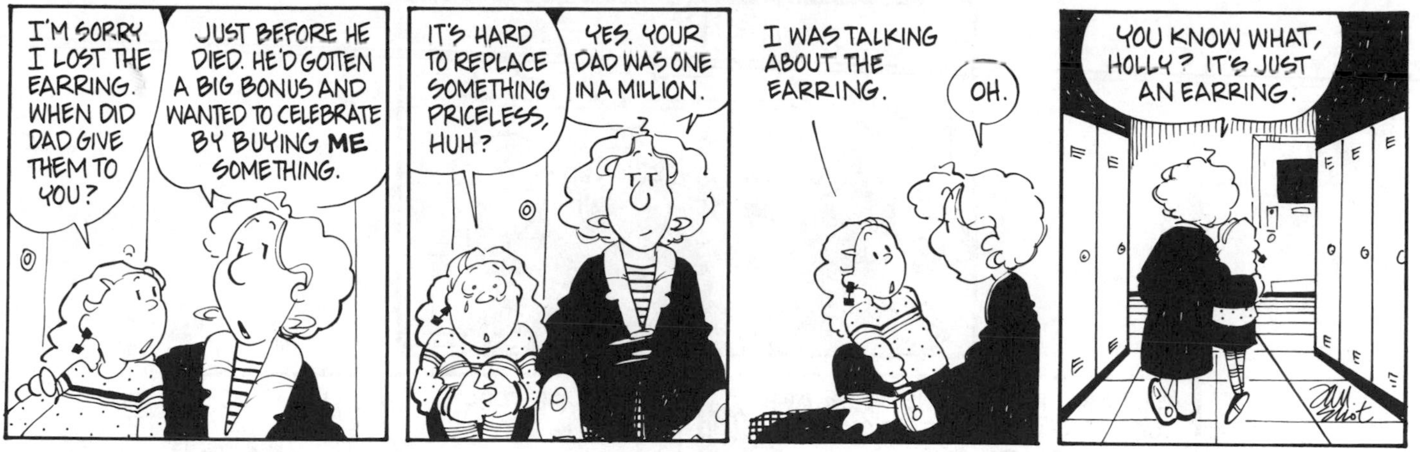
I'M SORRY I LOST THE EARRING. WHEN DID DAD GIVE THEM TO YOU?
JUST BEFORE HE DIED. HE'D GOTTEN A BIG BONUS AND WANTED TO CELEBRATE BY BUYING **ME** SOMETHING.
IT'S HARD TO REPLACE SOMETHING PRICELESS, HUH?
YES. YOUR DAD WAS ONE IN A MILLION.
I WAS TALKING ABOUT THE EARRING.
OH.
YOU KNOW WHAT, HOLLY? IT'S JUST AN EARRING.

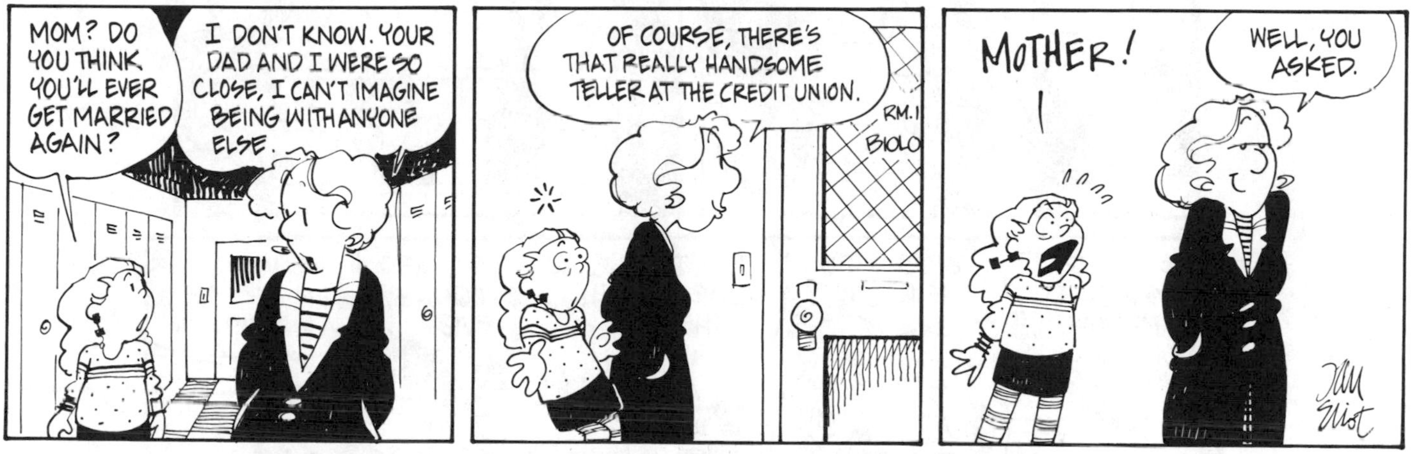
MOM? DO YOU THINK YOU'LL EVER GET MARRIED AGAIN?
I DON'T KNOW. YOUR DAD AND I WERE SO CLOSE, I CAN'T IMAGINE BEING WITH ANYONE ELSE.
OF COURSE, THERE'S THAT REALLY HANDSOME TELLER AT THE CREDIT UNION.
RM. 1
BIOLO
MOTHER!
WELL, YOU ASKED.

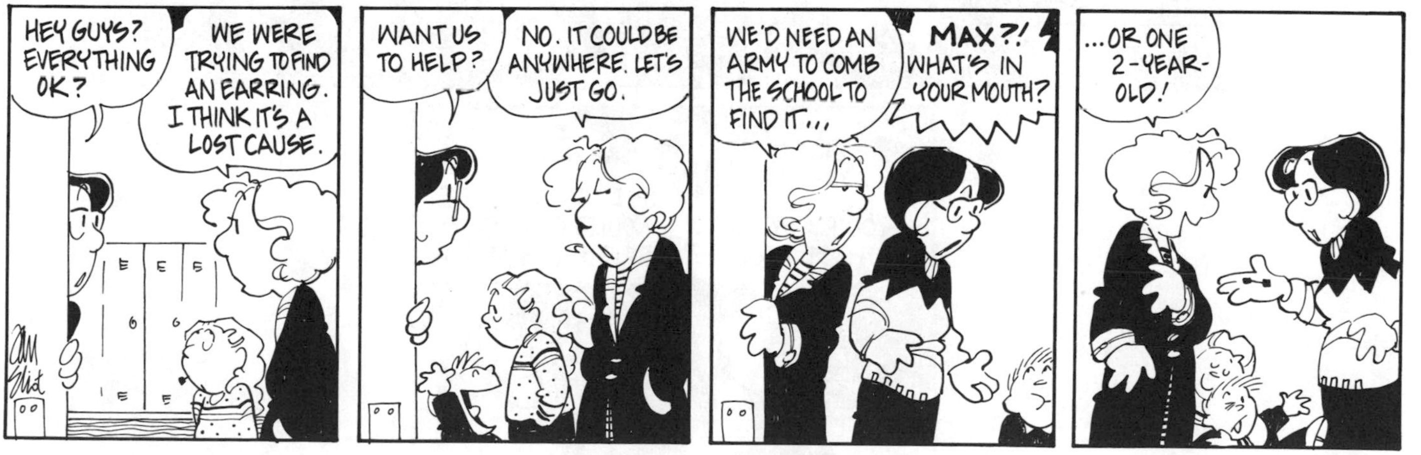
HEY GUYS? EVERYTHING OK?
WE WERE TRYING TO FIND AN EARRING. I THINK IT'S A LOST CAUSE.
WANT US TO HELP?
NO. IT COULD BE ANYWHERE. LET'S JUST GO.
WE'D NEED AN ARMY TO COMB THE SCHOOL TO FIND IT...
MAX?! WHAT'S IN YOUR MOUTH?
...OR ONE 2-YEAR-OLD!

ALIX AND HER KIDDIE PALS ARE SUCH DWEEBS. LET'S GO SIT WITH THE **ADULTS.**

MAYBE THEY'LL BUY US POPCORN.

HEY **REF?!** IT'S A GOOD GAME! WHY DON'T YOU WATCH IT?!

WHO DOES THEIR HAIR?!

THEY'RE AWFULLY **RUDE** TO EACH OTHER.

IT'S CALLED BLOCKING, EVIE.

WE WANT **JEN**-NY! WE WANT **JEN**-NY!

YOU'RE *RELATED* TO THESE PEOPLE?

IF I COULD DRIVE I WOULDN'T HAVE TO RELATE TO THEM AT ALL.

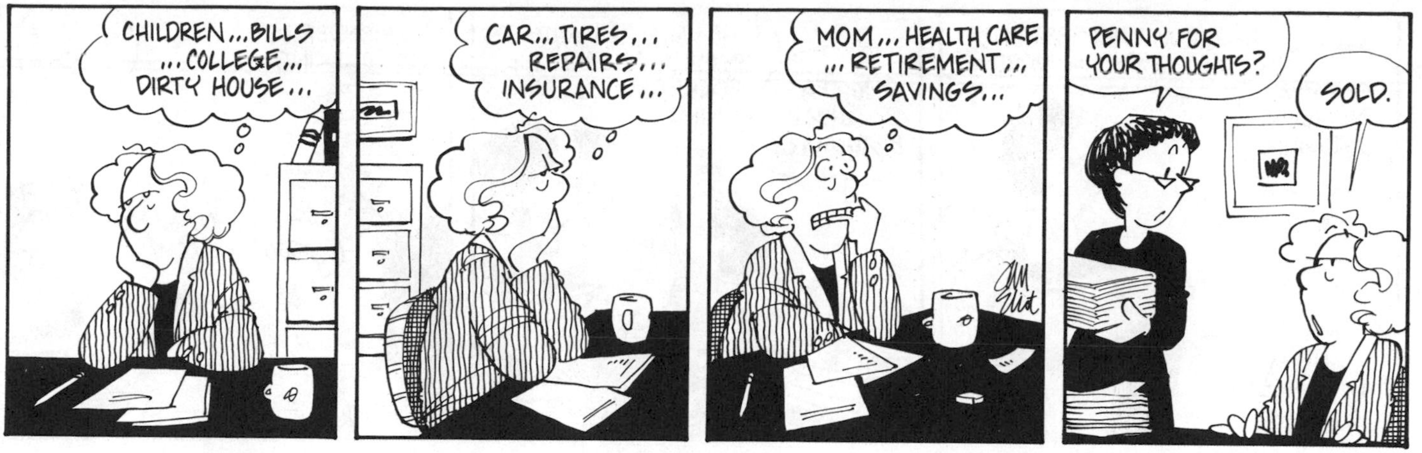
CHILDREN...BILLS ...COLLEGE... DIRTY HOUSE...
CAR... TIRES... REPAIRS... INSURANCE...
MOM... HEALTH CARE ...RETIREMENT... SAVINGS...
PENNY FOR YOUR THOUGHTS?
SOLD.

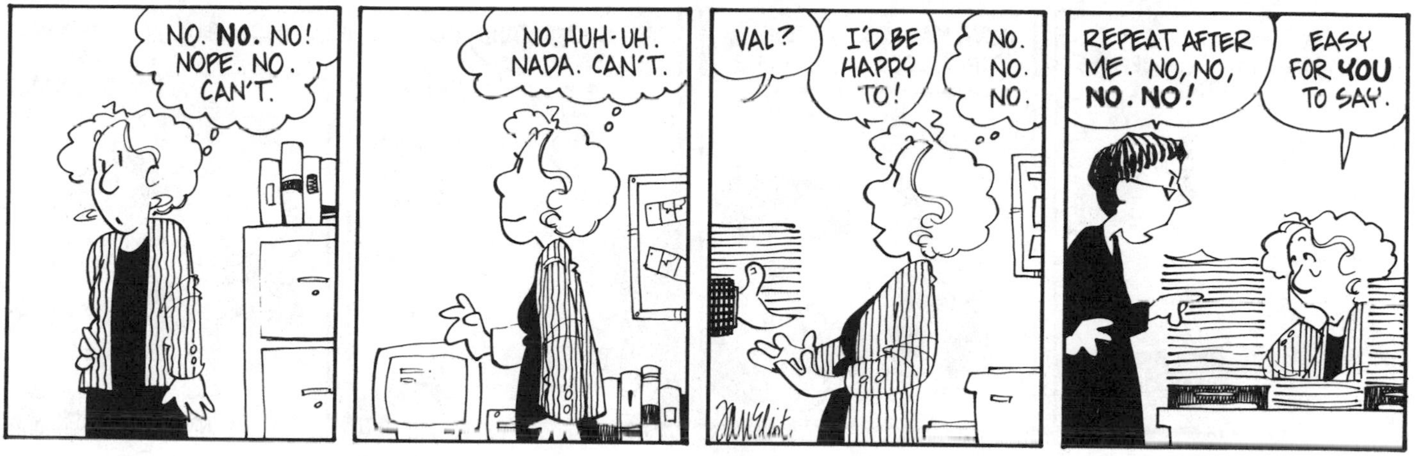
NO. NO. NO! NOPE. NO. CAN'T.
NO. HUH-UH. NADA. CAN'T.
VAL?
I'D BE HAPPY TO!
NO. NO. NO.
REPEAT AFTER ME. NO, NO, NO. NO!
EASY FOR YOU TO SAY.

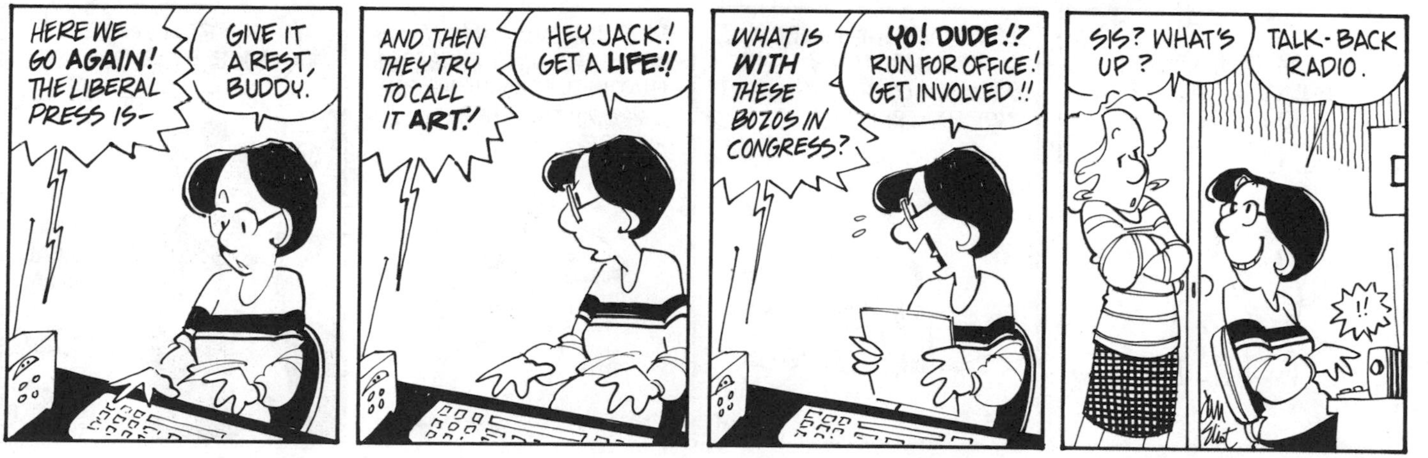
HERE WE GO AGAIN! THE LIBERAL PRESS IS-
GIVE IT A REST, BUDDY.
AND THEN THEY TRY TO CALL IT ART!
HEY JACK! GET A LIFE!!
WHAT IS WITH THESE BOZOS IN CONGRESS?
YO! DUDE!? RUN FOR OFFICE! GET INVOLVED!!
SIS? WHAT'S UP?
TALK-BACK RADIO.
!!

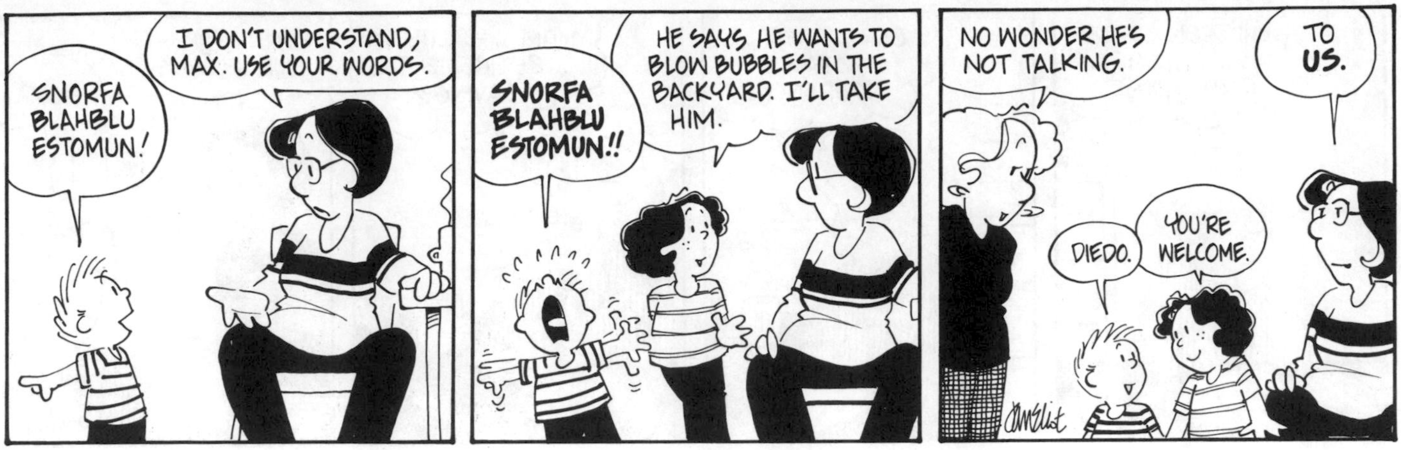
SNORFA BLAHBLU ESTOMUN!
I DON'T UNDERSTAND, MAX. USE YOUR WORDS.
SNORFA BLAHBLU ESTOMUN!!
HE SAYS HE WANTS TO BLOW BUBBLES IN THE BACKYARD. I'LL TAKE HIM.
NO WONDER HE'S NOT TALKING.
TO US.
DIEDO.
YOU'RE WELCOME.

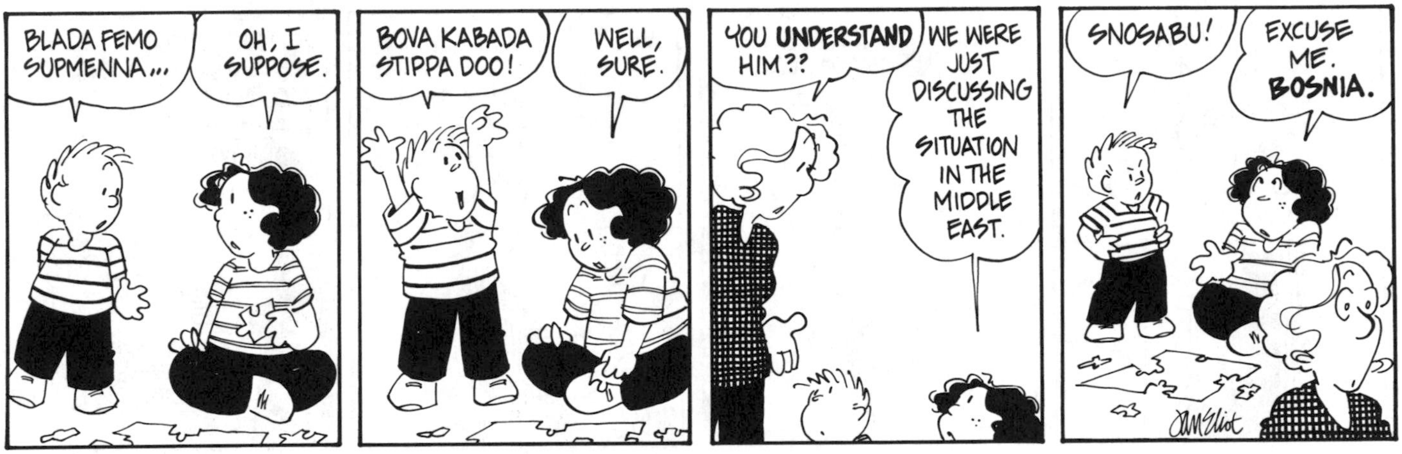
BLADA FEMO SUPMENNA...
OH, I SUPPOSE.
BOVA KABADA STIPPA DOO!
WELL, SURE.
YOU UNDERSTAND HIM??
WE WERE JUST DISCUSSING THE SITUATION IN THE MIDDLE EAST.
SNOSABU!
EXCUSE ME. BOSNIA.

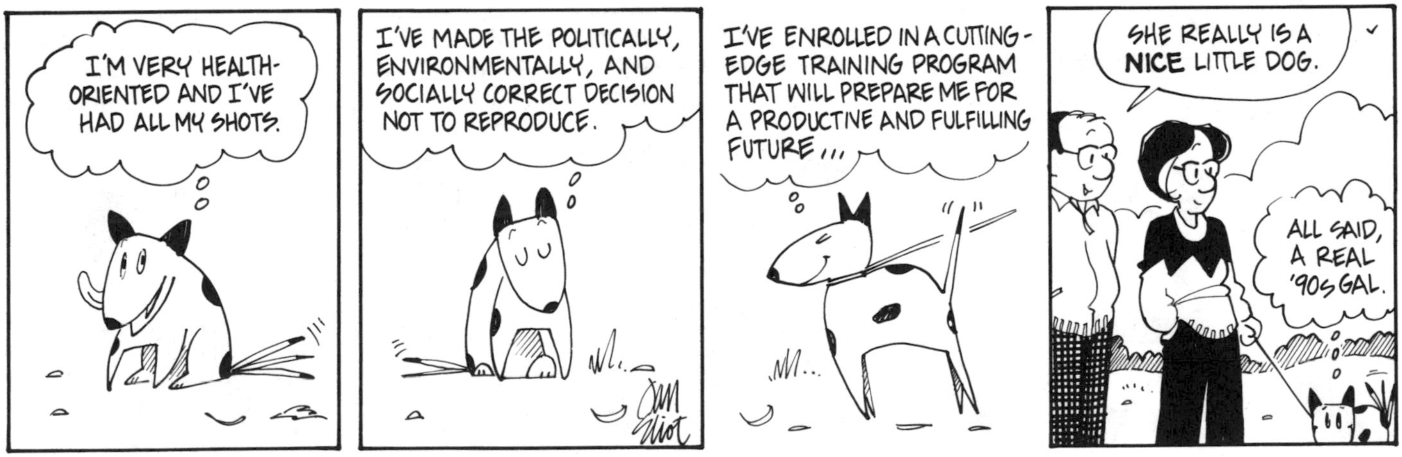
I'M VERY HEALTH-ORIENTED AND I'VE HAD ALL MY SHOTS.
I'VE MADE THE POLITICALLY, ENVIRONMENTALLY, AND SOCIALLY CORRECT DECISION NOT TO REPRODUCE.
I'VE ENROLLED IN A CUTTING-EDGE TRAINING PROGRAM THAT WILL PREPARE ME FOR A PRODUCTIVE AND FULFILLING FUTURE...
SHE REALLY IS A NICE LITTLE DOG.
ALL SAID, A REAL '90s GAL.

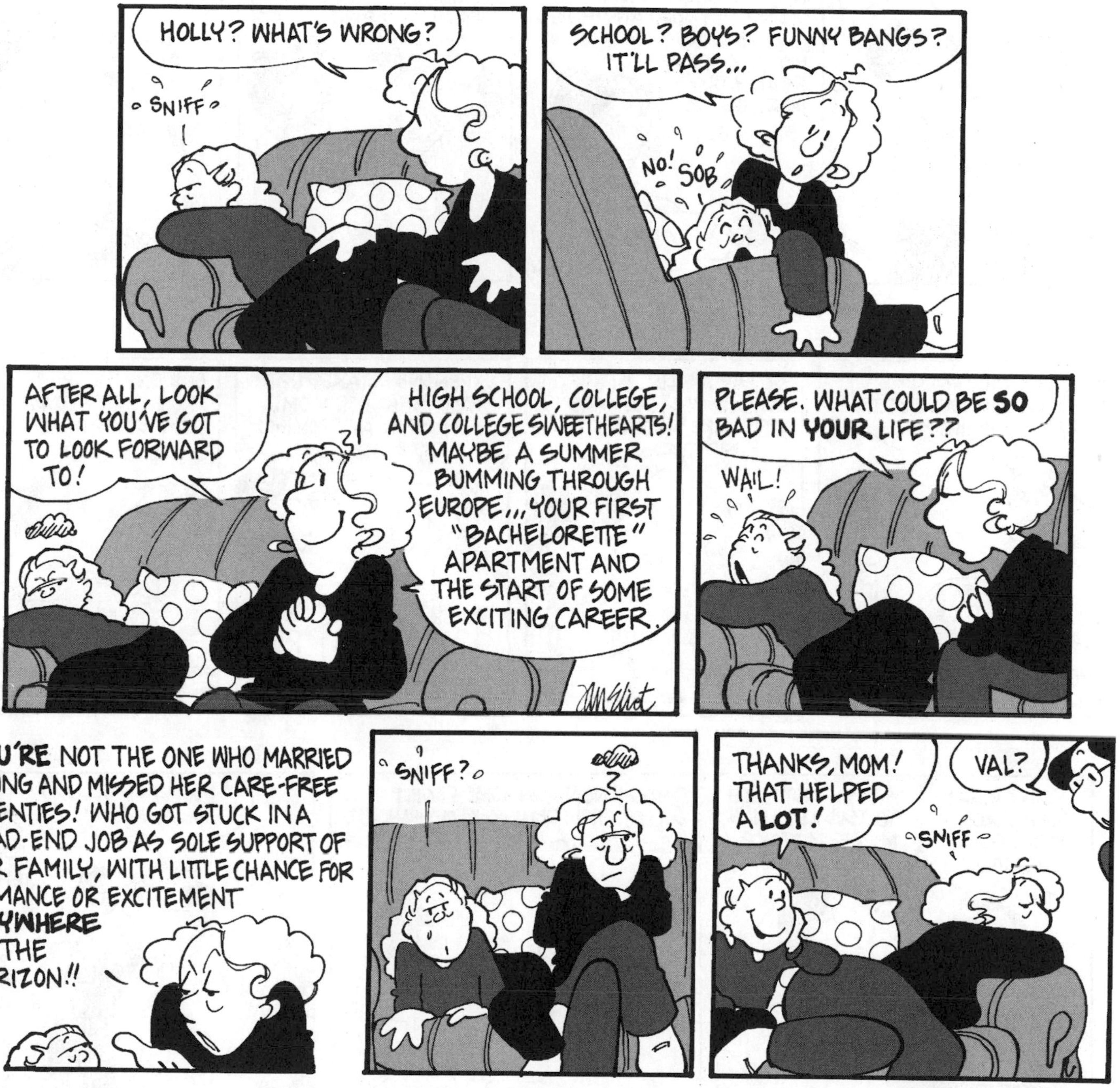
HOLLY? WHAT'S WRONG?
SNIFF
SCHOOL? BOYS? FUNNY BANGS? IT'LL PASS...
NO! SOB
AFTER ALL, LOOK WHAT YOU'VE GOT TO LOOK FORWARD TO!
HIGH SCHOOL, COLLEGE, AND COLLEGE SWEETHEARTS! MAYBE A SUMMER BUMMING THROUGH EUROPE... YOUR FIRST "BACHELORETTE" APARTMENT AND THE START OF SOME EXCITING CAREER.
PLEASE. WHAT COULD BE **SO** BAD IN **YOUR** LIFE??
WAIL!
YOU'RE NOT THE ONE WHO MARRIED YOUNG AND MISSED HER CARE-FREE TWENTIES! WHO GOT STUCK IN A DEAD-END JOB AS SOLE SUPPORT OF HER FAMILY, WITH LITTLE CHANCE FOR ROMANCE OR EXCITEMENT **ANYWHERE** ON THE HORIZON!!
SNIFF?
THANKS, MOM! THAT HELPED A **LOT**!
VAL?
SNIFF

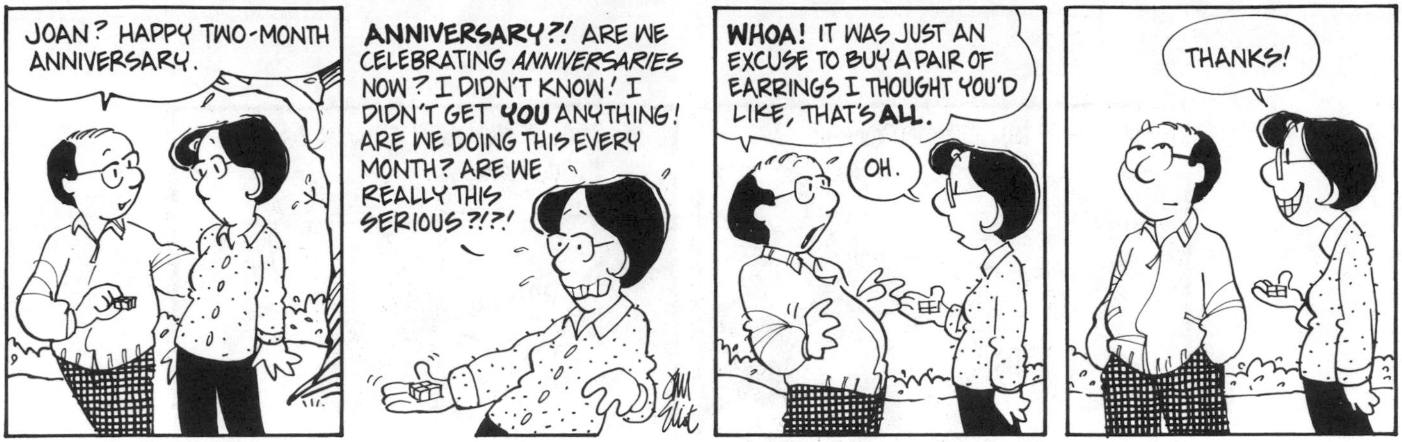
JOAN? HAPPY TWO-MONTH ANNIVERSARY.
ANNIVERSARY?! ARE WE CELEBRATING ANNIVERSARIES NOW? I DIDN'T KNOW! I DIDN'T GET YOU ANYTHING! ARE WE DOING THIS EVERY MONTH? ARE WE REALLY THIS SERIOUS?!?!
WHOA! IT WAS JUST AN EXCUSE TO BUY A PAIR OF EARRINGS I THOUGHT YOU'D LIKE, THAT'S ALL.
OH.
THANKS!

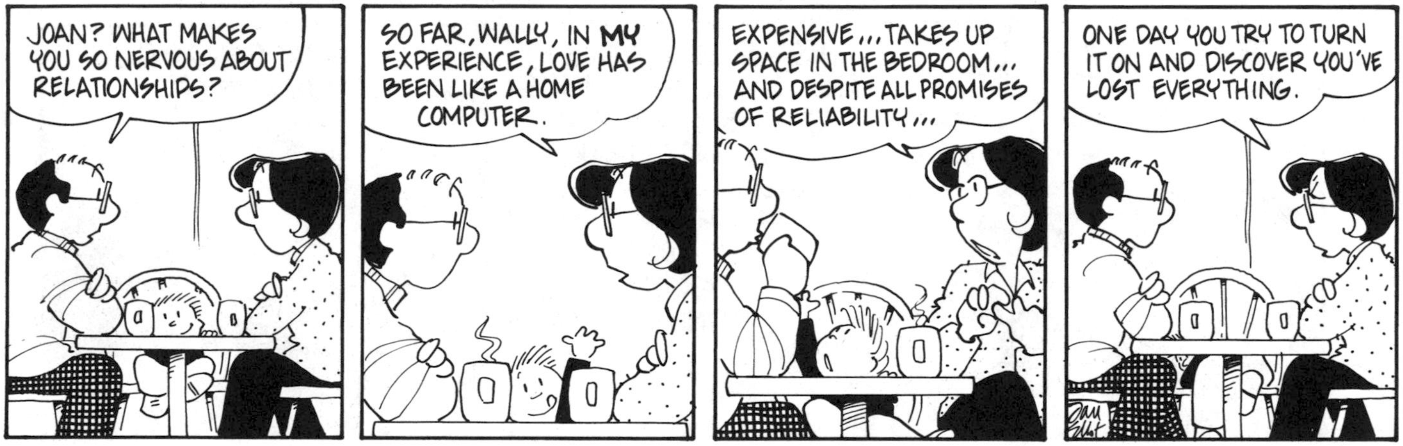
JOAN? WHAT MAKES YOU SO NERVOUS ABOUT RELATIONSHIPS?
SO FAR, WALLY, IN MY EXPERIENCE, LOVE HAS BEEN LIKE A HOME COMPUTER.
EXPENSIVE... TAKES UP SPACE IN THE BEDROOM... AND DESPITE ALL PROMISES OF RELIABILITY...
ONE DAY YOU TRY TO TURN IT ON AND DISCOVER YOU'VE LOST EVERYTHING.

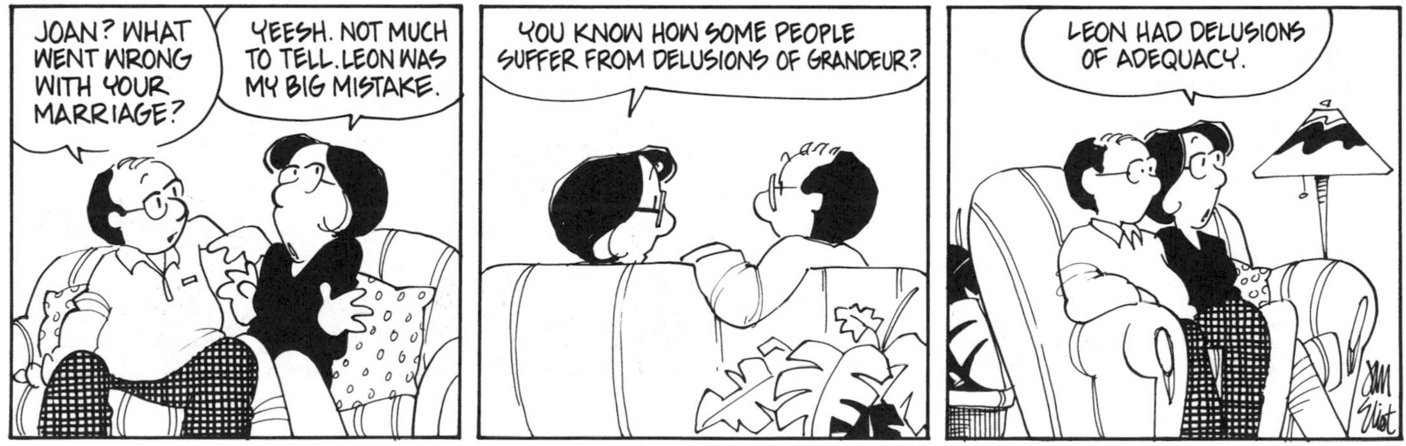
JOAN? WHAT WENT WRONG WITH YOUR MARRIAGE?
YEESH. NOT MUCH TO TELL. LEON WAS MY BIG MISTAKE.
YOU KNOW HOW SOME PEOPLE SUFFER FROM DELUSIONS OF GRANDEUR?
LEON HAD DELUSIONS OF ADEQUACY.

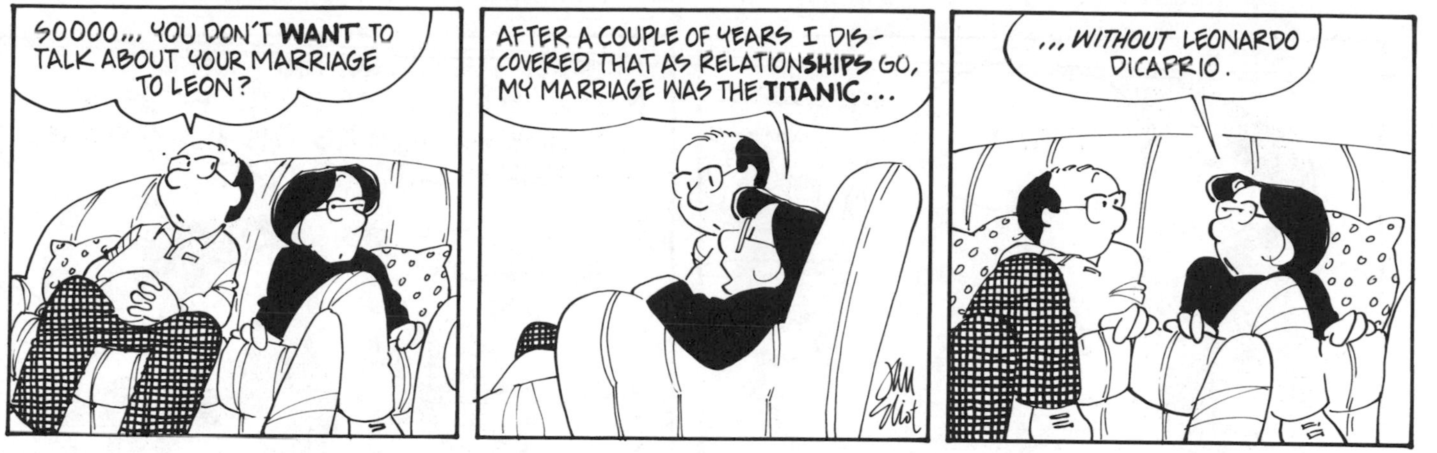
SOOOO... YOU DON'T WANT TO TALK ABOUT YOUR MARRIAGE TO LEON?
AFTER A COUPLE OF YEARS I DIS-COVERED THAT AS RELATIONSHIPS GO, MY MARRIAGE WAS THE TITANIC...
...WITHOUT LEONARDO DiCAPRIO.

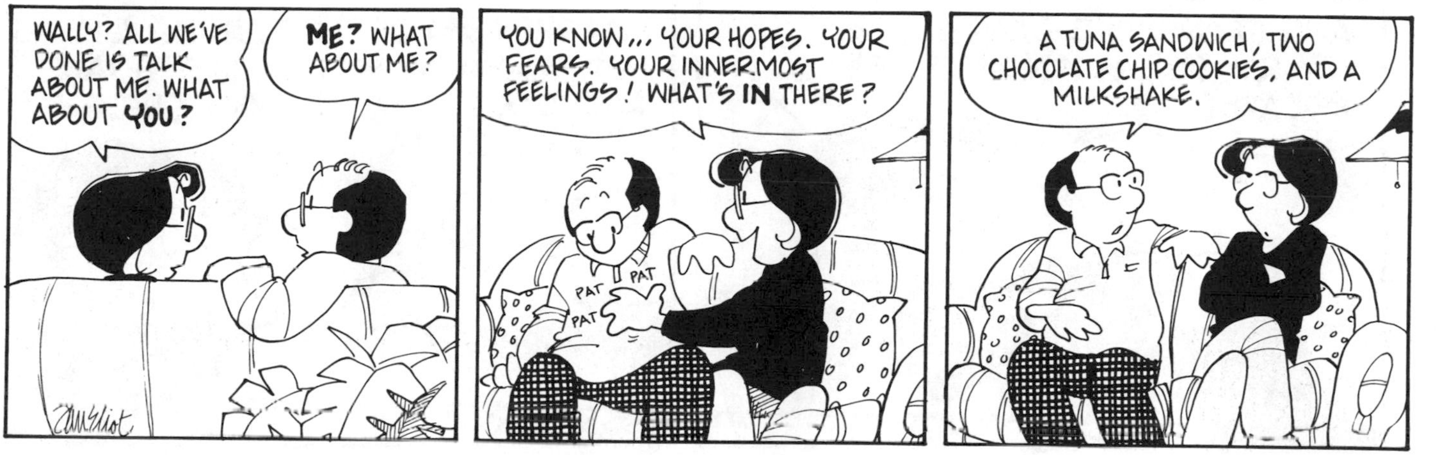
WALLY? ALL WE'VE DONE IS TALK ABOUT ME. WHAT ABOUT YOU?
ME? WHAT ABOUT ME?
YOU KNOW... YOUR HOPES. YOUR FEARS. YOUR INNERMOST FEELINGS! WHAT'S IN THERE?
PAT PAT PAT PAT
A TUNA SANDWICH, TWO CHOCOLATE CHIP COOKIES, AND A MILKSHAKE.

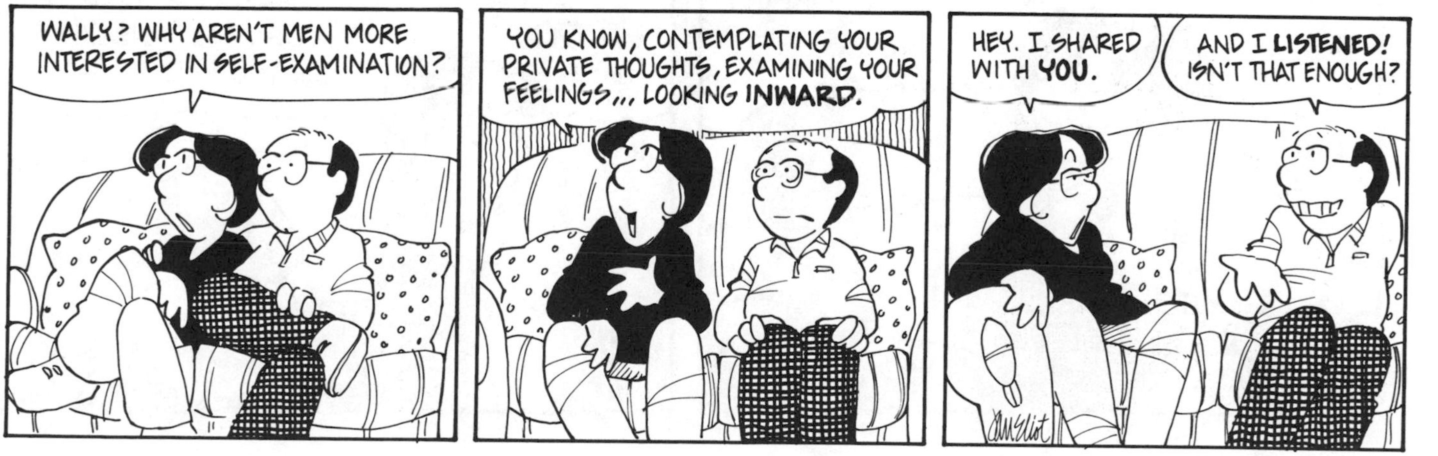
WALLY? WHY AREN'T MEN MORE INTERESTED IN SELF-EXAMINATION?
YOU KNOW, CONTEMPLATING YOUR PRIVATE THOUGHTS, EXAMINING YOUR FEELINGS... LOOKING INWARD.
HEY. I SHARED WITH YOU.
AND I LISTENED! ISN'T THAT ENOUGH?

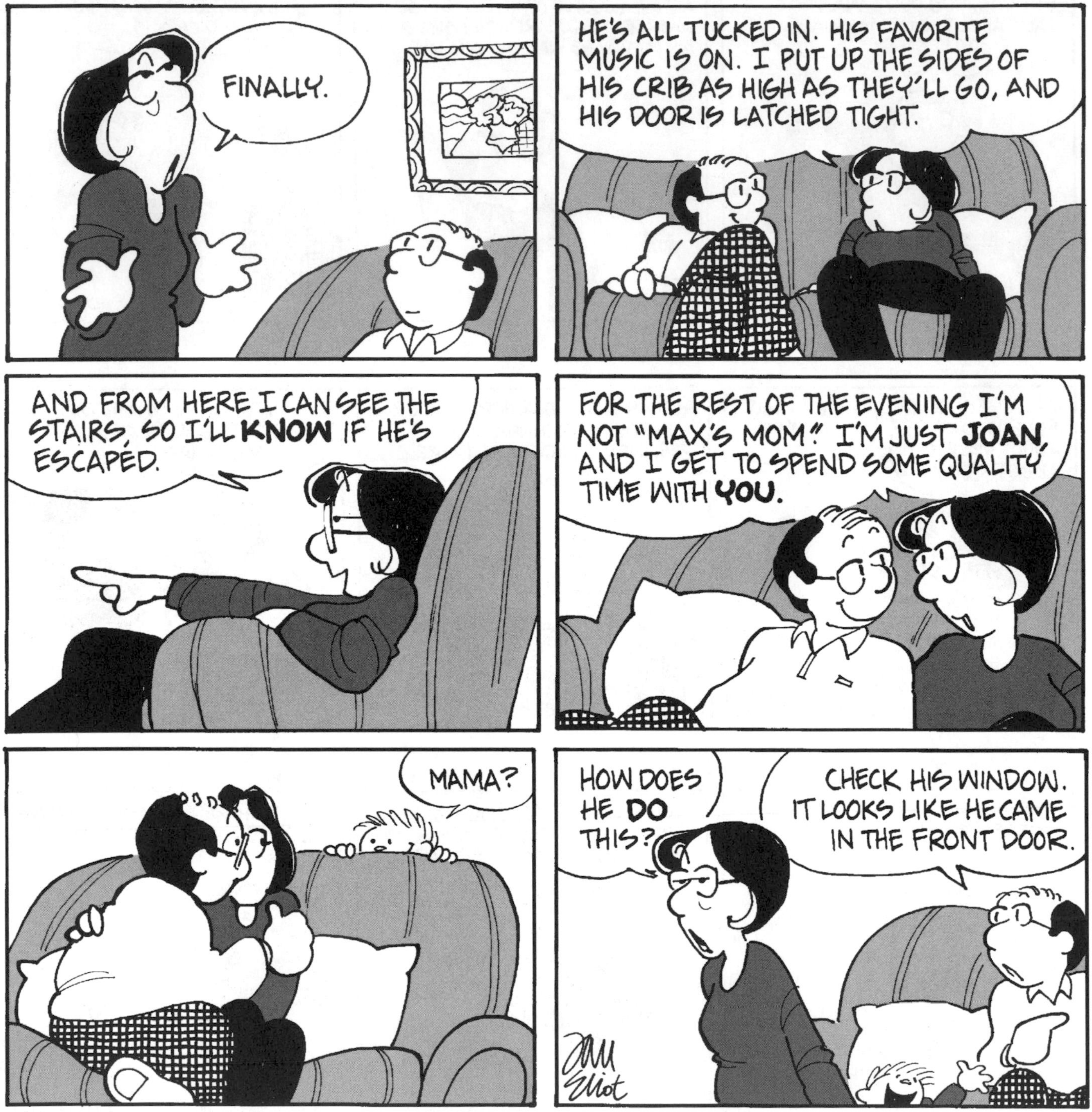
FINALLY.
HE'S ALL TUCKED IN. HIS FAVORITE MUSIC IS ON. I PUT UP THE SIDES OF HIS CRIB AS HIGH AS THEY'LL GO, AND HIS DOOR IS LATCHED TIGHT.
AND FROM HERE I CAN SEE THE STAIRS, SO I'LL **KNOW** IF HE'S ESCAPED.
FOR THE REST OF THE EVENING I'M NOT "MAX'S MOM." I'M JUST **JOAN**, AND I GET TO SPEND SOME QUALITY TIME WITH **YOU**.
MAMA?
HOW DOES HE **DO** THIS?
CHECK HIS WINDOW. IT LOOKS LIKE HE CAME IN THE FRONT DOOR.
JAN Eliot

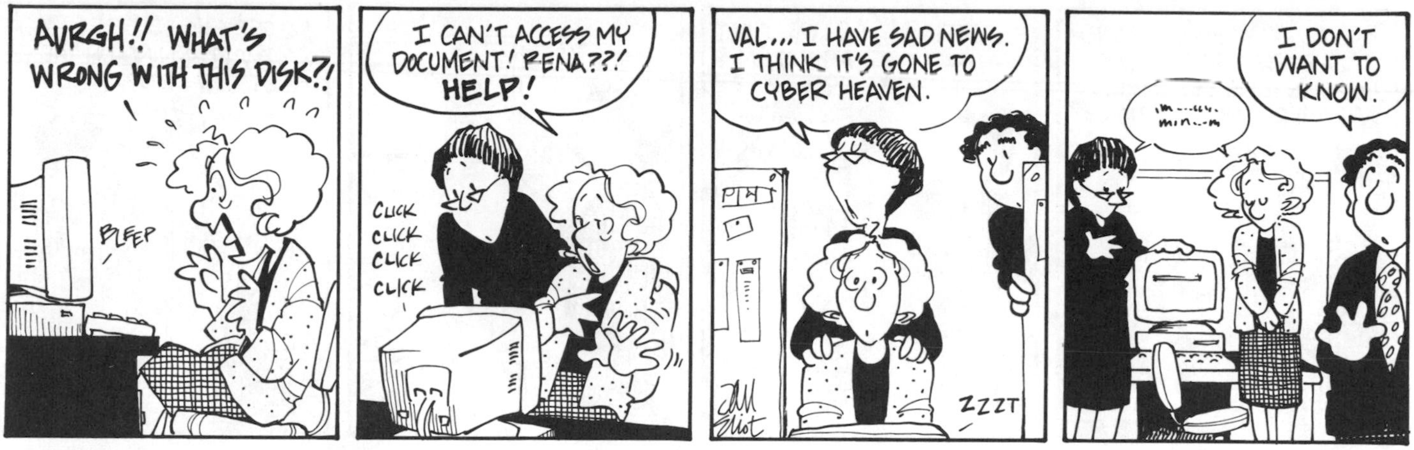
AVRGH!! WHAT'S WRONG WITH THIS DISK?!
BLEEP
I CAN'T ACCESS MY DOCUMENT! RENA??! HELP!
CLICK CLICK CLICK CLICK
VAL... I HAVE SAD NEWS. I THINK IT'S GONE TO CYBER HEAVEN.
ZZZT
I DON'T WANT TO KNOW.

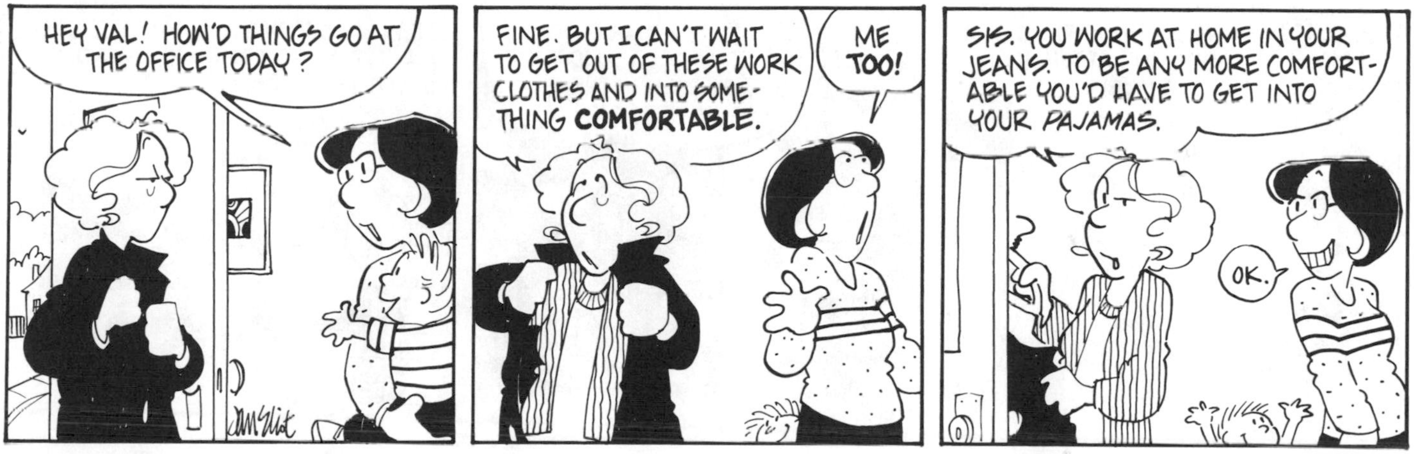
HEY VAL! HOW'D THINGS GO AT THE OFFICE TODAY?
FINE. BUT I CAN'T WAIT TO GET OUT OF THESE WORK CLOTHES AND INTO SOMETHING COMFORTABLE.
ME TOO!
SIS. YOU WORK AT HOME IN YOUR JEANS. TO BE ANY MORE COMFORTABLE YOU'D HAVE TO GET INTO YOUR PAJAMAS.
OK.

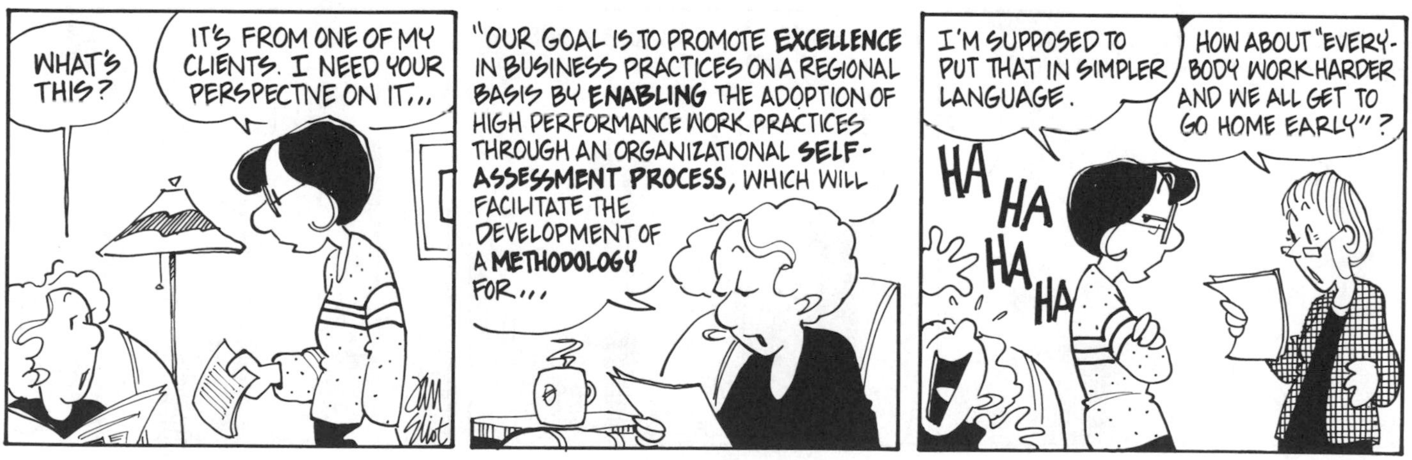
WHAT'S THIS?
IT'S FROM ONE OF MY CLIENTS. I NEED YOUR PERSPECTIVE ON IT...
"OUR GOAL IS TO PROMOTE EXCELLENCE IN BUSINESS PRACTICES ON A REGIONAL BASIS BY ENABLING THE ADOPTION OF HIGH PERFORMANCE WORK PRACTICES THROUGH AN ORGANIZATIONAL SELF-ASSESSMENT PROCESS, WHICH WILL FACILITATE THE DEVELOPMENT OF A METHODOLOGY FOR...
I'M SUPPOSED TO PUT THAT IN SIMPLER LANGUAGE.
HOW ABOUT "EVERYBODY WORK HARDER AND WE ALL GET TO GO HOME EARLY"?
HA HA HA HA

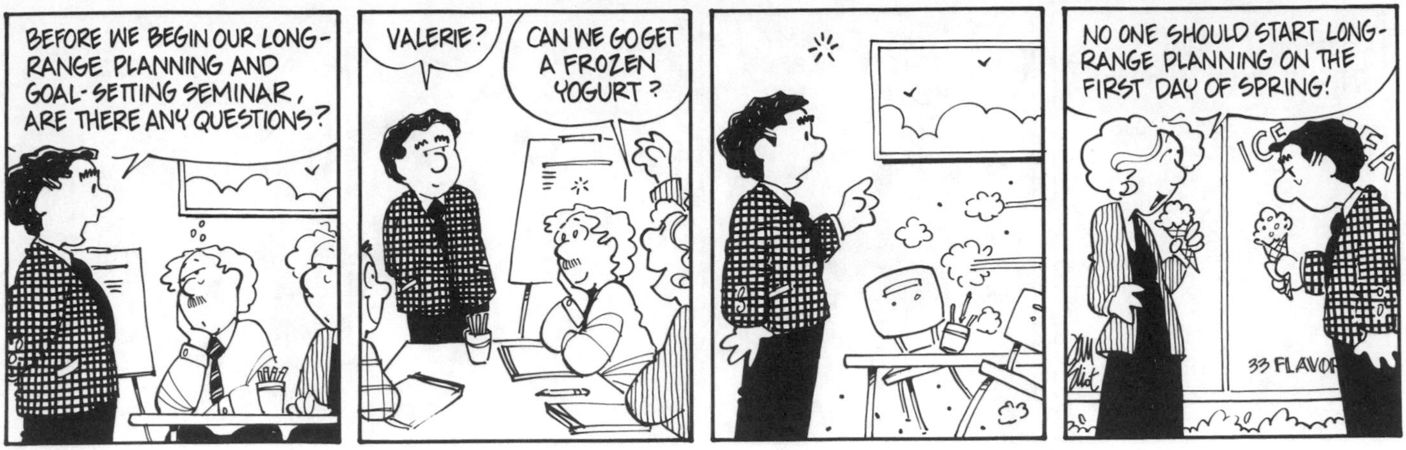
BEFORE WE BEGIN OUR LONG-RANGE PLANNING AND GOAL-SETTING SEMINAR, ARE THERE ANY QUESTIONS?
VALERIE?
CAN WE GO GET A FROZEN YOGURT?
NO ONE SHOULD START LONG-RANGE PLANNING ON THE FIRST DAY OF SPRING!

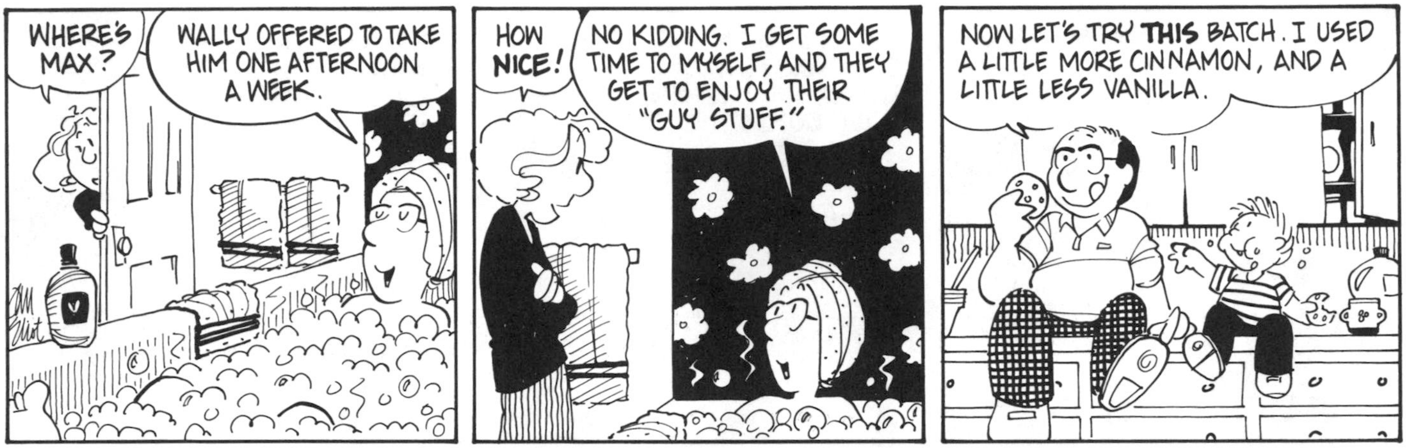
WHERE'S MAX?
WALLY OFFERED TO TAKE HIM ONE AFTERNOON A WEEK.
HOW **NICE**!
NO KIDDING. I GET SOME TIME TO MYSELF, AND THEY GET TO ENJOY THEIR "GUY STUFF."
NOW LET'S TRY **THIS** BATCH. I USED A LITTLE MORE CINNAMON, AND A LITTLE LESS VANILLA.

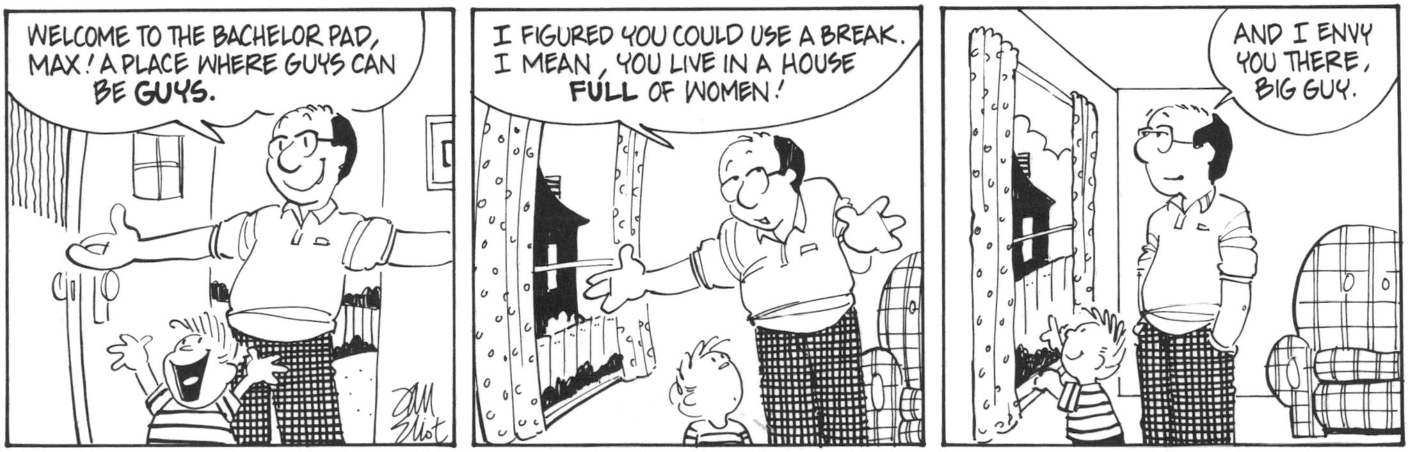
WELCOME TO THE BACHELOR PAD, MAX! A PLACE WHERE GUYS CAN BE **GUYS**.
I FIGURED YOU COULD USE A BREAK. I MEAN, YOU LIVE IN A HOUSE **FULL** OF WOMEN!
AND I ENVY YOU THERE, BIG GUY.

WHIMPER
WHIMPER
WHIMPER
FORGET IT.
EVERY DAY YOU WANT YOUR DINNER EARLIER. IT'S ONLY FOUR O'CLOCK.
BLAH
BLAH
BLAH
I WILL NOT HAVE A DOG WHO BEGS.
YOU'RE FIXING DINNER AT 4:15?
FOR SOME REASON I'M TOTALLY STARVED. FEED THE DOG, WILL YOU?
YIP!

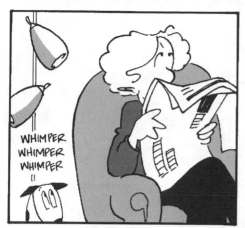

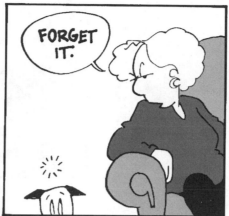

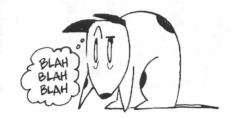

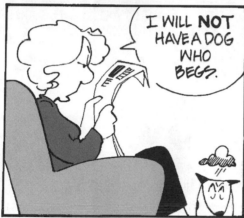

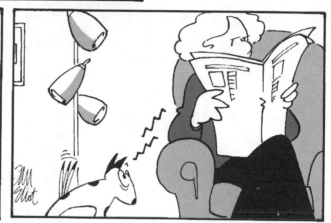

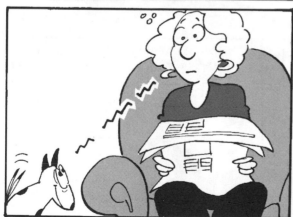

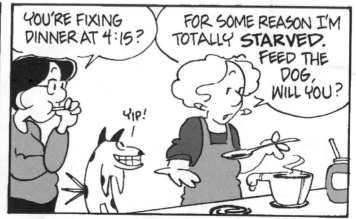

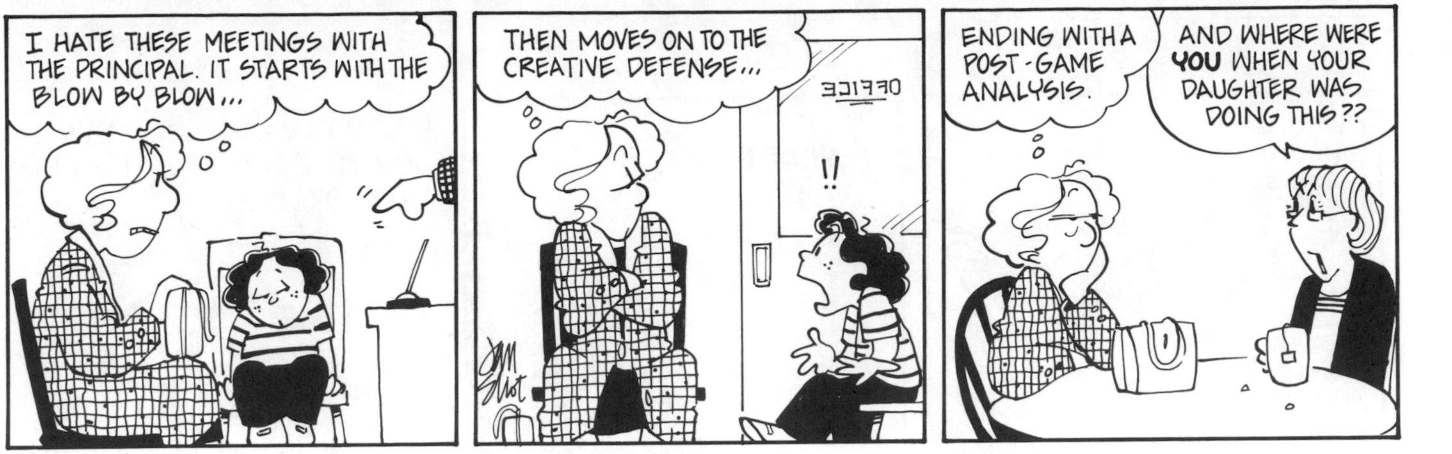
I HATE THESE MEETINGS WITH THE PRINCIPAL. IT STARTS WITH THE BLOW BY BLOW...
THEN MOVES ON TO THE CREATIVE DEFENSE...
!!
ENDING WITH A POST-GAME ANALYSIS.
AND WHERE WERE **YOU** WHEN YOUR DAUGHTER WAS DOING THIS??

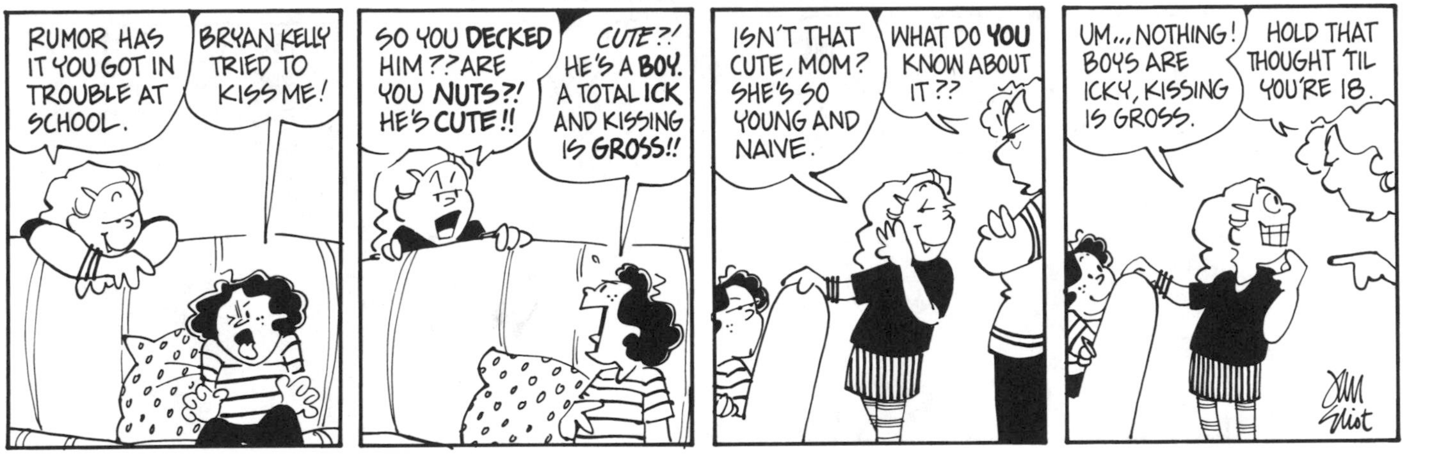
RUMOR HAS IT YOU GOT IN TROUBLE AT SCHOOL.
BRYAN KELLY TRIED TO KISS ME!
SO YOU **DECKED** HIM??ARE YOU **NUTS?!** HE'S **CUTE!!**
CUTE?! HE'S A **BOY.** A TOTAL **ICK** AND KISSING IS **GROSS!!**
ISN'T THAT CUTE, MOM? SHE'S SO YOUNG AND NAIVE.
WHAT DO **YOU** KNOW ABOUT IT??
UM... NOTHING! BOYS ARE ICKY, KISSING IS GROSS.
HOLD THAT THOUGHT 'TIL YOU'RE 18.

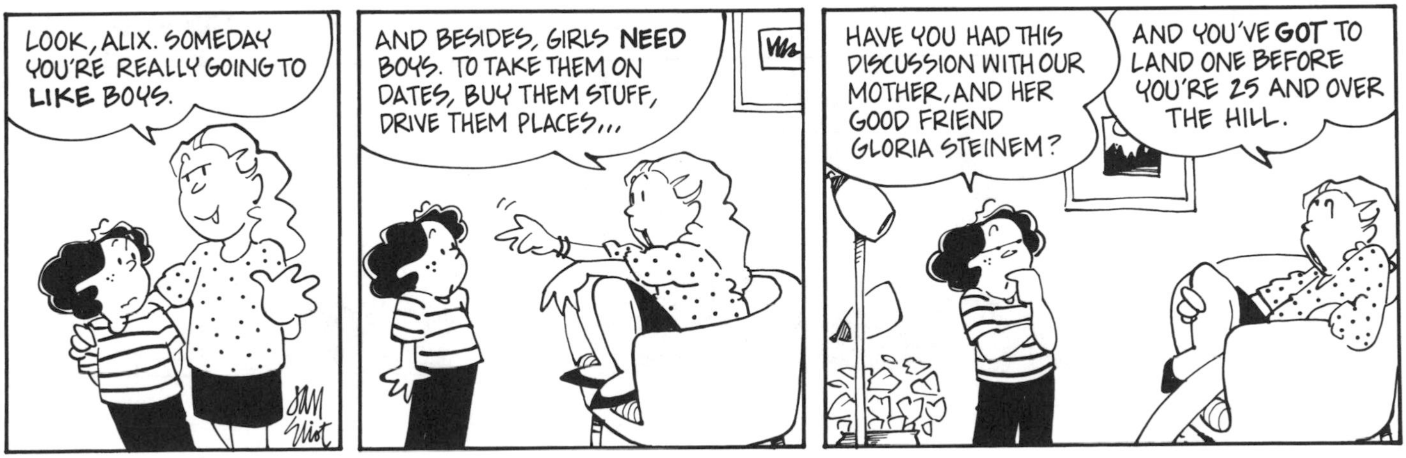
LOOK, ALIX. SOMEDAY YOU'RE REALLY GOING TO **LIKE** BOYS.
AND BESIDES, GIRLS **NEED** BOYS. TO TAKE THEM ON DATES, BUY THEM STUFF, DRIVE THEM PLACES...
HAVE YOU HAD THIS DISCUSSION WITH OUR MOTHER, AND HER GOOD FRIEND GLORIA STEINEM?
AND YOU'VE **GOT** TO LAND ONE BEFORE YOU'RE 25 AND OVER THE HILL.

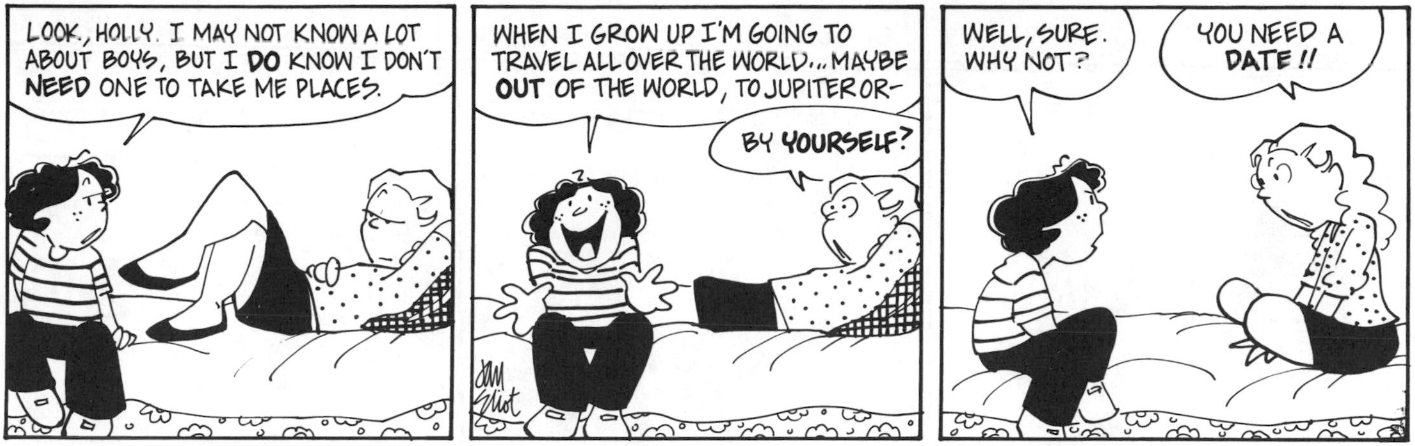
LOOK, HOLLY. I MAY NOT KNOW A LOT ABOUT BOYS, BUT I **DO** KNOW I DON'T **NEED** ONE TO TAKE ME PLACES.
WHEN I GROW UP I'M GOING TO TRAVEL ALL OVER THE WORLD... MAYBE **OUT** OF THE WORLD, TO JUPITER OR-
BY **YOURSELF**?
WELL, SURE. WHY NOT?
YOU NEED A **DATE**!!

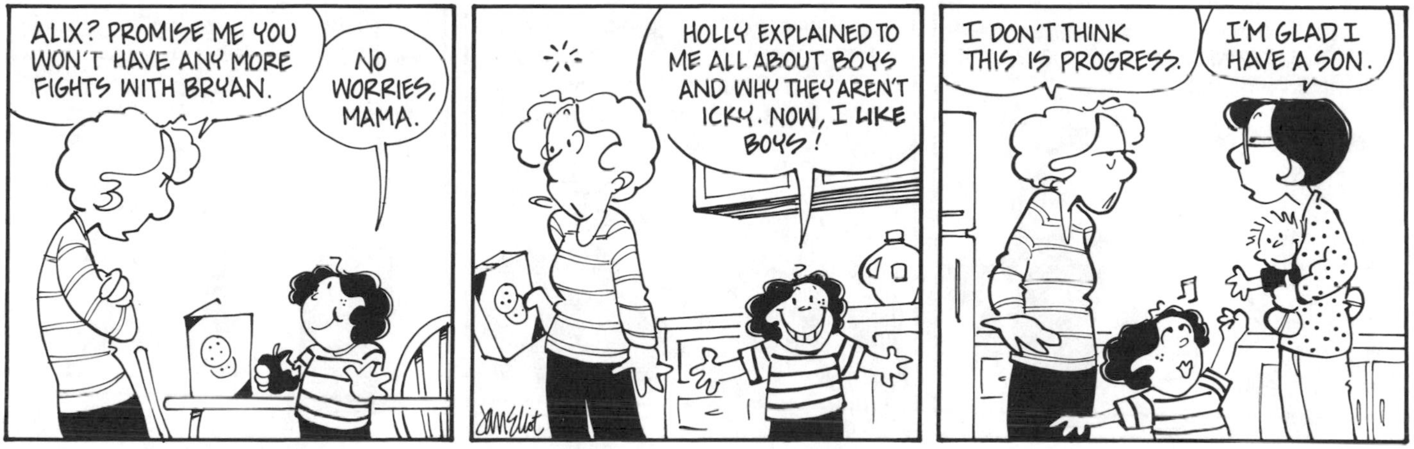
ALIX? PROMISE ME YOU WON'T HAVE ANY MORE FIGHTS WITH BRYAN.
NO WORRIES, MAMA.
HOLLY EXPLAINED TO ME ALL ABOUT BOYS AND WHY THEY AREN'T ICKY. NOW, I **LIKE** BOYS!
I DON'T THINK THIS IS PROGRESS.
I'M GLAD I HAVE A SON.

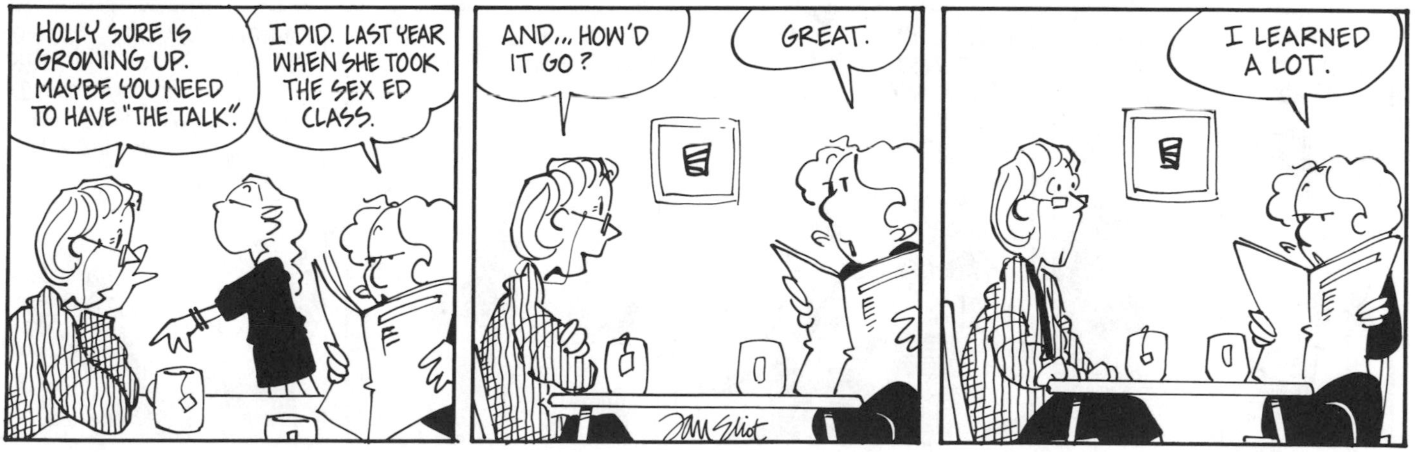
HOLLY SURE IS GROWING UP. MAYBE YOU NEED TO HAVE "THE TALK."
I DID. LAST YEAR WHEN SHE TOOK THE SEX ED CLASS.
AND... HOW'D IT GO?
GREAT.
I LEARNED A LOT.

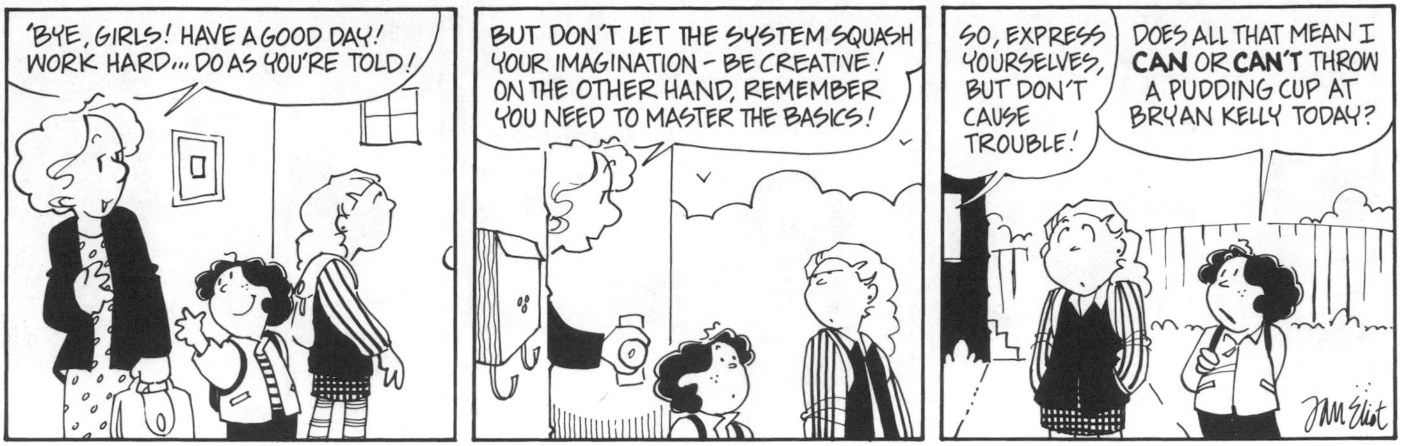
'BYE, GIRLS! HAVE A GOOD DAY! WORK HARD... DO AS YOU'RE TOLD!
BUT DON'T LET THE SYSTEM SQUASH YOUR IMAGINATION - BE CREATIVE! ON THE OTHER HAND, REMEMBER YOU NEED TO MASTER THE BASICS!
SO, EXPRESS YOURSELVES, BUT DON'T CAUSE TROUBLE!
DOES ALL THAT MEAN I **CAN** OR **CAN'T** THROW A PUDDING CUP AT BRYAN KELLY TODAY?

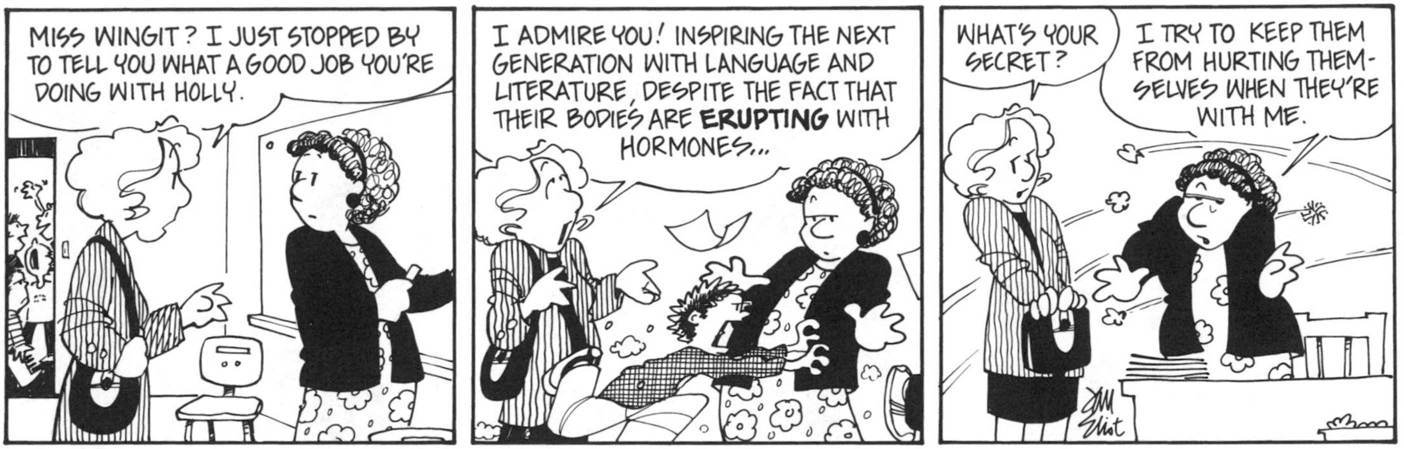
MISS WINGIT? I JUST STOPPED BY TO TELL YOU WHAT A GOOD JOB YOU'RE DOING WITH HOLLY.
I ADMIRE YOU! INSPIRING THE NEXT GENERATION WITH LANGUAGE AND LITERATURE, DESPITE THE FACT THAT THEIR BODIES ARE **ERUPTING** WITH HORMONES...
WHAT'S YOUR SECRET?
I TRY TO KEEP THEM FROM HURTING THEMSELVES WHEN THEY'RE WITH ME.

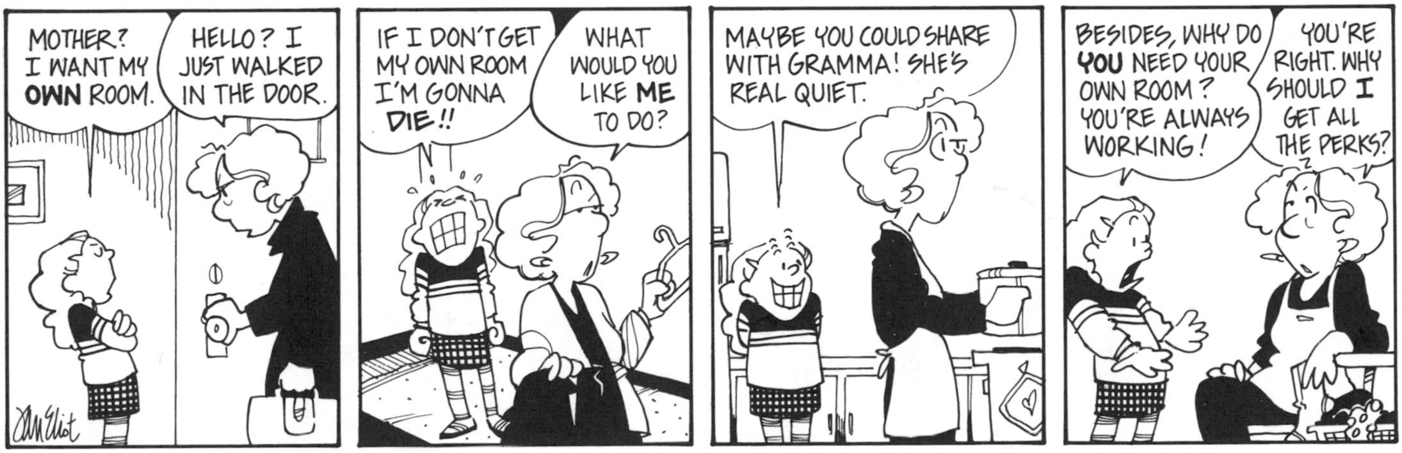
MOTHER? I WANT MY **OWN** ROOM.
HELLO? I JUST WALKED IN THE DOOR.
IF I DON'T GET MY OWN ROOM I'M GONNA **DIE**!!
WHAT WOULD YOU LIKE **ME** TO DO?
MAYBE YOU COULD SHARE WITH GRAMMA! SHE'S REAL QUIET.
BESIDES, WHY DO **YOU** NEED YOUR OWN ROOM? YOU'RE ALWAYS WORKING!
YOU'RE RIGHT. WHY SHOULD **I** GET ALL THE PERKS?

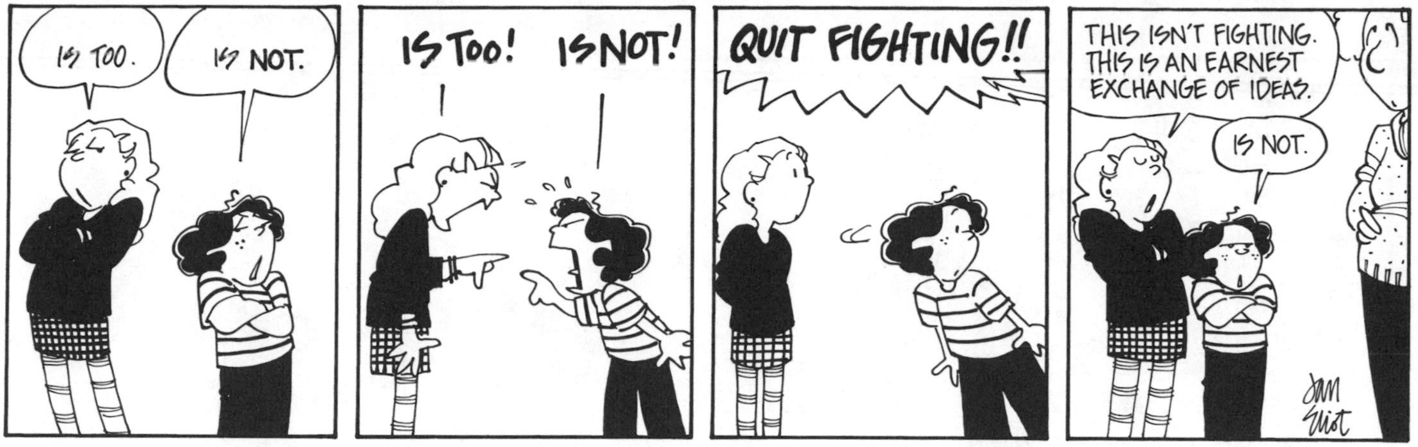
IS TOO.
IS NOT.
IS TOO!
IS NOT!
QUIT FIGHTING!!
THIS ISN'T FIGHTING. THIS IS AN EARNEST EXCHANGE OF IDEAS.
IS NOT.

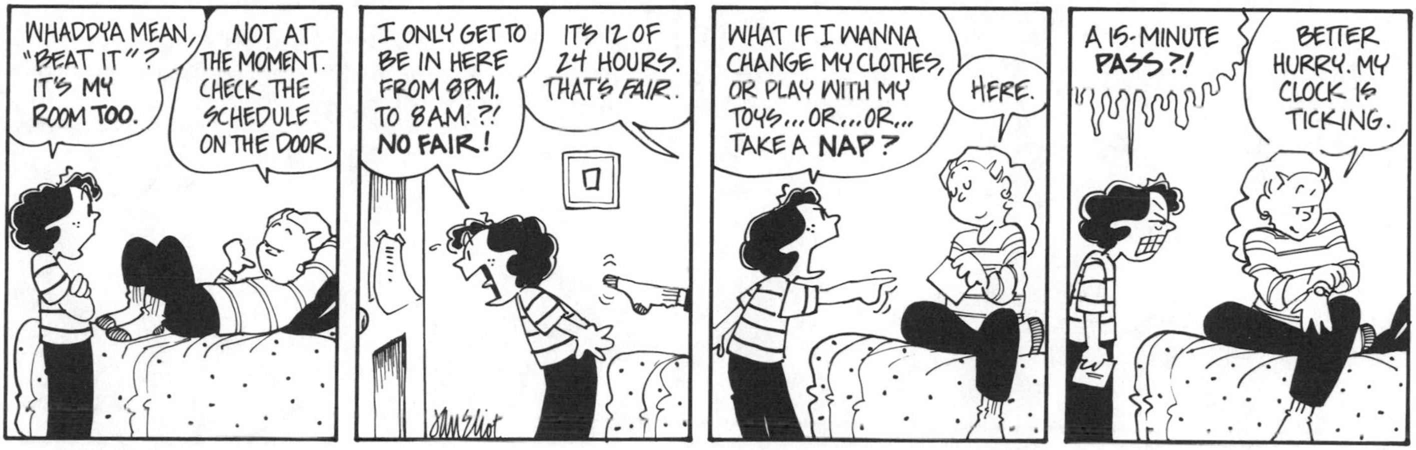
WHADDYA MEAN, "BEAT IT"? IT'S MY ROOM TOO.
NOT AT THE MOMENT. CHECK THE SCHEDULE ON THE DOOR.
I ONLY GET TO BE IN HERE FROM 8P.M. TO 8A.M.?! NO FAIR!
IT'S 12 OF 24 HOURS. THAT'S FAIR.
WHAT IF I WANNA CHANGE MY CLOTHES, OR PLAY WITH MY TOYS... OR... OR... TAKE A NAP?
HERE.
A 15-MINUTE PASS?!
BETTER HURRY. MY CLOCK IS TICKING.

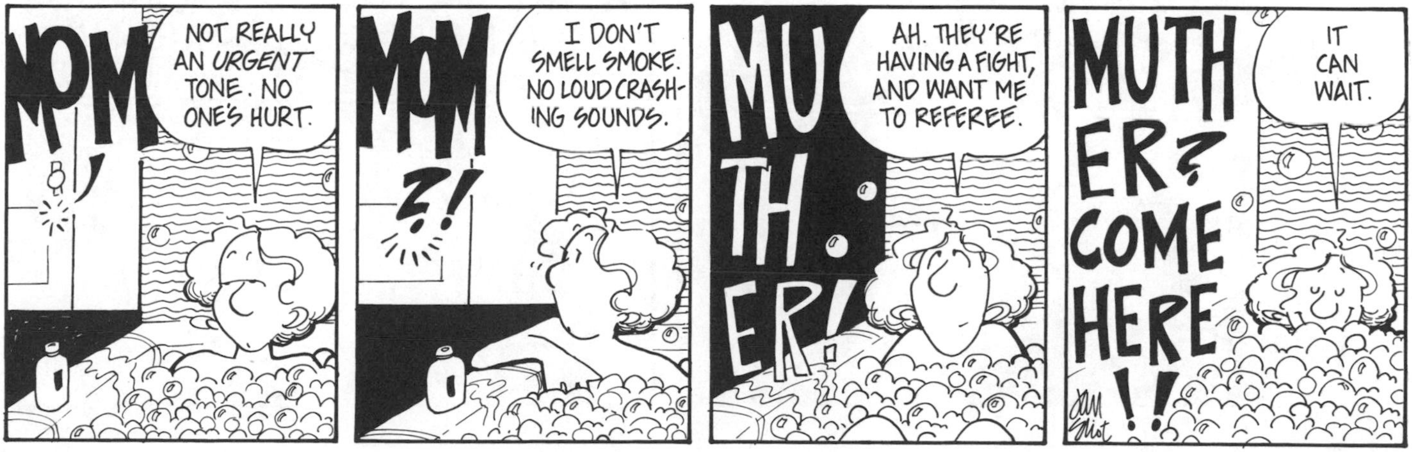
MOM!
NOT REALLY AN URGENT TONE. NO ONE'S HURT.
MOM?!
I DON'T SMELL SMOKE. NO LOUD CRASHING SOUNDS.
MUTHER!
AH. THEY'RE HAVING A FIGHT, AND WANT ME TO REFEREE.
MUTHER? COME HERE!!
IT CAN WAIT.

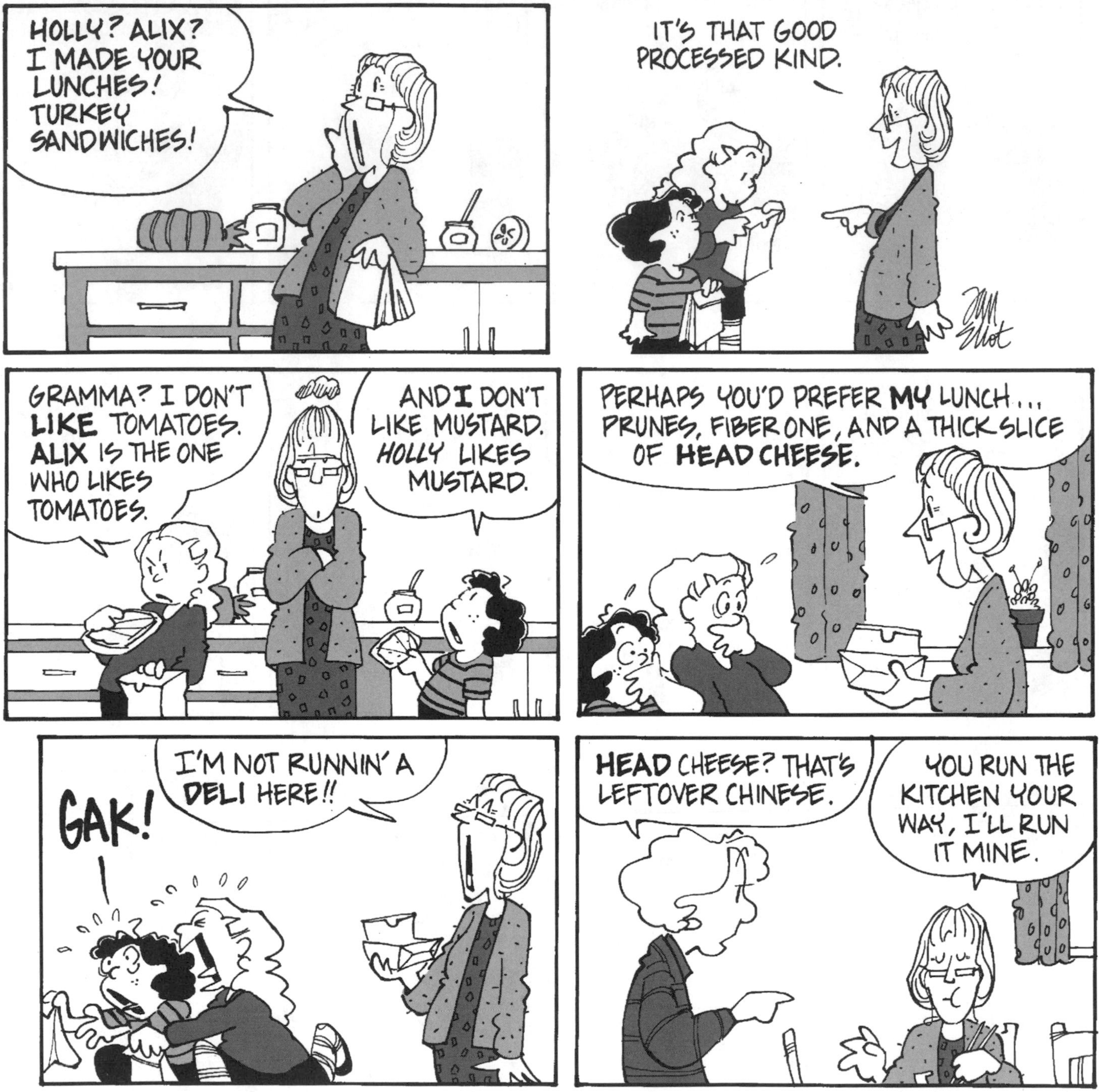
HOLLY? ALIX? I MADE YOUR LUNCHES! TURKEY SANDWICHES!
IT'S THAT GOOD PROCESSED KIND.
GRAMMA? I DON'T LIKE TOMATOES. ALIX IS THE ONE WHO LIKES TOMATOES.
AND I DON'T LIKE MUSTARD. HOLLY LIKES MUSTARD.
PERHAPS YOU'D PREFER MY LUNCH... PRUNES, FIBER ONE, AND A THICK SLICE OF HEAD CHEESE.
GAK!
I'M NOT RUNNIN' A DELI HERE!!
HEAD CHEESE? THAT'S LEFTOVER CHINESE.
YOU RUN THE KITCHEN YOUR WAY, I'LL RUN IT MINE.

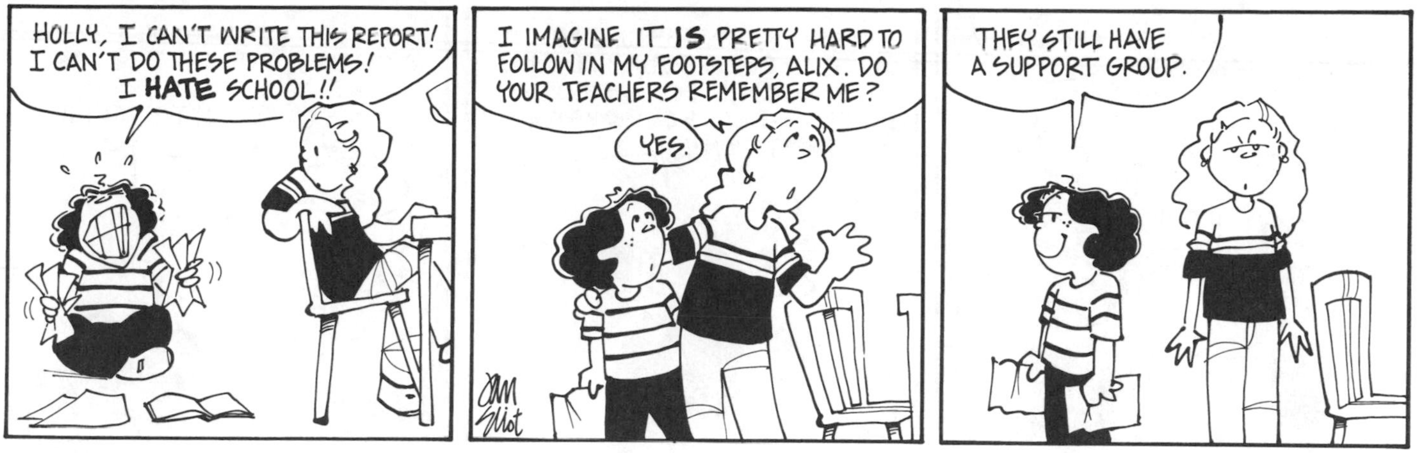
HOLLY, I CAN'T WRITE THIS REPORT! I CAN'T DO THESE PROBLEMS! I **HATE** SCHOOL!!
I IMAGINE IT **IS** PRETTY HARD TO FOLLOW IN MY FOOTSTEPS, ALIX. DO YOUR TEACHERS REMEMBER ME?
YES.
THEY STILL HAVE A SUPPORT GROUP.

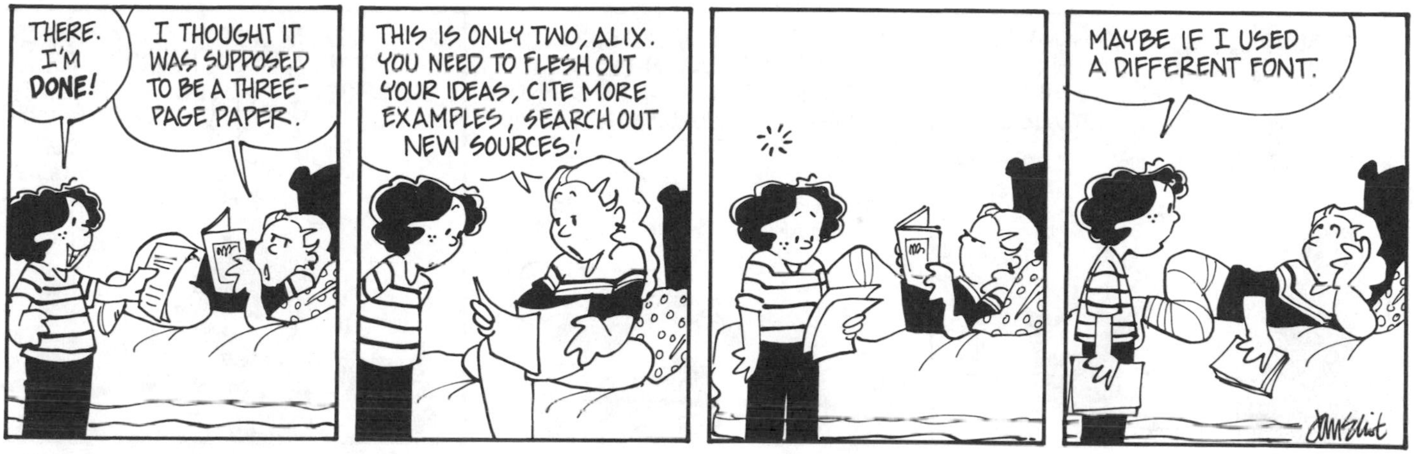
THERE. I'M **DONE!**
I THOUGHT IT WAS SUPPOSED TO BE A THREE-PAGE PAPER.
THIS IS ONLY TWO, ALIX. YOU NEED TO FLESH OUT YOUR IDEAS, CITE MORE EXAMPLES, SEARCH OUT NEW SOURCES!
MAYBE IF I USED A DIFFERENT FONT.

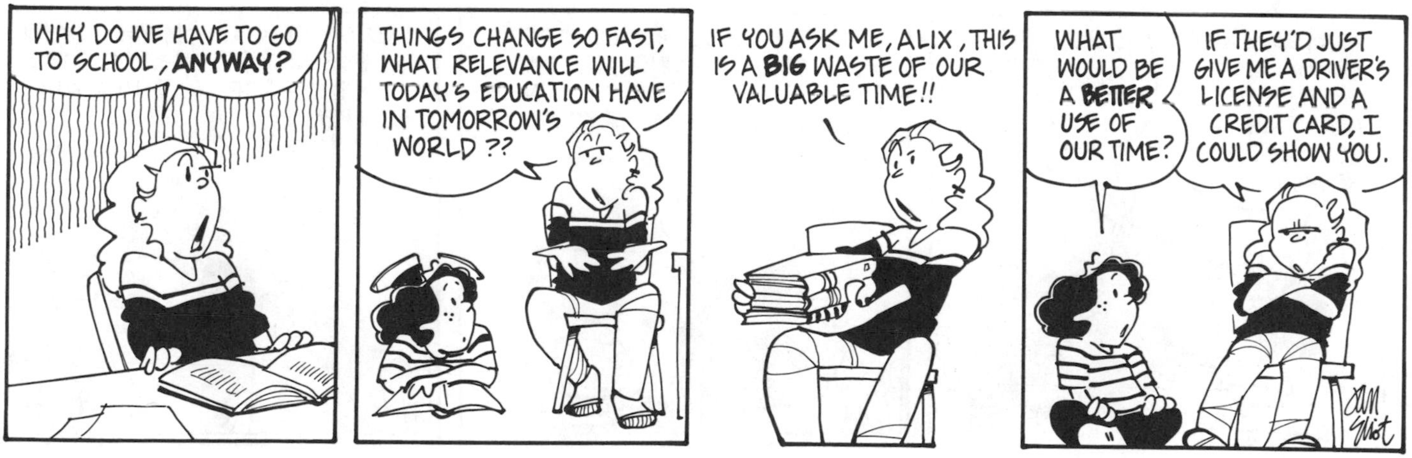
WHY DO WE HAVE TO GO TO SCHOOL, **ANYWAY?**
THINGS CHANGE SO FAST, WHAT RELEVANCE WILL TODAY'S EDUCATION HAVE IN TOMORROW'S WORLD??
IF YOU ASK ME, ALIX, THIS IS A **BIG** WASTE OF OUR VALUABLE TIME!!
WHAT WOULD BE A **BETTER** USE OF OUR TIME?
IF THEY'D JUST GIVE ME A DRIVER'S LICENSE AND A CREDIT CARD, I COULD SHOW YOU.

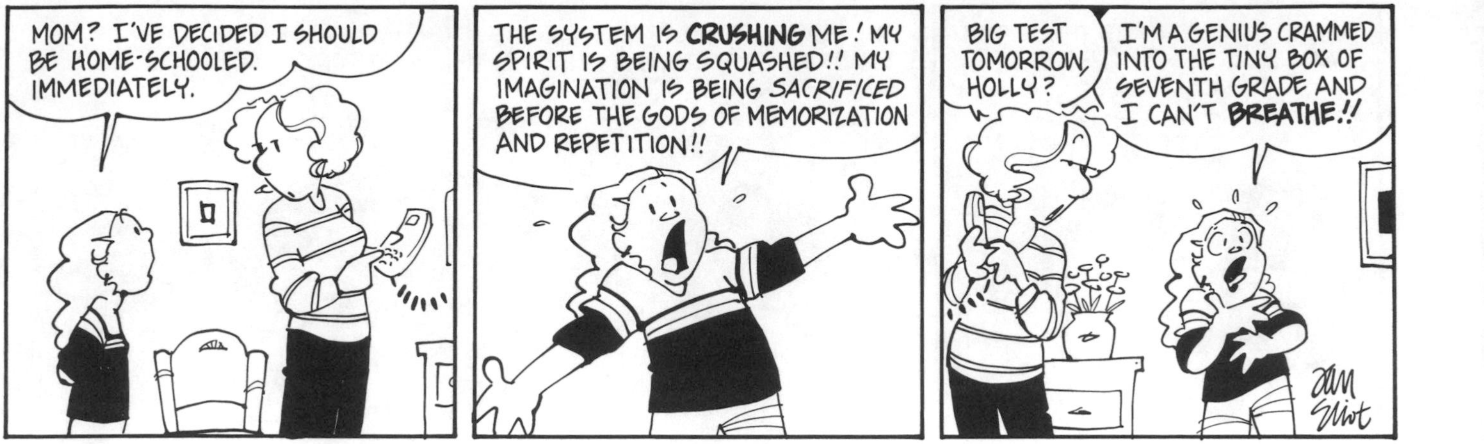
MOM? I'VE DECIDED I SHOULD BE HOME-SCHOOLED. IMMEDIATELY.
THE SYSTEM IS **CRUSHING** ME! MY SPIRIT IS BEING SQUASHED!! MY IMAGINATION IS BEING *SACRIFICED* BEFORE THE GODS OF MEMORIZATION AND REPETITION!!
BIG TEST TOMORROW, HOLLY?
I'M A GENIUS CRAMMED INTO THE TINY BOX OF SEVENTH GRADE AND I CAN'T **BREATHE**!!

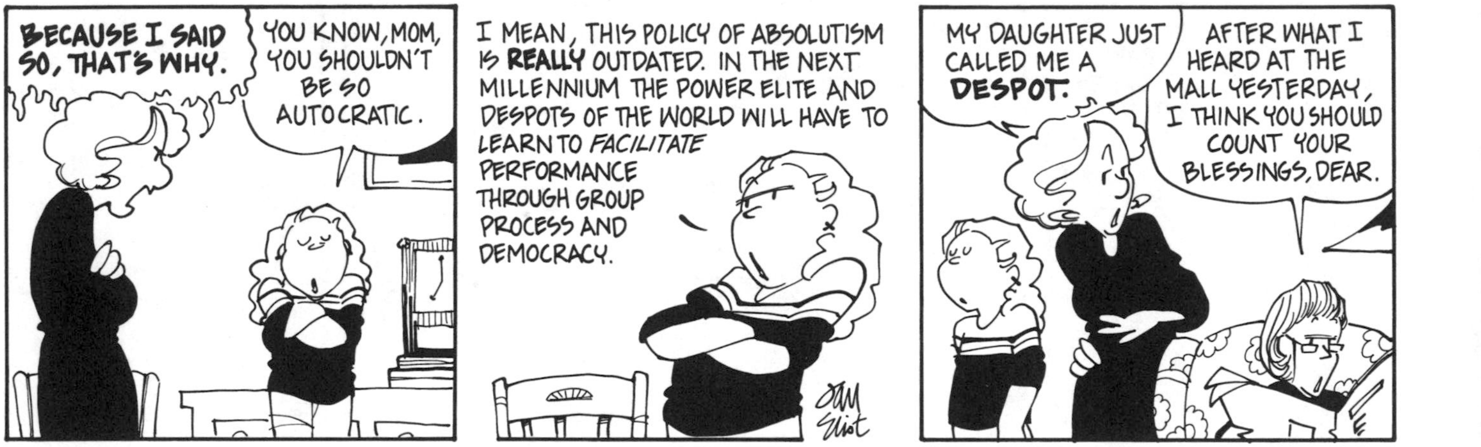
BECAUSE I SAID SO, THAT'S WHY.
YOU KNOW, MOM, YOU SHOULDN'T BE SO AUTOCRATIC.
I MEAN, THIS POLICY OF ABSOLUTISM IS **REALLY** OUTDATED. IN THE NEXT MILLENNIUM THE POWER ELITE AND DESPOTS OF THE WORLD WILL HAVE TO LEARN TO *FACILITATE* PERFORMANCE THROUGH GROUP PROCESS AND DEMOCRACY.
MY DAUGHTER JUST CALLED ME A **DESPOT**.
AFTER WHAT I HEARD AT THE MALL YESTERDAY, I THINK YOU SHOULD COUNT YOUR BLESSINGS, DEAR.

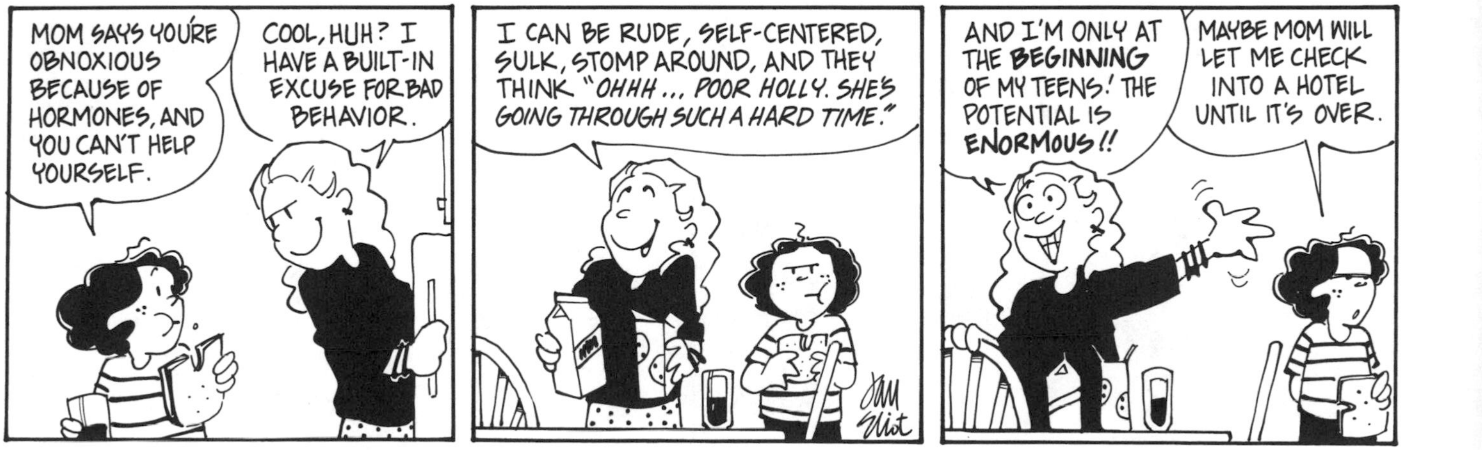
MOM SAYS YOU'RE OBNOXIOUS BECAUSE OF HORMONES, AND YOU CAN'T HELP YOURSELF.
COOL, HUH? I HAVE A BUILT-IN EXCUSE FOR BAD BEHAVIOR.
I CAN BE RUDE, SELF-CENTERED, SULK, STOMP AROUND, AND THEY THINK "*OHHH... POOR HOLLY. SHE'S GOING THROUGH SUCH A HARD TIME.*"
AND I'M ONLY AT THE **BEGINNING** OF MY TEENS! THE POTENTIAL IS **ENORMOUS**!!
MAYBE MOM WILL LET ME CHECK INTO A HOTEL UNTIL IT'S OVER.

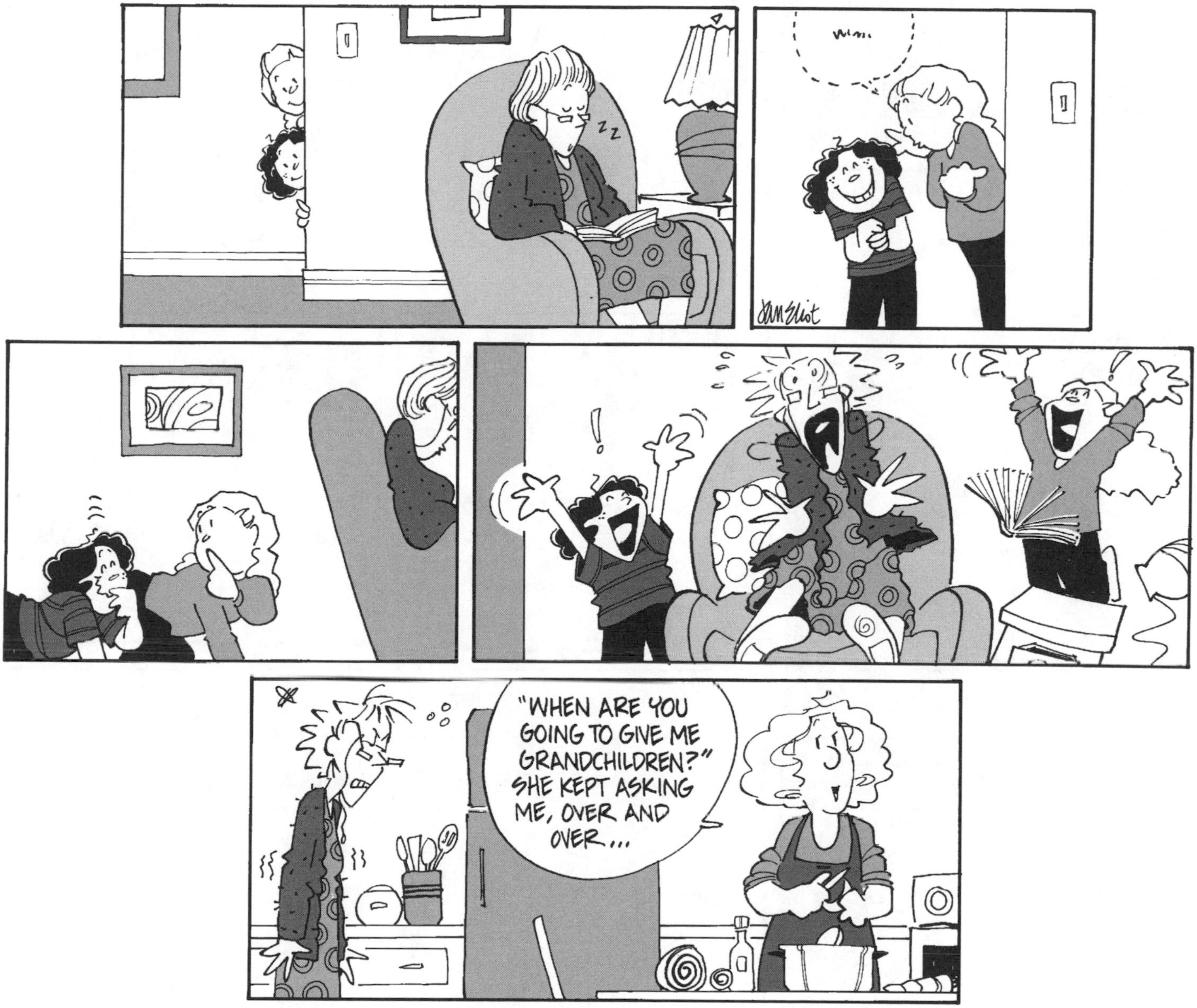
"WHEN ARE YOU GOING TO GIVE ME GRANDCHILDREN?" SHE KEPT ASKING ME, OVER AND OVER...

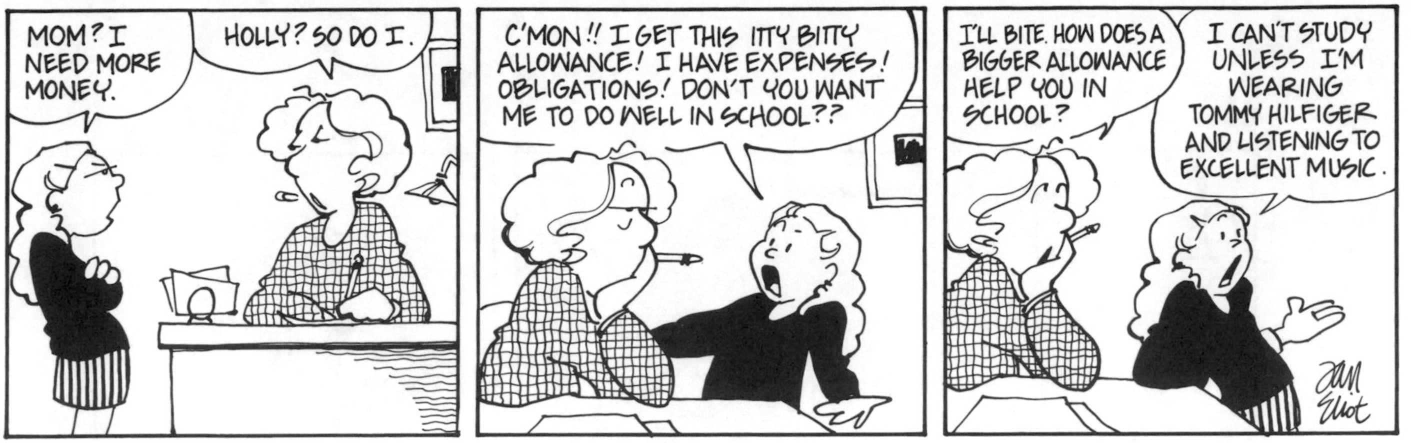
MOM? I NEED MORE MONEY.
HOLLY? SO DO I.
C'MON!! I GET THIS ITTY BITTY ALLOWANCE! I HAVE EXPENSES! OBLIGATIONS! DON'T YOU WANT ME TO DO WELL IN SCHOOL??
I'LL BITE. HOW DOES A BIGGER ALLOWANCE HELP YOU IN SCHOOL?
I CAN'T STUDY UNLESS I'M WEARING TOMMY HILFIGER AND LISTENING TO EXCELLENT MUSIC.
JAN Eliot

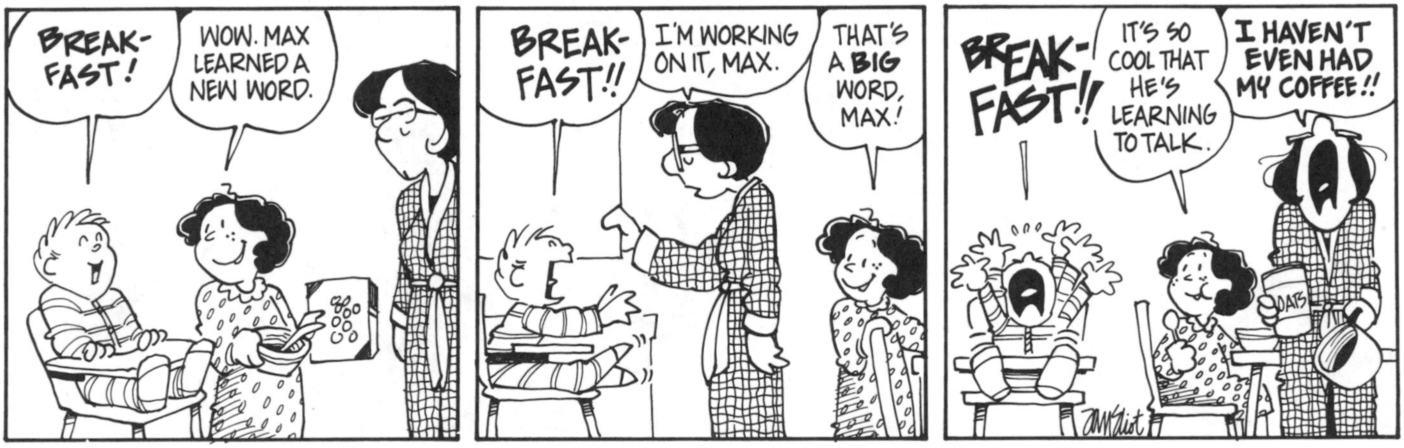
BREAK-FAST!
WOW. MAX LEARNED A NEW WORD.
BREAK-FAST!!
I'M WORKING ON IT, MAX.
THAT'S A **BIG** WORD, MAX!
BREAK-FAST!!
IT'S SO COOL THAT HE'S LEARNING TO TALK.
I HAVEN'T EVEN HAD MY COFFEE!!
OATS
JAN Eliot

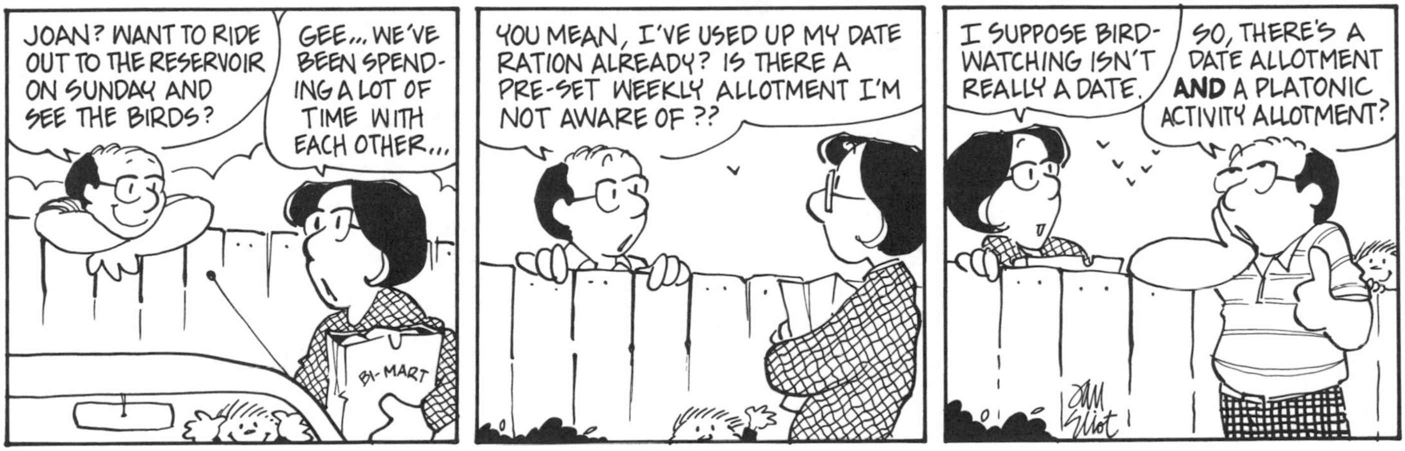
JOAN? WANT TO RIDE OUT TO THE RESERVOIR ON SUNDAY AND SEE THE BIRDS?
GEE... WE'VE BEEN SPENDING A LOT OF TIME WITH EACH OTHER...
BI-MART
YOU MEAN, I'VE USED UP MY DATE RATION ALREADY? IS THERE A PRE-SET WEEKLY ALLOTMENT I'M NOT AWARE OF??
I SUPPOSE BIRD-WATCHING ISN'T REALLY A DATE.
SO, THERE'S A DATE ALLOTMENT **AND** A PLATONIC ACTIVITY ALLOTMENT?
JAN Eliot

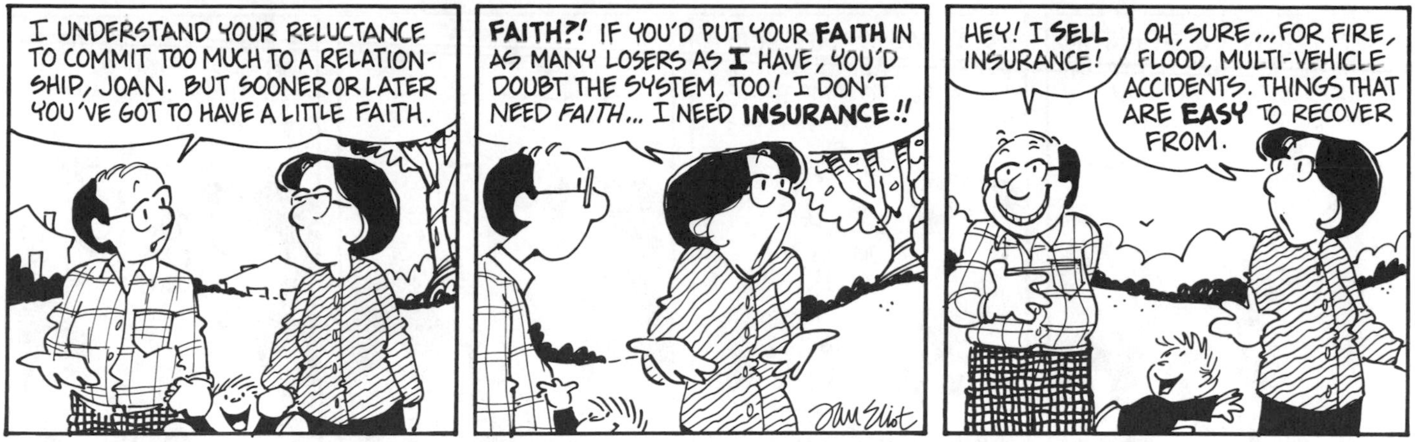
I UNDERSTAND YOUR RELUCTANCE TO COMMIT TOO MUCH TO A RELATIONSHIP, JOAN. BUT SOONER OR LATER YOU'VE GOT TO HAVE A LITTLE FAITH.
FAITH?! IF YOU'D PUT YOUR FAITH IN AS MANY LOSERS AS I HAVE, YOU'D DOUBT THE SYSTEM, TOO! I DON'T NEED FAITH... I NEED INSURANCE!!
HEY! I SELL INSURANCE!
OH, SURE... FOR FIRE, FLOOD, MULTI-VEHICLE ACCIDENTS. THINGS THAT ARE EASY TO RECOVER FROM.

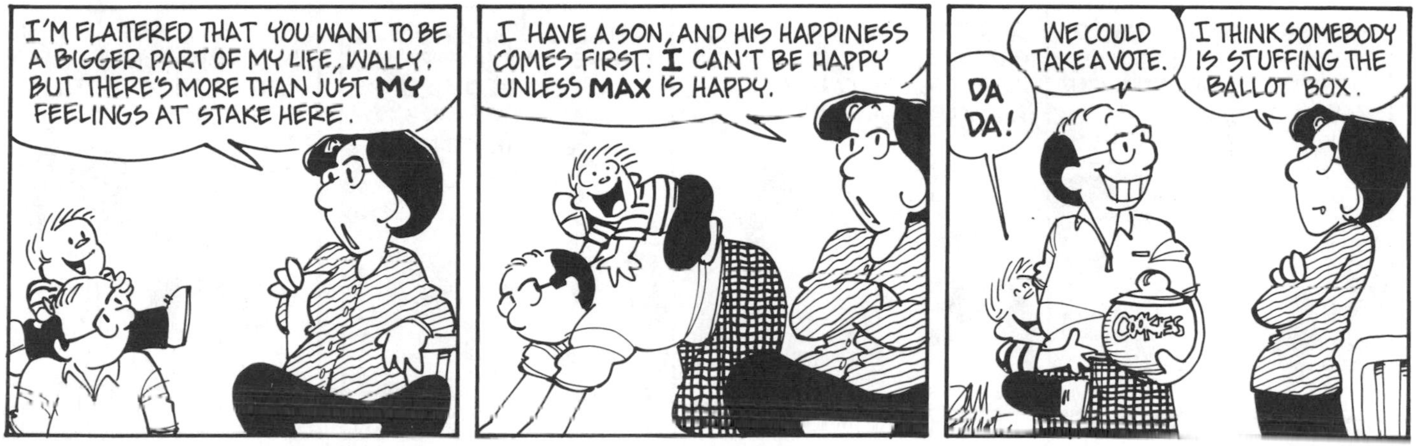
I'M FLATTERED THAT YOU WANT TO BE A BIGGER PART OF MY LIFE, WALLY. BUT THERE'S MORE THAN JUST MY FEELINGS AT STAKE HERE.
I HAVE A SON, AND HIS HAPPINESS COMES FIRST. I CAN'T BE HAPPY UNLESS MAX IS HAPPY.
DA DA!
WE COULD TAKE A VOTE.
I THINK SOMEBODY IS STUFFING THE BALLOT BOX.
COOKIES

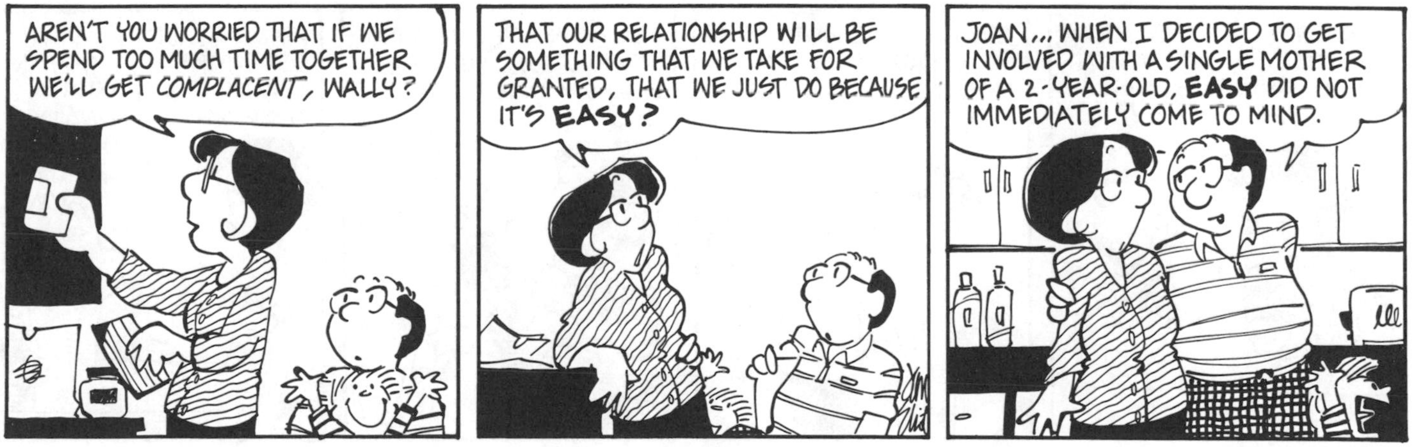
AREN'T YOU WORRIED THAT IF WE SPEND TOO MUCH TIME TOGETHER WE'LL GET COMPLACENT, WALLY?
THAT OUR RELATIONSHIP WILL BE SOMETHING THAT WE TAKE FOR GRANTED, THAT WE JUST DO BECAUSE IT'S EASY?
JOAN... WHEN I DECIDED TO GET INVOLVED WITH A SINGLE MOTHER OF A 2-YEAR-OLD, EASY DID NOT IMMEDIATELY COME TO MIND.

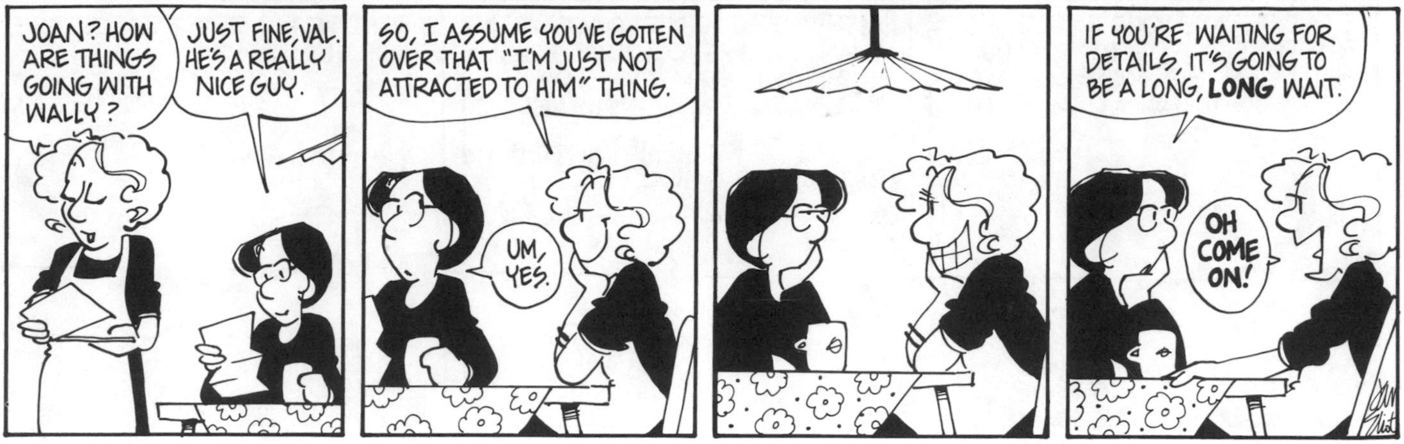
JOAN? HOW ARE THINGS GOING WITH WALLY?
JUST FINE, VAL. HE'S A REALLY NICE GUY.
SO, I ASSUME YOU'VE GOTTEN OVER THAT "I'M JUST NOT ATTRACTED TO HIM" THING.
UM, YES.
IF YOU'RE WAITING FOR DETAILS, IT'S GOING TO BE A LONG, **LONG** WAIT.
OH COME ON!

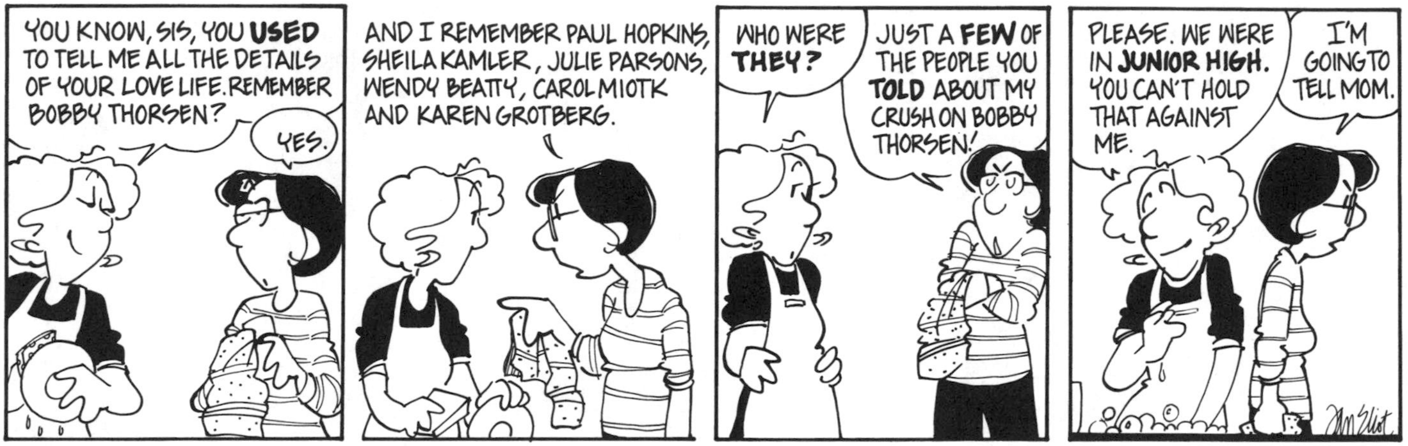
YOU KNOW, SIS, YOU **USED** TO TELL ME ALL THE DETAILS OF YOUR LOVE LIFE. REMEMBER BOBBY THORSEN?
YES.
AND I REMEMBER PAUL HOPKINS, SHEILA KAMLER, JULIE PARSONS, WENDY BEATTY, CAROL MIOTK AND KAREN GROTBERG.
WHO WERE **THEY?**
JUST A **FEW** OF THE PEOPLE YOU **TOLD** ABOUT MY CRUSH ON BOBBY THORSEN!
PLEASE. WE WERE IN **JUNIOR HIGH.** YOU CAN'T HOLD THAT AGAINST ME.
I'M GOING TO TELL MOM.

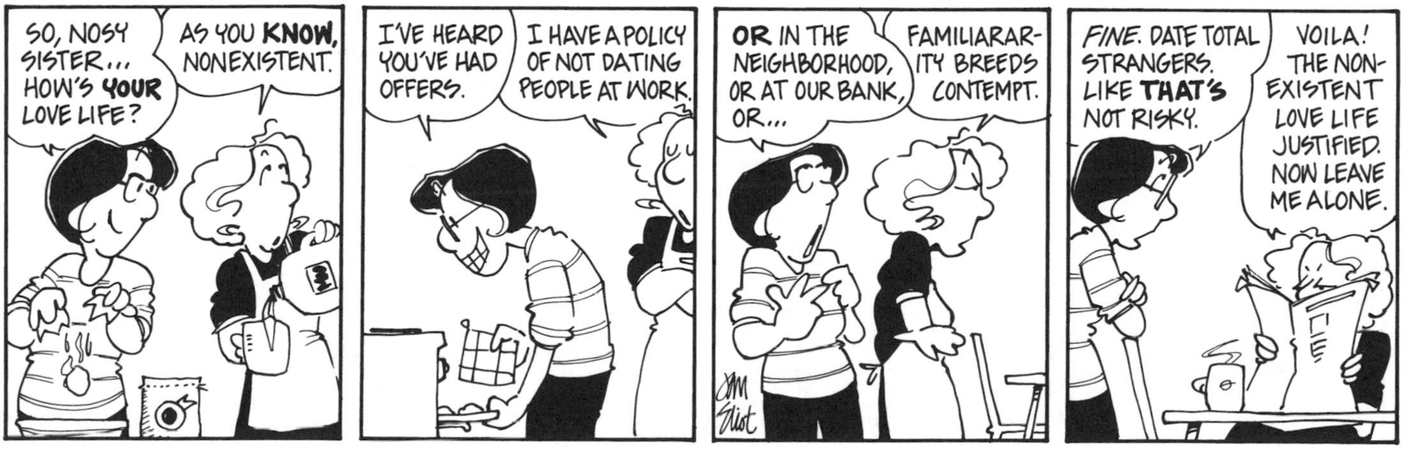
SO, NOSY SISTER... HOW'S **YOUR** LOVE LIFE?
AS YOU **KNOW,** NONEXISTENT.
I'VE HEARD YOU'VE HAD OFFERS.
I HAVE A POLICY OF NOT DATING PEOPLE AT WORK.
OR IN THE NEIGHBORHOOD, OR AT OUR BANK, OR...
FAMILIARARITY BREEDS CONTEMPT.
FINE. DATE TOTAL STRANGERS. LIKE **THAT'S** NOT RISKY.
VOILA! THE NON-EXISTENT LOVE LIFE JUSTIFIED. NOW LEAVE ME ALONE.

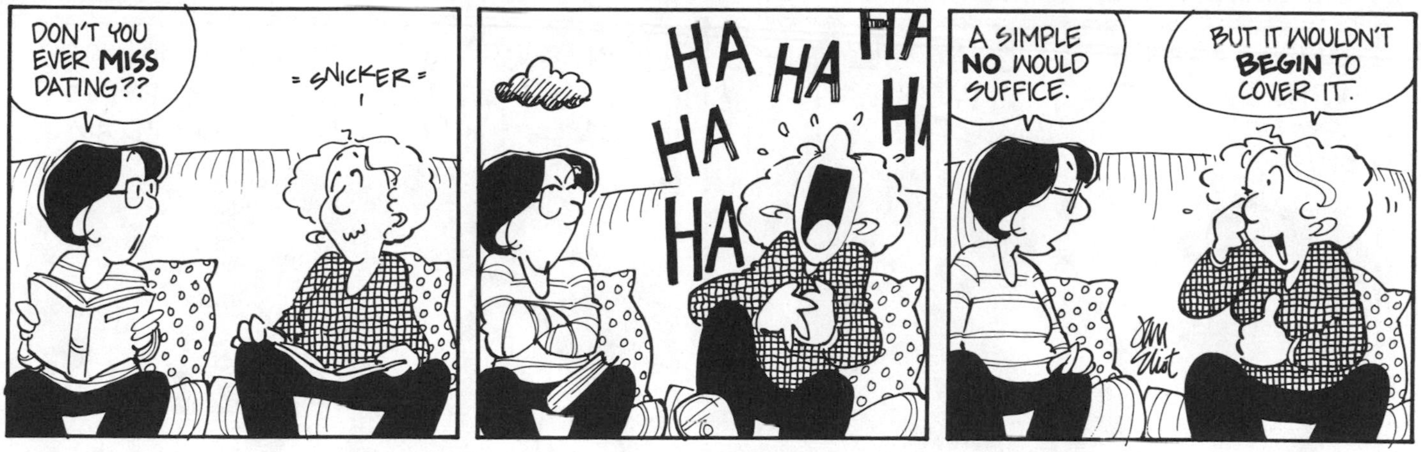
DON'T YOU EVER **MISS** DATING??
= SNICKER =
HA HA HA HA
A SIMPLE **NO** WOULD SUFFICE.
BUT IT WOULDN'T **BEGIN** TO COVER IT.

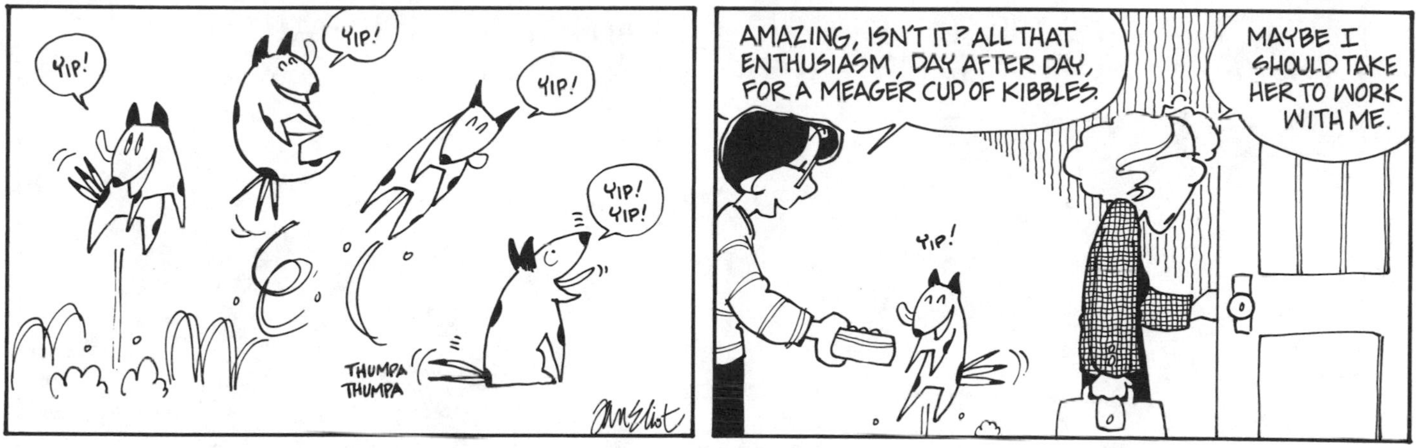
YIP!
YIP!
YIP!
YIP! YIP!
THUMPA THUMPA
AMAZING, ISN'T IT? ALL THAT ENTHUSIASM, DAY AFTER DAY, FOR A MEAGER CUP OF KIBBLES.
YIP!
MAYBE I SHOULD TAKE HER TO WORK WITH ME.

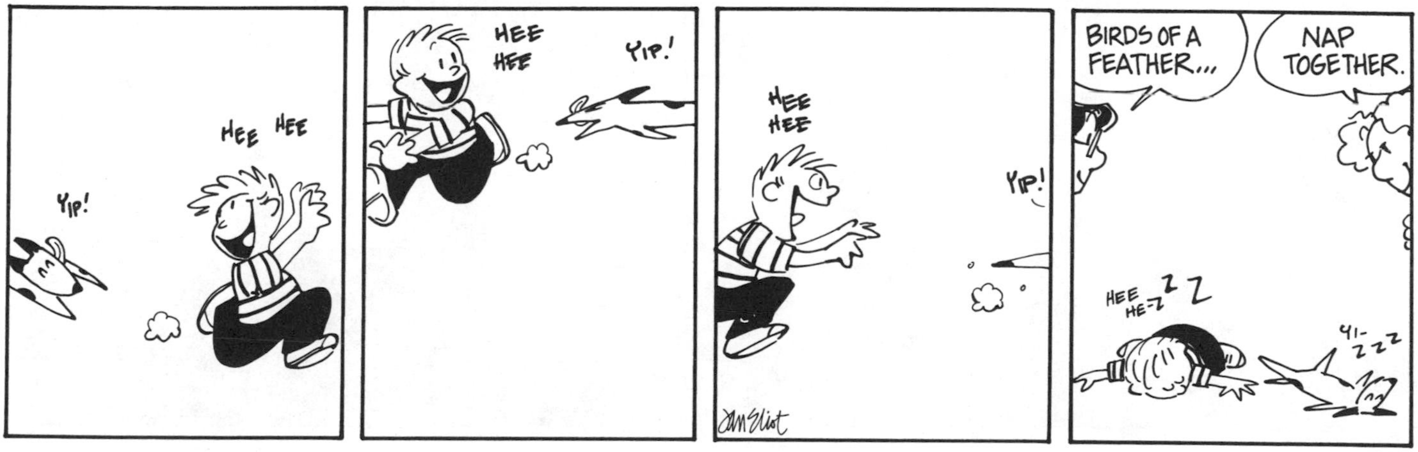
HEE HEE
YIP!
HEE HEE
YIP!
HEE HEE
YIP!
BIRDS OF A FEATHER...
NAP TOGETHER.
HEE HE-Z Z Z
YI- Z Z Z

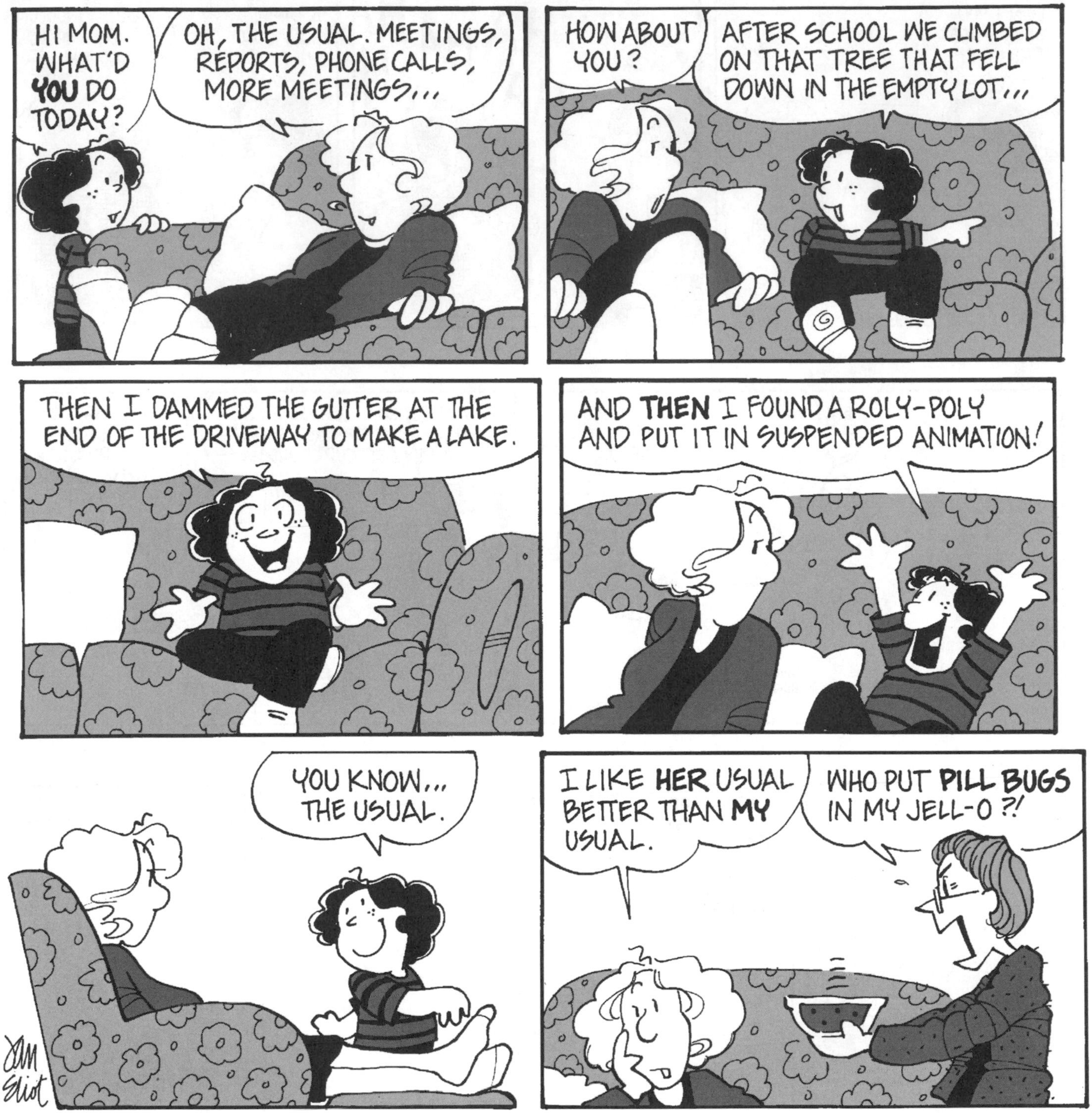
HI MOM. WHAT'D **YOU** DO TODAY?
OH, THE USUAL. MEETINGS, REPORTS, PHONE CALLS, MORE MEETINGS...
HOW ABOUT YOU?
AFTER SCHOOL WE CLIMBED ON THAT TREE THAT FELL DOWN IN THE EMPTY LOT...
THEN I DAMMED THE GUTTER AT THE END OF THE DRIVEWAY TO MAKE A LAKE.
AND **THEN** I FOUND A ROLY-POLY AND PUT IT IN SUSPENDED ANIMATION!
YOU KNOW... THE USUAL.
I LIKE **HER** USUAL BETTER THAN **MY** USUAL.
WHO PUT **PILL BUGS** IN MY JELL-O ?!

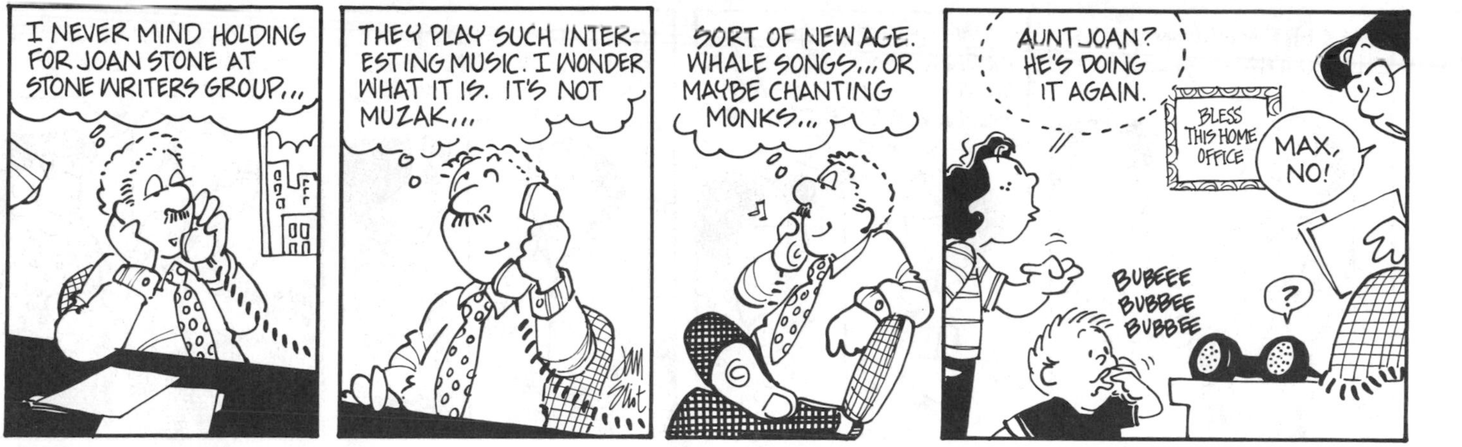
I NEVER MIND HOLDING FOR JOAN STONE AT STONE WRITERS GROUP...
THEY PLAY SUCH INTER-ESTING MUSIC. I WONDER WHAT IT IS. IT'S NOT MUZAK...
SORT OF NEW AGE. WHALE SONGS... OR MAYBE CHANTING MONKS...
AUNT JOAN? HE'S DOING IT AGAIN.
BLESS THIS HOME OFFICE
MAX, NO!
BUBEEE BUBBEE BUBBEE
?

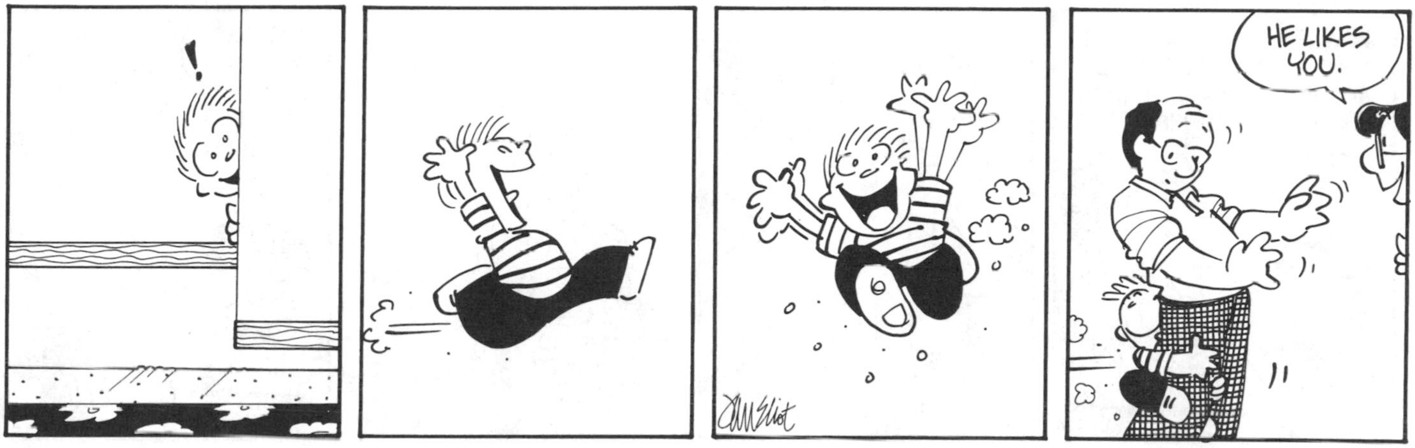
!
HE LIKES YOU.

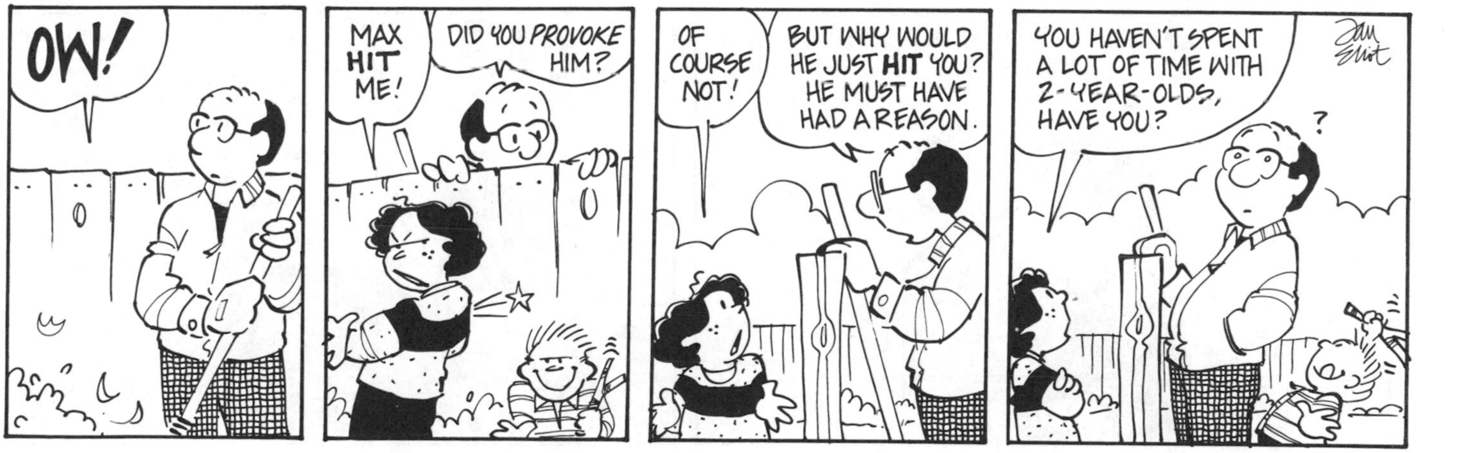
OW!
MAX HIT ME!
DID YOU PROVOKE HIM?
OF COURSE NOT!
BUT WHY WOULD HE JUST HIT YOU? HE MUST HAVE HAD A REASON.
YOU HAVEN'T SPENT A LOT OF TIME WITH 2-YEAR-OLDS, HAVE YOU?
?

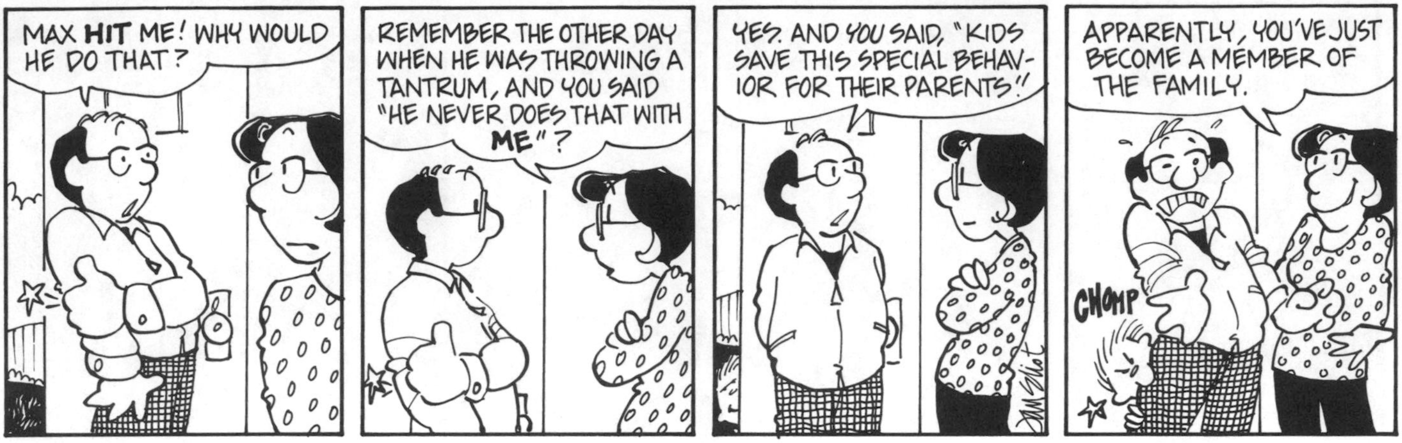
MAX **HIT** ME! WHY WOULD HE DO THAT?
REMEMBER THE OTHER DAY WHEN HE WAS THROWING A TANTRUM, AND YOU SAID "HE NEVER DOES THAT WITH **ME**"?
YES. AND *YOU* SAID, "KIDS SAVE THIS SPECIAL BEHAVIOR FOR THEIR PARENTS"!
APPARENTLY, YOU'VE JUST BECOME A MEMBER OF THE FAMILY.
CHOMP

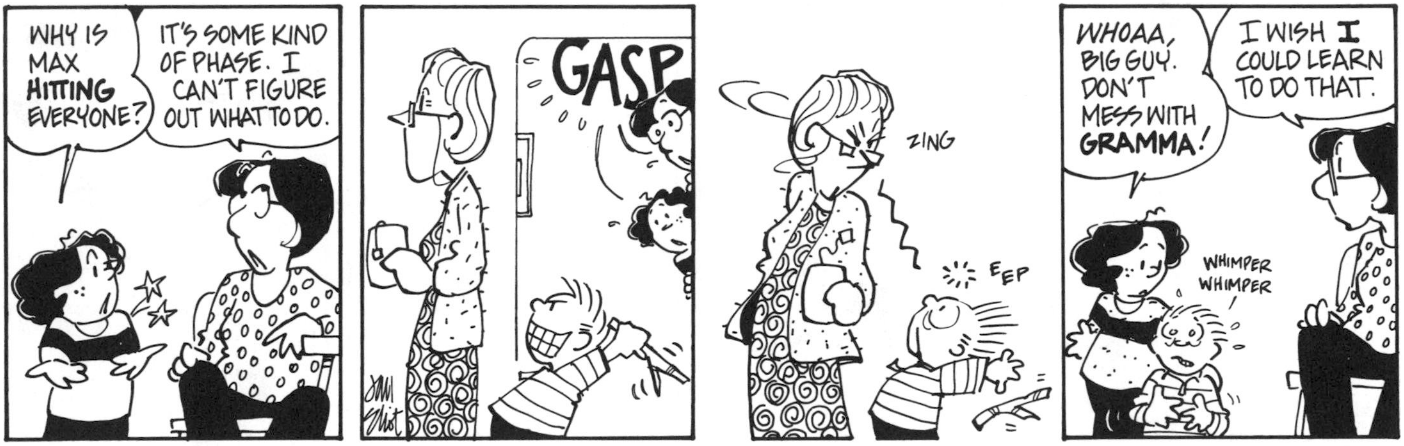
WHY IS MAX **HITTING** EVERYONE?
IT'S SOME KIND OF PHASE. I CAN'T FIGURE OUT WHAT TO DO.
GASP
ZING
EEP
WHOAA, BIG GUY. DON'T MESS WITH **GRAMMA**!
WHIMPER WHIMPER
I WISH **I** COULD LEARN TO DO THAT.

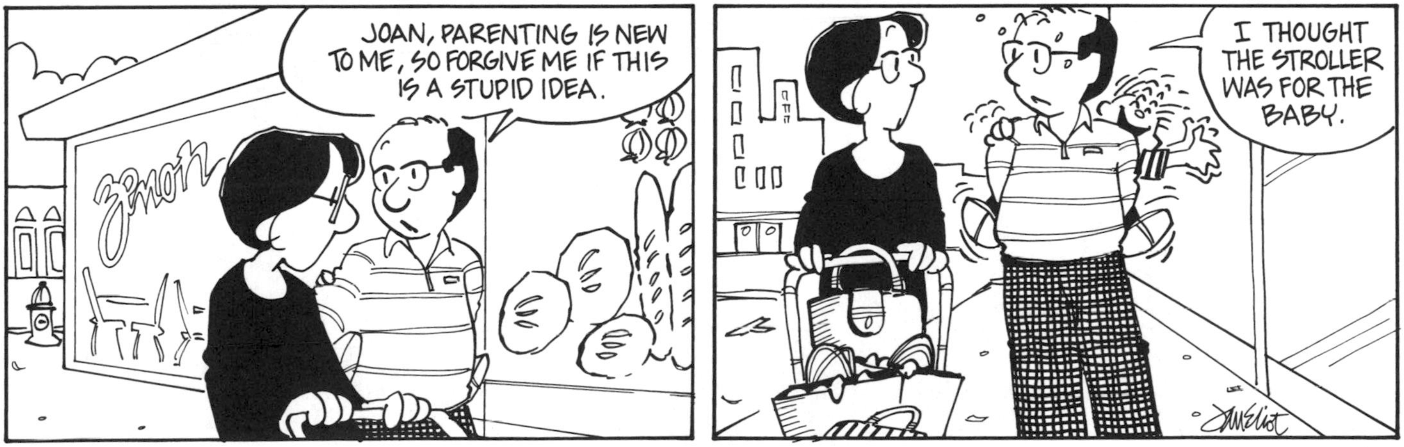
JOAN, PARENTING IS NEW TO ME, SO FORGIVE ME IF THIS IS A STUPID IDEA.
I THOUGHT THE STROLLER WAS FOR THE BABY.

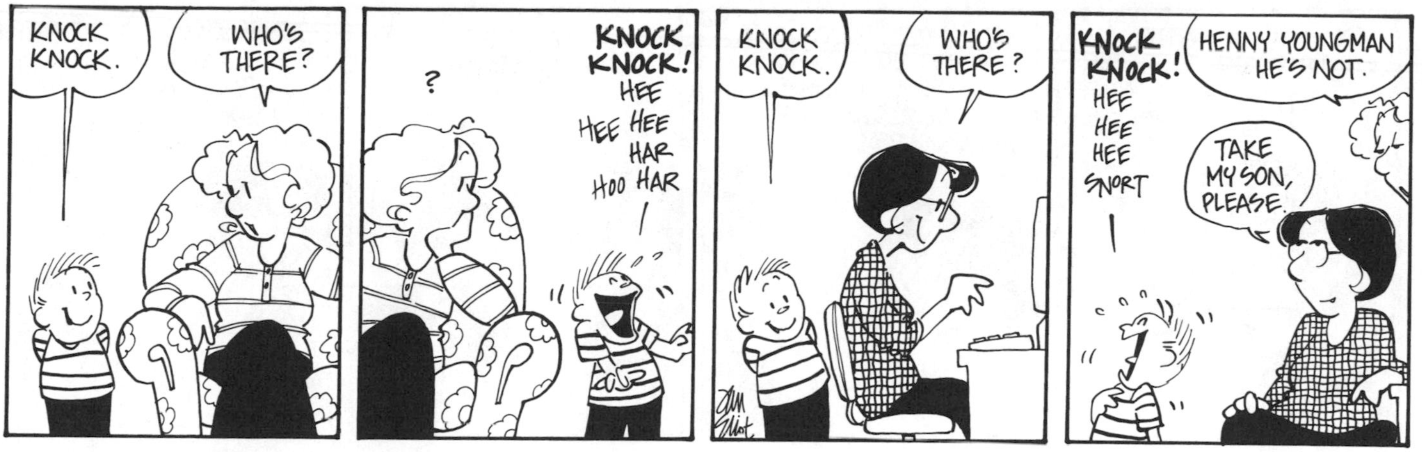
KNOCK KNOCK.
WHO'S THERE?
?
KNOCK KNOCK! HEE HEE HEE HAR HOO HAR
KNOCK KNOCK.
WHO'S THERE?
KNOCK KNOCK! HEE HEE HEE SNORT
HENNY YOUNGMAN HE'S NOT.
TAKE MY SON, PLEASE.

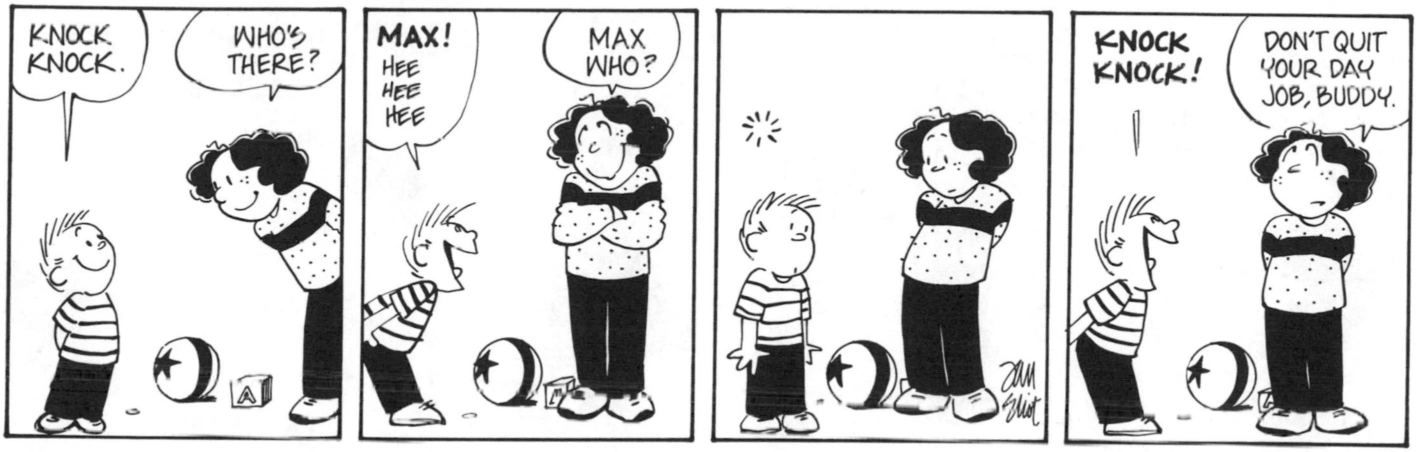
KNOCK KNOCK.
WHO'S THERE?
MAX! HEE HEE HEE
MAX WHO?
KNOCK KNOCK!
DON'T QUIT YOUR DAY JOB, BUDDY.

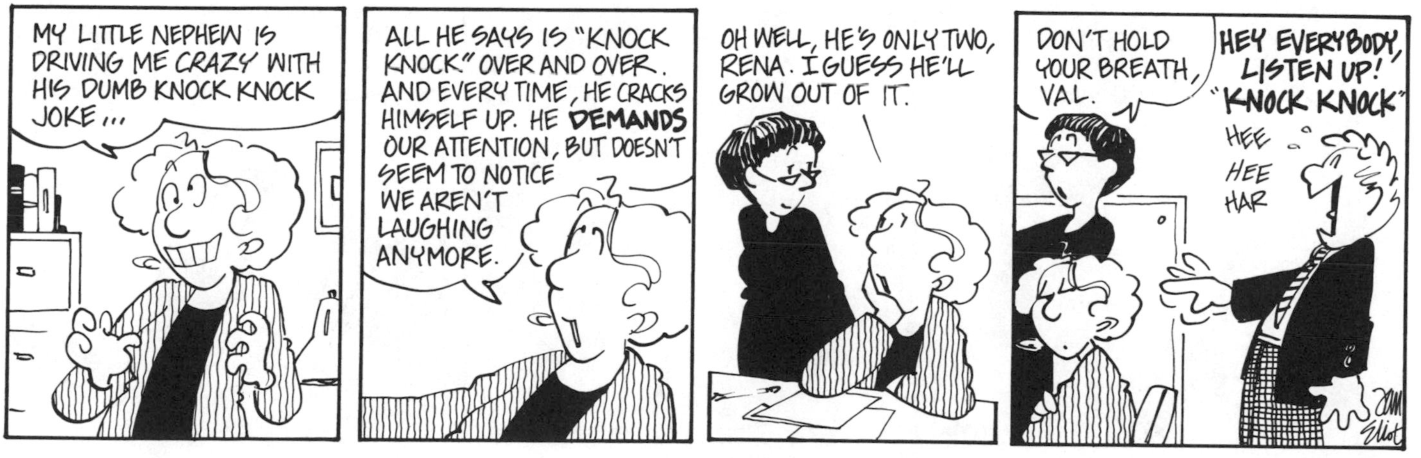
MY LITTLE NEPHEW IS DRIVING ME CRAZY WITH HIS DUMB KNOCK KNOCK JOKE...
ALL HE SAYS IS "KNOCK KNOCK" OVER AND OVER. AND EVERY TIME, HE CRACKS HIMSELF UP. HE DEMANDS OUR ATTENTION, BUT DOESN'T SEEM TO NOTICE WE AREN'T LAUGHING ANYMORE.
OH WELL, HE'S ONLY TWO, RENA. I GUESS HE'LL GROW OUT OF IT.
DON'T HOLD YOUR BREATH, VAL.
HEY EVERYBODY, LISTEN UP! "KNOCK KNOCK" HEE HEE HAR

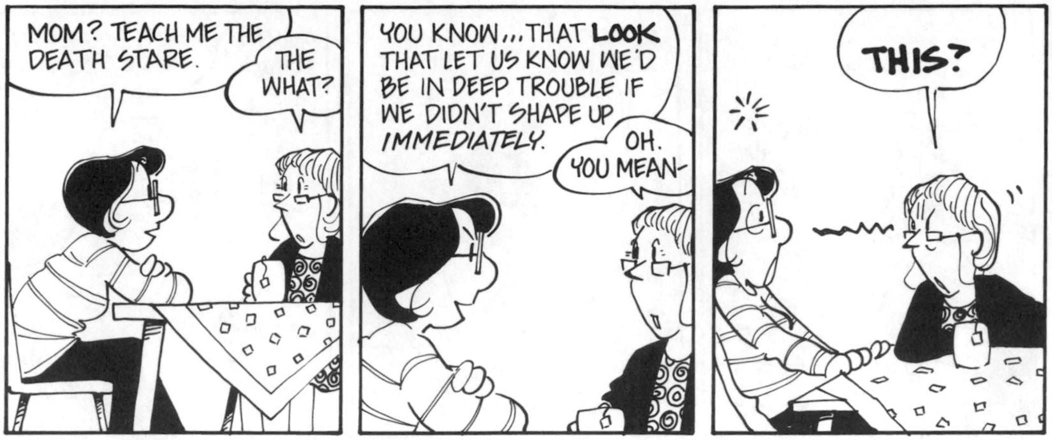
MOM? TEACH ME THE DEATH STARE.
THE WHAT?
YOU KNOW... THAT **LOOK** THAT LET US KNOW WE'D BE IN DEEP TROUBLE IF WE DIDN'T SHAPE UP *IMMEDIATELY*.
OH. YOU MEAN-
THIS?
STOP! I'M FEELING REALLY GUILTY FOR NO REASON!!
IT'S NICE TO KNOW I STILL HAVE THE TOUCH.

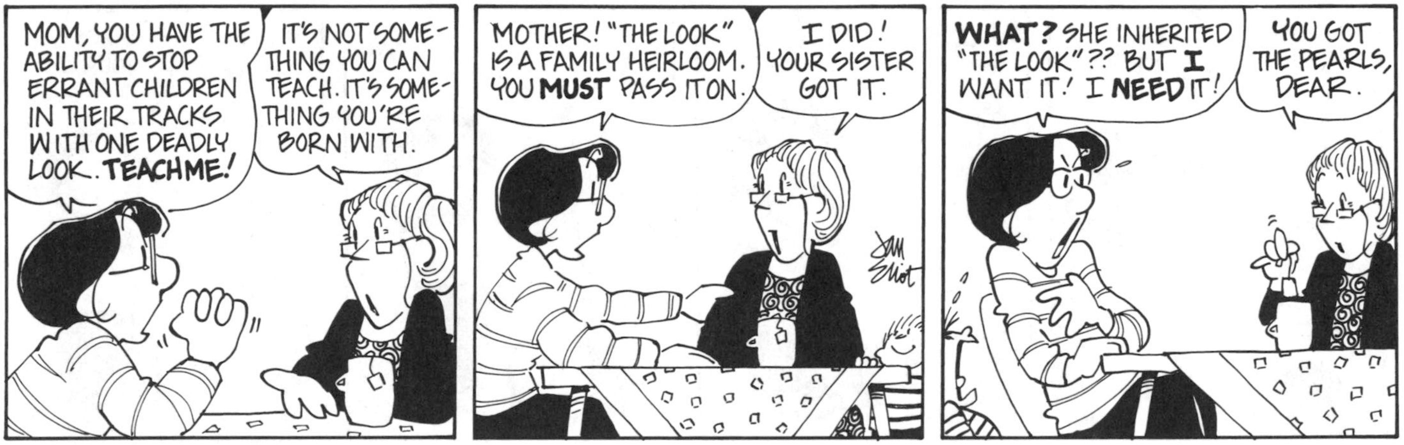
MOM, YOU HAVE THE ABILITY TO STOP ERRANT CHILDREN IN THEIR TRACKS WITH ONE DEADLY LOOK. **TEACH ME!**
IT'S NOT SOMETHING YOU CAN TEACH. IT'S SOMETHING YOU'RE BORN WITH.
MOTHER! "THE LOOK" IS A FAMILY HEIRLOOM. YOU **MUST** PASS IT ON.
I DID! YOUR SISTER GOT IT.
WHAT? SHE INHERITED "THE LOOK"?? BUT **I** WANT IT! I **NEED** IT!
YOU GOT THE PEARLS, DEAR.

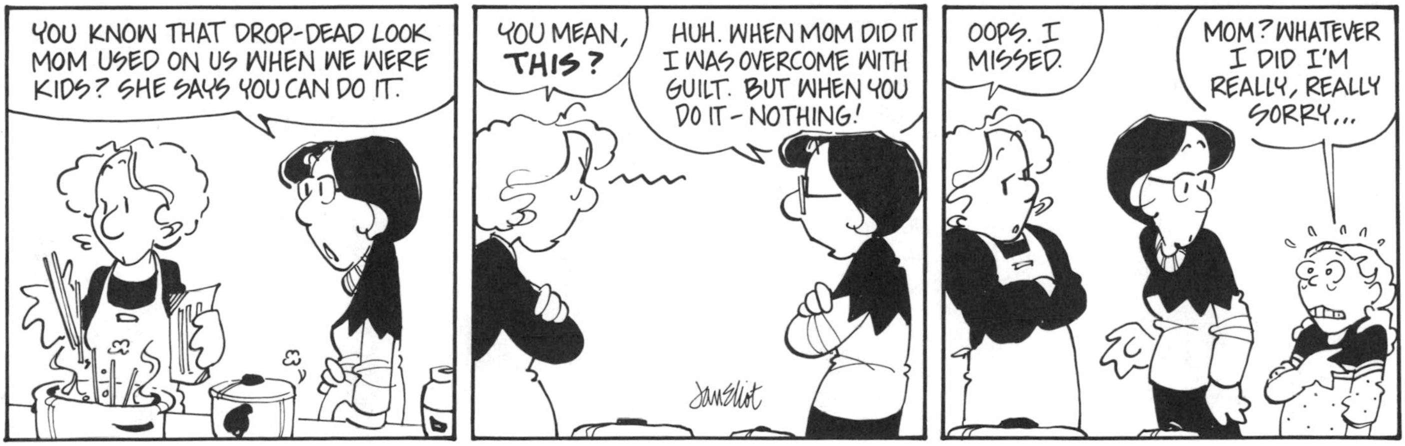
YOU KNOW THAT DROP-DEAD LOOK MOM USED ON US WHEN WE WERE KIDS? SHE SAYS YOU CAN DO IT.
YOU MEAN, **THIS?**
HUH. WHEN MOM DID IT I WAS OVERCOME WITH GUILT. BUT WHEN YOU DO IT - NOTHING!
OOPS. I MISSED.
MOM? WHATEVER I DID I'M REALLY, REALLY SORRY...

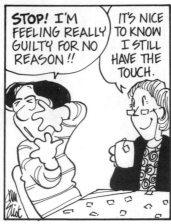

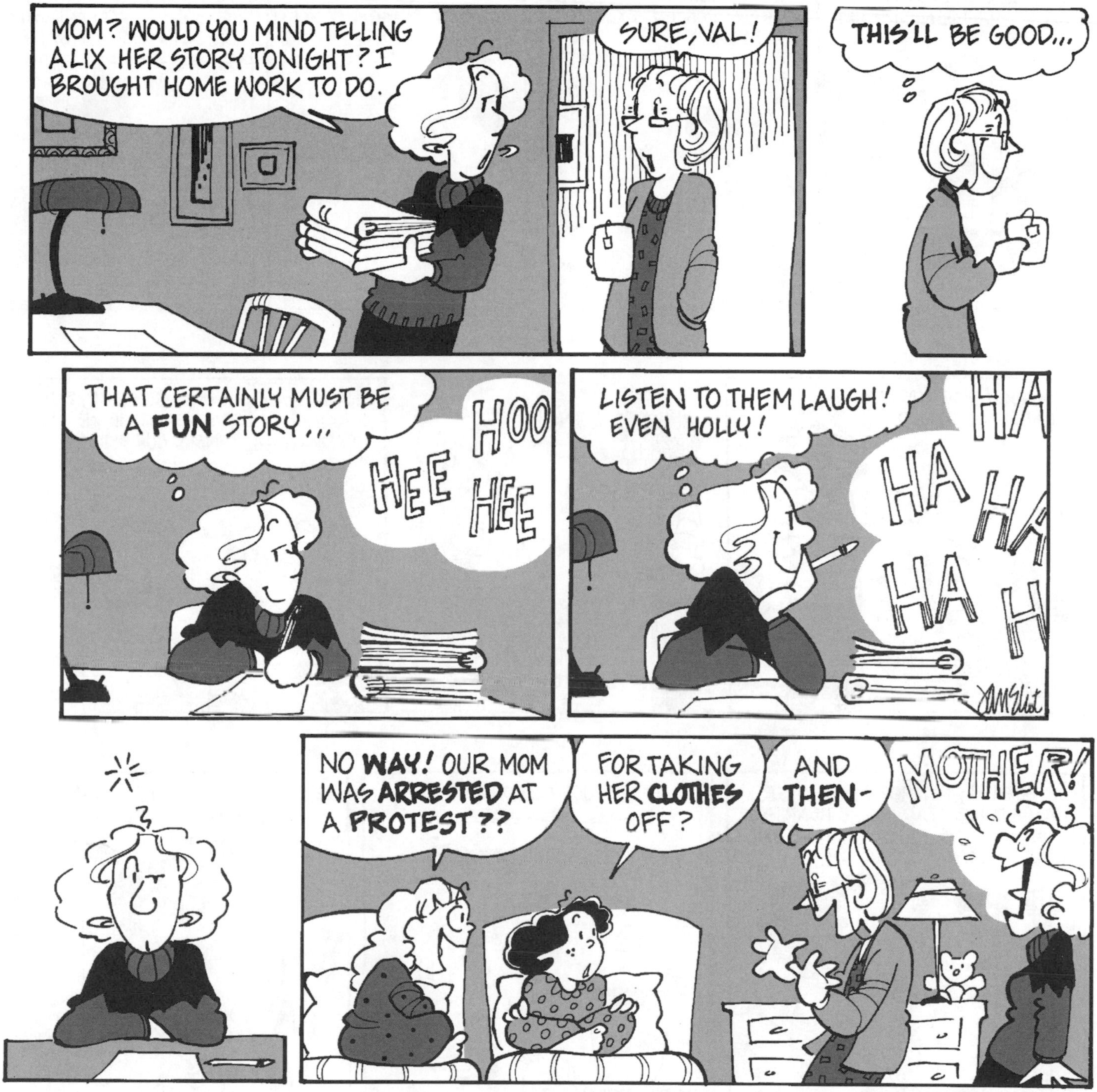
MOM? WOULD YOU MIND TELLING ALIX HER STORY TONIGHT? I BROUGHT HOME WORK TO DO.
SURE, VAL!
THIS'LL BE GOOD...
THAT CERTAINLY MUST BE A FUN STORY...
HEE HOO HEE
LISTEN TO THEM LAUGH! EVEN HOLLY!
HA HA HA HA HA H
NO WAY! OUR MOM WAS ARRESTED AT A PROTEST??
FOR TAKING HER CLOTHES OFF?
AND THEN-
MOTHER!

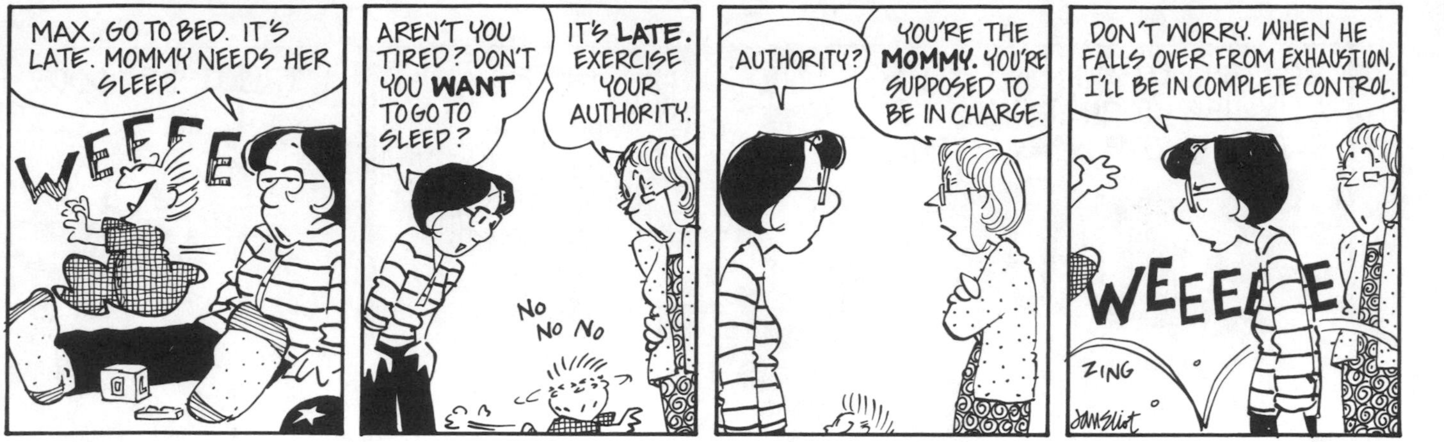
MAX, GO TO BED. IT'S LATE. MOMMY NEEDS HER SLEEP.
WEEEE
AREN'T YOU TIRED? DON'T YOU **WANT** TO GO TO SLEEP?
IT'S **LATE.** EXERCISE YOUR AUTHORITY.
NO NO NO
AUTHORITY?
YOU'RE THE **MOMMY.** YOU'RE SUPPOSED TO BE IN CHARGE.
DON'T WORRY. WHEN HE FALLS OVER FROM EXHAUSTION, I'LL BE IN COMPLETE CONTROL.
WEEEEE
ZING

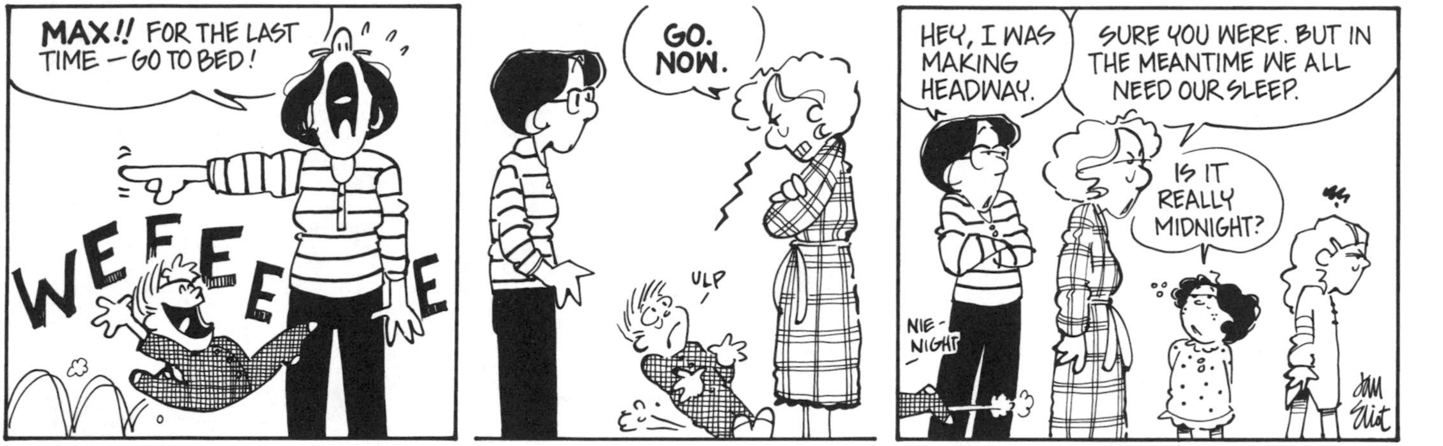
MAX!! FOR THE LAST TIME — GO TO BED!
WEEEEEE
GO. NOW.
ULP
HEY, I WAS MAKING HEADWAY.
SURE YOU WERE. BUT IN THE MEANTIME WE ALL NEED OUR SLEEP.
IS IT REALLY MIDNIGHT?
NIE-NIGHT

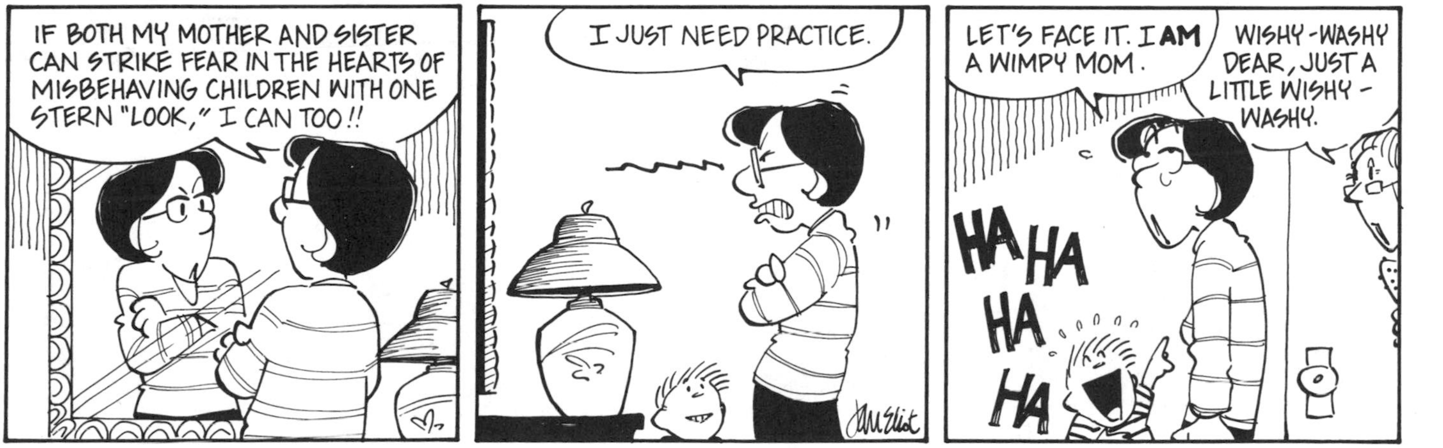
IF BOTH MY MOTHER AND SISTER CAN STRIKE FEAR IN THE HEARTS OF MISBEHAVING CHILDREN WITH ONE STERN "LOOK," I CAN TOO!!
I JUST NEED PRACTICE.
LET'S FACE IT. I **AM** A WIMPY MOM.
WISHY-WASHY DEAR, JUST A LITTLE WISHY-WASHY.
HA HA HA HA

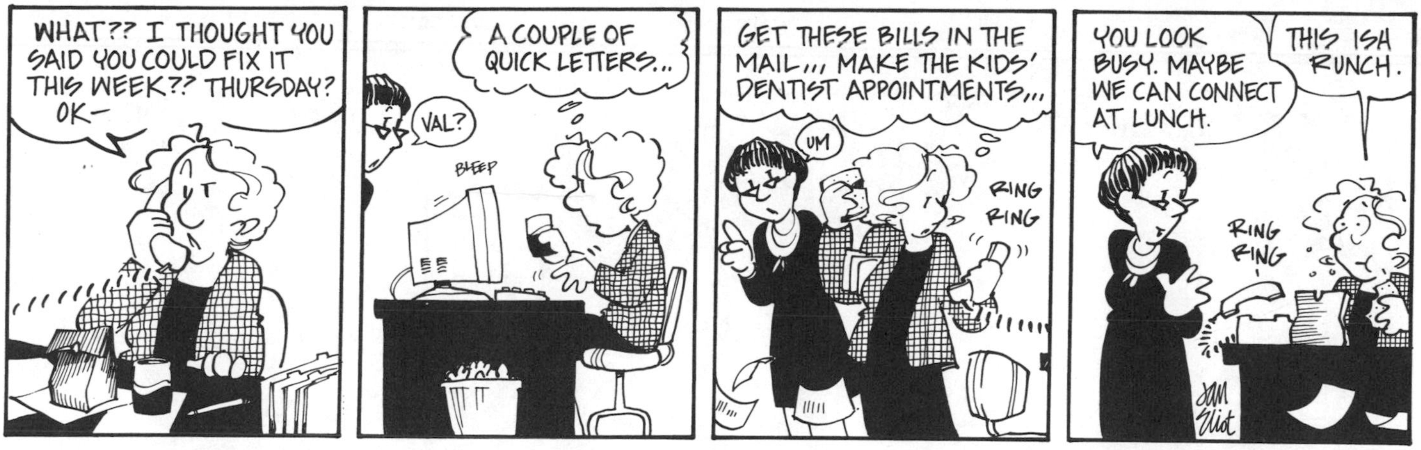
WHAT?? I THOUGHT YOU SAID YOU COULD FIX IT THIS WEEK?? THURSDAY? OK—
A COUPLE OF QUICK LETTERS...
VAL?
BLEEP
GET THESE BILLS IN THE MAIL,,, MAKE THE KIDS' DENTIST APPOINTMENTS,,,
UM
RING RING
YOU LOOK BUSY. MAYBE WE CAN CONNECT AT LUNCH.
THIS ISH RUNCH.
RING RING

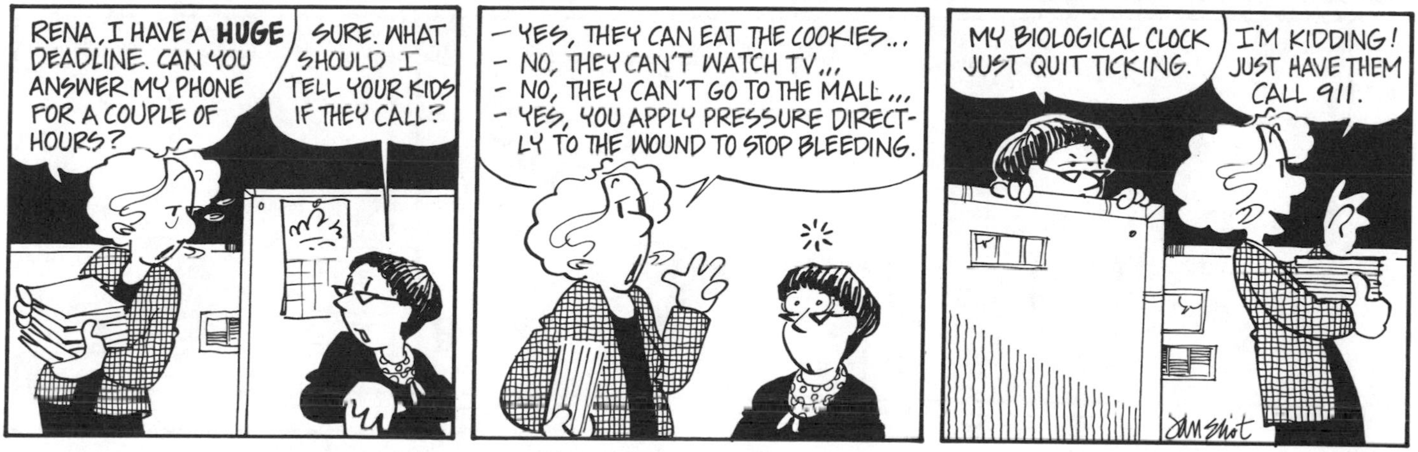
RENA, I HAVE A **HUGE** DEADLINE. CAN YOU ANSWER MY PHONE FOR A COUPLE OF HOURS?
SURE. WHAT SHOULD I TELL YOUR KIDS IF THEY CALL?
– YES, THEY CAN EAT THE COOKIES...
– NO, THEY CAN'T WATCH TV,,,
– NO, THEY CAN'T GO TO THE MALL,,,
– YES, YOU APPLY PRESSURE DIRECTLY TO THE WOUND TO STOP BLEEDING.
MY BIOLOGICAL CLOCK JUST QUIT TICKING.
I'M KIDDING! JUST HAVE THEM CALL 911.

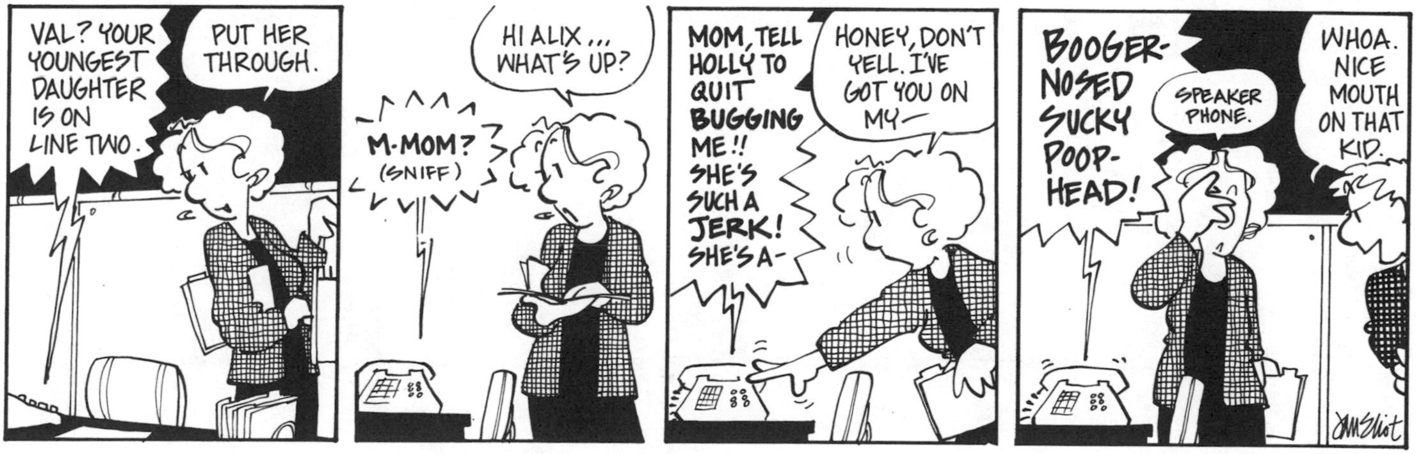
VAL? YOUR YOUNGEST DAUGHTER IS ON LINE TWO.
PUT HER THROUGH.
HI ALIX,,, WHAT'S UP?
M-MOM? (SNIFF)
MOM, TELL HOLLY TO QUIT BUGGING ME!! SHE'S SUCH A JERK! SHE'S A-
HONEY, DON'T YELL. I'VE GOT YOU ON MY—
BOOGER-NOSED SUCKY POOP-HEAD!
SPEAKER PHONE.
WHOA. NICE MOUTH ON THAT KID.

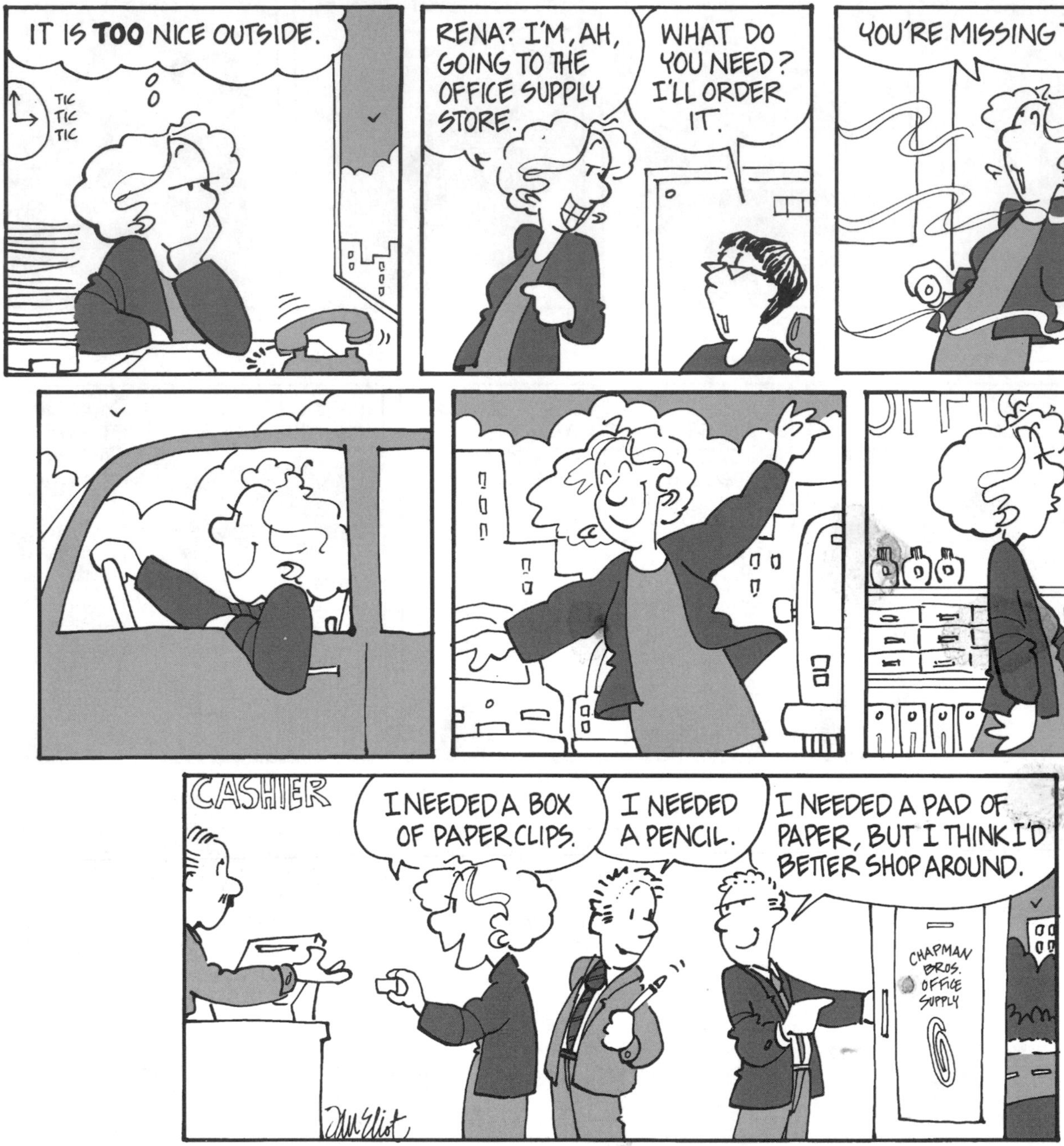
IT IS **TOO** NICE OUTSIDE.
TIC
TIC
TIC
RENA? I'M, AH, GOING TO THE OFFICE SUPPLY STORE.
WHAT DO YOU NEED? I'LL ORDER IT.
YOU'RE MISSING THE POINT.
CASHIER
I NEEDED A BOX OF PAPER CLIPS.
I NEEDED A PENCIL.
I NEEDED A PAD OF PAPER, BUT I THINK I'D BETTER SHOP AROUND.
CHAPMAN BROS. OFFICE SUPPLY

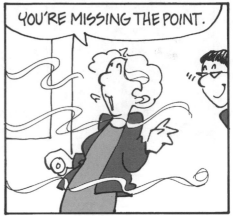

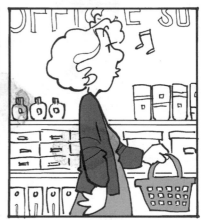

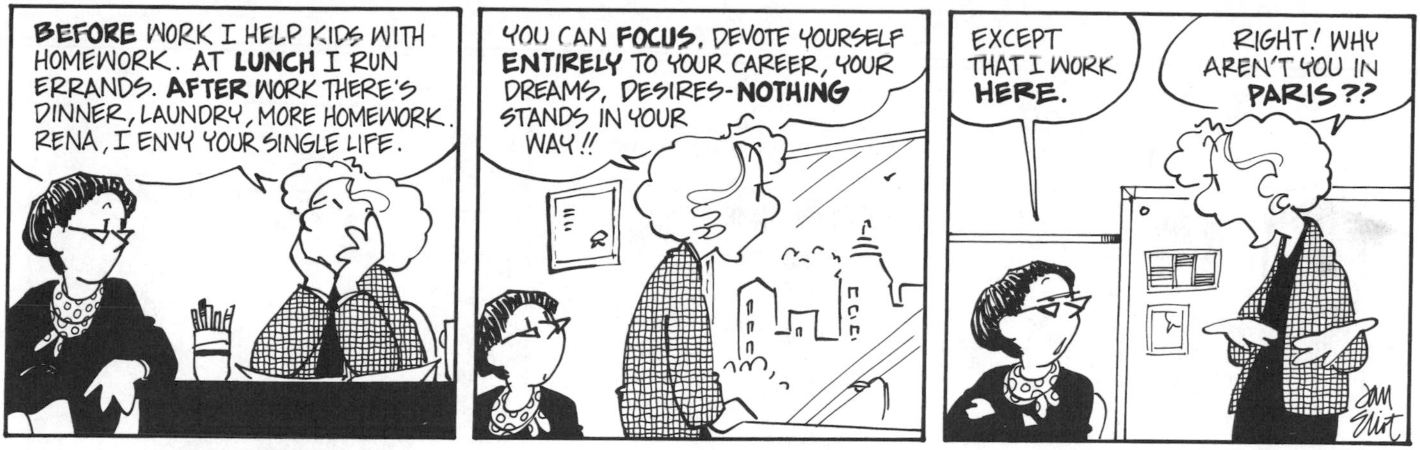
BEFORE WORK I HELP KIDS WITH HOMEWORK. AT LUNCH I RUN ERRANDS. AFTER WORK THERE'S DINNER, LAUNDRY, MORE HOMEWORK. RENA, I ENVY YOUR SINGLE LIFE.
YOU CAN FOCUS. DEVOTE YOURSELF ENTIRELY TO YOUR CAREER, YOUR DREAMS, DESIRES-NOTHING STANDS IN YOUR WAY!!
EXCEPT THAT I WORK HERE.
RIGHT! WHY AREN'T YOU IN PARIS??
Jan Eliot

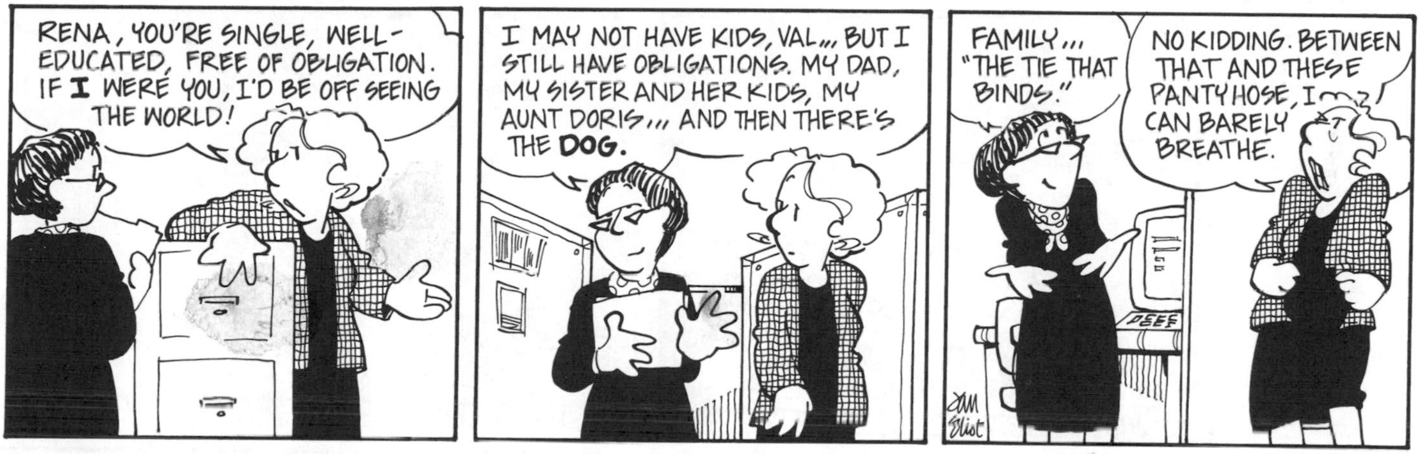
RENA, YOU'RE SINGLE, WELL-EDUCATED, FREE OF OBLIGATION. IF I WERE YOU, I'D BE OFF SEEING THE WORLD!
I MAY NOT HAVE KIDS, VAL,,, BUT I STILL HAVE OBLIGATIONS. MY DAD, MY SISTER AND HER KIDS, MY AUNT DORIS,,, AND THEN THERE'S THE DOG.
FAMILY,,, "THE TIE THAT BINDS."
NO KIDDING. BETWEEN THAT AND THESE PANTYHOSE, I CAN BARELY BREATHE.
Jan Eliot

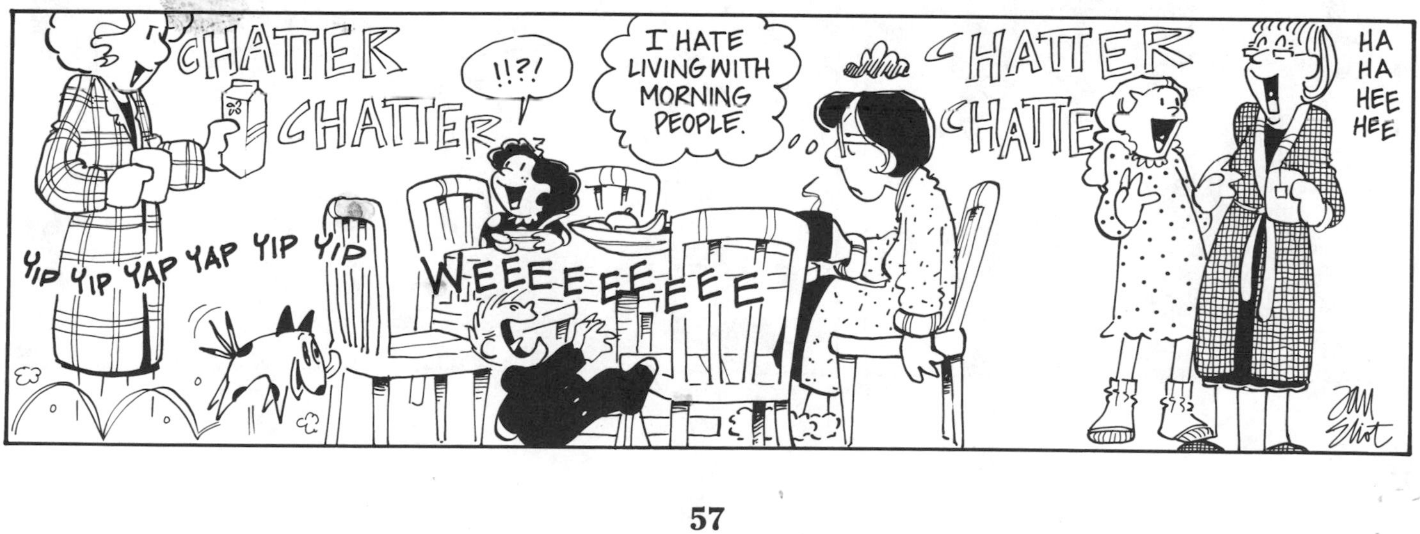
CHATTER
CHATTER
!!?!
I HATE LIVING WITH MORNING PEOPLE.
CHATTER
CHATTE
HA HA HEE HEE
YIP YIP YAP YAP YIP YIP
WEEEEEEEEEE
Jan Eliot

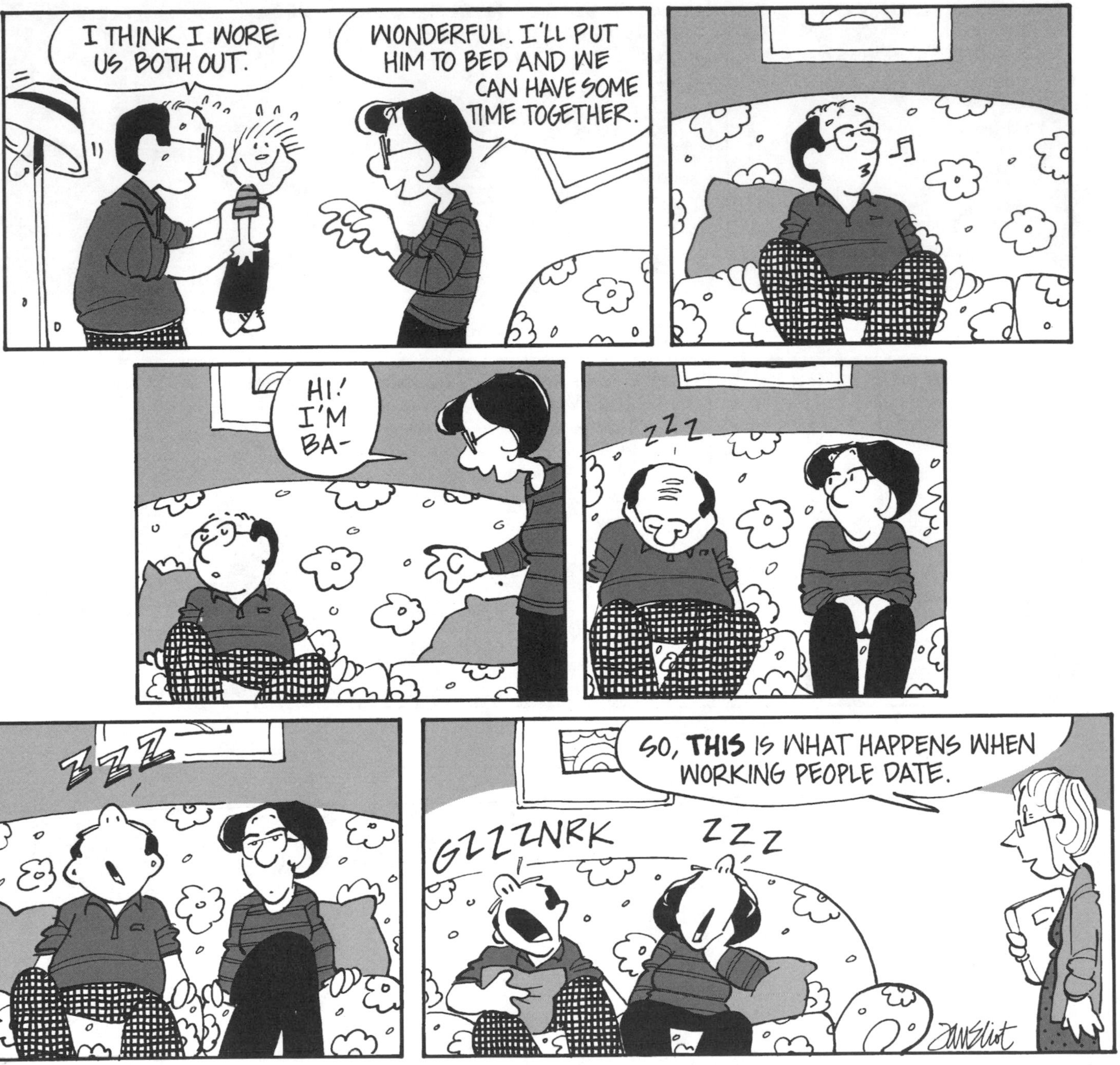
I THINK I WORE US BOTH OUT.
WONDERFUL. I'LL PUT HIM TO BED AND WE CAN HAVE SOME TIME TOGETHER.
HI! I'M BA-
Z Z Z
Z Z Z
SO, **THIS** IS WHAT HAPPENS WHEN WORKING PEOPLE DATE.
GZZZNRK
Z Z Z

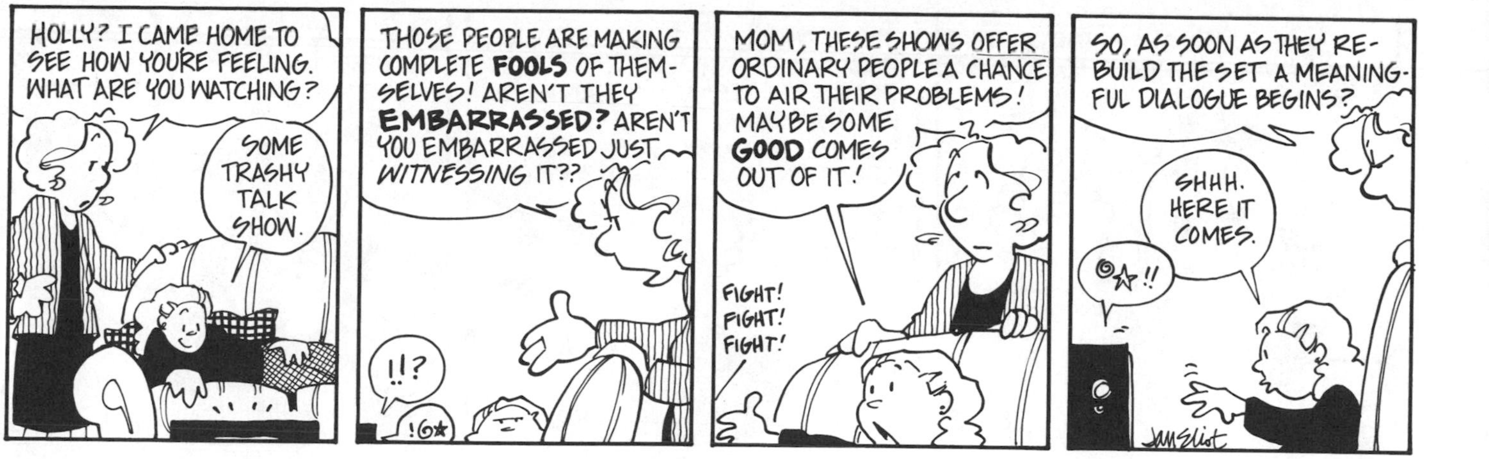
HOLLY? I CAME HOME TO SEE HOW YOU'RE FEELING. WHAT ARE YOU WATCHING?
SOME TRASHY TALK SHOW.
THOSE PEOPLE ARE MAKING COMPLETE **FOOLS** OF THEMSELVES! AREN'T THEY **EMBARRASSED?** AREN'T YOU EMBARRASSED JUST *WITNESSING* IT??
!!?
MOM, THESE SHOWS OFFER ORDINARY PEOPLE A CHANCE TO AIR THEIR PROBLEMS! MAYBE SOME **GOOD** COMES OUT OF IT!
FIGHT! FIGHT! FIGHT!
SO, AS SOON AS THEY REBUILD THE SET A MEANINGFUL DIALOGUE BEGINS?
SHHH. HERE IT COMES.

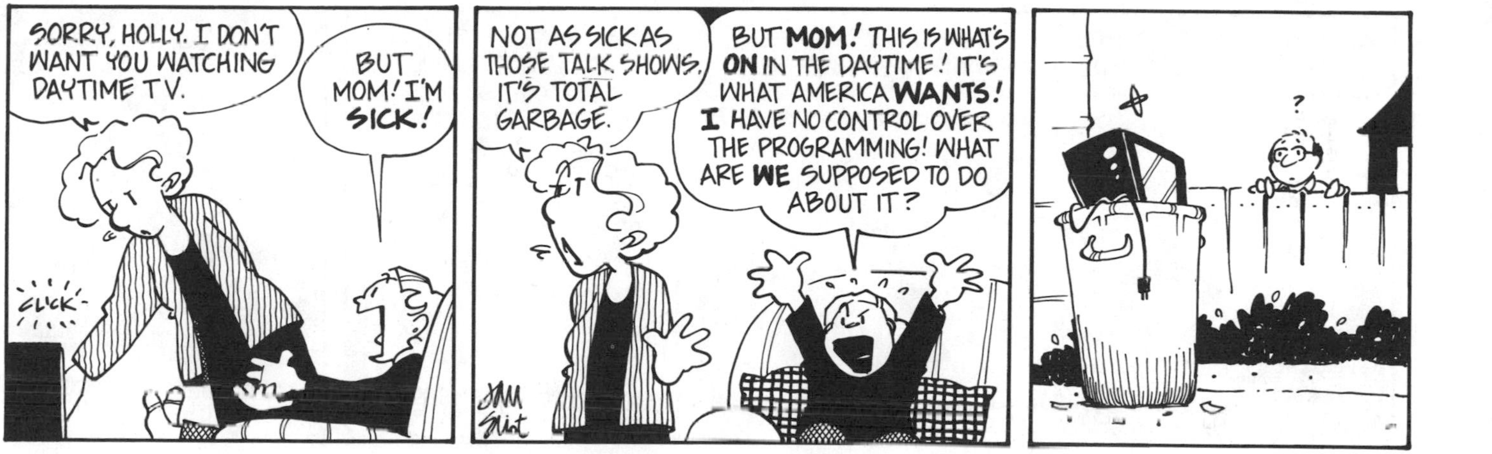
SORRY, HOLLY. I DON'T WANT YOU WATCHING DAYTIME T.V.
BUT MOM! I'M **SICK**!
CLICK
NOT AS SICK AS THOSE TALK SHOWS. IT'S TOTAL GARBAGE.
BUT **MOM!** THIS IS WHAT'S **ON** IN THE DAYTIME! IT'S WHAT AMERICA **WANTS**! **I** HAVE NO CONTROL OVER THE PROGRAMMING! WHAT ARE **WE** SUPPOSED TO DO ABOUT IT?
?

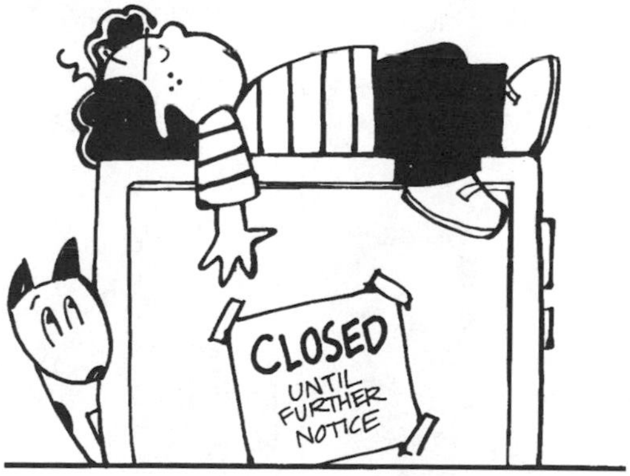
CLOSED
UNTIL FURTHER NOTICE

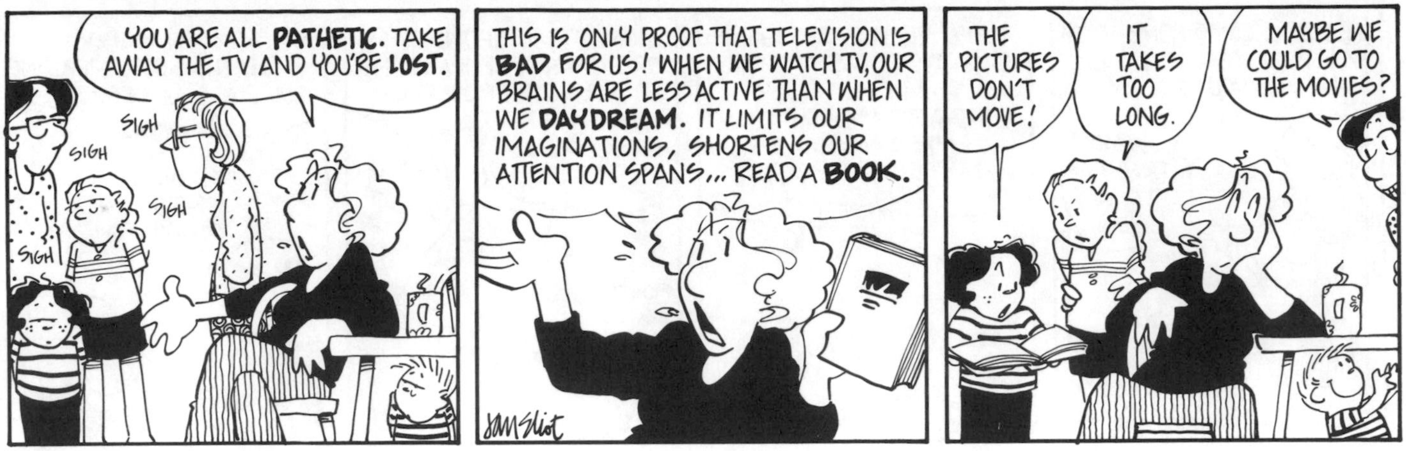
YOU ARE ALL **PATHETIC**. TAKE AWAY THE TV AND YOU'RE **LOST**.
SIGH
SIGH
SIGH
SIGH
THIS IS ONLY PROOF THAT TELEVISION IS **BAD** FOR US! WHEN WE WATCH TV, OUR BRAINS ARE LESS ACTIVE THAN WHEN WE **DAYDREAM**. IT LIMITS OUR IMAGINATIONS, SHORTENS OUR ATTENTION SPANS... READ A **BOOK**.
THE PICTURES DON'T MOVE!
IT TAKES TOO LONG.
MAYBE WE COULD GO TO THE MOVIES?

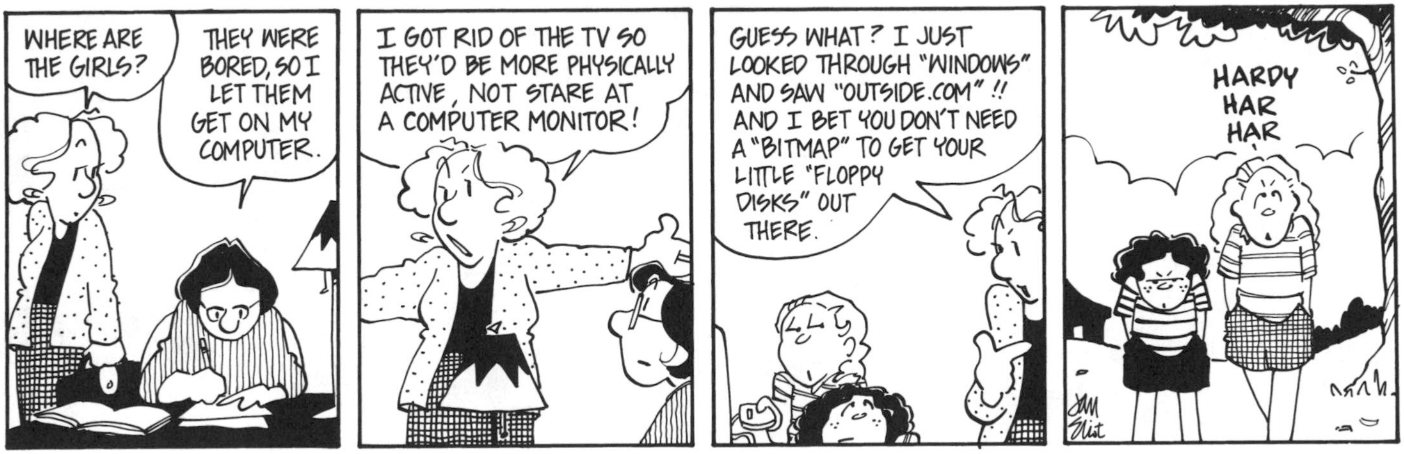
WHERE ARE THE GIRLS?
THEY WERE BORED, SO I LET THEM GET ON MY COMPUTER.
I GOT RID OF THE TV SO THEY'D BE MORE PHYSICALLY ACTIVE, NOT STARE AT A COMPUTER MONITOR!
GUESS WHAT? I JUST LOOKED THROUGH "WINDOWS" AND SAW "OUTSIDE.COM"!! AND I BET YOU DON'T NEED A "BITMAP" TO GET YOUR LITTLE "FLOPPY DISKS" OUT THERE.
HARDY HAR HAR

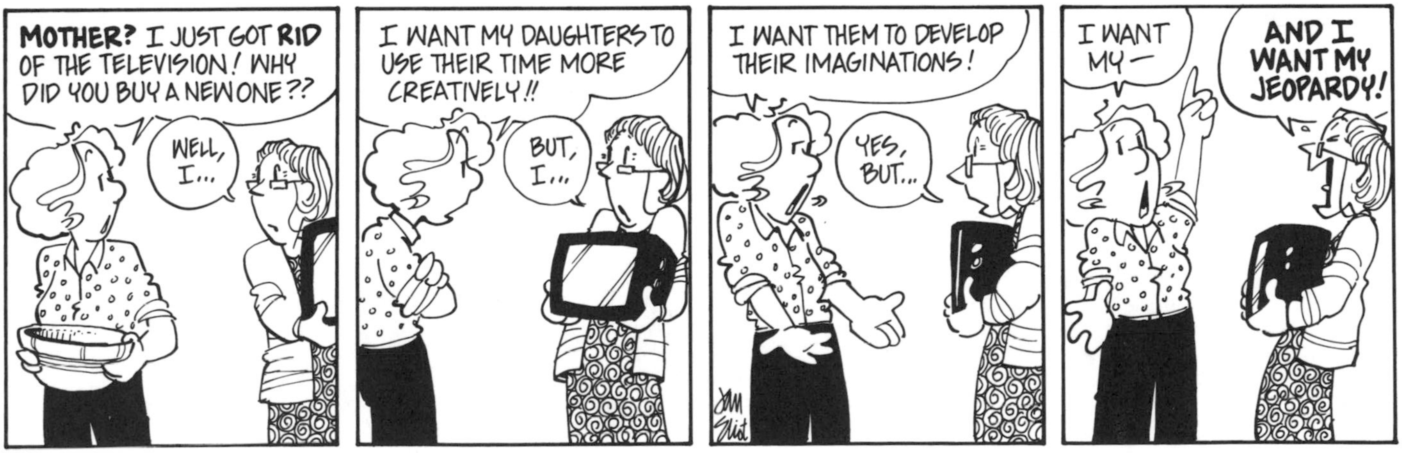
MOTHER? I JUST GOT **RID** OF THE TELEVISION! WHY DID YOU BUY A NEW ONE??
WELL, I...
I WANT MY DAUGHTERS TO USE THEIR TIME MORE CREATIVELY!!
BUT, I...
I WANT THEM TO DEVELOP THEIR IMAGINATIONS!
YES, BUT...
I WANT MY—
AND I WANT MY JEOPARDY!

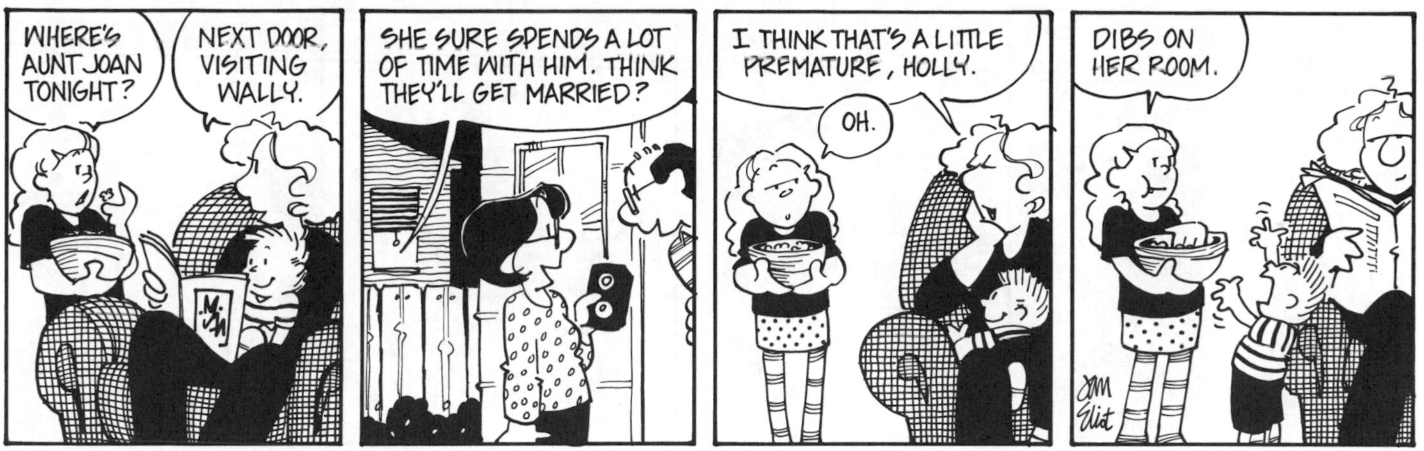
WHERE'S AUNT JOAN TONIGHT?
NEXT DOOR, VISITING WALLY.
SHE SURE SPENDS A LOT OF TIME WITH HIM. THINK THEY'LL GET MARRIED?
I THINK THAT'S A LITTLE PREMATURE, HOLLY.
OH.
DIBS ON HER ROOM.

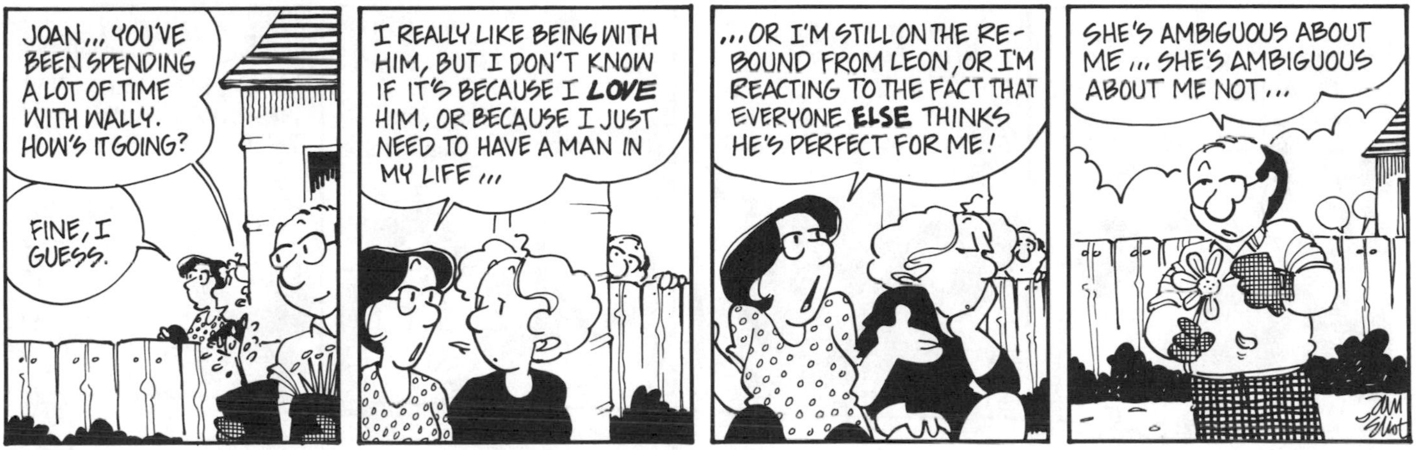
JOAN... YOU'VE BEEN SPENDING A LOT OF TIME WITH WALLY. HOW'S IT GOING?
FINE, I GUESS.
I REALLY LIKE BEING WITH HIM, BUT I DON'T KNOW IF IT'S BECAUSE I LOVE HIM, OR BECAUSE I JUST NEED TO HAVE A MAN IN MY LIFE...
...OR I'M STILL ON THE RE-BOUND FROM LEON, OR I'M REACTING TO THE FACT THAT EVERYONE ELSE THINKS HE'S PERFECT FOR ME!
SHE'S AMBIGUOUS ABOUT ME... SHE'S AMBIGUOUS ABOUT ME NOT...

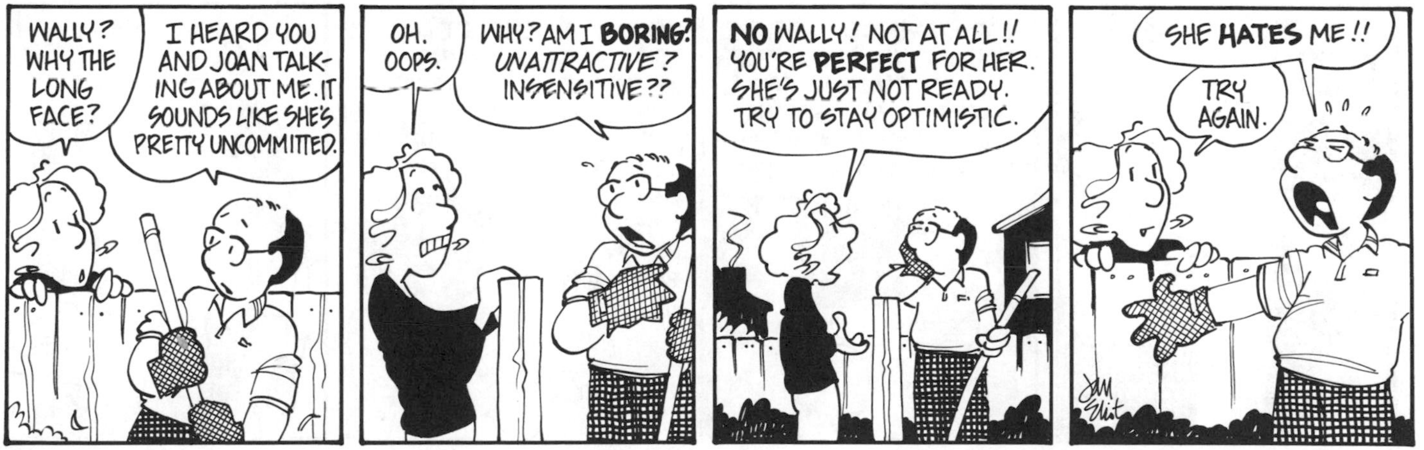
WALLY? WHY THE LONG FACE?
I HEARD YOU AND JOAN TALK-ING ABOUT ME. IT SOUNDS LIKE SHE'S PRETTY UNCOMMITTED.
OH. OOPS.
WHY? AM I BORING? UNATTRACTIVE? INSENSITIVE??
NO WALLY! NOT AT ALL!! YOU'RE PERFECT FOR HER. SHE'S JUST NOT READY. TRY TO STAY OPTIMISTIC.
SHE HATES ME!!
TRY AGAIN.

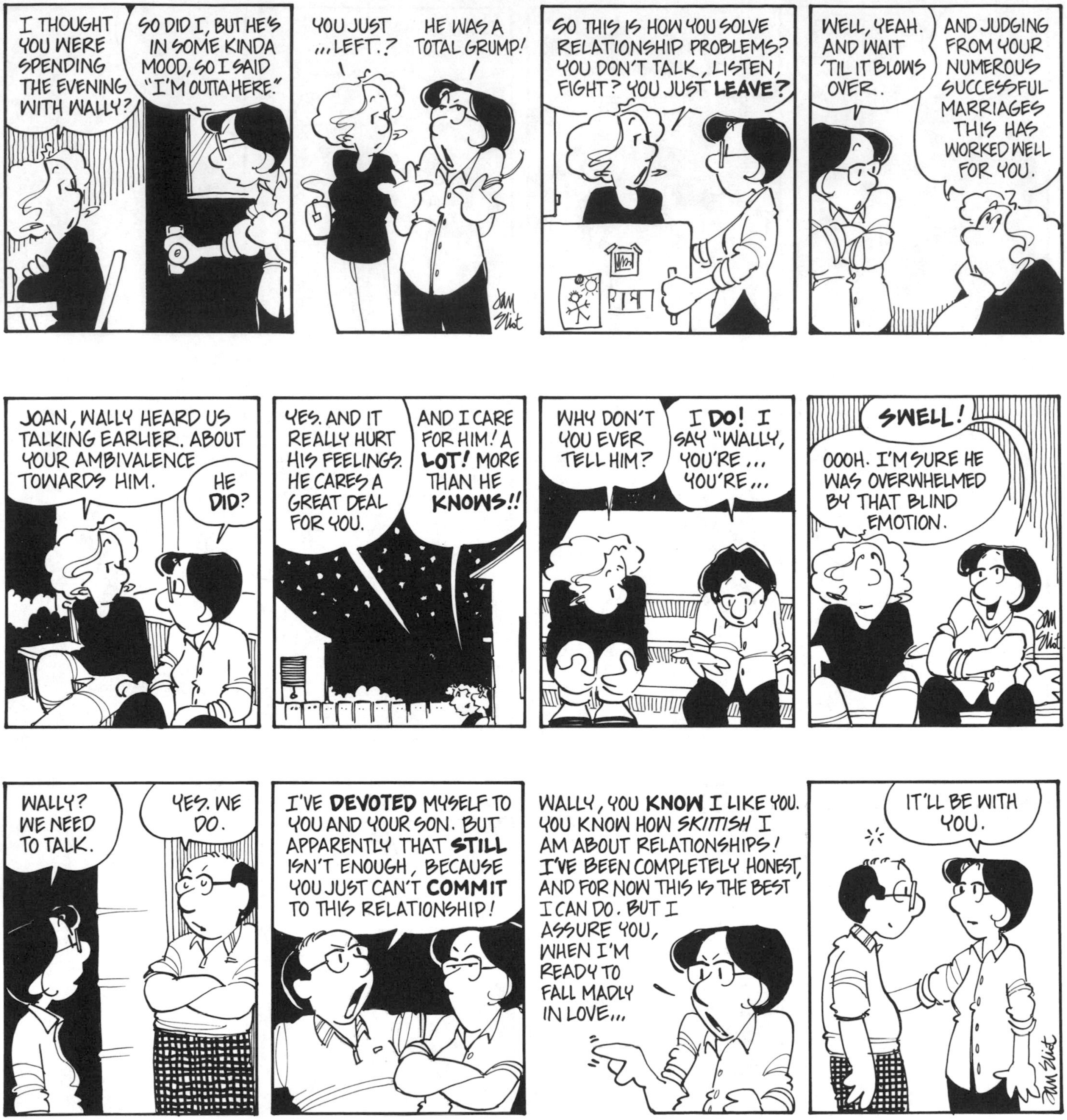
I THOUGHT YOU WERE SPENDING THE EVENING WITH WALLY?
SO DID I, BUT HE'S IN SOME KINDA MOOD, SO I SAID "I'M OUTTA HERE."
YOU JUST ...LEFT.?
HE WAS A TOTAL GRUMP!
SO THIS IS HOW YOU SOLVE RELATIONSHIP PROBLEMS? YOU DON'T TALK, LISTEN, FIGHT? YOU JUST LEAVE?
WELL, YEAH. AND WAIT 'TIL IT BLOWS OVER.
AND JUDGING FROM YOUR NUMEROUS SUCCESSFUL MARRIAGES THIS HAS WORKED WELL FOR YOU.
JOAN, WALLY HEARD US TALKING EARLIER. ABOUT YOUR AMBIVALENCE TOWARDS HIM.
HE DID?
YES. AND IT REALLY HURT HIS FEELINGS. HE CARES A GREAT DEAL FOR YOU.
AND I CARE FOR HIM! A LOT! MORE THAN HE KNOWS!!
WHY DON'T YOU EVER TELL HIM?
I DO! I SAY "WALLY, YOU'RE ... YOU'RE ...
SWELL!
OOOH. I'M SURE HE WAS OVERWHELMED BY THAT BLIND EMOTION.
WALLY? WE NEED TO TALK.
YES. WE DO.
I'VE DEVOTED MYSELF TO YOU AND YOUR SON. BUT APPARENTLY THAT STILL ISN'T ENOUGH, BECAUSE YOU JUST CAN'T COMMIT TO THIS RELATIONSHIP!
WALLY, YOU KNOW I LIKE YOU. YOU KNOW HOW SKITTISH I AM ABOUT RELATIONSHIPS! I'VE BEEN COMPLETELY HONEST, AND FOR NOW THIS IS THE BEST I CAN DO. BUT I ASSURE YOU, WHEN I'M READY TO FALL MADLY IN LOVE...
IT'LL BE WITH YOU.

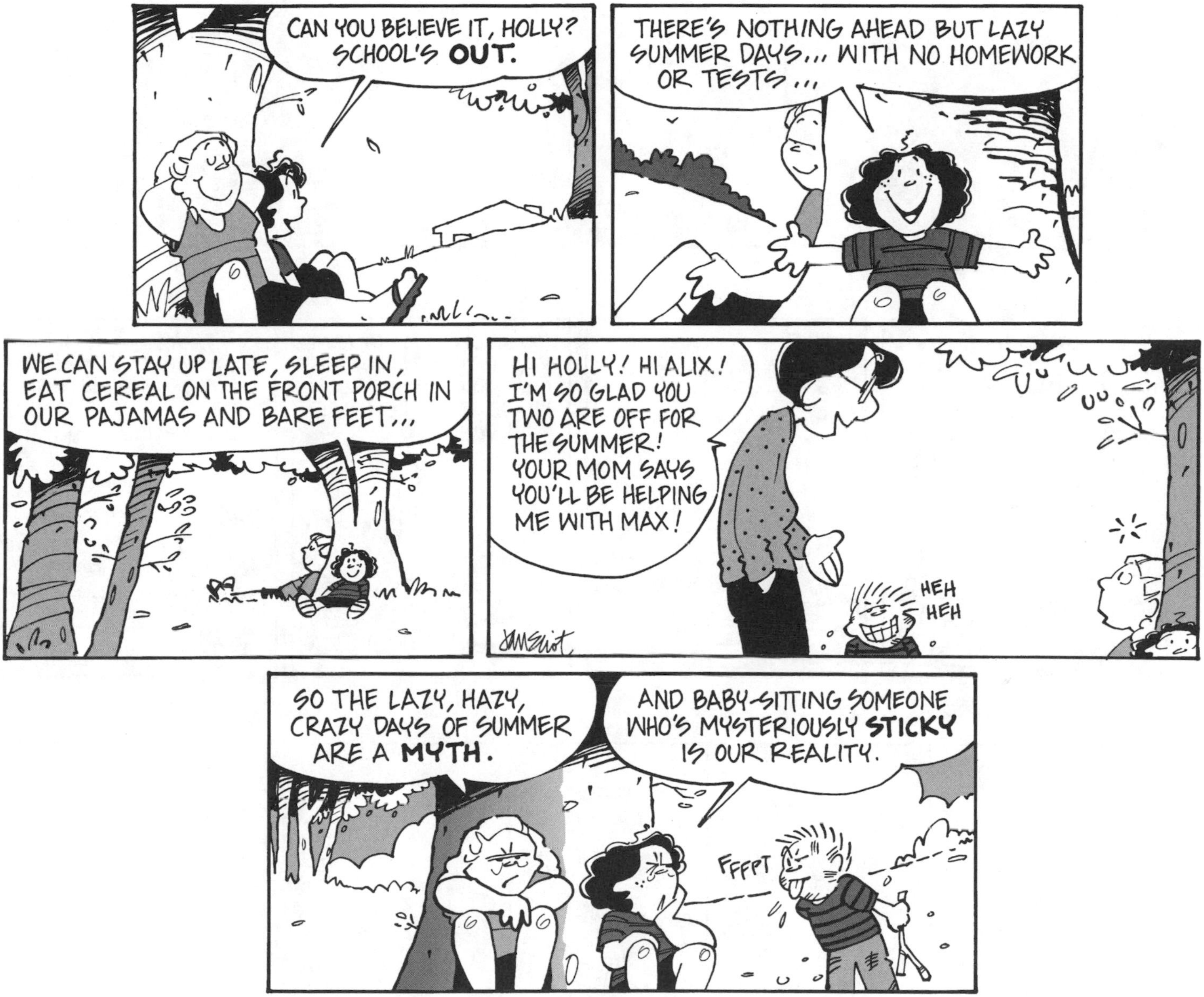
CAN YOU BELIEVE IT, HOLLY? SCHOOL'S **OUT**.
THERE'S NOTHING AHEAD BUT LAZY SUMMER DAYS... WITH NO HOMEWORK OR TESTS...
WE CAN STAY UP LATE, SLEEP IN, EAT CEREAL ON THE FRONT PORCH IN OUR PAJAMAS AND BARE FEET...
HI HOLLY! HI ALIX! I'M SO GLAD YOU TWO ARE OFF FOR THE SUMMER! YOUR MOM SAYS YOU'LL BE HELPING ME WITH MAX!
HEH HEH
SO THE LAZY, HAZY, CRAZY DAYS OF SUMMER ARE A **MYTH**.
AND BABY-SITTING SOMEONE WHO'S MYSTERIOUSLY **STICKY** IS OUR REALITY.
FFFPT

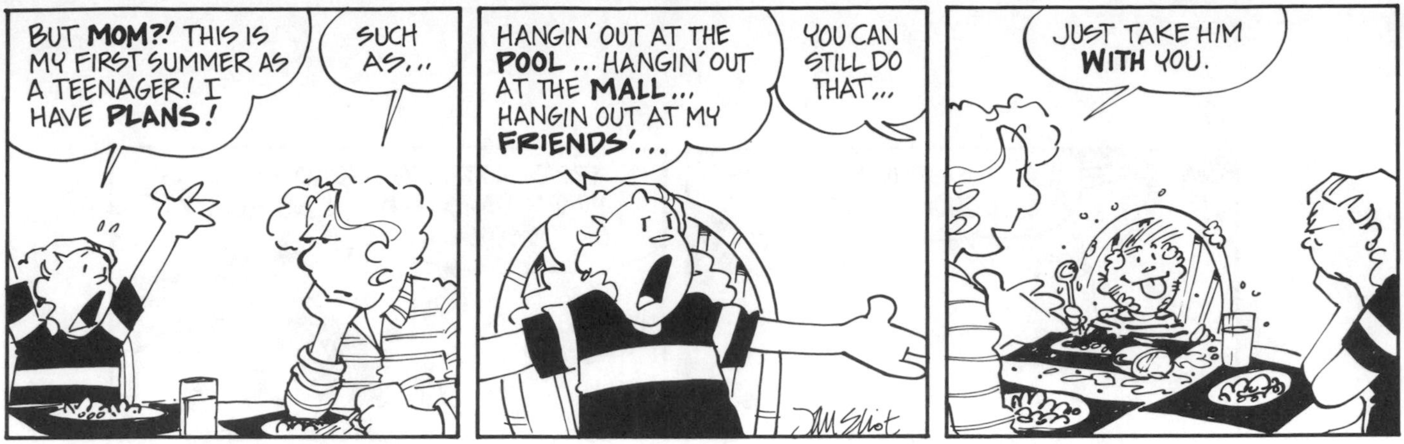
BUT MOM?! THIS IS MY FIRST SUMMER AS A TEENAGER! I HAVE PLANS!
SUCH AS...
HANGIN' OUT AT THE POOL ... HANGIN' OUT AT THE MALL... HANGIN OUT AT MY FRIENDS'...
YOU CAN STILL DO THAT,...
JUST TAKE HIM WITH YOU.

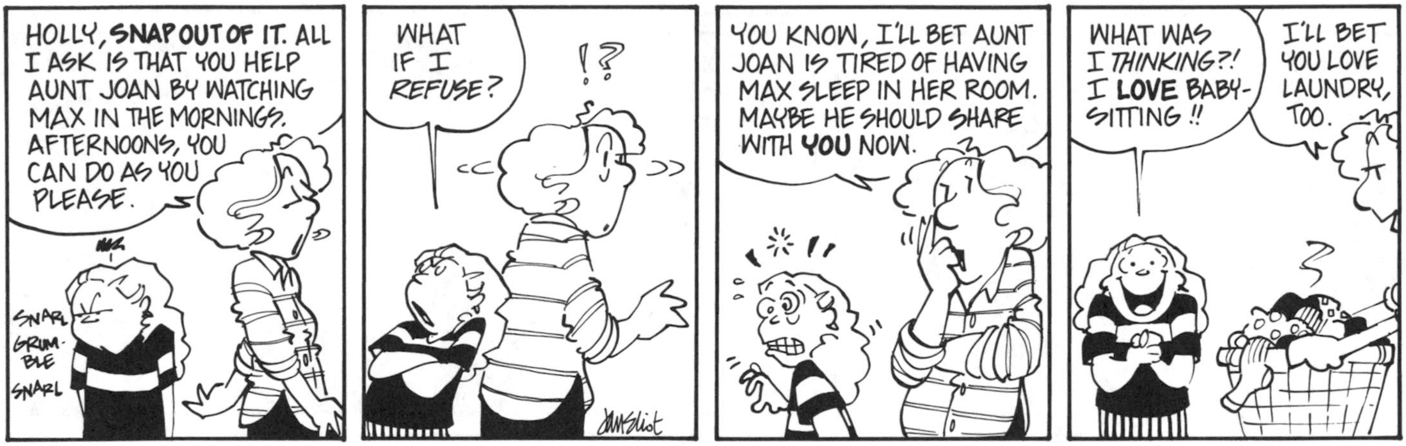
HOLLY, SNAP OUT OF IT. ALL I ASK IS THAT YOU HELP AUNT JOAN BY WATCHING MAX IN THE MORNINGS. AFTERNOONS, YOU CAN DO AS YOU PLEASE.
SNARL
GRUMBLE
SNARL
WHAT IF I REFUSE?
!?
YOU KNOW, I'LL BET AUNT JOAN IS TIRED OF HAVING MAX SLEEP IN HER ROOM. MAYBE HE SHOULD SHARE WITH YOU NOW.
WHAT WAS I THINKING?! I LOVE BABY-SITTING!!
I'LL BET YOU LOVE LAUNDRY, TOO.

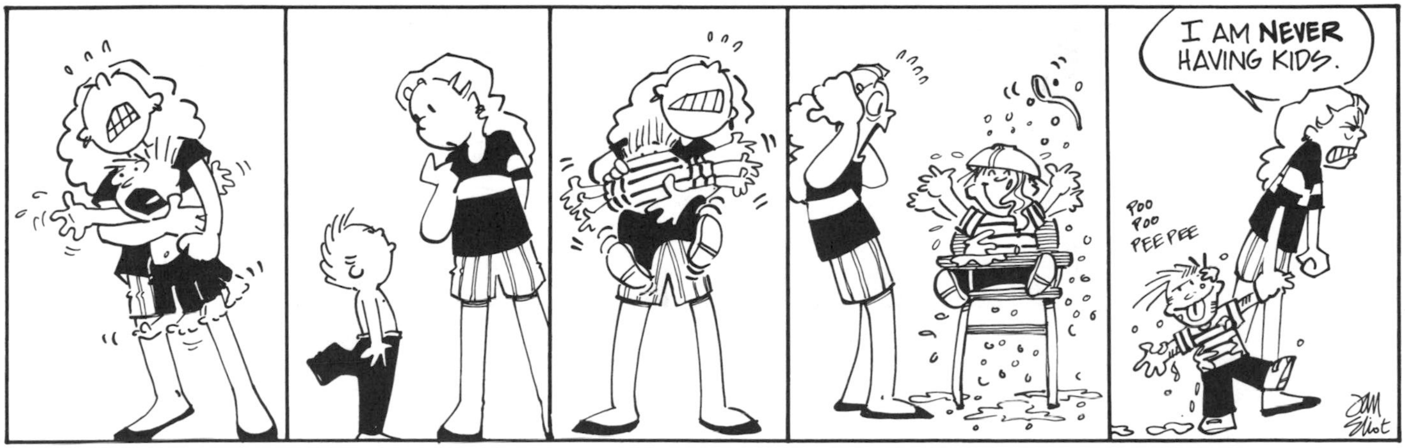
POO POO PEE PEE
I AM NEVER HAVING KIDS.

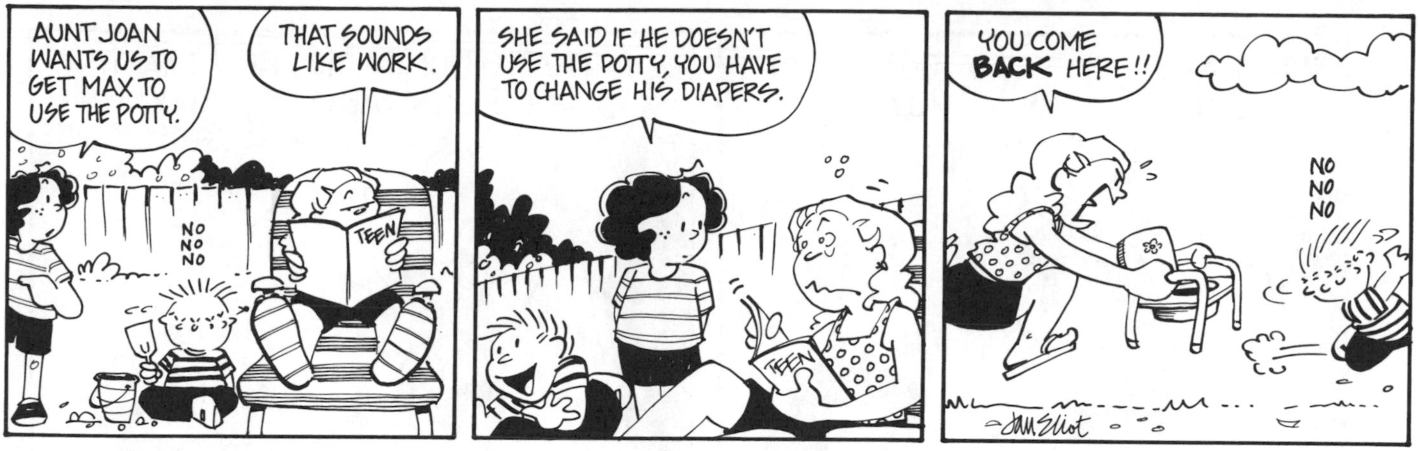
AUNT JOAN WANTS US TO GET MAX TO USE THE POTTY.
NO NO NO
THAT SOUNDS LIKE WORK.
TEEN
SHE SAID IF HE DOESN'T USE THE POTTY, YOU HAVE TO CHANGE HIS DIAPERS.
TEEN
YOU COME BACK HERE!!
NO NO NO

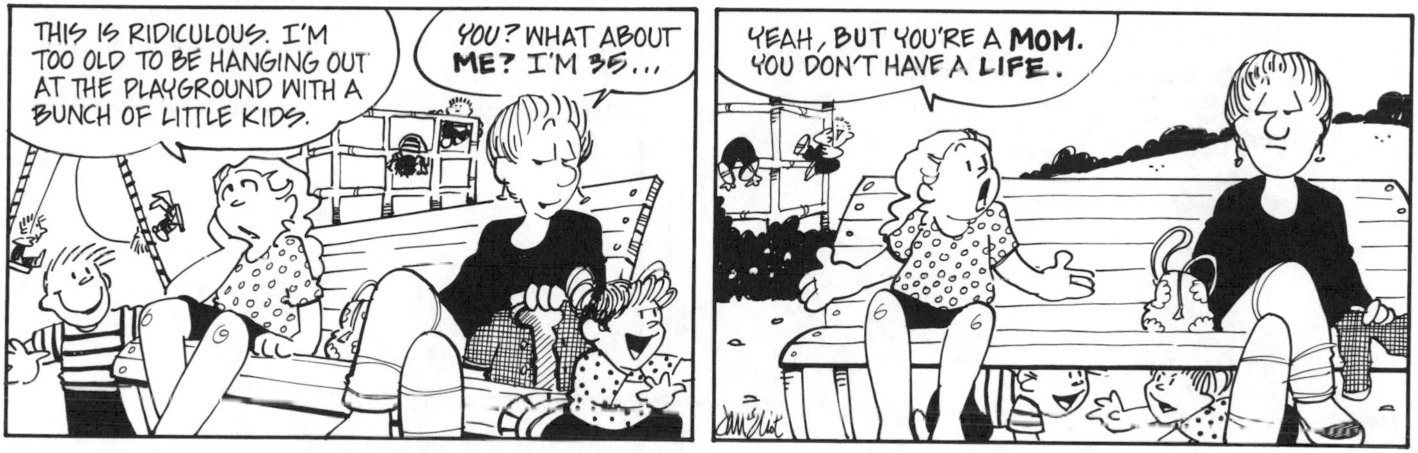
THIS IS RIDICULOUS. I'M TOO OLD TO BE HANGING OUT AT THE PLAYGROUND WITH A BUNCH OF LITTLE KIDS.
YOU? WHAT ABOUT ME? I'M 35...
YEAH, BUT YOU'RE A MOM. YOU DON'T HAVE A LIFE.

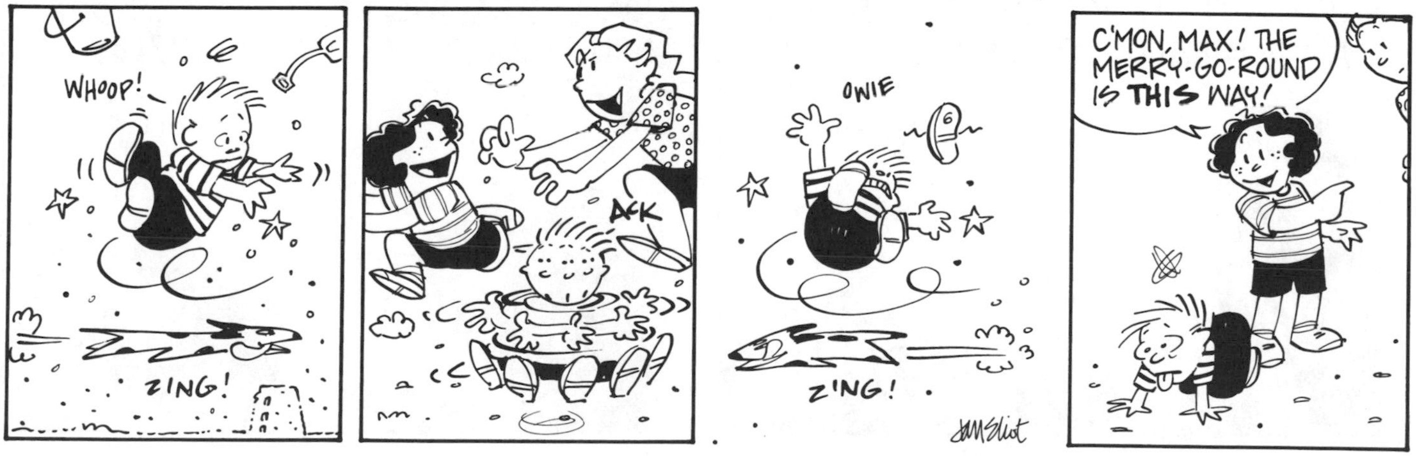
WHOOP!
ZING!
ACK
OWIE
ZING!
C'MON, MAX! THE MERRY-GO-ROUND IS THIS WAY!

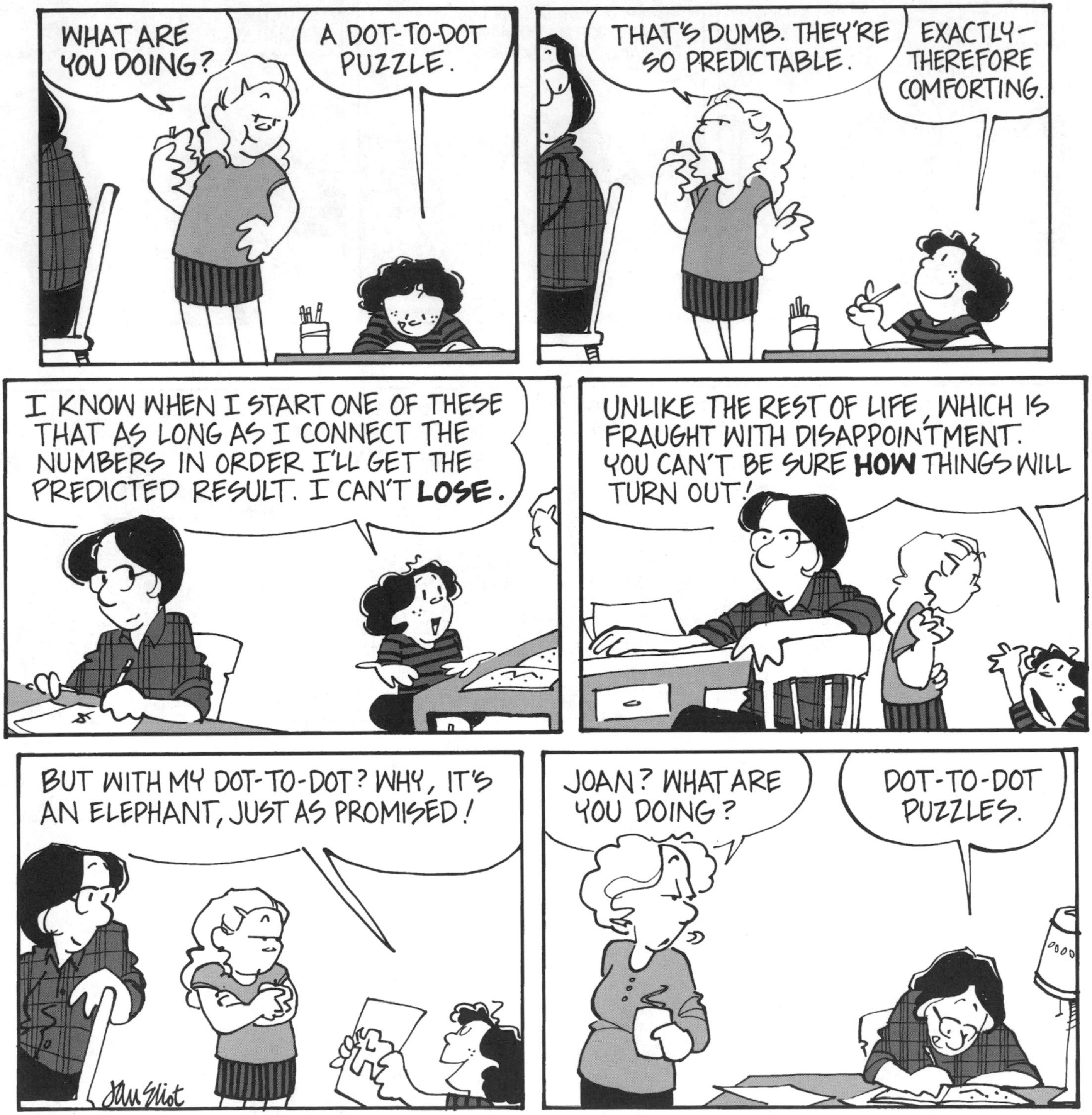
WHAT ARE YOU DOING?
A DOT-TO-DOT PUZZLE.
THAT'S DUMB. THEY'RE SO PREDICTABLE.
EXACTLY– THEREFORE COMFORTING.
I KNOW WHEN I START ONE OF THESE THAT AS LONG AS I CONNECT THE NUMBERS IN ORDER I'LL GET THE PREDICTED RESULT. I CAN'T **LOSE**.
UNLIKE THE REST OF LIFE, WHICH IS FRAUGHT WITH DISAPPOINTMENT. YOU CAN'T BE SURE **HOW** THINGS WILL TURN OUT!
BUT WITH MY DOT-TO-DOT? WHY, IT'S AN ELEPHANT, JUST AS PROMISED!
JOAN? WHAT ARE YOU DOING?
DOT-TO-DOT PUZZLES.

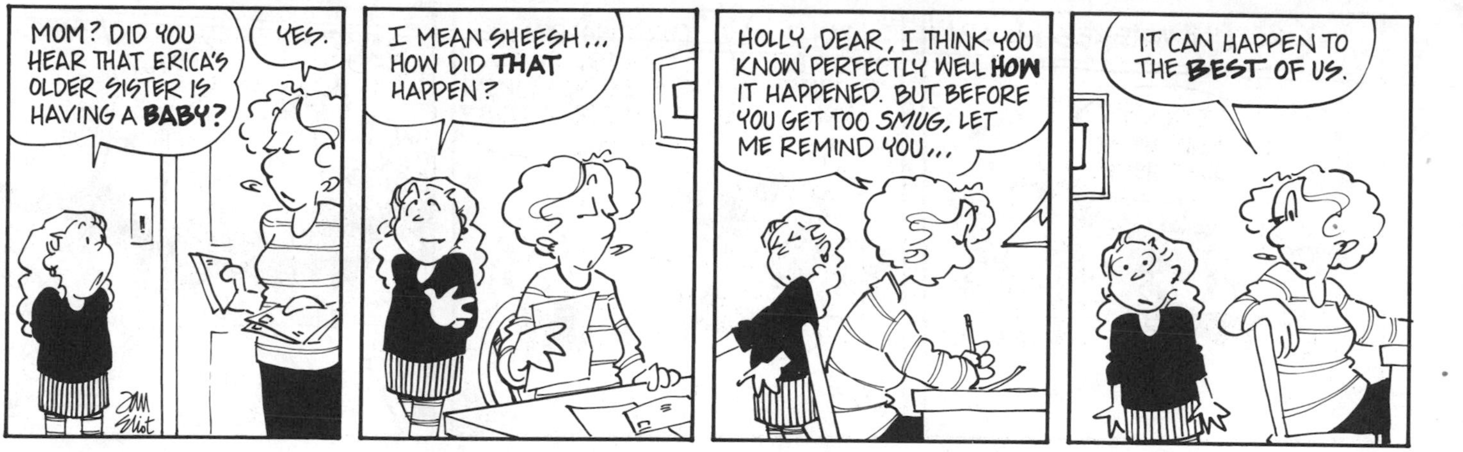
MOM? DID YOU HEAR THAT ERICA'S OLDER SISTER IS HAVING A BABY?
YES.
I MEAN SHEESH... HOW DID THAT HAPPEN?
HOLLY, DEAR, I THINK YOU KNOW PERFECTLY WELL HOW IT HAPPENED. BUT BEFORE YOU GET TOO SMUG, LET ME REMIND YOU...
IT CAN HAPPEN TO THE BEST OF US.

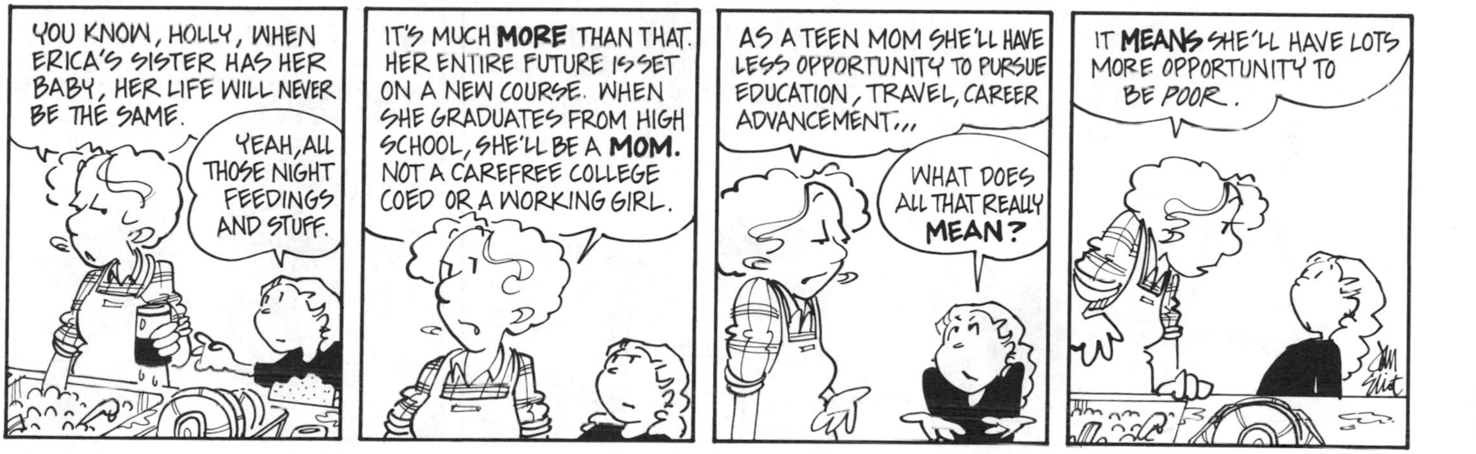
YOU KNOW, HOLLY, WHEN ERICA'S SISTER HAS HER BABY, HER LIFE WILL NEVER BE THE SAME.
YEAH, ALL THOSE NIGHT FEEDINGS AND STUFF.
IT'S MUCH MORE THAN THAT. HER ENTIRE FUTURE IS SET ON A NEW COURSE. WHEN SHE GRADUATES FROM HIGH SCHOOL, SHE'LL BE A MOM. NOT A CAREFREE COLLEGE COED OR A WORKING GIRL.
AS A TEEN MOM SHE'LL HAVE LESS OPPORTUNITY TO PURSUE EDUCATION, TRAVEL, CAREER ADVANCEMENT...
WHAT DOES ALL THAT REALLY MEAN?
IT MEANS SHE'LL HAVE LOTS MORE OPPORTUNITY TO BE POOR.

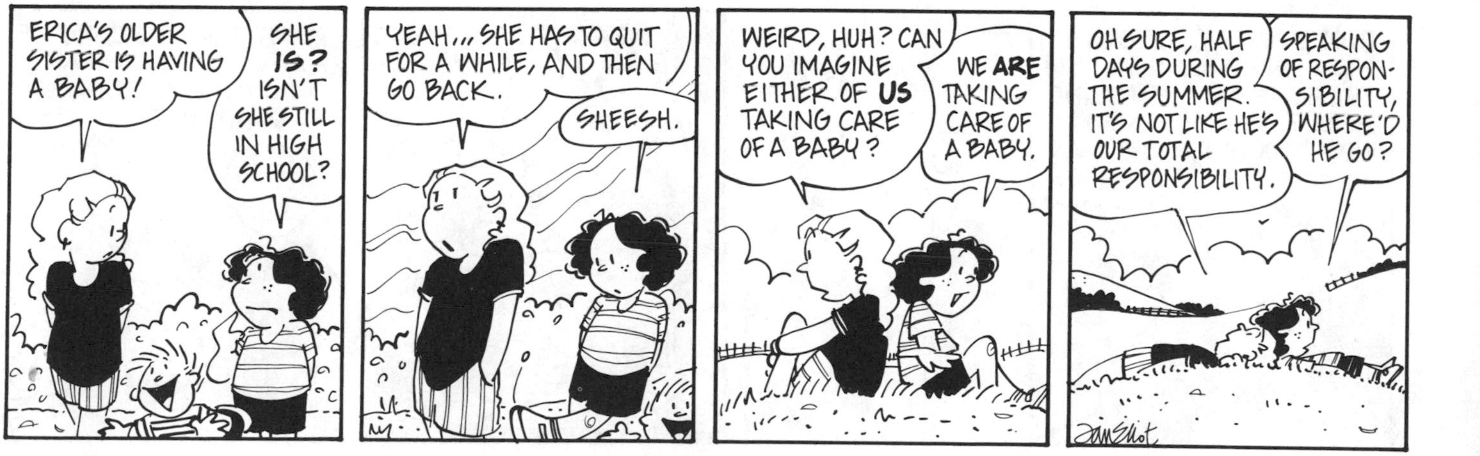
ERICA'S OLDER SISTER IS HAVING A BABY!
SHE IS? ISN'T SHE STILL IN HIGH SCHOOL?
YEAH... SHE HAS TO QUIT FOR A WHILE, AND THEN GO BACK.
SHEESH.
WEIRD, HUH? CAN YOU IMAGINE EITHER OF US TAKING CARE OF A BABY?
WE ARE TAKING CARE OF A BABY.
OH SURE, HALF DAYS DURING THE SUMMER. IT'S NOT LIKE HE'S OUR TOTAL RESPONSIBILITY.
SPEAKING OF RESPONSIBILITY, WHERE'D HE GO?

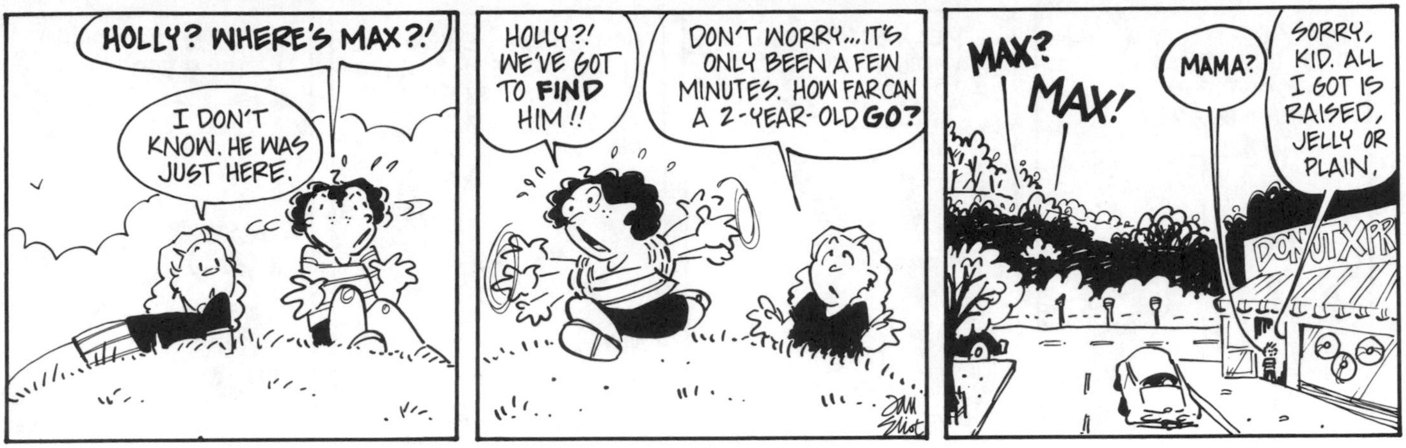
HOLLY? WHERE'S MAX?!
I DON'T KNOW. HE WAS JUST HERE.
HOLLY?! WE'VE GOT TO FIND HIM!!
DON'T WORRY... IT'S ONLY BEEN A FEW MINUTES. HOW FAR CAN A 2-YEAR-OLD GO?
MAX?
MAX!
MAMA?
SORRY, KID. ALL I GOT IS RAISED, JELLY OR PLAIN.

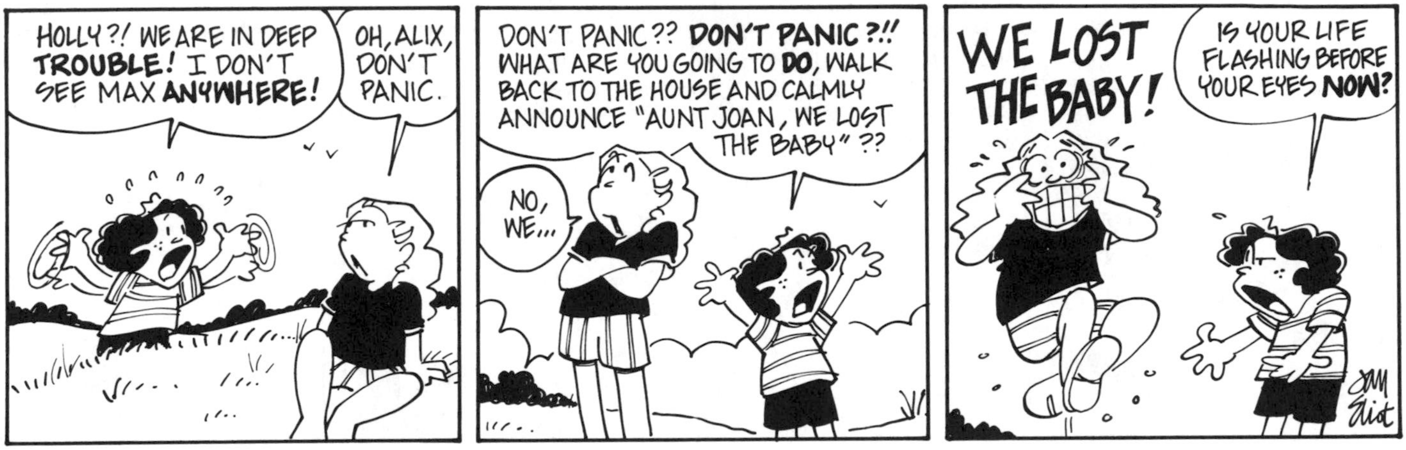
HOLLY?! WE ARE IN DEEP TROUBLE! I DON'T SEE MAX ANYWHERE!
OH, ALIX, DON'T PANIC.
DON'T PANIC?? DON'T PANIC?!! WHAT ARE YOU GOING TO DO, WALK BACK TO THE HOUSE AND CALMLY ANNOUNCE "AUNT JOAN, WE LOST THE BABY"??
NO, WE...
WE LOST THE BABY!
IS YOUR LIFE FLASHING BEFORE YOUR EYES NOW?

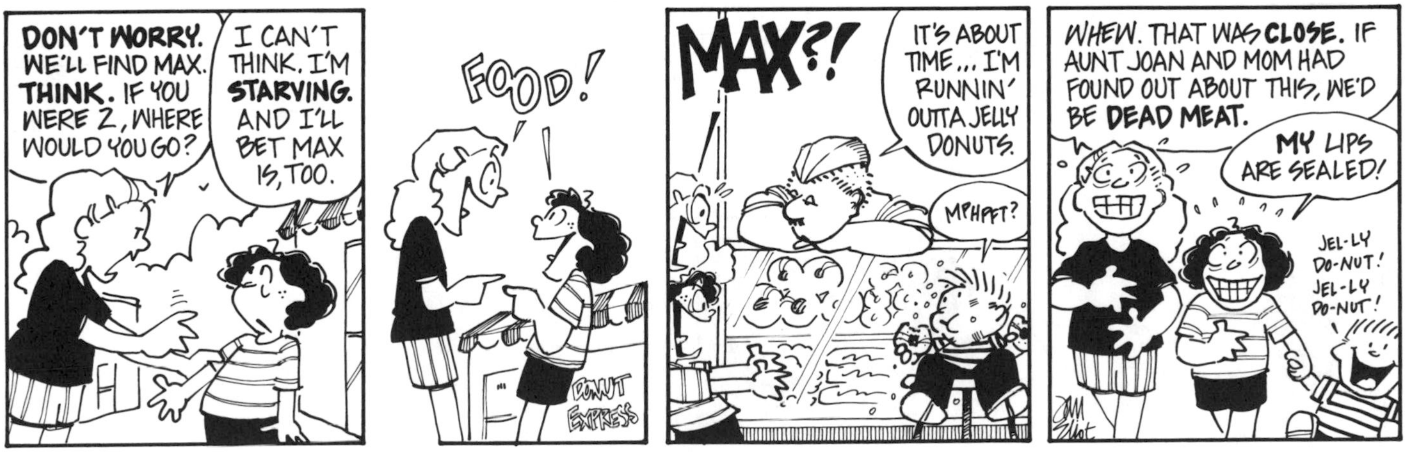
DON'T WORRY. WE'LL FIND MAX. THINK. IF YOU WERE 2, WHERE WOULD YOU GO?
I CAN'T THINK. I'M STARVING. AND I'LL BET MAX IS, TOO.
FOOD!
DONUT EXPRESS
MAX?!
IT'S ABOUT TIME... I'M RUNNIN' OUTTA JELLY DONUTS.
MPHFFT?
WHEW. THAT WAS CLOSE. IF AUNT JOAN AND MOM HAD FOUND OUT ABOUT THIS, WE'D BE DEAD MEAT.
MY LIPS ARE SEALED!
JEL-LY DO-NUT! JEL-LY DO-NUT!

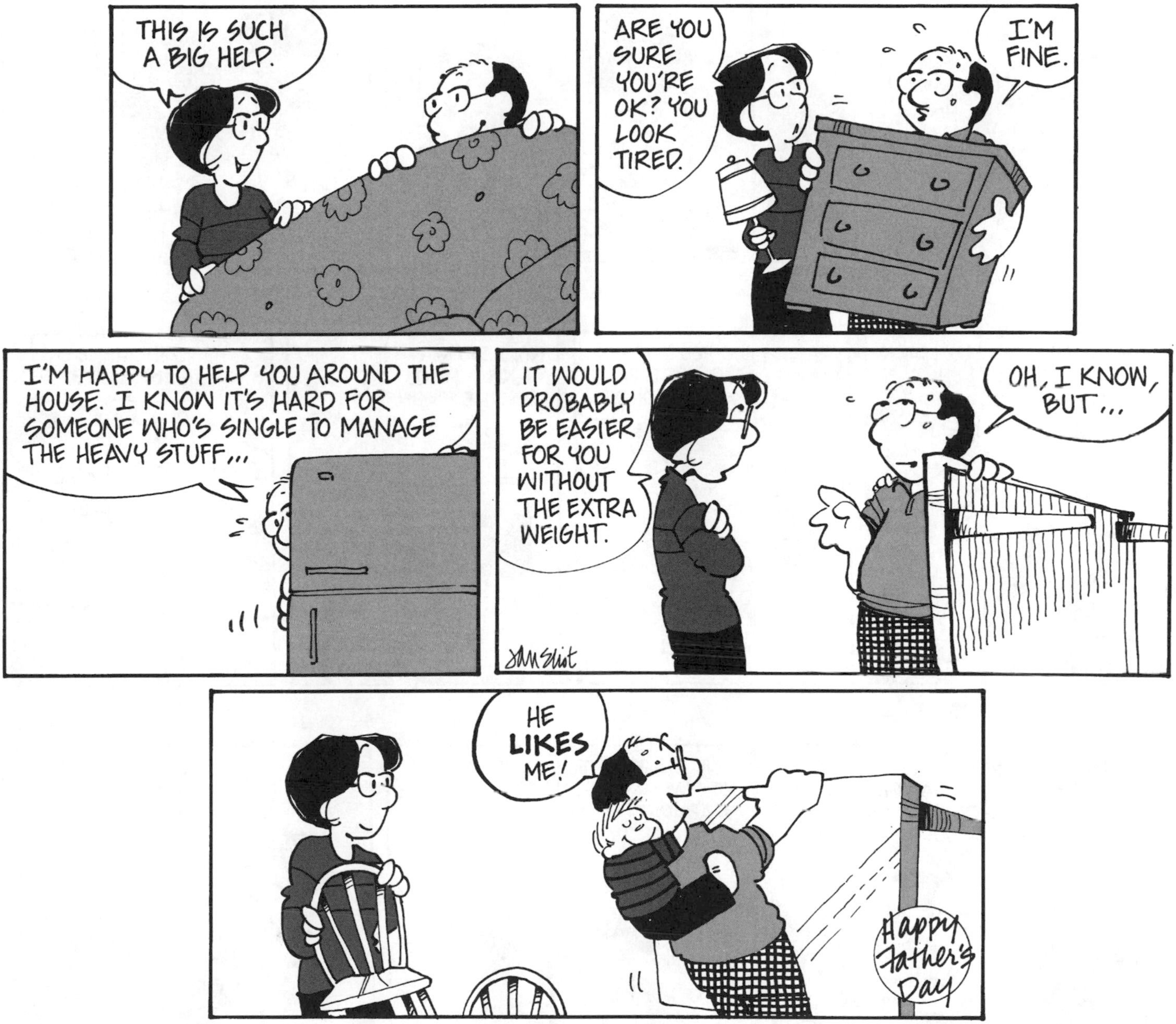
THIS IS SUCH A BIG HELP.
ARE YOU SURE YOU'RE OK? YOU LOOK TIRED.
I'M FINE.
I'M HAPPY TO HELP YOU AROUND THE HOUSE. I KNOW IT'S HARD FOR SOMEONE WHO'S SINGLE TO MANAGE THE HEAVY STUFF...
IT WOULD PROBABLY BE EASIER FOR YOU WITHOUT THE EXTRA WEIGHT.
OH, I KNOW, BUT...
HE **LIKES** ME!
Happy Father's Day

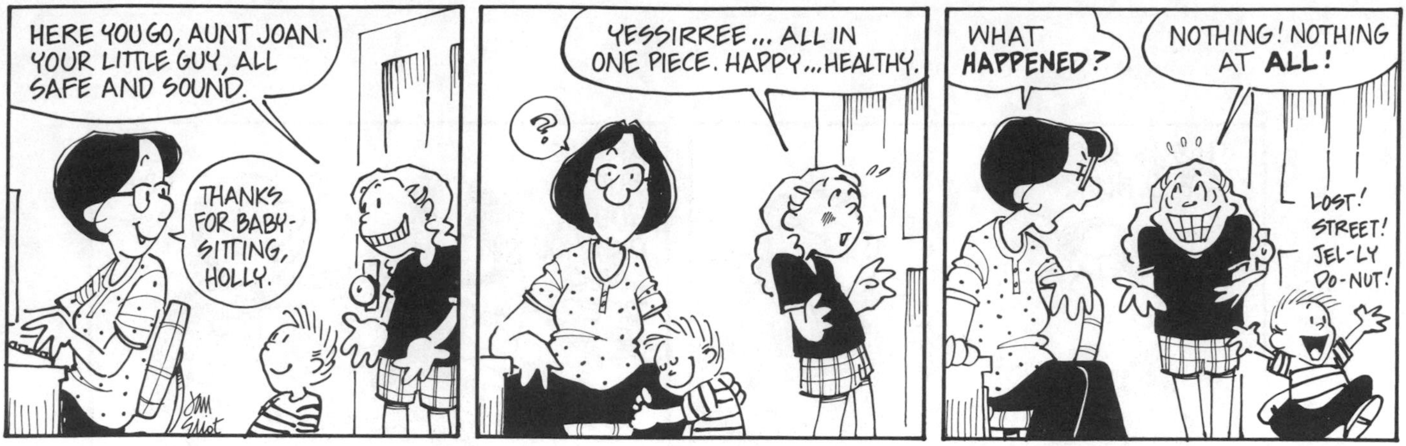
HERE YOU GO, AUNT JOAN. YOUR LITTLE GUY, ALL SAFE AND SOUND.
THANKS FOR BABY-SITTING, HOLLY.
YESSIRREE ... ALL IN ONE PIECE. HAPPY ... HEALTHY.
?
WHAT HAPPENED?
NOTHING! NOTHING AT ALL!
LOST! STREET! JEL-LY DO-NUT!

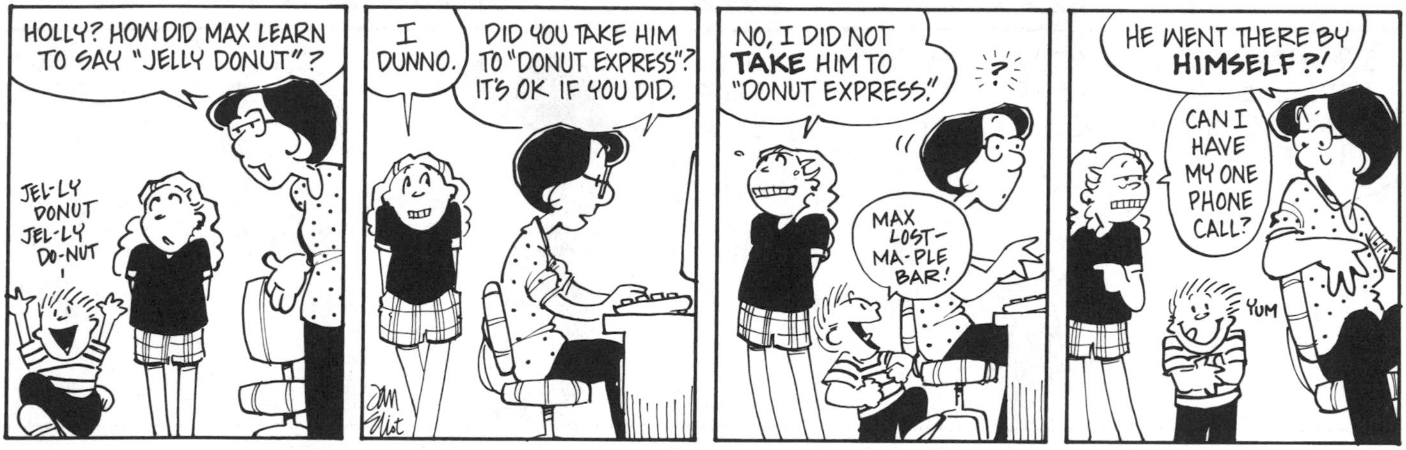
HOLLY? HOW DID MAX LEARN TO SAY "JELLY DONUT"?
JEL-LY DONUT JEL-LY DO-NUT!
I DUNNO.
DID YOU TAKE HIM TO "DONUT EXPRESS"? IT'S OK IF YOU DID.
NO, I DID NOT TAKE HIM TO "DONUT EXPRESS."
?
MAX LOST-MA-PLE BAR!
HE WENT THERE BY HIMSELF?!
CAN I HAVE MY ONE PHONE CALL?
YUM

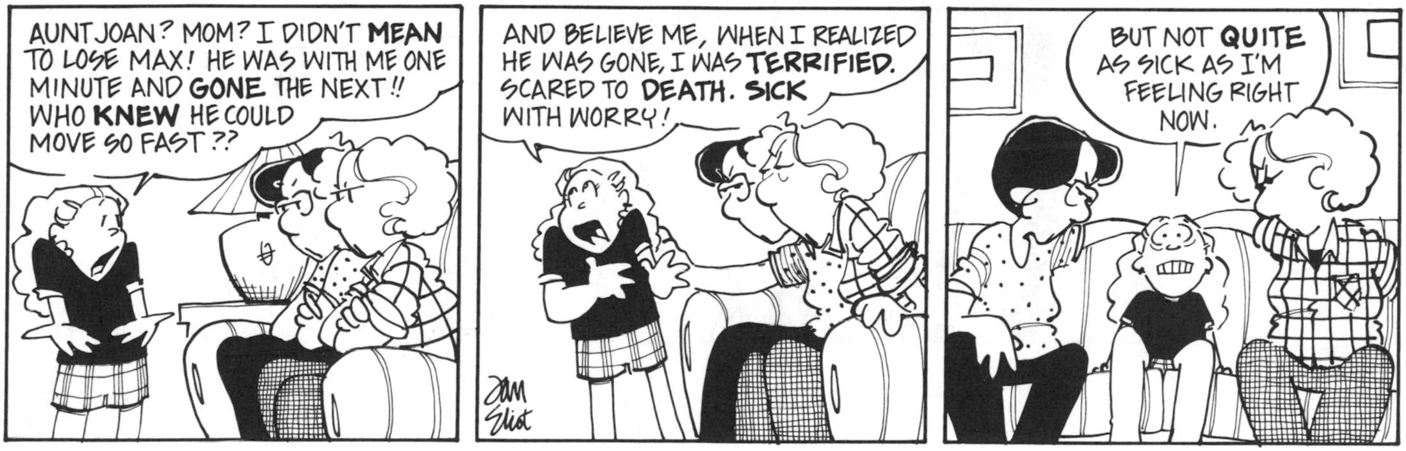
AUNT JOAN? MOM? I DIDN'T MEAN TO LOSE MAX! HE WAS WITH ME ONE MINUTE AND GONE THE NEXT!! WHO KNEW HE COULD MOVE SO FAST??
AND BELIEVE ME, WHEN I REALIZED HE WAS GONE, I WAS TERRIFIED. SCARED TO DEATH. SICK WITH WORRY!
BUT NOT QUITE AS SICK AS I'M FEELING RIGHT NOW.

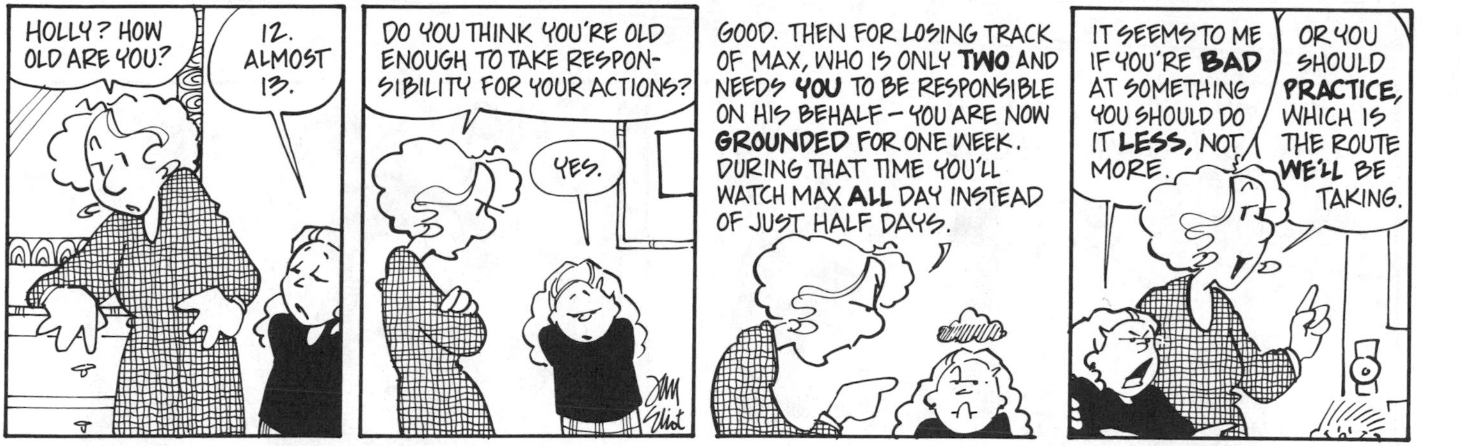
HOLLY? HOW OLD ARE YOU?
12. ALMOST 13.
DO YOU THINK YOU'RE OLD ENOUGH TO TAKE RESPONSIBILITY FOR YOUR ACTIONS?
YES.
GOOD. THEN FOR LOSING TRACK OF MAX, WHO IS ONLY **TWO** AND NEEDS **YOU** TO BE RESPONSIBLE ON HIS BEHALF – YOU ARE NOW **GROUNDED** FOR ONE WEEK. DURING THAT TIME YOU'LL WATCH MAX **ALL** DAY INSTEAD OF JUST HALF DAYS.
IT SEEMS TO ME IF YOU'RE **BAD** AT SOMETHING YOU SHOULD DO IT **LESS,** NOT MORE.
OR YOU SHOULD **PRACTICE,** WHICH IS THE ROUTE **WE'LL** BE TAKING.

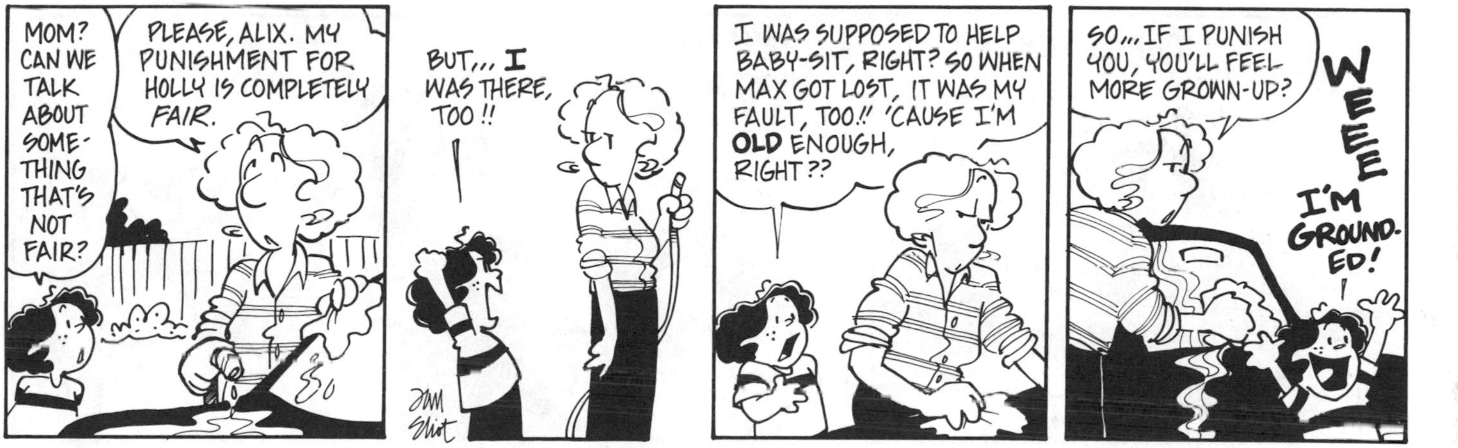
MOM? CAN WE TALK ABOUT SOMETHING THAT'S NOT FAIR?
PLEASE, ALIX. MY PUNISHMENT FOR HOLLY IS COMPLETELY *FAIR*.
BUT,,, **I** WAS THERE, TOO!!
I WAS SUPPOSED TO HELP BABY-SIT, RIGHT? SO WHEN MAX GOT LOST, IT WAS MY FAULT, TOO!! 'CAUSE I'M **OLD** ENOUGH, RIGHT??
SO,,, IF I PUNISH YOU, YOU'LL FEEL MORE GROWN-UP?
WEEE
I'M GROUNDED!

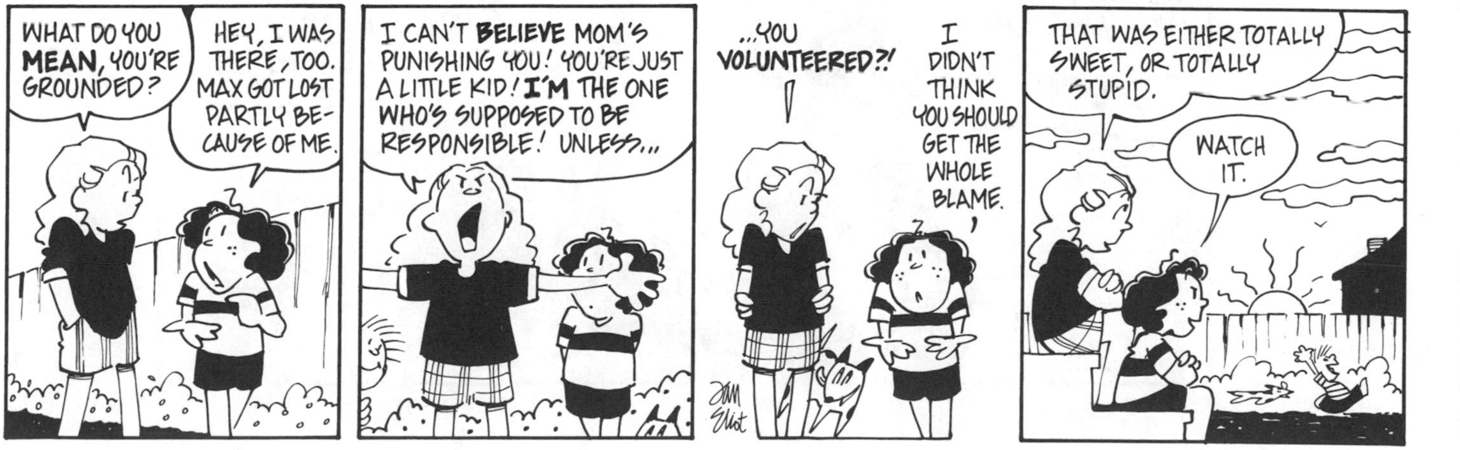
WHAT DO YOU **MEAN,** YOU'RE GROUNDED?
HEY, I WAS THERE, TOO. MAX GOT LOST PARTLY BECAUSE OF ME.
I CAN'T **BELIEVE** MOM'S PUNISHING YOU! YOU'RE JUST A LITTLE KID! **I'M** THE ONE WHO'S SUPPOSED TO BE RESPONSIBLE! UNLESS,,,
,,,YOU **VOLUNTEERED?!**
I DIDN'T THINK YOU SHOULD GET THE WHOLE BLAME.
THAT WAS EITHER TOTALLY SWEET, OR TOTALLY STUPID.
WATCH IT.

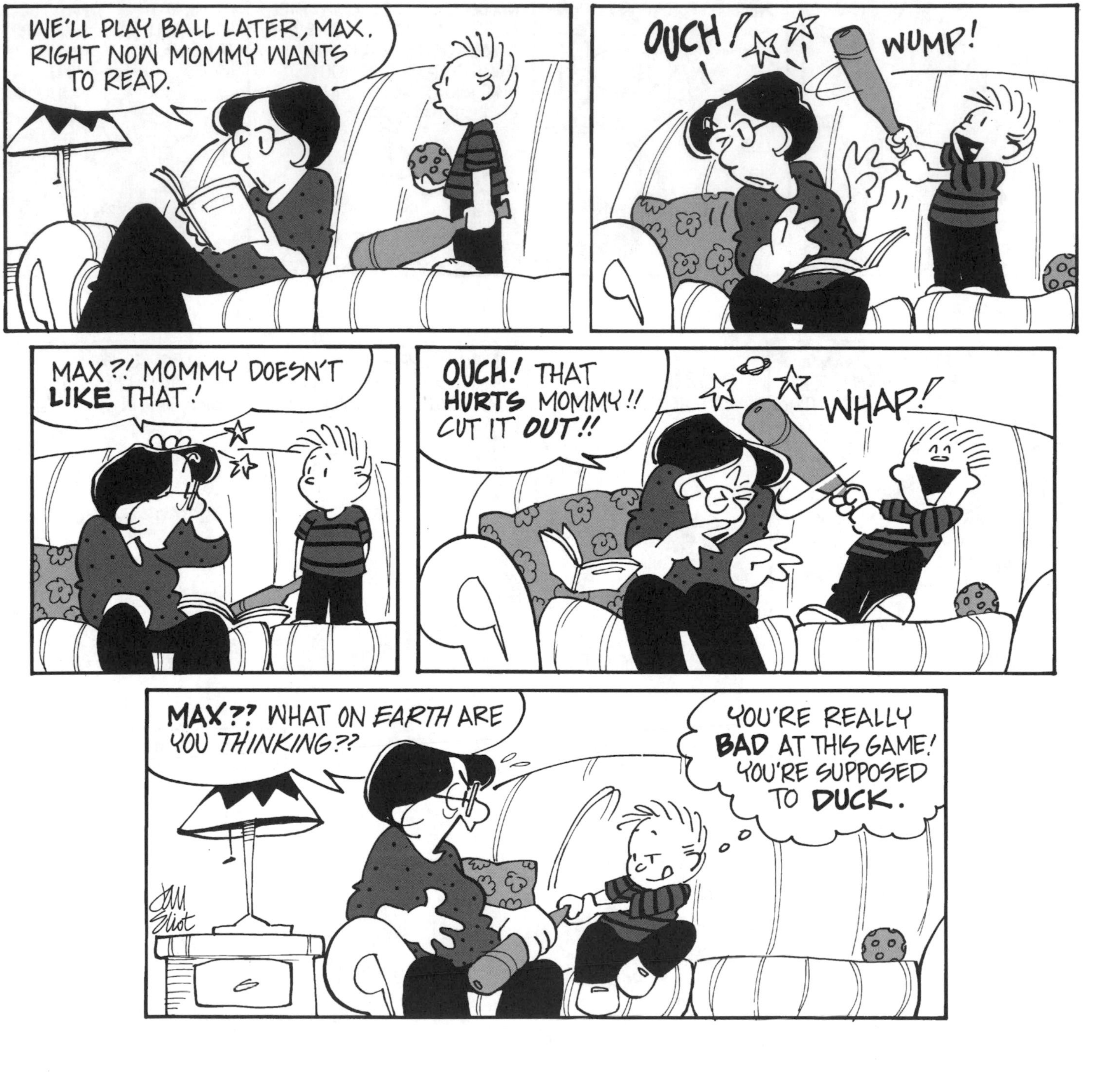
WE'LL PLAY BALL LATER, MAX. RIGHT NOW MOMMY WANTS TO READ.
OUCH!
WUMP!
MAX?! MOMMY DOESN'T **LIKE** THAT!
OUCH! THAT **HURTS** MOMMY!! CUT IT ***OUT***!!
WHAP!
MAX?? WHAT ON *EARTH* ARE YOU *THINKING??*
YOU'RE REALLY **BAD** AT THIS GAME! YOU'RE SUPPOSED TO **DUCK**.

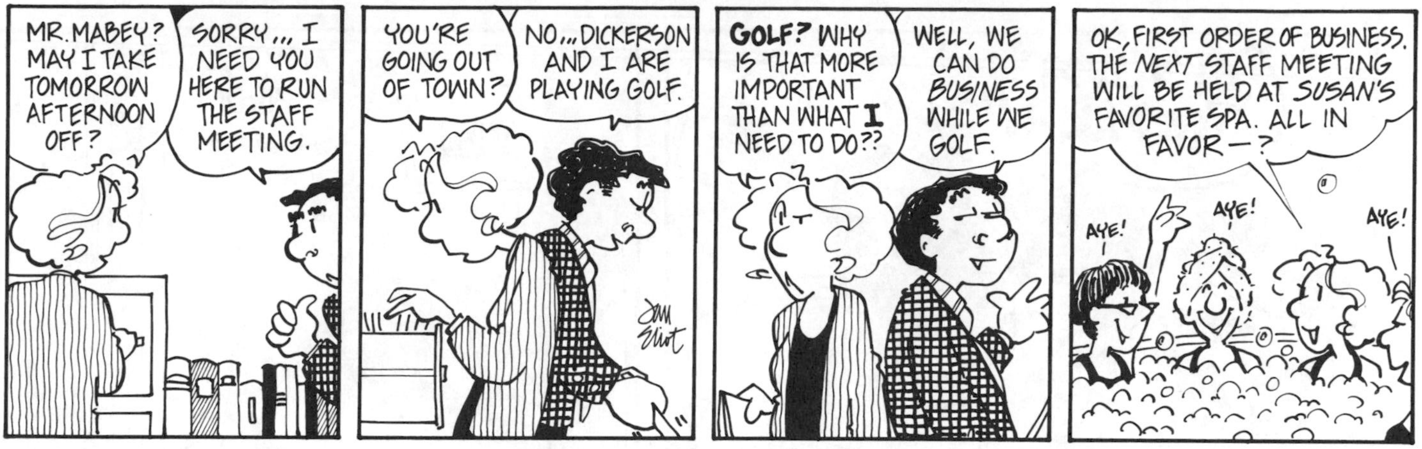
MR. MABEY? MAY I TAKE TOMORROW AFTERNOON OFF?
SORRY... I NEED YOU HERE TO RUN THE STAFF MEETING.
YOU'RE GOING OUT OF TOWN?
NO... DICKERSON AND I ARE PLAYING GOLF.
GOLF? WHY IS THAT MORE IMPORTANT THAN WHAT I NEED TO DO??
WELL, WE CAN DO BUSINESS WHILE WE GOLF.
OK, FIRST ORDER OF BUSINESS. THE NEXT STAFF MEETING WILL BE HELD AT SUSAN'S FAVORITE SPA. ALL IN FAVOR—?
AYE!
AYE!
AYE!

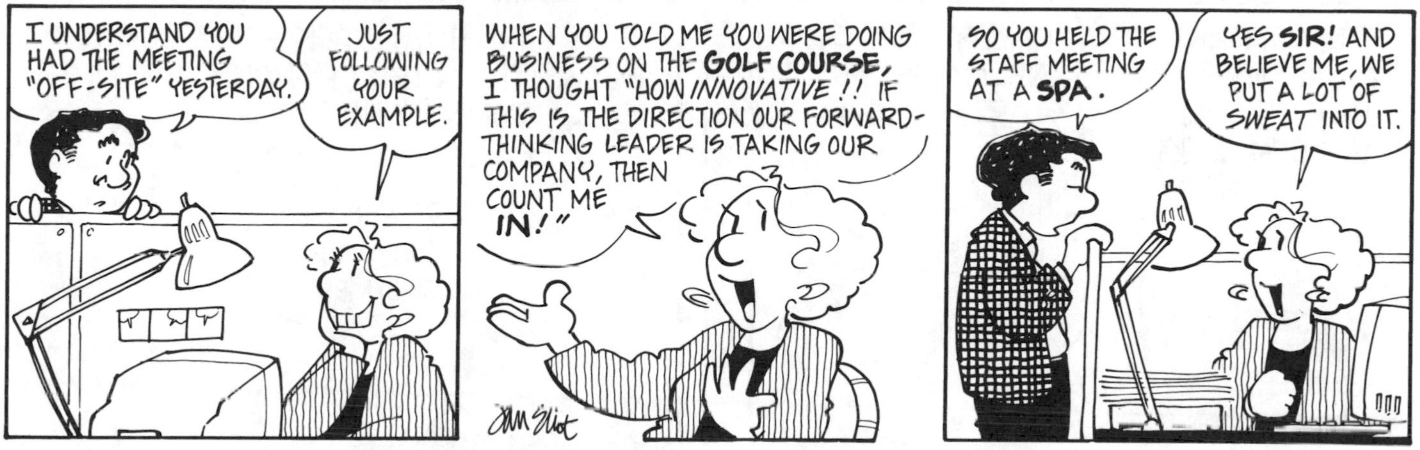
I UNDERSTAND YOU HAD THE MEETING "OFF-SITE" YESTERDAY.
JUST FOLLOWING YOUR EXAMPLE.
WHEN YOU TOLD ME YOU WERE DOING BUSINESS ON THE GOLF COURSE, I THOUGHT "HOW INNOVATIVE!! IF THIS IS THE DIRECTION OUR FORWARD-THINKING LEADER IS TAKING OUR COMPANY, THEN COUNT ME IN!"
SO YOU HELD THE STAFF MEETING AT A SPA.
YES SIR! AND BELIEVE ME, WE PUT A LOT OF SWEAT INTO IT.

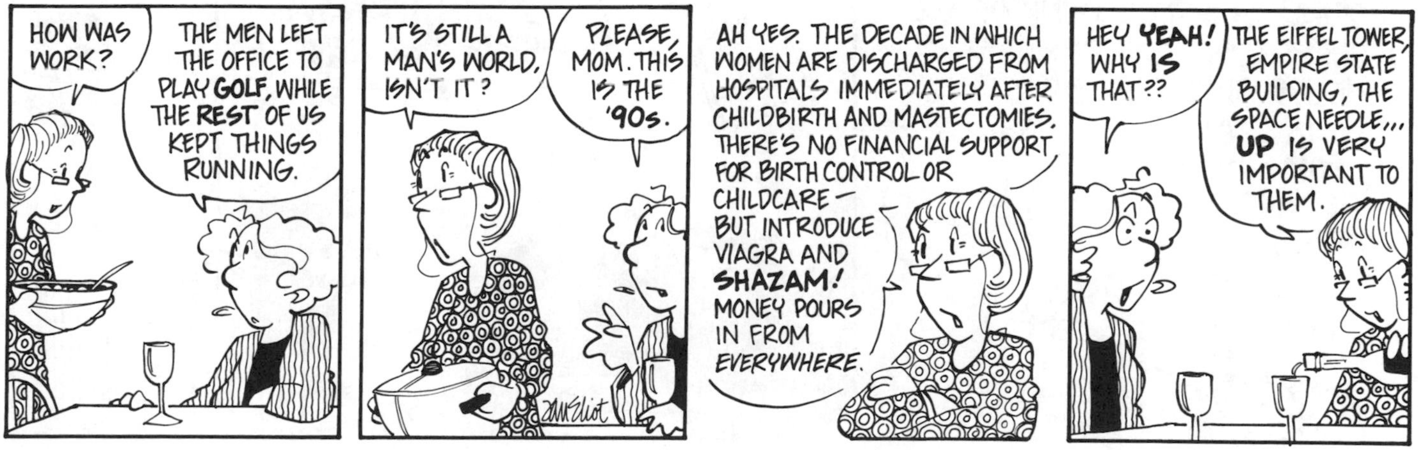
HOW WAS WORK?
THE MEN LEFT THE OFFICE TO PLAY GOLF, WHILE THE REST OF US KEPT THINGS RUNNING.
IT'S STILL A MAN'S WORLD, ISN'T IT?
PLEASE, MOM. THIS IS THE '90s.
AH YES. THE DECADE IN WHICH WOMEN ARE DISCHARGED FROM HOSPITALS IMMEDIATELY AFTER CHILDBIRTH AND MASTECTOMIES. THERE'S NO FINANCIAL SUPPORT FOR BIRTH CONTROL OR CHILDCARE— BUT INTRODUCE VIAGRA AND SHAZAM! MONEY POURS IN FROM EVERYWHERE.
HEY YEAH! WHY IS THAT??
THE EIFFEL TOWER, EMPIRE STATE BUILDING, THE SPACE NEEDLE... UP IS VERY IMPORTANT TO THEM.

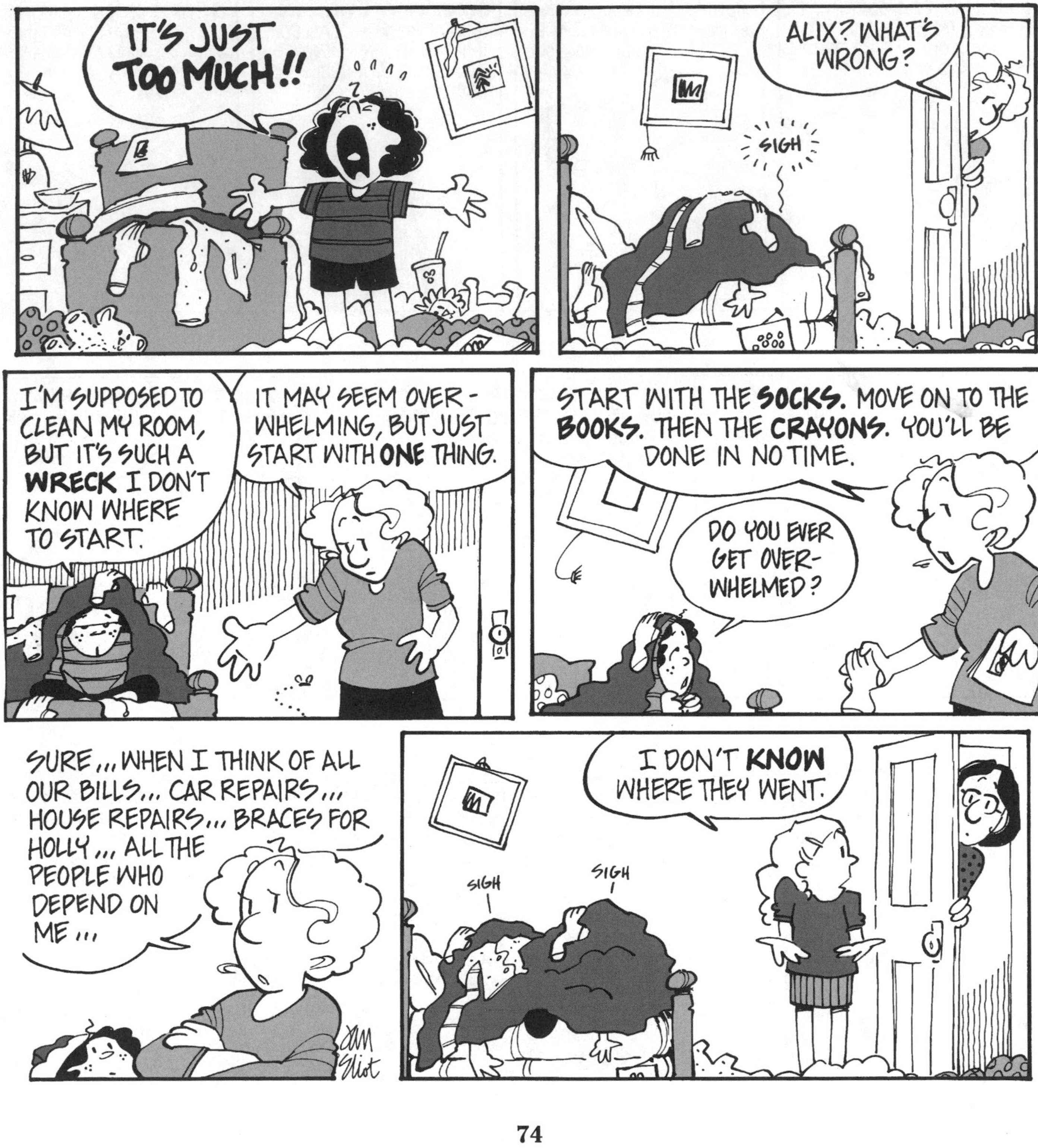
IT'S JUST TOO MUCH!!
ALIX? WHAT'S WRONG?
SIGH
I'M SUPPOSED TO CLEAN MY ROOM, BUT IT'S SUCH A WRECK I DON'T KNOW WHERE TO START.
IT MAY SEEM OVER-WHELMING, BUT JUST START WITH ONE THING.
START WITH THE SOCKS. MOVE ON TO THE BOOKS. THEN THE CRAYONS. YOU'LL BE DONE IN NO TIME.
DO YOU EVER GET OVER-WHELMED?
SURE... WHEN I THINK OF ALL OUR BILLS... CAR REPAIRS... HOUSE REPAIRS... BRACES FOR HOLLY... ALL THE PEOPLE WHO DEPEND ON ME...
I DON'T KNOW WHERE THEY WENT.
SIGH
SIGH
JAN Eliot

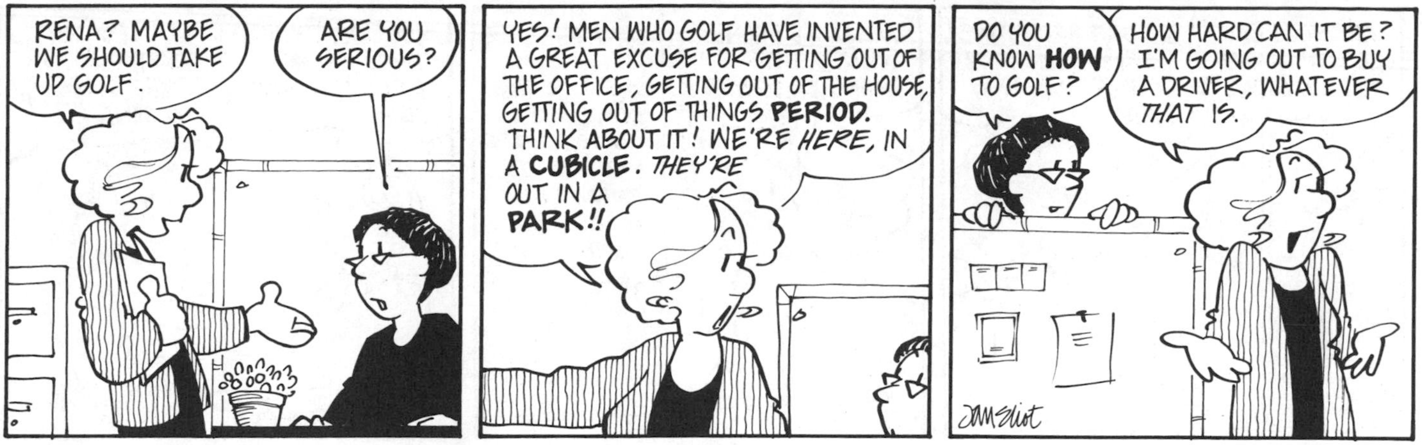
RENA? MAYBE WE SHOULD TAKE UP GOLF.
ARE YOU SERIOUS?
YES! MEN WHO GOLF HAVE INVENTED A GREAT EXCUSE FOR GETTING OUT OF THE OFFICE, GETTING OUT OF THE HOUSE, GETTING OUT OF THINGS **PERIOD.** THINK ABOUT IT! WE'RE *HERE*, IN A **CUBICLE**. *THEY'RE* OUT IN A **PARK!!**
DO YOU KNOW **HOW** TO GOLF?
HOW HARD CAN IT BE? I'M GOING OUT TO BUY A DRIVER, WHATEVER *THAT* IS.

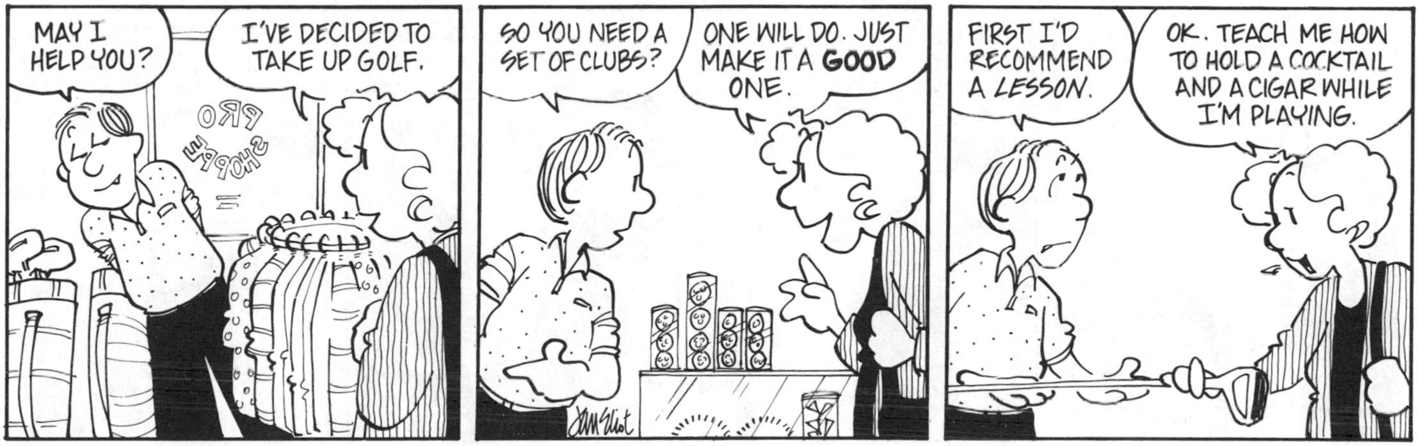
MAY I HELP YOU?
I'VE DECIDED TO TAKE UP GOLF.
PRO SHOPPE
SO YOU NEED A SET OF CLUBS?
ONE WILL DO. JUST MAKE IT A **GOOD** ONE.
FIRST I'D RECOMMEND A *LESSON*.
OK. TEACH ME HOW TO HOLD A COCKTAIL AND A CIGAR WHILE I'M PLAYING.

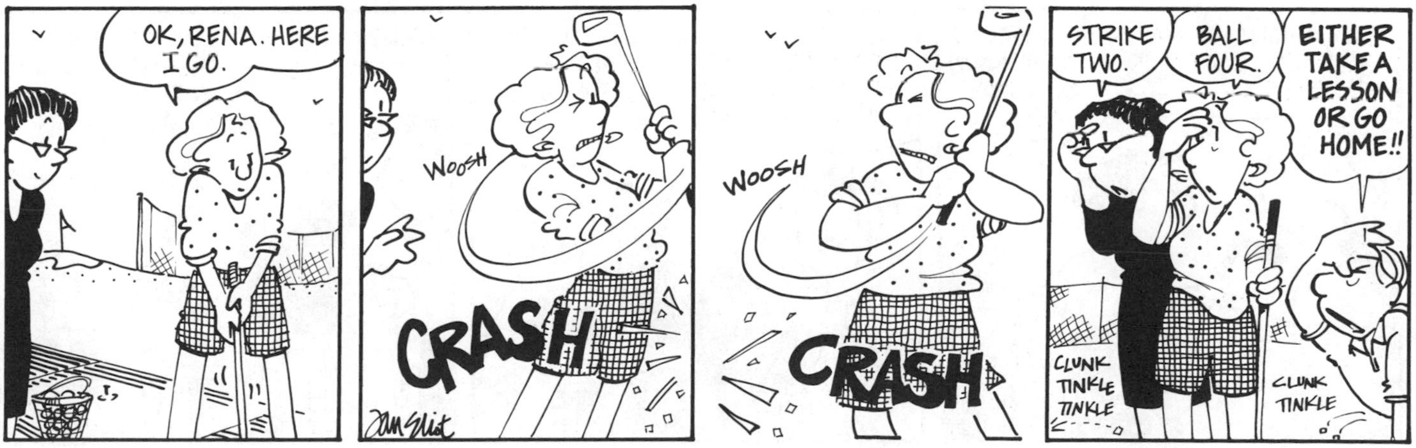
OK, RENA. HERE I GO.
WOOSH
CRASH
WOOSH
CRASH
STRIKE TWO.
BALL FOUR.
EITHER TAKE A LESSON OR GO HOME!!
CLUNK TINKLE TINKLE
CLUNK TINKLE

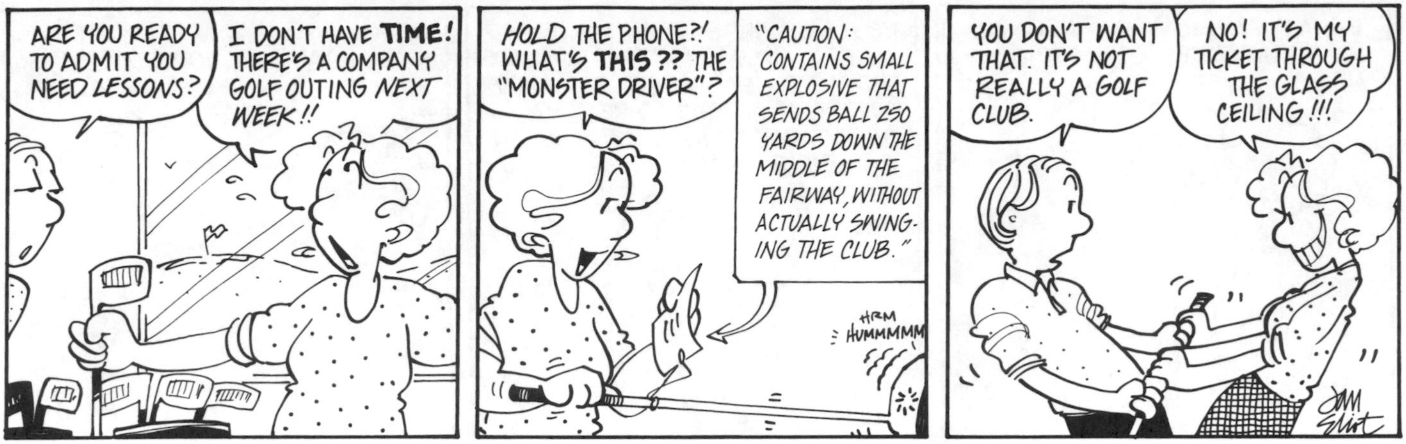
ARE YOU READY TO ADMIT YOU NEED LESSONS?
I DON'T HAVE TIME! THERE'S A COMPANY GOLF OUTING NEXT WEEK!!
HOLD THE PHONE?! WHAT'S THIS?? THE "MONSTER DRIVER"?
"CAUTION: CONTAINS SMALL EXPLOSIVE THAT SENDS BALL 250 YARDS DOWN THE MIDDLE OF THE FAIRWAY, WITHOUT ACTUALLY SWINGING THE CLUB."
HRM HUMMMMM
YOU DON'T WANT THAT. IT'S NOT REALLY A GOLF CLUB.
NO! IT'S MY TICKET THROUGH THE GLASS CEILING!!!

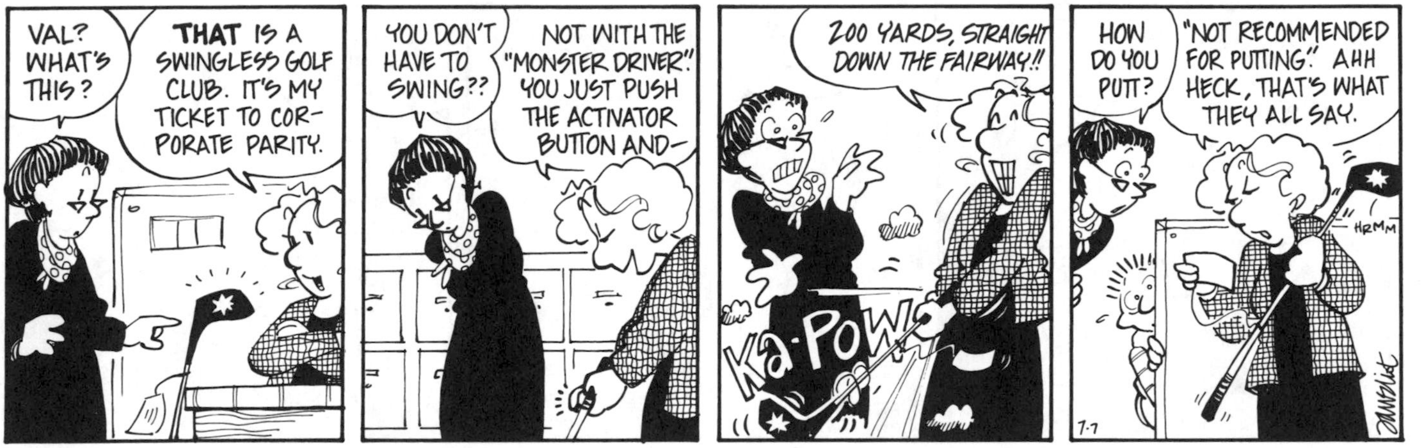
VAL? WHAT'S THIS?
THAT IS A SWINGLESS GOLF CLUB. IT'S MY TICKET TO CORPORATE PARITY.
YOU DON'T HAVE TO SWING??
NOT WITH THE "MONSTER DRIVER." YOU JUST PUSH THE ACTIVATOR BUTTON AND-
200 YARDS, STRAIGHT DOWN THE FAIRWAY!!
KA-POW!
HOW DO YOU PUTT?
"NOT RECOMMENDED FOR PUTTING." AHH HECK, THAT'S WHAT THEY ALL SAY.
HRMM
7-7

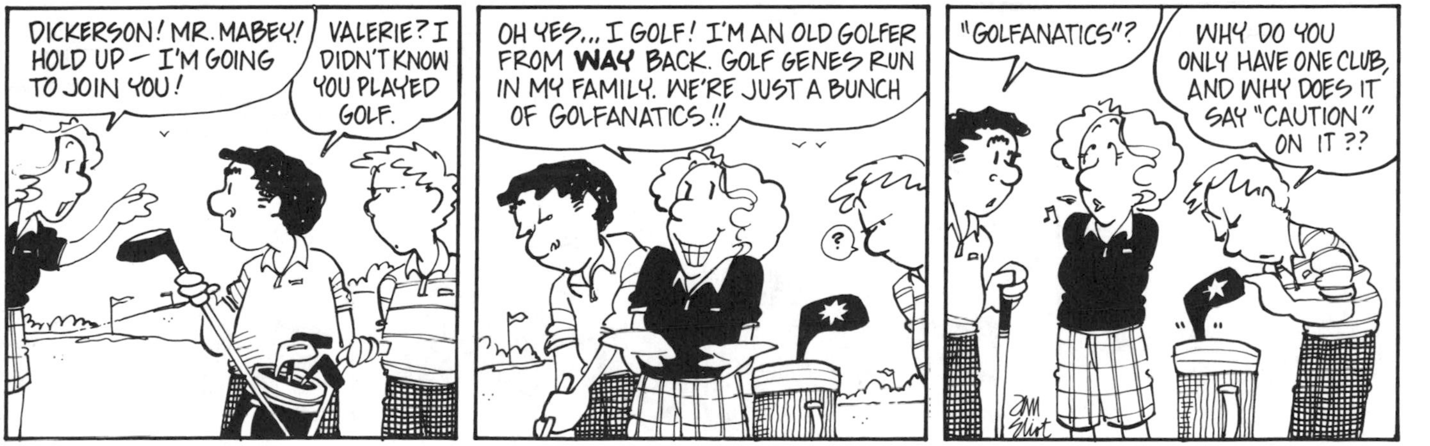
DICKERSON! MR. MABEY! HOLD UP — I'M GOING TO JOIN YOU!
VALERIE? I DIDN'T KNOW YOU PLAYED GOLF.
OH YES... I GOLF! I'M AN OLD GOLFER FROM WAY BACK. GOLF GENES RUN IN MY FAMILY. WE'RE JUST A BUNCH OF GOLFANATICS!!
?
"GOLFANATICS"?
WHY DO YOU ONLY HAVE ONE CLUB, AND WHY DOES IT SAY "CAUTION" ON IT??

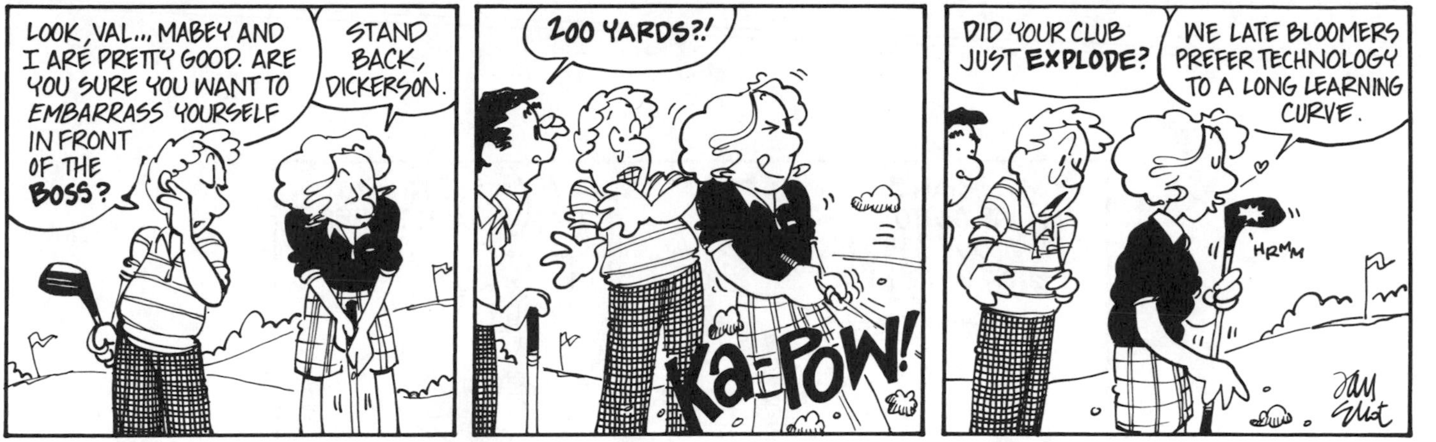
LOOK, VAL... MABEY AND I ARE PRETTY GOOD. ARE YOU SURE YOU WANT TO EMBARRASS YOURSELF IN FRONT OF THE BOSS?
STAND BACK, DICKERSON.
200 YARDS?!
KA-POW!
DID YOUR CLUB JUST EXPLODE?
WE LATE BLOOMERS PREFER TECHNOLOGY TO A LONG LEARNING CURVE.
HRMM

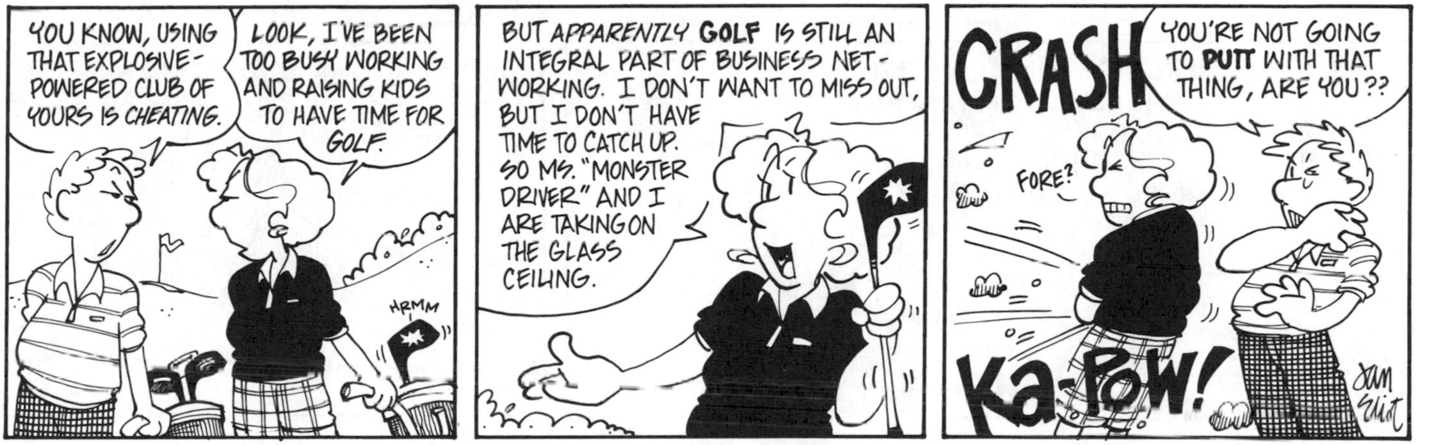
YOU KNOW, USING THAT EXPLOSIVE-POWERED CLUB OF YOURS IS CHEATING.
LOOK, I'VE BEEN TOO BUSY WORKING AND RAISING KIDS TO HAVE TIME FOR GOLF.
HRMM
BUT APPARENTLY GOLF IS STILL AN INTEGRAL PART OF BUSINESS NET-WORKING. I DON'T WANT TO MISS OUT, BUT I DON'T HAVE TIME TO CATCH UP. SO MS. "MONSTER DRIVER" AND I ARE TAKING ON THE GLASS CEILING.
CRASH
YOU'RE NOT GOING TO PUTT WITH THAT THING, ARE YOU??
FORE?
KA-POW!

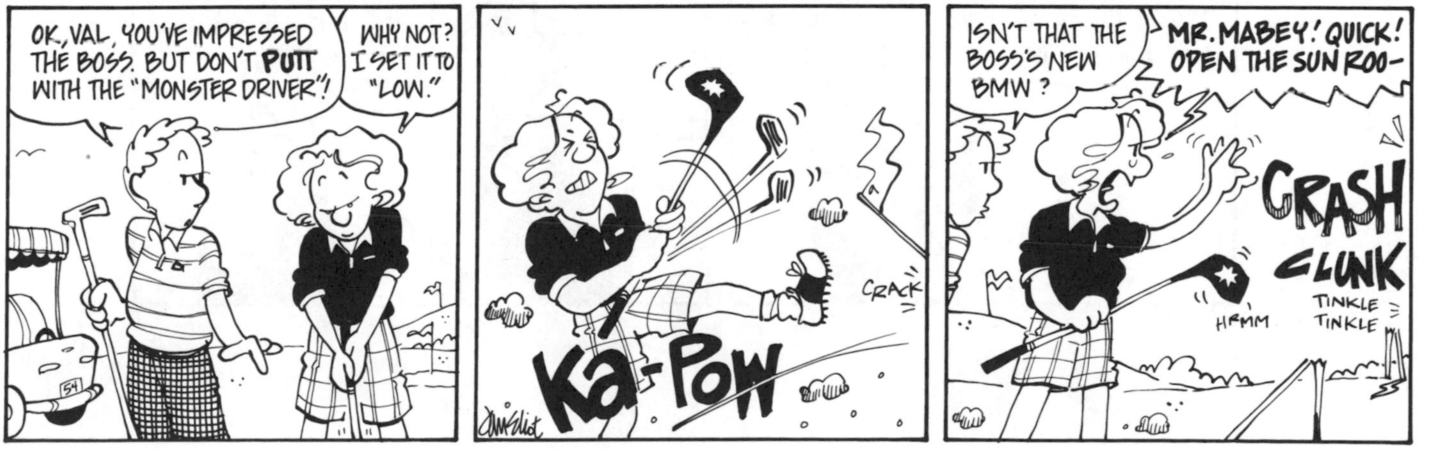
OK, VAL, YOU'VE IMPRESSED THE BOSS. BUT DON'T PUTT WITH THE "MONSTER DRIVER"!
WHY NOT? I SET IT TO "LOW."
KA-POW
CRACK
ISN'T THAT THE BOSS'S NEW BMW?
MR. MABEY! QUICK! OPEN THE SUN ROO-
CRASH
CLUNK
HRMM
TINKLE
TINKLE

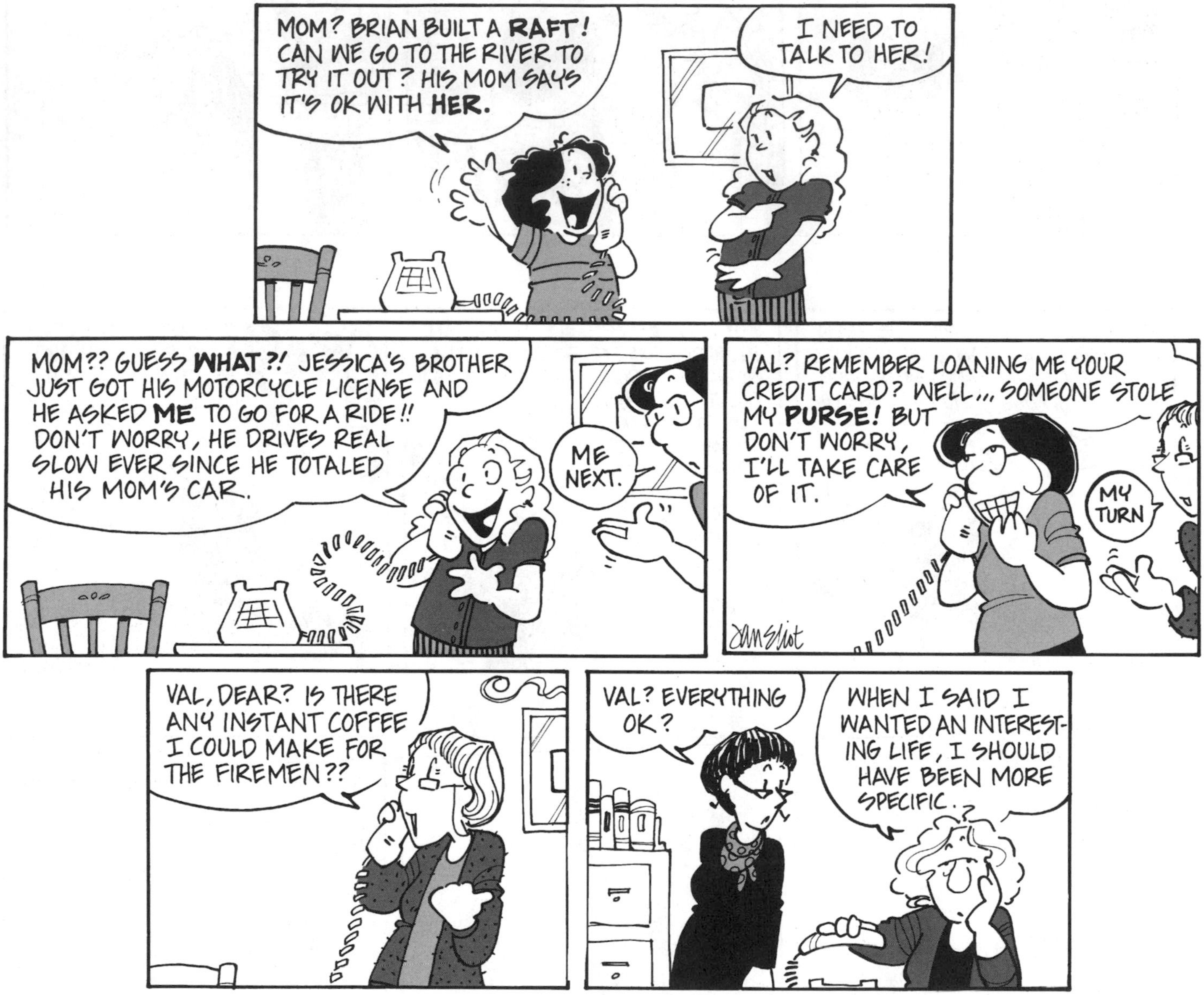
MOM? BRIAN BUILT A RAFT! CAN WE GO TO THE RIVER TO TRY IT OUT? HIS MOM SAYS IT'S OK WITH HER.
I NEED TO TALK TO HER!
MOM?? GUESS WHAT?! JESSICA'S BROTHER JUST GOT HIS MOTORCYCLE LICENSE AND HE ASKED ME TO GO FOR A RIDE!! DON'T WORRY, HE DRIVES REAL SLOW EVER SINCE HE TOTALED HIS MOM'S CAR.
ME NEXT.
VAL? REMEMBER LOANING ME YOUR CREDIT CARD? WELL,,, SOMEONE STOLE MY PURSE! BUT DON'T WORRY, I'LL TAKE CARE OF IT.
MY TURN
VAL, DEAR? IS THERE ANY INSTANT COFFEE I COULD MAKE FOR THE FIREMEN??
VAL? EVERYTHING OK?
WHEN I SAID I WANTED AN INTERESTING LIFE, I SHOULD HAVE BEEN MORE SPECIFIC.

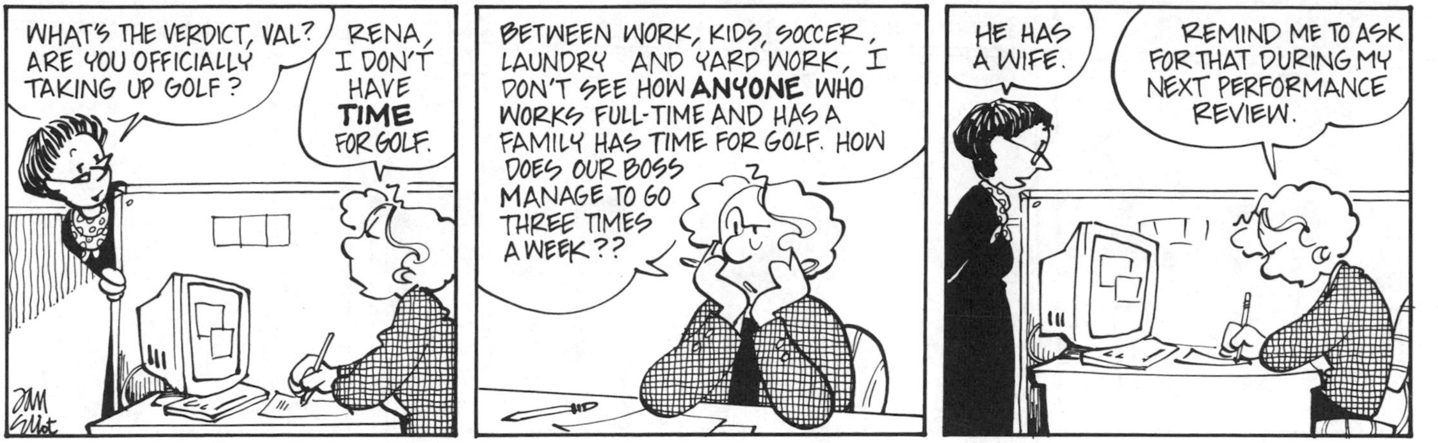
WHAT'S THE VERDICT, VAL? ARE YOU OFFICIALLY TAKING UP GOLF?
RENA, I DON'T HAVE TIME FOR GOLF.
BETWEEN WORK, KIDS, SOCCER, LAUNDRY AND YARD WORK, I DON'T SEE HOW ANYONE WHO WORKS FULL-TIME AND HAS A FAMILY HAS TIME FOR GOLF. HOW DOES OUR BOSS MANAGE TO GO THREE TIMES A WEEK??
HE HAS A WIFE.
REMIND ME TO ASK FOR THAT DURING MY NEXT PERFORMANCE REVIEW.

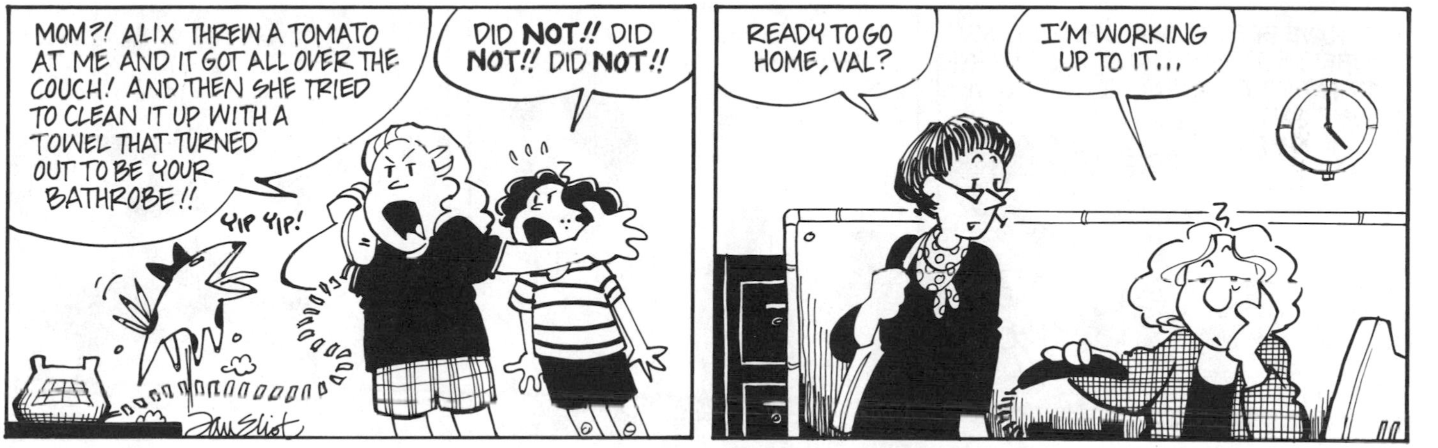
MOM?! ALIX THREW A TOMATO AT ME AND IT GOT ALL OVER THE COUCH! AND THEN SHE TRIED TO CLEAN IT UP WITH A TOWEL THAT TURNED OUT TO BE YOUR BATHROBE!!
DID NOT!! DID NOT!! DID NOT!!
YIP YIP!
READY TO GO HOME, VAL?
I'M WORKING UP TO IT...

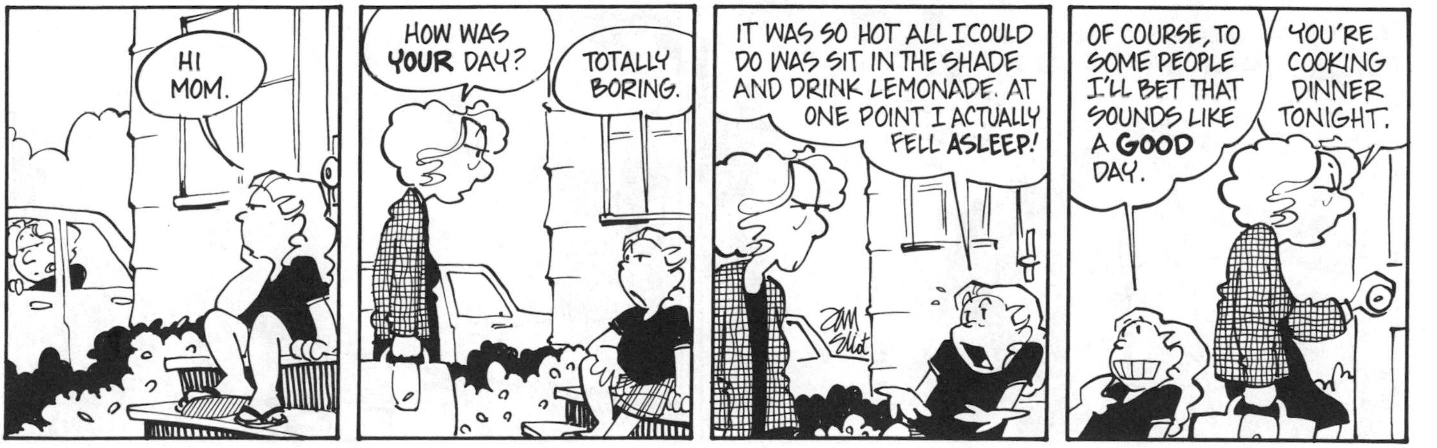
HI MOM.
HOW WAS YOUR DAY?
TOTALLY BORING.
IT WAS SO HOT ALL I COULD DO WAS SIT IN THE SHADE AND DRINK LEMONADE. AT ONE POINT I ACTUALLY FELL ASLEEP!
OF COURSE, TO SOME PEOPLE I'LL BET THAT SOUNDS LIKE A GOOD DAY.
YOU'RE COOKING DINNER TONIGHT.

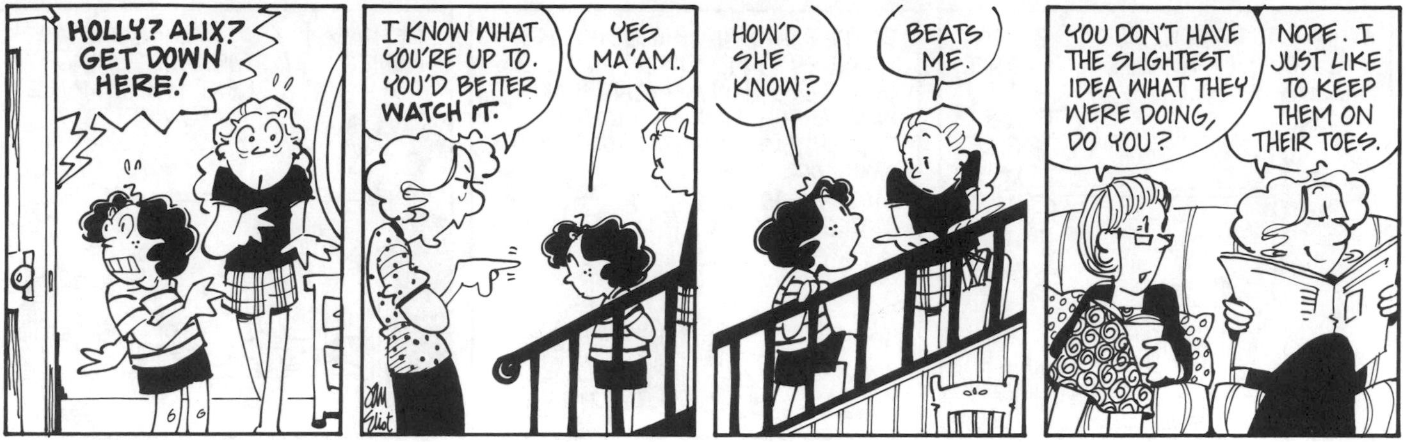
HOLLY? ALIX? GET DOWN HERE!
I KNOW WHAT YOU'RE UP TO. YOU'D BETTER **WATCH IT.**
YES MA'AM.
HOW'D SHE KNOW?
BEATS ME.
YOU DON'T HAVE THE SLIGHTEST IDEA WHAT THEY WERE DOING, DO YOU?
NOPE. I JUST LIKE TO KEEP THEM ON THEIR TOES.

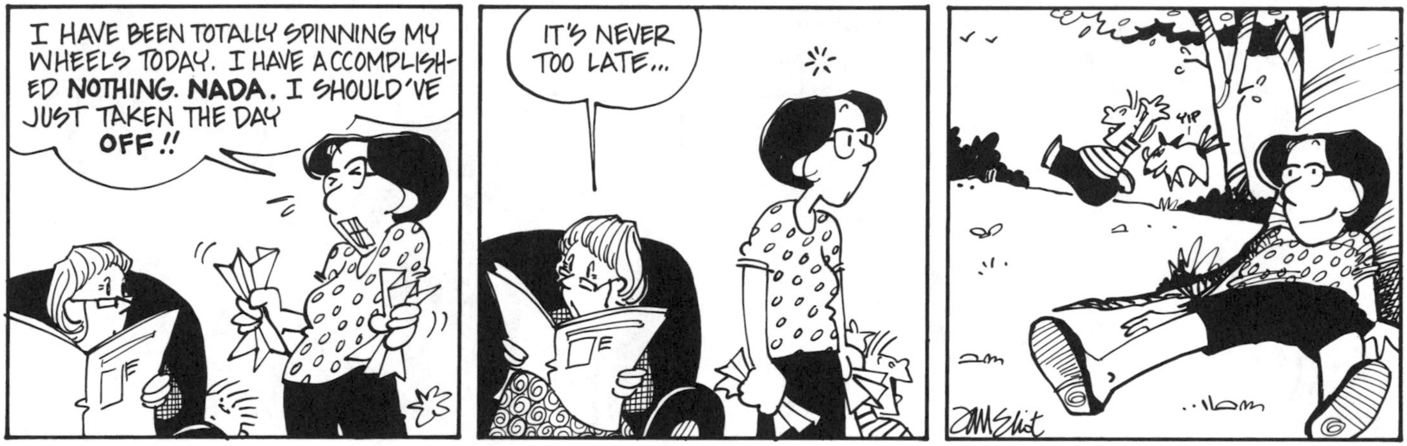
I HAVE BEEN TOTALLY SPINNING MY WHEELS TODAY. I HAVE ACCOMPLISHED **NOTHING. NADA.** I SHOULD'VE JUST TAKEN THE DAY **OFF!!**
IT'S NEVER TOO LATE...
YIP

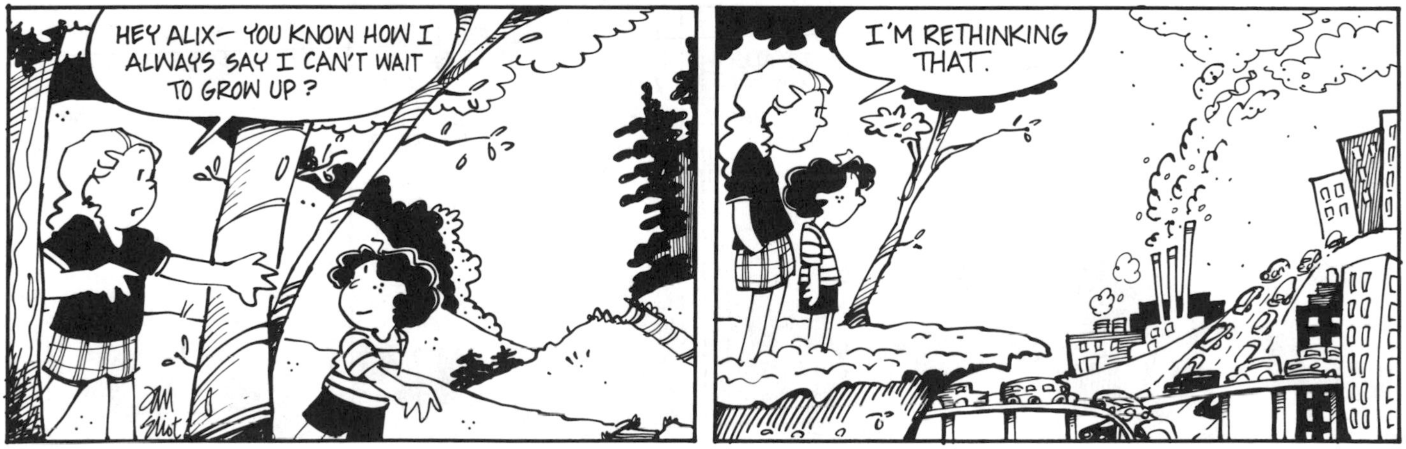
HEY ALIX— YOU KNOW HOW I ALWAYS SAY I CAN'T WAIT TO GROW UP?
I'M RETHINKING THAT.

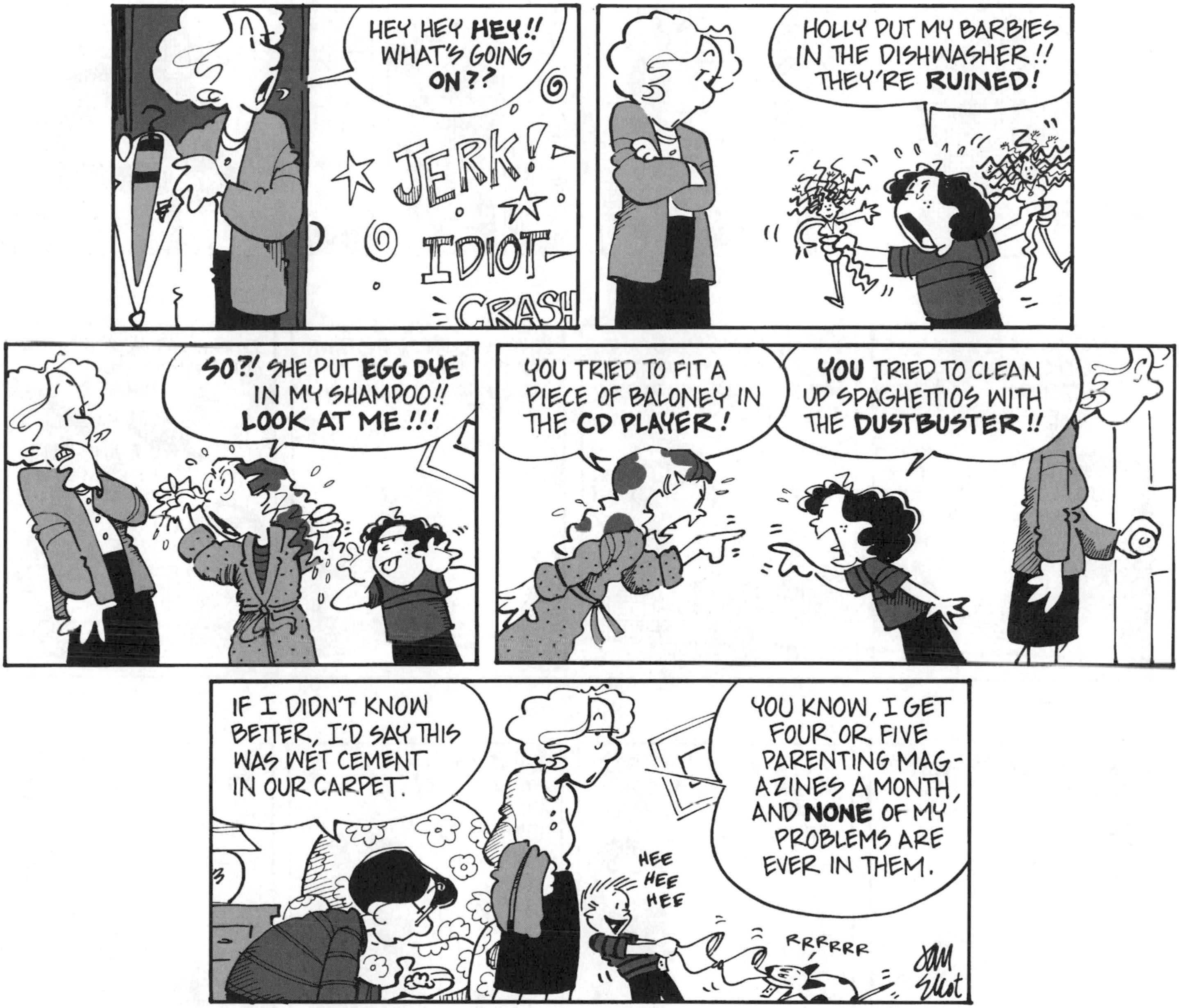
HEY HEY HEY!! WHAT'S GOING ON??
JERK!
IDIOT
CRASH
HOLLY PUT MY BARBIES IN THE DISHWASHER!! THEY'RE RUINED!
SO?! SHE PUT EGG DYE IN MY SHAMPOO!! LOOK AT ME!!!
YOU TRIED TO FIT A PIECE OF BALONEY IN THE CD PLAYER!
YOU TRIED TO CLEAN UP SPAGHETTIOS WITH THE DUSTBUSTER!!
IF I DIDN'T KNOW BETTER, I'D SAY THIS WAS WET CEMENT IN OUR CARPET.
YOU KNOW, I GET FOUR OR FIVE PARENTING MAGAZINES A MONTH, AND NONE OF MY PROBLEMS ARE EVER IN THEM.
HEE HEE HEE
RRRRRR

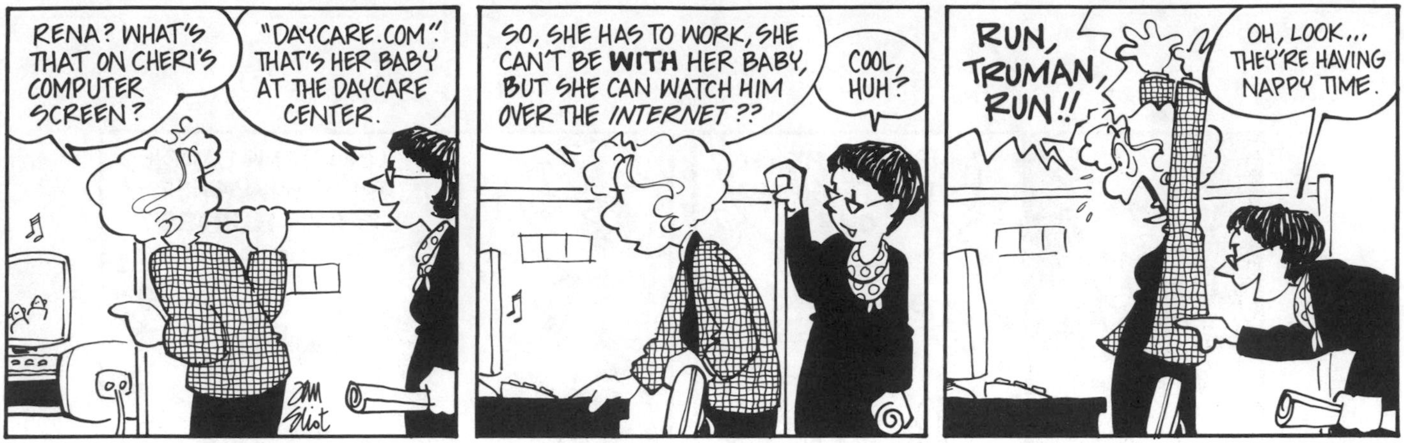
RENA? WHAT'S THAT ON CHERI'S COMPUTER SCREEN?
"DAYCARE.COM". THAT'S HER BABY AT THE DAYCARE CENTER.
SO, SHE HAS TO WORK, SHE CAN'T BE **WITH** HER BABY, BUT SHE CAN WATCH HIM OVER THE *INTERNET*??
COOL, HUH?
RUN, TRUMAN, RUN!!
OH, LOOK... THEY'RE HAVING NAPPY TIME.

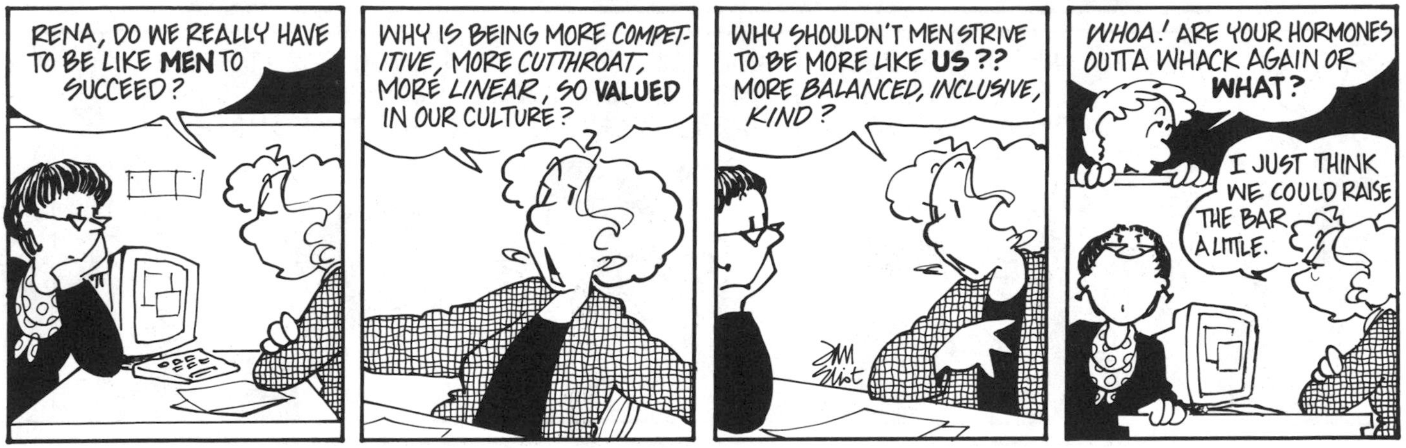
RENA, DO WE REALLY HAVE TO BE LIKE **MEN** TO SUCCEED?
WHY IS BEING MORE *COMPETITIVE*, MORE *CUTTHROAT*, MORE *LINEAR*, SO **VALUED** IN OUR CULTURE?
WHY SHOULDN'T MEN STRIVE TO BE MORE LIKE **US**?? MORE *BALANCED, INCLUSIVE, KIND*?
WHOA! ARE YOUR HORMONES OUTTA WHACK AGAIN OR **WHAT**?
I JUST THINK WE COULD RAISE THE BAR A LITTLE.

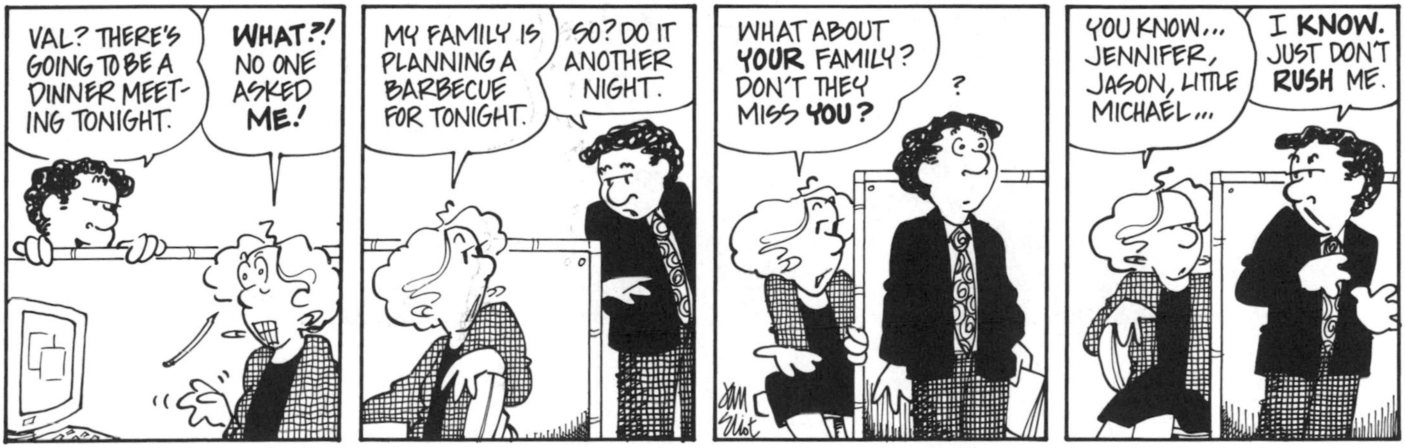
VAL? THERE'S GOING TO BE A DINNER MEETING TONIGHT.
WHAT?! NO ONE ASKED **ME!**
MY FAMILY IS PLANNING A BARBECUE FOR TONIGHT.
SO? DO IT ANOTHER NIGHT.
WHAT ABOUT **YOUR** FAMILY? DON'T THEY MISS **YOU**?
?
YOU KNOW... JENNIFER, JASON, LITTLE MICHAEL...
I **KNOW**. JUST DON'T **RUSH** ME.

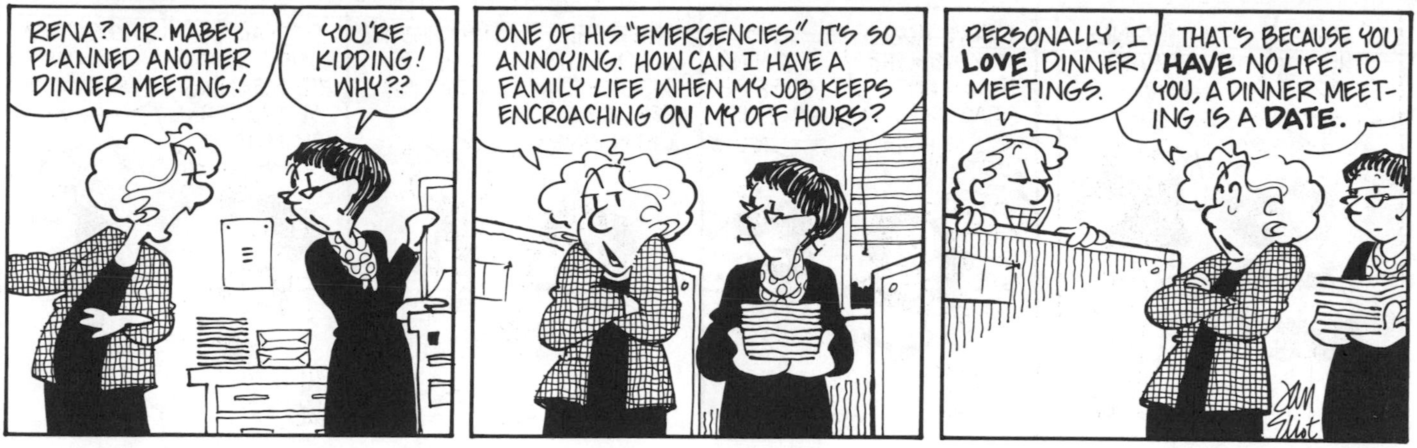
RENA? MR. MABEY PLANNED ANOTHER DINNER MEETING!
YOU'RE KIDDING! WHY??
ONE OF HIS "EMERGENCIES." IT'S SO ANNOYING. HOW CAN I HAVE A FAMILY LIFE WHEN MY JOB KEEPS ENCROACHING ON MY OFF HOURS?
PERSONALLY, I **LOVE** DINNER MEETINGS.
THAT'S BECAUSE YOU **HAVE** NO LIFE. TO YOU, A DINNER MEETING IS A **DATE.**
JAN Eliot

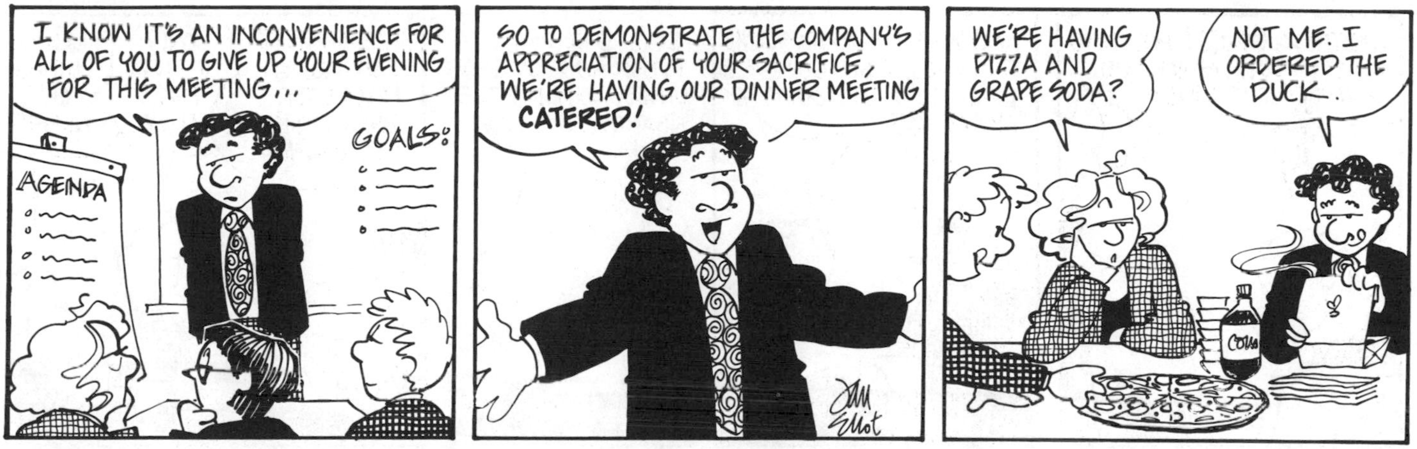
I KNOW IT'S AN INCONVENIENCE FOR ALL OF YOU TO GIVE UP YOUR EVENING FOR THIS MEETING...
AGENDA
GOALS:
SO TO DEMONSTRATE THE COMPANY'S APPRECIATION OF YOUR SACRIFICE, WE'RE HAVING OUR DINNER MEETING **CATERED!**
JAN Eliot
WE'RE HAVING PIZZA AND GRAPE SODA?
NOT ME. I ORDERED THE DUCK.

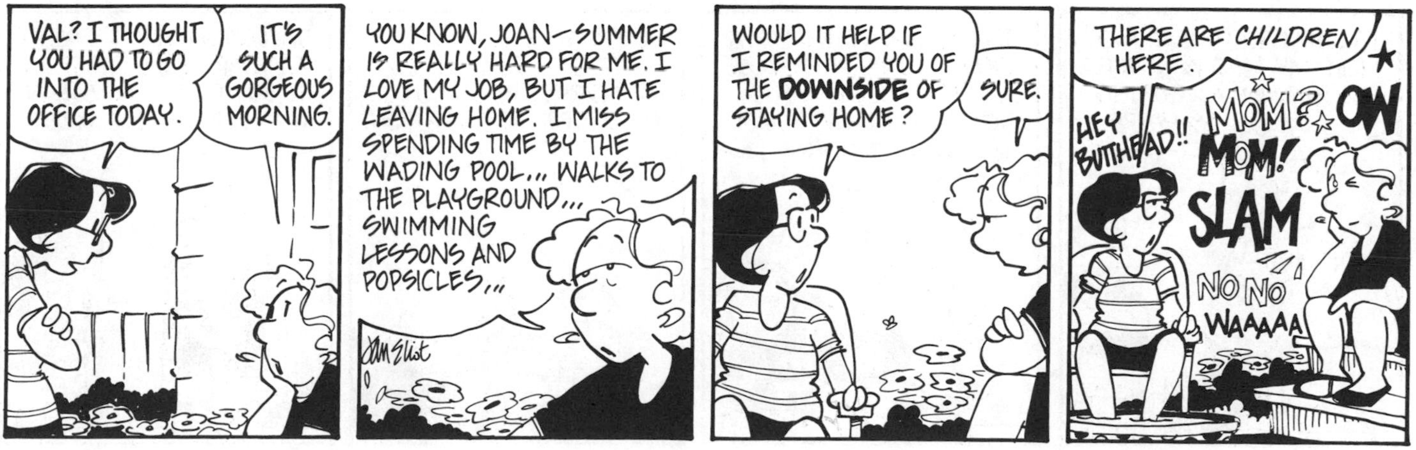
VAL? I THOUGHT YOU HAD TO GO INTO THE OFFICE TODAY.
IT'S SUCH A GORGEOUS MORNING.
YOU KNOW, JOAN—SUMMER IS REALLY HARD FOR ME. I LOVE MY JOB, BUT I HATE LEAVING HOME. I MISS SPENDING TIME BY THE WADING POOL... WALKS TO THE PLAYGROUND... SWIMMING LESSONS AND POPSICLES...
JAN Eliot
WOULD IT HELP IF I REMINDED YOU OF THE **DOWNSIDE** OF STAYING HOME?
SURE.
THERE ARE CHILDREN HERE.
HEY BUTTHEAD!!
MOM?
OW
MOM!
SLAM
NO NO
WAAAAA

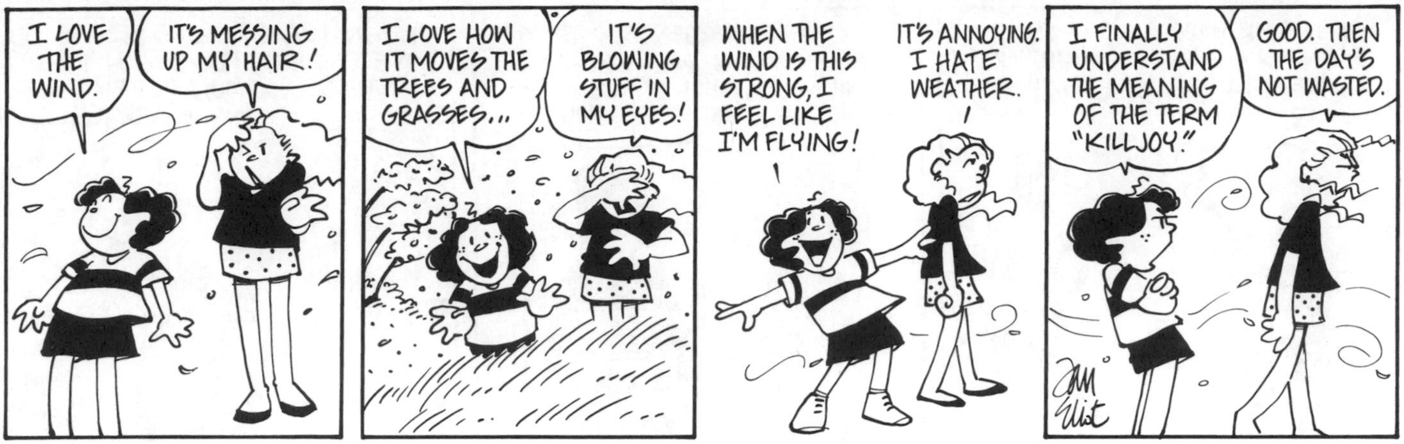
I LOVE THE WIND.
IT'S MESSING UP MY HAIR!
I LOVE HOW IT MOVES THE TREES AND GRASSES...
IT'S BLOWING STUFF IN MY EYES!
WHEN THE WIND IS THIS STRONG, I FEEL LIKE I'M FLYING!
IT'S ANNOYING. I HATE WEATHER.
I FINALLY UNDERSTAND THE MEANING OF THE TERM "KILLJOY."
GOOD. THEN THE DAY'S NOT WASTED.
JAN Eliot

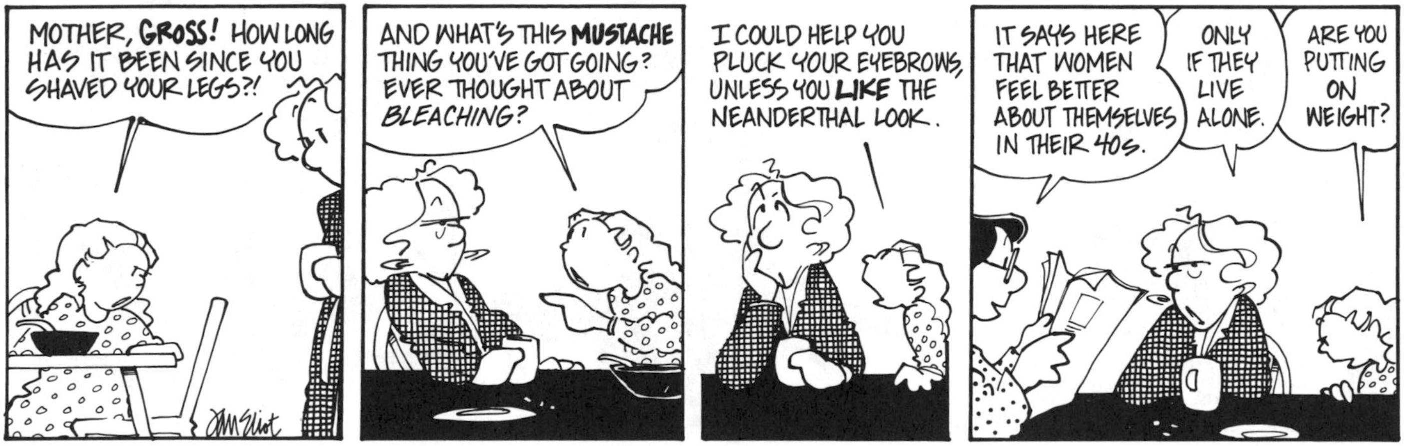
MOTHER, GROSS! HOW LONG HAS IT BEEN SINCE YOU SHAVED YOUR LEGS?!
JAN Eliot
AND WHAT'S THIS MUSTACHE THING YOU'VE GOT GOING? EVER THOUGHT ABOUT BLEACHING?
I COULD HELP YOU PLUCK YOUR EYEBROWS, UNLESS YOU LIKE THE NEANDERTHAL LOOK.
IT SAYS HERE THAT WOMEN FEEL BETTER ABOUT THEMSELVES IN THEIR 40s.
ONLY IF THEY LIVE ALONE.
ARE YOU PUTTING ON WEIGHT?

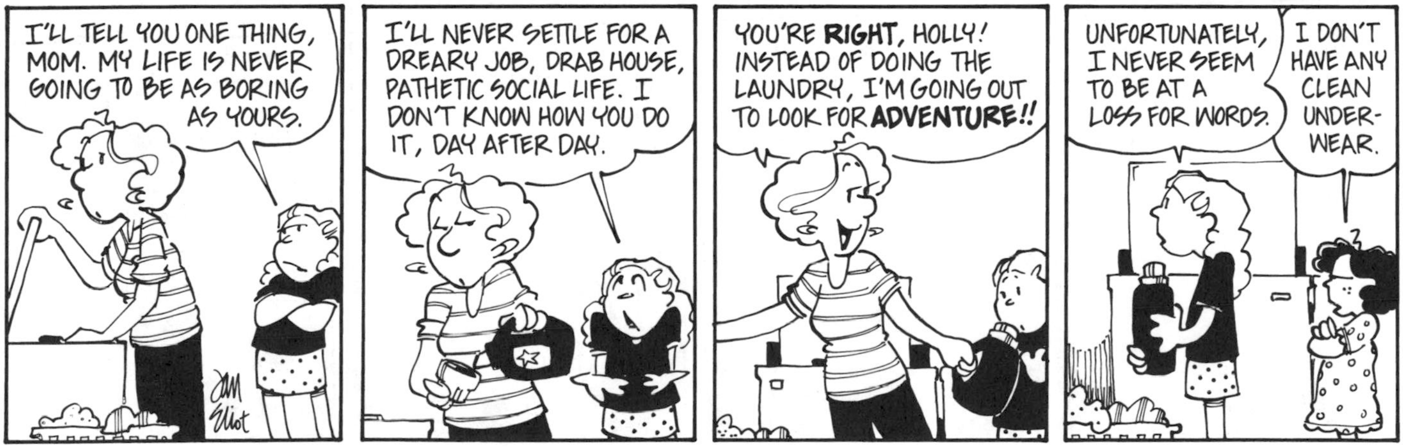
I'LL TELL YOU ONE THING, MOM. MY LIFE IS NEVER GOING TO BE AS BORING AS YOURS.
JAN Eliot
I'LL NEVER SETTLE FOR A DREARY JOB, DRAB HOUSE, PATHETIC SOCIAL LIFE. I DON'T KNOW HOW YOU DO IT, DAY AFTER DAY.
YOU'RE RIGHT, HOLLY! INSTEAD OF DOING THE LAUNDRY, I'M GOING OUT TO LOOK FOR ADVENTURE!!
UNFORTUNATELY, I NEVER SEEM TO BE AT A LOSS FOR WORDS.
I DON'T HAVE ANY CLEAN UNDER-WEAR.

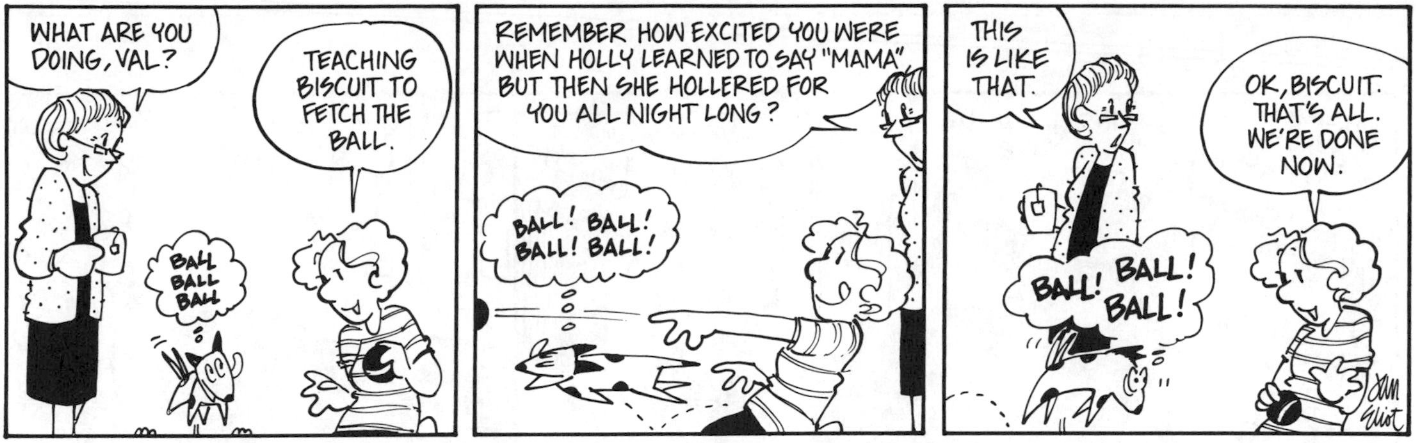
WHAT ARE YOU DOING, VAL?
TEACHING BISCUIT TO FETCH THE BALL.
BALL BALL BALL
REMEMBER HOW EXCITED YOU WERE WHEN HOLLY LEARNED TO SAY "MAMA" BUT THEN SHE HOLLERED FOR YOU ALL NIGHT LONG?
BALL! BALL! BALL! BALL!
THIS IS LIKE THAT.
OK, BISCUIT. THAT'S ALL. WE'RE DONE NOW.
BALL! BALL! BALL!

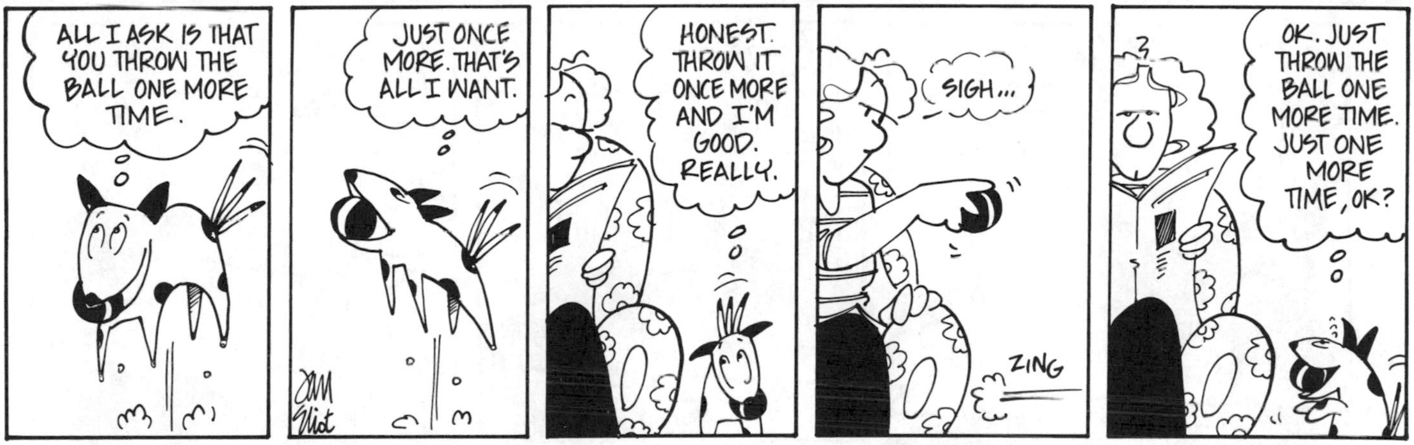
ALL I ASK IS THAT YOU THROW THE BALL ONE MORE TIME.
JUST ONCE MORE. THAT'S ALL I WANT.
HONEST. THROW IT ONCE MORE AND I'M GOOD. REALLY.
SIGH...
ZING
OK. JUST THROW THE BALL ONE MORE TIME. JUST ONE MORE TIME, OK?

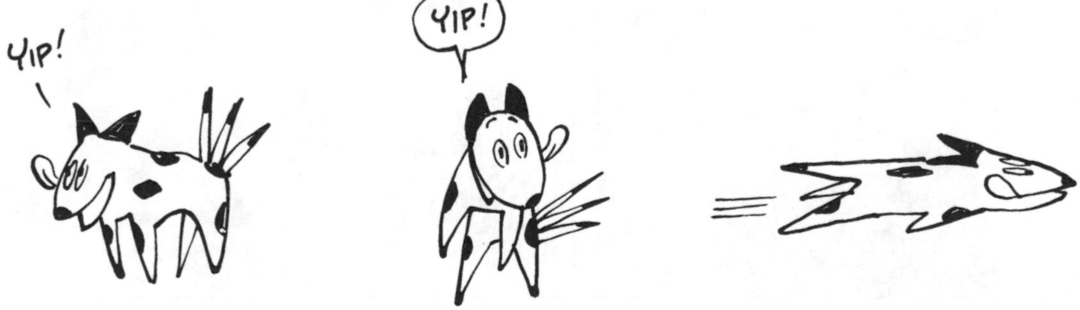
YIP!
YIP!

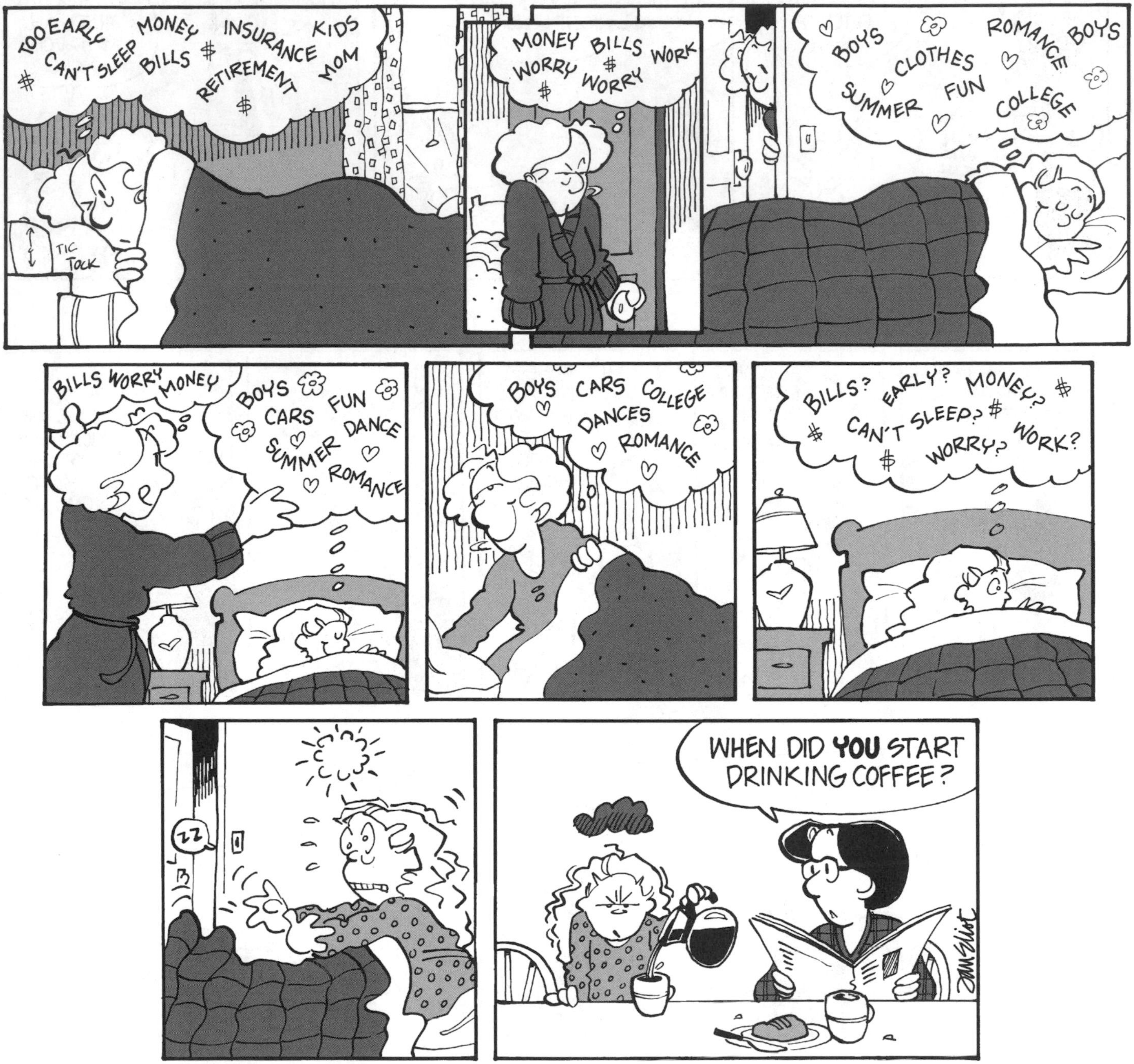
TOO EARLY
CAN'T SLEEP
MONEY
BILLS
INSURANCE
RETIREMENT
KIDS
MOM
TIC
TOCK
MONEY
BILLS
WORK
WORRY
WORRY
BOYS
CLOTHES
ROMANCE
BOYS
SUMMER
FUN
COLLEGE
BILLS WORRY MONEY
BOYS
CARS
FUN
SUMMER
DANCE
ROMANCE
BOYS
CARS
COLLEGE
DANCES
ROMANCE
BILLS?
EARLY?
MONEY?
CAN'T SLEEP?
WORK?
WORRY?
ZZ
WHEN DID **YOU** START DRINKING COFFEE?

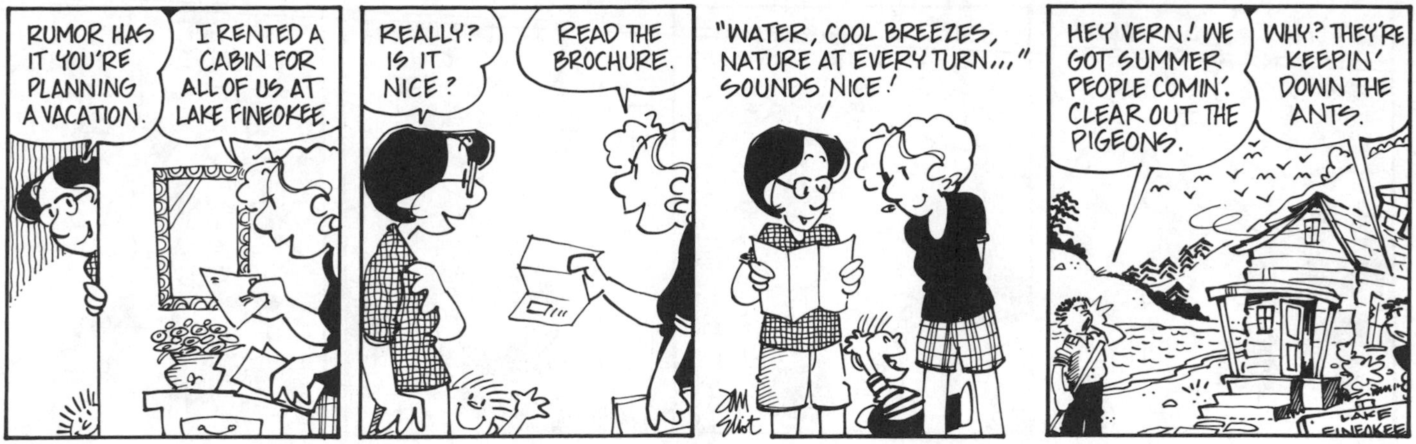
RUMOR HAS IT YOU'RE PLANNING A VACATION.
I RENTED A CABIN FOR ALL OF US AT LAKE FINEOKEE.
REALLY? IS IT NICE?
READ THE BROCHURE.
"WATER, COOL BREEZES, NATURE AT EVERY TURN..." SOUNDS NICE!
HEY VERN! WE GOT SUMMER PEOPLE COMIN'. CLEAR OUT THE PIGEONS.
WHY? THEY'RE KEEPIN' DOWN THE ANTS.
LAKE FINEOKEE

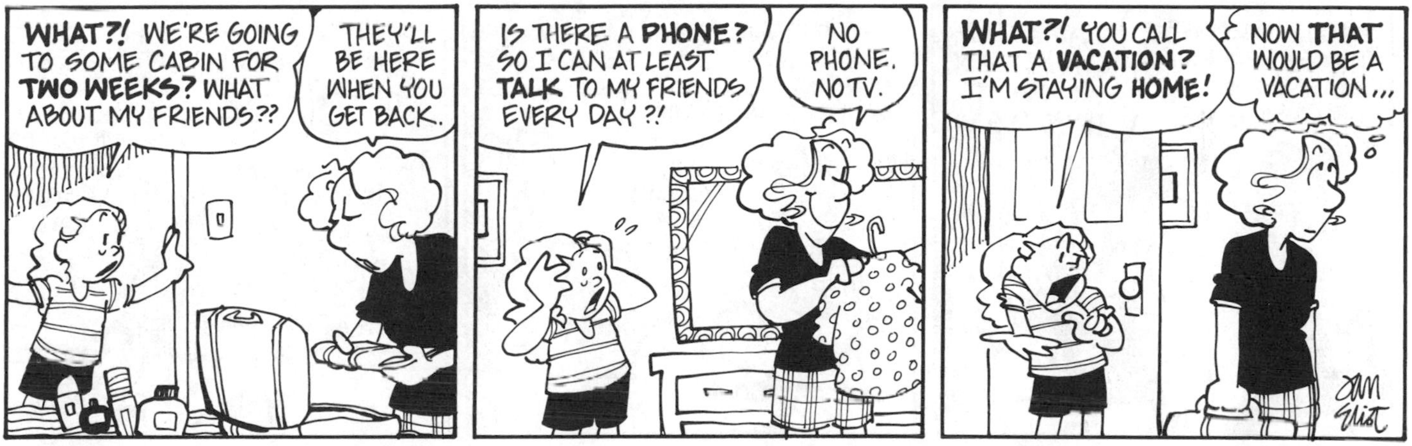
WHAT?! WE'RE GOING TO SOME CABIN FOR TWO WEEKS? WHAT ABOUT MY FRIENDS??
THEY'LL BE HERE WHEN YOU GET BACK.
IS THERE A PHONE? SO I CAN AT LEAST TALK TO MY FRIENDS EVERY DAY?!
NO PHONE. NO TV.
WHAT?! YOU CALL THAT A VACATION? I'M STAYING HOME!
NOW THAT WOULD BE A VACATION...

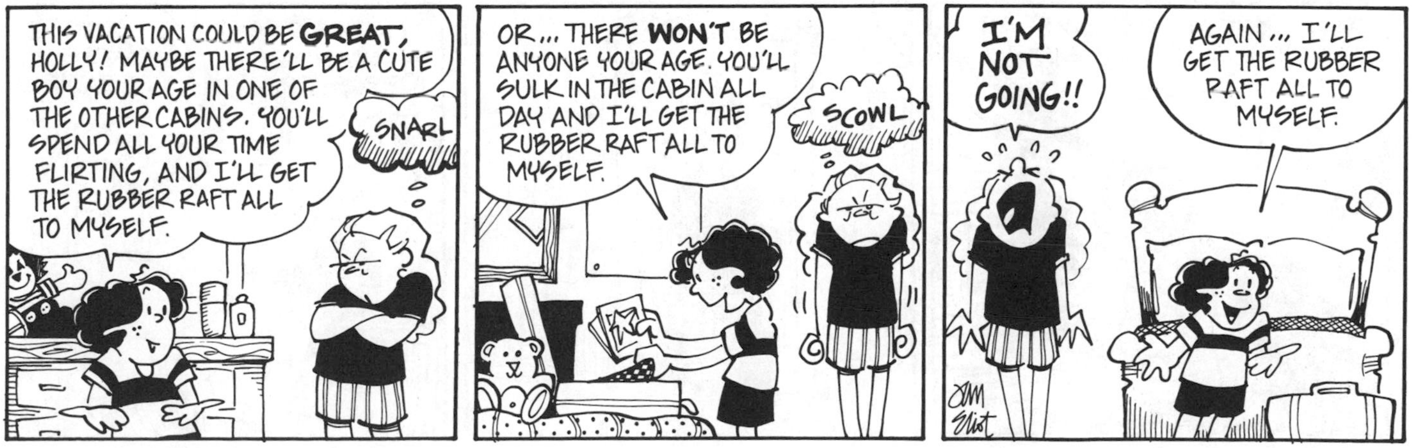
THIS VACATION COULD BE GREAT, HOLLY! MAYBE THERE'LL BE A CUTE BOY YOUR AGE IN ONE OF THE OTHER CABINS. YOU'LL SPEND ALL YOUR TIME FLIRTING, AND I'LL GET THE RUBBER RAFT ALL TO MYSELF.
SNARL
OR... THERE WON'T BE ANYONE YOUR AGE. YOU'LL SULK IN THE CABIN ALL DAY AND I'LL GET THE RUBBER RAFT ALL TO MYSELF.
SCOWL
I'M NOT GOING!!
AGAIN... I'LL GET THE RUBBER RAFT ALL TO MYSELF.

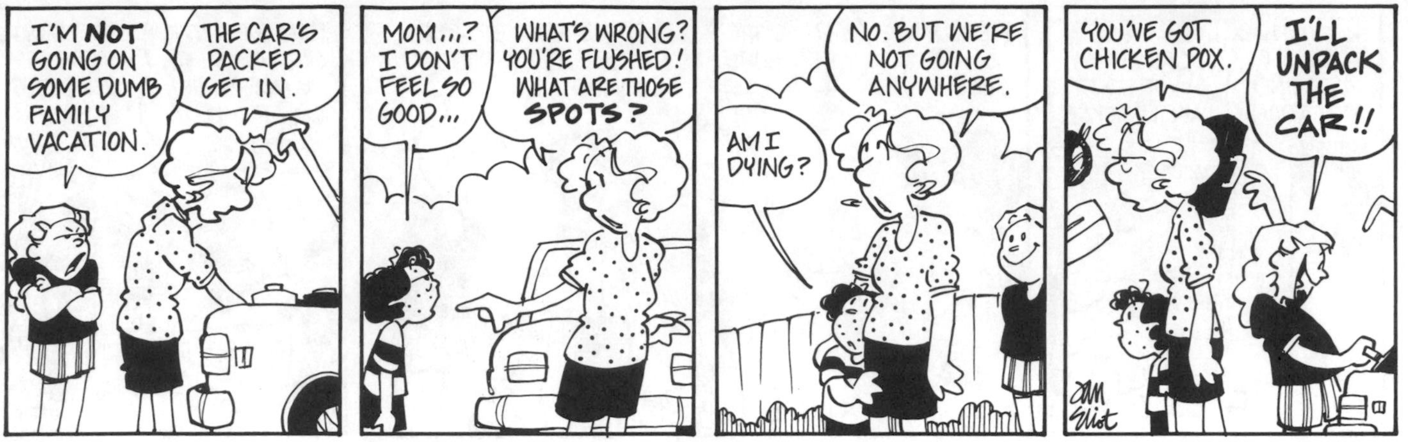
I'M NOT GOING ON SOME DUMB FAMILY VACATION.
THE CAR'S PACKED. GET IN.
MOM...? I DON'T FEEL SO GOOD...
WHAT'S WRONG? YOU'RE FLUSHED! WHAT ARE THOSE SPOTS?
AM I DYING?
NO. BUT WE'RE NOT GOING ANYWHERE.
YOU'VE GOT CHICKEN POX.
I'LL UNPACK THE CAR!!
JAN ELIOT

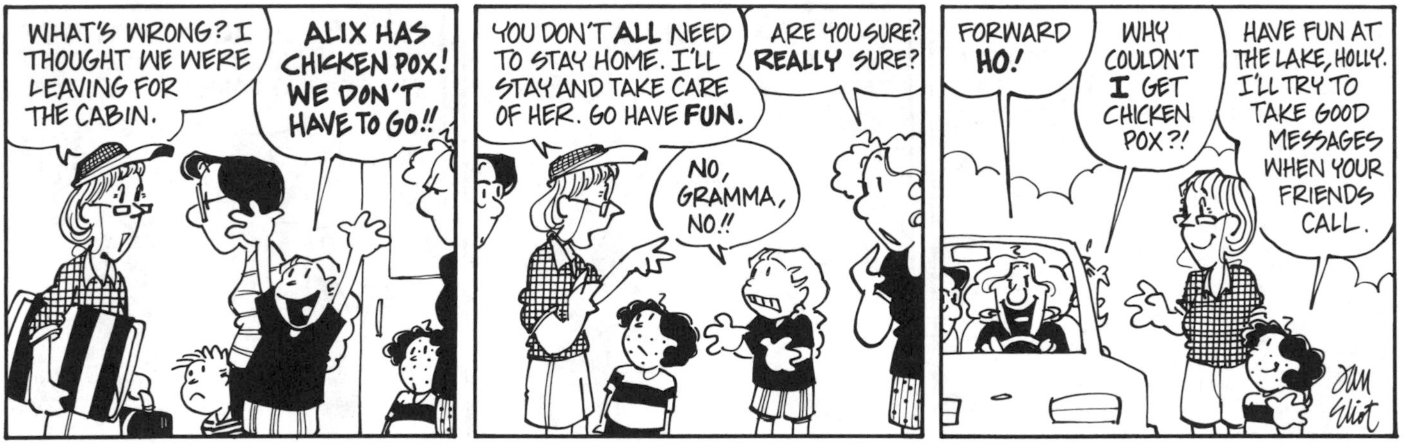
WHAT'S WRONG? I THOUGHT WE WERE LEAVING FOR THE CABIN.
ALIX HAS CHICKEN POX! WE DON'T HAVE TO GO!!
YOU DON'T ALL NEED TO STAY HOME. I'LL STAY AND TAKE CARE OF HER. GO HAVE FUN.
ARE YOU SURE? REALLY SURE?
NO, GRAMMA, NO!!
FORWARD HO!
WHY COULDN'T I GET CHICKEN POX?!
HAVE FUN AT THE LAKE, HOLLY. I'LL TRY TO TAKE GOOD MESSAGES WHEN YOUR FRIENDS CALL.
JAN ELIOT

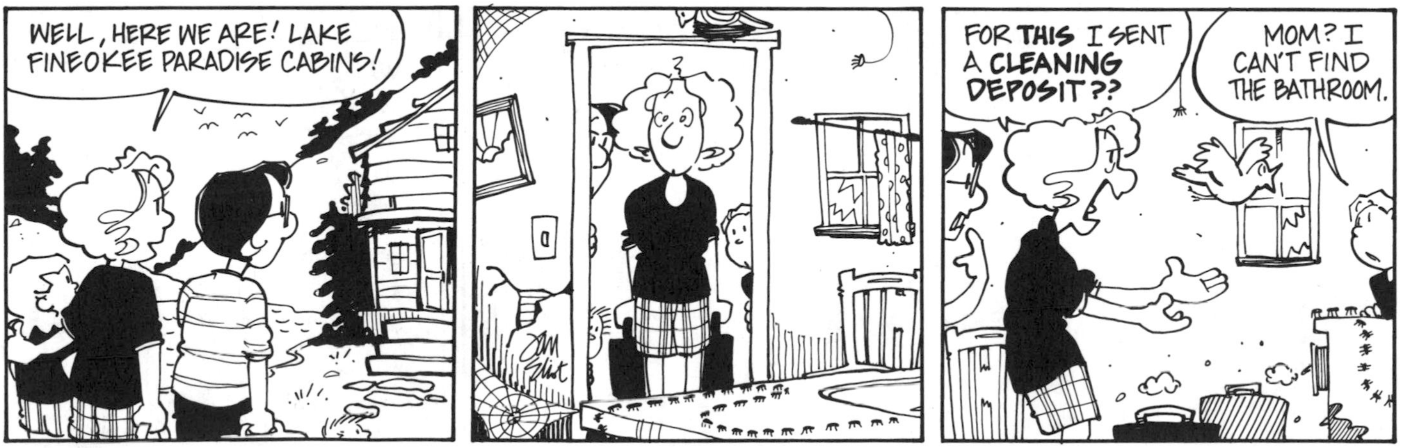
WELL, HERE WE ARE! LAKE FINEOKEE PARADISE CABINS!
JAN ELIOT
FOR THIS I SENT A CLEANING DEPOSIT??
MOM? I CAN'T FIND THE BATHROOM.

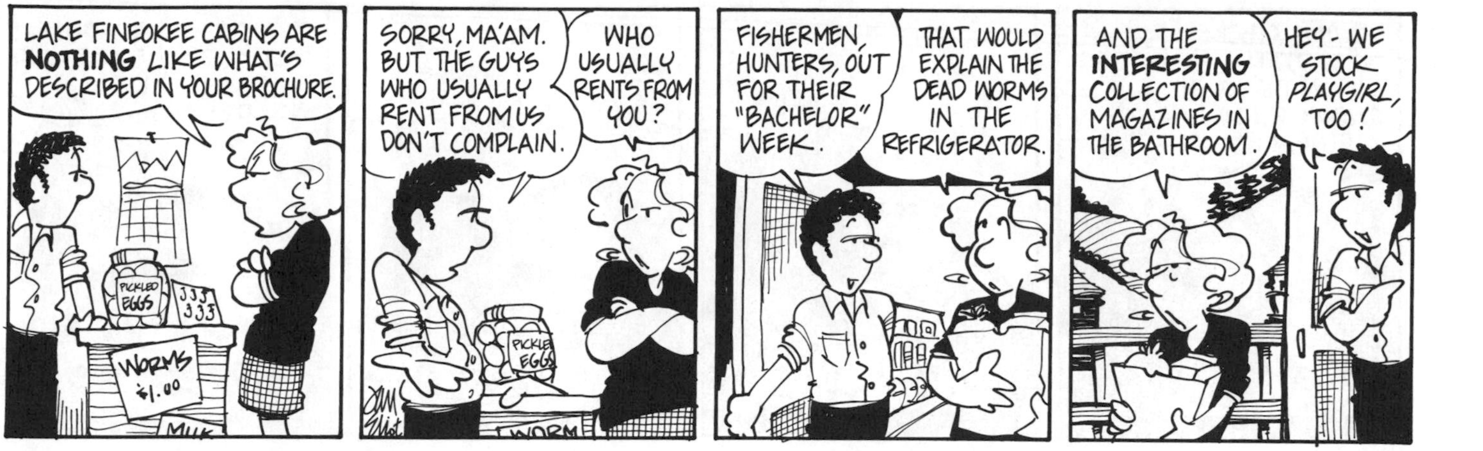
LAKE FINEOKEE CABINS ARE **NOTHING** LIKE WHAT'S DESCRIBED IN YOUR BROCHURE.
PICKLED EGGS
WORMS $1.00
SORRY, MA'AM. BUT THE GUYS WHO USUALLY RENT FROM US DON'T COMPLAIN.
WHO USUALLY RENTS FROM YOU?
FISHERMEN, HUNTERS, OUT FOR THEIR "BACHELOR" WEEK.
THAT WOULD EXPLAIN THE DEAD WORMS IN THE REFRIGERATOR.
AND THE **INTERESTING** COLLECTION OF MAGAZINES IN THE BATHROOM.
HEY - WE STOCK *PLAYGIRL*, TOO!

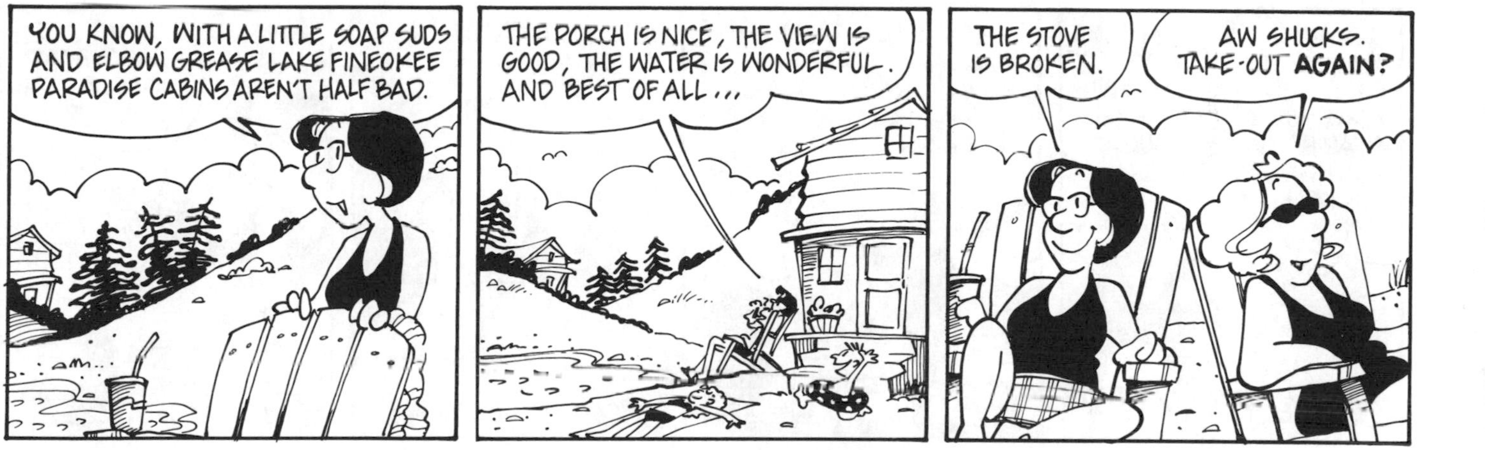
YOU KNOW, WITH A LITTLE SOAP SUDS AND ELBOW GREASE LAKE FINEOKEE PARADISE CABINS AREN'T HALF BAD.
THE PORCH IS NICE, THE VIEW IS GOOD, THE WATER IS WONDERFUL. AND BEST OF ALL...
THE STOVE IS BROKEN.
AW SHUCKS. TAKE-OUT **AGAIN?**

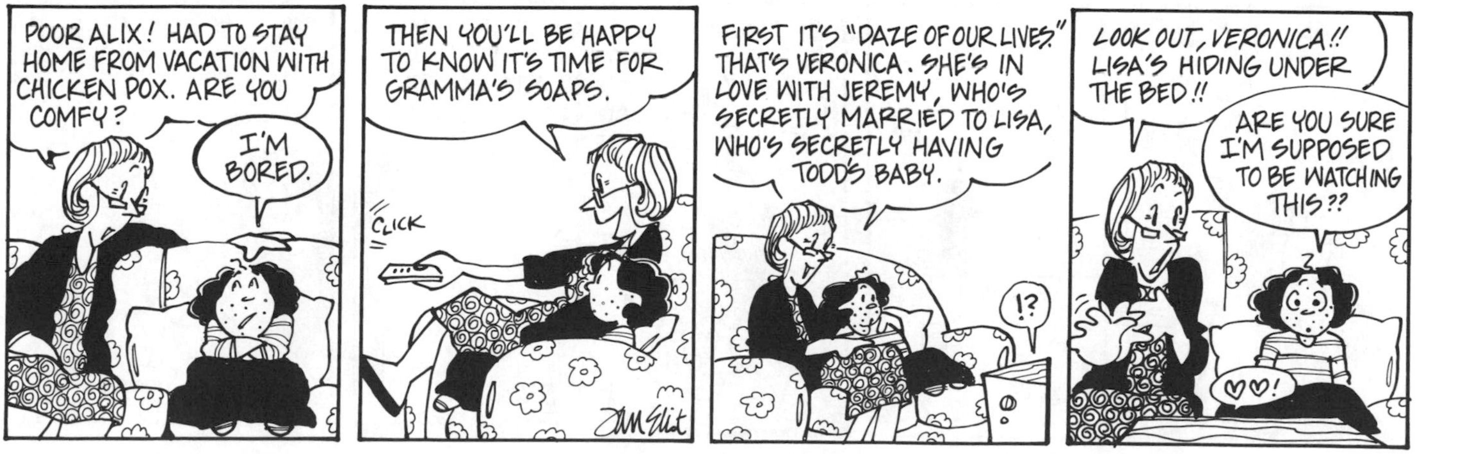
POOR ALIX! HAD TO STAY HOME FROM VACATION WITH CHICKEN POX. ARE YOU COMFY?
I'M BORED.
THEN YOU'LL BE HAPPY TO KNOW IT'S TIME FOR GRAMMA'S SOAPS.
CLICK
FIRST IT'S "DAZE OF OUR LIVES." THAT'S VERONICA. SHE'S IN LOVE WITH JEREMY, WHO'S SECRETLY MARRIED TO LISA, WHO'S SECRETLY HAVING TODD'S BABY.
!?
LOOK OUT, VERONICA!! LISA'S HIDING UNDER THE BED!!
ARE YOU SURE I'M SUPPOSED TO BE WATCHING THIS??
♡♡!

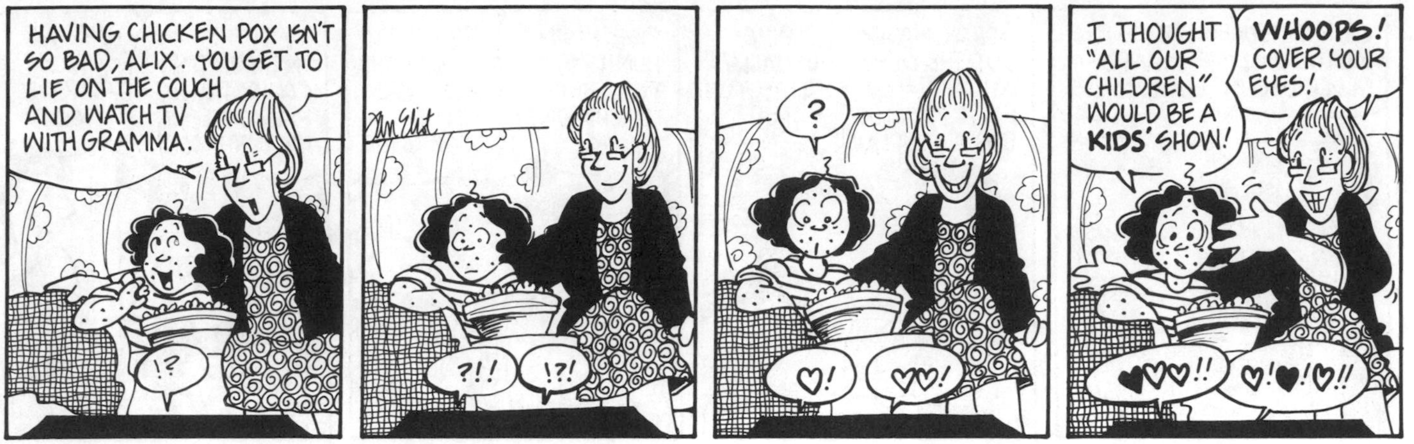
HAVING CHICKEN POX ISN'T SO BAD, ALIX. YOU GET TO LIE ON THE COUCH AND WATCH TV WITH GRAMMA.
!?
?!!
!?!
?
♡!
♡♡!
I THOUGHT "ALL OUR CHILDREN" WOULD BE A **KIDS'** SHOW!
WHOOPS! COVER YOUR EYES!
♥♡♡!!
♡!♥!♡!!

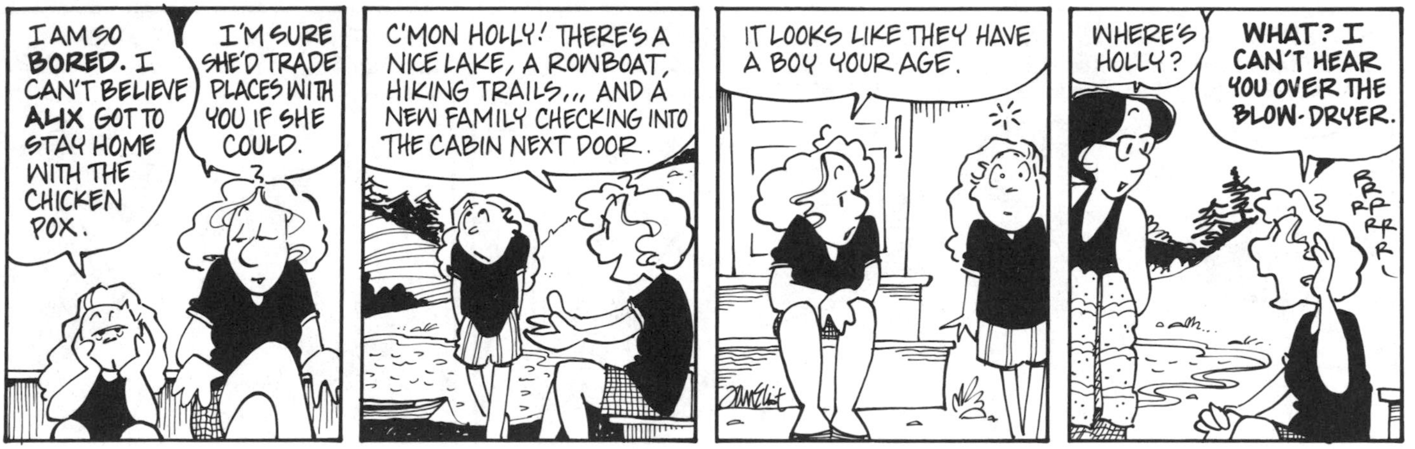
I AM SO **BORED.** I CAN'T BELIEVE **ALIX** GOT TO STAY HOME WITH THE CHICKEN POX.
I'M SURE SHE'D TRADE PLACES WITH YOU IF SHE COULD.
C'MON HOLLY! THERE'S A NICE LAKE, A ROWBOAT, HIKING TRAILS,,, AND A NEW FAMILY CHECKING INTO THE CABIN NEXT DOOR.
IT LOOKS LIKE THEY HAVE A BOY YOUR AGE.
WHERE'S HOLLY?
WHAT? I CAN'T HEAR YOU OVER THE BLOW-DRYER.
RRRRRRR

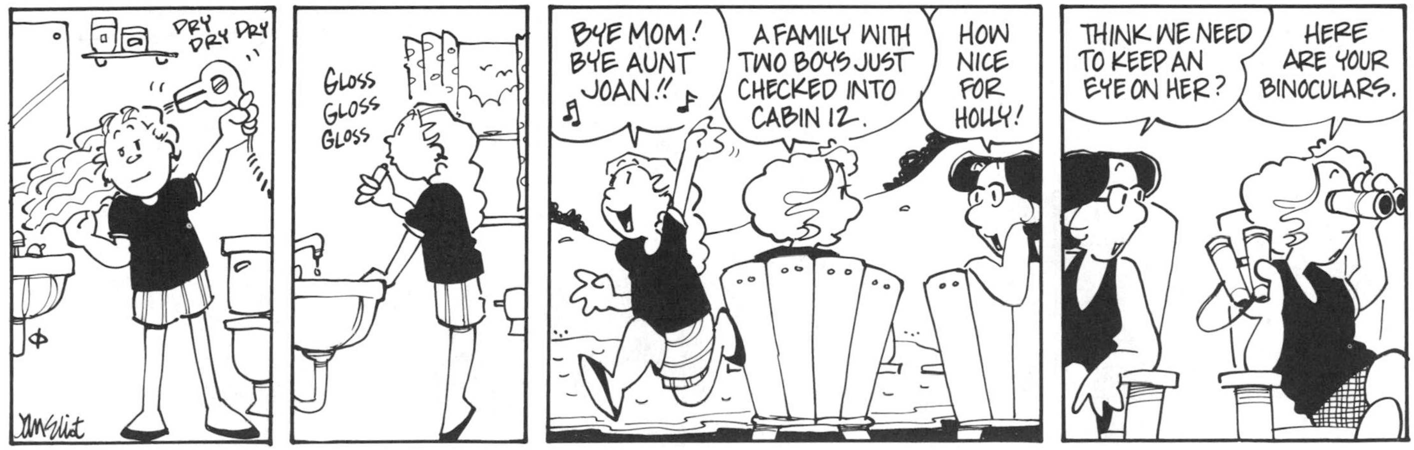
DRY DRY DRY
GLOSS GLOSS GLOSS
BYE MOM! BYE AUNT JOAN!!
A FAMILY WITH TWO BOYS JUST CHECKED INTO CABIN 12.
HOW NICE FOR HOLLY!
THINK WE NEED TO KEEP AN EYE ON HER?
HERE ARE YOUR BINOCULARS.

WHAT A GORGEOUS DAY!
I'M HOT.
LOOK! A BUTTERFLY!
OW! I THINK A BUG BIT ME!!
WOW! A FOUR-LEAF CLOVER!
MY SKIN ITCHES, THESE WEEDS ARE SCRATCHY. IS THAT POISON OAK?!
COOL! THERE MUST BE A GAZILLON LADYBUGS ON THIS BUSH!
I AM SO BORED.
YOU KNOW WHAT MOM HAD THE NERVE TO SAY TO ME THIS MORNING?
SHE SAID I HAVE AN ATTITUDE PROBLEM.
I BROUGHT YOU A GLASS OF LEMONADE. HALF EMPTY, JUST LIKE YOU LIKE IT.

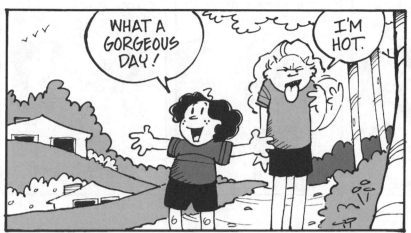

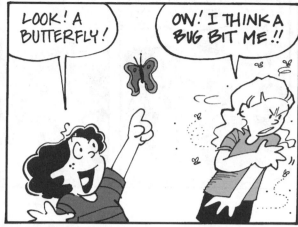

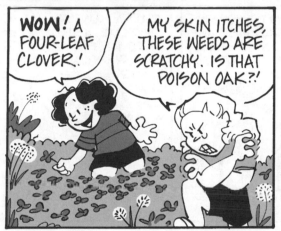

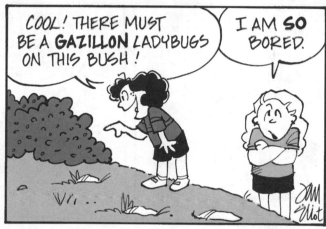

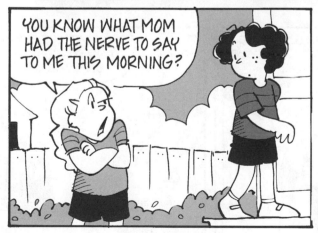

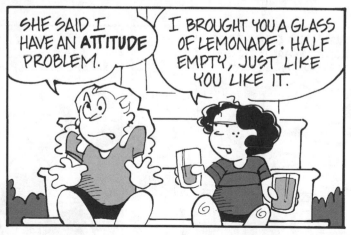

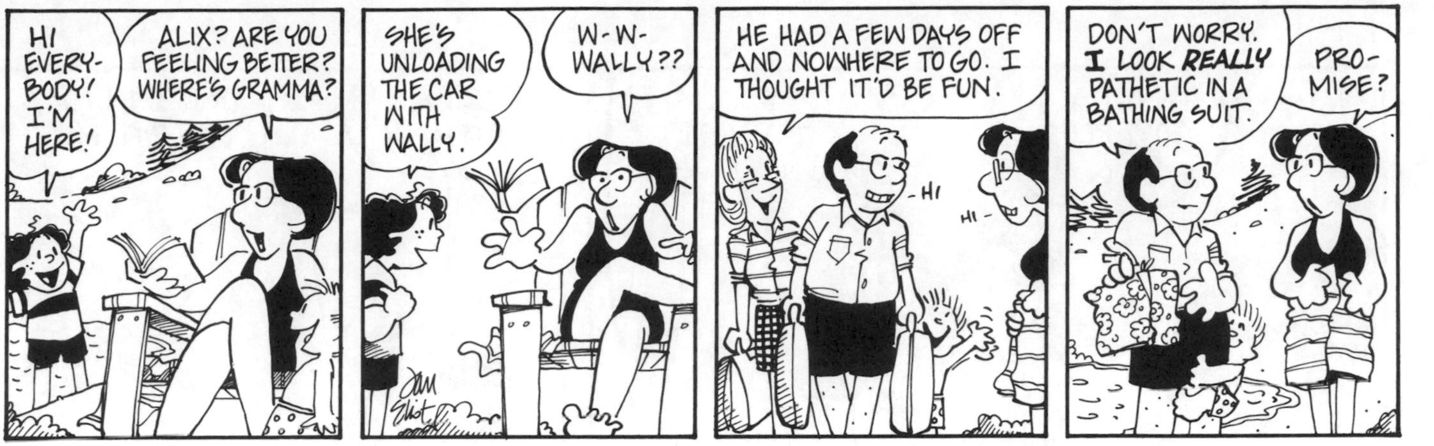
HI EVERY-BODY! I'M HERE!
ALIX? ARE YOU FEELING BETTER? WHERE'S GRAMMA?
SHE'S UNLOADING THE CAR WITH WALLY.
W-W-WALLY??
HE HAD A FEW DAYS OFF AND NOWHERE TO GO. I THOUGHT IT'D BE FUN.
- HI
HI -
DON'T WORRY. I LOOK REALLY PATHETIC IN A BATHING SUIT.
PRO-MISE?

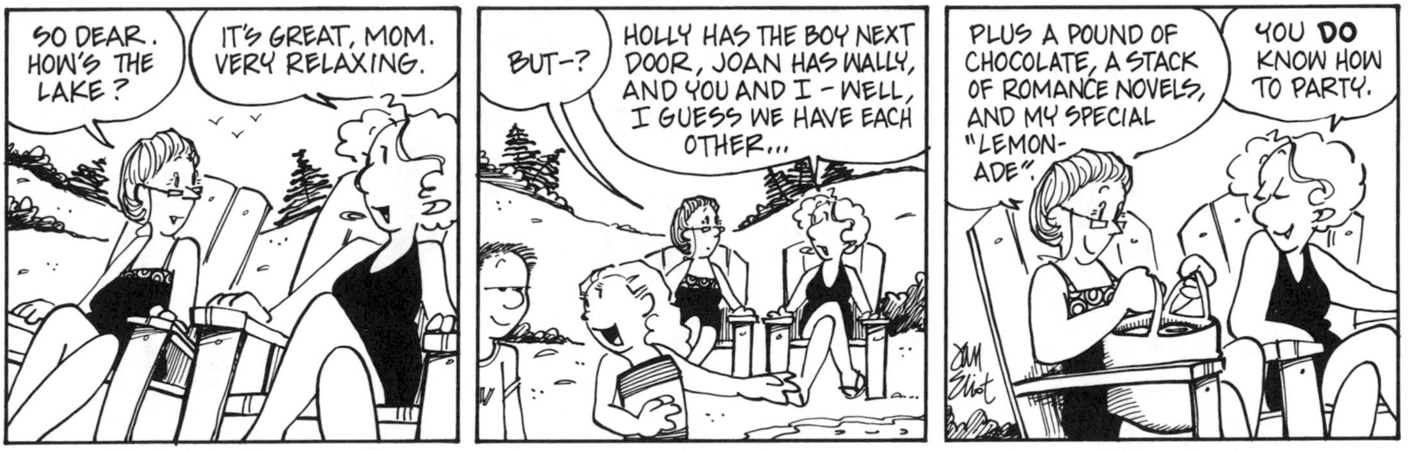
SO DEAR. HOW'S THE LAKE?
IT'S GREAT, MOM. VERY RELAXING.
BUT-?
HOLLY HAS THE BOY NEXT DOOR, JOAN HAS WALLY, AND YOU AND I - WELL, I GUESS WE HAVE EACH OTHER...
PLUS A POUND OF CHOCOLATE, A STACK OF ROMANCE NOVELS, AND MY SPECIAL "LEMON-ADE".
YOU DO KNOW HOW TO PARTY.

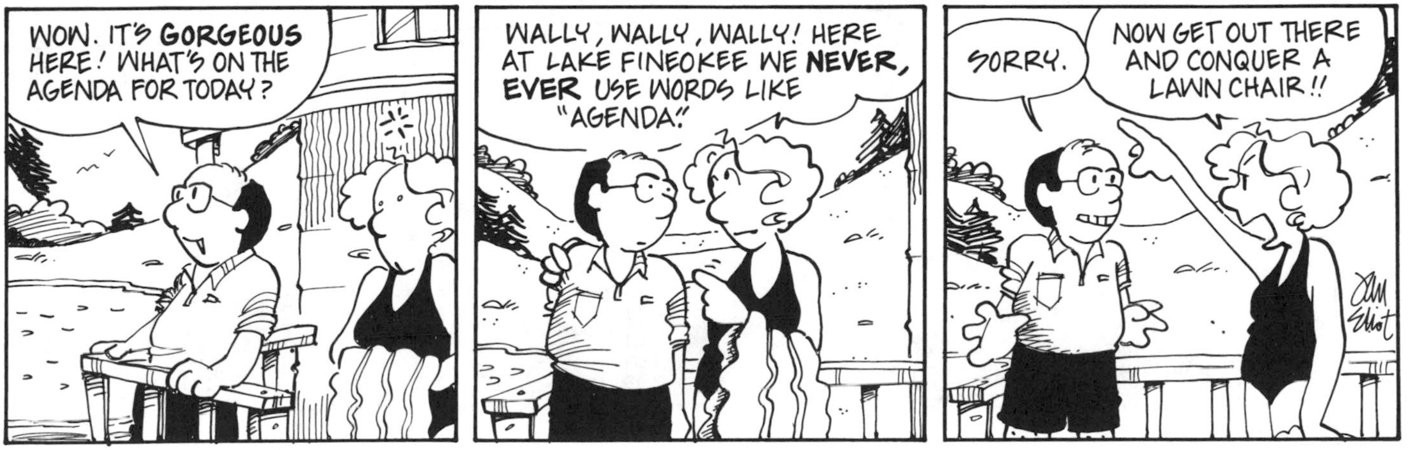
WOW. IT'S GORGEOUS HERE! WHAT'S ON THE AGENDA FOR TODAY?
WALLY, WALLY, WALLY! HERE AT LAKE FINEOKEE WE NEVER, EVER USE WORDS LIKE "AGENDA."
SORRY.
NOW GET OUT THERE AND CONQUER A LAWN CHAIR!!

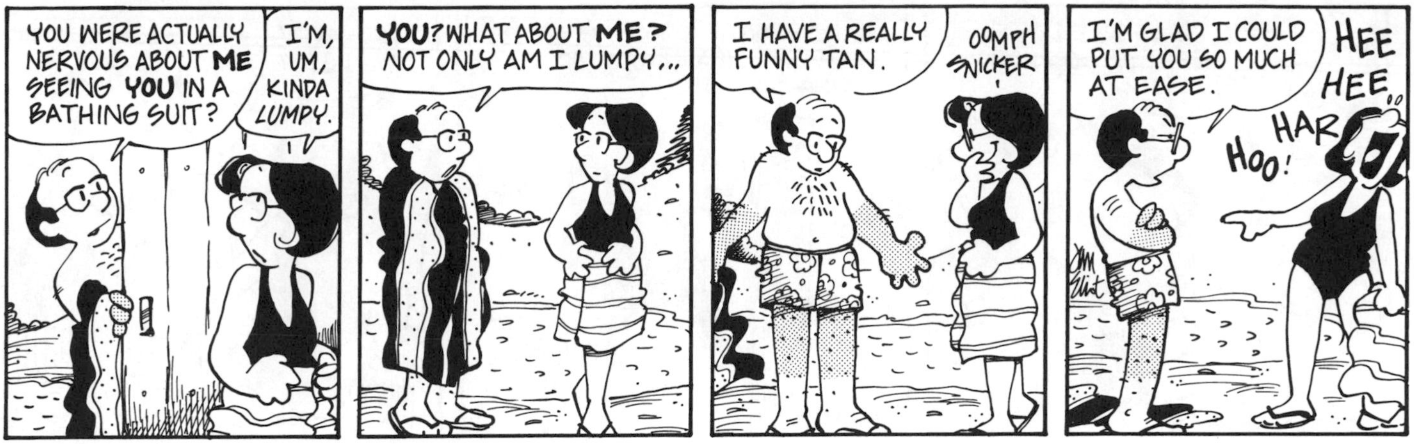
YOU WERE ACTUALLY NERVOUS ABOUT ME SEEING YOU IN A BATHING SUIT?
I'M, UM, KINDA LUMPY.
YOU? WHAT ABOUT ME? NOT ONLY AM I LUMPY...
I HAVE A REALLY FUNNY TAN.
OOMPH SNICKER
I'M GLAD I COULD PUT YOU SO MUCH AT EASE.
HEE HEE
HAR
HOO!

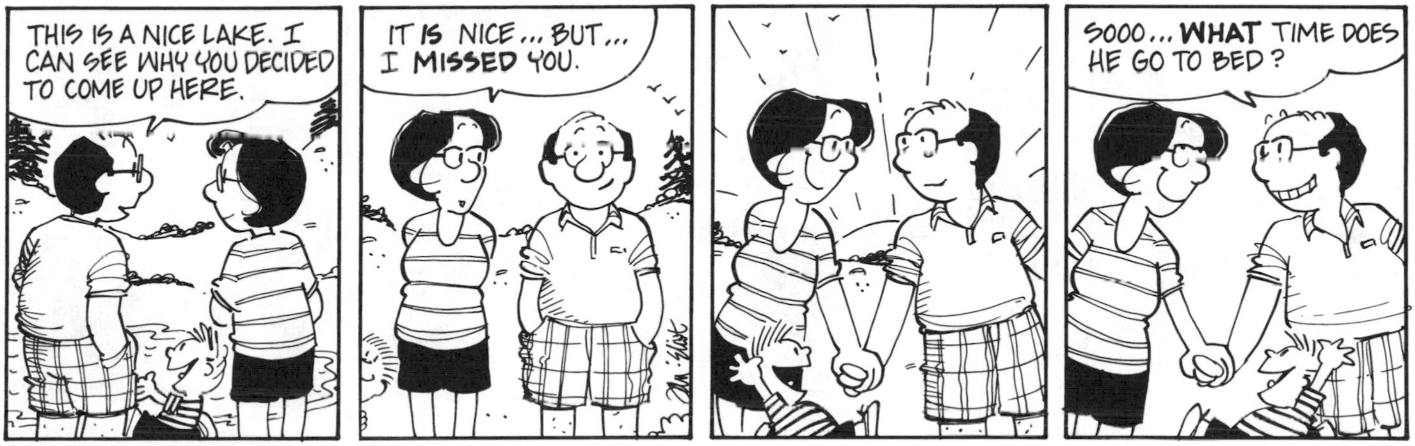
THIS IS A NICE LAKE. I CAN SEE WHY YOU DECIDED TO COME UP HERE.
IT IS NICE... BUT... I MISSED YOU.
SOOO... WHAT TIME DOES HE GO TO BED?

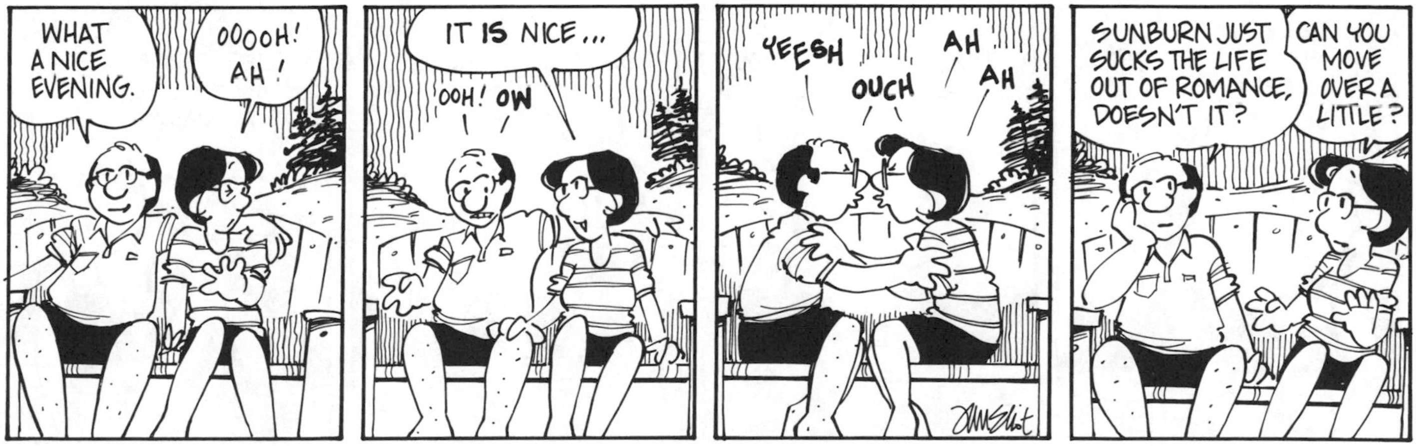
WHAT A NICE EVENING.
OOOOH! AH!
IT IS NICE...
OOH! OW
YEESH
OUCH
AH
AH
SUNBURN JUST SUCKS THE LIFE OUT OF ROMANCE, DOESN'T IT?
CAN YOU MOVE OVER A LITTLE?

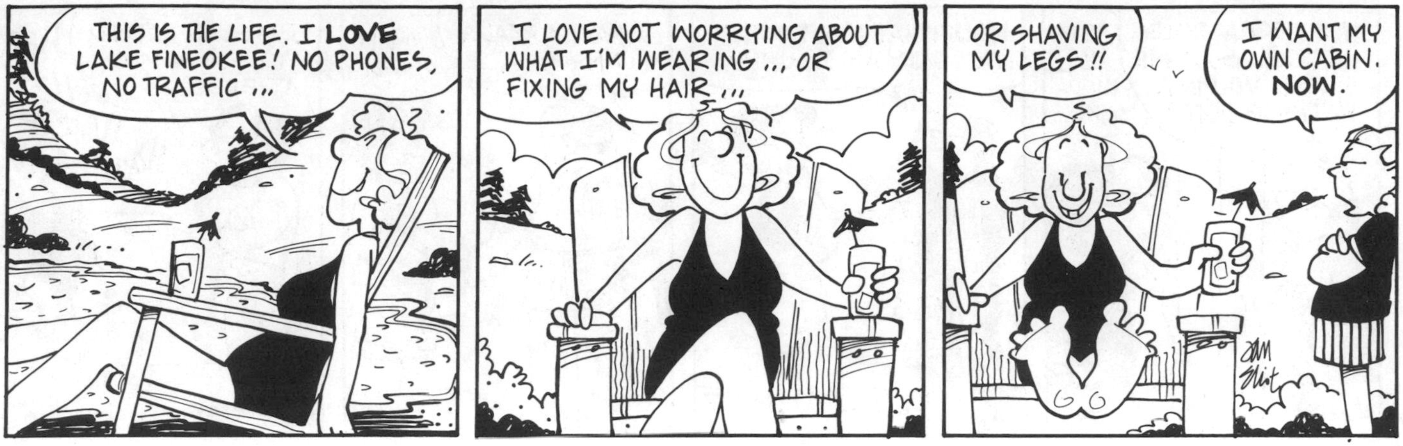
THIS IS THE LIFE. I **LOVE** LAKE FINEOKEE! NO PHONES, NO TRAFFIC ...
I LOVE NOT WORRYING ABOUT WHAT I'M WEARING ... OR FIXING MY HAIR ...
OR SHAVING MY LEGS !!
I WANT MY OWN CABIN. **NOW**.

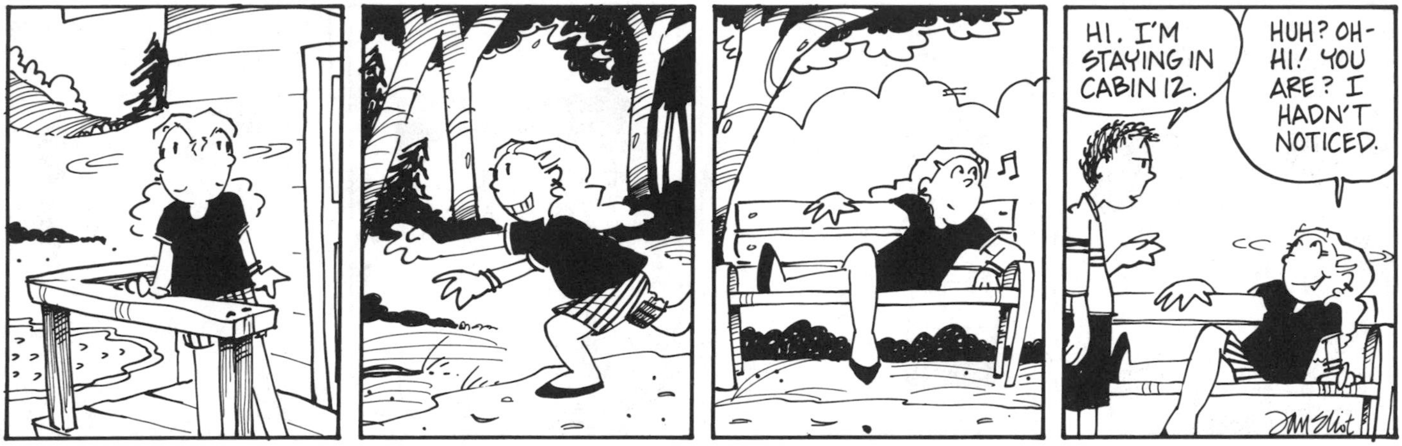
HI. I'M STAYING IN CABIN 12.
HUH? OH- HI! YOU ARE? I HADN'T NOTICED.

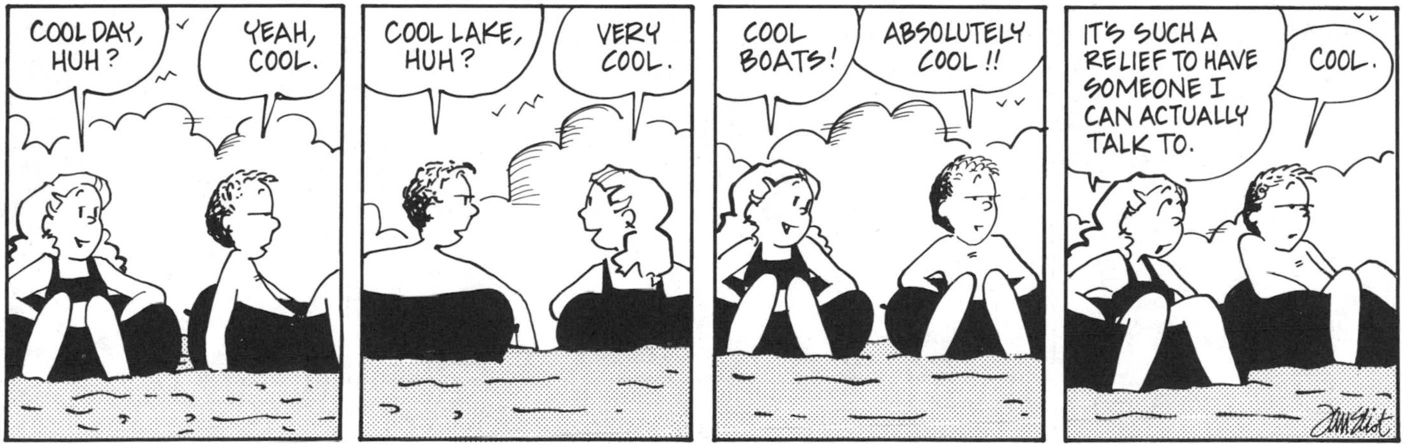
COOL DAY, HUH?
YEAH, COOL.
COOL LAKE, HUH?
VERY COOL.
COOL BOATS!
ABSOLUTELY COOL !!
IT'S SUCH A RELIEF TO HAVE SOMEONE I CAN ACTUALLY TALK TO.
COOL.

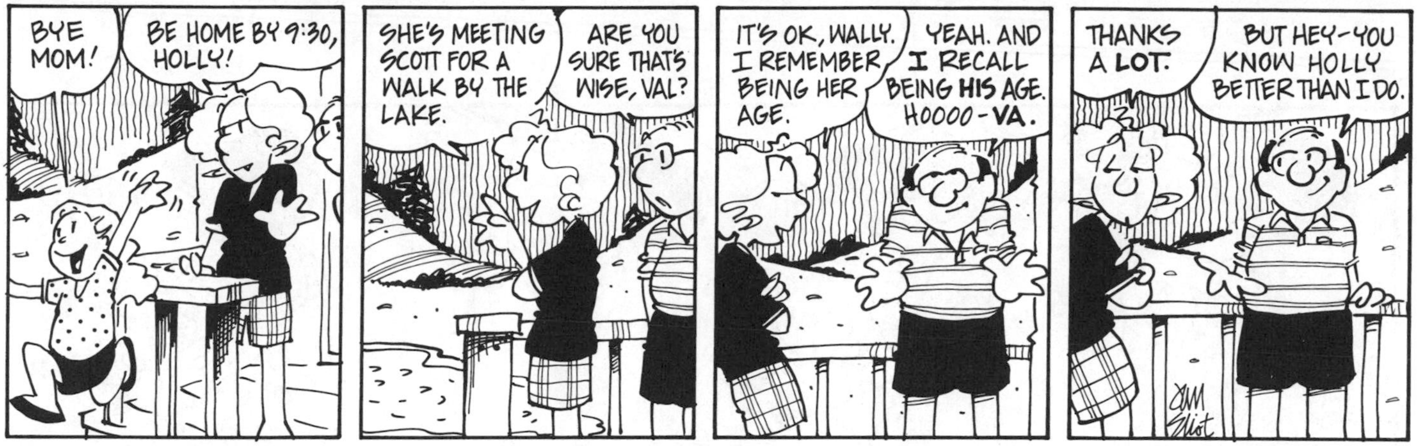
BYE MOM!
BE HOME BY 9:30, HOLLY!
SHE'S MEETING SCOTT FOR A WALK BY THE LAKE.
ARE YOU SURE THAT'S WISE, VAL?
IT'S OK, WALLY. I REMEMBER BEING HER AGE.
YEAH. AND I RECALL BEING HIS AGE. HOOOO-VA.
THANKS A LOT.
BUT HEY-YOU KNOW HOLLY BETTER THAN I DO.

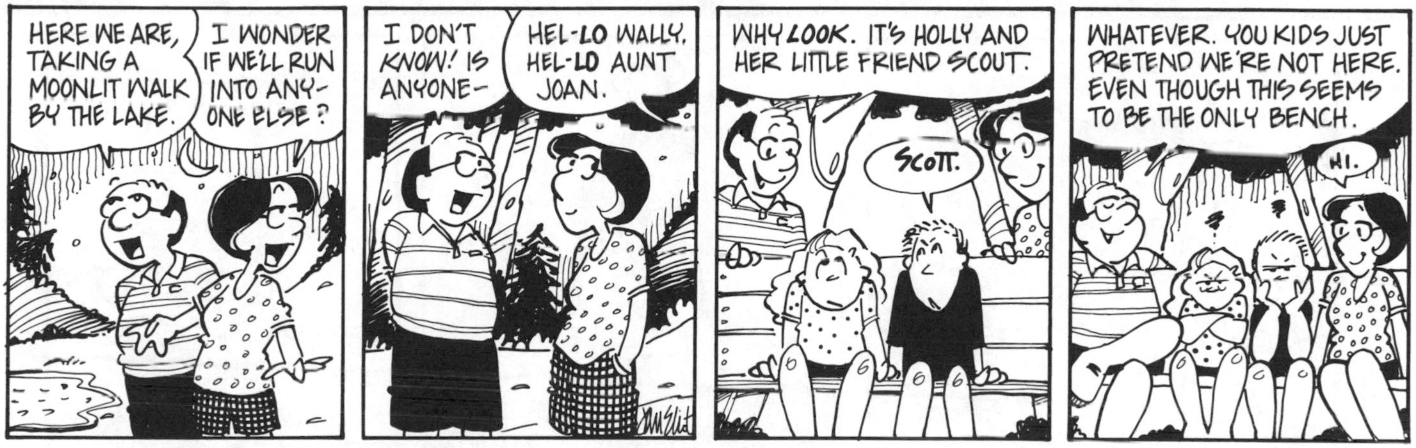
HERE WE ARE, TAKING A MOONLIT WALK BY THE LAKE.
I WONDER IF WE'LL RUN INTO ANY-ONE ELSE?
I DON'T KNOW! IS ANYONE-
HEL-LO WALLY. HEL-LO AUNT JOAN.
WHY LOOK. IT'S HOLLY AND HER LITTLE FRIEND SCOUT.
SCOTT.
WHATEVER. YOU KIDS JUST PRETEND WE'RE NOT HERE. EVEN THOUGH THIS SEEMS TO BE THE ONLY BENCH.
HI.

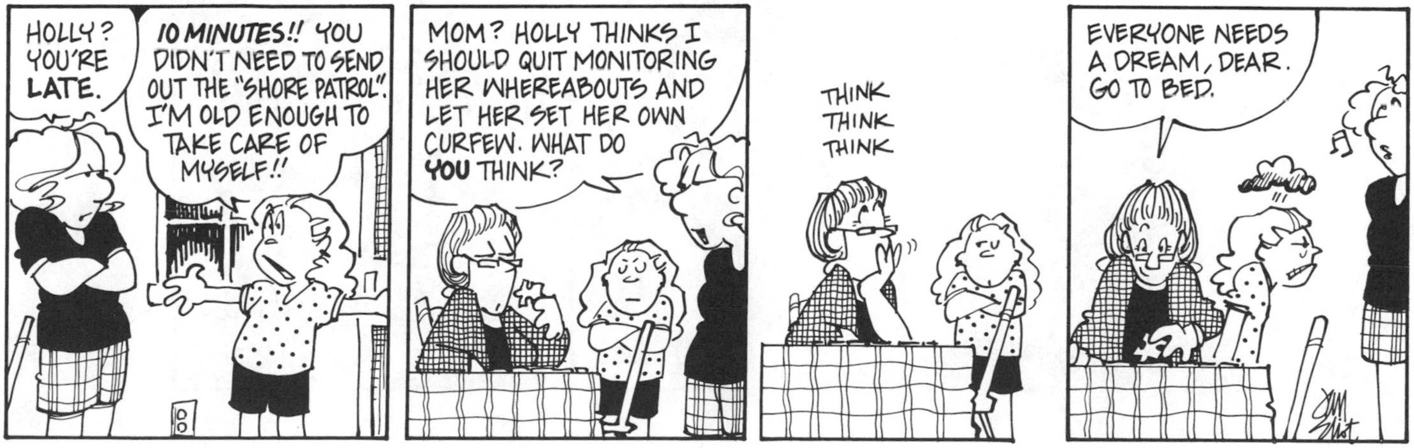
HOLLY? YOU'RE LATE.
10 MINUTES!! YOU DIDN'T NEED TO SEND OUT THE "SHORE PATROL". I'M OLD ENOUGH TO TAKE CARE OF MYSELF!!
MOM? HOLLY THINKS I SHOULD QUIT MONITORING HER WHEREABOUTS AND LET HER SET HER OWN CURFEW. WHAT DO YOU THINK?
THINK THINK THINK
EVERYONE NEEDS A DREAM, DEAR. GO TO BED.

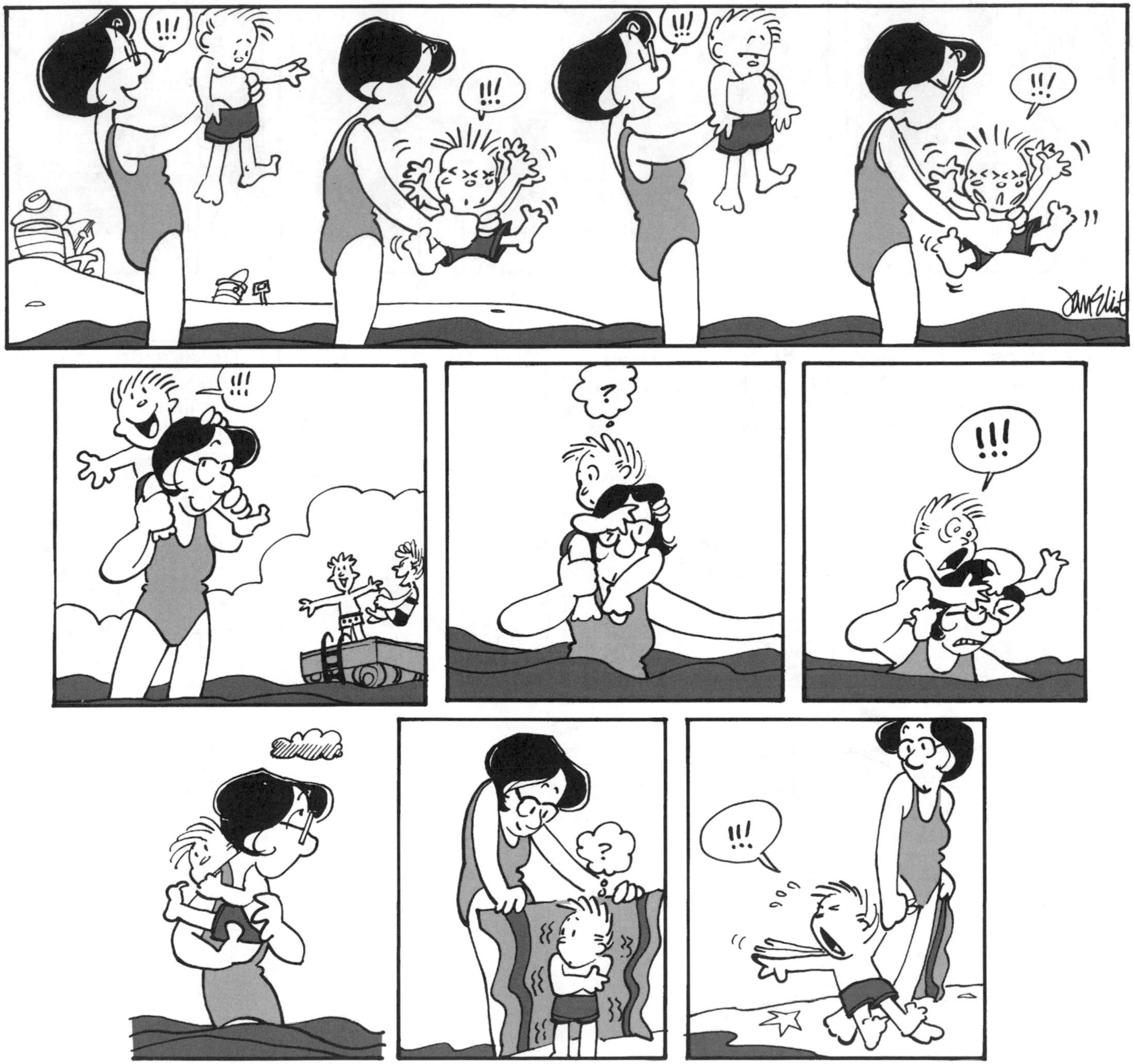
!!!
!!!
!!!
!!!
!!!
?
!!!
?
!!!

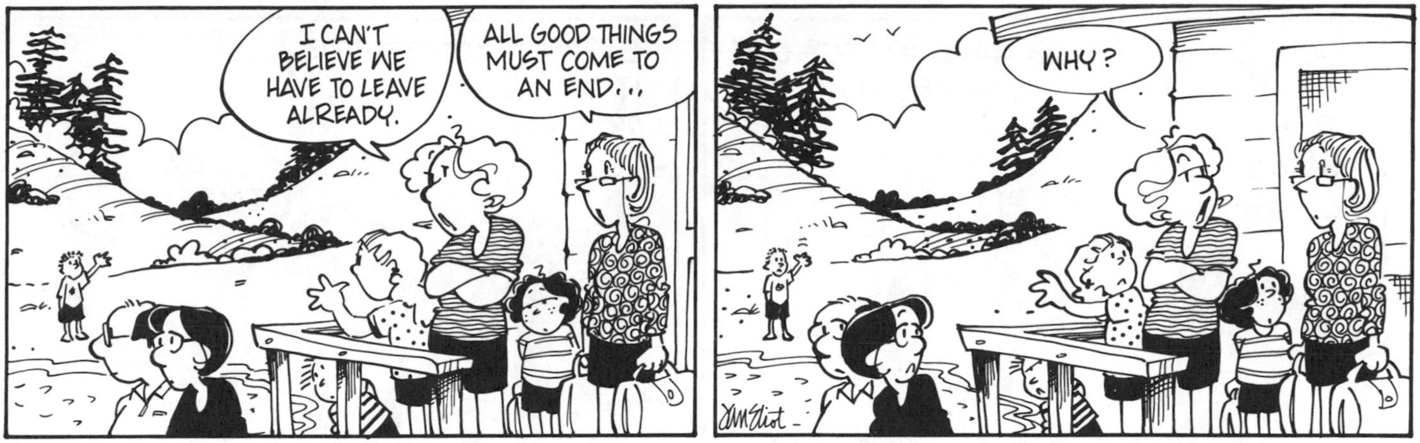
I CAN'T BELIEVE WE HAVE TO LEAVE ALREADY.
ALL GOOD THINGS MUST COME TO AN END...
WHY?

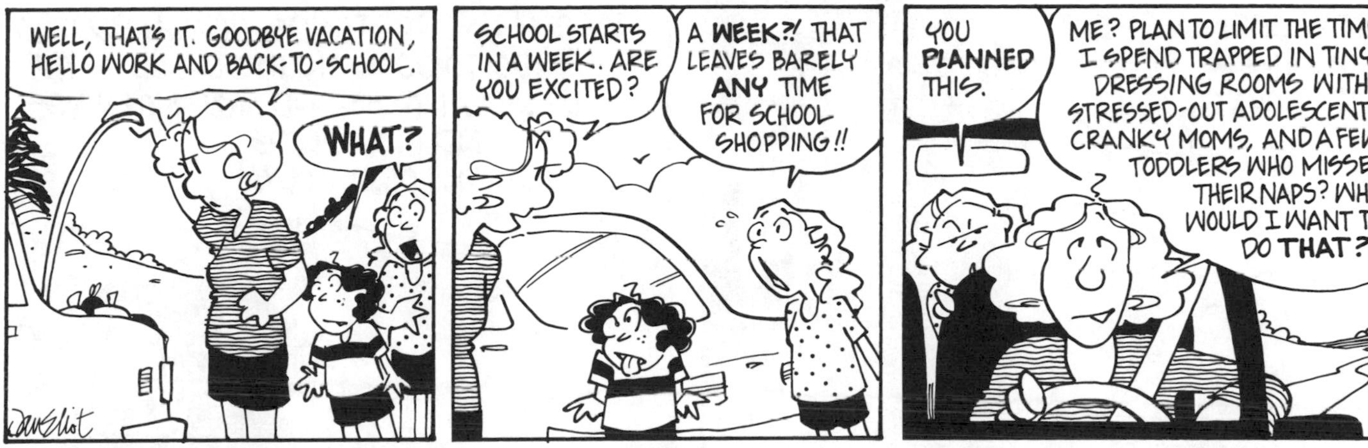
WELL, THAT'S IT. GOODBYE VACATION, HELLO WORK AND BACK-TO-SCHOOL.
WHAT?
SCHOOL STARTS IN A WEEK. ARE YOU EXCITED?
A WEEK?! THAT LEAVES BARELY ANY TIME FOR SCHOOL SHOPPING!!
YOU PLANNED THIS.
ME? PLAN TO LIMIT THE TIME I SPEND TRAPPED IN TINY DRESSING ROOMS WITH STRESSED-OUT ADOLESCENTS, CRANKY MOMS, AND A FEW TODDLERS WHO MISSED THEIR NAPS? WHY WOULD I WANT TO DO THAT?

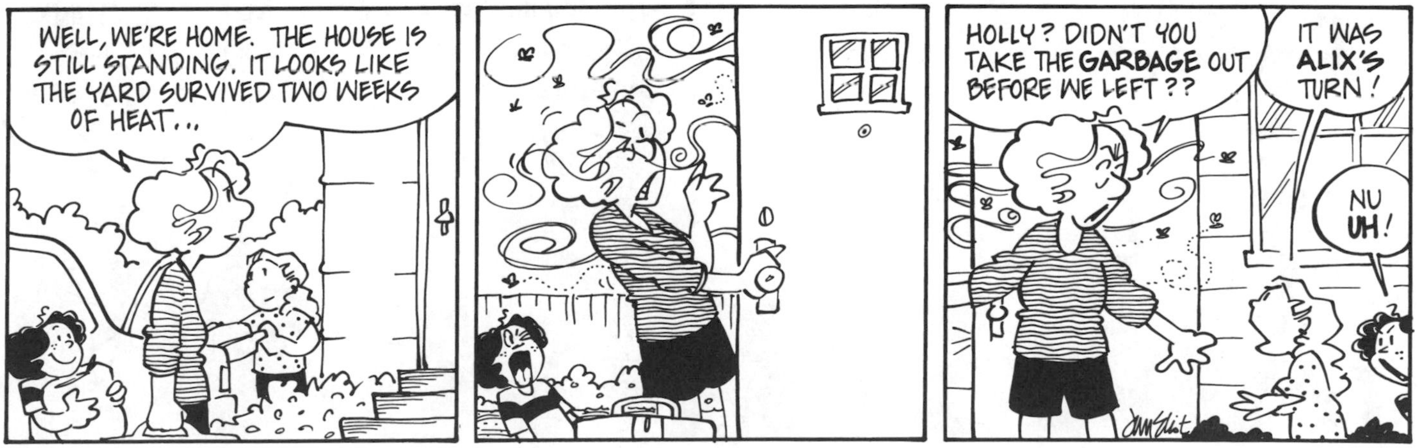
WELL, WE'RE HOME. THE HOUSE IS STILL STANDING. IT LOOKS LIKE THE YARD SURVIVED TWO WEEKS OF HEAT...
HOLLY? DIDN'T YOU TAKE THE GARBAGE OUT BEFORE WE LEFT??
IT WAS ALIX'S TURN!
NU UH!

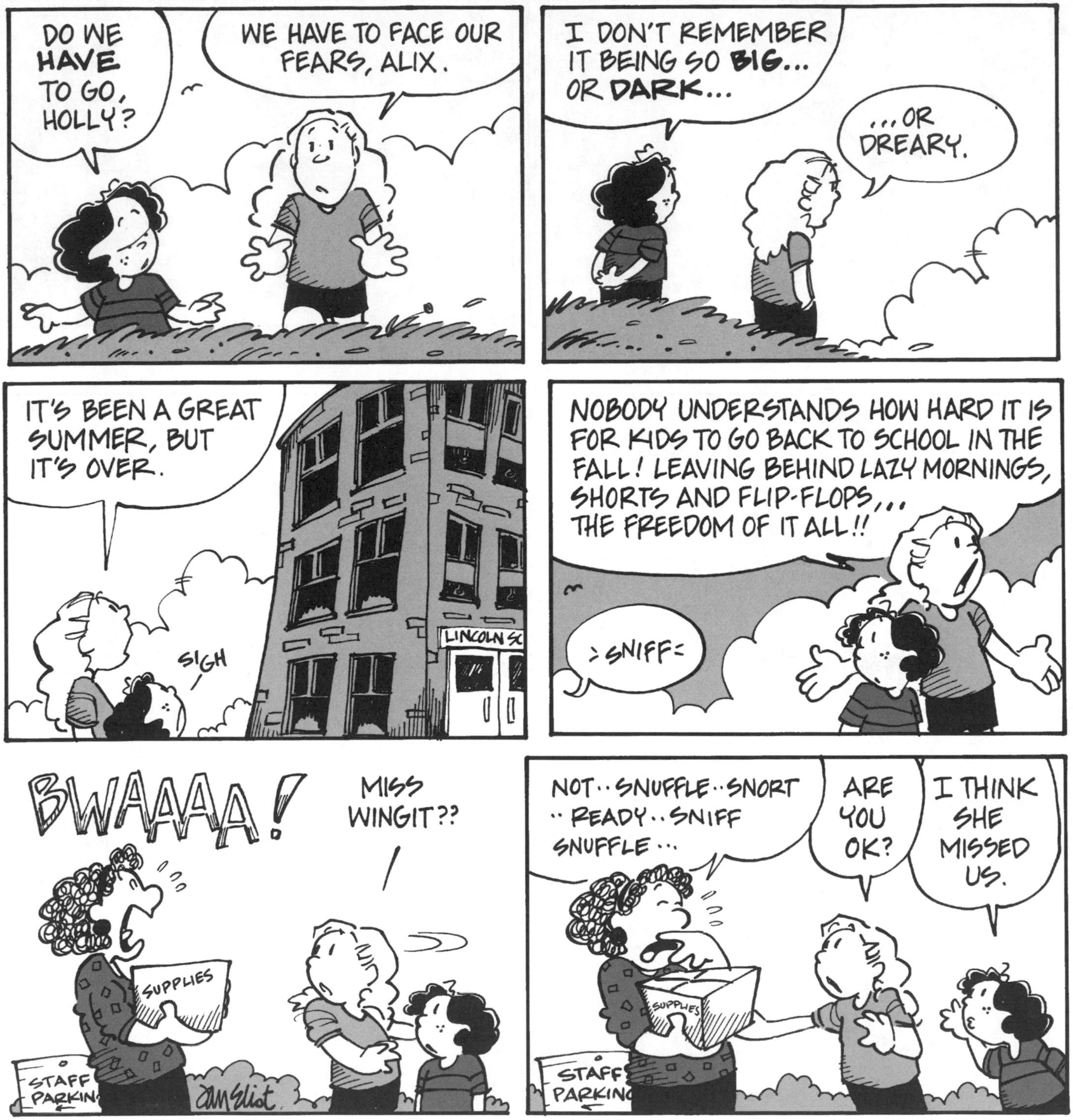
DO WE HAVE TO GO, HOLLY?
WE HAVE TO FACE OUR FEARS, ALIX.
I DON'T REMEMBER IT BEING SO BIG... OR DARK...
...OR DREARY.
IT'S BEEN A GREAT SUMMER, BUT IT'S OVER.
SIGH
LINCOLN SC
NOBODY UNDERSTANDS HOW HARD IT IS FOR KIDS TO GO BACK TO SCHOOL IN THE FALL! LEAVING BEHIND LAZY MORNINGS, SHORTS AND FLIP-FLOPS,,, THE FREEDOM OF IT ALL!!
SNIFF
BWAAAA!
MISS WINGIT??
SUPPLIES
STAFF PARKING
NOT.. SNUFFLE.. SNORT .. READY.. SNIFF SNUFFLE...
ARE YOU OK?
I THINK SHE MISSED US.
SUPPLIES
STAFF PARKING

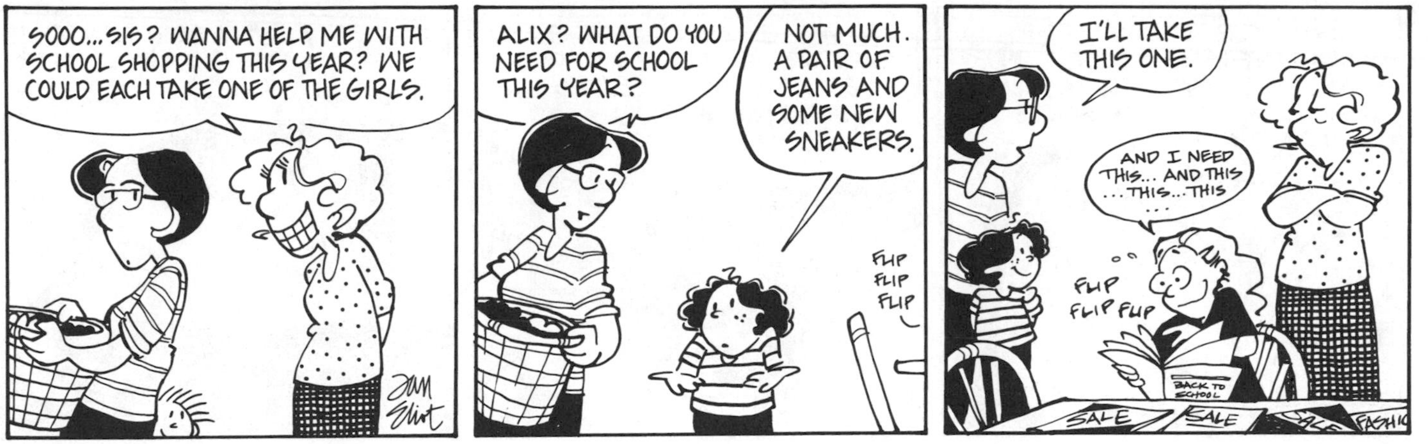
SOOO...SIS? WANNA HELP ME WITH SCHOOL SHOPPING THIS YEAR? WE COULD EACH TAKE ONE OF THE GIRLS.
ALIX? WHAT DO YOU NEED FOR SCHOOL THIS YEAR?
NOT MUCH. A PAIR OF JEANS AND SOME NEW SNEAKERS.
FLIP FLIP FLIP
I'LL TAKE THIS ONE.
AND I NEED THIS... AND THIS ...THIS...THIS ...
FLIP FLIP FLIP
BACK TO SCHOOL
SALE
SALE
SALE
FASHIO

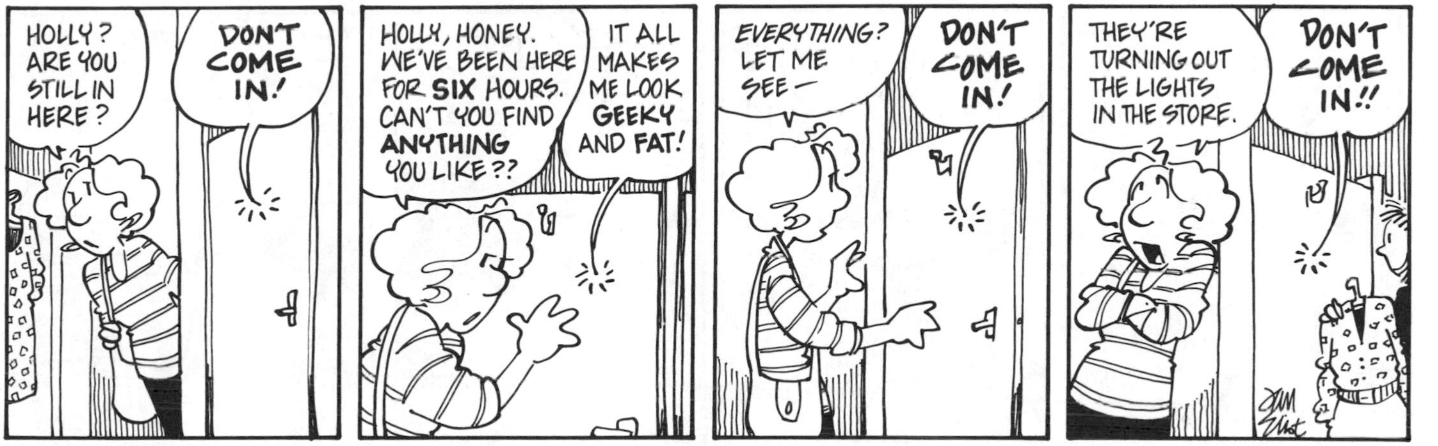
HOLLY? ARE YOU STILL IN HERE?
DON'T COME IN!
HOLLY, HONEY. WE'VE BEEN HERE FOR **SIX** HOURS. CAN'T YOU FIND **ANYTHING** YOU LIKE??
IT ALL MAKES ME LOOK **GEEKY** AND **FAT**!
EVERYTHING? LET ME SEE—
DON'T COME IN!
THEY'RE TURNING OUT THE LIGHTS IN THE STORE.
DON'T COME IN!!

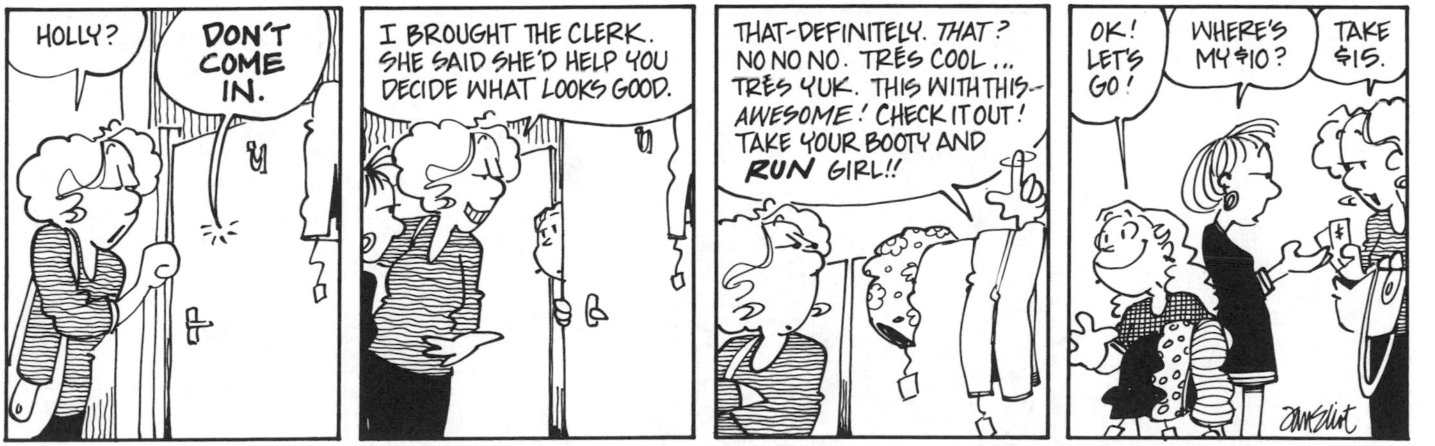
HOLLY?
DON'T COME IN.
I BROUGHT THE CLERK. SHE SAID SHE'D HELP YOU DECIDE WHAT LOOKS GOOD.
THAT-DEFINITELY. *THAT?* NO NO NO. TRÉS COOL... TRÉS YUK. THIS WITH THIS- *AWESOME!* CHECK IT OUT! TAKE YOUR BOOTY AND ***RUN*** GIRL!!
OK! LET'S GO!
WHERE'S MY $10?
TAKE $15.

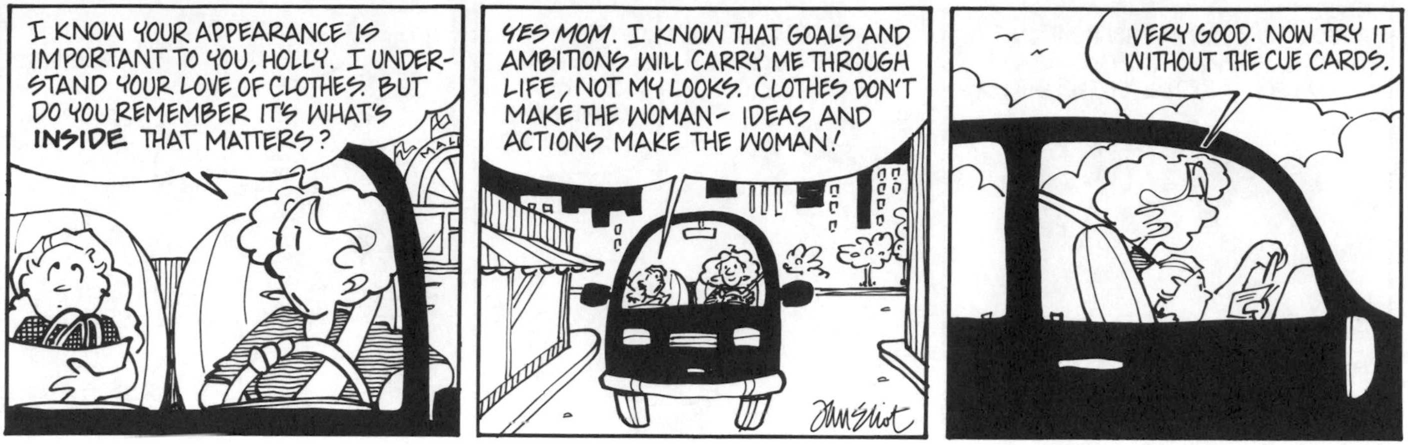
I KNOW YOUR APPEARANCE IS IMPORTANT TO YOU, HOLLY. I UNDERSTAND YOUR LOVE OF CLOTHES. BUT DO YOU REMEMBER IT'S WHAT'S **INSIDE** THAT MATTERS?
MALL
YES MOM. I KNOW THAT GOALS AND AMBITIONS WILL CARRY ME THROUGH LIFE, NOT MY LOOKS. CLOTHES DON'T MAKE THE WOMAN- IDEAS AND ACTIONS MAKE THE WOMAN!
VERY GOOD. NOW TRY IT WITHOUT THE CUE CARDS.

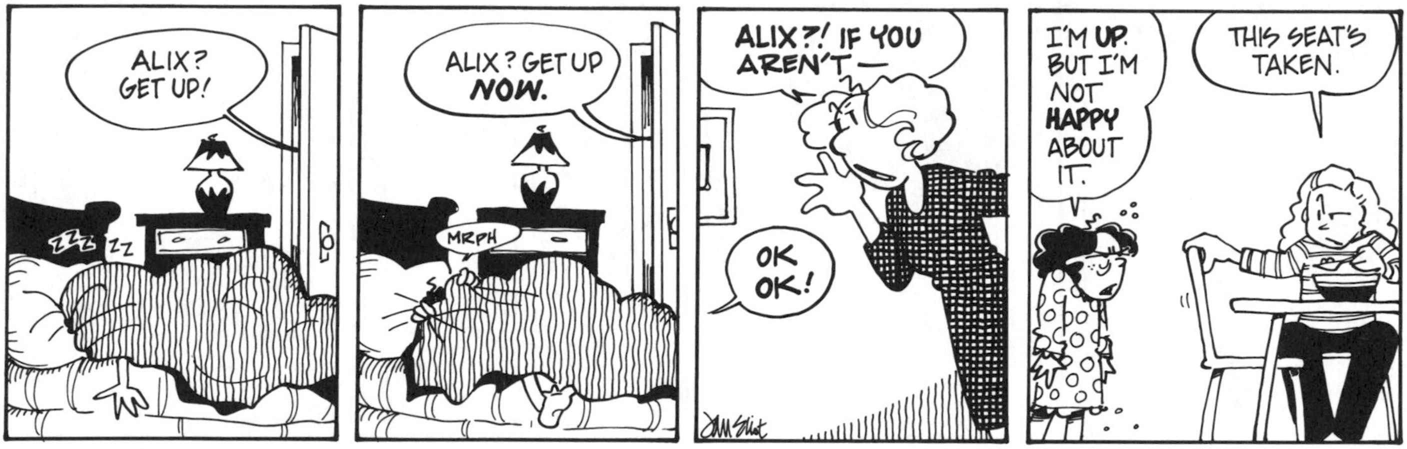
ALIX? GET UP!
ZZZ ZZ
ALIX? GET UP **NOW.**
MRPH
ALIX?! IF YOU AREN'T—
OK OK!
I'M **UP.** BUT I'M NOT **HAPPY** ABOUT IT.
THIS SEAT'S TAKEN.

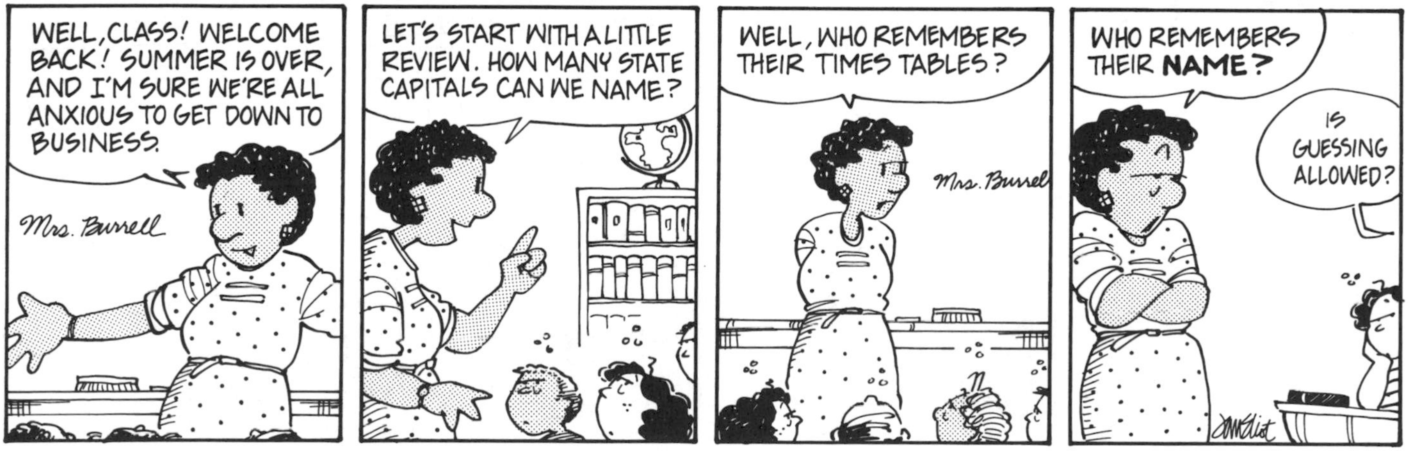
WELL, CLASS! WELCOME BACK! SUMMER IS OVER, AND I'M SURE WE'RE ALL ANXIOUS TO GET DOWN TO BUSINESS.
Mrs. Burrell
LET'S START WITH A LITTLE REVIEW. HOW MANY STATE CAPITALS CAN WE NAME?
WELL, WHO REMEMBERS THEIR TIMES TABLES?
Mrs. Burrell
WHO REMEMBERS THEIR **NAME?**
IS GUESSING ALLOWED?

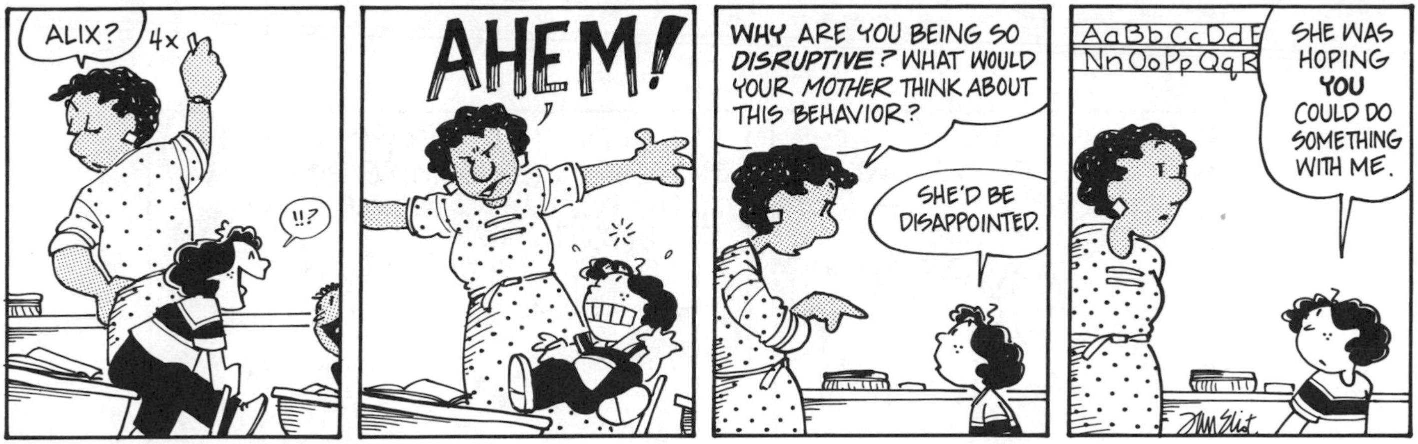
ALIX?
!!?
AHEM!
WHY ARE YOU BEING SO DISRUPTIVE? WHAT WOULD YOUR MOTHER THINK ABOUT THIS BEHAVIOR?
SHE'D BE DISAPPOINTED.
SHE WAS HOPING YOU COULD DO SOMETHING WITH ME.

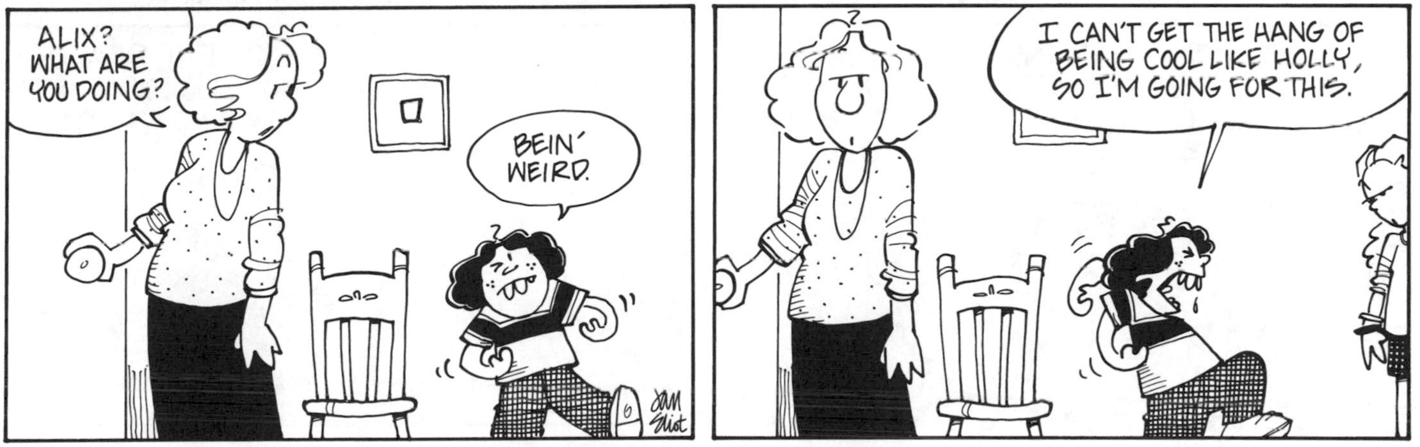
ALIX? WHAT ARE YOU DOING?
BEIN' WEIRD.
I CAN'T GET THE HANG OF BEING COOL LIKE HOLLY, SO I'M GOING FOR THIS.

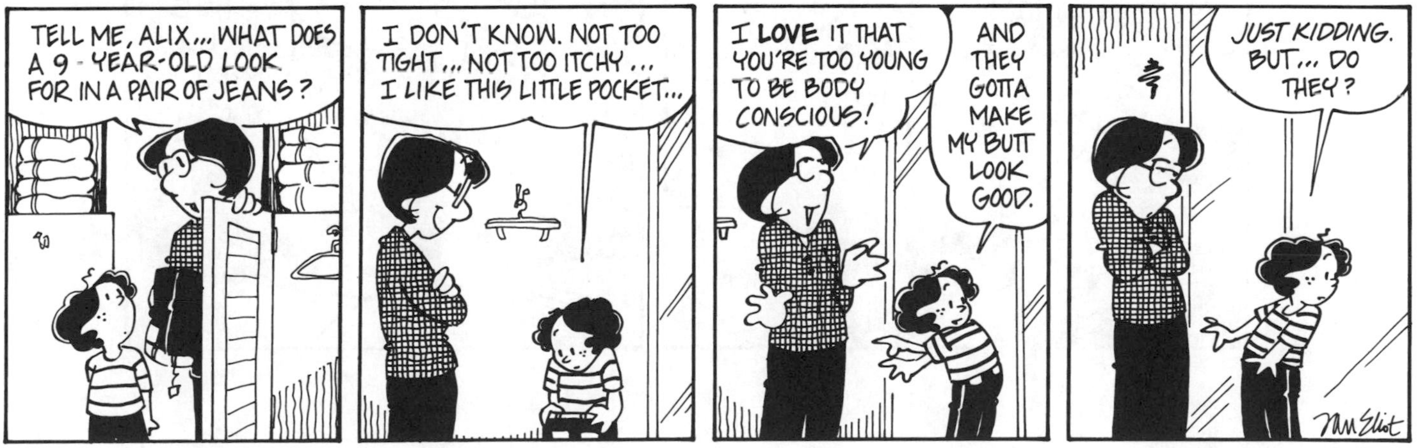
TELL ME, ALIX... WHAT DOES A 9-YEAR-OLD LOOK FOR IN A PAIR OF JEANS?
I DON'T KNOW. NOT TOO TIGHT... NOT TOO ITCHY... I LIKE THIS LITTLE POCKET...
I LOVE IT THAT YOU'RE TOO YOUNG TO BE BODY CONSCIOUS!
AND THEY GOTTA MAKE MY BUTT LOOK GOOD.
JUST KIDDING. BUT... DO THEY?

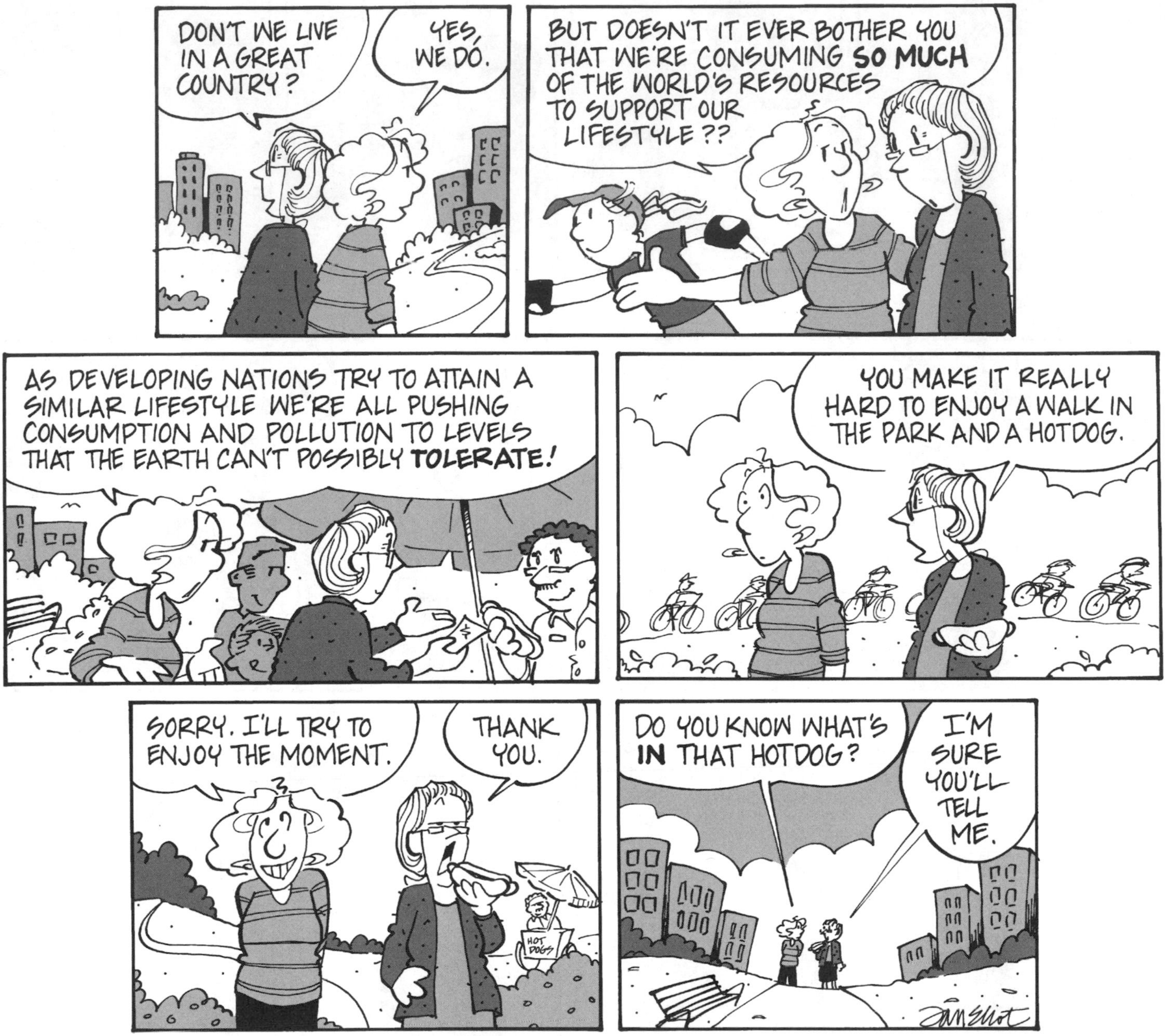
DON'T WE LIVE IN A GREAT COUNTRY?
YES, WE DO.
BUT DOESN'T IT EVER BOTHER YOU THAT WE'RE CONSUMING **SO MUCH** OF THE WORLD'S RESOURCES TO SUPPORT OUR LIFESTYLE??
AS DEVELOPING NATIONS TRY TO ATTAIN A SIMILAR LIFESTYLE WE'RE ALL PUSHING CONSUMPTION AND POLLUTION TO LEVELS THAT THE EARTH CAN'T POSSIBLY **TOLERATE**!
YOU MAKE IT REALLY HARD TO ENJOY A WALK IN THE PARK AND A HOTDOG.
SORRY. I'LL TRY TO ENJOY THE MOMENT.
THANK YOU.
HOT DOGS
DO YOU KNOW WHAT'S **IN** THAT HOTDOG?
I'M SURE YOU'LL TELL ME.
Jan Eliot

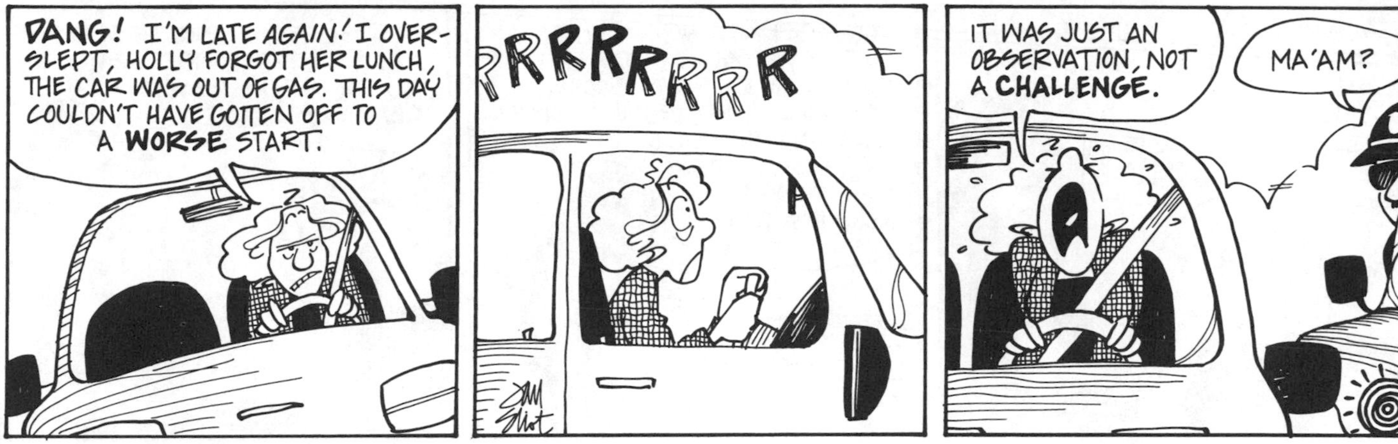
DANG! I'M LATE AGAIN! I OVERSLEPT, HOLLY FORGOT HER LUNCH, THE CAR WAS OUT OF GAS. THIS DAY COULDN'T HAVE GOTTEN OFF TO A WORSE START.
RRRRRRRRR
IT WAS JUST AN OBSERVATION, NOT A CHALLENGE.
MA'AM?

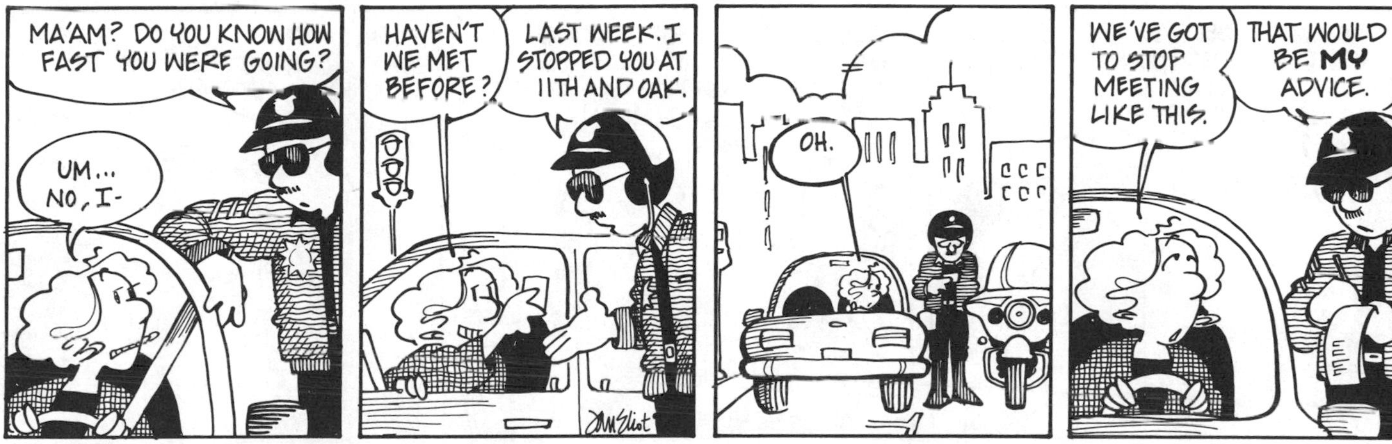
MA'AM? DO YOU KNOW HOW FAST YOU WERE GOING?
UM... NO, I-
HAVEN'T WE MET BEFORE?
LAST WEEK. I STOPPED YOU AT 11TH AND OAK.
OH.
WE'VE GOT TO STOP MEETING LIKE THIS.
THAT WOULD BE MY ADVICE.

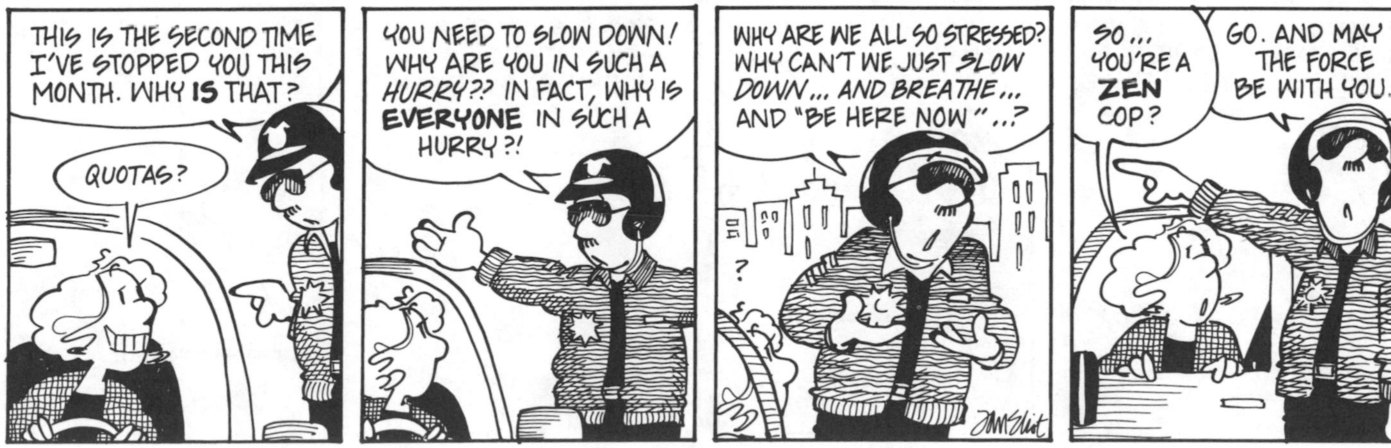
THIS IS THE SECOND TIME I'VE STOPPED YOU THIS MONTH. WHY IS THAT?
QUOTAS?
YOU NEED TO SLOW DOWN! WHY ARE YOU IN SUCH A HURRY?? IN FACT, WHY IS EVERYONE IN SUCH A HURRY?!
WHY ARE WE ALL SO STRESSED? WHY CAN'T WE JUST SLOW DOWN... AND BREATHE... AND "BE HERE NOW"...?
SO... YOU'RE A ZEN COP?
GO. AND MAY THE FORCE BE WITH YOU.

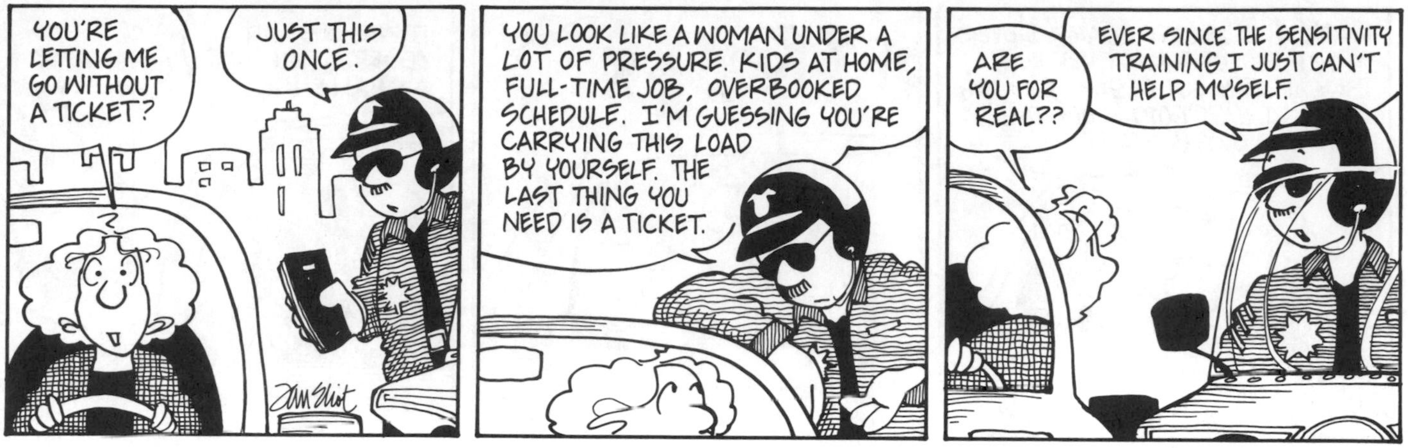
YOU'RE LETTING ME GO WITHOUT A TICKET?
JUST THIS ONCE.
YOU LOOK LIKE A WOMAN UNDER A LOT OF PRESSURE. KIDS AT HOME, FULL-TIME JOB, OVERBOOKED SCHEDULE. I'M GUESSING YOU'RE CARRYING THIS LOAD BY YOURSELF. THE LAST THING YOU NEED IS A TICKET.
ARE YOU FOR REAL??
EVER SINCE THE SENSITIVITY TRAINING I JUST CAN'T HELP MYSELF.

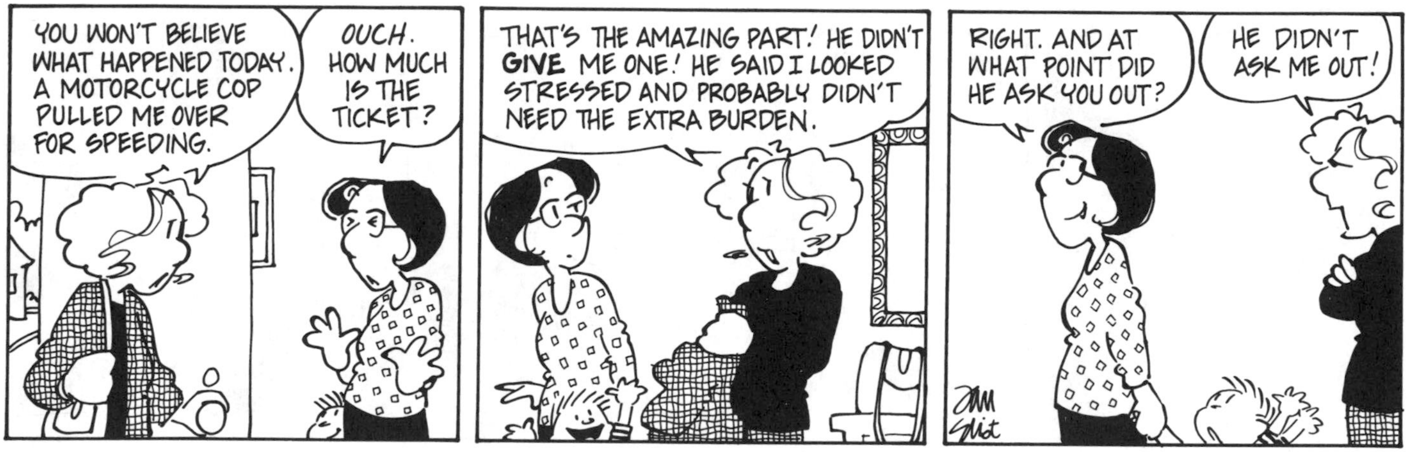
YOU WON'T BELIEVE WHAT HAPPENED TODAY. A MOTORCYCLE COP PULLED ME OVER FOR SPEEDING.
OUCH. HOW MUCH IS THE TICKET?
THAT'S THE AMAZING PART! HE DIDN'T **GIVE** ME ONE! HE SAID I LOOKED STRESSED AND PROBABLY DIDN'T NEED THE EXTRA BURDEN.
RIGHT. AND AT WHAT POINT DID HE ASK YOU OUT?
HE DIDN'T ASK ME OUT!

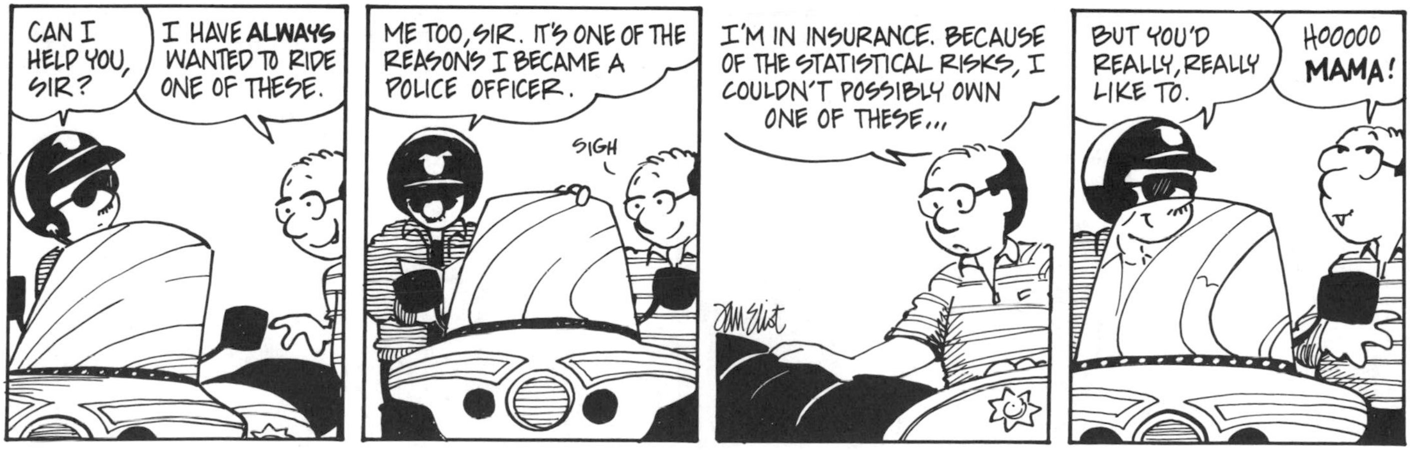
CAN I HELP YOU, SIR?
I HAVE **ALWAYS** WANTED TO RIDE ONE OF THESE.
ME TOO, SIR. IT'S ONE OF THE REASONS I BECAME A POLICE OFFICER.
SIGH
I'M IN INSURANCE. BECAUSE OF THE STATISTICAL RISKS, I COULDN'T POSSIBLY OWN ONE OF THESE...
BUT YOU'D REALLY, REALLY LIKE TO.
HOOOOO **MAMA**!

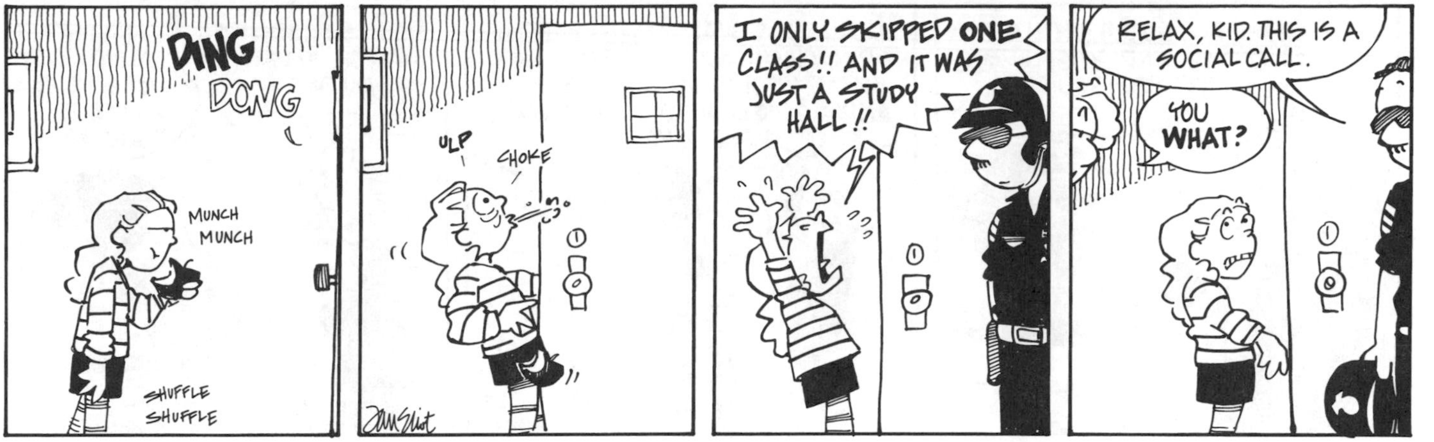
DING
DONG
MUNCH
MUNCH
SHUFFLE
SHUFFLE
ULP
CHOKE
I ONLY SKIPPED ONE CLASS!! AND IT WAS JUST A STUDY HALL!!
RELAX, KID. THIS IS A SOCIAL CALL.
YOU WHAT?

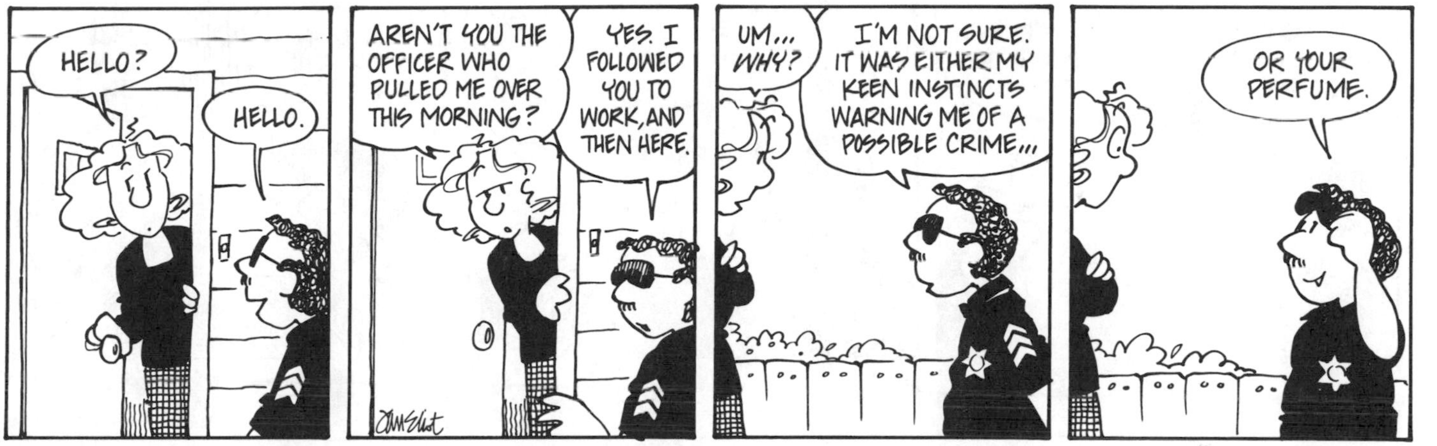
HELLO?
HELLO.
AREN'T YOU THE OFFICER WHO PULLED ME OVER THIS MORNING?
YES. I FOLLOWED YOU TO WORK, AND THEN HERE.
UM... WHY?
I'M NOT SURE. IT WAS EITHER MY KEEN INSTINCTS WARNING ME OF A POSSIBLE CRIME...
OR YOUR PERFUME.

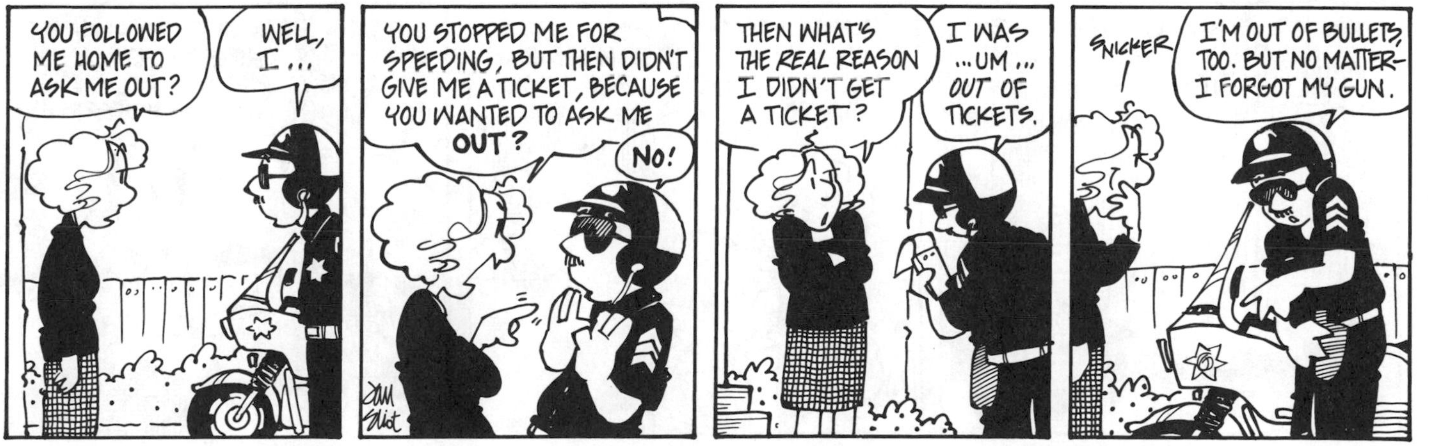
YOU FOLLOWED ME HOME TO ASK ME OUT?
WELL, I...
YOU STOPPED ME FOR SPEEDING, BUT THEN DIDN'T GIVE ME A TICKET, BECAUSE YOU WANTED TO ASK ME OUT?
NO!
THEN WHAT'S THE REAL REASON I DIDN'T GET A TICKET?
I WAS ...UM... OUT OF TICKETS.
SNICKER
I'M OUT OF BULLETS, TOO. BUT NO MATTER– I FORGOT MY GUN.

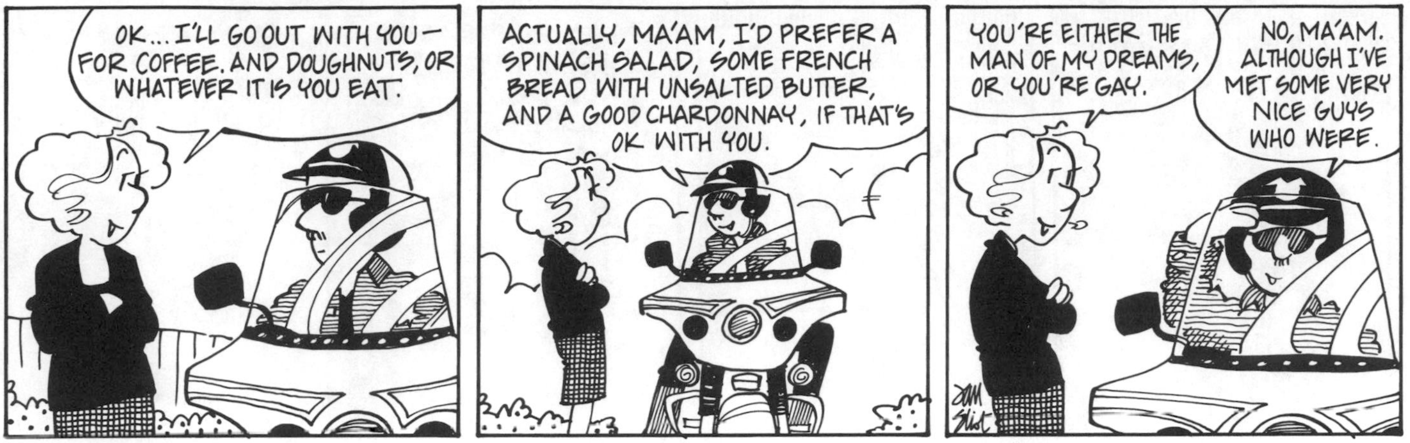
OK... I'LL GO OUT WITH YOU— FOR COFFEE. AND DOUGHNUTS, OR WHATEVER IT IS YOU EAT.
ACTUALLY, MA'AM, I'D PREFER A SPINACH SALAD, SOME FRENCH BREAD WITH UNSALTED BUTTER, AND A GOOD CHARDONNAY, IF THAT'S OK WITH YOU.
YOU'RE EITHER THE MAN OF MY DREAMS, OR YOU'RE GAY.
NO, MA'AM. ALTHOUGH I'VE MET SOME VERY NICE GUYS WHO WERE.

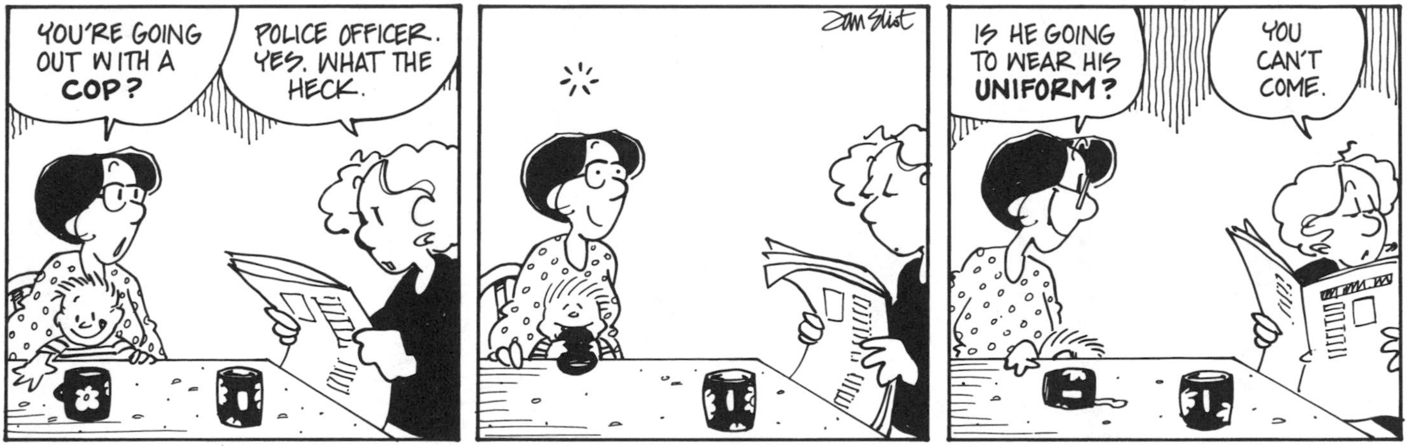
YOU'RE GOING OUT WITH A **COP**?
POLICE OFFICER. YES. WHAT THE HECK.
IS HE GOING TO WEAR HIS **UNIFORM**?
YOU CAN'T COME.

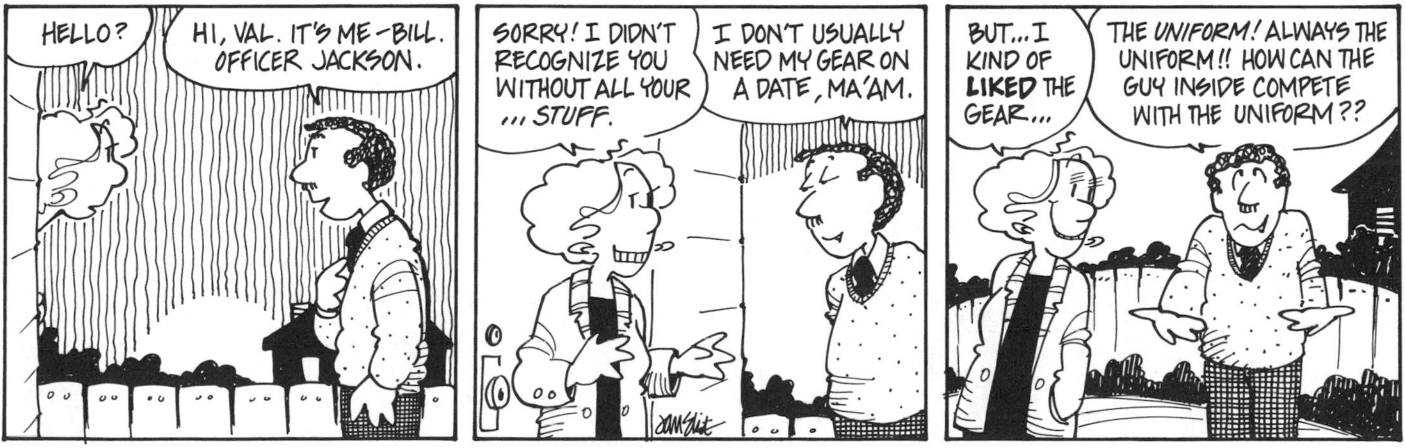
HELLO?
HI, VAL. IT'S ME-BILL. OFFICER JACKSON.
SORRY! I DIDN'T RECOGNIZE YOU WITHOUT ALL YOUR ... *STUFF*.
I DON'T USUALLY NEED MY GEAR ON A DATE, MA'AM.
BUT... I KIND OF **LIKED** THE GEAR...
THE *UNIFORM*! ALWAYS THE UNIFORM!! HOW CAN THE GUY INSIDE COMPETE WITH THE UNIFORM??

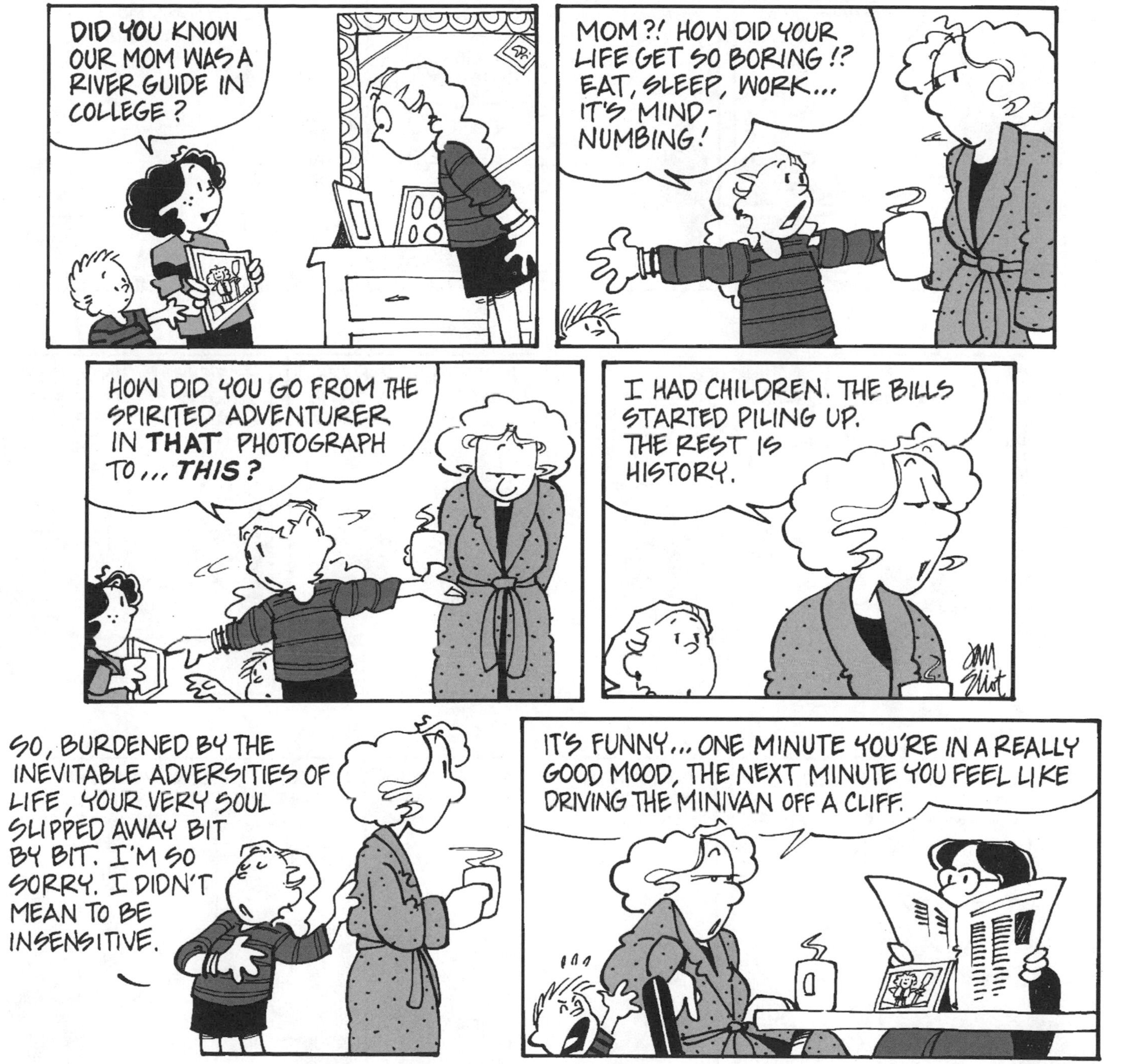
DID YOU KNOW OUR MOM WAS A RIVER GUIDE IN COLLEGE?
MOM?! HOW DID YOUR LIFE GET SO BORING!? EAT, SLEEP, WORK... IT'S MIND-NUMBING!
HOW DID YOU GO FROM THE SPIRITED ADVENTURER IN THAT PHOTOGRAPH TO... THIS?
I HAD CHILDREN. THE BILLS STARTED PILING UP. THE REST IS HISTORY.
SO, BURDENED BY THE INEVITABLE ADVERSITIES OF LIFE, YOUR VERY SOUL SLIPPED AWAY BIT BY BIT. I'M SO SORRY. I DIDN'T MEAN TO BE INSENSITIVE.
IT'S FUNNY... ONE MINUTE YOU'RE IN A REALLY GOOD MOOD, THE NEXT MINUTE YOU FEEL LIKE DRIVING THE MINIVAN OFF A CLIFF.

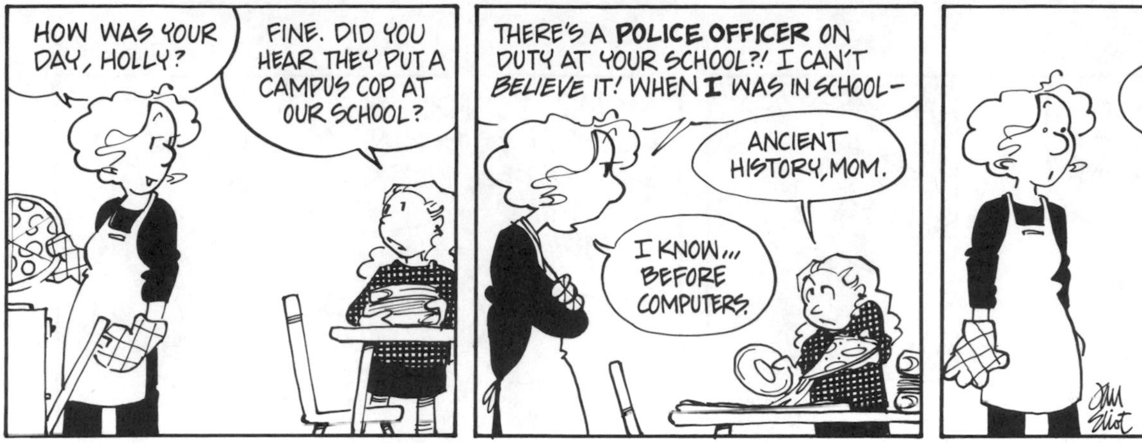
HOW WAS YOUR DAY, HOLLY?
FINE. DID YOU HEAR THEY PUT A CAMPUS COP AT OUR SCHOOL?
THERE'S A POLICE OFFICER ON DUTY AT YOUR SCHOOL?! I CAN'T BELIEVE IT! WHEN I WAS IN SCHOOL—
ANCIENT HISTORY, MOM.
I KNOW... BEFORE COMPUTERS.
AND METAL DETECTORS.

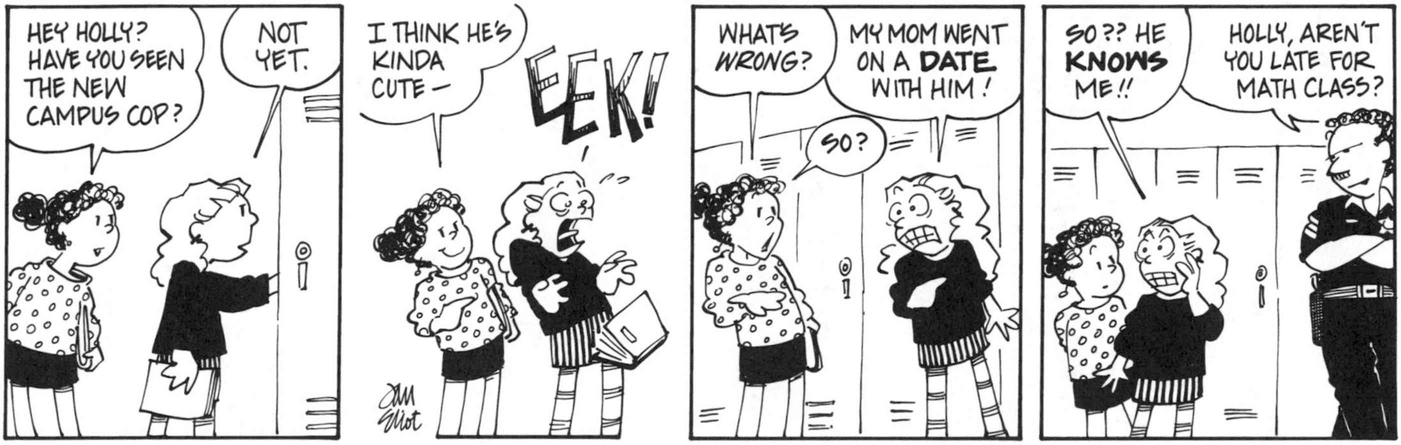
HEY HOLLY? HAVE YOU SEEN THE NEW CAMPUS COP?
NOT YET.
I THINK HE'S KINDA CUTE —
EEK!
WHAT'S WRONG?
MY MOM WENT ON A DATE WITH HIM!
SO?
SO?? HE KNOWS ME!!
HOLLY, AREN'T YOU LATE FOR MATH CLASS?

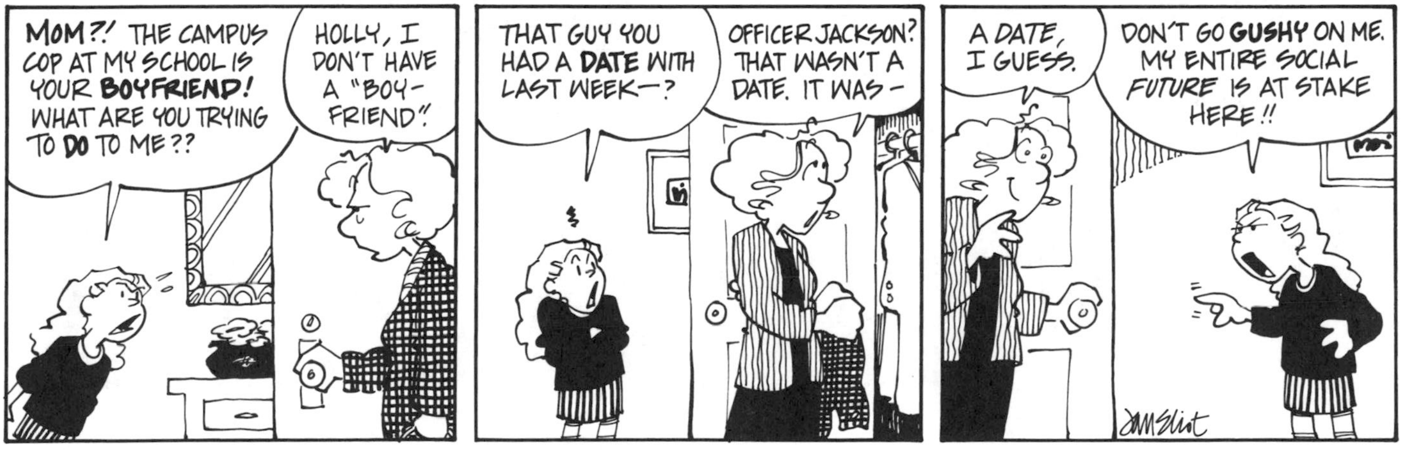
MOM?! THE CAMPUS COP AT MY SCHOOL IS YOUR BOYFRIEND! WHAT ARE YOU TRYING TO DO TO ME??
HOLLY, I DON'T HAVE A "BOY-FRIEND"!
THAT GUY YOU HAD A DATE WITH LAST WEEK—?
OFFICER JACKSON? THAT WASN'T A DATE. IT WAS—
A DATE, I GUESS.
DON'T GO GUSHY ON ME. MY ENTIRE SOCIAL FUTURE IS AT STAKE HERE!!

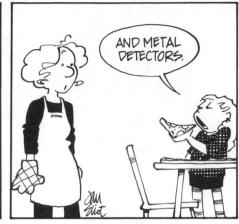

I THINK THE **REAL** REASON YOU DISLIKE ME KNOWING THE CAMPUS COP AT YOUR SCHOOL IS THAT YOU'RE AFRAID I'LL ASK HIM TO KEEP TABS ON YOU.

NO.

HE TOLD ME YOU WERE LATE FOR MATH YESTERDAY.

THIS IS GOING TO BE A **HORRIBLE** YEAR!!

YOUR GIRLS ALL SETTLED INTO THE NEW SCHOOL YEAR?

YES. BUT HOLLY'S A LITTLE TWEEKED THAT THE CAMPUS COP IS A GUY I KNOW.

SHE'S WORRIED THAT I'LL USE HIM TO KEEP TABS ON HER BEHAVIOR AT SCHOOL...

AND WILL YOU?

WHAT KIND OF MOTHER DO YOU THINK I **AM**? OF **COURSE** I WILL.

109

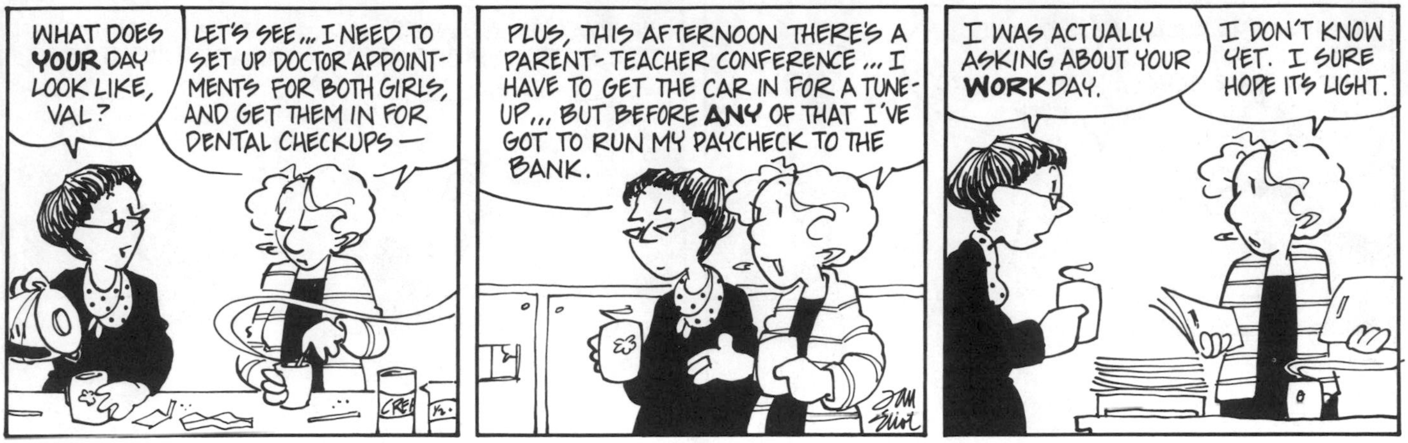
WHAT DOES **YOUR** DAY LOOK LIKE, VAL?
LET'S SEE... I NEED TO SET UP DOCTOR APPOINTMENTS FOR BOTH GIRLS, AND GET THEM IN FOR DENTAL CHECKUPS —
PLUS, THIS AFTERNOON THERE'S A PARENT-TEACHER CONFERENCE... I HAVE TO GET THE CAR IN FOR A TUNE-UP... BUT BEFORE **ANY** OF THAT I'VE GOT TO RUN MY PAYCHECK TO THE BANK.
I WAS ACTUALLY ASKING ABOUT YOUR **WORK**DAY.
I DON'T KNOW YET. I SURE HOPE IT'S LIGHT.

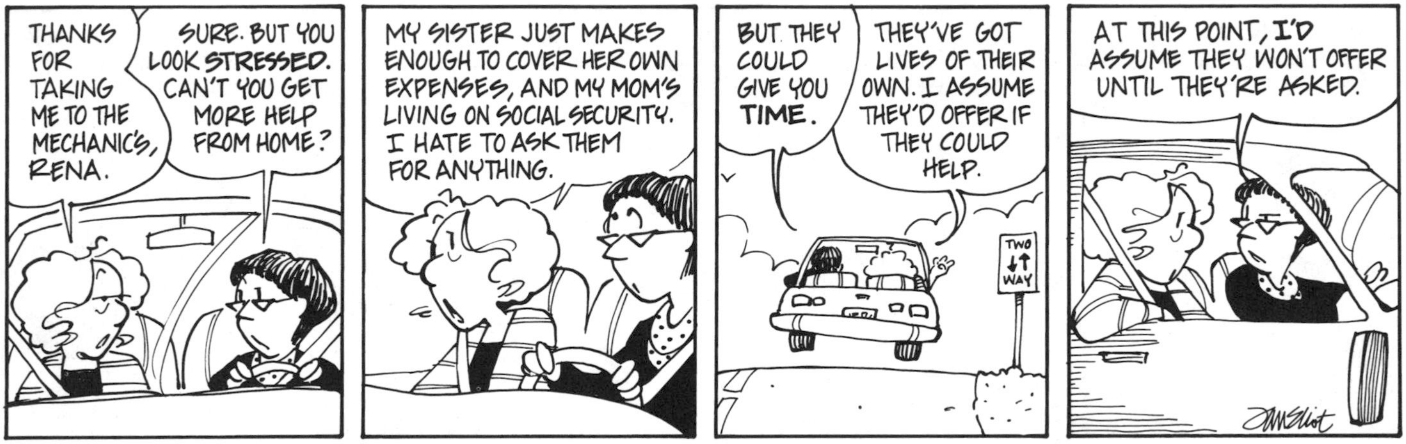
THANKS FOR TAKING ME TO THE MECHANIC'S, RENA.
SURE. BUT YOU LOOK **STRESSED**. CAN'T YOU GET MORE HELP FROM HOME?
MY SISTER JUST MAKES ENOUGH TO COVER HER OWN EXPENSES, AND MY MOM'S LIVING ON SOCIAL SECURITY. I HATE TO ASK THEM FOR ANYTHING.
BUT THEY COULD GIVE YOU **TIME**.
THEY'VE GOT LIVES OF THEIR OWN. I ASSUME THEY'D OFFER IF THEY COULD HELP.
TWO WAY
AT THIS POINT, **I'D** ASSUME THEY WON'T OFFER UNTIL THEY'RE ASKED.

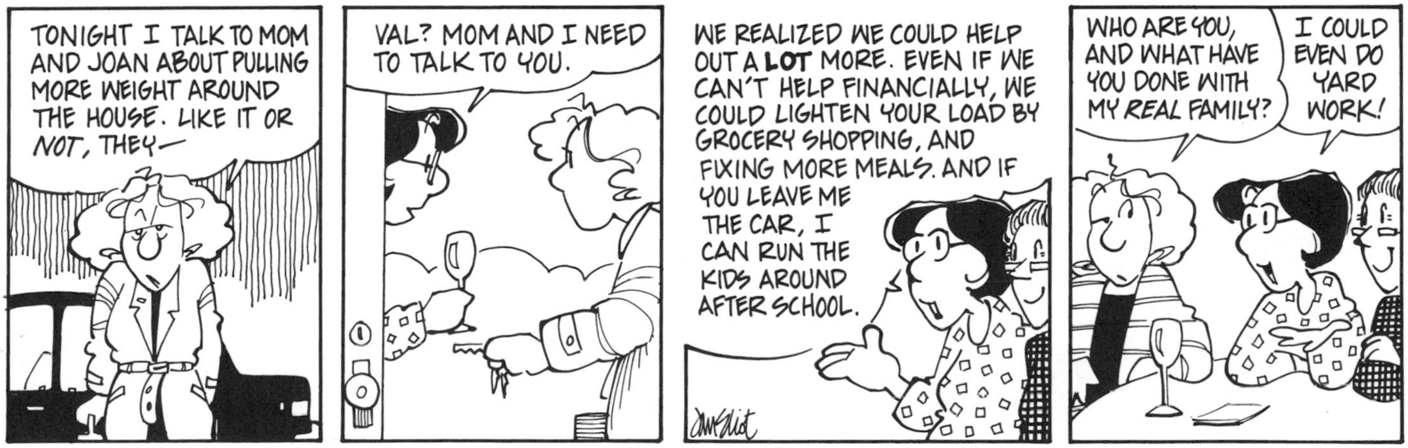
TONIGHT I TALK TO MOM AND JOAN ABOUT PULLING MORE WEIGHT AROUND THE HOUSE. LIKE IT OR *NOT*, THEY—
VAL? MOM AND I NEED TO TALK TO YOU.
WE REALIZED WE COULD HELP OUT A **LOT** MORE. EVEN IF WE CAN'T HELP FINANCIALLY, WE COULD LIGHTEN YOUR LOAD BY GROCERY SHOPPING, AND FIXING MORE MEALS. AND IF YOU LEAVE ME THE CAR, I CAN RUN THE KIDS AROUND AFTER SCHOOL.
WHO ARE YOU, AND WHAT HAVE YOU DONE WITH MY *REAL* FAMILY?
I COULD EVEN DO YARD WORK!

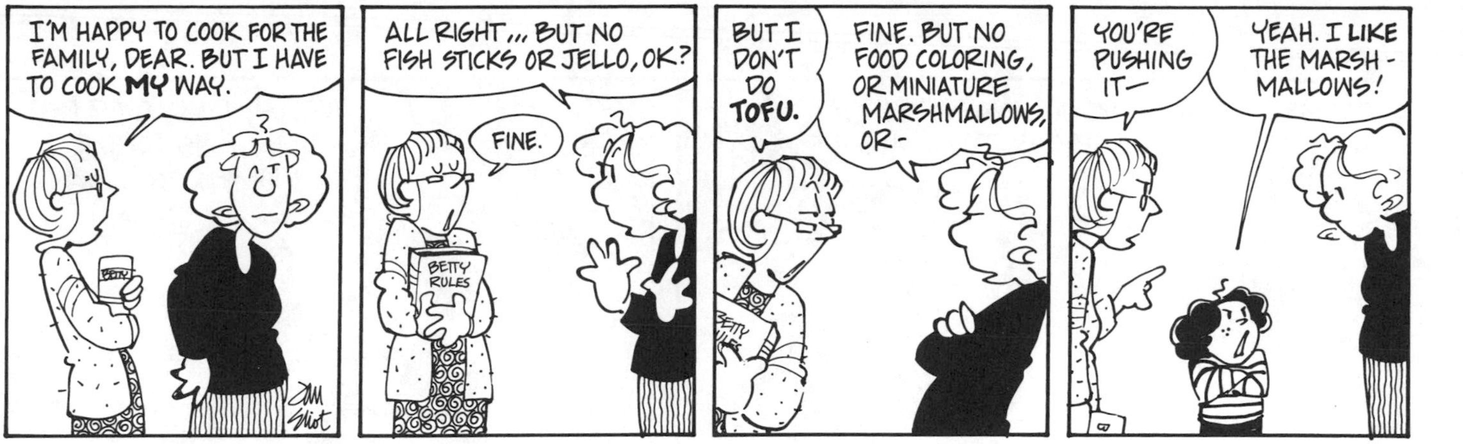
I'M HAPPY TO COOK FOR THE FAMILY, DEAR. BUT I HAVE TO COOK **MY** WAY.
ALL RIGHT,,, BUT NO FISH STICKS OR JELLO, OK?
FINE.
BETTY RULES
BUT I DON'T DO **TOFU.**
FINE. BUT NO FOOD COLORING, OR MINIATURE MARSHMALLOWS, OR-
YOU'RE PUSHING IT—
YEAH. I **LIKE** THE MARSH-MALLOWS!

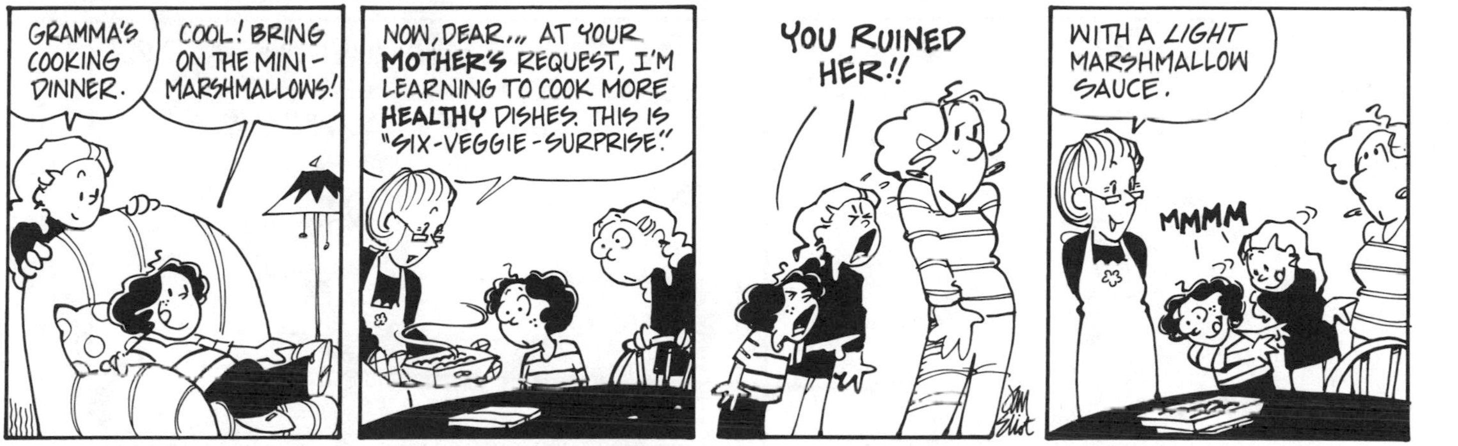
GRAMMA'S COOKING DINNER.
COOL! BRING ON THE MINI-MARSHMALLOWS!
NOW, DEAR,,, AT YOUR **MOTHER'S** REQUEST, I'M LEARNING TO COOK MORE **HEALTHY** DISHES. THIS IS "SIX-VEGGIE-SURPRISE."
YOU RUINED HER!!
WITH A *LIGHT* MARSHMALLOW SAUCE.
MMMM

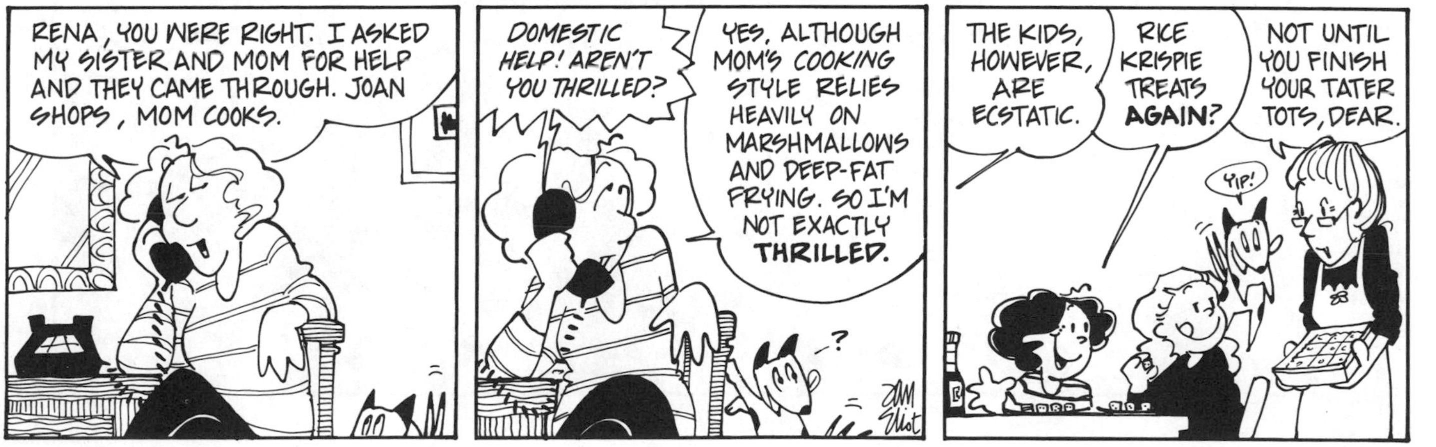
RENA, YOU WERE RIGHT. I ASKED MY SISTER AND MOM FOR HELP AND THEY CAME THROUGH. JOAN SHOPS, MOM COOKS.
DOMESTIC HELP! AREN'T YOU THRILLED?
YES, ALTHOUGH MOM'S *COOKING* STYLE RELIES HEAVILY ON MARSHMALLOWS AND DEEP-FAT FRYING. SO I'M NOT EXACTLY **THRILLED.**
THE KIDS, HOWEVER, ARE ECSTATIC.
RICE KRISPIE TREATS **AGAIN?**
NOT UNTIL YOU FINISH YOUR TATER TOTS, DEAR.
YIP!

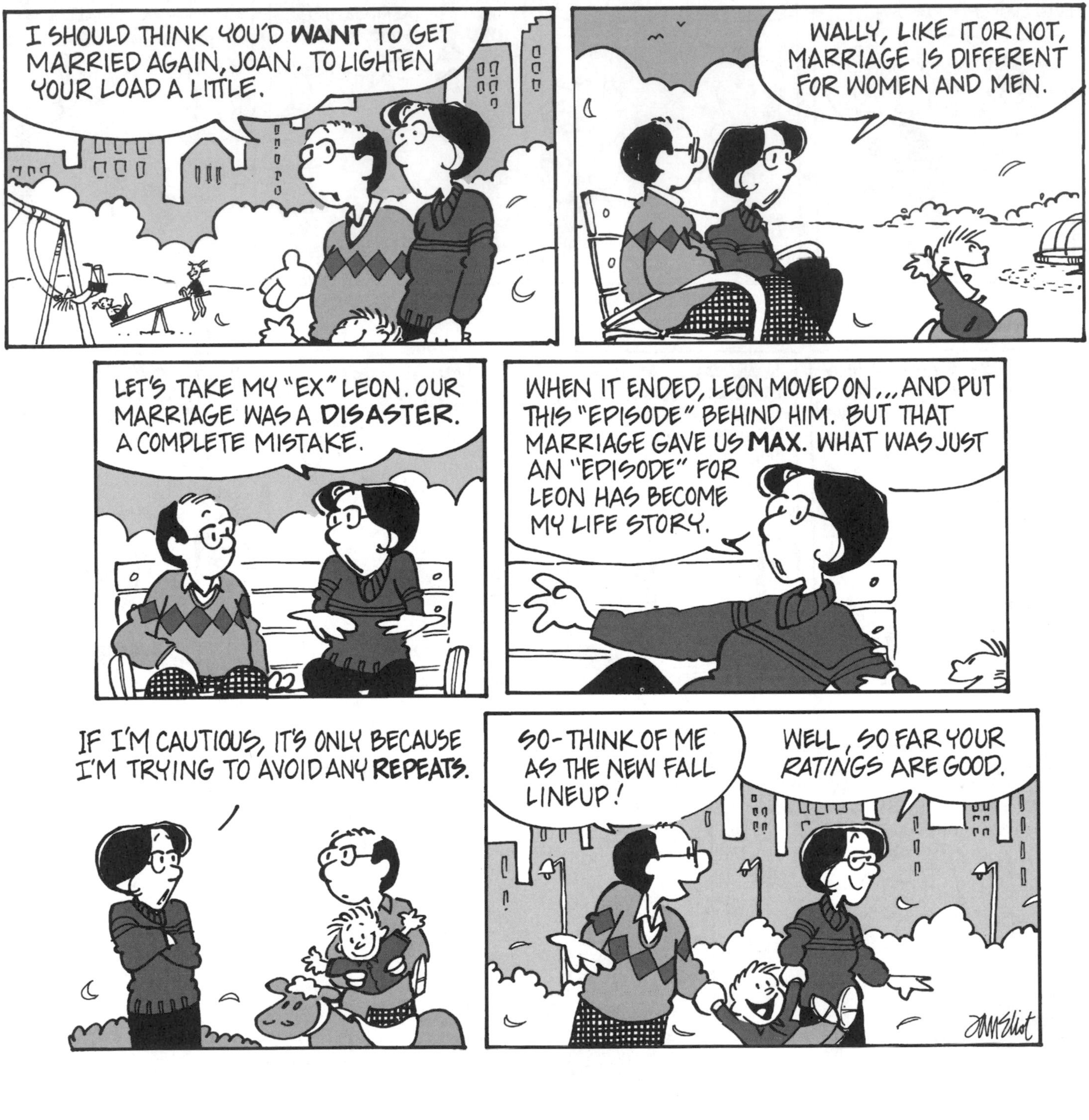
I SHOULD THINK YOU'D **WANT** TO GET MARRIED AGAIN, JOAN. TO LIGHTEN YOUR LOAD A LITTLE.
WALLY, LIKE IT OR NOT, MARRIAGE IS DIFFERENT FOR WOMEN AND MEN.
LET'S TAKE MY "EX" LEON. OUR MARRIAGE WAS A **DISASTER**. A COMPLETE MISTAKE.
WHEN IT ENDED, LEON MOVED ON,.. AND PUT THIS "EPISODE" BEHIND HIM. BUT THAT MARRIAGE GAVE US **MAX**. WHAT WAS JUST AN "EPISODE" FOR LEON HAS BECOME MY LIFE STORY.
IF I'M CAUTIOUS, IT'S ONLY BECAUSE I'M TRYING TO AVOID ANY **REPEATS**.
SO- THINK OF ME AS THE NEW FALL LINEUP!
WELL, SO FAR YOUR *RATINGS* ARE GOOD.
JAN Eliot

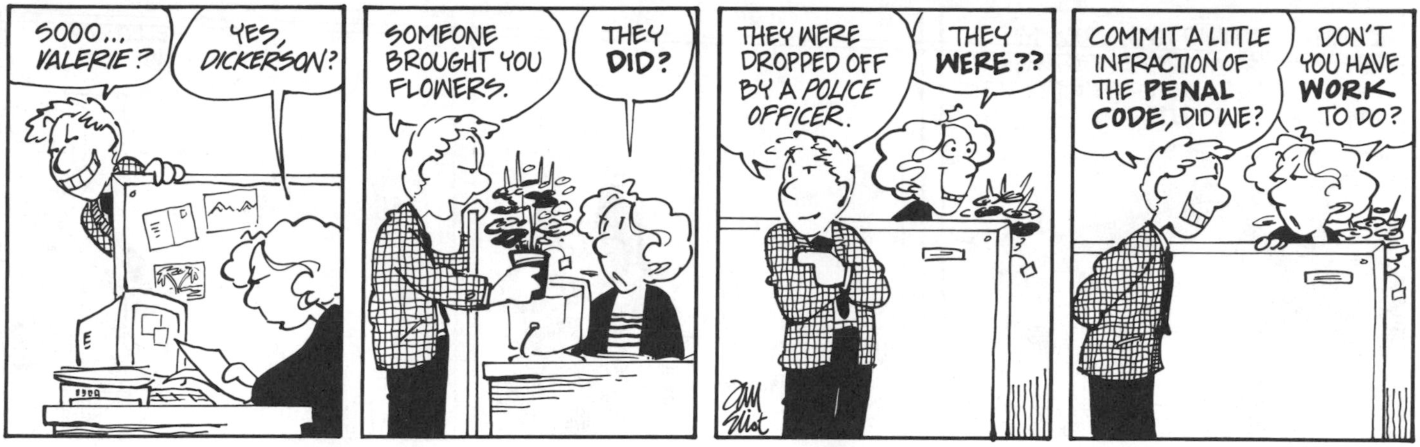
SOOO... VALERIE?
YES, DICKERSON?
SOMEONE BROUGHT YOU FLOWERS.
THEY DID?
THEY WERE DROPPED OFF BY A POLICE OFFICER.
THEY WERE??
COMMIT A LITTLE INFRACTION OF THE PENAL CODE, DID WE?
DON'T YOU HAVE WORK TO DO?

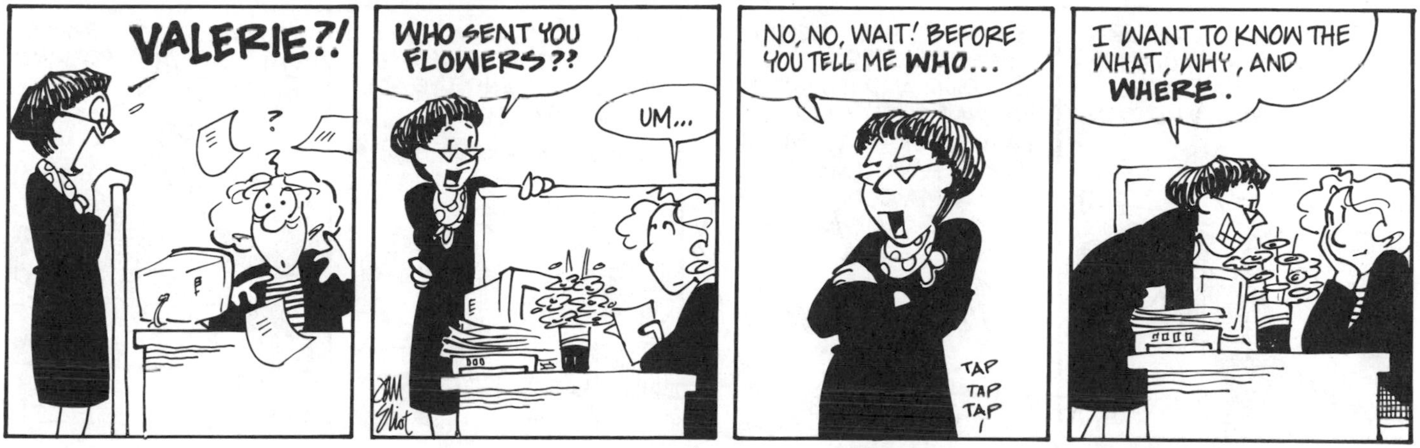
VALERIE?!
WHO SENT YOU FLOWERS??
UM...
NO, NO, WAIT! BEFORE YOU TELL ME WHO...
TAP TAP TAP
I WANT TO KNOW THE WHAT, WHY, AND WHERE.

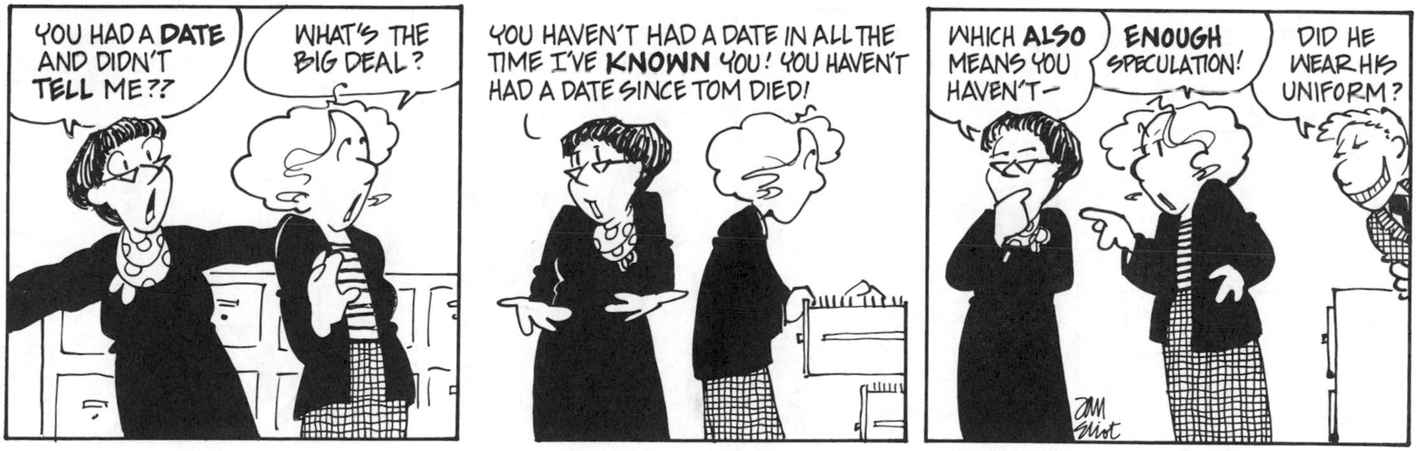
YOU HAD A DATE AND DIDN'T TELL ME??
WHAT'S THE BIG DEAL?
YOU HAVEN'T HAD A DATE IN ALL THE TIME I'VE KNOWN YOU! YOU HAVEN'T HAD A DATE SINCE TOM DIED!
WHICH ALSO MEANS YOU HAVEN'T—
ENOUGH SPECULATION!
DID HE WEAR HIS UNIFORM?

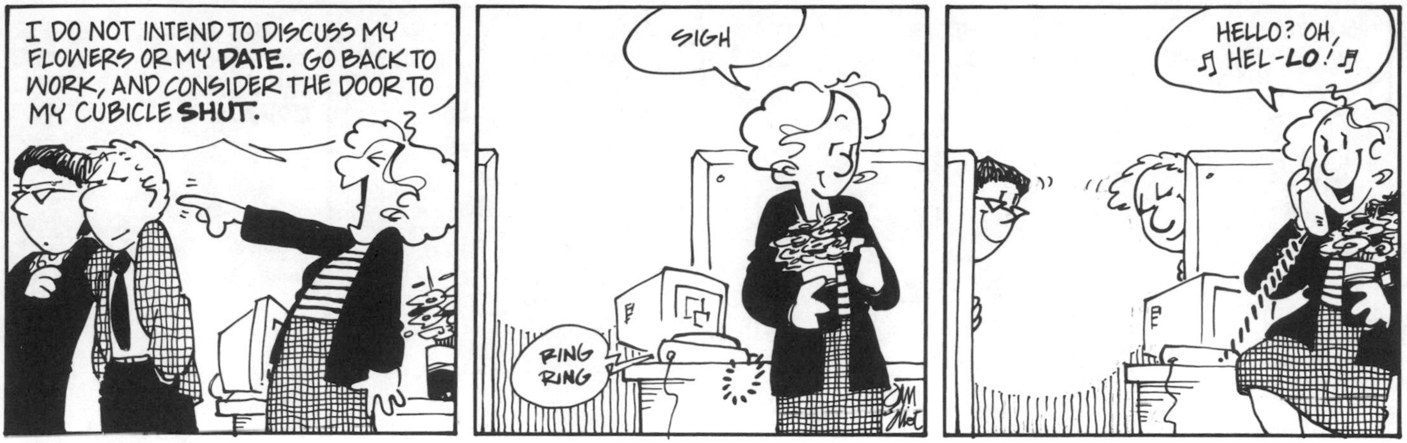
I DO NOT INTEND TO DISCUSS MY FLOWERS OR MY **DATE.** GO BACK TO WORK, AND CONSIDER THE DOOR TO MY CUBICLE **SHUT.**
SIGH
RING RING
HELLO? OH, ♬ HEL-**LO**! ♬

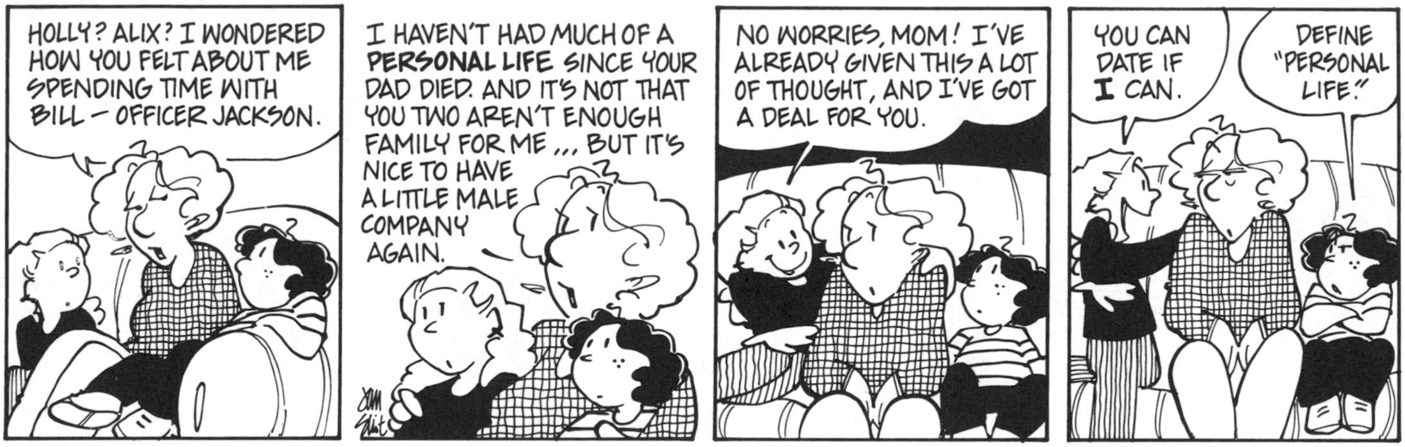
HOLLY? ALIX? I WONDERED HOW YOU FELT ABOUT ME SPENDING TIME WITH BILL – OFFICER JACKSON.
I HAVEN'T HAD MUCH OF A **PERSONAL LIFE** SINCE YOUR DAD DIED. AND IT'S NOT THAT YOU TWO AREN'T ENOUGH FAMILY FOR ME ... BUT IT'S NICE TO HAVE A LITTLE MALE COMPANY AGAIN.
NO WORRIES, MOM! I'VE ALREADY GIVEN THIS A LOT OF THOUGHT, AND I'VE GOT A DEAL FOR YOU.
YOU CAN DATE IF **I** CAN.
DEFINE "PERSONAL LIFE."

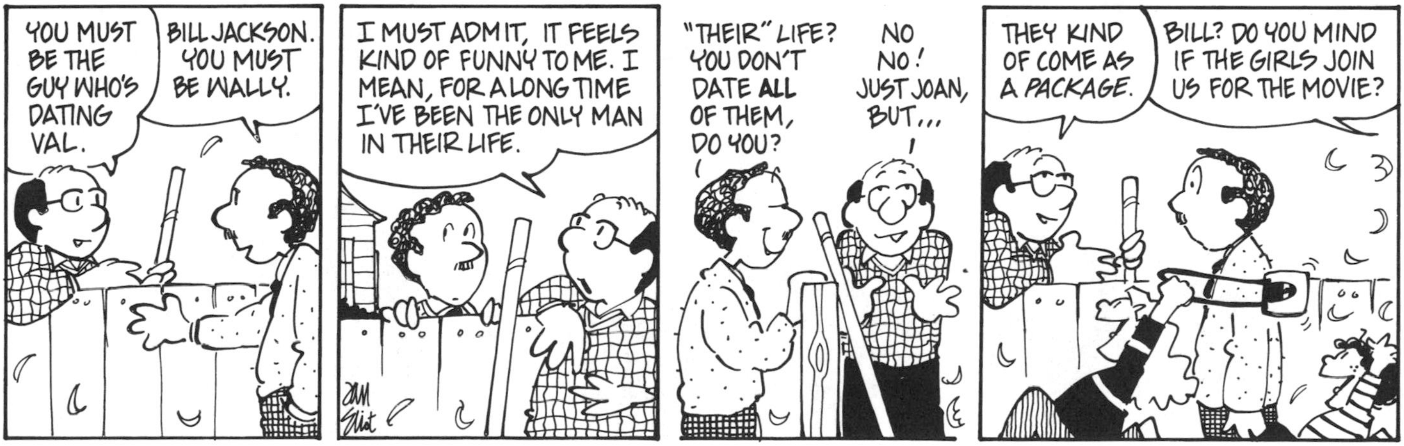
YOU MUST BE THE GUY WHO'S DATING VAL.
BILL JACKSON. YOU MUST BE WALLY.
I MUST ADMIT IT, IT FEELS KIND OF FUNNY TO ME. I MEAN, FOR A LONG TIME I'VE BEEN THE ONLY MAN IN THEIR LIFE.
"THEIR" LIFE? YOU DON'T DATE **ALL** OF THEM, DO YOU?
NO NO! JUST JOAN, BUT...
THEY KIND OF COME AS A *PACKAGE*.
BILL? DO YOU MIND IF THE GIRLS JOIN US FOR THE MOVIE?

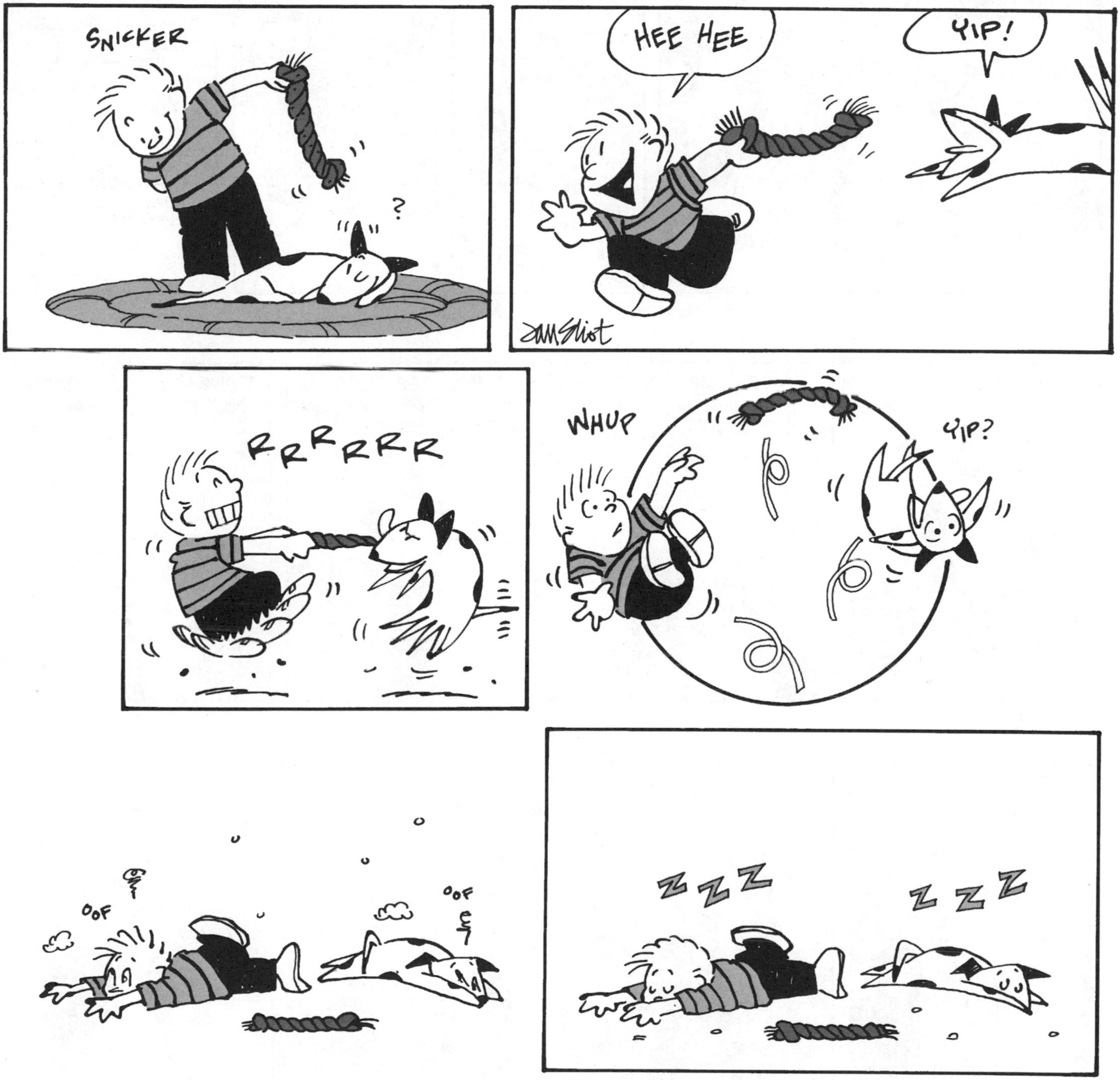
SNICKER
?
HEE HEE
YIP!
RRRRRRR
WHUP
YIP?
OOF
OOF
Z Z Z
Z Z Z

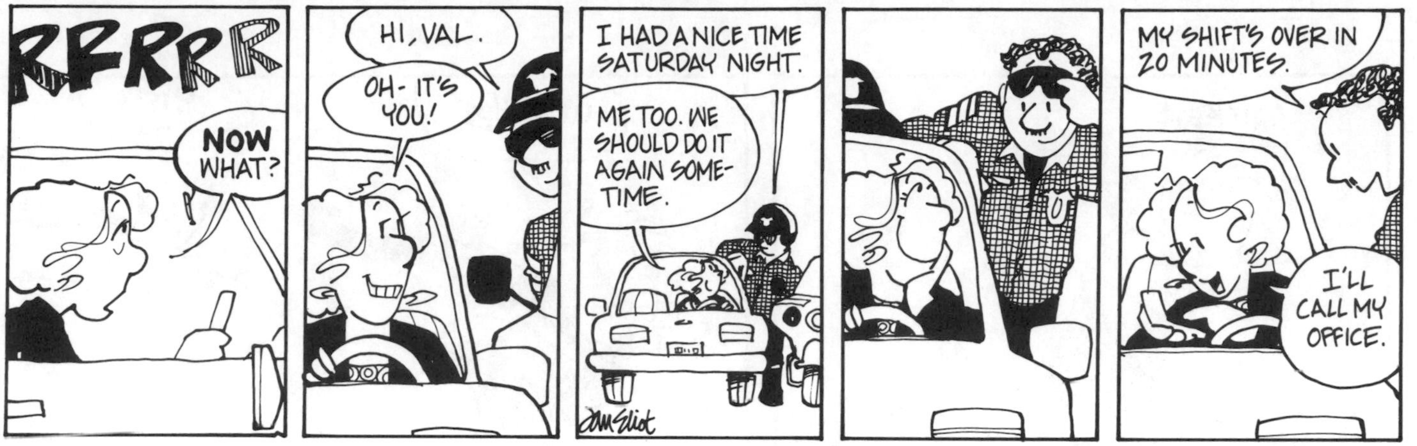
RRRRR
NOW WHAT?
HI, VAL.
OH- IT'S YOU!
I HAD A NICE TIME SATURDAY NIGHT.
ME TOO. WE SHOULD DO IT AGAIN SOMETIME.
MY SHIFT'S OVER IN 20 MINUTES.
I'LL CALL MY OFFICE.

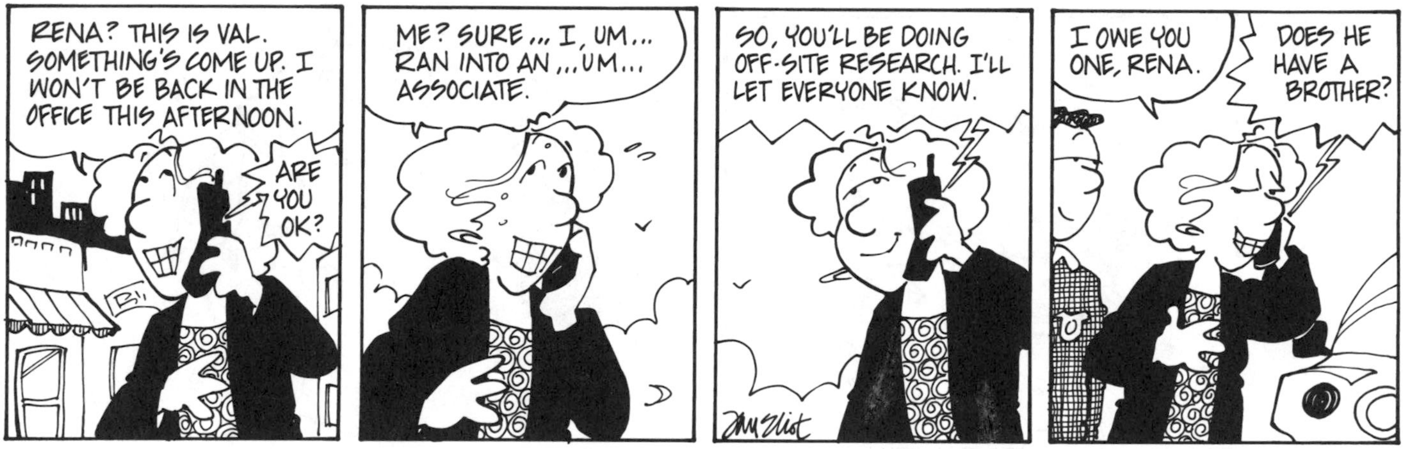
RENA? THIS IS VAL. SOMETHING'S COME UP. I WON'T BE BACK IN THE OFFICE THIS AFTERNOON.
ARE YOU OK?
ME? SURE ... I, UM... RAN INTO AN ... UM... ASSOCIATE.
SO, YOU'LL BE DOING OFF-SITE RESEARCH. I'LL LET EVERYONE KNOW.
I OWE YOU ONE, RENA.
DOES HE HAVE A BROTHER?

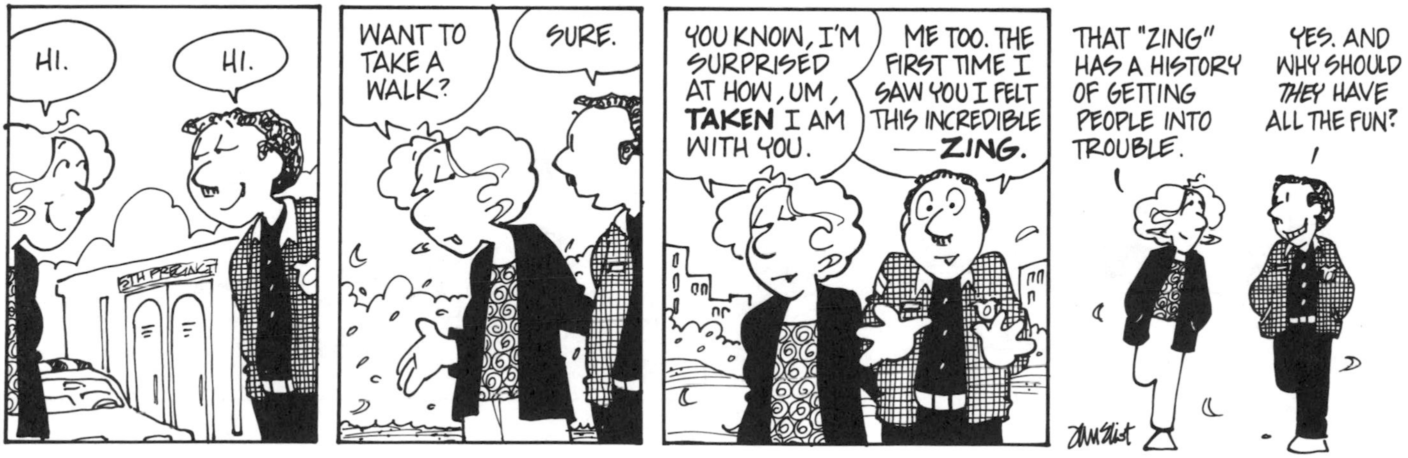
HI.
HI.
WANT TO TAKE A WALK?
SURE.
YOU KNOW, I'M SURPRISED AT HOW, UM, **TAKEN** I AM WITH YOU.
ME TOO. THE FIRST TIME I SAW YOU I FELT THIS INCREDIBLE —**ZING.**
THAT "ZING" HAS A HISTORY OF GETTING PEOPLE INTO TROUBLE.
YES. AND WHY SHOULD *THEY* HAVE ALL THE FUN?

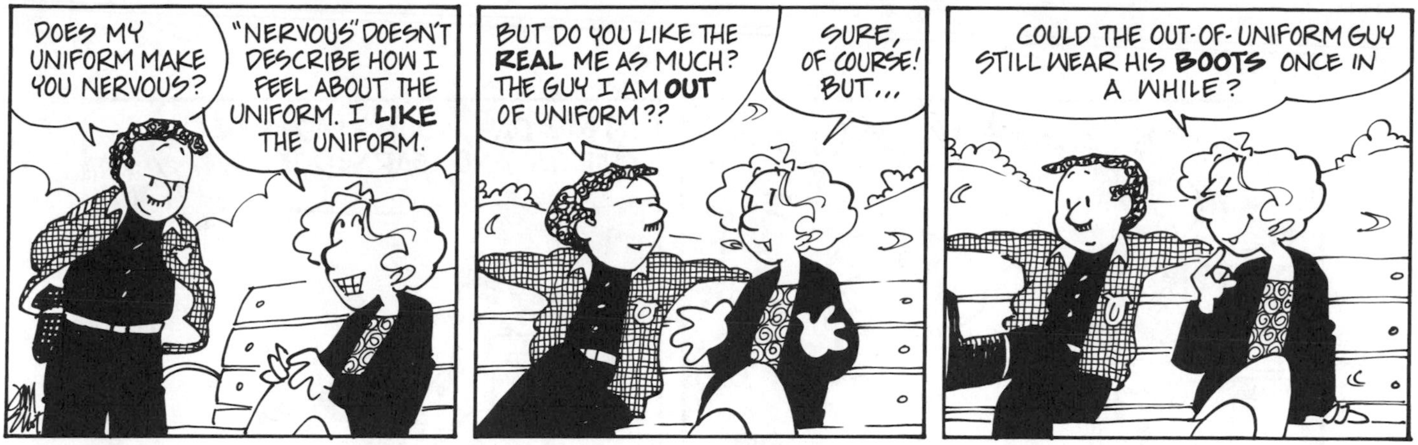
DOES MY UNIFORM MAKE YOU NERVOUS?
"NERVOUS" DOESN'T DESCRIBE HOW I FEEL ABOUT THE UNIFORM. I LIKE THE UNIFORM.
BUT DO YOU LIKE THE REAL ME AS MUCH? THE GUY I AM OUT OF UNIFORM??
SURE, OF COURSE! BUT...
COULD THE OUT-OF-UNIFORM GUY STILL WEAR HIS BOOTS ONCE IN A WHILE?

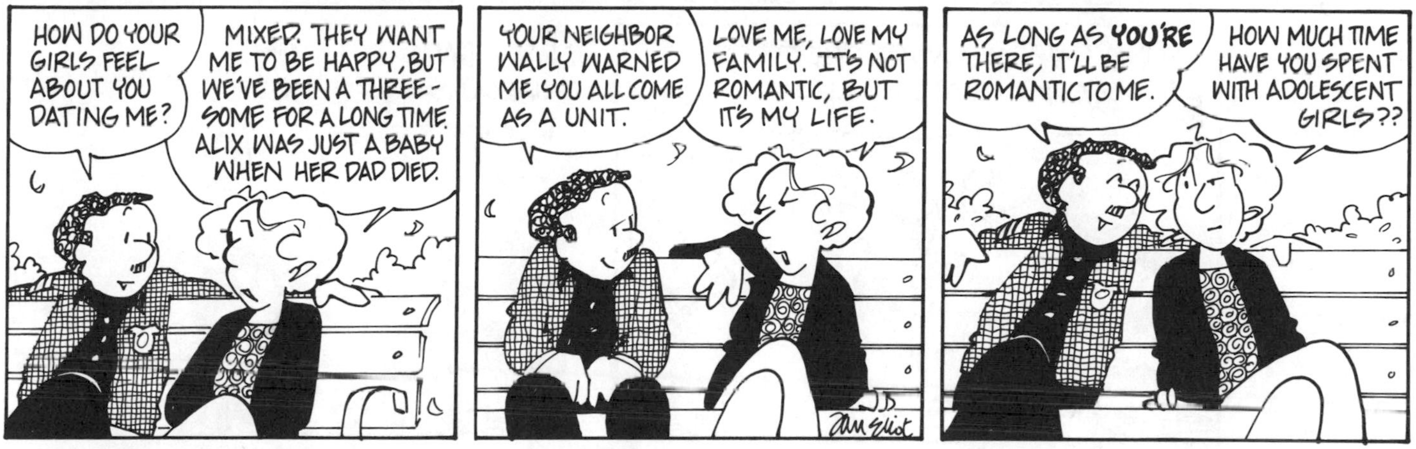
HOW DO YOUR GIRLS FEEL ABOUT YOU DATING ME?
MIXED. THEY WANT ME TO BE HAPPY, BUT WE'VE BEEN A THREESOME FOR A LONG TIME. ALIX WAS JUST A BABY WHEN HER DAD DIED.
YOUR NEIGHBOR WALLY WARNED ME YOU ALL COME AS A UNIT.
LOVE ME, LOVE MY FAMILY. IT'S NOT ROMANTIC, BUT IT'S MY LIFE.
AS LONG AS YOU'RE THERE, IT'LL BE ROMANTIC TO ME.
HOW MUCH TIME HAVE YOU SPENT WITH ADOLESCENT GIRLS??

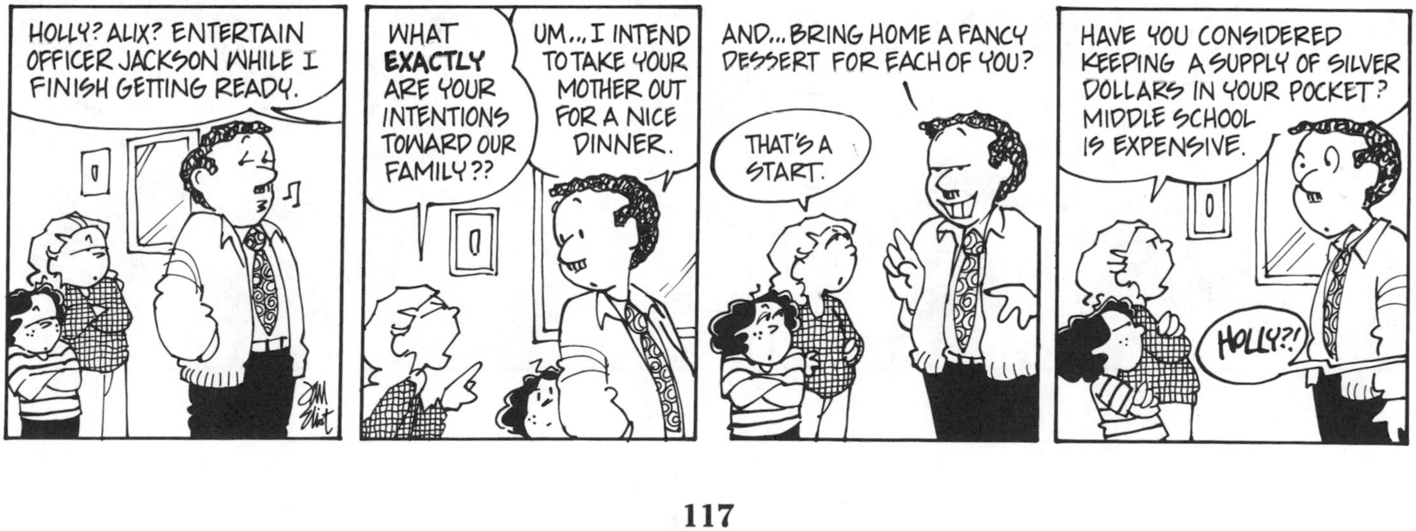
HOLLY? ALIX? ENTERTAIN OFFICER JACKSON WHILE I FINISH GETTING READY.
WHAT EXACTLY ARE YOUR INTENTIONS TOWARD OUR FAMILY??
UM... I INTEND TO TAKE YOUR MOTHER OUT FOR A NICE DINNER.
AND... BRING HOME A FANCY DESSERT FOR EACH OF YOU?
THAT'S A START.
HAVE YOU CONSIDERED KEEPING A SUPPLY OF SILVER DOLLARS IN YOUR POCKET? MIDDLE SCHOOL IS EXPENSIVE.
HOLLY?!

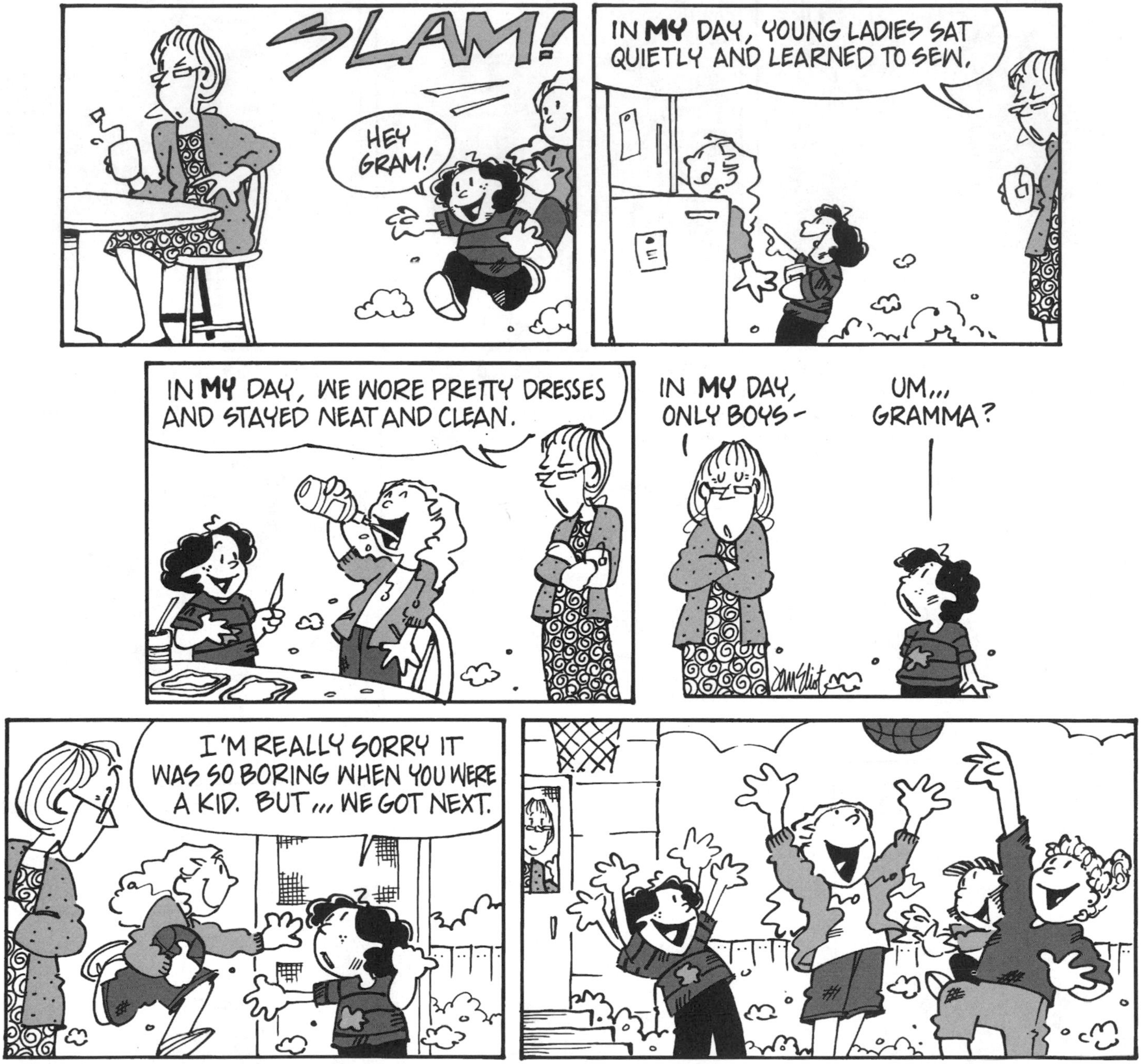
SLAM!
HEY GRAM!
IN MY DAY, YOUNG LADIES SAT QUIETLY AND LEARNED TO SEW.
IN MY DAY, WE WORE PRETTY DRESSES AND STAYED NEAT AND CLEAN.
IN MY DAY, ONLY BOYS-
UM,,, GRAMMA?
I'M REALLY SORRY IT WAS SO BORING WHEN YOU WERE A KID. BUT,,, WE GOT NEXT.

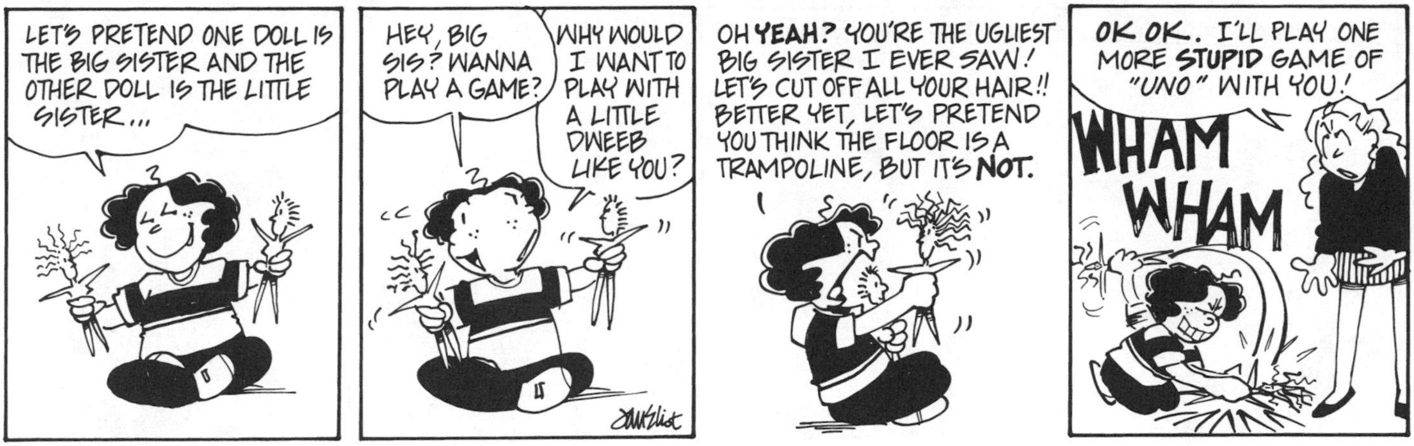
LET'S PRETEND ONE DOLL IS THE BIG SISTER AND THE OTHER DOLL IS THE LITTLE SISTER...
HEY, BIG SIS? WANNA PLAY A GAME?
WHY WOULD I WANT TO PLAY WITH A LITTLE DWEEB LIKE YOU?
OH **YEAH?** YOU'RE THE UGLIEST BIG SISTER I EVER SAW! LET'S CUT OFF ALL YOUR HAIR!! BETTER YET, LET'S PRETEND YOU THINK THE FLOOR IS A TRAMPOLINE, BUT IT'S **NOT.**
WHAM
WHAM
OK OK. I'LL PLAY ONE MORE **STUPID** GAME OF "UNO" WITH YOU!

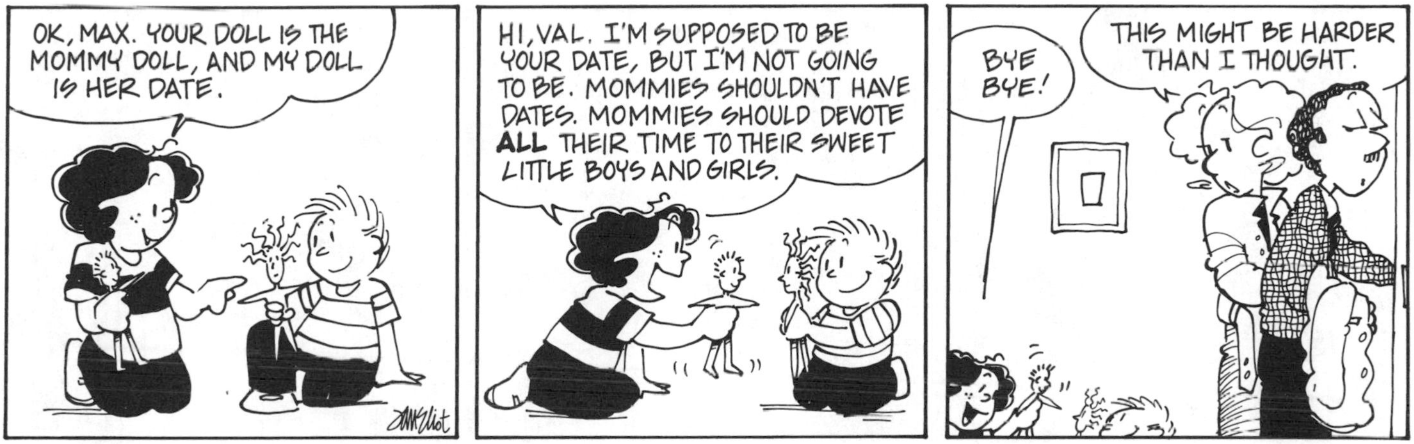
OK, MAX. YOUR DOLL IS THE MOMMY DOLL, AND MY DOLL IS HER DATE.
HI, VAL. I'M SUPPOSED TO BE YOUR DATE, BUT I'M NOT GOING TO BE. MOMMIES SHOULDN'T HAVE DATES. MOMMIES SHOULD DEVOTE **ALL** THEIR TIME TO THEIR SWEET LITTLE BOYS AND GIRLS.
BYE BYE!
THIS MIGHT BE HARDER THAN I THOUGHT.

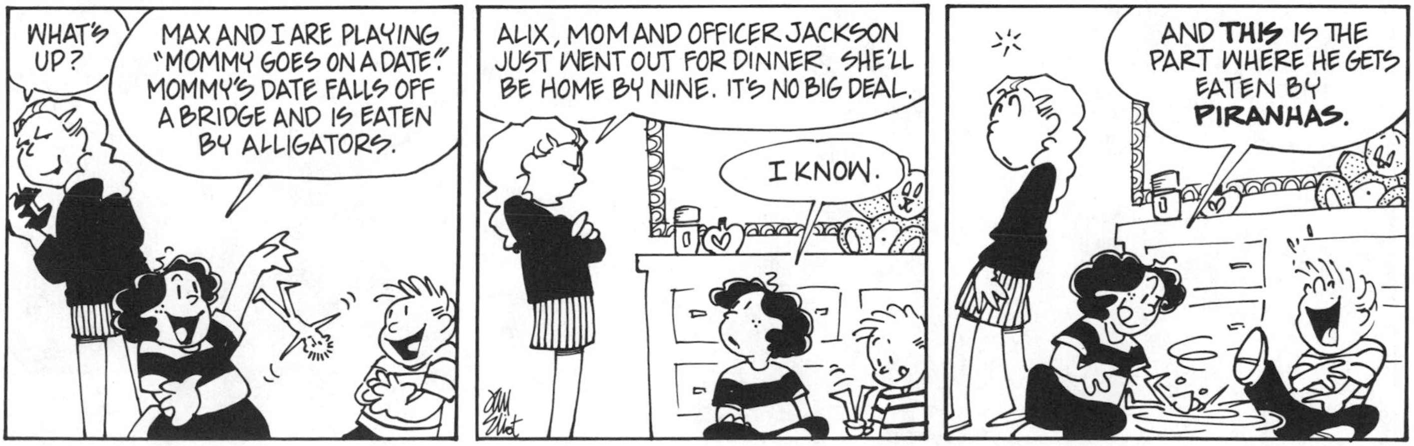
WHAT'S UP?
MAX AND I ARE PLAYING "MOMMY GOES ON A DATE." MOMMY'S DATE FALLS OFF A BRIDGE AND IS EATEN BY ALLIGATORS.
ALIX, MOM AND OFFICER JACKSON JUST WENT OUT FOR DINNER. SHE'LL BE HOME BY NINE. IT'S NO BIG DEAL.
I KNOW.
AND **THIS** IS THE PART WHERE HE GETS EATEN BY **PIRANHAS.**

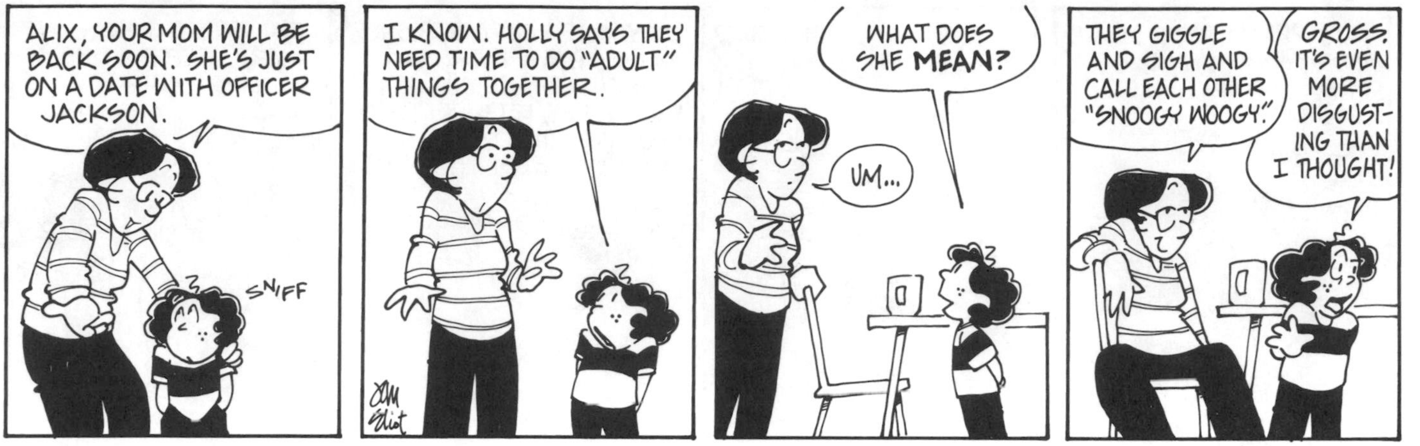
ALIX, YOUR MOM WILL BE BACK SOON. SHE'S JUST ON A DATE WITH OFFICER JACKSON.
SNIFF
I KNOW. HOLLY SAYS THEY NEED TIME TO DO "ADULT" THINGS TOGETHER.
WHAT DOES SHE **MEAN?**
UM...
THEY GIGGLE AND SIGH AND CALL EACH OTHER "SNOOGY WOOGY."
GROSS. IT'S EVEN MORE DISGUSTING THAN I THOUGHT!

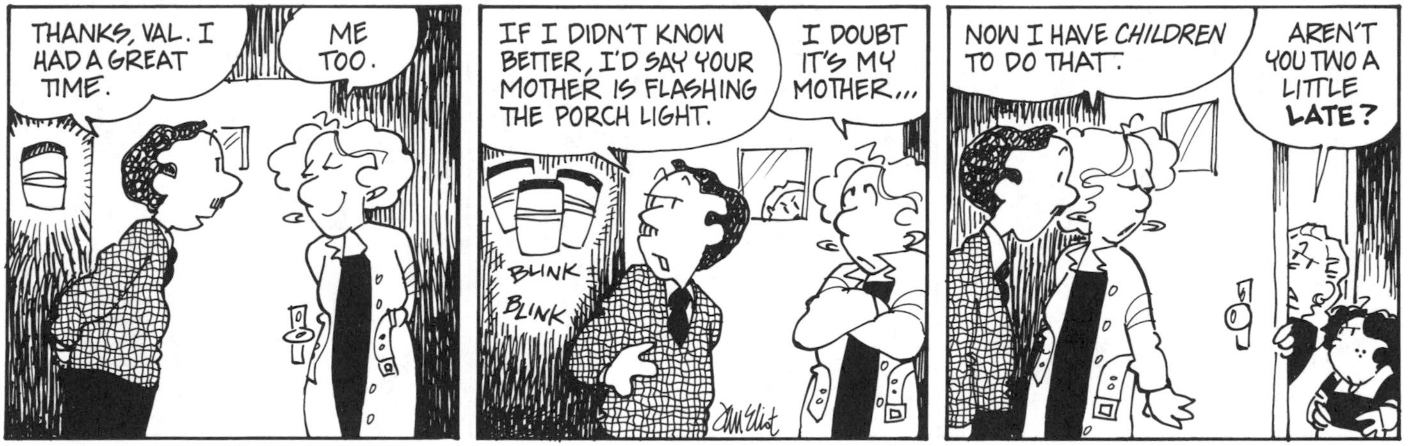
THANKS, VAL. I HAD A GREAT TIME.
ME TOO.
IF I DIDN'T KNOW BETTER, I'D SAY YOUR MOTHER IS FLASHING THE PORCH LIGHT.
BLINK
BLINK
I DOUBT IT'S MY MOTHER...
NOW I HAVE *CHILDREN* TO DO THAT.
AREN'T YOU TWO A LITTLE **LATE?**

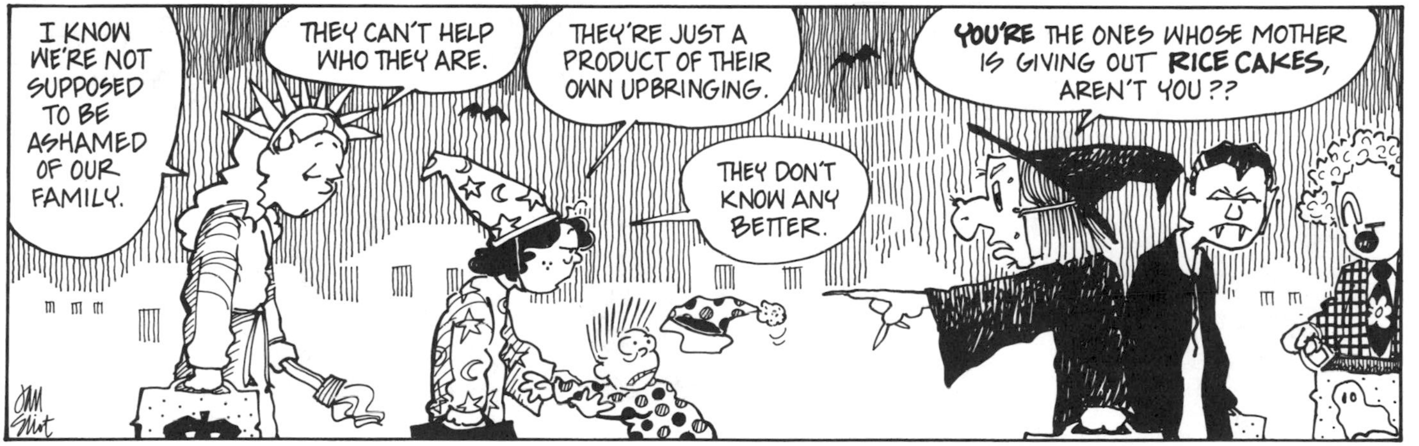
I KNOW WE'RE NOT SUPPOSED TO BE ASHAMED OF OUR FAMILY.
THEY CAN'T HELP WHO THEY ARE.
THEY'RE JUST A PRODUCT OF THEIR OWN UPBRINGING.
THEY DON'T KNOW ANY BETTER.
YOU'RE THE ONES WHOSE MOTHER IS GIVING OUT **RICE CAKES**, AREN'T YOU??

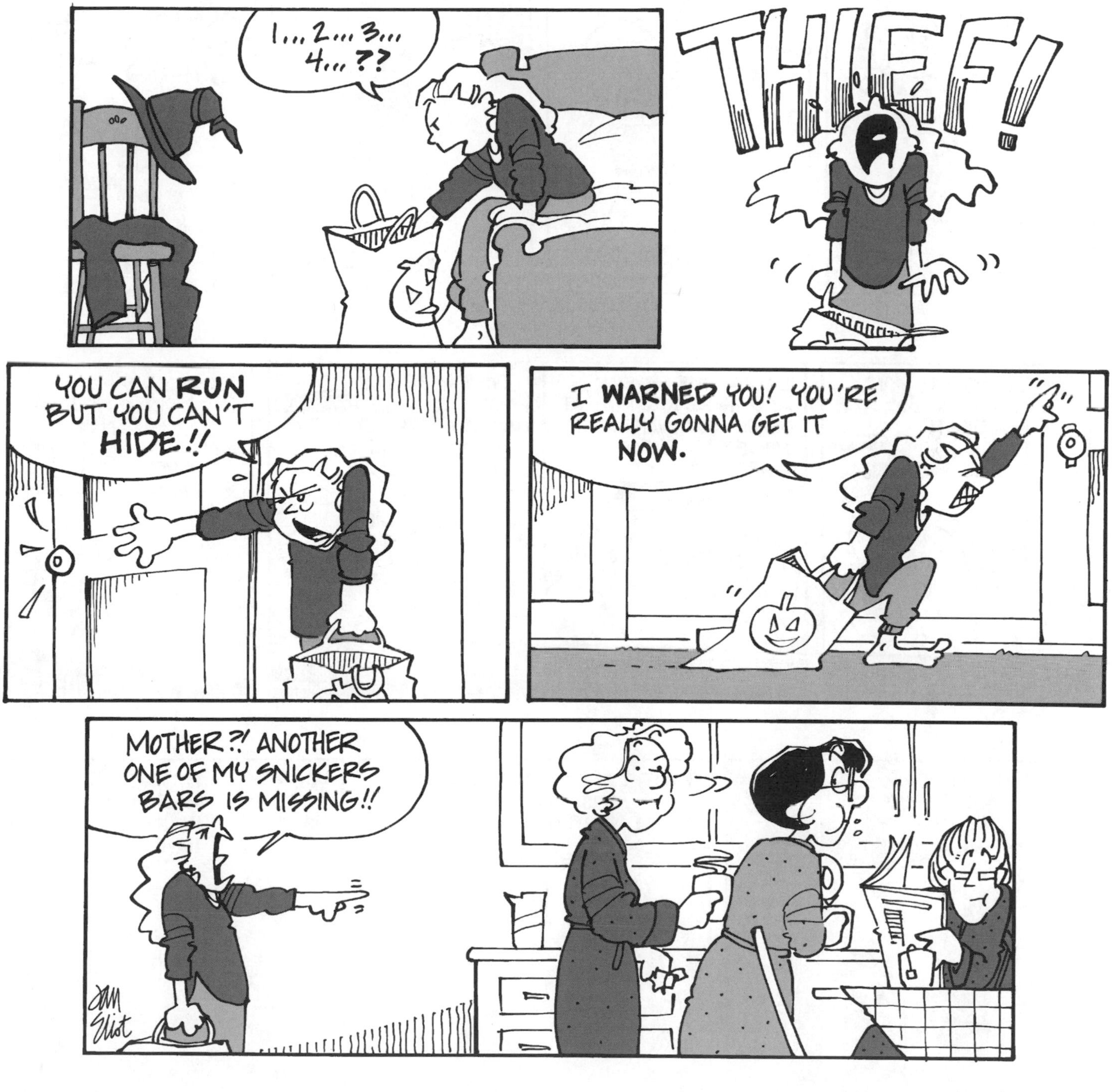
1... 2... 3... 4... ??
THIEF!
YOU CAN RUN BUT YOU CAN'T HIDE!!
I WARNED YOU! YOU'RE REALLY GONNA GET IT NOW.
MOTHER?! ANOTHER ONE OF MY SNICKERS BARS IS MISSING!!

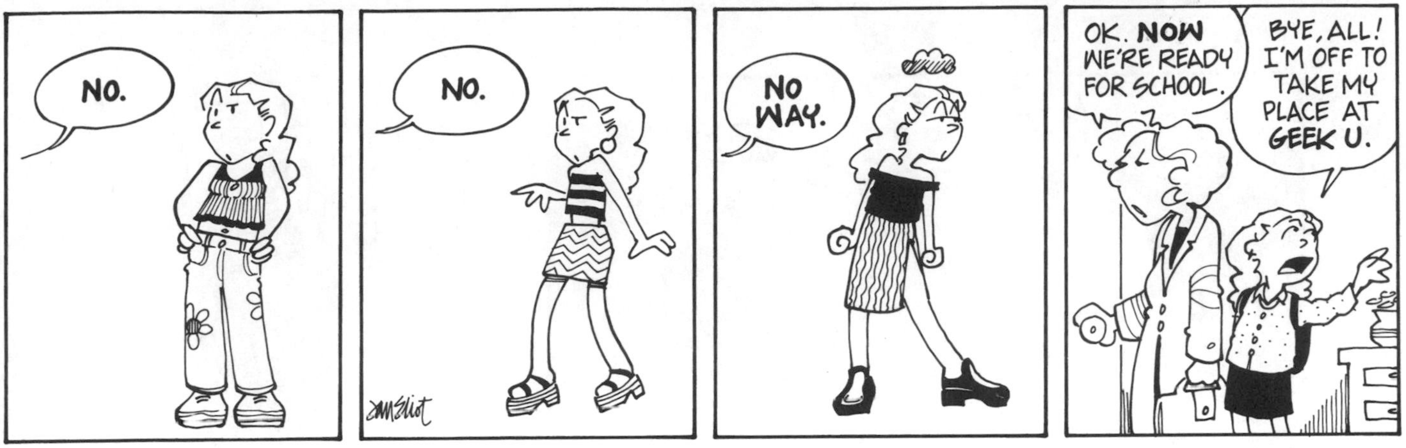
NO.
NO.
NO WAY.
OK. NOW WE'RE READY FOR SCHOOL.
BYE, ALL! I'M OFF TO TAKE MY PLACE AT GEEK U.

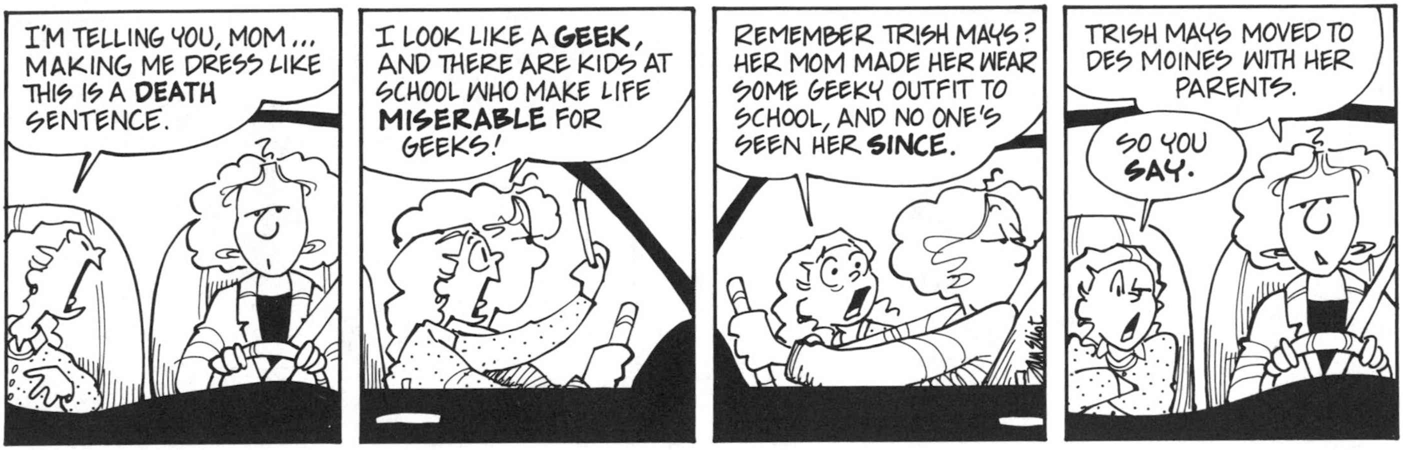
I'M TELLING YOU, MOM... MAKING ME DRESS LIKE THIS IS A DEATH SENTENCE.
I LOOK LIKE A GEEK, AND THERE ARE KIDS AT SCHOOL WHO MAKE LIFE MISERABLE FOR GEEKS!
REMEMBER TRISH MAYS? HER MOM MADE HER WEAR SOME GEEKY OUTFIT TO SCHOOL, AND NO ONE'S SEEN HER SINCE.
TRISH MAYS MOVED TO DES MOINES WITH HER PARENTS.
SO YOU SAY.

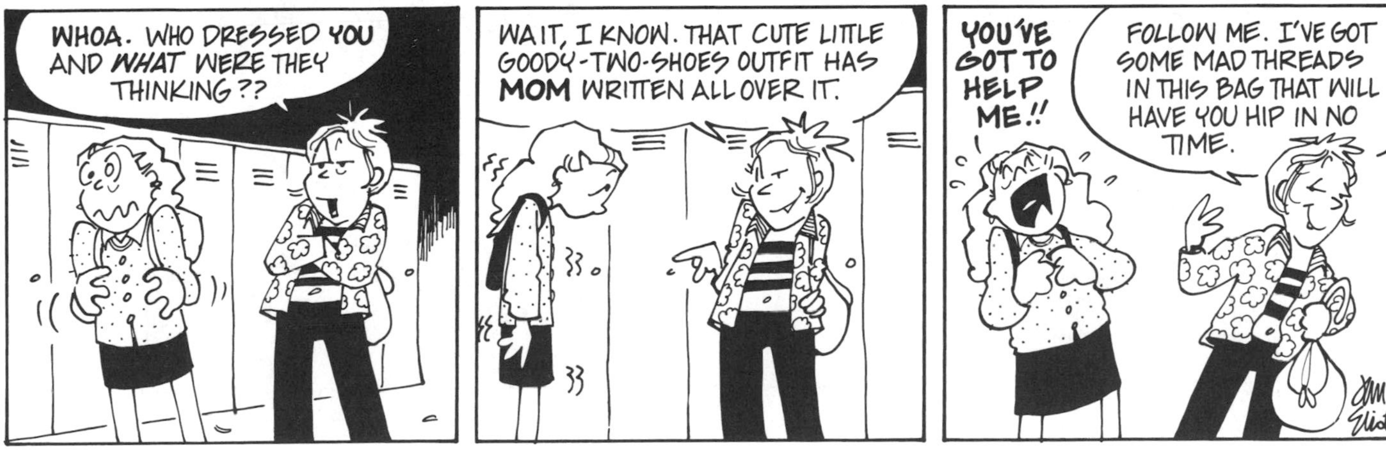
WHOA. WHO DRESSED YOU AND WHAT WERE THEY THINKING??
WAIT, I KNOW. THAT CUTE LITTLE GOODY-TWO-SHOES OUTFIT HAS MOM WRITTEN ALL OVER IT.
YOU'VE GOT TO HELP ME!!
FOLLOW ME. I'VE GOT SOME MAD THREADS IN THIS BAG THAT WILL HAVE YOU HIP IN NO TIME.

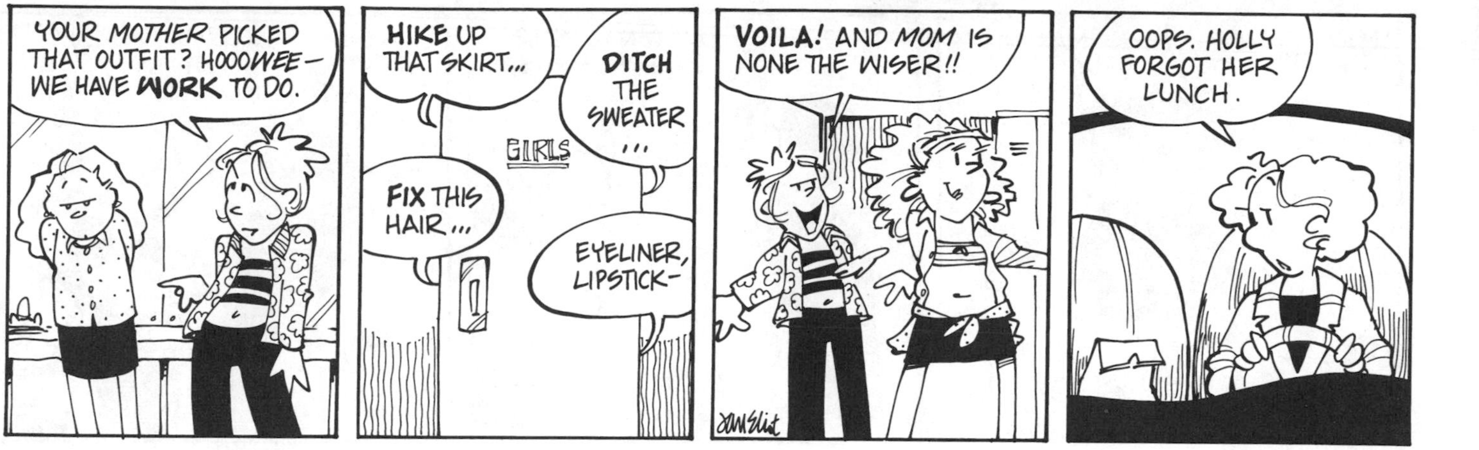
YOUR MOTHER PICKED THAT OUTFIT? HOOOWEE— WE HAVE WORK TO DO.
HIKE UP THAT SKIRT...
DITCH THE SWEATER ...
GIRLS
FIX THIS HAIR...
EYELINER, LIPSTICK-
VOILA! AND MOM IS NONE THE WISER!!
OOPS. HOLLY FORGOT HER LUNCH.

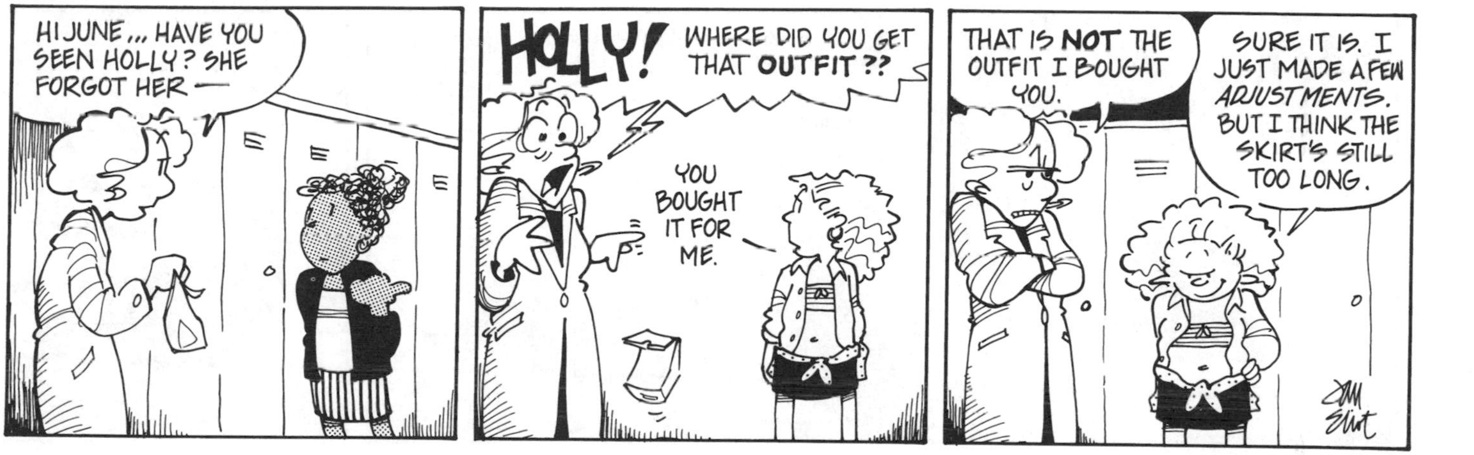
HI JUNE... HAVE YOU SEEN HOLLY? SHE FORGOT HER—
HOLLY!
WHERE DID YOU GET THAT OUTFIT??
YOU BOUGHT IT FOR ME.
THAT IS NOT THE OUTFIT I BOUGHT YOU.
SURE IT IS. I JUST MADE A FEW ADJUSTMENTS. BUT I THINK THE SKIRT'S STILL TOO LONG.

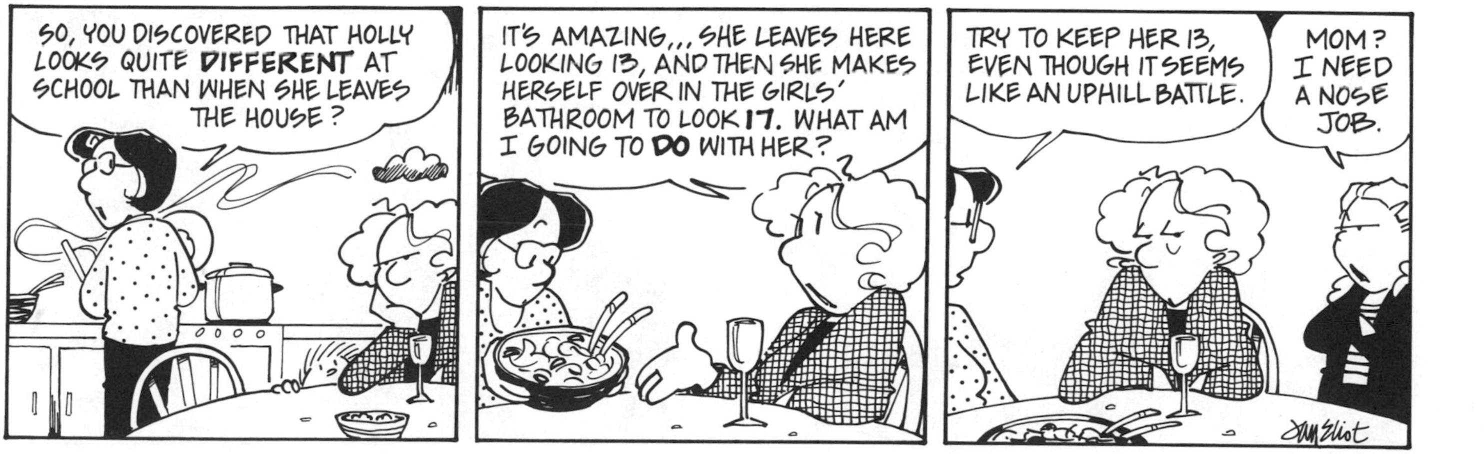
SO, YOU DISCOVERED THAT HOLLY LOOKS QUITE DIFFERENT AT SCHOOL THAN WHEN SHE LEAVES THE HOUSE?
IT'S AMAZING... SHE LEAVES HERE LOOKING 13, AND THEN SHE MAKES HERSELF OVER IN THE GIRLS' BATHROOM TO LOOK 17. WHAT AM I GOING TO DO WITH HER?
TRY TO KEEP HER 13, EVEN THOUGH IT SEEMS LIKE AN UPHILL BATTLE.
MOM? I NEED A NOSE JOB.

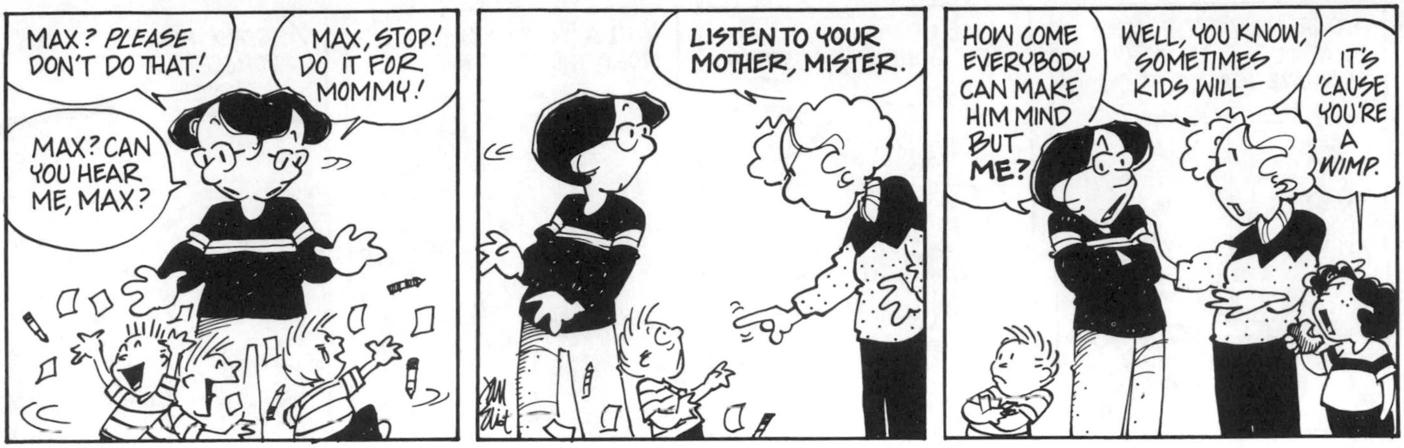
MAX? *PLEASE* DON'T DO THAT!
MAX? CAN YOU HEAR ME, MAX?
MAX, STOP! DO IT FOR MOMMY!
LISTEN TO YOUR MOTHER, MISTER.
HOW COME EVERYBODY CAN MAKE HIM MIND BUT **ME?**
WELL, YOU KNOW, SOMETIMES KIDS WILL—
IT'S 'CAUSE YOU'RE A WIMP.

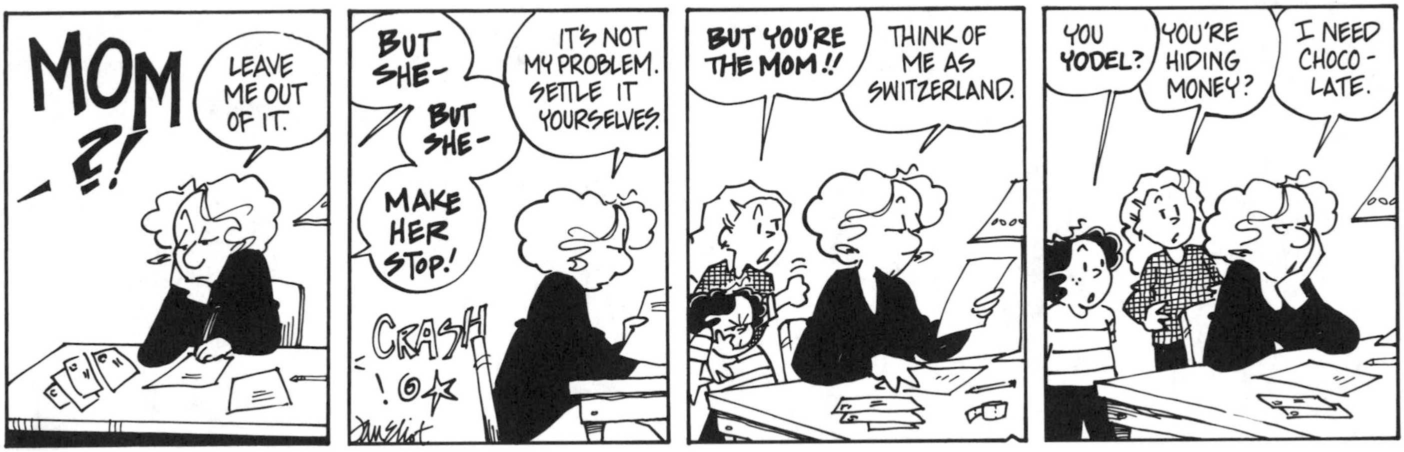
MOM
-?!
LEAVE ME OUT OF IT.
BUT SHE-
BUT SHE-
MAKE HER STOP!
IT'S NOT MY PROBLEM. SETTLE IT YOURSELVES.
CRASH
BUT YOU'RE THE MOM!!
THINK OF ME AS SWITZERLAND.
YOU **YODEL?**
YOU'RE HIDING MONEY?
I NEED CHOCO-LATE.

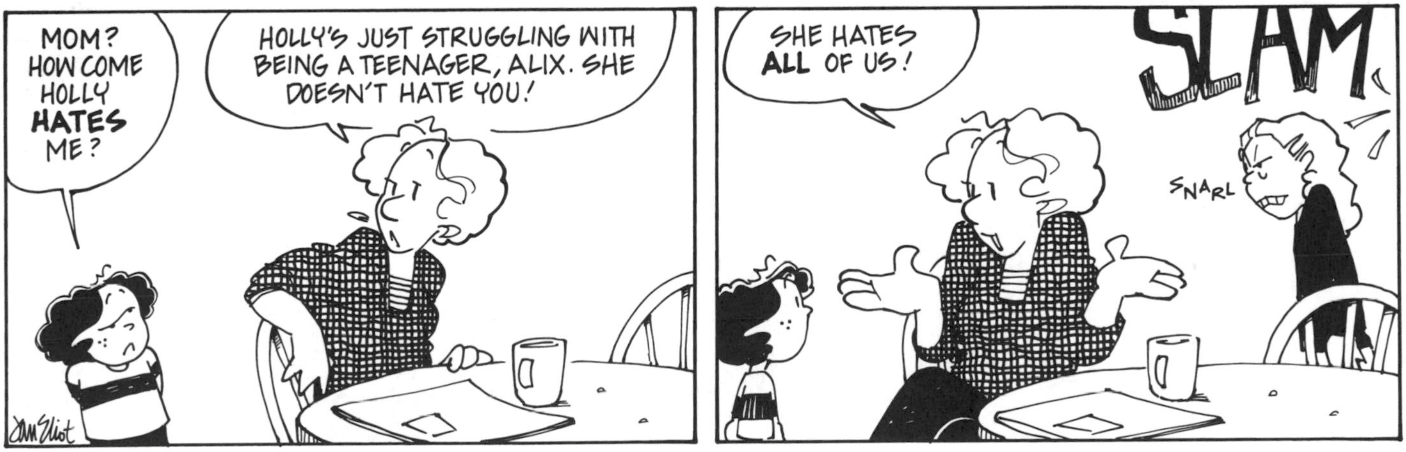
MOM? HOW COME HOLLY **HATES** ME?
HOLLY'S JUST STRUGGLING WITH BEING A TEENAGER, ALIX. SHE DOESN'T HATE YOU!
SHE HATES **ALL** OF US!
SLAM
SNARL

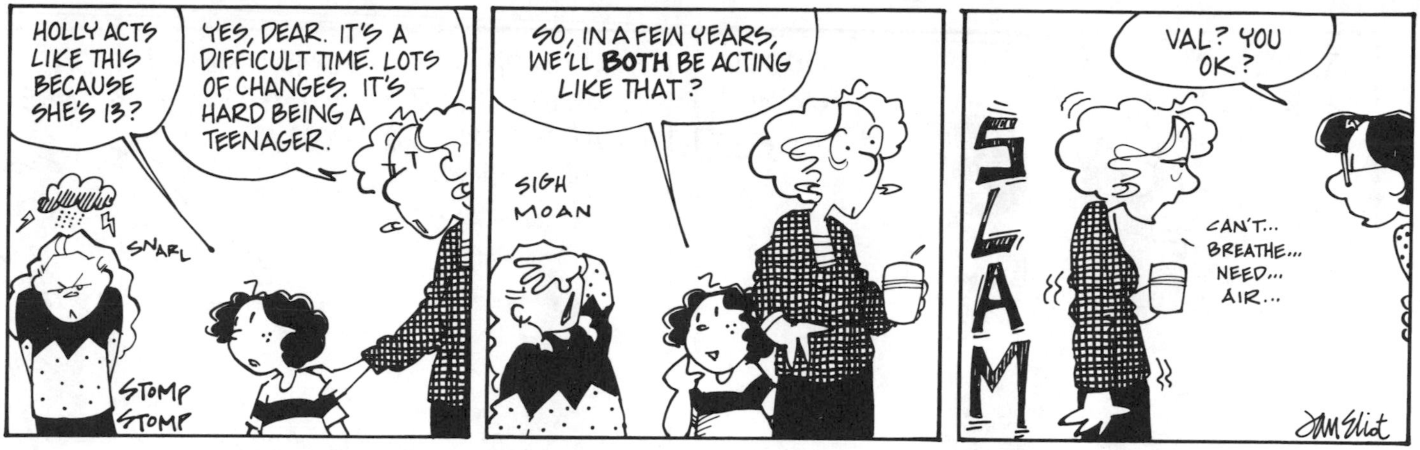
HOLLY ACTS LIKE THIS BECAUSE SHE'S 13?
YES, DEAR. IT'S A DIFFICULT TIME. LOTS OF CHANGES. IT'S HARD BEING A TEENAGER.
SNARL
STOMP STOMP
SO, IN A FEW YEARS, WE'LL **BOTH** BE ACTING LIKE THAT?
SIGH MOAN
VAL? YOU OK?
SLAM
CAN'T... BREATHE... NEED... AIR...

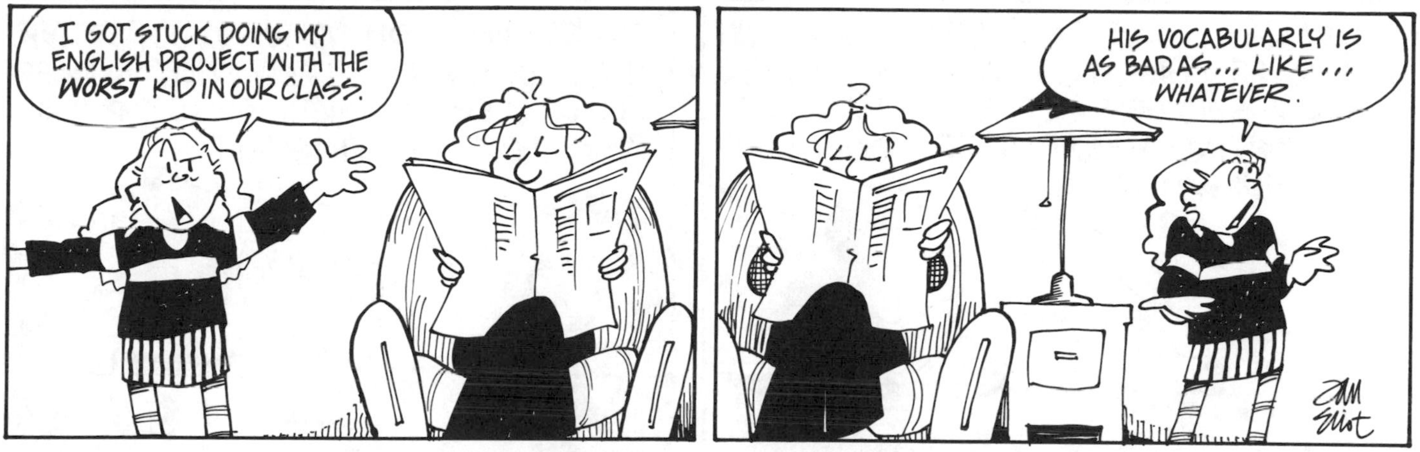
I GOT STUCK DOING MY ENGLISH PROJECT WITH THE *WORST* KID IN OUR CLASS.
HIS VOCABULARLY IS AS BAD AS... LIKE... WHATEVER.

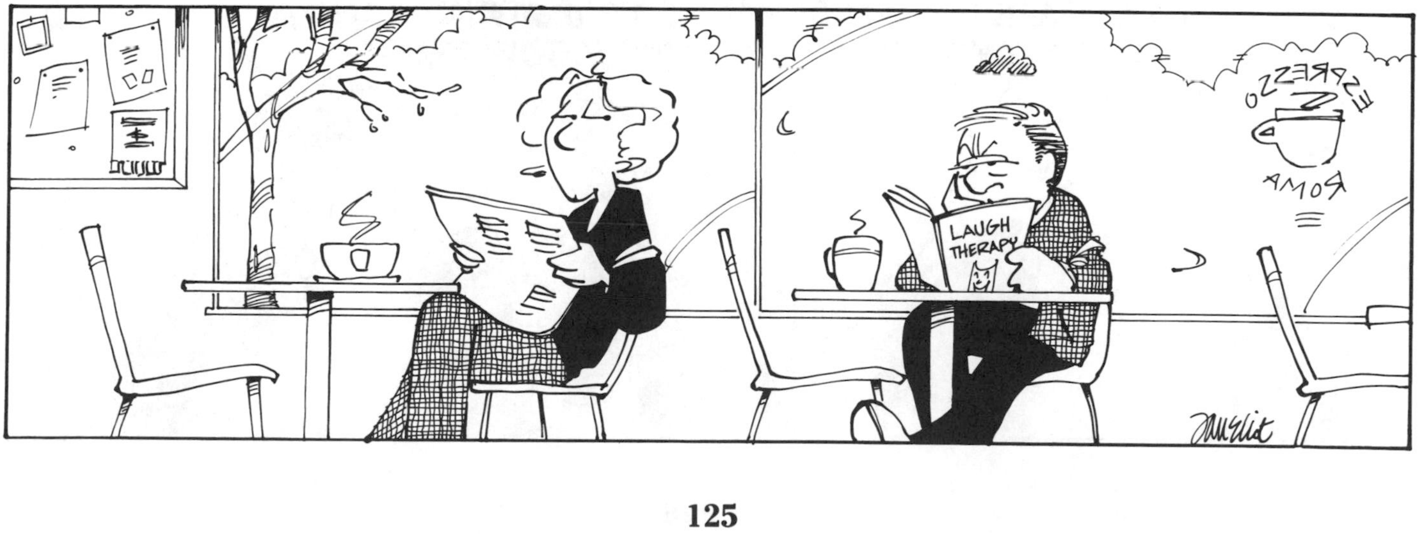
ESPRESSO
ROMA
LAUGH THERAPY

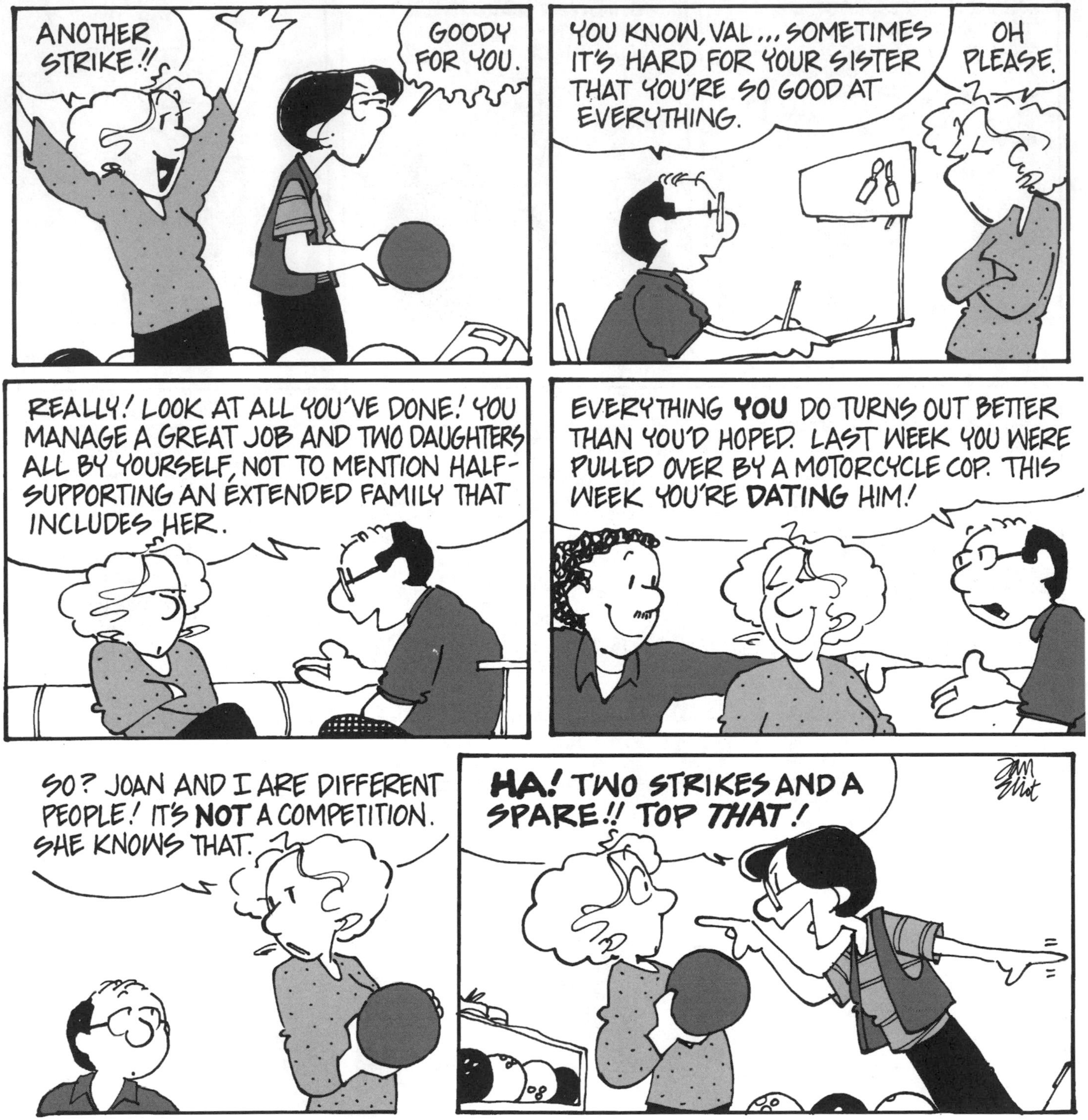
ANOTHER STRIKE!!
GOODY FOR YOU.
YOU KNOW, VAL... SOMETIMES IT'S HARD FOR YOUR SISTER THAT YOU'RE SO GOOD AT EVERYTHING.
OH PLEASE.
REALLY! LOOK AT ALL YOU'VE DONE! YOU MANAGE A GREAT JOB AND TWO DAUGHTERS ALL BY YOURSELF, NOT TO MENTION HALF-SUPPORTING AN EXTENDED FAMILY THAT INCLUDES HER.
EVERYTHING **YOU** DO TURNS OUT BETTER THAN YOU'D HOPED. LAST WEEK YOU WERE PULLED OVER BY A MOTORCYCLE COP. THIS WEEK YOU'RE **DATING** HIM!
SO? JOAN AND I ARE DIFFERENT PEOPLE! IT'S **NOT** A COMPETITION. SHE KNOWS THAT.
HA! TWO STRIKES AND A SPARE!! **TOP THAT!**
JAN Eliot

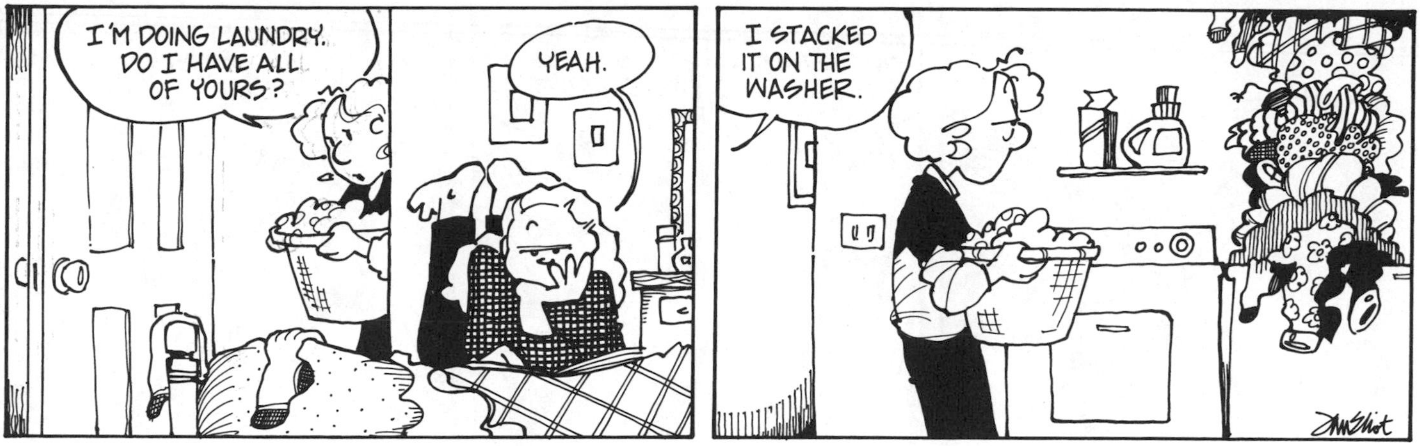
I'M DOING LAUNDRY. DO I HAVE ALL OF YOURS?
YEAH.
I STACKED IT ON THE WASHER.

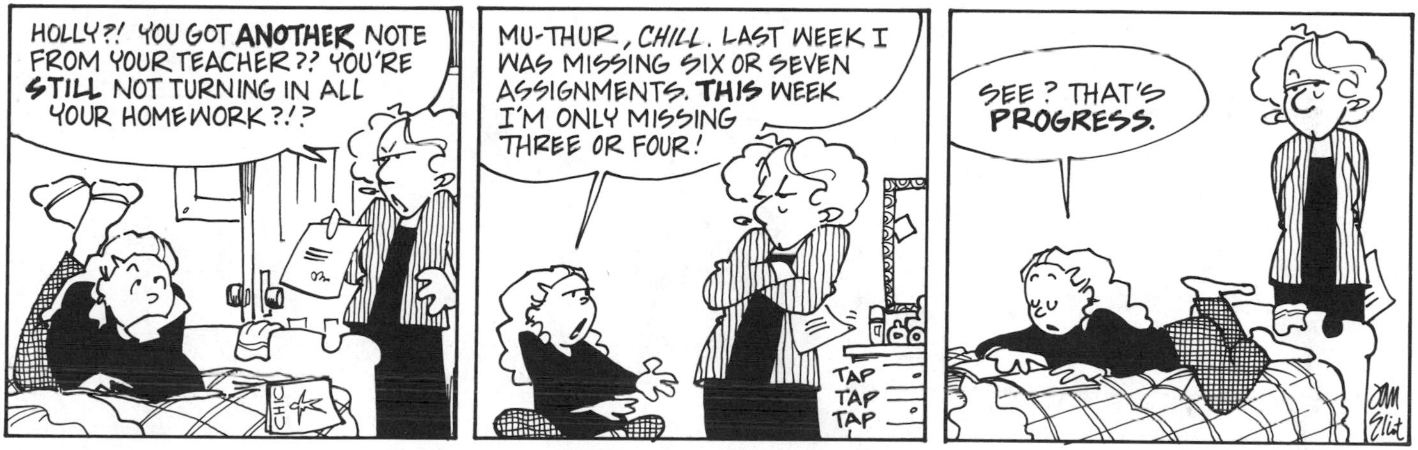
HOLLY?! YOU GOT **ANOTHER** NOTE FROM YOUR TEACHER?? YOU'RE **STILL** NOT TURNING IN ALL YOUR HOMEWORK?!?
MU-THUR, *CHILL*. LAST WEEK I WAS MISSING SIX OR SEVEN ASSIGNMENTS. **THIS** WEEK I'M ONLY MISSING THREE OR FOUR!
TAP TAP TAP
SEE? THAT'S **PROGRESS.**

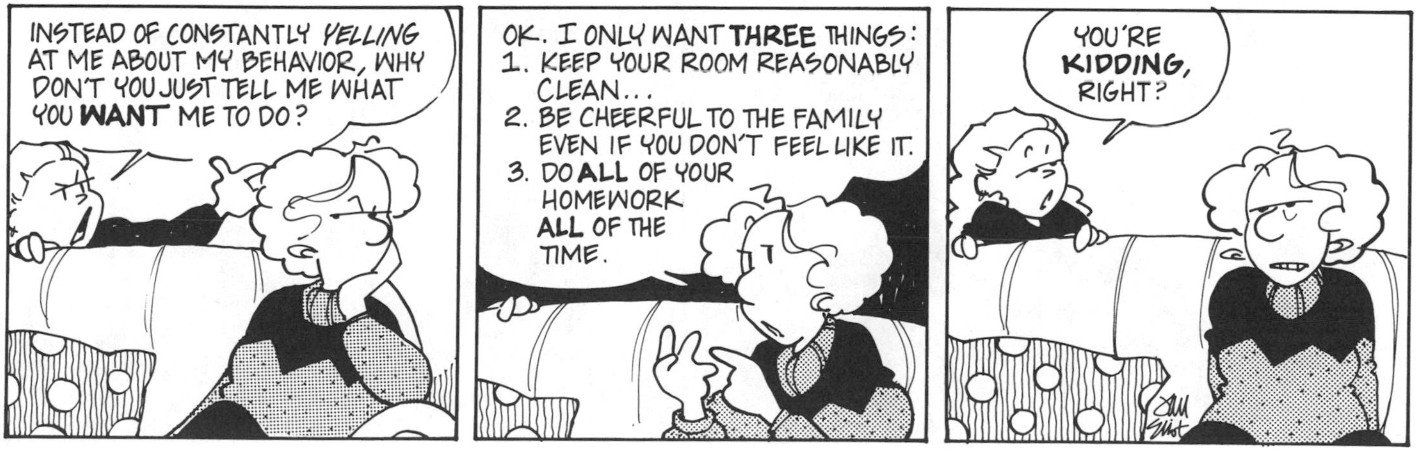
INSTEAD OF CONSTANTLY *YELLING* AT ME ABOUT MY BEHAVIOR, WHY DON'T YOU JUST TELL ME WHAT YOU **WANT** ME TO DO?
OK. I ONLY WANT **THREE** THINGS: 1. KEEP YOUR ROOM REASONABLY CLEAN... 2. BE CHEERFUL TO THE FAMILY EVEN IF YOU DON'T FEEL LIKE IT. 3. DO **ALL** OF YOUR HOMEWORK **ALL** OF THE TIME.
YOU'RE **KIDDING,** RIGHT?

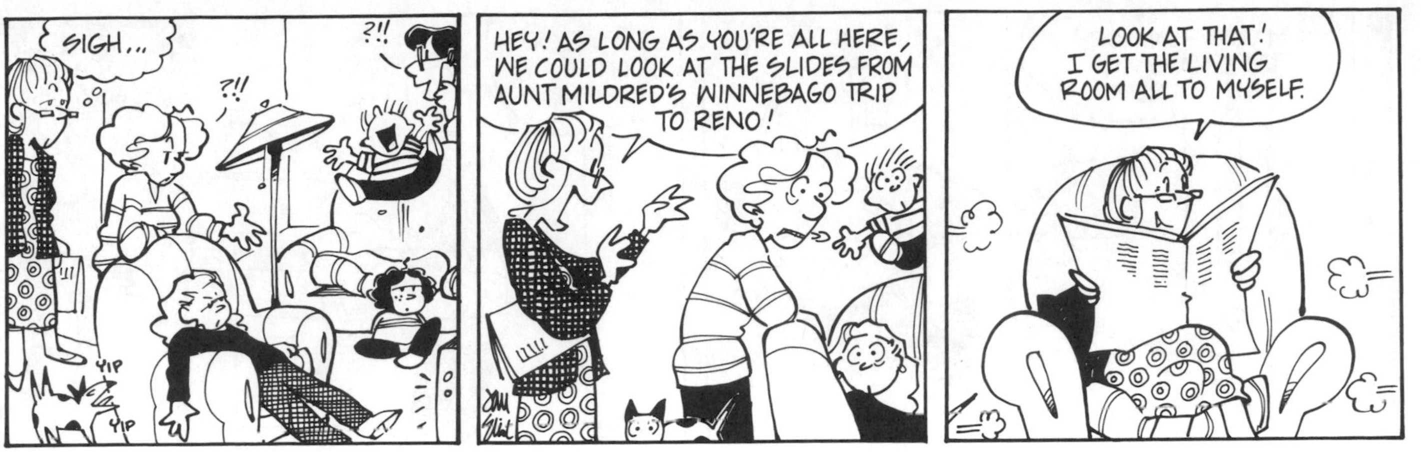
SIGH...
?!!
?!!
YIP
YIP
HEY! AS LONG AS YOU'RE ALL HERE, WE COULD LOOK AT THE SLIDES FROM AUNT MILDRED'S WINNEBAGO TRIP TO RENO!
LOOK AT THAT! I GET THE LIVING ROOM ALL TO MYSELF.

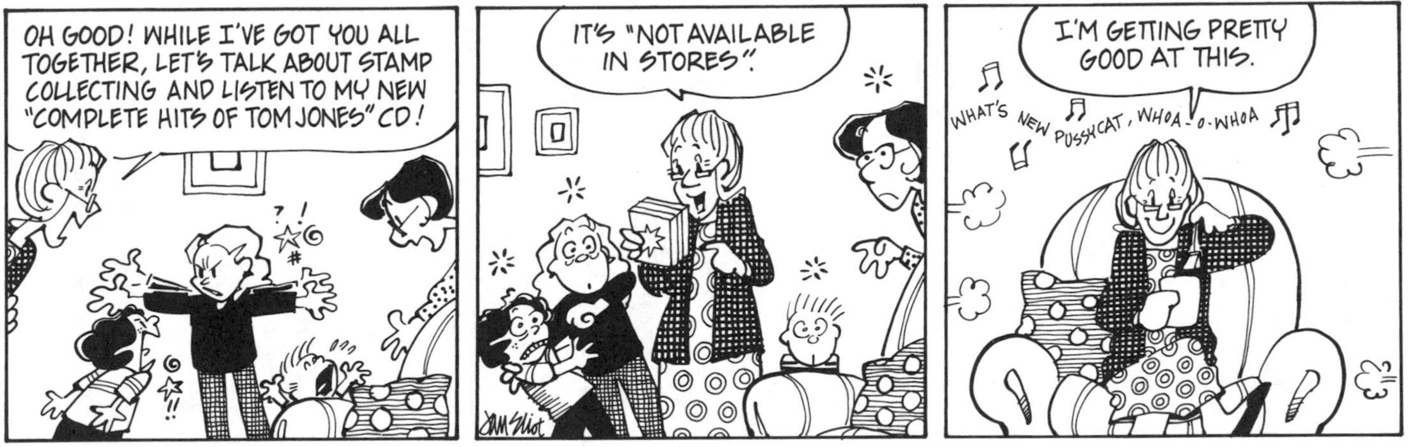
OH GOOD! WHILE I'VE GOT YOU ALL TOGETHER, LET'S TALK ABOUT STAMP COLLECTING AND LISTEN TO MY NEW "COMPLETE HITS OF TOM JONES" CD!
IT'S "NOT AVAILABLE IN STORES".
I'M GETTING PRETTY GOOD AT THIS.
WHAT'S NEW PUSSYCAT, WHOA-O-WHOA

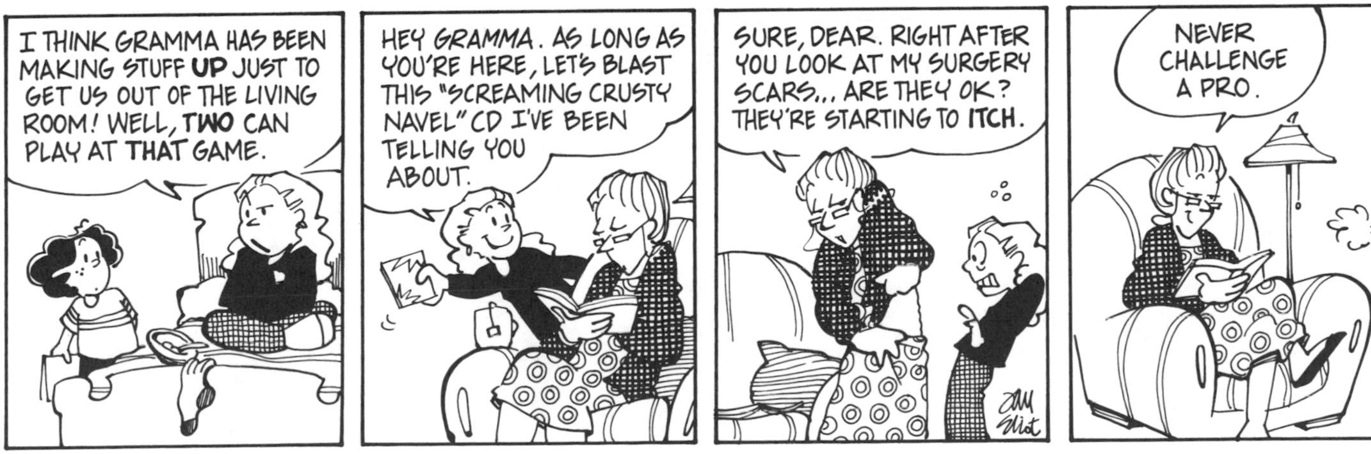
I THINK GRAMMA HAS BEEN MAKING STUFF **UP** JUST TO GET US OUT OF THE LIVING ROOM! WELL, **TWO** CAN PLAY AT **THAT** GAME.
HEY GRAMMA. AS LONG AS YOU'RE HERE, LET'S BLAST THIS "SCREAMING CRUSTY NAVEL" CD I'VE BEEN TELLING YOU ABOUT.
SURE, DEAR. RIGHT AFTER YOU LOOK AT MY SURGERY SCARS... ARE THEY OK? THEY'RE STARTING TO **ITCH**.
NEVER CHALLENGE A PRO.

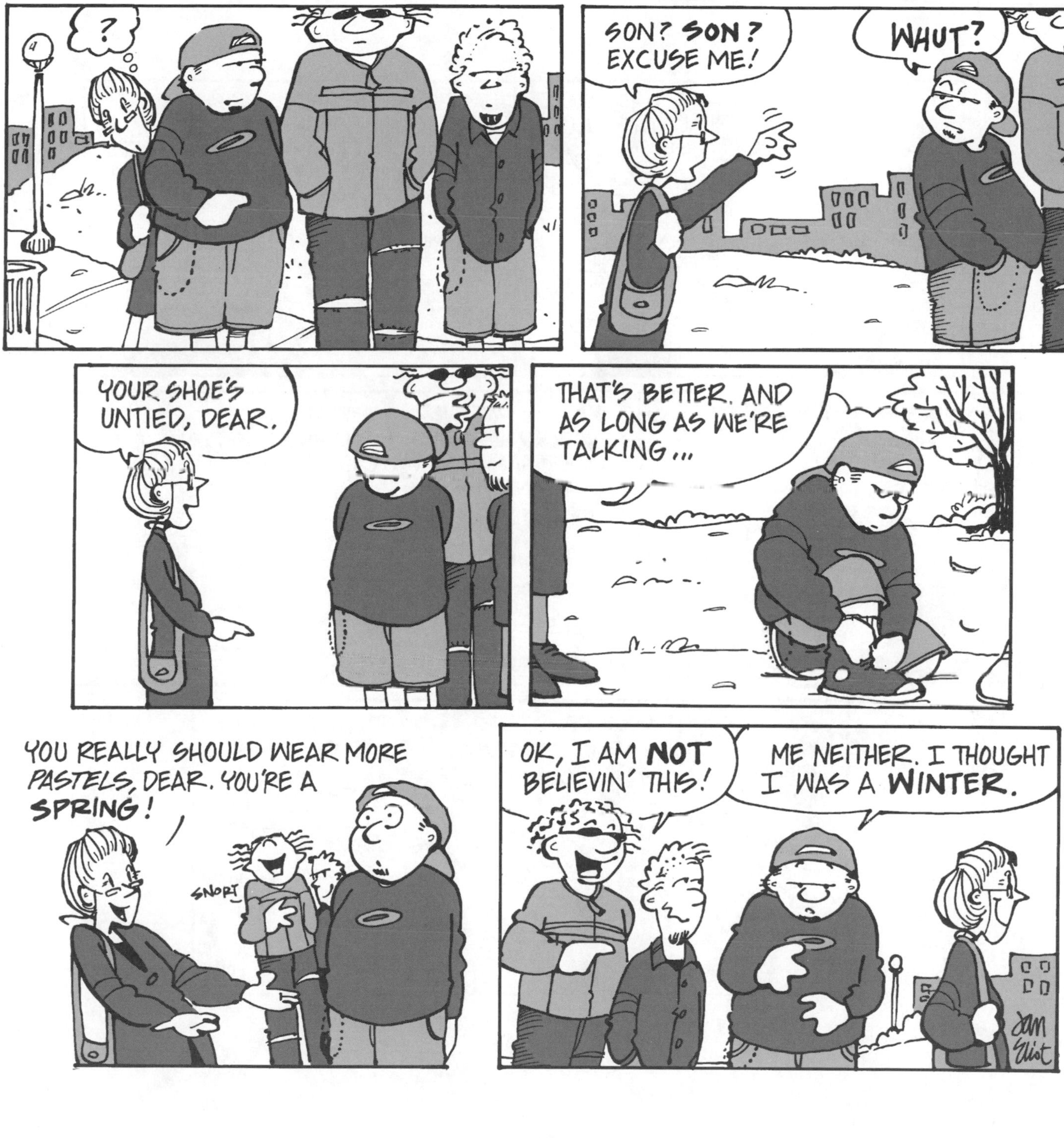
?
SON? SON? EXCUSE ME!
WHUT?
YOUR SHOE'S UNTIED, DEAR.
THAT'S BETTER. AND AS LONG AS WE'RE TALKING...
YOU REALLY SHOULD WEAR MORE PASTELS, DEAR. YOU'RE A SPRING!
SNORT
OK, I AM NOT BELIEVIN' THIS!
ME NEITHER. I THOUGHT I WAS A WINTER.
Jan Eliot

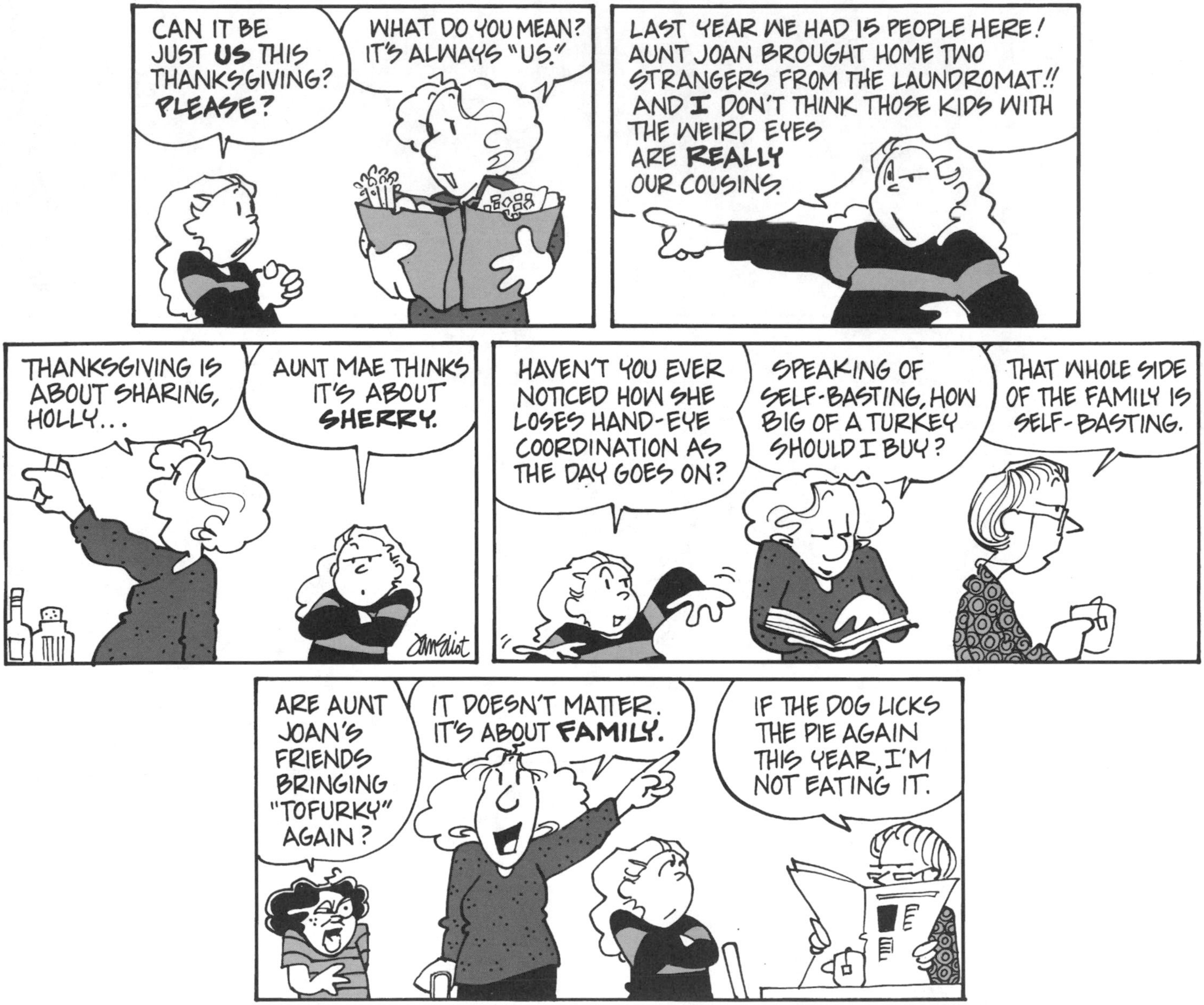
CAN IT BE JUST US THIS THANKSGIVING? PLEASE?
WHAT DO YOU MEAN? IT'S ALWAYS "US."
LAST YEAR WE HAD 15 PEOPLE HERE! AUNT JOAN BROUGHT HOME TWO STRANGERS FROM THE LAUNDROMAT!! AND I DON'T THINK THOSE KIDS WITH THE WEIRD EYES ARE REALLY OUR COUSINS.
THANKSGIVING IS ABOUT SHARING, HOLLY...
AUNT MAE THINKS IT'S ABOUT SHERRY.
HAVEN'T YOU EVER NOTICED HOW SHE LOSES HAND-EYE COORDINATION AS THE DAY GOES ON?
SPEAKING OF SELF-BASTING, HOW BIG OF A TURKEY SHOULD I BUY?
THAT WHOLE SIDE OF THE FAMILY IS SELF-BASTING.
ARE AUNT JOAN'S FRIENDS BRINGING "TOFURKY" AGAIN?
IT DOESN'T MATTER. IT'S ABOUT FAMILY.
IF THE DOG LICKS THE PIE AGAIN THIS YEAR, I'M NOT EATING IT.

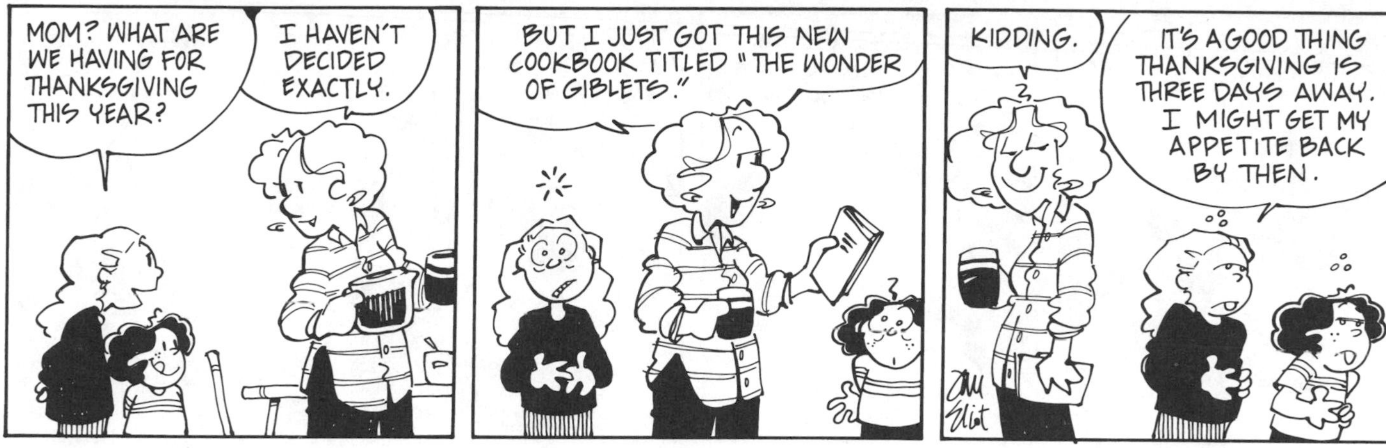
MOM? WHAT ARE WE HAVING FOR THANKSGIVING THIS YEAR?
I HAVEN'T DECIDED EXACTLY.
BUT I JUST GOT THIS NEW COOKBOOK TITLED "THE WONDER OF GIBLETS."
KIDDING.
IT'S A GOOD THING THANKSGIVING IS THREE DAYS AWAY. I MIGHT GET MY APPETITE BACK BY THEN.

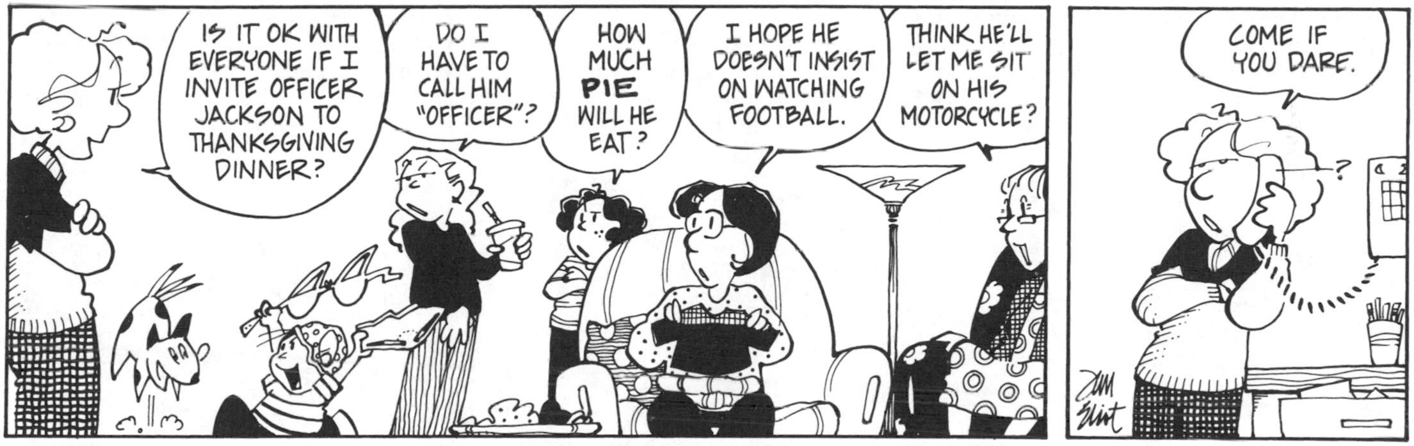
IS IT OK WITH EVERYONE IF I INVITE OFFICER JACKSON TO THANKSGIVING DINNER?
DO I HAVE TO CALL HIM "OFFICER"?
HOW MUCH PIE WILL HE EAT?
I HOPE HE DOESN'T INSIST ON WATCHING FOOTBALL.
THINK HE'LL LET ME SIT ON HIS MOTORCYCLE?
COME IF YOU DARE.

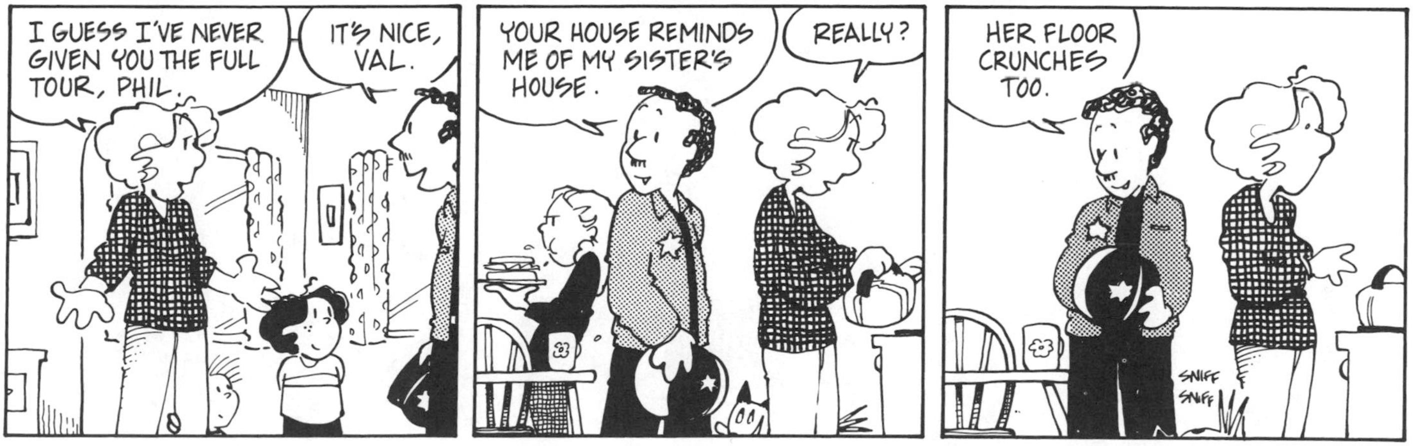
I GUESS I'VE NEVER GIVEN YOU THE FULL TOUR, PHIL.
IT'S NICE, VAL.
YOUR HOUSE REMINDS ME OF MY SISTER'S HOUSE.
REALLY?
HER FLOOR CRUNCHES TOO.
SNIFF
SNIFF

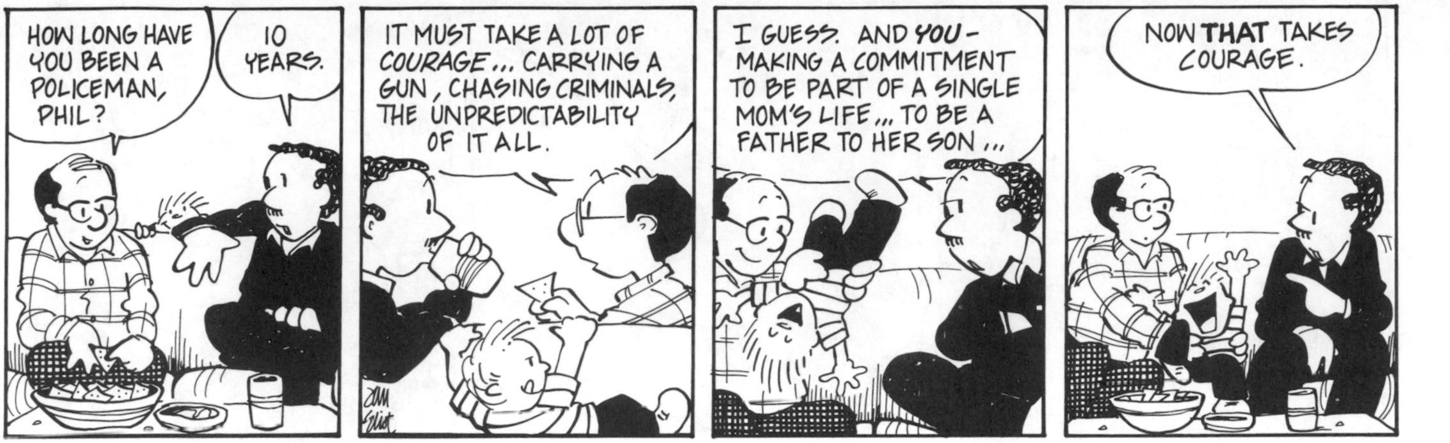
HOW LONG HAVE YOU BEEN A POLICEMAN, PHIL?
10 YEARS.
IT MUST TAKE A LOT OF COURAGE... CARRYING A GUN, CHASING CRIMINALS, THE UNPREDICTABILITY OF IT ALL.
I GUESS. AND YOU - MAKING A COMMITMENT TO BE PART OF A SINGLE MOM'S LIFE... TO BE A FATHER TO HER SON...
NOW THAT TAKES COURAGE.

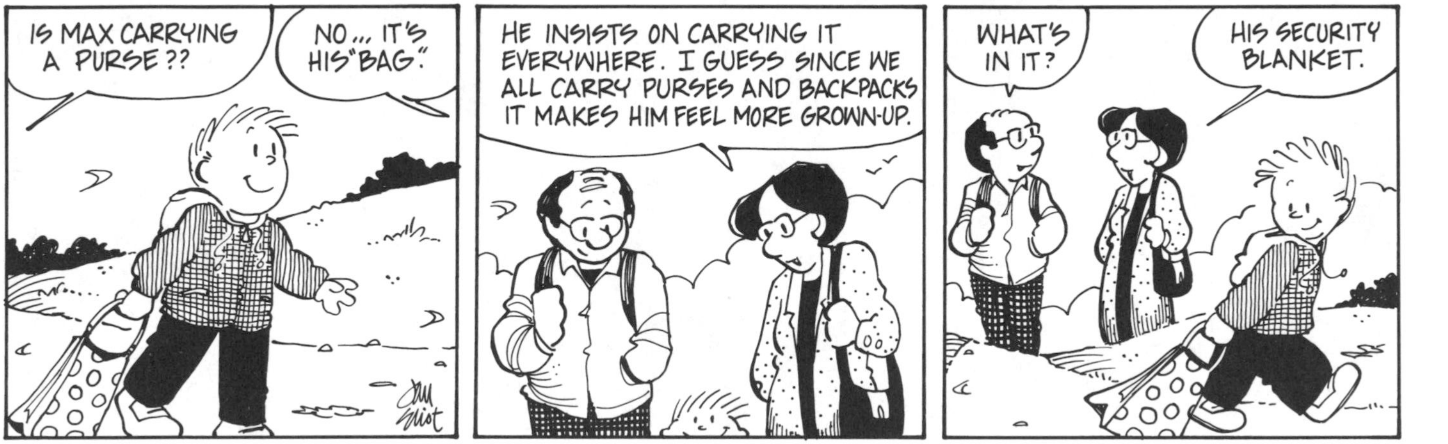
IS MAX CARRYING A PURSE??
NO... IT'S HIS "BAG."
HE INSISTS ON CARRYING IT EVERYWHERE. I GUESS SINCE WE ALL CARRY PURSES AND BACKPACKS IT MAKES HIM FEEL MORE GROWN-UP.
WHAT'S IN IT?
HIS SECURITY BLANKET.

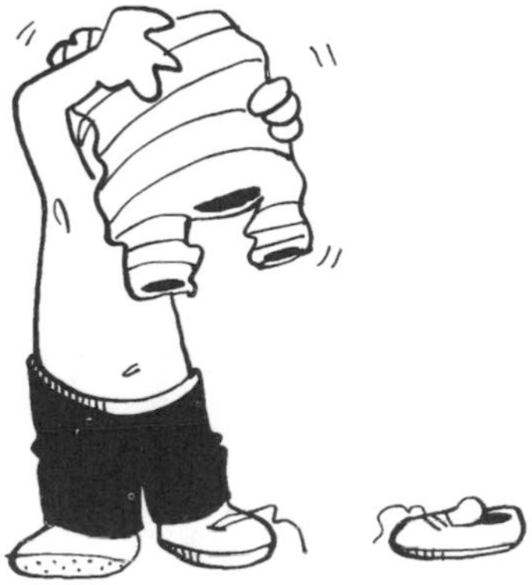

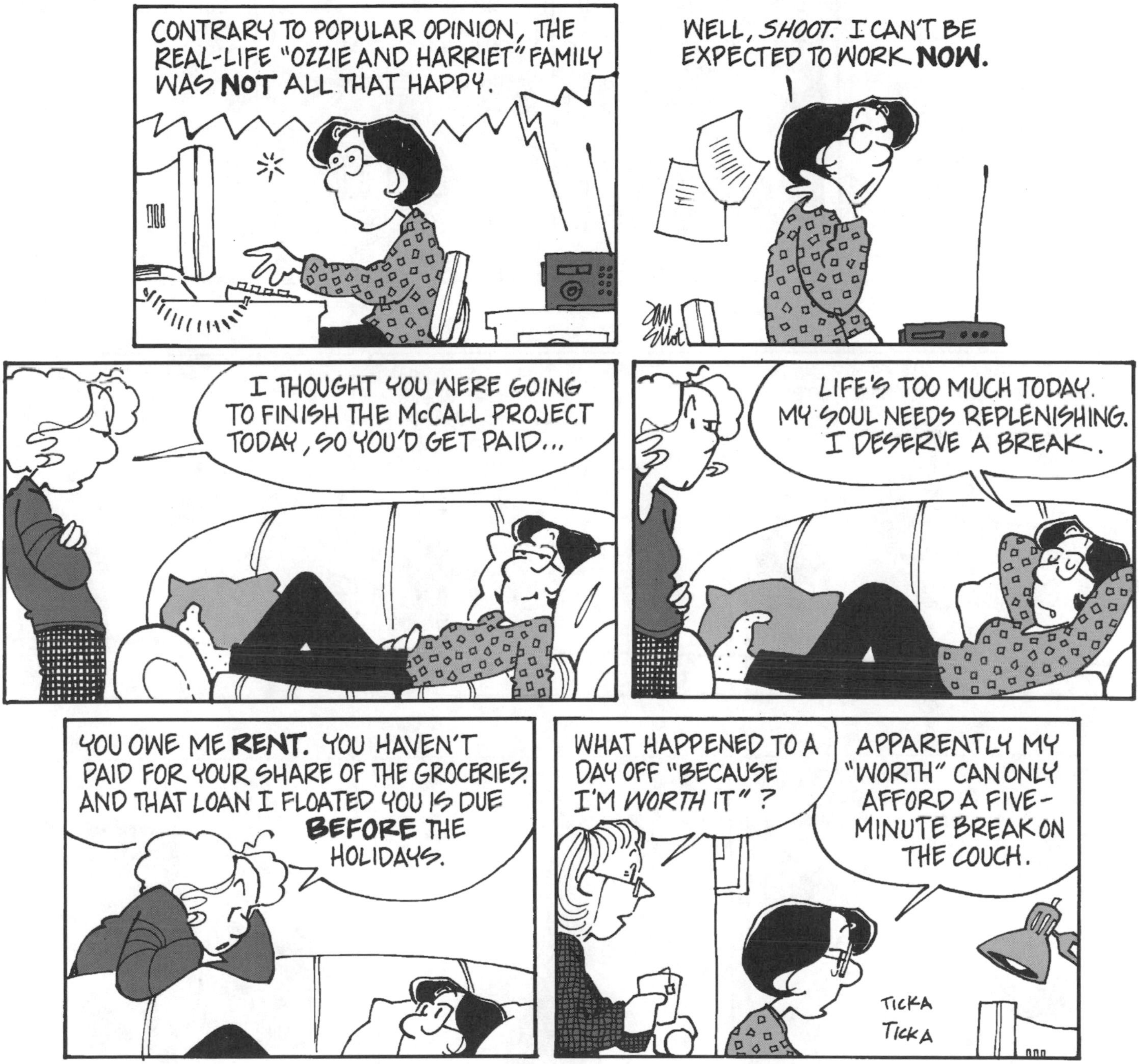
CONTRARY TO POPULAR OPINION, THE REAL-LIFE "OZZIE AND HARRIET" FAMILY WAS **NOT** ALL THAT HAPPY.
WELL, *SHOOT.* I CAN'T BE EXPECTED TO WORK **NOW.**
I THOUGHT YOU WERE GOING TO FINISH THE McCALL PROJECT TODAY, SO YOU'D GET PAID...
LIFE'S TOO MUCH TODAY. MY SOUL NEEDS REPLENISHING. I DESERVE A BREAK.
YOU OWE ME **RENT.** YOU HAVEN'T PAID FOR YOUR SHARE OF THE GROCERIES. AND THAT LOAN I FLOATED YOU IS DUE **BEFORE** THE HOLIDAYS.
WHAT HAPPENED TO A DAY OFF "BECAUSE I'M *WORTH* IT"?
APPARENTLY MY "WORTH" CAN ONLY AFFORD A FIVE-MINUTE BREAK ON THE COUCH.
TICKA TICKA

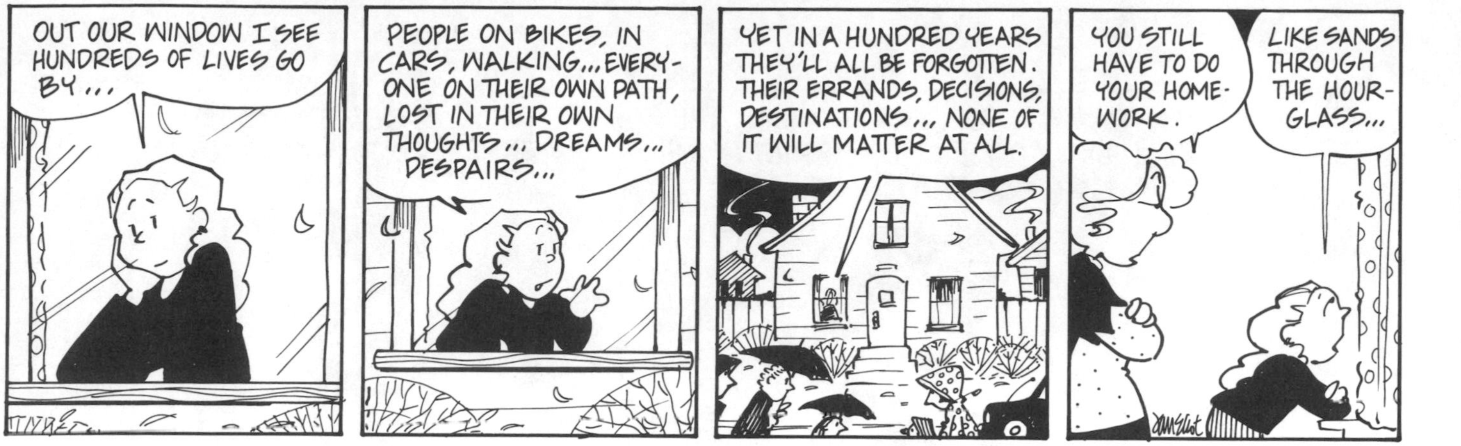
OUT OUR WINDOW I SEE HUNDREDS OF LIVES GO BY...
PEOPLE ON BIKES, IN CARS, WALKING... EVERY-ONE ON THEIR OWN PATH, LOST IN THEIR OWN THOUGHTS... DREAMS... DESPAIRS...
YET IN A HUNDRED YEARS THEY'LL ALL BE FORGOTTEN. THEIR ERRANDS, DECISIONS, DESTINATIONS... NONE OF IT WILL MATTER AT ALL.
LIKE SANDS THROUGH THE HOUR-GLASS...
YOU STILL HAVE TO DO YOUR HOME-WORK.

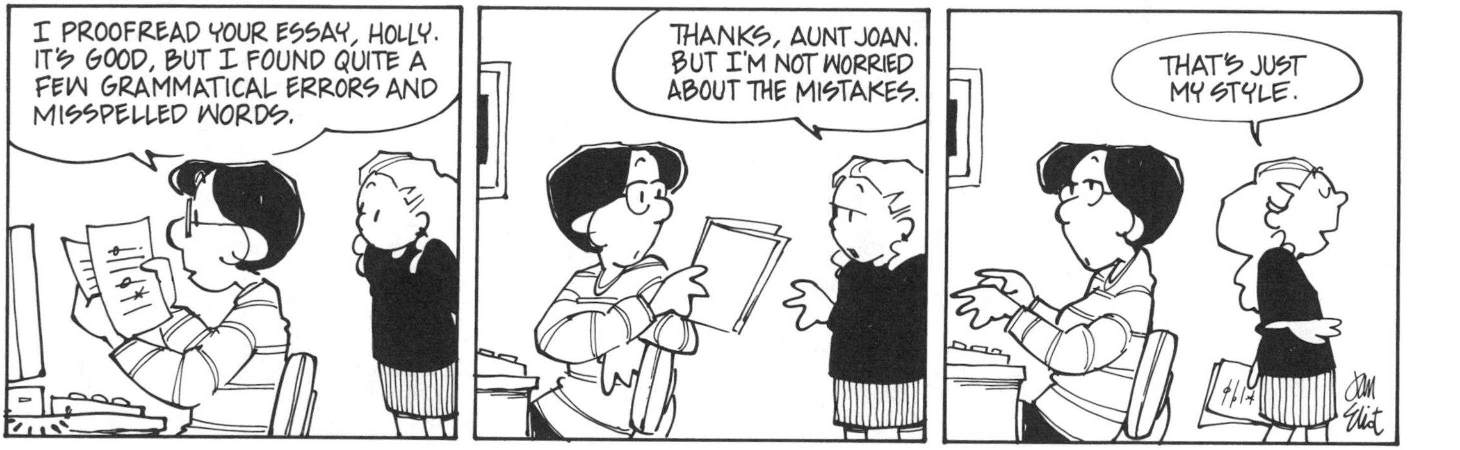
I PROOFREAD YOUR ESSAY, HOLLY. IT'S GOOD, BUT I FOUND QUITE A FEW GRAMMATICAL ERRORS AND MISSPELLED WORDS.
THANKS, AUNT JOAN. BUT I'M NOT WORRIED ABOUT THE MISTAKES.
THAT'S JUST MY STYLE.

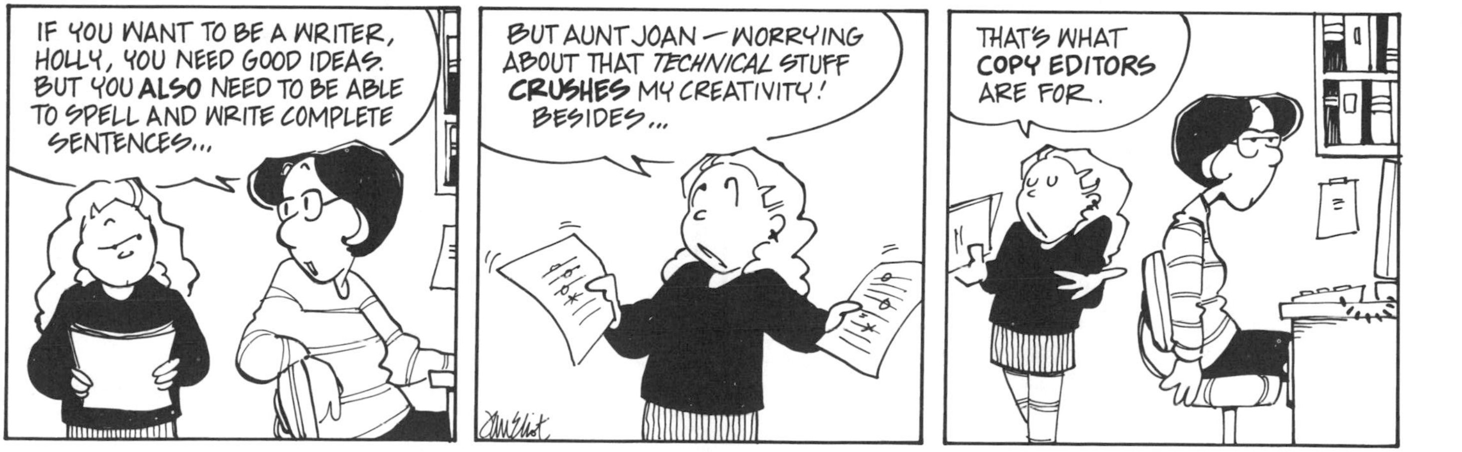
IF YOU WANT TO BE A WRITER, HOLLY, YOU NEED GOOD IDEAS. BUT YOU **ALSO** NEED TO BE ABLE TO SPELL AND WRITE COMPLETE SENTENCES...
BUT AUNT JOAN — WORRYING ABOUT THAT *TECHNICAL* STUFF **CRUSHES** MY CREATIVITY! BESIDES...
THAT'S WHAT **COPY EDITORS** ARE FOR.

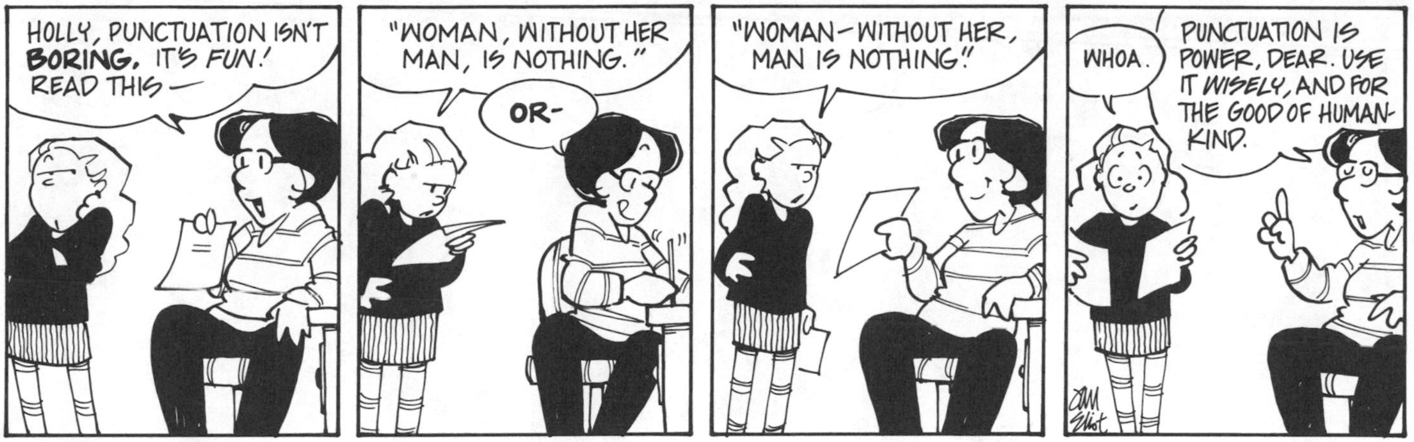
HOLLY, PUNCTUATION ISN'T **BORING.** IT'S *FUN!* READ THIS —
"WOMAN, WITHOUT HER MAN, IS NOTHING."
OR-
"WOMAN - WITHOUT HER, MAN IS NOTHING."
WHOA.
PUNCTUATION IS POWER, DEAR. USE IT *WISELY*, AND FOR THE GOOD OF HUMAN-KIND.

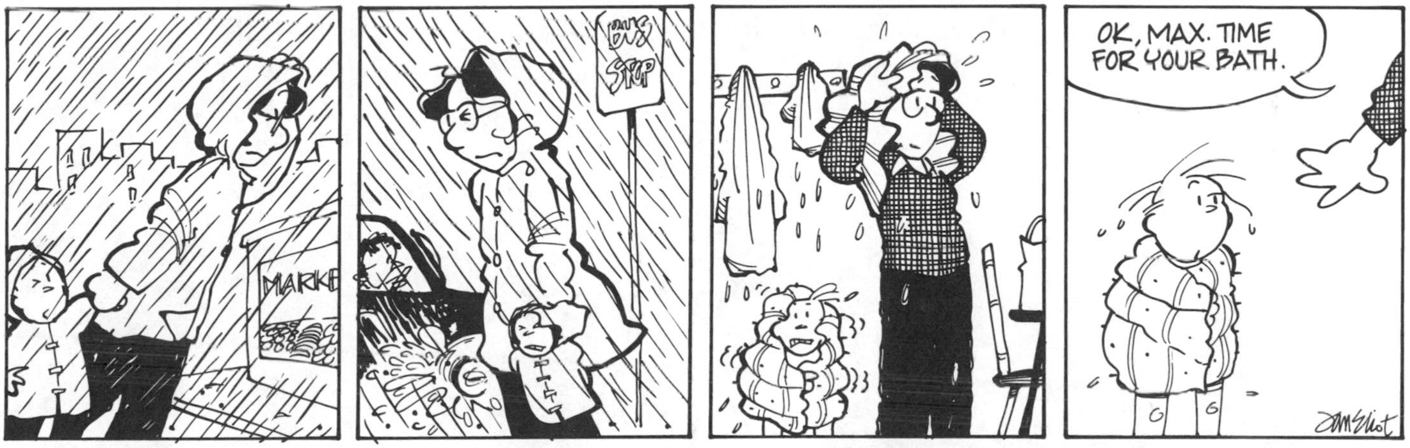
MARKE
BUS STOP
OK, MAX. TIME FOR YOUR BATH.

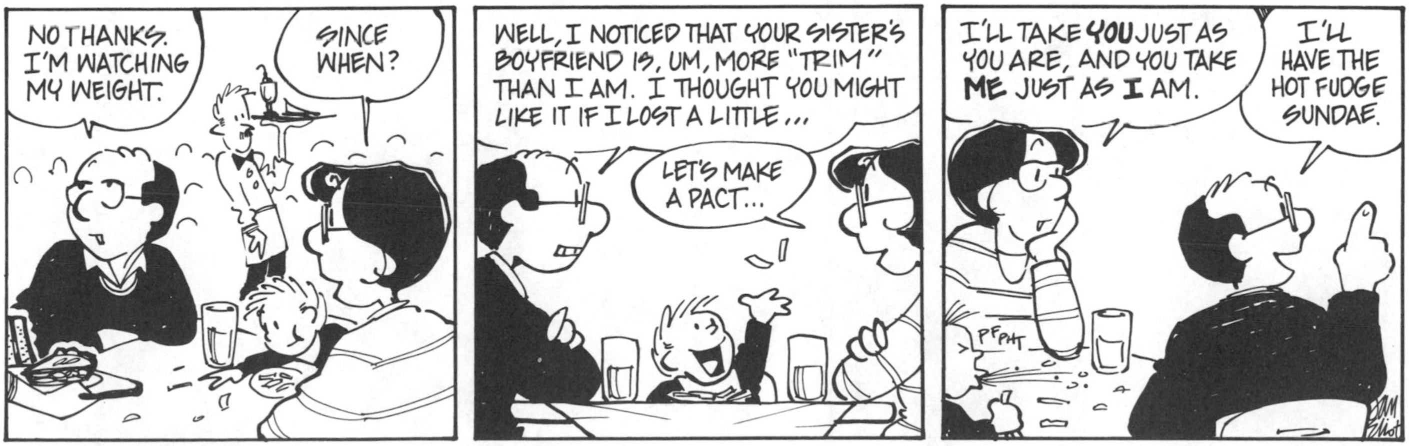
NO THANKS. I'M WATCHING MY WEIGHT.
SINCE WHEN?
WELL, I NOTICED THAT YOUR SISTER'S BOYFRIEND IS, UM, MORE "TRIM" THAN I AM. I THOUGHT YOU MIGHT LIKE IT IF I LOST A LITTLE...
LET'S MAKE A PACT...
I'LL TAKE **YOU** JUST AS YOU ARE, AND YOU TAKE **ME** JUST AS **I** AM.
I'LL HAVE THE HOT FUDGE SUNDAE.
PFPHT

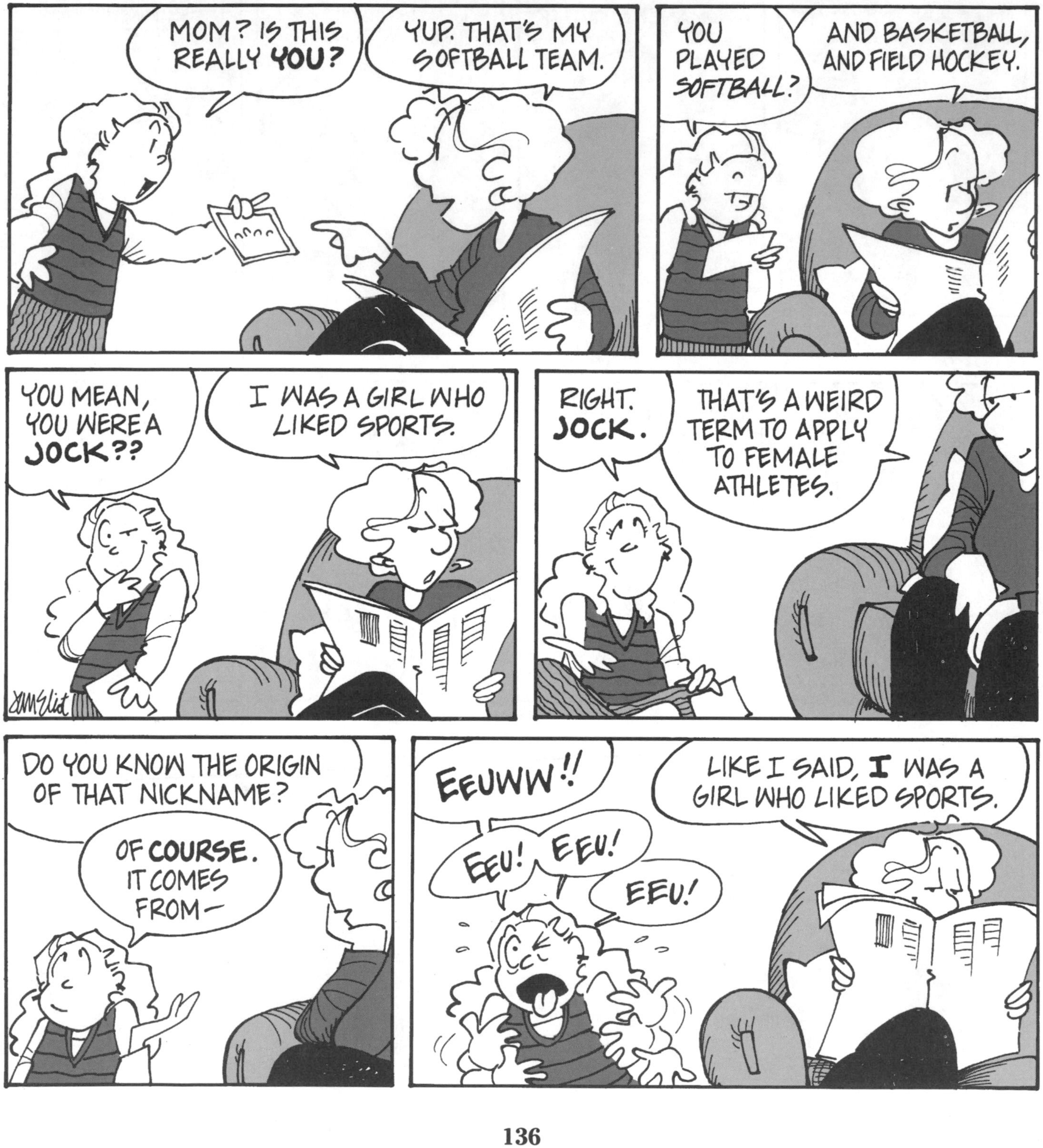
MOM? IS THIS REALLY **YOU**?
YUP. THAT'S MY SOFTBALL TEAM.
YOU PLAYED SOFTBALL?
AND BASKETBALL, AND FIELD HOCKEY.
YOU MEAN, YOU WERE A **JOCK**??
I WAS A GIRL WHO LIKED SPORTS.
RIGHT. **JOCK**.
THAT'S A WEIRD TERM TO APPLY TO FEMALE ATHLETES.
DO YOU KNOW THE ORIGIN OF THAT NICKNAME?
OF **COURSE**. IT COMES FROM—
EEUWW!!
EEU! EEU!
EEU!
LIKE I SAID, **I** WAS A GIRL WHO LIKED SPORTS.

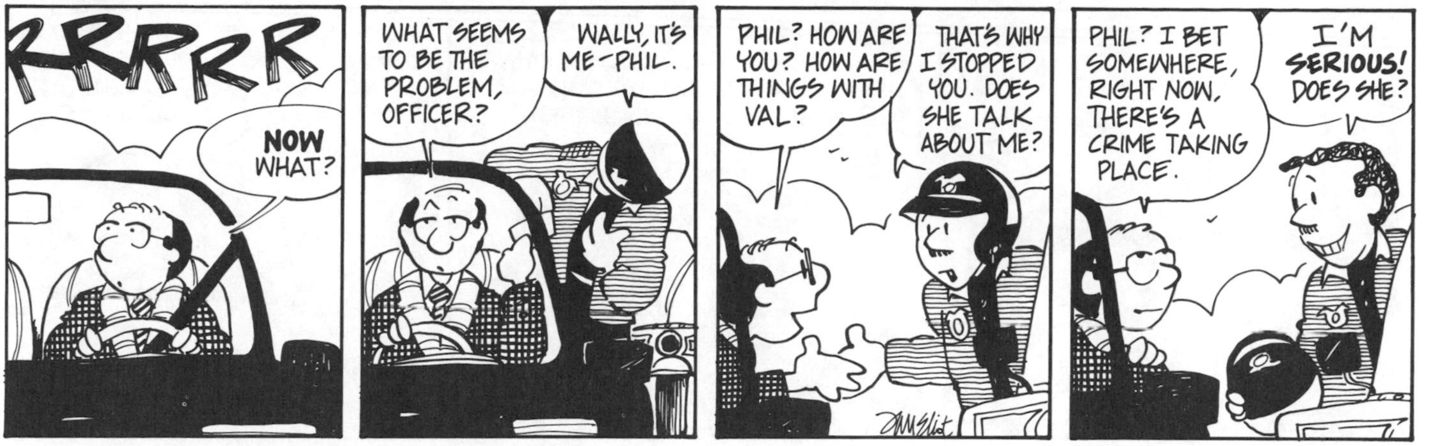
RRRRR
NOW WHAT?
WHAT SEEMS TO BE THE PROBLEM, OFFICER?
WALLY, IT'S ME-PHIL.
PHIL? HOW ARE YOU? HOW ARE THINGS WITH VAL?
THAT'S WHY I STOPPED YOU. DOES SHE TALK ABOUT ME?
PHIL? I BET SOMEWHERE, RIGHT NOW, THERE'S A CRIME TAKING PLACE.
I'M SERIOUS! DOES SHE?

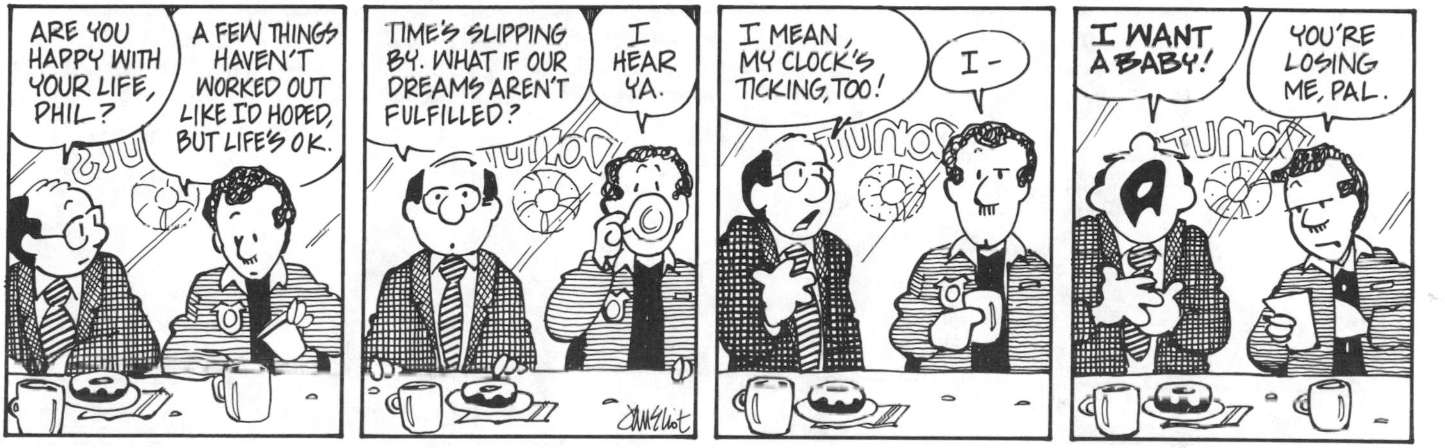
ARE YOU HAPPY WITH YOUR LIFE, PHIL?
A FEW THINGS HAVEN'T WORKED OUT LIKE I'D HOPED, BUT LIFE'S OK.
TIME'S SLIPPING BY. WHAT IF OUR DREAMS AREN'T FULFILLED?
I HEAR YA.
I MEAN, MY CLOCK'S TICKING, TOO!
I -
I WANT A BABY!
YOU'RE LOSING ME, PAL.

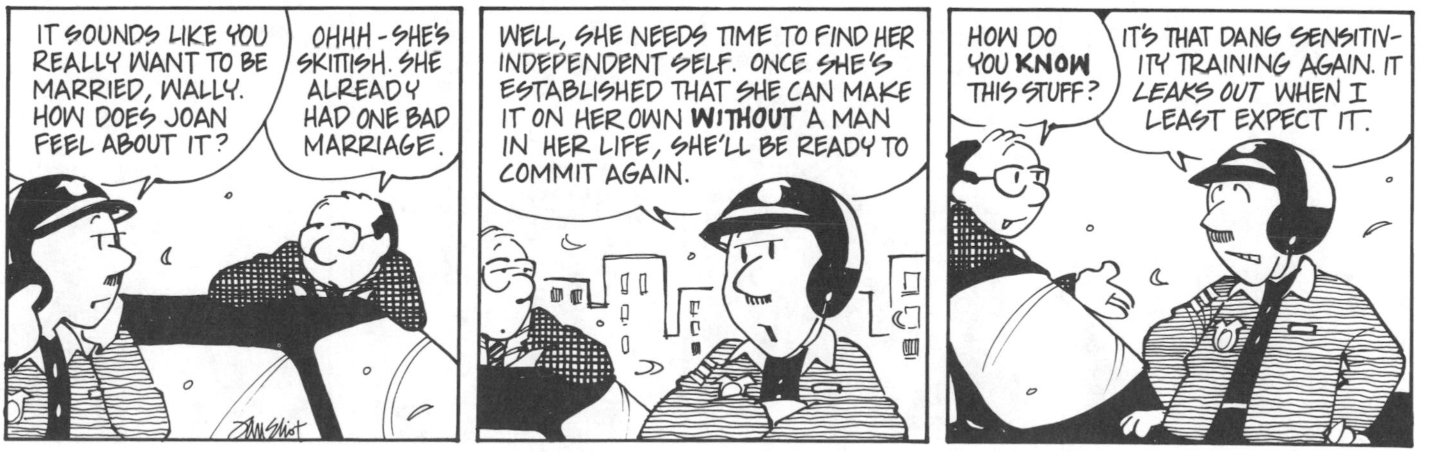
IT SOUNDS LIKE YOU REALLY WANT TO BE MARRIED, WALLY. HOW DOES JOAN FEEL ABOUT IT?
OHHH - SHE'S SKITTISH. SHE ALREADY HAD ONE BAD MARRIAGE.
WELL, SHE NEEDS TIME TO FIND HER INDEPENDENT SELF. ONCE SHE'S ESTABLISHED THAT SHE CAN MAKE IT ON HER OWN WITHOUT A MAN IN HER LIFE, SHE'LL BE READY TO COMMIT AGAIN.
HOW DO YOU KNOW THIS STUFF?
IT'S THAT DANG SENSITIVITY TRAINING AGAIN. IT LEAKS OUT WHEN I LEAST EXPECT IT.

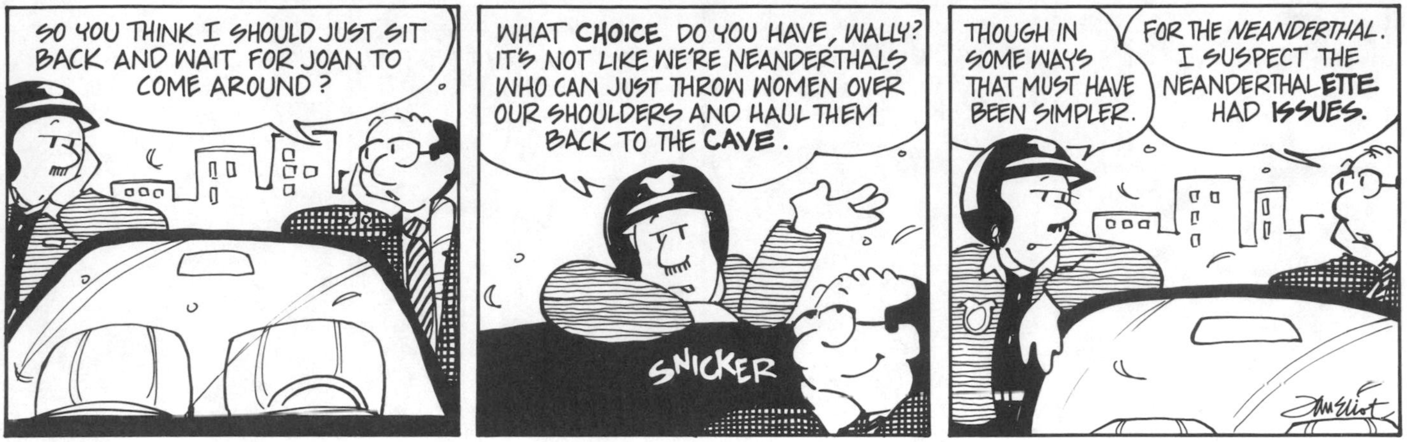
SO YOU THINK I SHOULD JUST SIT BACK AND WAIT FOR JOAN TO COME AROUND?
WHAT CHOICE DO YOU HAVE, WALLY? IT'S NOT LIKE WE'RE NEANDERTHALS WHO CAN JUST THROW WOMEN OVER OUR SHOULDERS AND HAUL THEM BACK TO THE CAVE.
SNICKER
THOUGH IN SOME WAYS THAT MUST HAVE BEEN SIMPLER.
FOR THE NEANDERTHAL. I SUSPECT THE NEANDERTHALETTE HAD ISSUES.

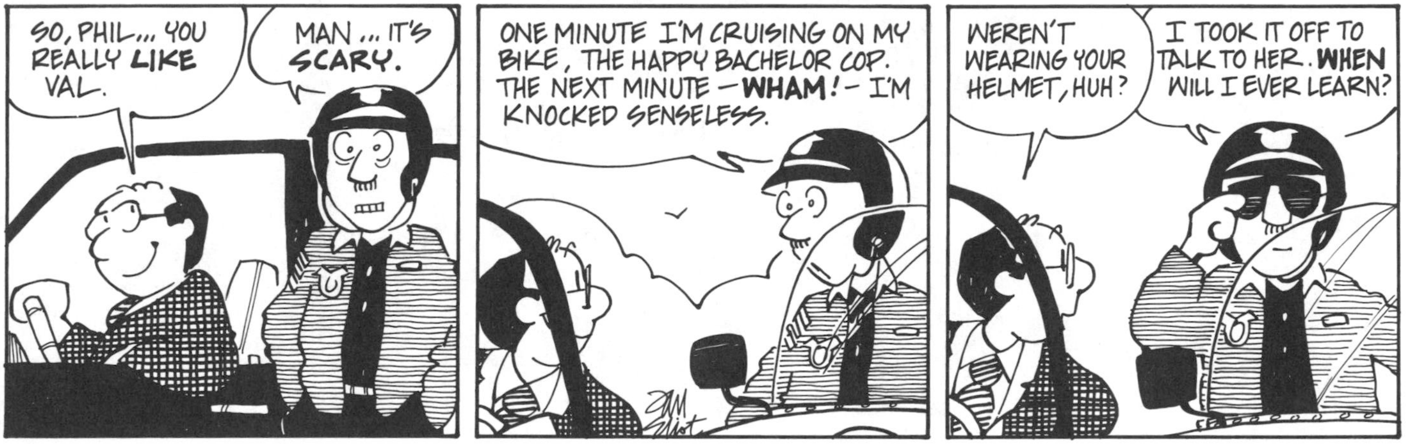
SO, PHIL... YOU REALLY LIKE VAL.
MAN... IT'S SCARY.
ONE MINUTE I'M CRUISING ON MY BIKE, THE HAPPY BACHELOR COP. THE NEXT MINUTE — WHAM! — I'M KNOCKED SENSELESS.
WEREN'T WEARING YOUR HELMET, HUH?
I TOOK IT OFF TO TALK TO HER. WHEN WILL I EVER LEARN?

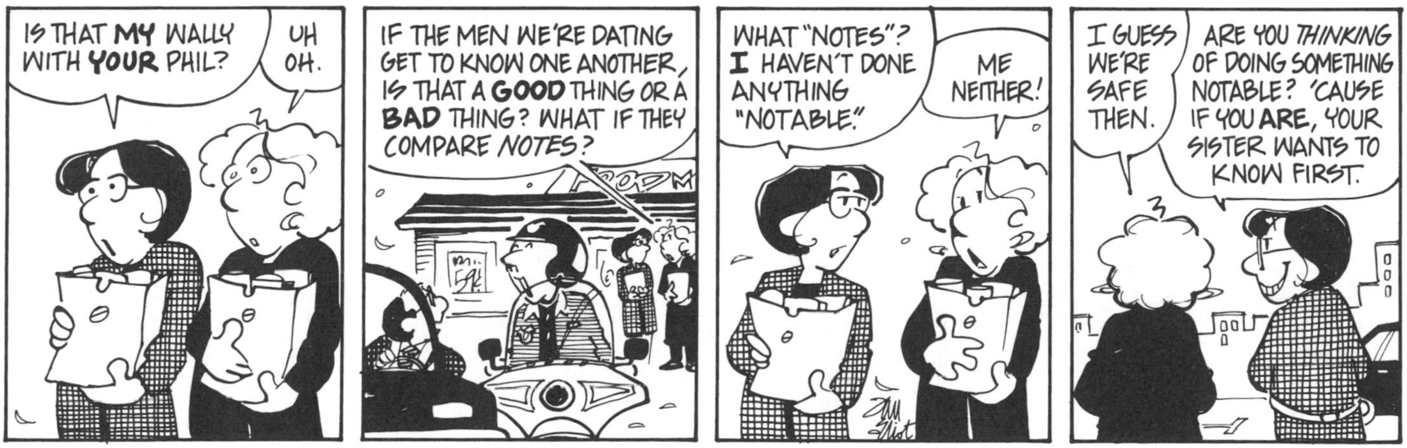
IS THAT MY WALLY WITH YOUR PHIL?
UH OH.
IF THE MEN WE'RE DATING GET TO KNOW ONE ANOTHER, IS THAT A GOOD THING OR A BAD THING? WHAT IF THEY COMPARE NOTES?
WHAT "NOTES"? I HAVEN'T DONE ANYTHING "NOTABLE."
ME NEITHER!
I GUESS WE'RE SAFE THEN.
ARE YOU THINKING OF DOING SOMETHING NOTABLE? 'CAUSE IF YOU ARE, YOUR SISTER WANTS TO KNOW FIRST.

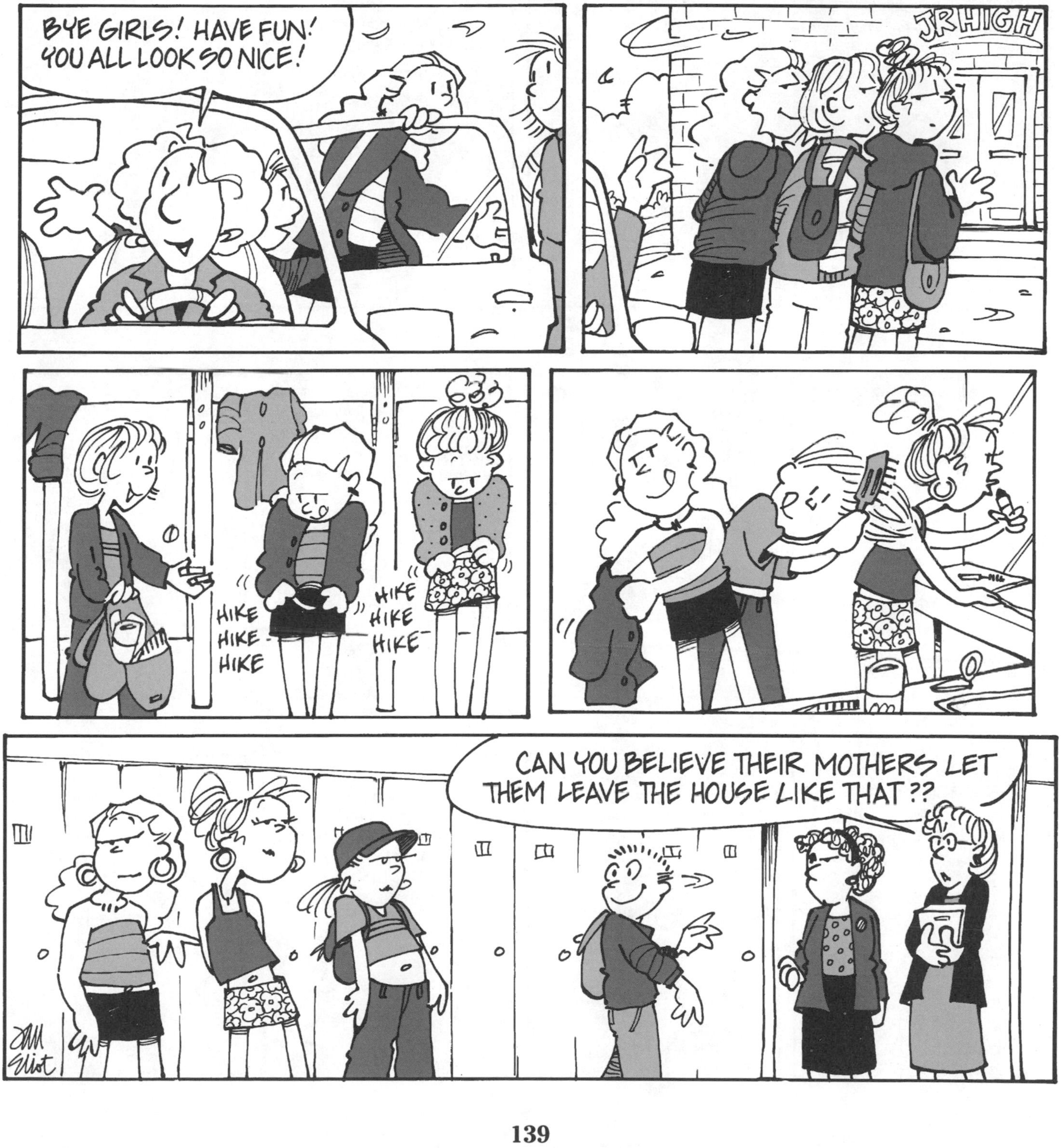
BYE GIRLS! HAVE FUN! YOU ALL LOOK SO NICE!
JR HIGH
HIKE HIKE HIKE
HIKE HIKE HIKE
CAN YOU BELIEVE THEIR MOTHERS LET THEM LEAVE THE HOUSE LIKE THAT??

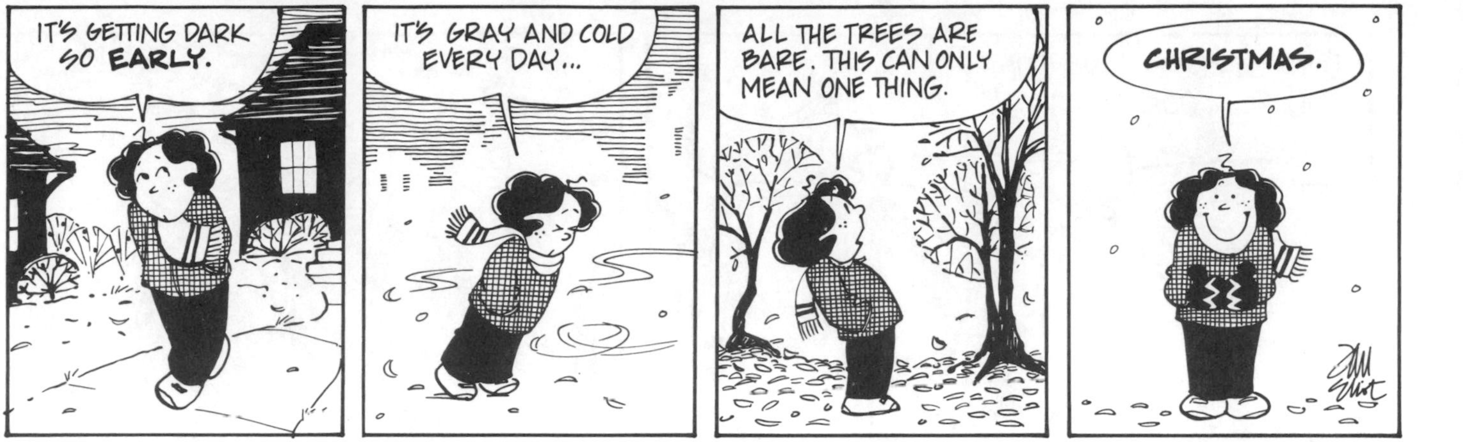
IT'S GETTING DARK SO EARLY.
IT'S GRAY AND COLD EVERY DAY...
ALL THE TREES ARE BARE. THIS CAN ONLY MEAN ONE THING.
CHRISTMAS.

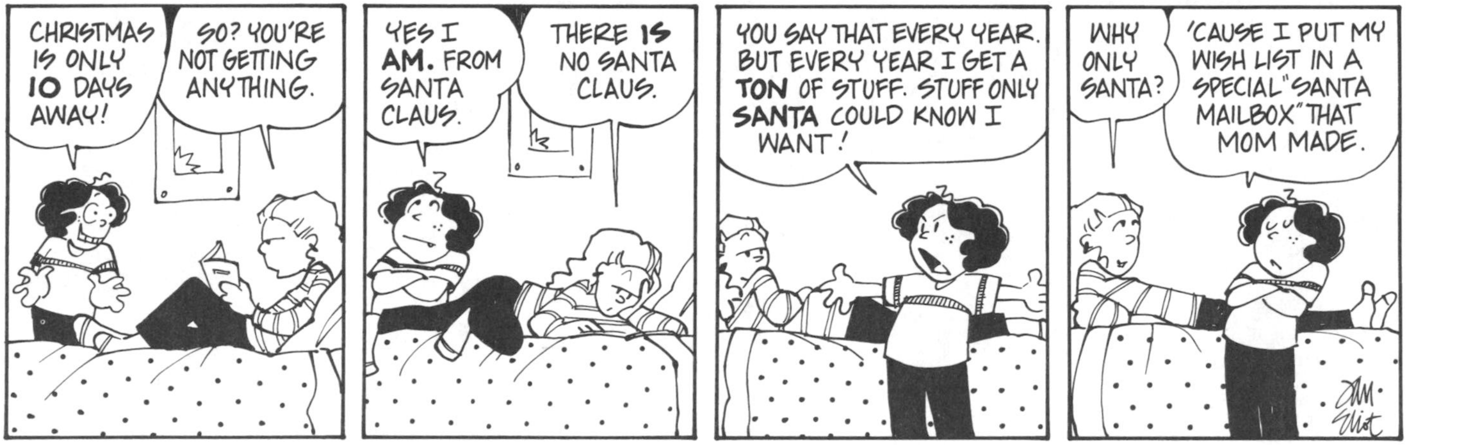
CHRISTMAS IS ONLY 10 DAYS AWAY!
SO? YOU'RE NOT GETTING ANYTHING.
YES I AM. FROM SANTA CLAUS.
THERE IS NO SANTA CLAUS.
YOU SAY THAT EVERY YEAR. BUT EVERY YEAR I GET A TON OF STUFF. STUFF ONLY SANTA COULD KNOW I WANT!
WHY ONLY SANTA?
'CAUSE I PUT MY WISH LIST IN A SPECIAL "SANTA MAILBOX" THAT MOM MADE.

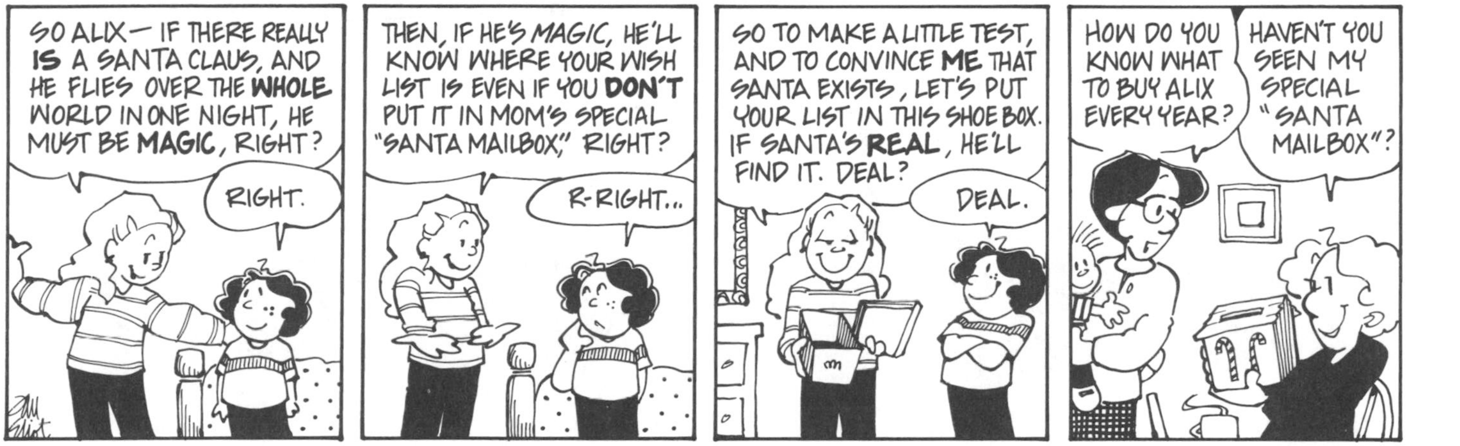
SO ALIX— IF THERE REALLY IS A SANTA CLAUS, AND HE FLIES OVER THE WHOLE WORLD IN ONE NIGHT, HE MUST BE MAGIC, RIGHT?
RIGHT.
THEN, IF HE'S MAGIC, HE'LL KNOW WHERE YOUR WISH LIST IS EVEN IF YOU DON'T PUT IT IN MOM'S SPECIAL "SANTA MAILBOX," RIGHT?
R-RIGHT...
SO TO MAKE A LITTLE TEST, AND TO CONVINCE ME THAT SANTA EXISTS, LET'S PUT YOUR LIST IN THIS SHOE BOX. IF SANTA'S REAL, HE'LL FIND IT. DEAL?
DEAL.
HOW DO YOU KNOW WHAT TO BUY ALIX EVERY YEAR?
HAVEN'T YOU SEEN MY SPECIAL "SANTA MAILBOX"?

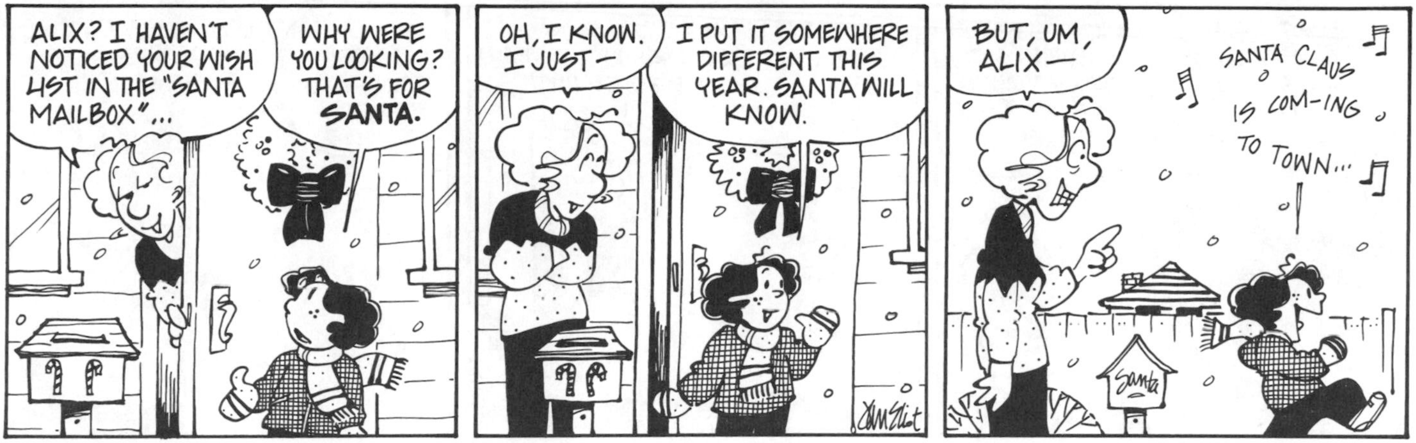
ALIX? I HAVEN'T NOTICED YOUR WISH LIST IN THE "SANTA MAILBOX"...
WHY WERE YOU LOOKING? THAT'S FOR SANTA.
OH, I KNOW. I JUST—
I PUT IT SOMEWHERE DIFFERENT THIS YEAR. SANTA WILL KNOW.
BUT, UM, ALIX—
SANTA CLAUS IS COM-ING TO TOWN...
SANTA

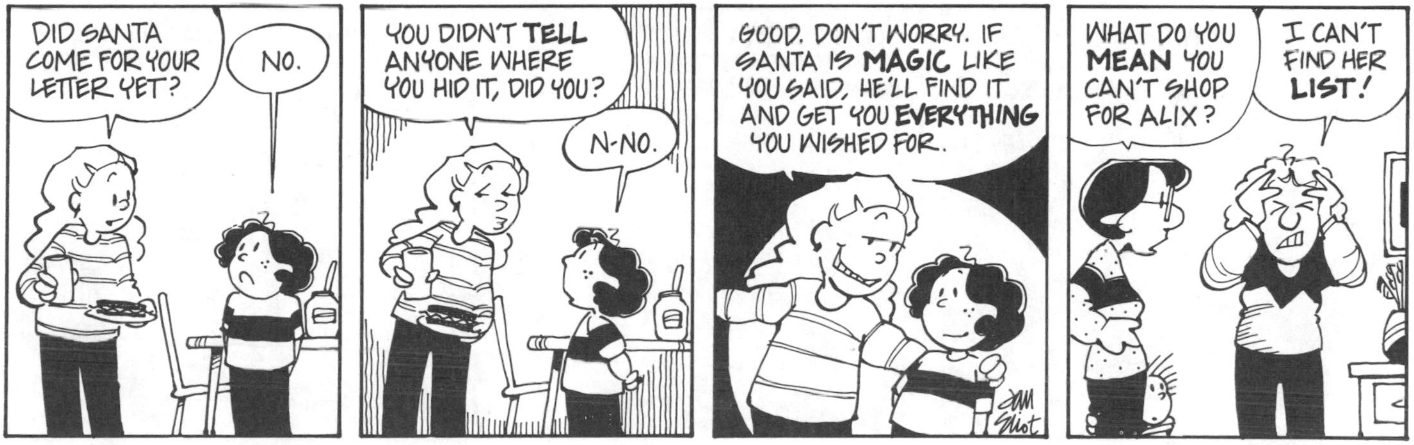
DID SANTA COME FOR YOUR LETTER YET?
NO.
YOU DIDN'T TELL ANYONE WHERE YOU HID IT, DID YOU?
N-NO.
GOOD. DON'T WORRY. IF SANTA IS MAGIC LIKE YOU SAID, HE'LL FIND IT AND GET YOU EVERYTHING YOU WISHED FOR.
WHAT DO YOU MEAN YOU CAN'T SHOP FOR ALIX?
I CAN'T FIND HER LIST!

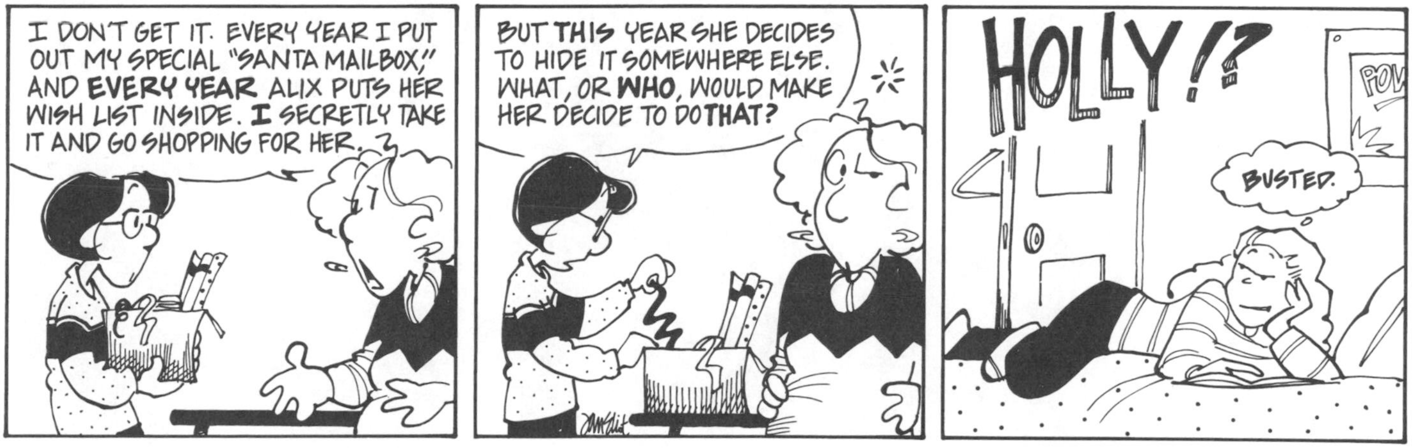
I DON'T GET IT. EVERY YEAR I PUT OUT MY SPECIAL "SANTA MAILBOX," AND EVERY YEAR ALIX PUTS HER WISH LIST INSIDE. I SECRETLY TAKE IT AND GO SHOPPING FOR HER.
BUT THIS YEAR SHE DECIDES TO HIDE IT SOMEWHERE ELSE. WHAT, OR WHO, WOULD MAKE HER DECIDE TO DO THAT?
HOLLY!?
BUSTED.

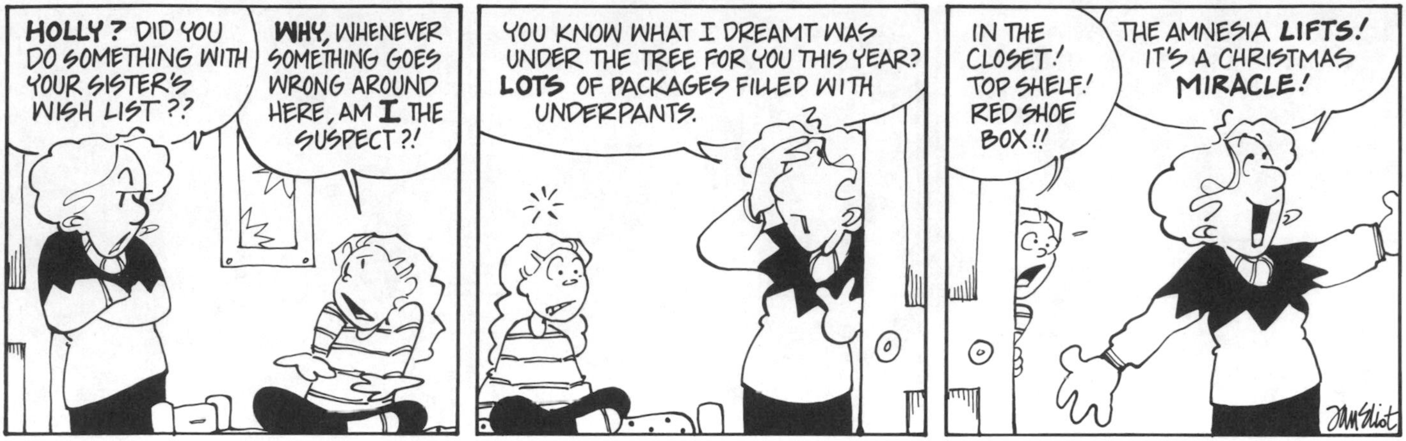
HOLLY? DID YOU DO SOMETHING WITH YOUR SISTER'S WISH LIST??
WHY, WHENEVER SOMETHING GOES WRONG AROUND HERE, AM I THE SUSPECT?!
YOU KNOW WHAT I DREAMT WAS UNDER THE TREE FOR YOU THIS YEAR? LOTS OF PACKAGES FILLED WITH UNDERPANTS.
IN THE CLOSET! TOP SHELF! RED SHOE BOX!!
THE AMNESIA LIFTS! IT'S A CHRISTMAS MIRACLE!

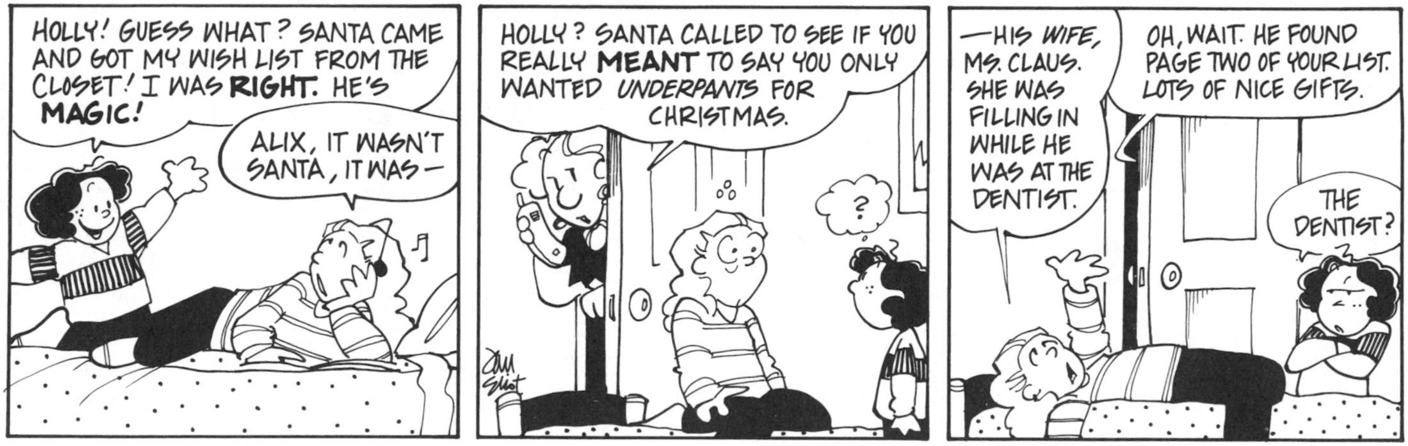
HOLLY! GUESS WHAT? SANTA CAME AND GOT MY WISH LIST FROM THE CLOSET! I WAS RIGHT. HE'S MAGIC!
ALIX, IT WASN'T SANTA, IT WAS—
HOLLY? SANTA CALLED TO SEE IF YOU REALLY MEANT TO SAY YOU ONLY WANTED UNDERPANTS FOR CHRISTMAS.
?
—HIS WIFE, MS. CLAUS. SHE WAS FILLING IN WHILE HE WAS AT THE DENTIST.
OH, WAIT. HE FOUND PAGE TWO OF YOUR LIST. LOTS OF NICE GIFTS.
THE DENTIST?

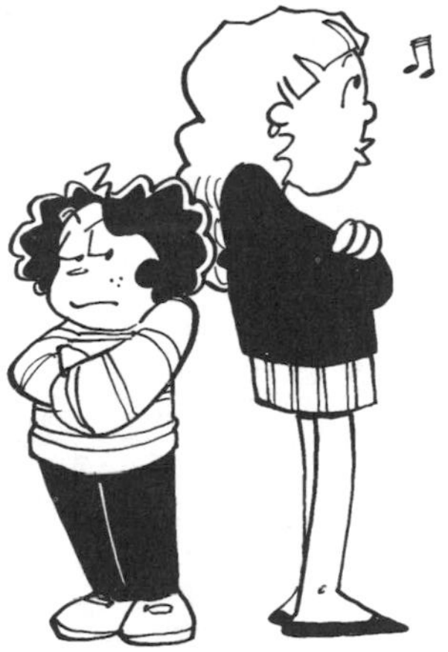

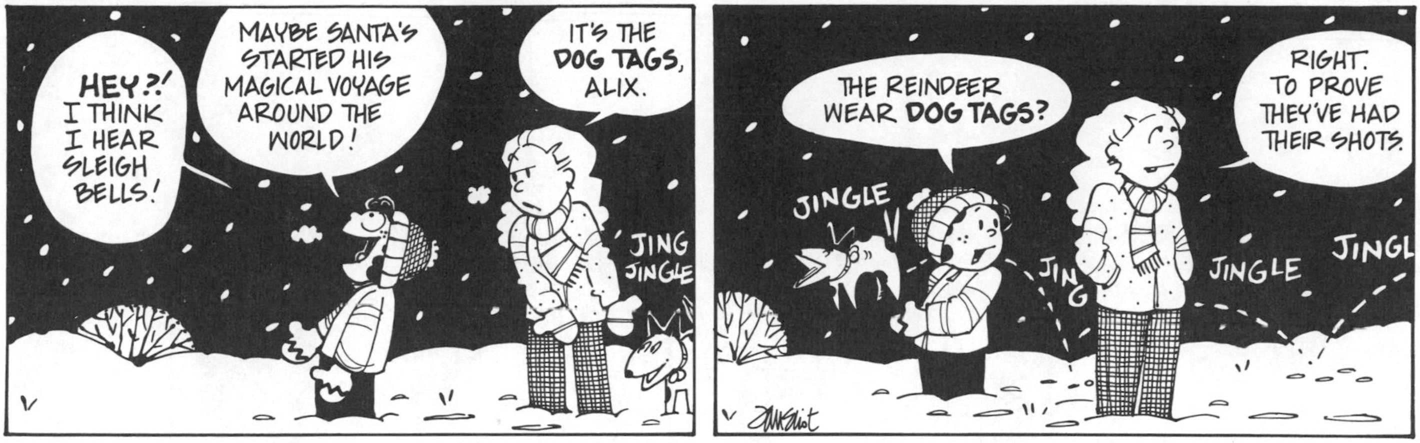
HEY?! I THINK I HEAR SLEIGH BELLS!
MAYBE SANTA'S STARTED HIS MAGICAL VOYAGE AROUND THE WORLD!
IT'S THE DOG TAGS, ALIX.
JING JINGLE
THE REINDEER WEAR DOG TAGS?
RIGHT. TO PROVE THEY'VE HAD THEIR SHOTS.
JINGLE
JING
JINGLE
JINGL

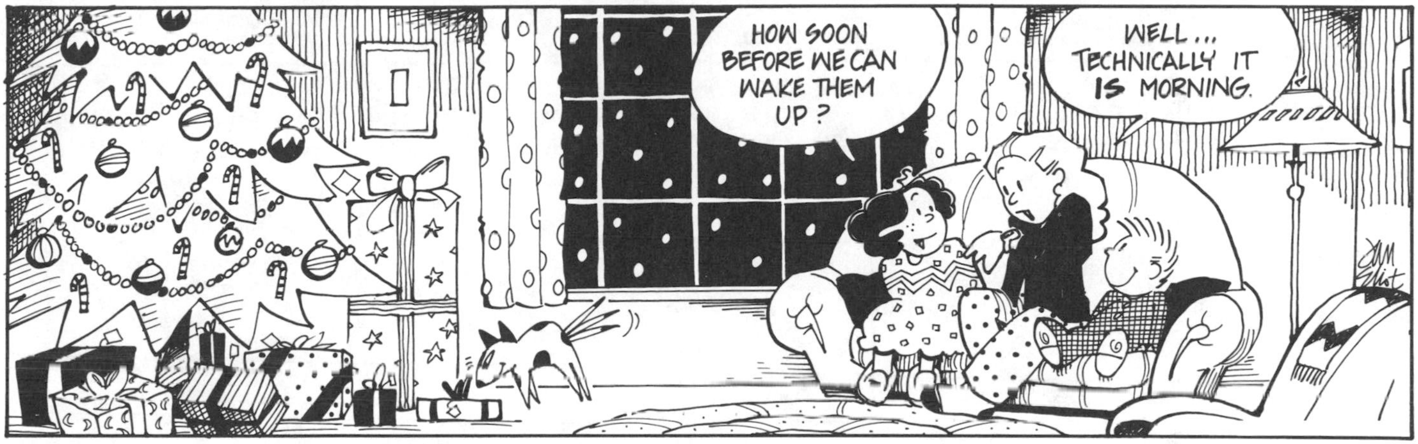
HOW SOON BEFORE WE CAN WAKE THEM UP?
WELL... TECHNICALLY IT IS MORNING.

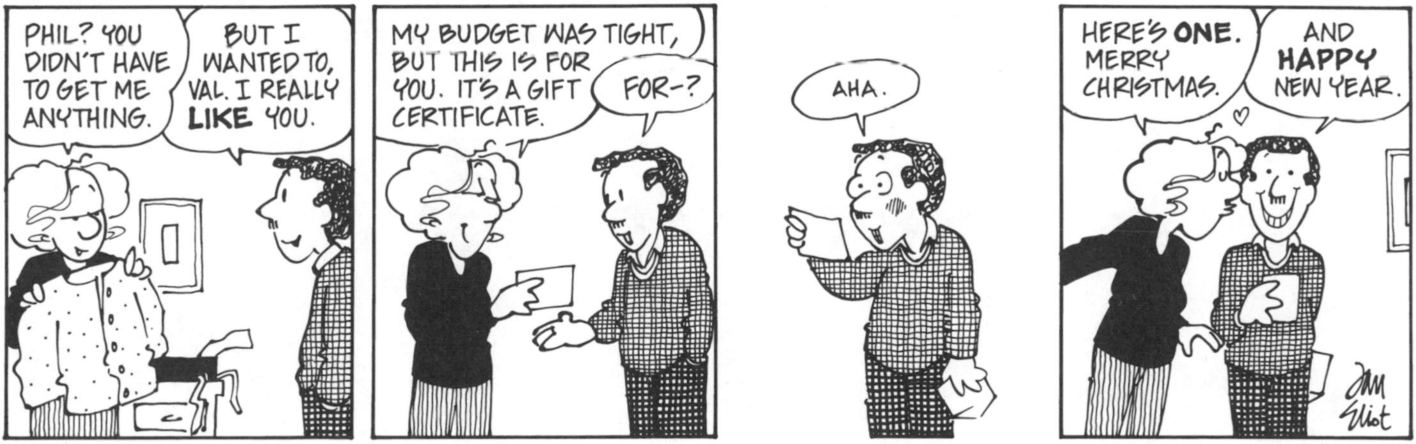
PHIL? YOU DIDN'T HAVE TO GET ME ANYTHING.
BUT I WANTED TO, VAL. I REALLY LIKE YOU.
MY BUDGET WAS TIGHT, BUT THIS IS FOR YOU. IT'S A GIFT CERTIFICATE.
FOR-?
AHA.
HERE'S ONE. MERRY CHRISTMAS.
AND HAPPY NEW YEAR.

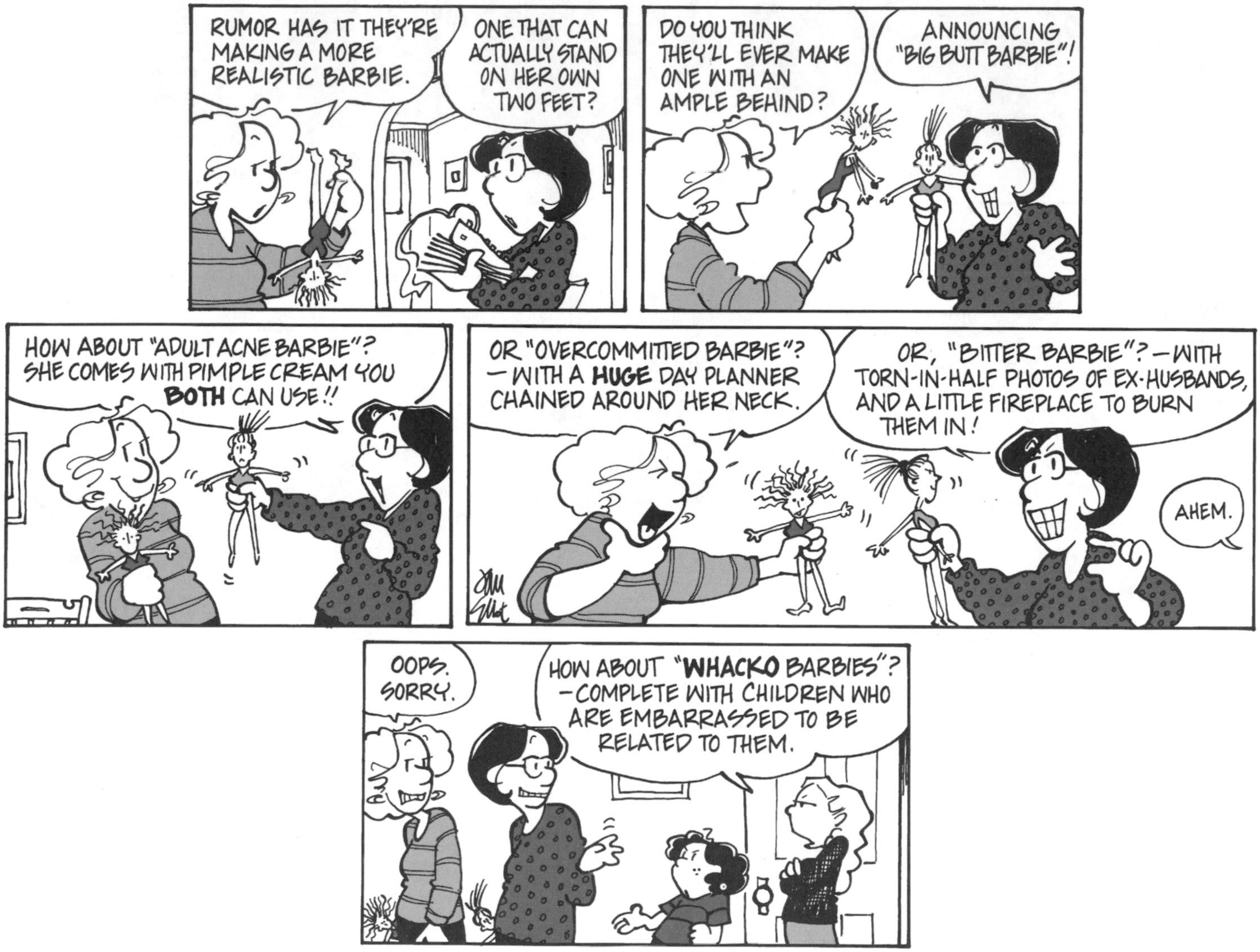
RUMOR HAS IT THEY'RE MAKING A MORE REALISTIC BARBIE.
ONE THAT CAN ACTUALLY STAND ON HER OWN TWO FEET?
DO YOU THINK THEY'LL EVER MAKE ONE WITH AN AMPLE BEHIND?
ANNOUNCING "BIG BUTT BARBIE"!
HOW ABOUT "ADULT ACNE BARBIE"? SHE COMES WITH PIMPLE CREAM YOU BOTH CAN USE!!
OR "OVERCOMMITTED BARBIE"? —WITH A HUGE DAY PLANNER CHAINED AROUND HER NECK.
OR, "BITTER BARBIE"? —WITH TORN-IN-HALF PHOTOS OF EX-HUSBANDS, AND A LITTLE FIREPLACE TO BURN THEM IN!
AHEM.
OOPS. SORRY.
HOW ABOUT "WHACKO BARBIES"? —COMPLETE WITH CHILDREN WHO ARE EMBARRASSED TO BE RELATED TO THEM.

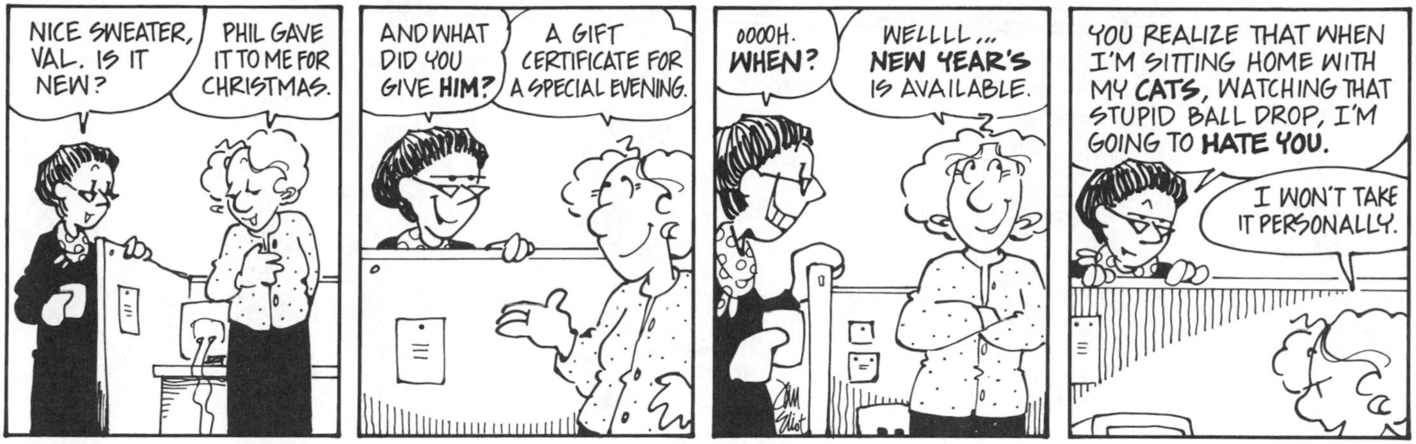
NICE SWEATER, VAL. IS IT NEW?
PHIL GAVE IT TO ME FOR CHRISTMAS.
AND WHAT DID YOU GIVE HIM?
A GIFT CERTIFICATE FOR A SPECIAL EVENING.
OOOOH. WHEN?
WELLLL... NEW YEAR'S IS AVAILABLE.
YOU REALIZE THAT WHEN I'M SITTING HOME WITH MY CATS, WATCHING THAT STUPID BALL DROP, I'M GOING TO HATE YOU.
I WON'T TAKE IT PERSONALLY.

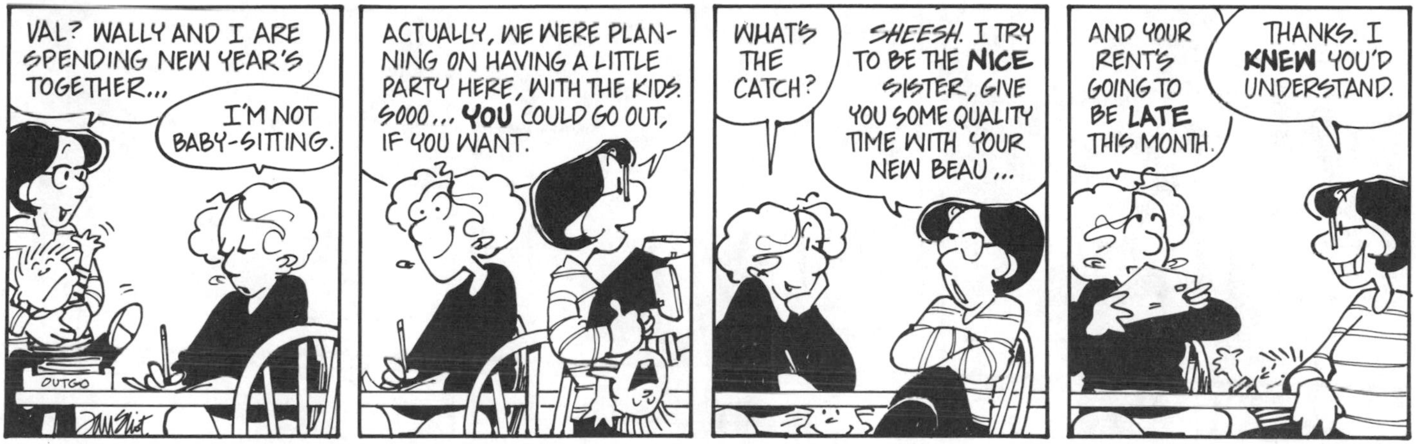
VAL? WALLY AND I ARE SPENDING NEW YEAR'S TOGETHER...
I'M NOT BABY-SITTING.
OUTGO
ACTUALLY, WE WERE PLANNING ON HAVING A LITTLE PARTY HERE, WITH THE KIDS. SOOO... YOU COULD GO OUT, IF YOU WANT.
WHAT'S THE CATCH?
SHEESH. I TRY TO BE THE NICE SISTER, GIVE YOU SOME QUALITY TIME WITH YOUR NEW BEAU...
AND YOUR RENT'S GOING TO BE LATE THIS MONTH.
THANKS. I KNEW YOU'D UNDERSTAND.

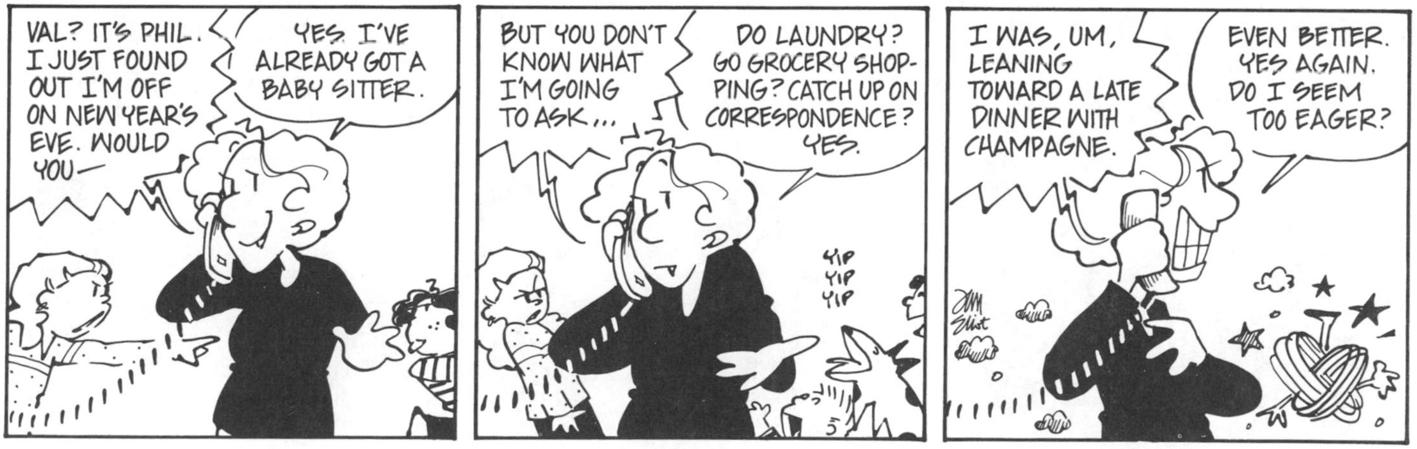
VAL? IT'S PHIL. I JUST FOUND OUT I'M OFF ON NEW YEAR'S EVE. WOULD YOU—
YES. I'VE ALREADY GOT A BABY SITTER.
BUT YOU DON'T KNOW WHAT I'M GOING TO ASK...
DO LAUNDRY? GO GROCERY SHOPPING? CATCH UP ON CORRESPONDENCE? YES.
YIP YIP YIP
I WAS, UM, LEANING TOWARD A LATE DINNER WITH CHAMPAGNE.
EVEN BETTER. YES AGAIN. DO I SEEM TOO EAGER?

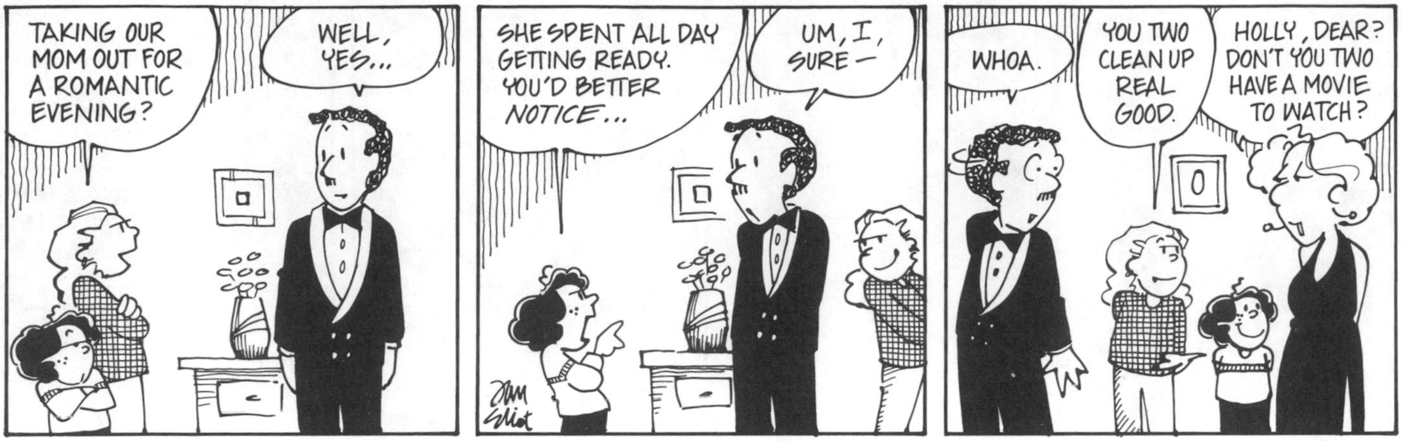
TAKING OUR MOM OUT FOR A ROMANTIC EVENING?
WELL, YES...
SHE SPENT ALL DAY GETTING READY. YOU'D BETTER *NOTICE*...
UM, I, SURE –
WHOA.
YOU TWO CLEAN UP REAL GOOD.
HOLLY, DEAR? DON'T YOU TWO HAVE A MOVIE TO WATCH?

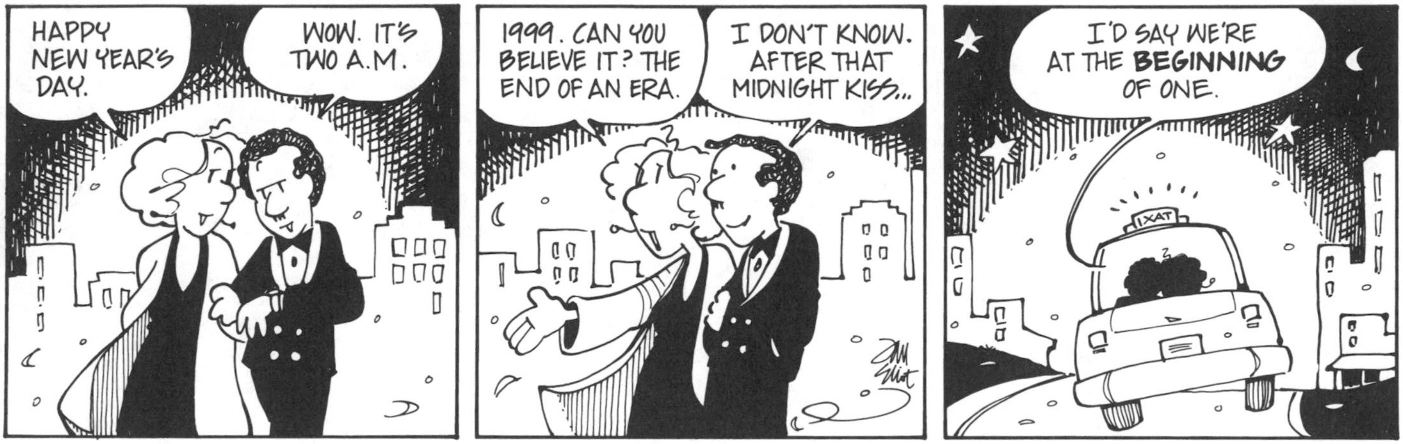
HAPPY NEW YEAR'S DAY.
WOW. IT'S TWO A.M.
1999. CAN YOU BELIEVE IT? THE END OF AN ERA.
I DON'T KNOW. AFTER THAT MIDNIGHT KISS...
I'D SAY WE'RE AT THE **BEGINNING** OF ONE.

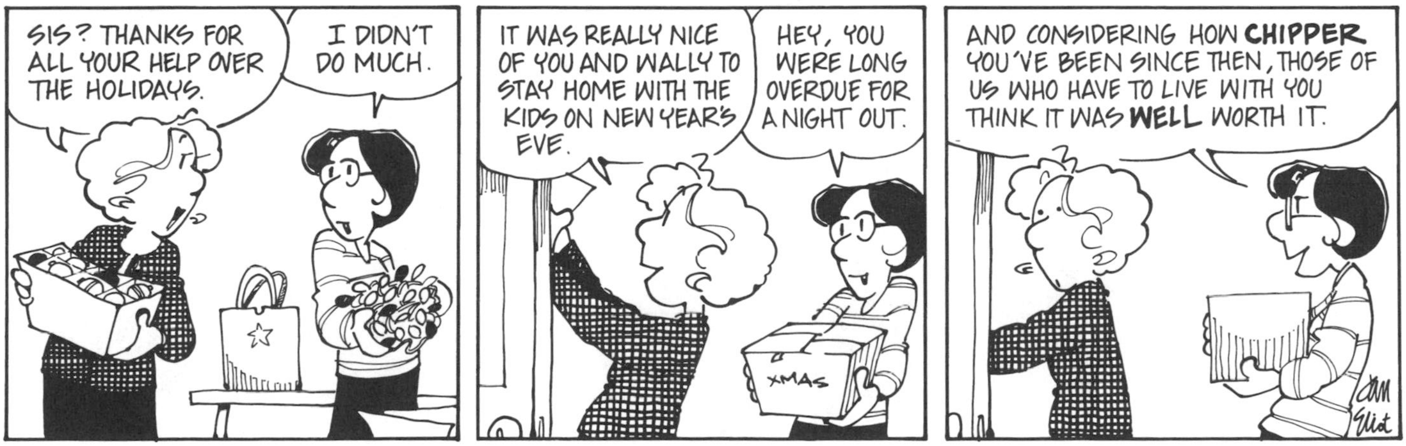
SIS? THANKS FOR ALL YOUR HELP OVER THE HOLIDAYS.
I DIDN'T DO MUCH.
IT WAS REALLY NICE OF YOU AND WALLY TO STAY HOME WITH THE KIDS ON NEW YEAR'S EVE.
HEY, YOU WERE LONG OVERDUE FOR A NIGHT OUT.
XMAS
AND CONSIDERING HOW **CHIPPER** YOU'VE BEEN SINCE THEN, THOSE OF US WHO HAVE TO LIVE WITH YOU THINK IT WAS **WELL** WORTH IT.

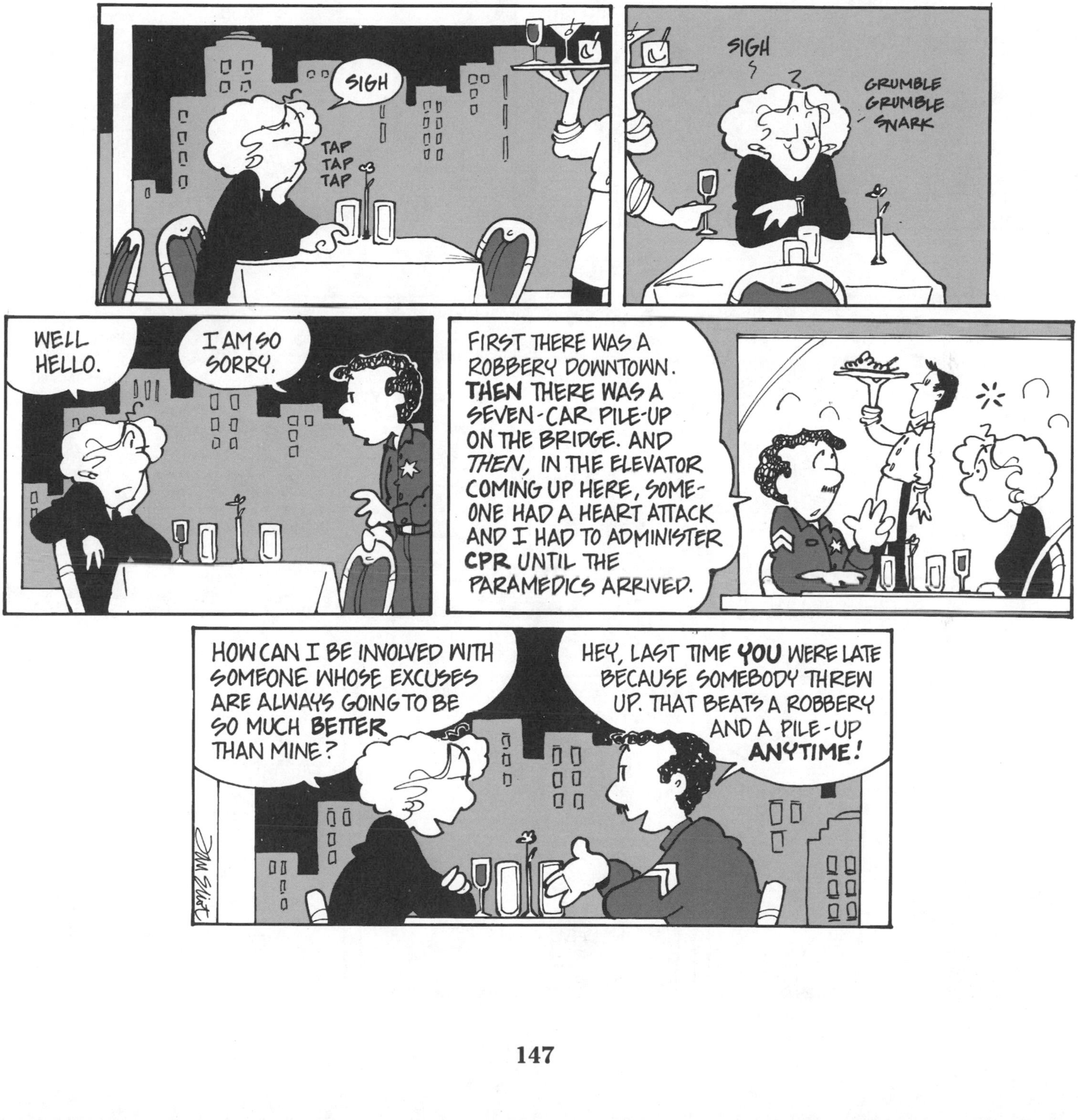
SIGH
TAP TAP TAP
SIGH
GRUMBLE GRUMBLE SNARK
WELL HELLO.
I AM SO SORRY.
FIRST THERE WAS A ROBBERY DOWNTOWN. THEN THERE WAS A SEVEN-CAR PILE-UP ON THE BRIDGE. AND THEN, IN THE ELEVATOR COMING UP HERE, SOMEONE HAD A HEART ATTACK AND I HAD TO ADMINISTER CPR UNTIL THE PARAMEDICS ARRIVED.
HOW CAN I BE INVOLVED WITH SOMEONE WHOSE EXCUSES ARE ALWAYS GOING TO BE SO MUCH BETTER THAN MINE?
HEY, LAST TIME YOU WERE LATE BECAUSE SOMEBODY THREW UP. THAT BEATS A ROBBERY AND A PILE-UP ANYTIME!

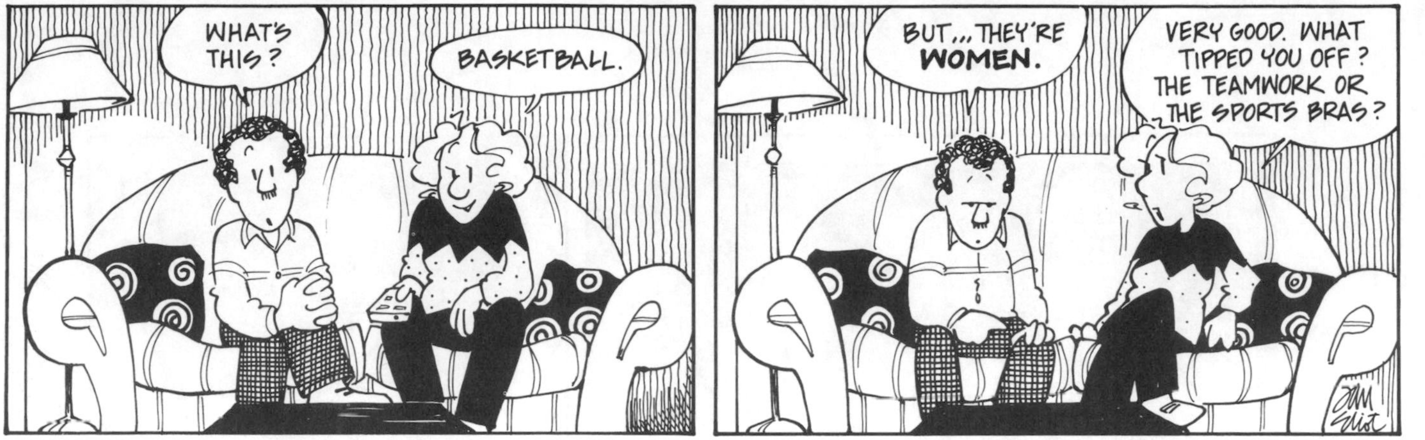
WHAT'S THIS?
BASKETBALL.
BUT... THEY'RE WOMEN.
VERY GOOD. WHAT TIPPED YOU OFF? THE TEAMWORK OR THE SPORTS BRAS?

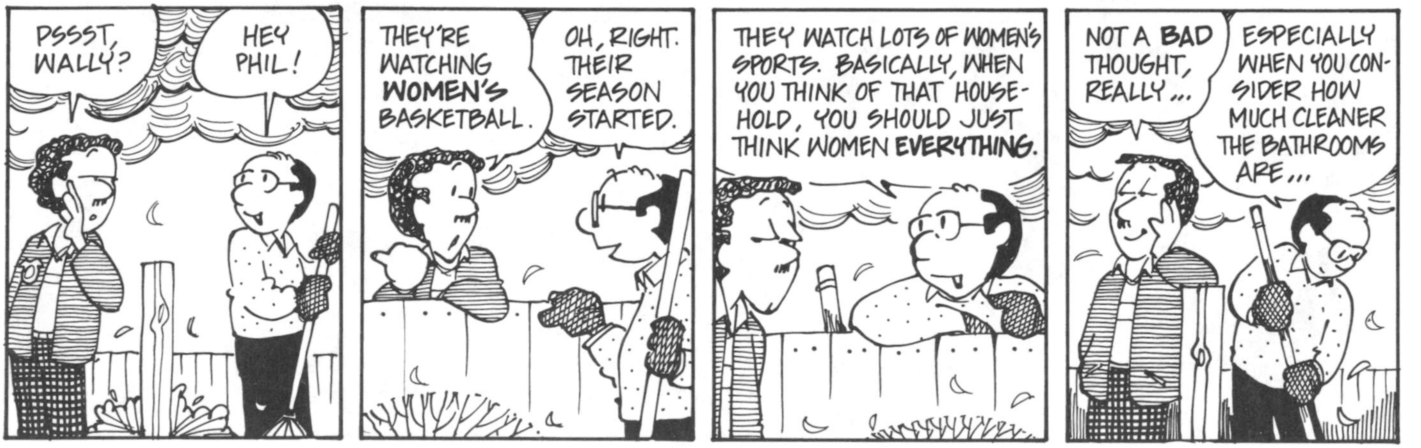
PSSST, WALLY?
HEY PHIL!
THEY'RE WATCHING WOMEN'S BASKETBALL.
OH, RIGHT. THEIR SEASON STARTED.
THEY WATCH LOTS OF WOMEN'S SPORTS. BASICALLY, WHEN YOU THINK OF THAT HOUSEHOLD, YOU SHOULD JUST THINK WOMEN EVERYTHING.
NOT A BAD THOUGHT, REALLY...
ESPECIALLY WHEN YOU CONSIDER HOW MUCH CLEANER THE BATHROOMS ARE...

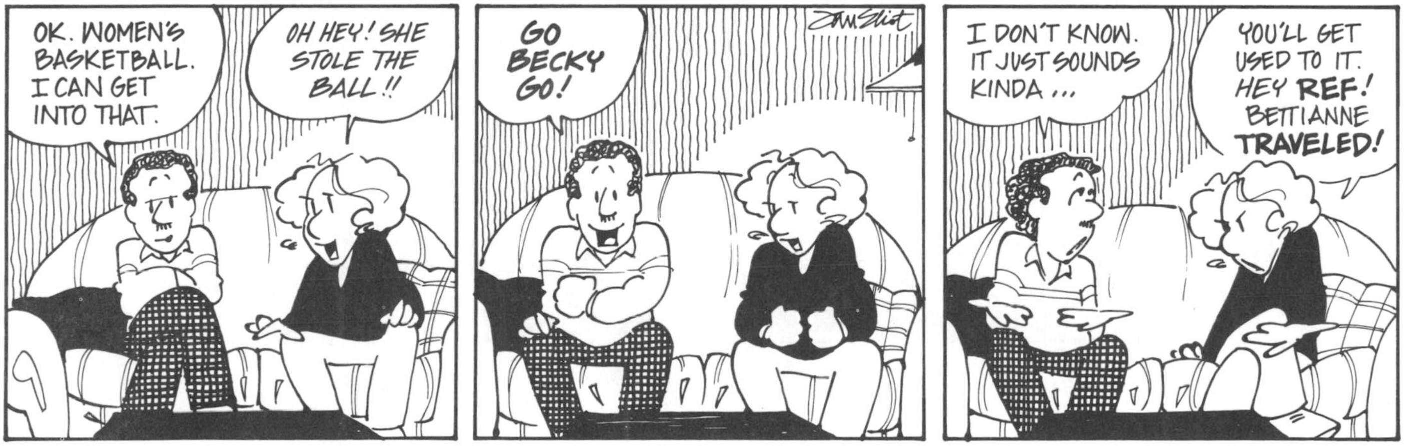
OK. WOMEN'S BASKETBALL. I CAN GET INTO THAT.
OH HEY! SHE STOLE THE BALL!!
GO BECKY GO!
I DON'T KNOW. IT JUST SOUNDS KINDA...
YOU'LL GET USED TO IT. HEY REF! BETTIANNE TRAVELED!

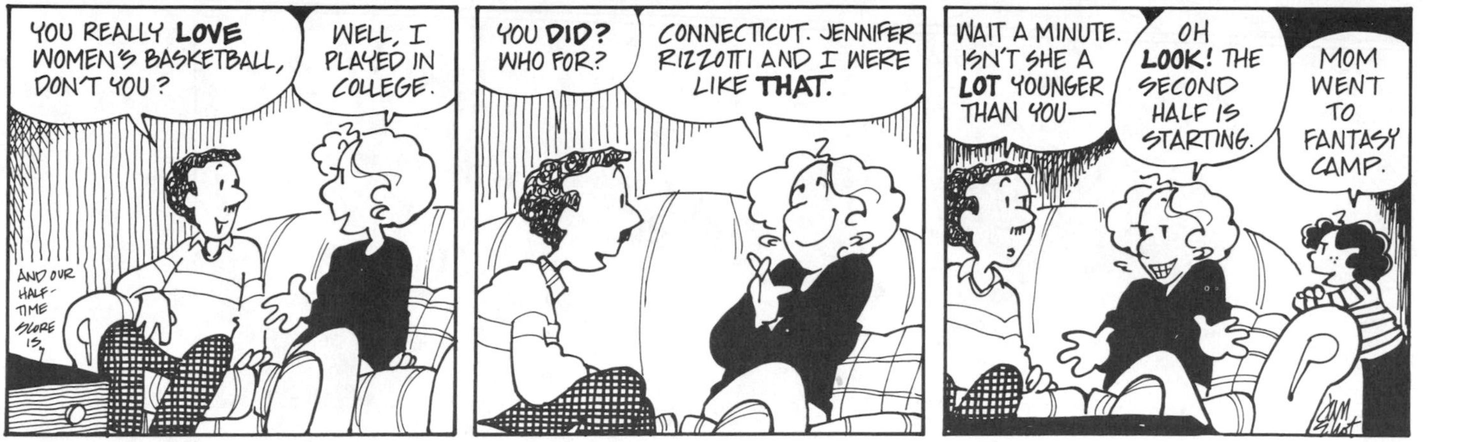
YOU REALLY **LOVE** WOMEN'S BASKETBALL, DON'T YOU?
WELL, I PLAYED IN COLLEGE.
AND OUR HALF-TIME SCORE IS,
YOU **DID?** WHO FOR?
CONNECTICUT. JENNIFER RIZZOTTI AND I WERE LIKE **THAT.**
WAIT A MINUTE. ISN'T SHE A **LOT** YOUNGER THAN YOU—
OH **LOOK!** THE SECOND HALF IS STARTING.
MOM WENT TO FANTASY CAMP.

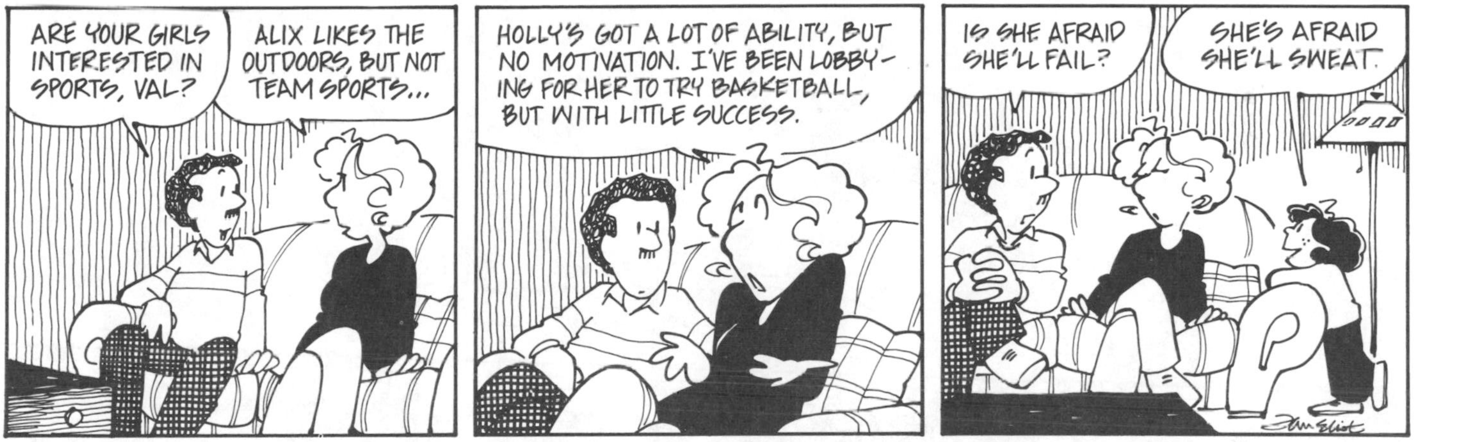
ARE YOUR GIRLS INTERESTED IN SPORTS, VAL?
ALIX LIKES THE OUTDOORS, BUT NOT TEAM SPORTS...
HOLLY'S GOT A LOT OF ABILITY, BUT NO MOTIVATION. I'VE BEEN LOBBYING FOR HER TO TRY BASKETBALL, BUT WITH LITTLE SUCCESS.
IS SHE AFRAID SHE'LL FAIL?
SHE'S AFRAID SHE'LL SWEAT.

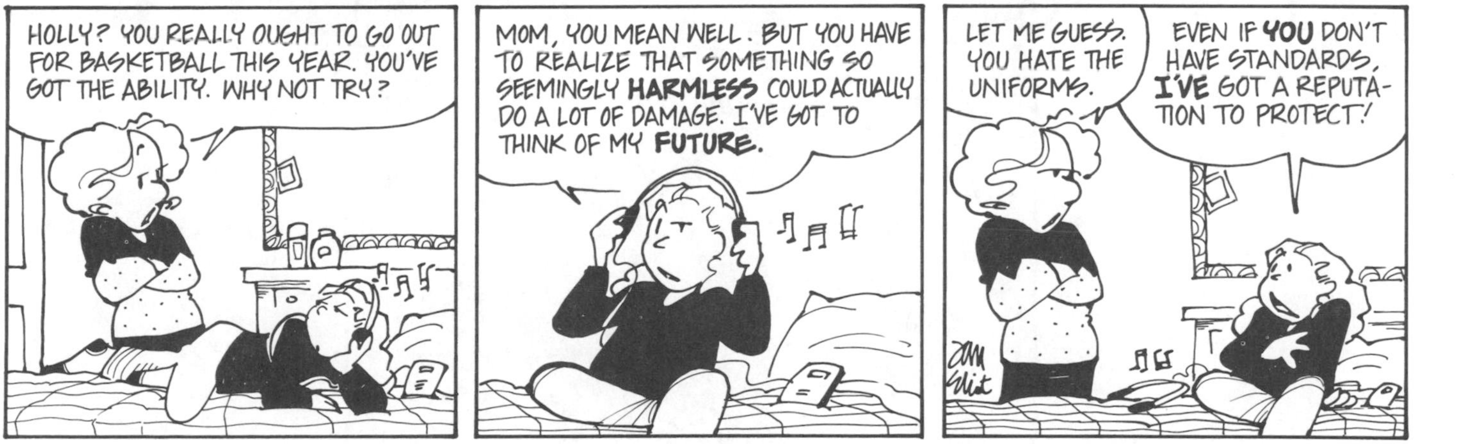
HOLLY? YOU REALLY OUGHT TO GO OUT FOR BASKETBALL THIS YEAR. YOU'VE GOT THE ABILITY. WHY NOT TRY?
MOM, YOU MEAN WELL. BUT YOU HAVE TO REALIZE THAT SOMETHING SO SEEMINGLY **HARMLESS** COULD ACTUALLY DO A LOT OF DAMAGE. I'VE GOT TO THINK OF MY **FUTURE.**
LET ME GUESS. YOU HATE THE UNIFORMS.
EVEN IF **YOU** DON'T HAVE STANDARDS, **I'VE** GOT A REPUTATION TO PROTECT!

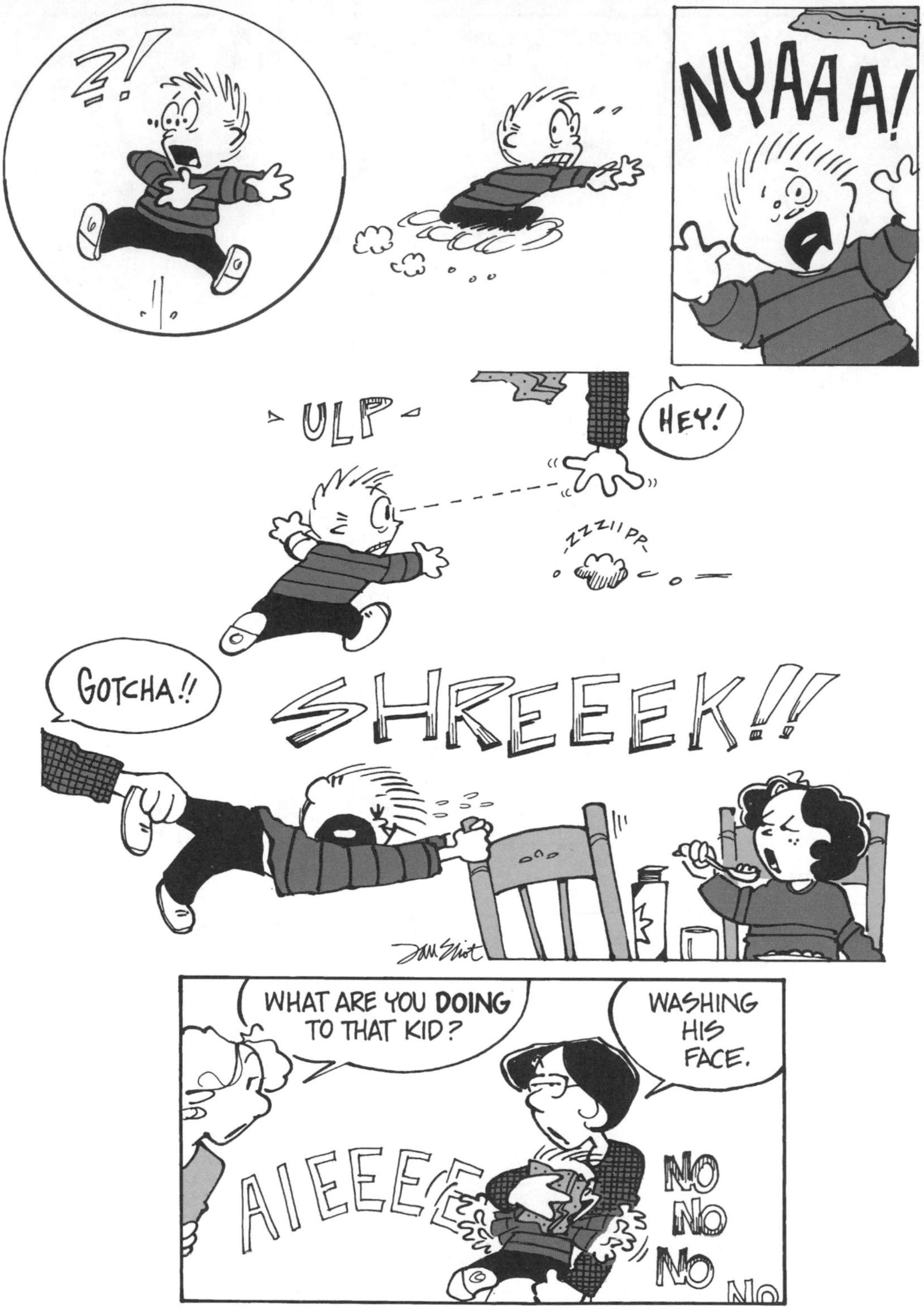
?!
NYAAA!
ULP
HEY!
ZZZIIPP
GOTCHA!!
SHREEEK!!
WHAT ARE YOU DOING TO THAT KID?
WASHING HIS FACE.
AIEEEE
NO
NO
NO
NO

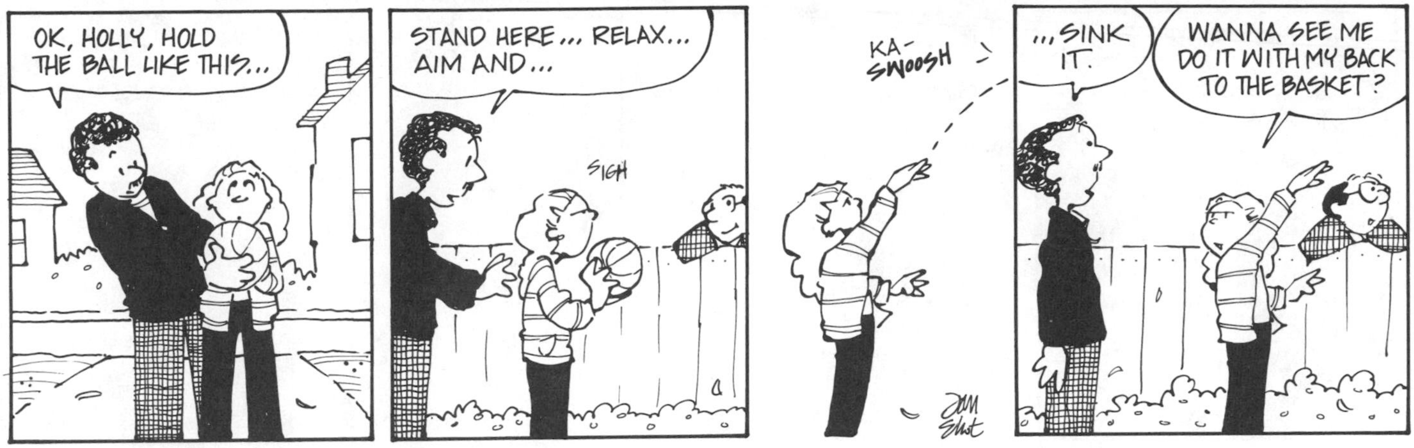
OK, HOLLY, HOLD THE BALL LIKE THIS...
STAND HERE... RELAX... AIM AND...
SIGH
KA-SWOOSH
...SINK IT.
WANNA SEE ME DO IT WITH MY BACK TO THE BASKET?

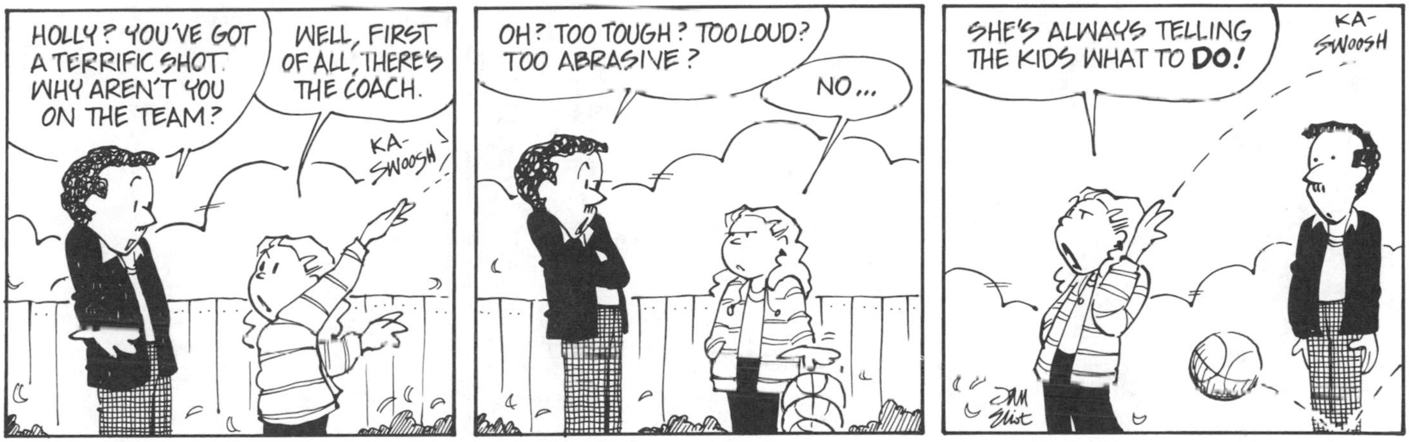
HOLLY? YOU'VE GOT A TERRIFIC SHOT. WHY AREN'T YOU ON THE TEAM?
WELL, FIRST OF ALL, THERE'S THE COACH.
KA-SWOOSH
OH? TOO TOUGH? TOO LOUD? TOO ABRASIVE?
NO...
SHE'S ALWAYS TELLING THE KIDS WHAT TO DO!
KA-SWOOSH

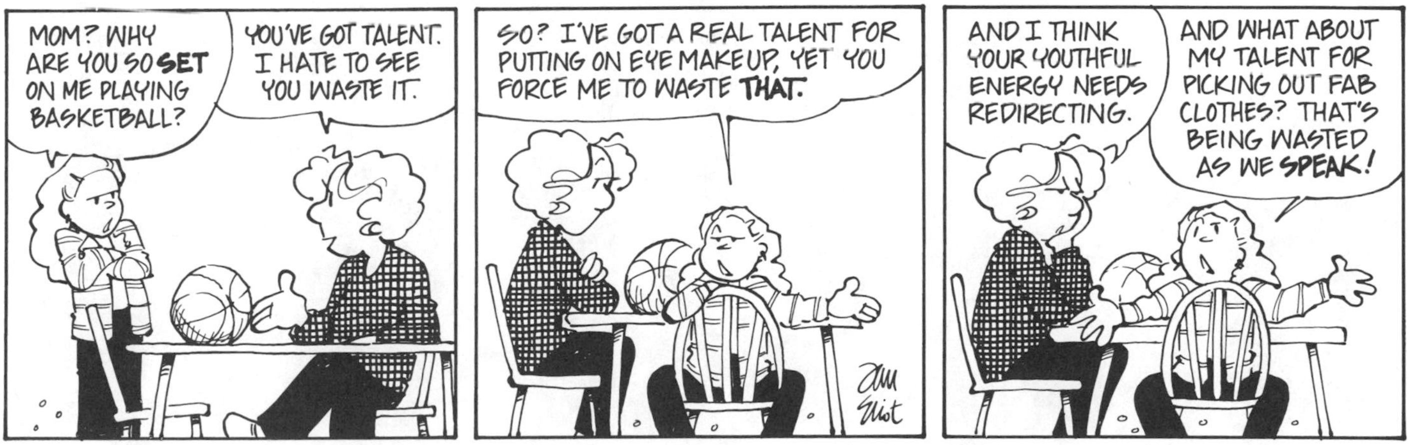
MOM? WHY ARE YOU SO SET ON ME PLAYING BASKETBALL?
YOU'VE GOT TALENT. I HATE TO SEE YOU WASTE IT.
SO? I'VE GOT A REAL TALENT FOR PUTTING ON EYE MAKEUP, YET YOU FORCE ME TO WASTE THAT.
AND I THINK YOUR YOUTHFUL ENERGY NEEDS REDIRECTING.
AND WHAT ABOUT MY TALENT FOR PICKING OUT FAB CLOTHES? THAT'S BEING WASTED AS WE SPEAK!

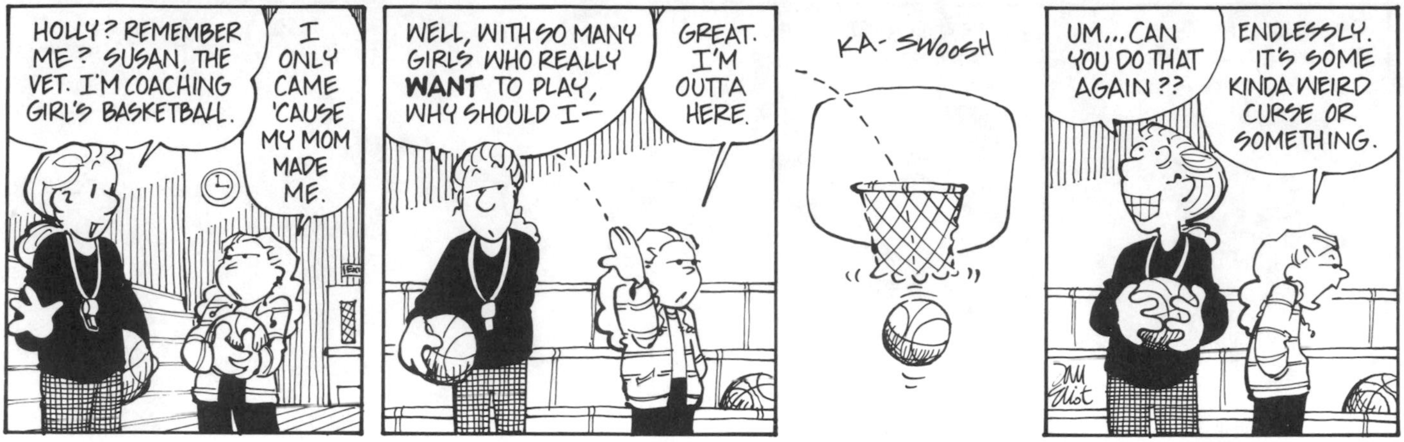
HOLLY? REMEMBER ME? SUSAN, THE VET. I'M COACHING GIRL'S BASKETBALL.
I ONLY CAME 'CAUSE MY MOM MADE ME.
WELL, WITH SO MANY GIRLS WHO REALLY **WANT** TO PLAY, WHY SHOULD I—
GREAT. I'M OUTTA HERE.
KA-SWOOSH
UM... CAN YOU DO THAT AGAIN??
ENDLESSLY. IT'S SOME KINDA WEIRD CURSE OR SOMETHING.

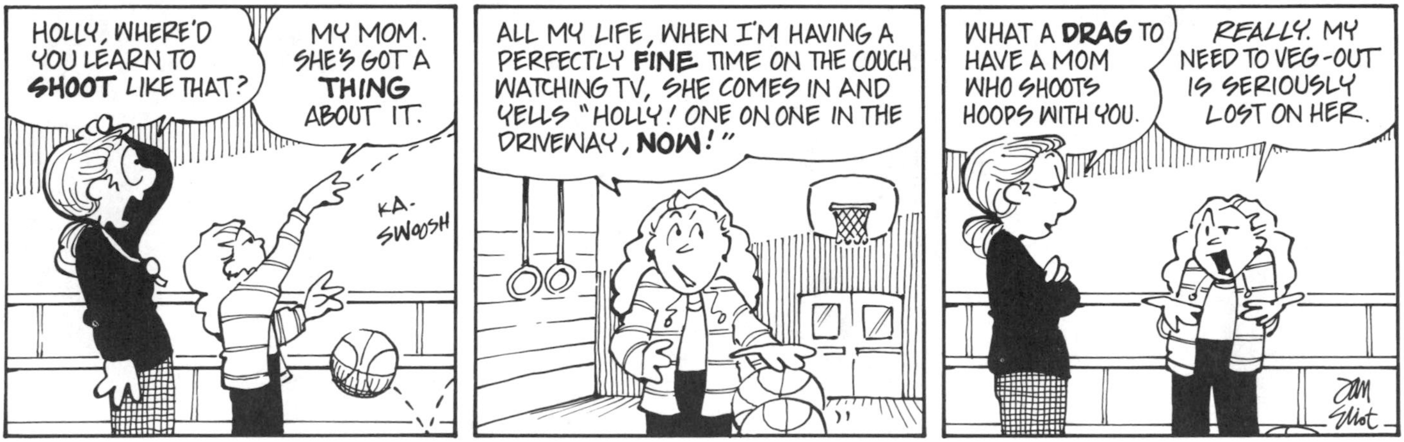
HOLLY, WHERE'D YOU LEARN TO **SHOOT** LIKE THAT?
MY MOM. SHE'S GOT A **THING** ABOUT IT.
KA-SWOOSH
ALL MY LIFE, WHEN I'M HAVING A PERFECTLY **FINE** TIME ON THE COUCH WATCHING TV, SHE COMES IN AND YELLS "HOLLY! ONE ON ONE IN THE DRIVEWAY, **NOW**!"
WHAT A **DRAG** TO HAVE A MOM WHO SHOOTS HOOPS WITH YOU.
REALLY. MY NEED TO VEG-OUT IS SERIOUSLY LOST ON HER.

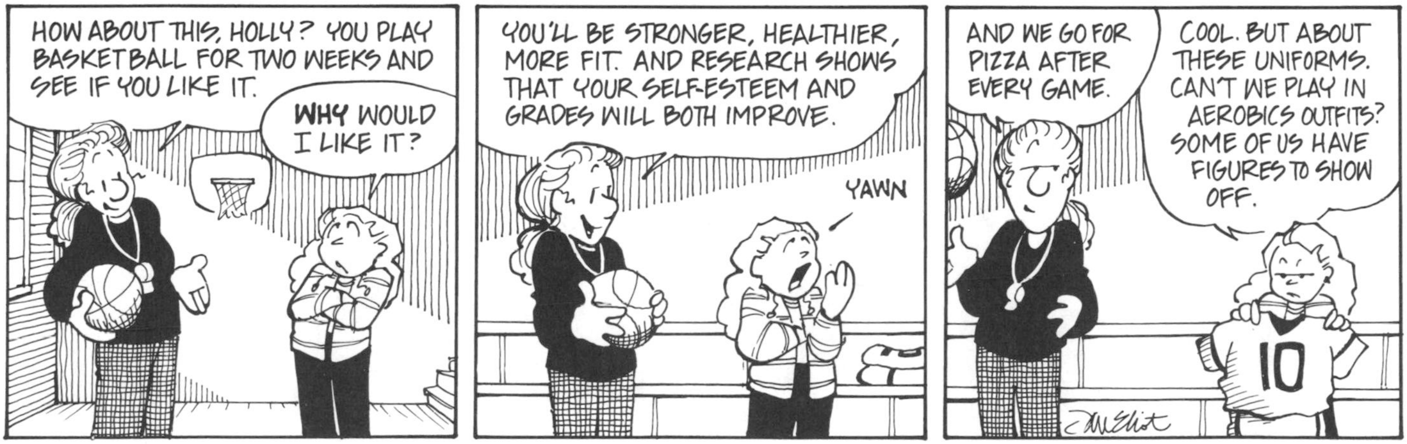
HOW ABOUT THIS, HOLLY? YOU PLAY BASKETBALL FOR TWO WEEKS AND SEE IF YOU LIKE IT.
WHY WOULD I LIKE IT?
YOU'LL BE STRONGER, HEALTHIER, MORE FIT. AND RESEARCH SHOWS THAT YOUR SELF-ESTEEM AND GRADES WILL BOTH IMPROVE.
YAWN
AND WE GO FOR PIZZA AFTER EVERY GAME.
COOL. BUT ABOUT THESE UNIFORMS. CAN'T WE PLAY IN AEROBICS OUTFITS? SOME OF US HAVE FIGURES TO SHOW OFF.
10

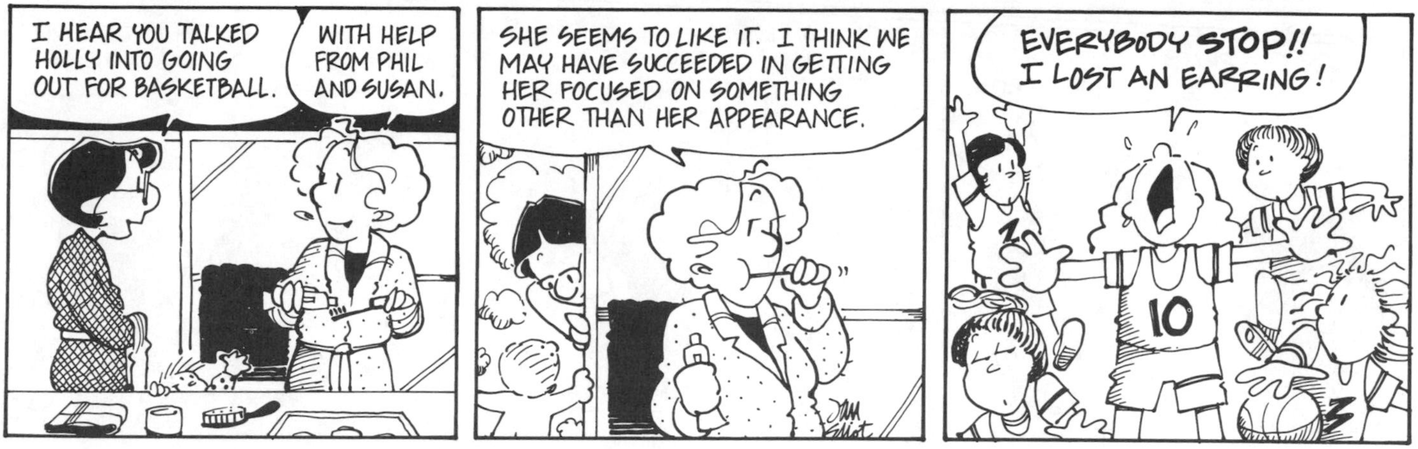
I HEAR YOU TALKED HOLLY INTO GOING OUT FOR BASKETBALL.
WITH HELP FROM PHIL AND SUSAN.
SHE SEEMS TO LIKE IT. I THINK WE MAY HAVE SUCCEEDED IN GETTING HER FOCUSED ON SOMETHING OTHER THAN HER APPEARANCE.
EVERYBODY STOP!! I LOST AN EARRING!
10

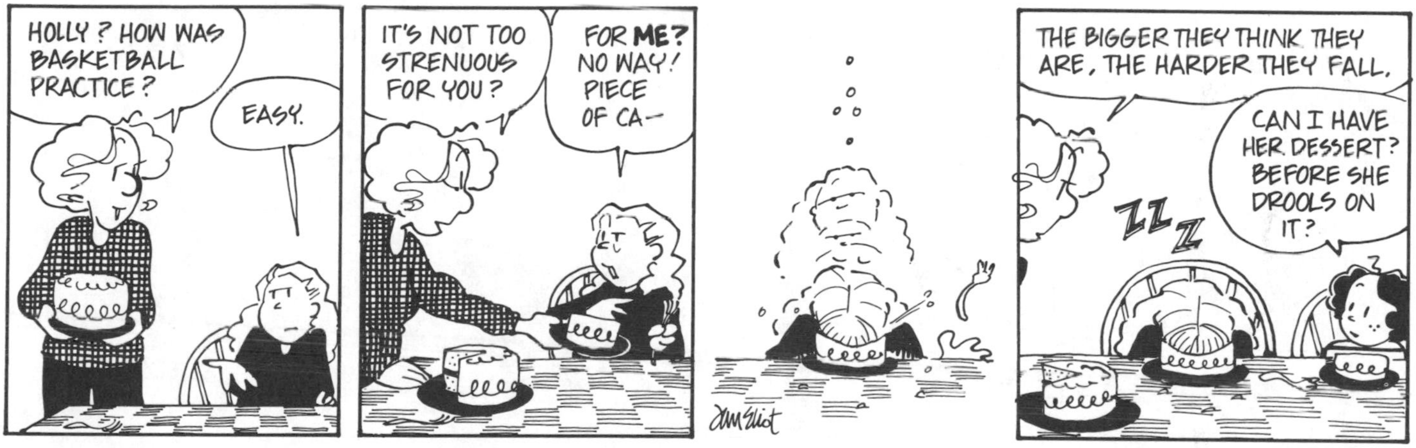
HOLLY? HOW WAS BASKETBALL PRACTICE?
EASY.
IT'S NOT TOO STRENUOUS FOR YOU?
FOR ME? NO WAY! PIECE OF CA—
THE BIGGER THEY THINK THEY ARE, THE HARDER THEY FALL.
ZZZ
CAN I HAVE HER DESSERT? BEFORE SHE DROOLS ON IT?

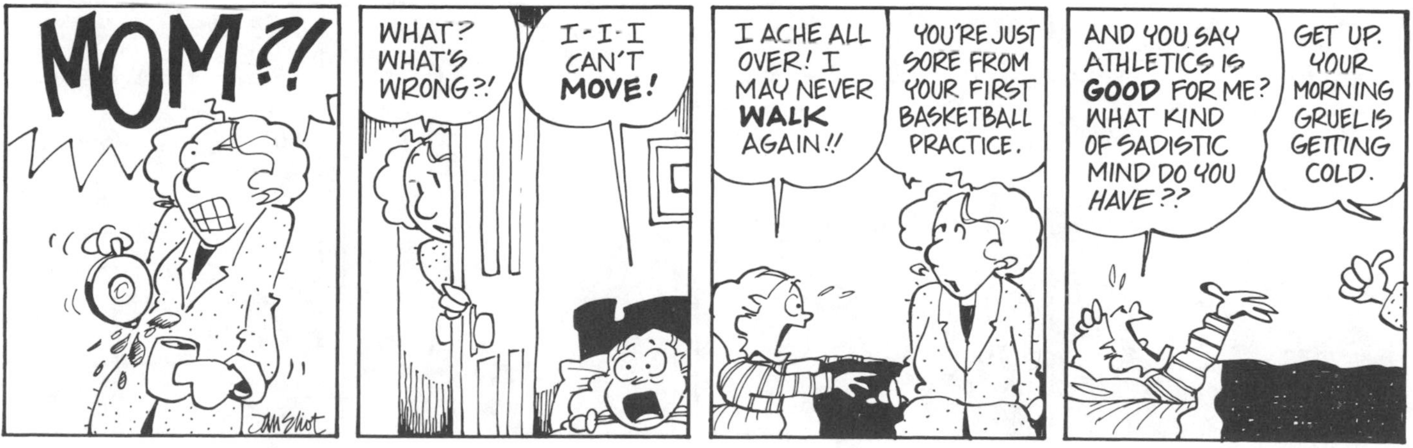
MOM?!
WHAT? WHAT'S WRONG?!
I-I-I CAN'T MOVE!
I ACHE ALL OVER! I MAY NEVER WALK AGAIN!!
YOU'RE JUST SORE FROM YOUR FIRST BASKETBALL PRACTICE.
AND YOU SAY ATHLETICS IS GOOD FOR ME? WHAT KIND OF SADISTIC MIND DO YOU HAVE??
GET UP. YOUR MORNING GRUEL IS GETTING COLD.

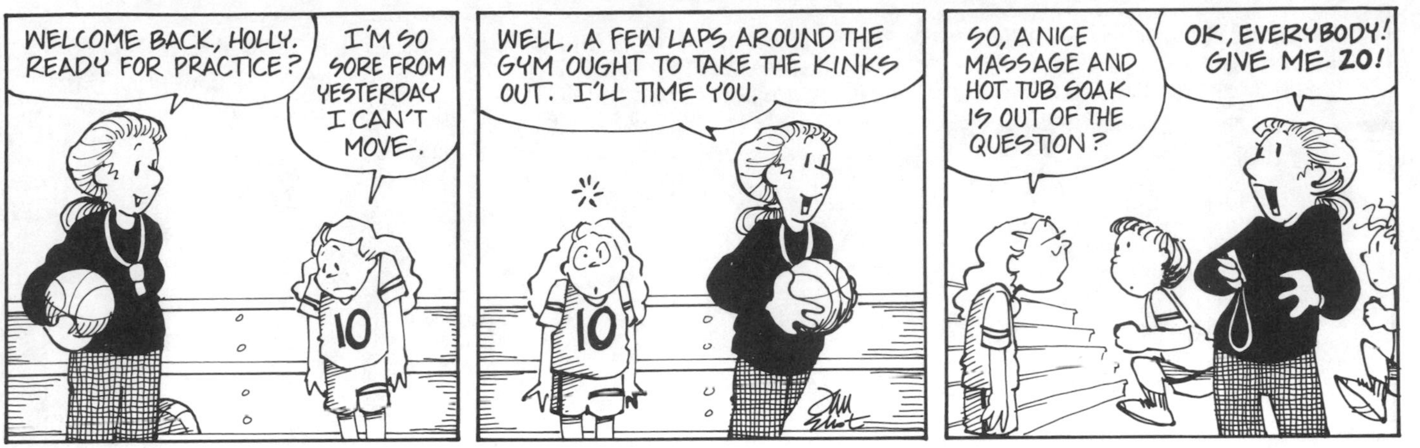
WELCOME BACK, HOLLY. READY FOR PRACTICE?
I'M SO SORE FROM YESTERDAY I CAN'T MOVE.
WELL, A FEW LAPS AROUND THE GYM OUGHT TO TAKE THE KINKS OUT. I'LL TIME YOU.
SO, A NICE MASSAGE AND HOT TUB SOAK IS OUT OF THE QUESTION?
OK, EVERYBODY! GIVE ME 20!

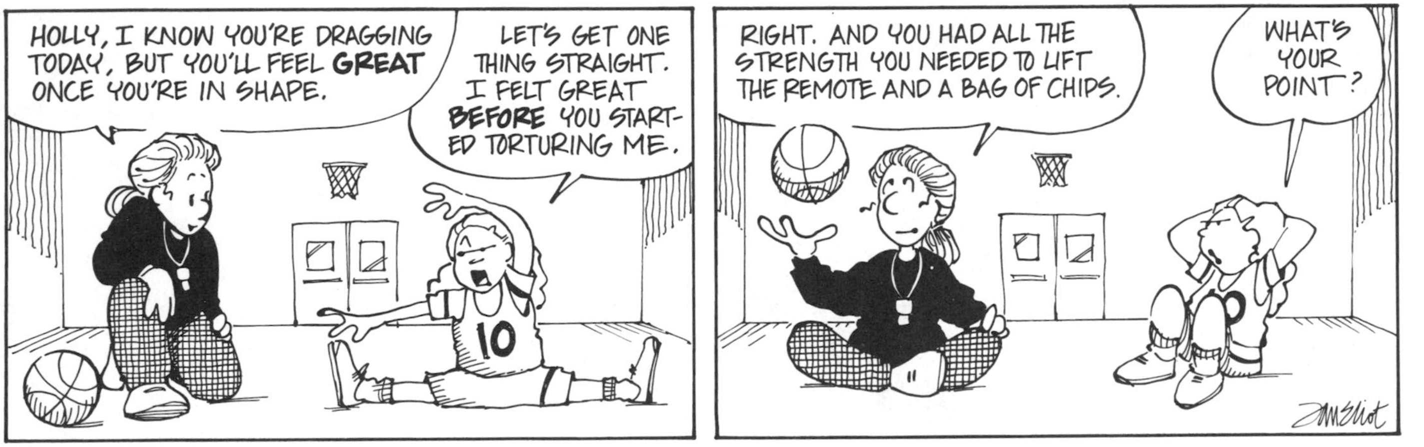
HOLLY, I KNOW YOU'RE DRAGGING TODAY, BUT YOU'LL FEEL GREAT ONCE YOU'RE IN SHAPE.
LET'S GET ONE THING STRAIGHT. I FELT GREAT BEFORE YOU STARTED TORTURING ME.
RIGHT. AND YOU HAD ALL THE STRENGTH YOU NEEDED TO LIFT THE REMOTE AND A BAG OF CHIPS.
WHAT'S YOUR POINT?

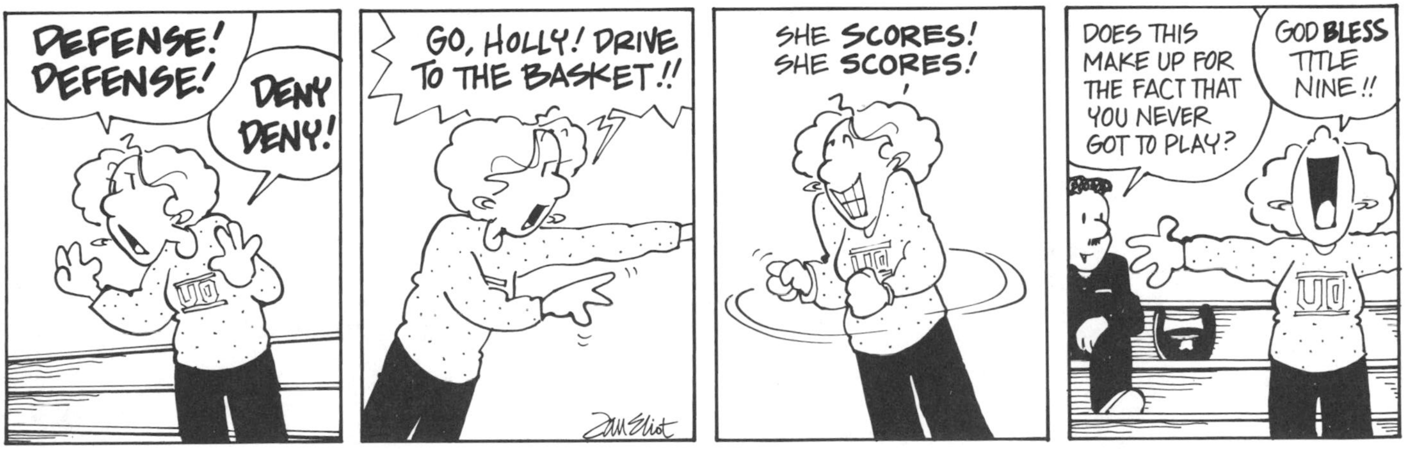
DEFENSE! DEFENSE!
DENY DENY!
GO, HOLLY! DRIVE TO THE BASKET!!
SHE SCORES! SHE SCORES!
DOES THIS MAKE UP FOR THE FACT THAT YOU NEVER GOT TO PLAY?
GOD BLESS TITLE NINE!!

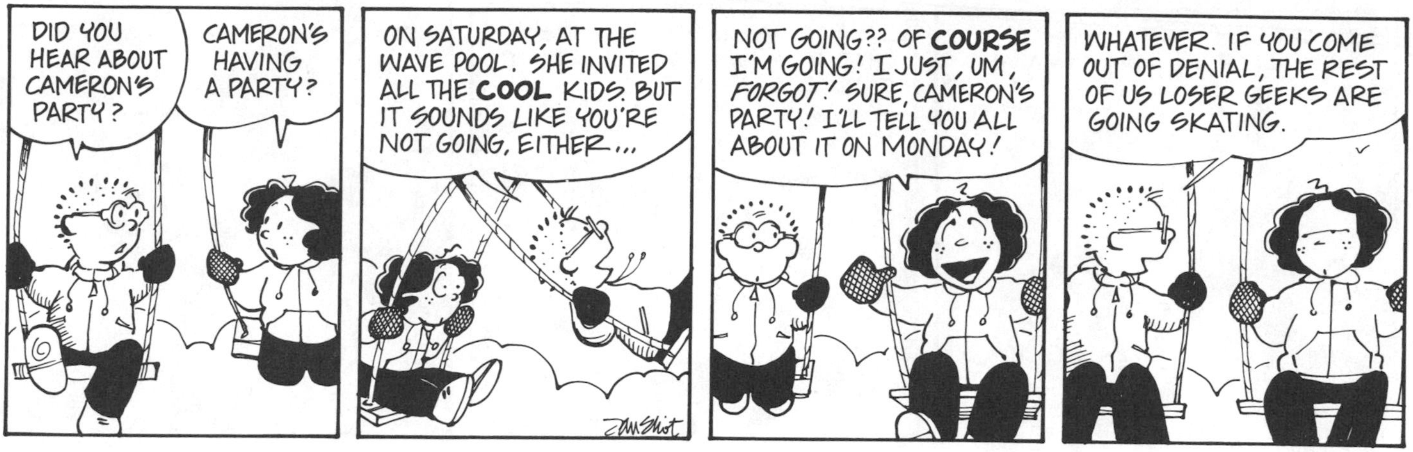
DID YOU HEAR ABOUT CAMERON'S PARTY?
CAMERON'S HAVING A PARTY?
ON SATURDAY, AT THE WAVE POOL. SHE INVITED ALL THE COOL KIDS. BUT IT SOUNDS LIKE YOU'RE NOT GOING, EITHER...
NOT GOING?? OF COURSE I'M GOING! I JUST, UM, FORGOT! SURE, CAMERON'S PARTY! I'LL TELL YOU ALL ABOUT IT ON MONDAY!
WHATEVER. IF YOU COME OUT OF DENIAL, THE REST OF US LOSER GEEKS ARE GOING SKATING.

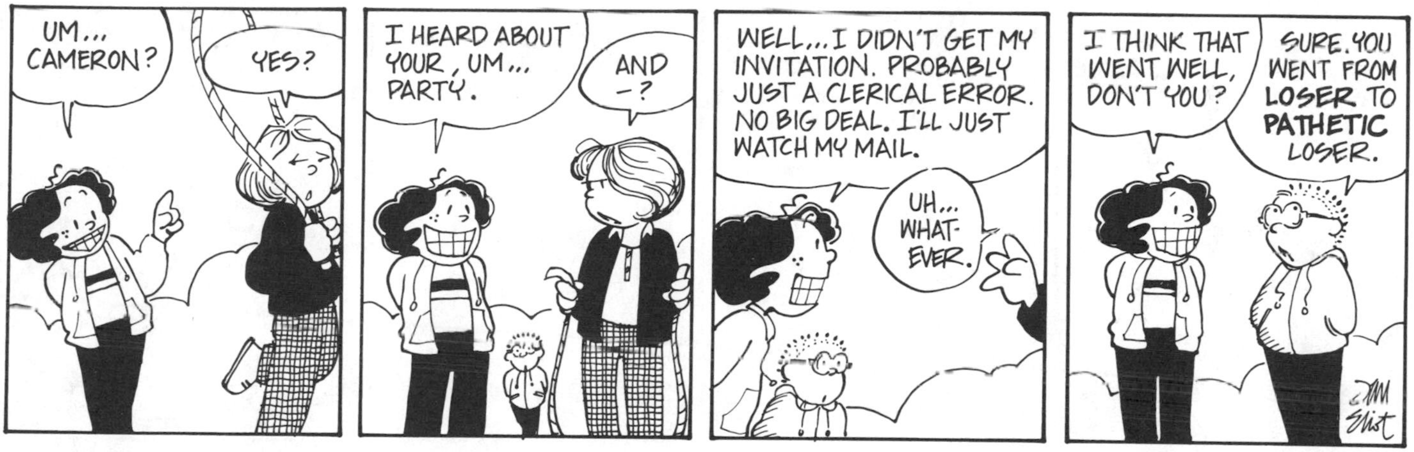
UM... CAMERON?
YES?
I HEARD ABOUT YOUR, UM... PARTY.
AND -?
WELL... I DIDN'T GET MY INVITATION. PROBABLY JUST A CLERICAL ERROR. NO BIG DEAL. I'LL JUST WATCH MY MAIL.
UH... WHAT-EVER.
I THINK THAT WENT WELL, DON'T YOU?
SURE. YOU WENT FROM LOSER TO PATHETIC LOSER.

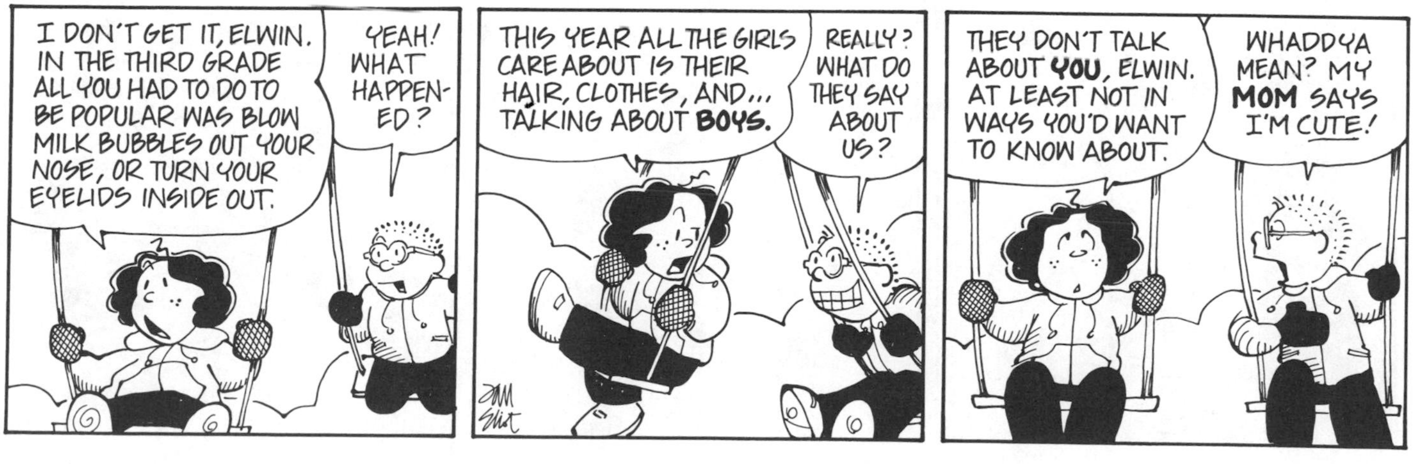
I DON'T GET IT, ELWIN. IN THE THIRD GRADE ALL YOU HAD TO DO TO BE POPULAR WAS BLOW MILK BUBBLES OUT YOUR NOSE, OR TURN YOUR EYELIDS INSIDE OUT.
YEAH! WHAT HAPPEN-ED?
THIS YEAR ALL THE GIRLS CARE ABOUT IS THEIR HAIR, CLOTHES, AND... TALKING ABOUT BOYS.
REALLY? WHAT DO THEY SAY ABOUT US?
THEY DON'T TALK ABOUT YOU, ELWIN. AT LEAST NOT IN WAYS YOU'D WANT TO KNOW ABOUT.
WHADDYA MEAN? MY MOM SAYS I'M CUTE!

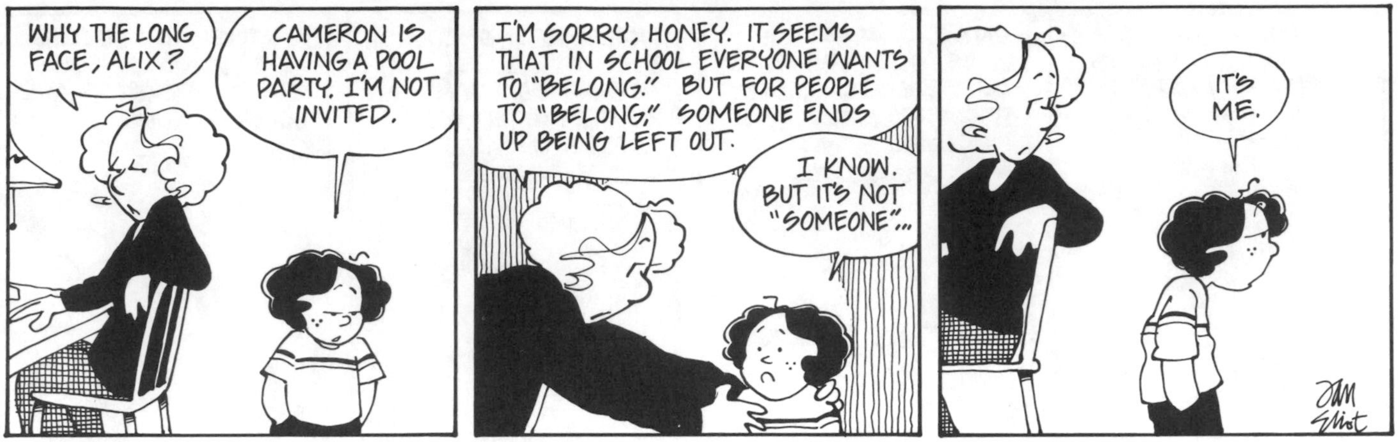
WHY THE LONG FACE, ALIX?
CAMERON IS HAVING A POOL PARTY. I'M NOT INVITED.
I'M SORRY, HONEY. IT SEEMS THAT IN SCHOOL EVERYONE WANTS TO "BELONG." BUT FOR PEOPLE TO "BELONG," SOMEONE ENDS UP BEING LEFT OUT.
I KNOW. BUT IT'S NOT "SOMEONE"...
IT'S ME.

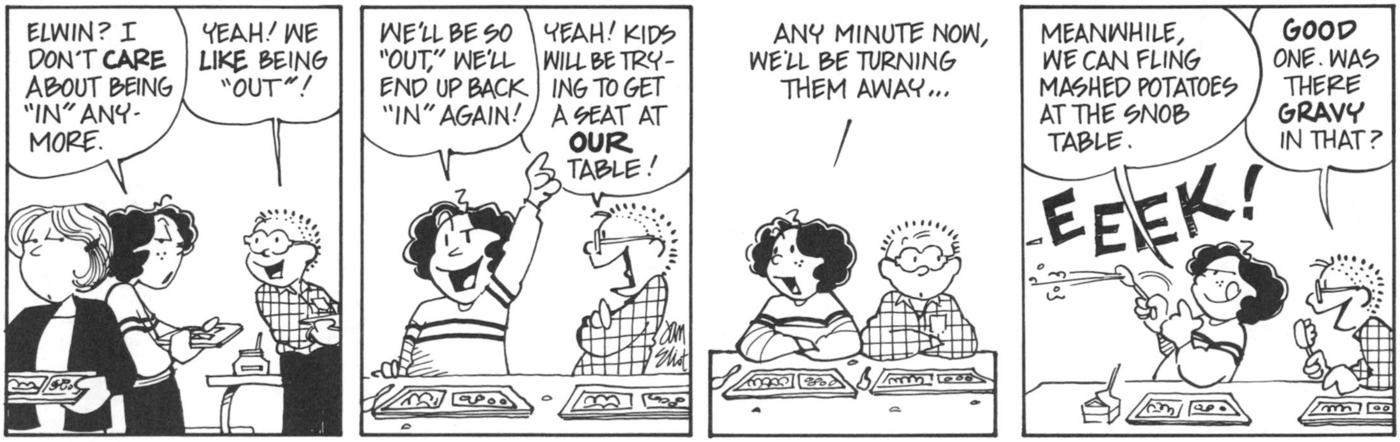
ELWIN? I DON'T **CARE** ABOUT BEING "IN" ANY-MORE.
YEAH! WE **LIKE** BEING "OUT"!
WE'LL BE SO "OUT," WE'LL END UP BACK "IN" AGAIN!
YEAH! KIDS WILL BE TRY-ING TO GET A SEAT AT **OUR** TABLE!
ANY MINUTE NOW, WE'LL BE TURNING THEM AWAY...
MEANWHILE, WE CAN FLING MASHED POTATOES AT THE SNOB TABLE.
EEEK!
GOOD ONE. WAS THERE **GRAVY** IN THAT?

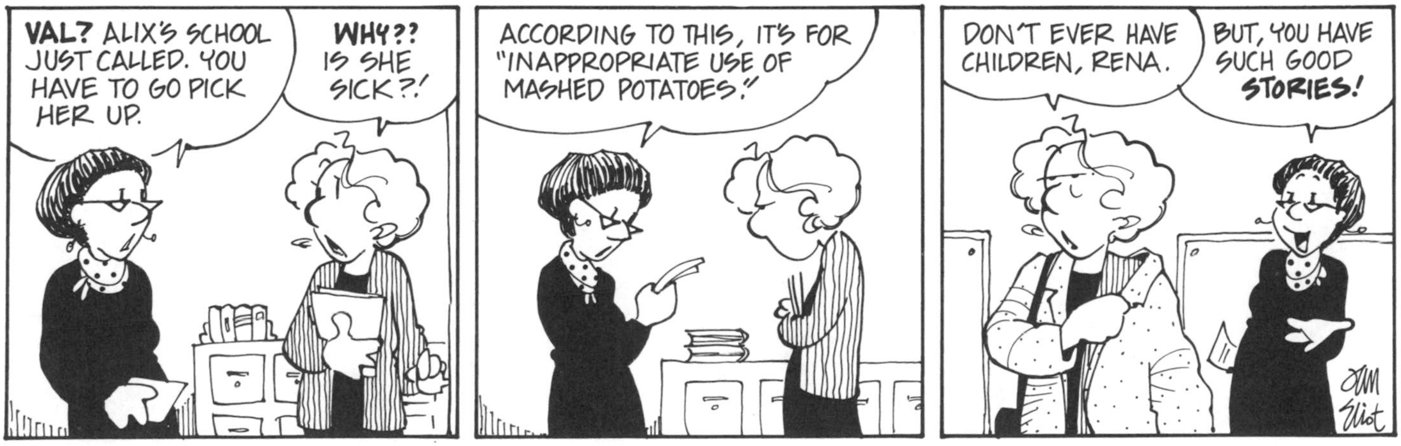
VAL? ALIX'S SCHOOL JUST CALLED. YOU HAVE TO GO PICK HER UP.
WHY?? IS SHE SICK?!
ACCORDING TO THIS, IT'S FOR "INAPPROPRIATE USE OF MASHED POTATOES."
DON'T EVER HAVE CHILDREN, RENA.
BUT, YOU HAVE SUCH GOOD **STORIES!**

WHAT'S WITH ALIX?

THE "POPULAR" GIRL AT HER SCHOOL HAD A PARTY AND DIDN'T INVITE HER.

OUCH. SHUT OUT AT **NINE**. THAT'S BITTER.

MAYBE **YOU** CAN CHEER HER UP.

HEY, ALIX? WHAT'S THE NAME OF THE GIRL WHO SNUBBED YOU?

CAMERON.

OK, WELL, **CAMERON** IS GOING TO GROW UP THINKING THE WORLD REVOLVES AROUND HER. SHE'LL FIND HER WAY INTO COUNTRY CLUBS, MARRY A RICH GUY, HAVE TWO KIDS AND A LEXUS...

ONLY TO SOON FIND HERSELF DEPRESSED, DIETING, FACE-LIFTING AND TUCKING, TRYING TO HANG ONTO THE ONLY THING SHE'S HAD TO CARRY HER THROUGH LIFE—HER NOW-FADING GOOD LOOKS.

FEEL BETTER?

HUH??

I WAS THINKING MORE ALONG THE LINES OF YOU TAKING HER OUT FOR ICE CREAM.

157

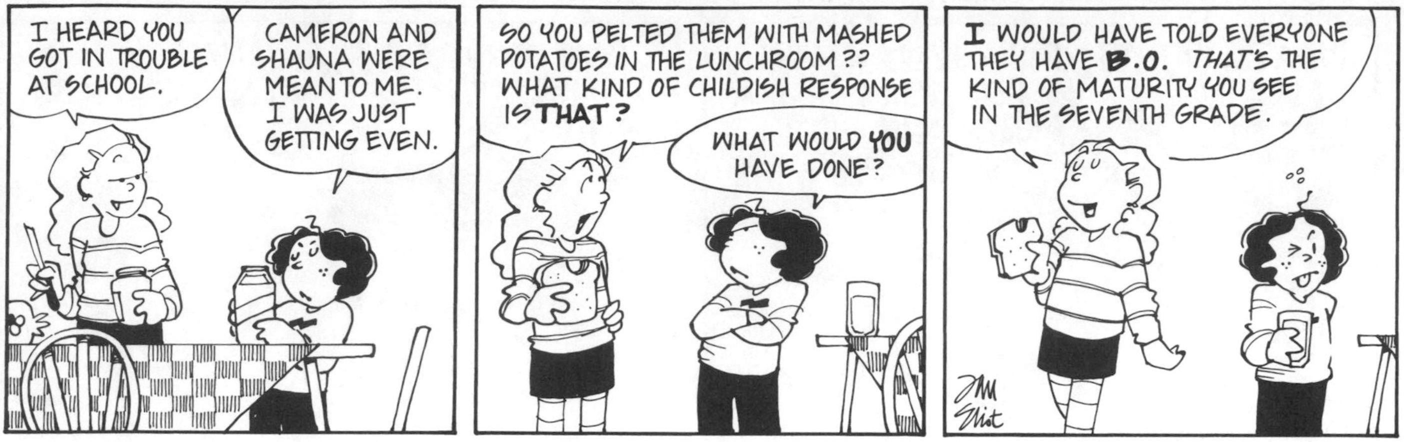
I HEARD YOU GOT IN TROUBLE AT SCHOOL.
CAMERON AND SHAUNA WERE MEAN TO ME. I WAS JUST GETTING EVEN.
SO YOU PELTED THEM WITH MASHED POTATOES IN THE LUNCHROOM?? WHAT KIND OF CHILDISH RESPONSE IS THAT?
WHAT WOULD YOU HAVE DONE?
I WOULD HAVE TOLD EVERYONE THEY HAVE B.O. THAT'S THE KIND OF MATURITY YOU SEE IN THE SEVENTH GRADE.

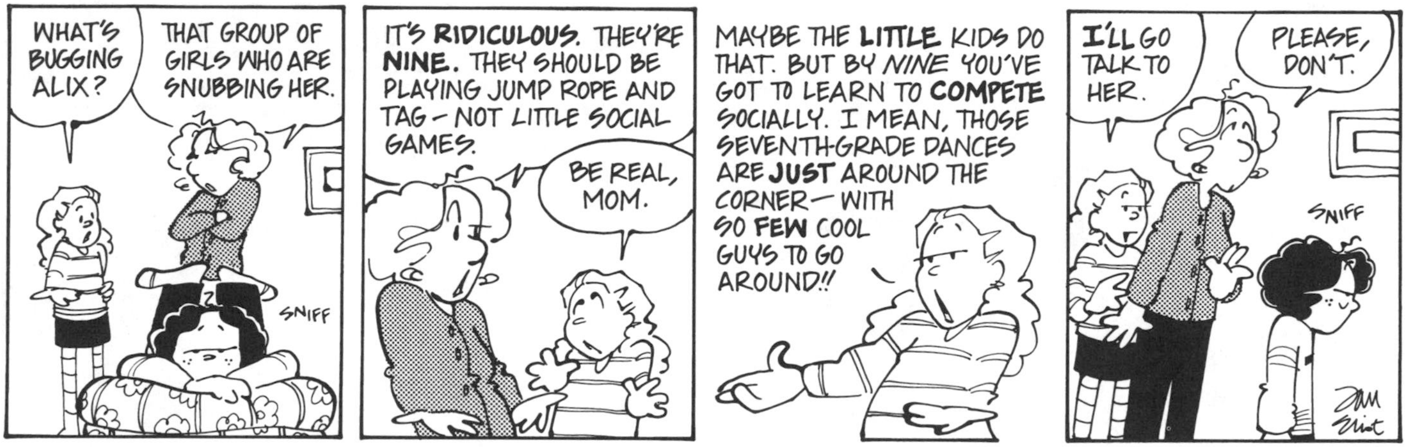
WHAT'S BUGGING ALIX?
THAT GROUP OF GIRLS WHO ARE SNUBBING HER.
SNIFF
IT'S RIDICULOUS. THEY'RE NINE. THEY SHOULD BE PLAYING JUMP ROPE AND TAG – NOT LITTLE SOCIAL GAMES.
BE REAL, MOM.
MAYBE THE LITTLE KIDS DO THAT. BUT BY NINE YOU'VE GOT TO LEARN TO COMPETE SOCIALLY. I MEAN, THOSE SEVENTH-GRADE DANCES ARE JUST AROUND THE CORNER– WITH SO FEW COOL GUYS TO GO AROUND!!
I'LL GO TALK TO HER.
PLEASE, DON'T.
SNIFF

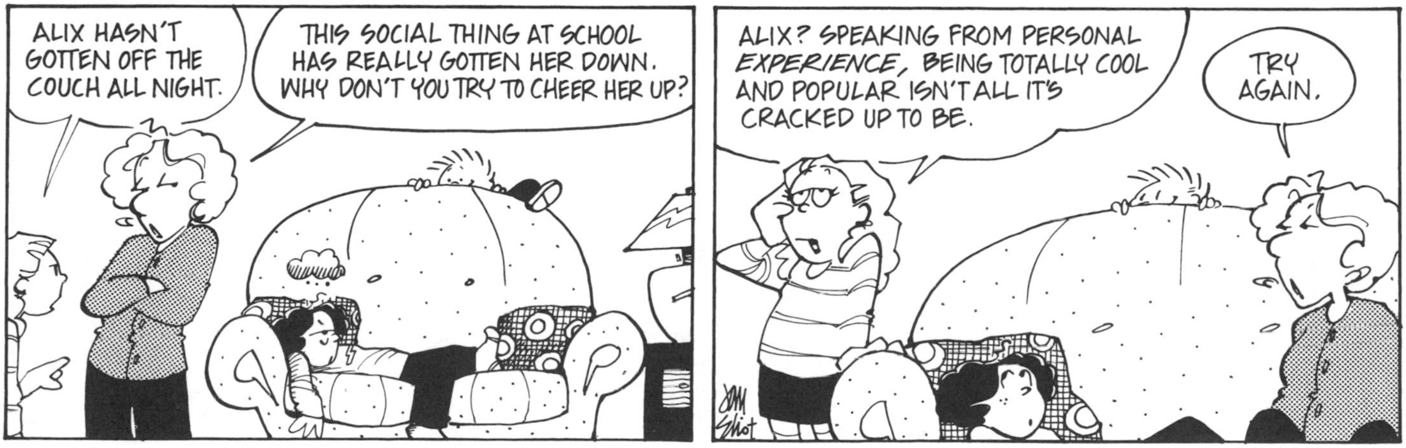
ALIX HASN'T GOTTEN OFF THE COUCH ALL NIGHT.
THIS SOCIAL THING AT SCHOOL HAS REALLY GOTTEN HER DOWN. WHY DON'T YOU TRY TO CHEER HER UP?
ALIX? SPEAKING FROM PERSONAL EXPERIENCE, BEING TOTALLY COOL AND POPULAR ISN'T ALL IT'S CRACKED UP TO BE.
TRY AGAIN.

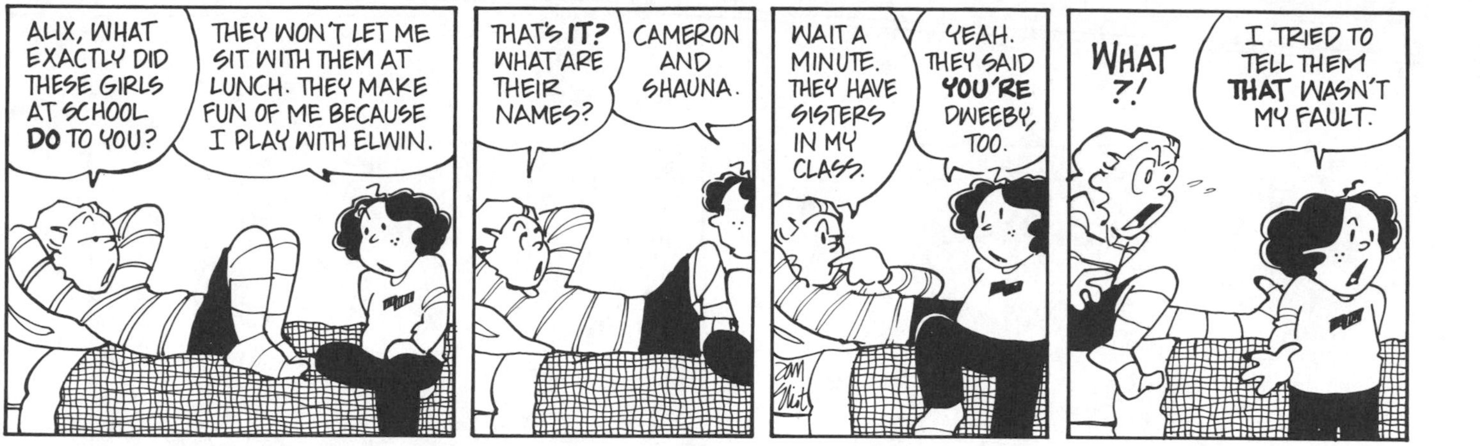
ALIX, WHAT EXACTLY DID THESE GIRLS AT SCHOOL **DO** TO YOU?
THEY WON'T LET ME SIT WITH THEM AT LUNCH. THEY MAKE FUN OF ME BECAUSE I PLAY WITH ELWIN.
THAT'S **IT?** WHAT ARE THEIR NAMES?
CAMERON AND SHAUNA.
WAIT A MINUTE. THEY HAVE SISTERS IN MY CLASS.
YEAH. THEY SAID **YOU'RE** DWEEBY, TOO.
WHAT?!
I TRIED TO TELL THEM **THAT** WASN'T MY FAULT.

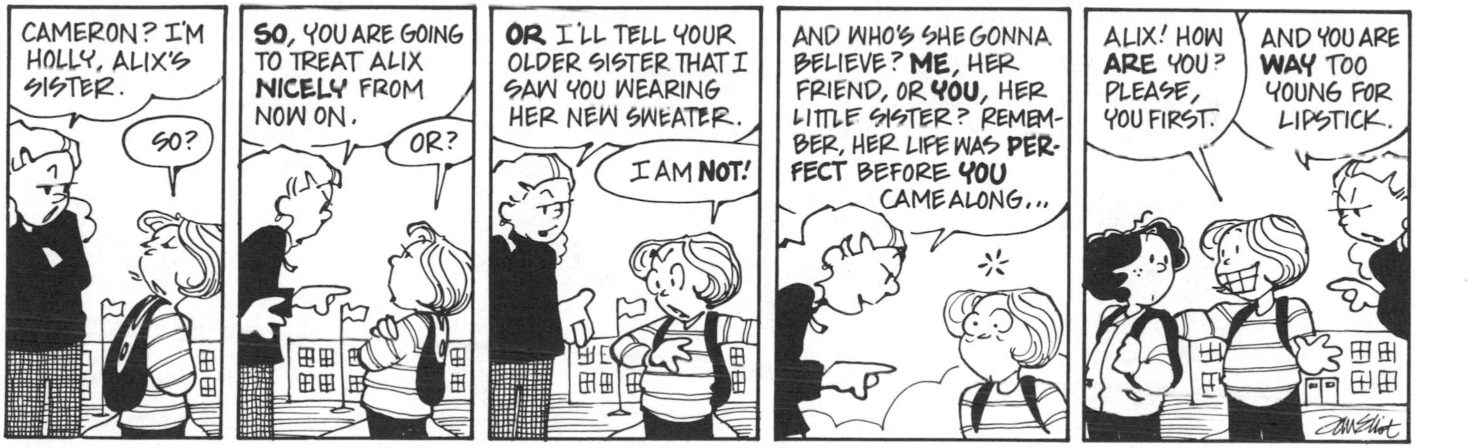
CAMERON? I'M HOLLY, ALIX'S SISTER.
SO?
SO, YOU ARE GOING TO TREAT ALIX **NICELY** FROM NOW ON.
OR?
OR I'LL TELL YOUR OLDER SISTER THAT I SAW YOU WEARING HER NEW SWEATER.
I AM **NOT!**
AND WHO'S SHE GONNA BELIEVE? **ME**, HER FRIEND, OR **YOU**, HER LITTLE SISTER? REMEMBER, HER LIFE WAS **PERFECT** BEFORE **YOU** CAME ALONG...
ALIX! HOW **ARE** YOU? PLEASE, YOU FIRST.
AND YOU ARE **WAY** TOO YOUNG FOR LIPSTICK.

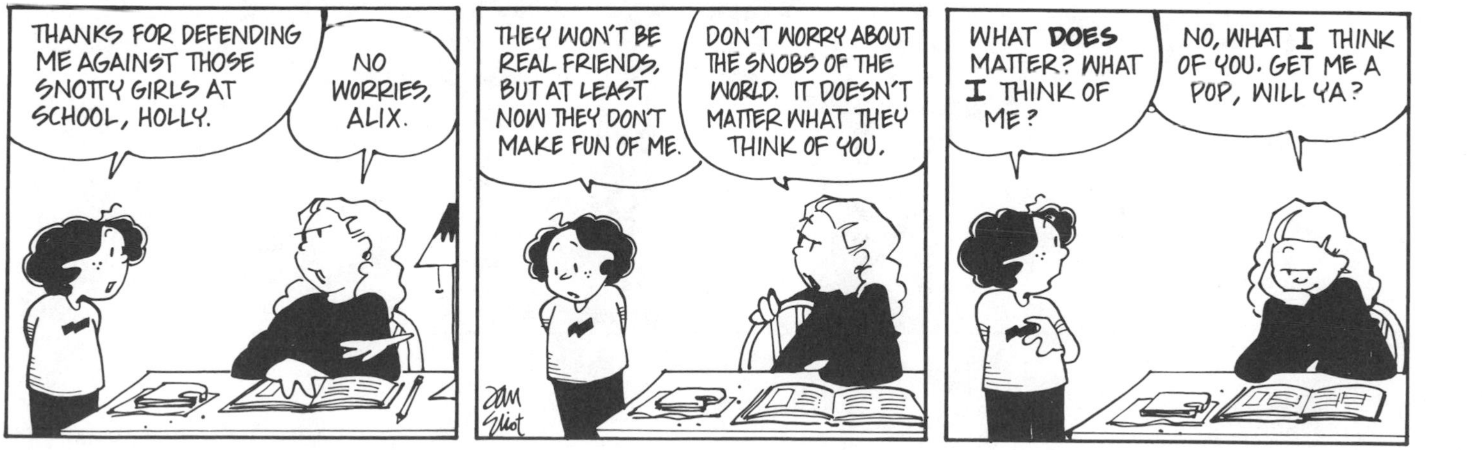
THANKS FOR DEFENDING ME AGAINST THOSE SNOTTY GIRLS AT SCHOOL, HOLLY.
NO WORRIES, ALIX.
THEY WON'T BE REAL FRIENDS, BUT AT LEAST NOW THEY DON'T MAKE FUN OF ME.
DON'T WORRY ABOUT THE SNOBS OF THE WORLD. IT DOESN'T MATTER WHAT THEY THINK OF YOU.
WHAT **DOES** MATTER? WHAT **I** THINK OF ME?
NO, WHAT **I** THINK OF YOU. GET ME A POP, WILL YA?

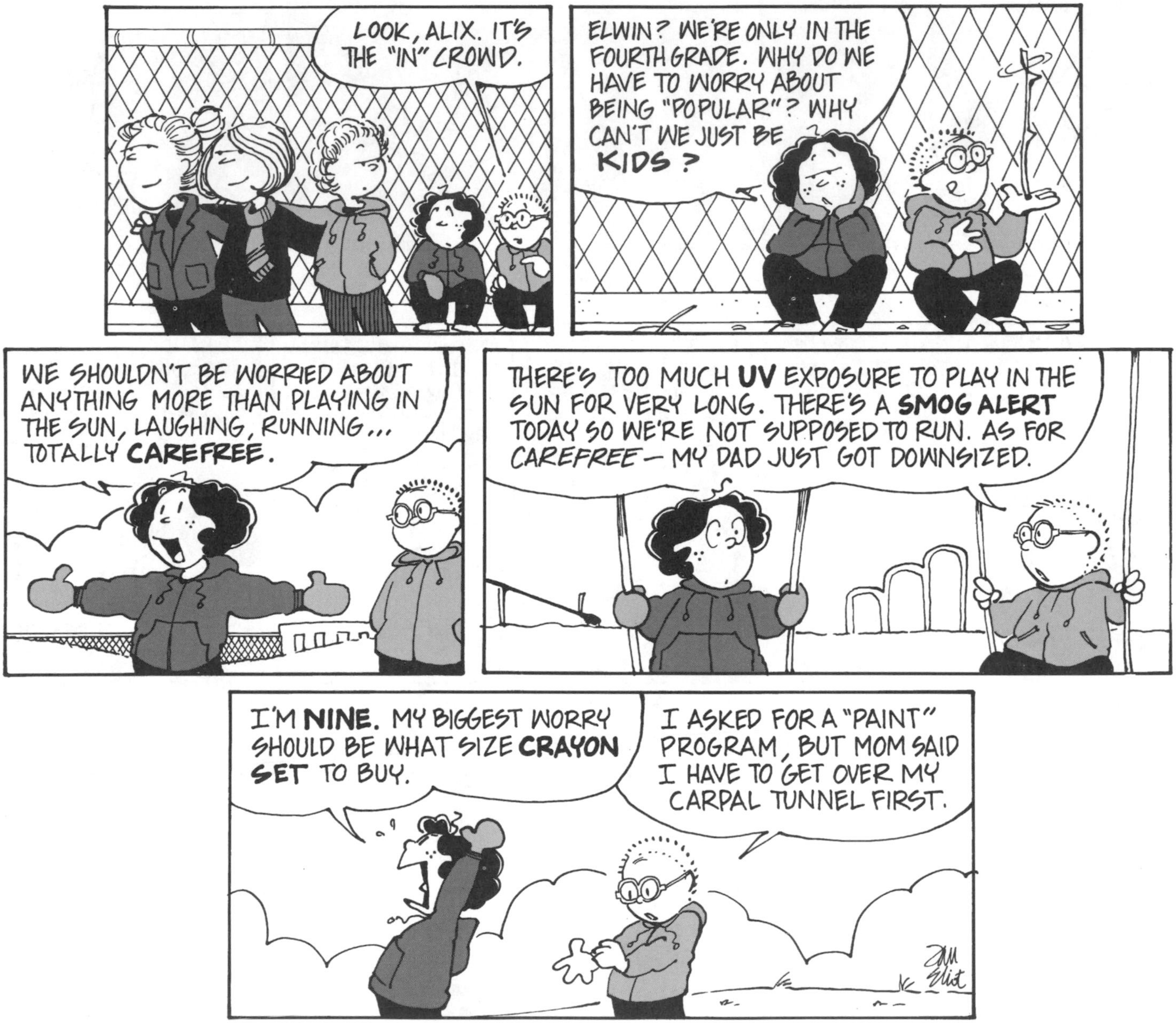
LOOK, ALIX. IT'S THE "IN" CROWD.
ELWIN? WE'RE ONLY IN THE FOURTH GRADE. WHY DO WE HAVE TO WORRY ABOUT BEING "POPULAR"? WHY CAN'T WE JUST BE KIDS ?
WE SHOULDN'T BE WORRIED ABOUT ANYTHING MORE THAN PLAYING IN THE SUN, LAUGHING, RUNNING... TOTALLY CAREFREE.
THERE'S TOO MUCH UV EXPOSURE TO PLAY IN THE SUN FOR VERY LONG. THERE'S A SMOG ALERT TODAY SO WE'RE NOT SUPPOSED TO RUN. AS FOR CAREFREE – MY DAD JUST GOT DOWNSIZED.
I'M NINE. MY BIGGEST WORRY SHOULD BE WHAT SIZE CRAYON SET TO BUY.
I ASKED FOR A "PAINT" PROGRAM, BUT MOM SAID I HAVE TO GET OVER MY CARPAL TUNNEL FIRST.

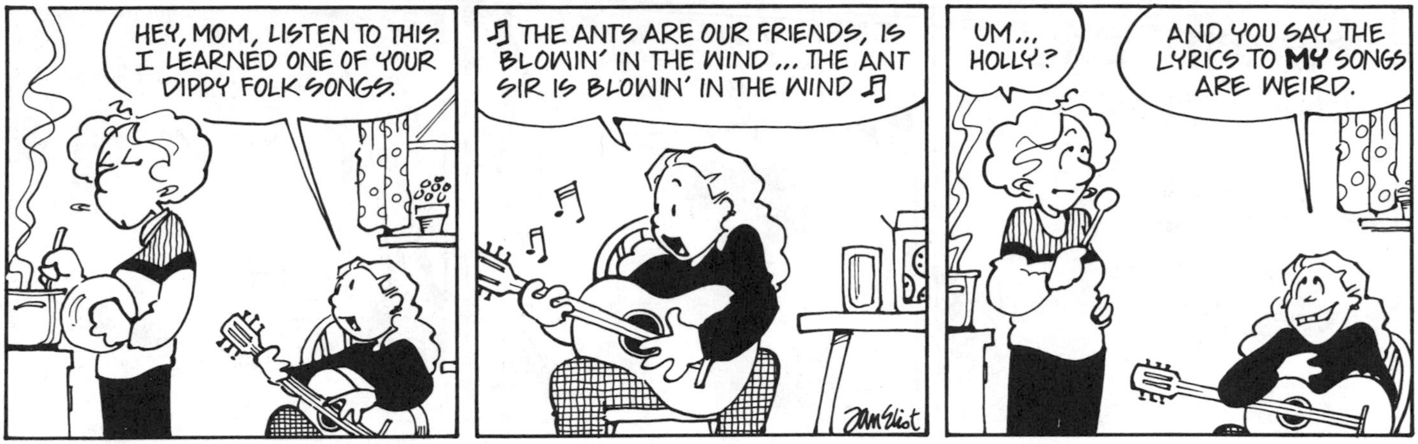
HEY, MOM, LISTEN TO THIS. I LEARNED ONE OF YOUR DIPPY FOLK SONGS.
THE ANTS ARE OUR FRIENDS, IS BLOWIN' IN THE WIND ... THE ANT SIR IS BLOWIN' IN THE WIND
UM... HOLLY?
AND YOU SAY THE LYRICS TO **MY** SONGS ARE WEIRD.

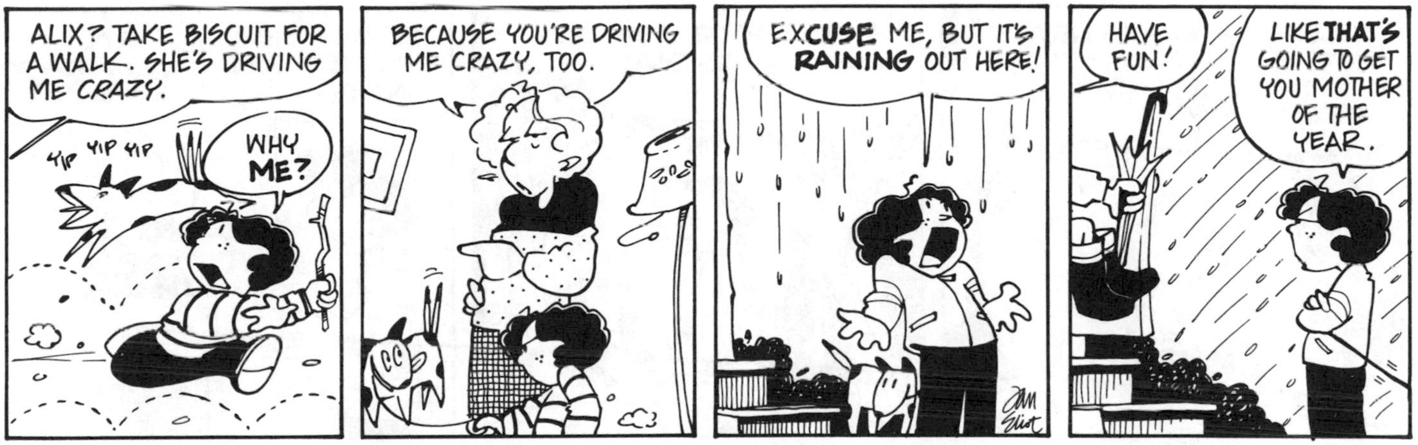
ALIX? TAKE BISCUIT FOR A WALK. SHE'S DRIVING ME *CRAZY*.
YIP YIP YIP
WHY **ME?**
BECAUSE YOU'RE DRIVING ME CRAZY, TOO.
EX**CUSE** ME, BUT IT'S **RAINING** OUT HERE!
HAVE FUN!
LIKE **THAT'S** GOING TO GET YOU MOTHER OF THE YEAR.

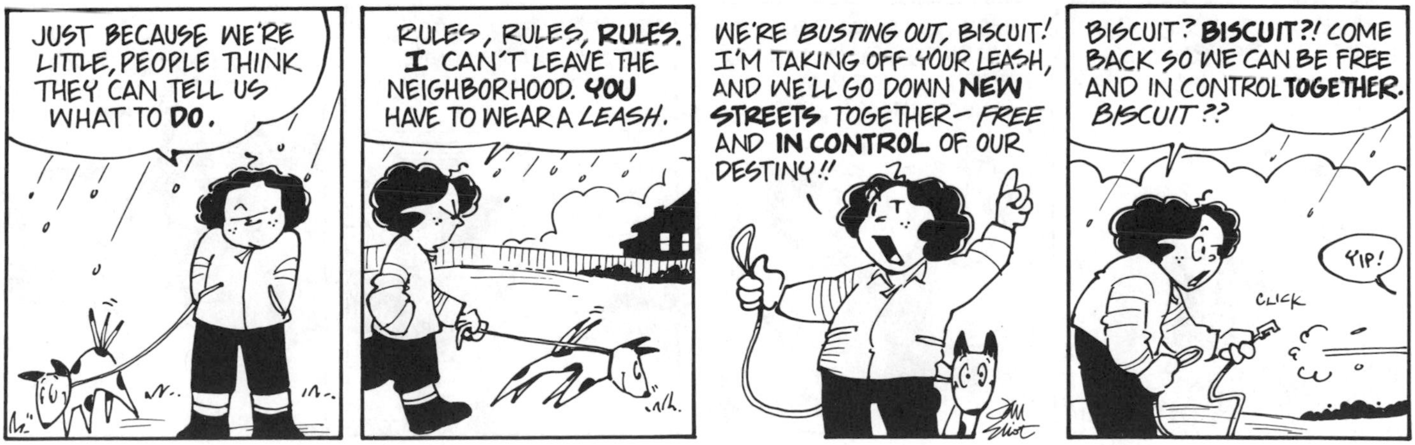
JUST BECAUSE WE'RE LITTLE, PEOPLE THINK THEY CAN TELL US WHAT TO **DO**.
RULES, RULES, **RULES**. **I** CAN'T LEAVE THE NEIGHBORHOOD. **YOU** HAVE TO WEAR A *LEASH*.
WE'RE *BUSTING OUT*, BISCUIT! I'M TAKING OFF YOUR LEASH, AND WE'LL GO DOWN **NEW STREETS** TOGETHER– *FREE* AND **IN CONTROL** OF OUR DESTINY!!
BISCUIT? **BISCUIT?!** COME BACK SO WE CAN BE FREE AND IN CONTROL **TOGETHER**. *BISCUIT??*
YIP!
CLICK

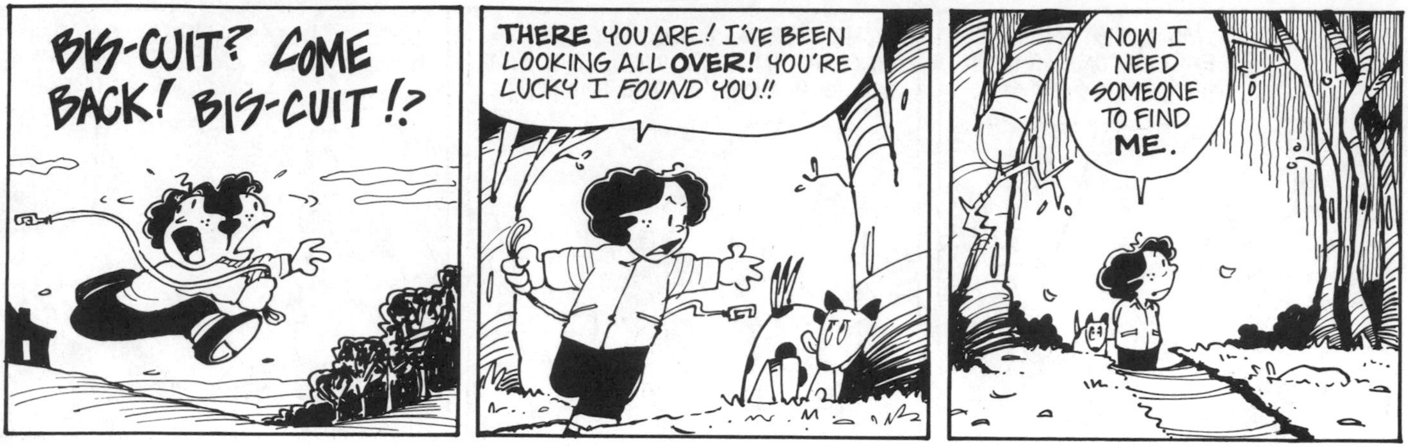
BIS-CUIT? COME BACK! BIS-CUIT!?
THERE YOU ARE! I'VE BEEN LOOKING ALL OVER! YOU'RE LUCKY I FOUND YOU!!
NOW I NEED SOMEONE TO FIND ME.

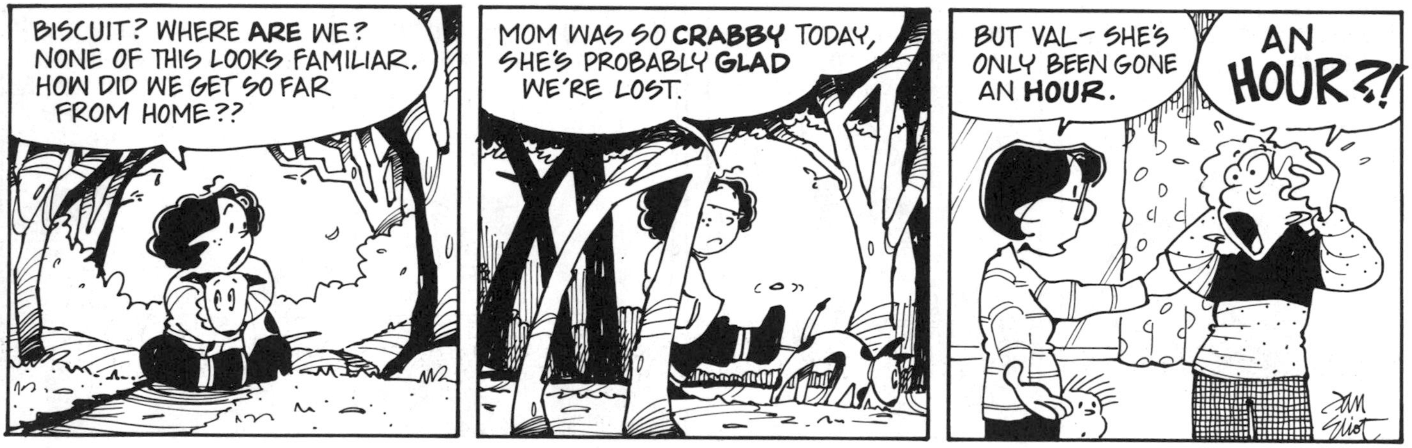
BISCUIT? WHERE ARE WE? NONE OF THIS LOOKS FAMILIAR. HOW DID WE GET SO FAR FROM HOME??
MOM WAS SO CRABBY TODAY, SHE'S PROBABLY GLAD WE'RE LOST.
BUT VAL- SHE'S ONLY BEEN GONE AN HOUR.
AN HOUR?!

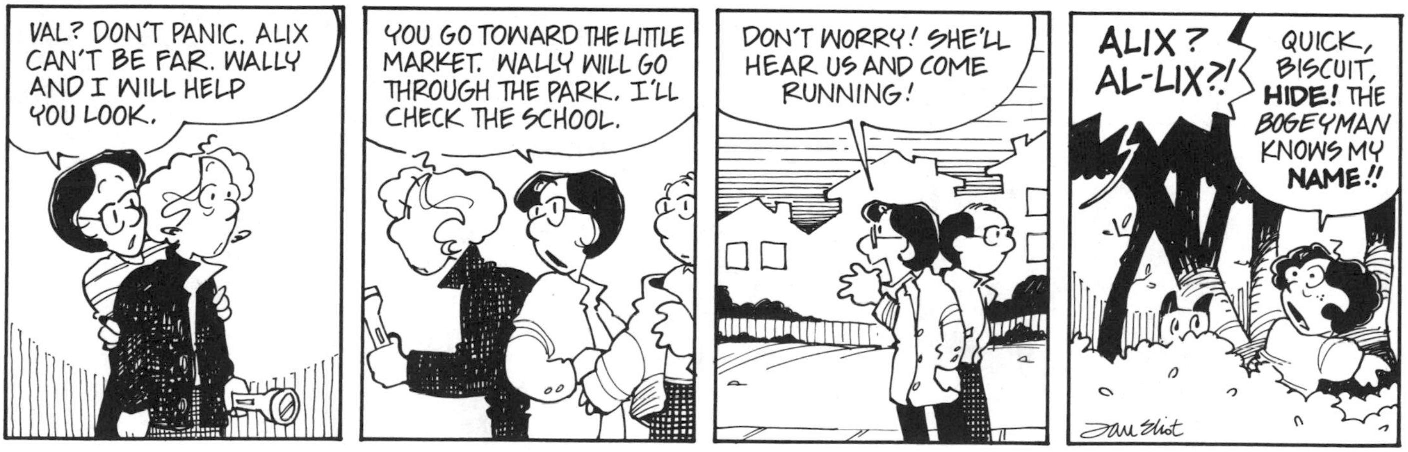
VAL? DON'T PANIC. ALIX CAN'T BE FAR. WALLY AND I WILL HELP YOU LOOK.
YOU GO TOWARD THE LITTLE MARKET. WALLY WILL GO THROUGH THE PARK. I'LL CHECK THE SCHOOL.
DON'T WORRY! SHE'LL HEAR US AND COME RUNNING!
ALIX? AL-LIX?!
QUICK, BISCUIT, HIDE! THE BOGEYMAN KNOWS MY NAME!!

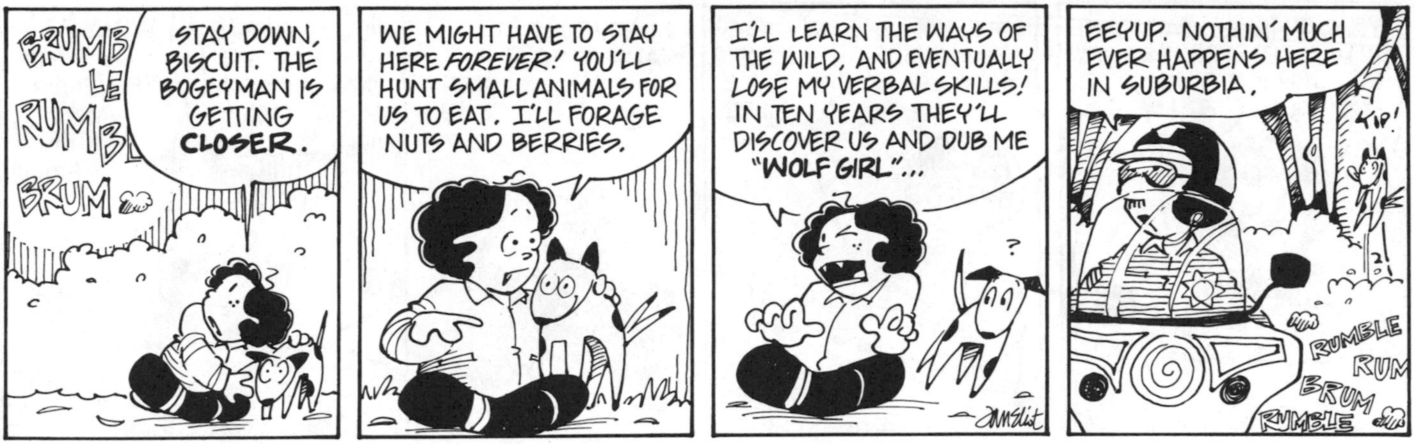
BRUMBLE RUMBLE BRUM
STAY DOWN, BISCUIT. THE BOGEYMAN IS GETTING **CLOSER**.
WE MIGHT HAVE TO STAY HERE *FOREVER!* YOU'LL HUNT SMALL ANIMALS FOR US TO EAT. I'LL FORAGE NUTS AND BERRIES.
I'LL LEARN THE WAYS OF THE WILD, AND EVENTUALLY *LOSE* MY VERBAL SKILLS! IN TEN YEARS THEY'LL DISCOVER US AND DUB ME "**WOLF GIRL**"...
?
EEYUP. NOTHIN' MUCH EVER HAPPENS HERE IN SUBURBIA.
YIP!
RUMBLE RUM BRUM RUMBLE

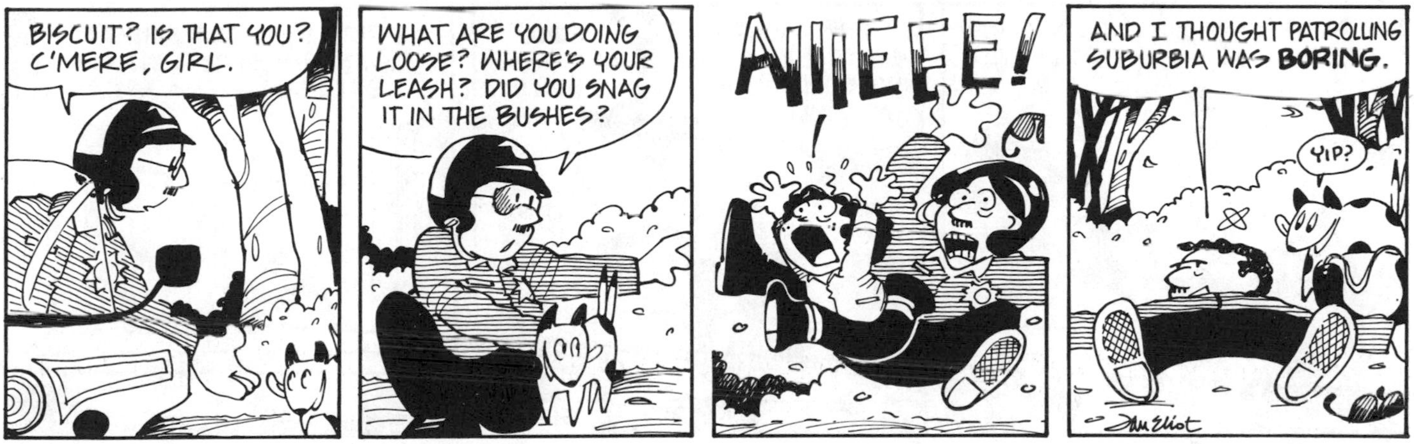
BISCUIT? IS THAT YOU? C'MERE, GIRL.
WHAT ARE YOU DOING LOOSE? WHERE'S YOUR LEASH? DID YOU SNAG IT IN THE BUSHES?
AIIEEE!
AND I THOUGHT PATROLLING SUBURBIA WAS **BORING**.
YIP?

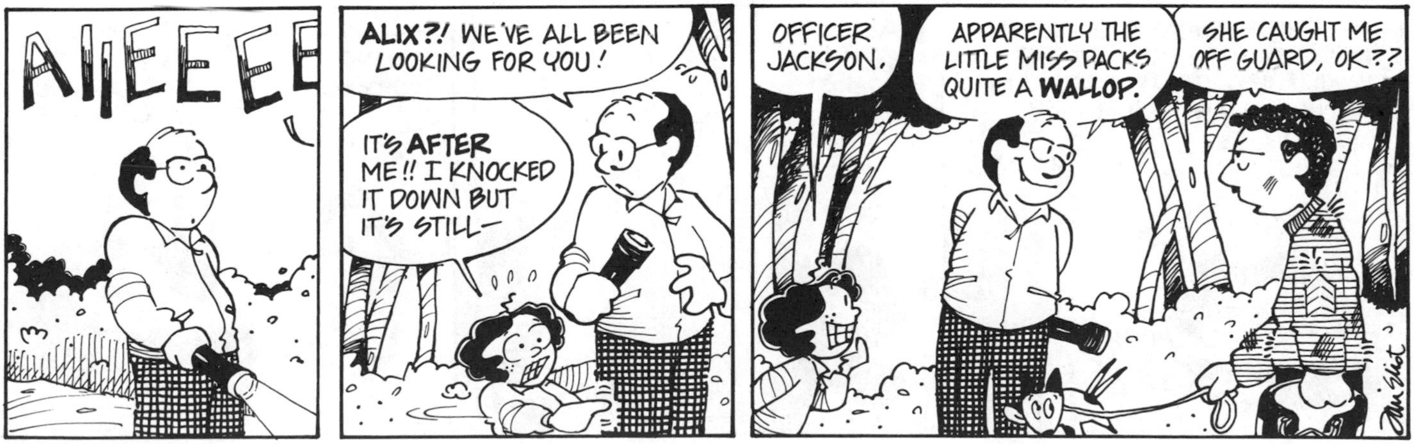
AIIEEEE
ALIX?! WE'VE ALL BEEN LOOKING FOR YOU!
IT'S **AFTER** ME!! I KNOCKED IT DOWN BUT IT'S STILL—
OFFICER JACKSON.
APPARENTLY THE LITTLE MISS PACKS QUITE A **WALLOP**.
SHE CAUGHT ME OFF GUARD, OK??

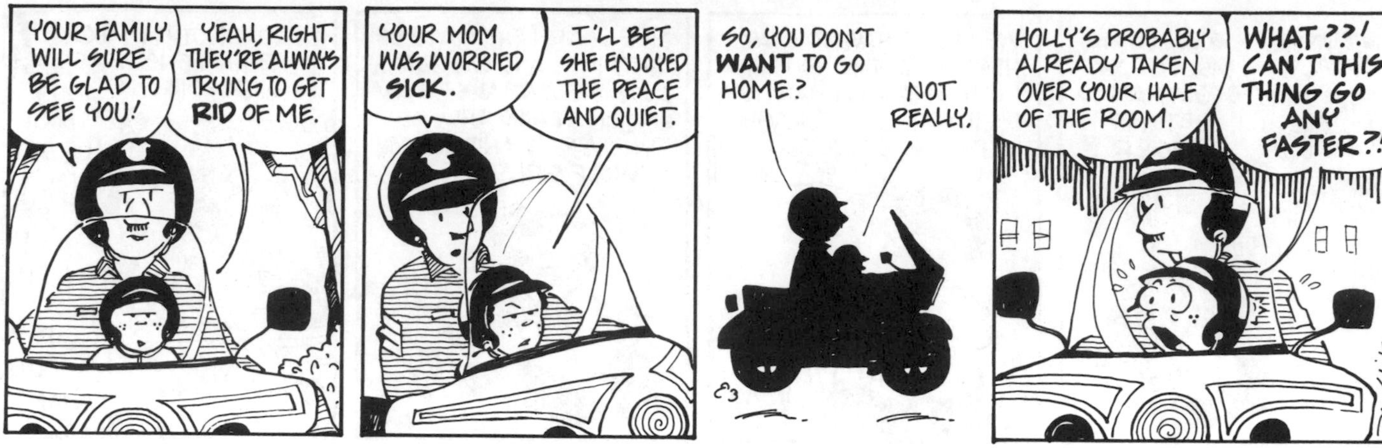
YOUR FAMILY WILL SURE BE GLAD TO SEE YOU!
YEAH, RIGHT. THEY'RE ALWAYS TRYING TO GET RID OF ME.
YOUR MOM WAS WORRIED SICK.
I'LL BET SHE ENJOYED THE PEACE AND QUIET.
SO, YOU DON'T WANT TO GO HOME?
NOT REALLY.
HOLLY'S PROBABLY ALREADY TAKEN OVER YOUR HALF OF THE ROOM.
WHAT??! CAN'T THIS THING GO ANY FASTER?!

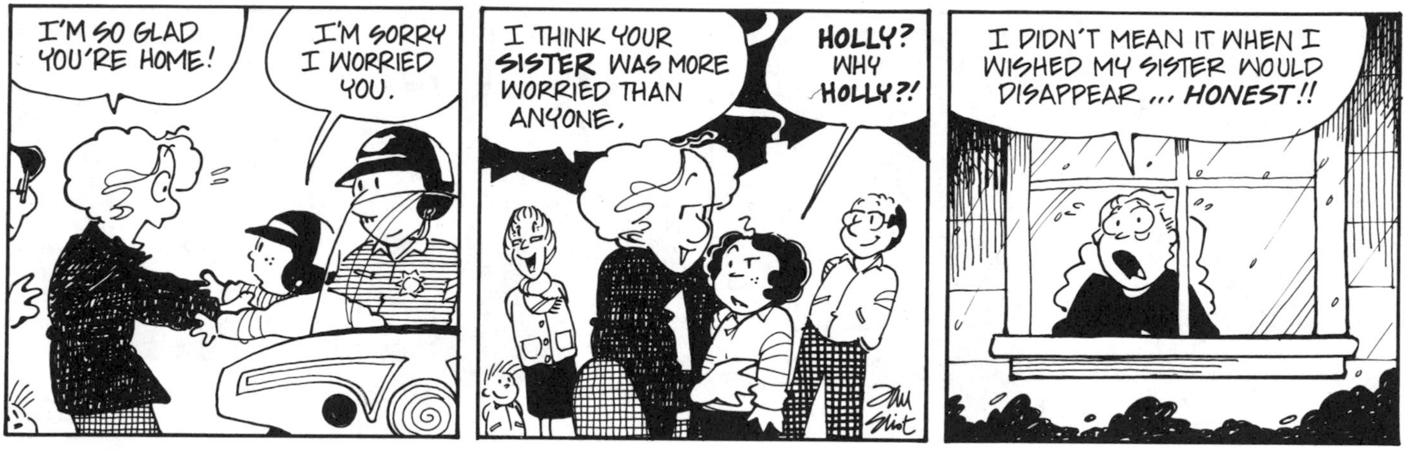
I'M SO GLAD YOU'RE HOME!
I'M SORRY I WORRIED YOU.
I THINK YOUR SISTER WAS MORE WORRIED THAN ANYONE.
HOLLY? WHY HOLLY?!
I DIDN'T MEAN IT WHEN I WISHED MY SISTER WOULD DISAPPEAR ... HONEST!!

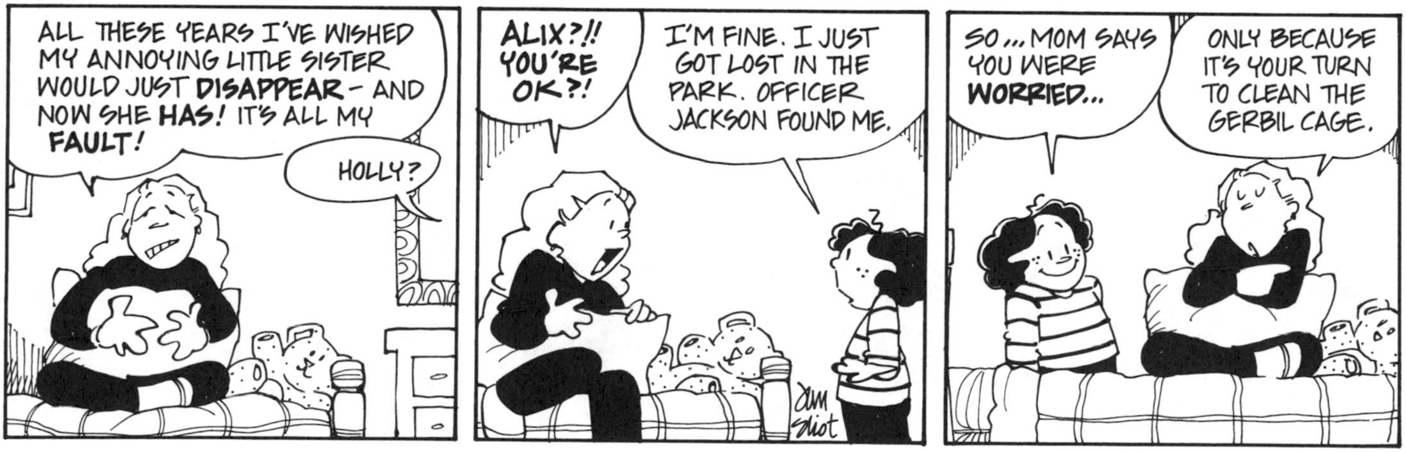
ALL THESE YEARS I'VE WISHED MY ANNOYING LITTLE SISTER WOULD JUST DISAPPEAR – AND NOW SHE HAS! IT'S ALL MY FAULT!
HOLLY?
ALIX?!! YOU'RE OK?!
I'M FINE. I JUST GOT LOST IN THE PARK. OFFICER JACKSON FOUND ME.
SO... MOM SAYS YOU WERE WORRIED...
ONLY BECAUSE IT'S YOUR TURN TO CLEAN THE GERBIL CAGE.

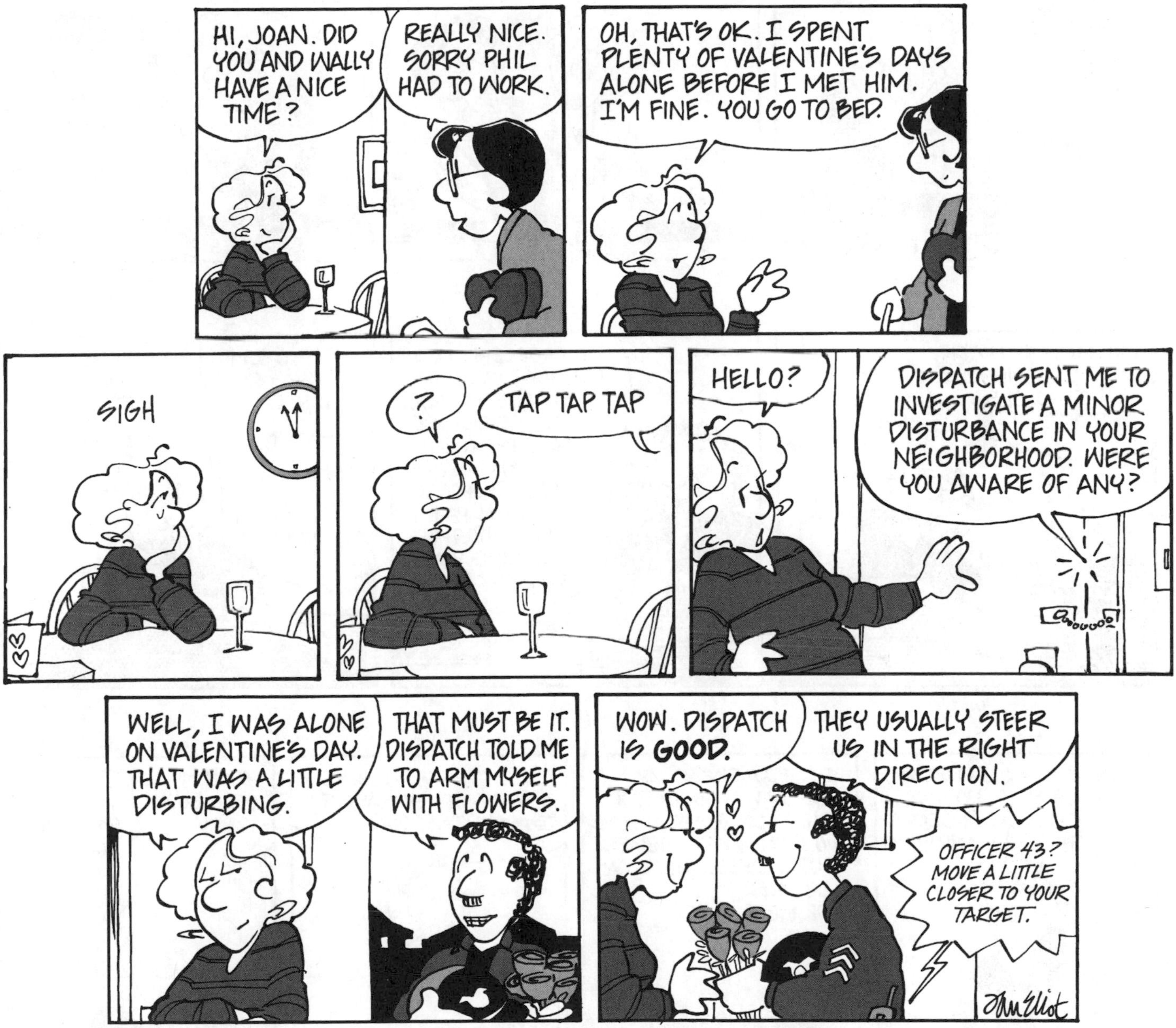

HI, JOAN. DID YOU AND WALLY HAVE A NICE TIME?
REALLY NICE. SORRY PHIL HAD TO WORK.
OH, THAT'S OK. I SPENT PLENTY OF VALENTINE'S DAYS ALONE BEFORE I MET HIM. I'M FINE. YOU GO TO BED.
SIGH
?
TAP TAP TAP
HELLO?
DISPATCH SENT ME TO INVESTIGATE A MINOR DISTURBANCE IN YOUR NEIGHBORHOOD. WERE YOU AWARE OF ANY?
WELL, I WAS ALONE ON VALENTINE'S DAY. THAT WAS A LITTLE DISTURBING.
THAT MUST BE IT. DISPATCH TOLD ME TO ARM MYSELF WITH FLOWERS.
WOW. DISPATCH IS **GOOD**.
THEY USUALLY STEER US IN THE RIGHT DIRECTION.
OFFICER 43? MOVE A LITTLE CLOSER TO YOUR TARGET.
Jan Eliot

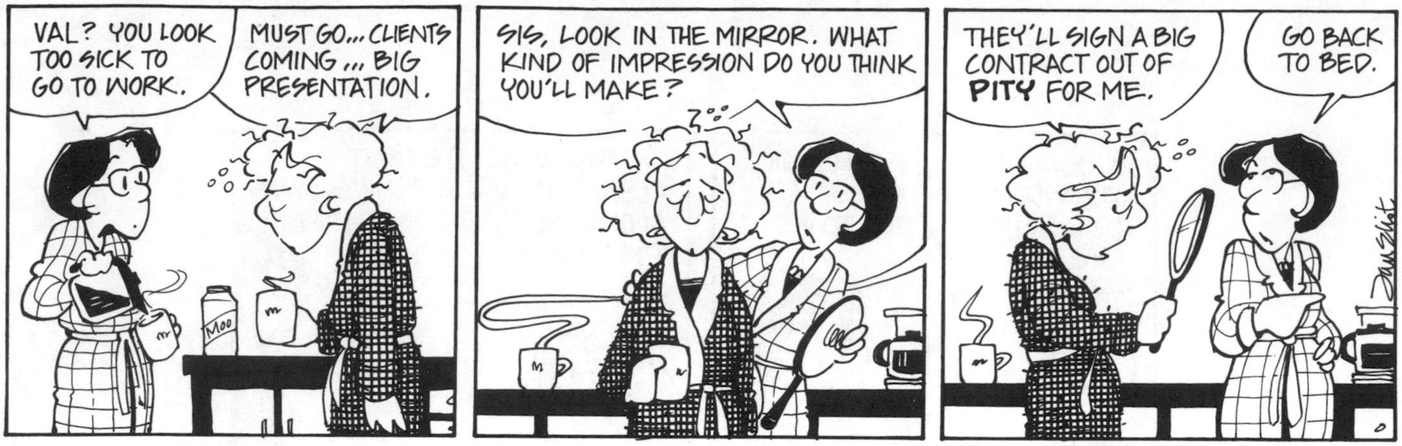
VAL? YOU LOOK TOO SICK TO GO TO WORK.
MUST GO... CLIENTS COMING ... BIG PRESENTATION.
SIS, LOOK IN THE MIRROR. WHAT KIND OF IMPRESSION DO YOU THINK YOU'LL MAKE?
THEY'LL SIGN A BIG CONTRACT OUT OF **PITY** FOR ME.
GO BACK TO BED.

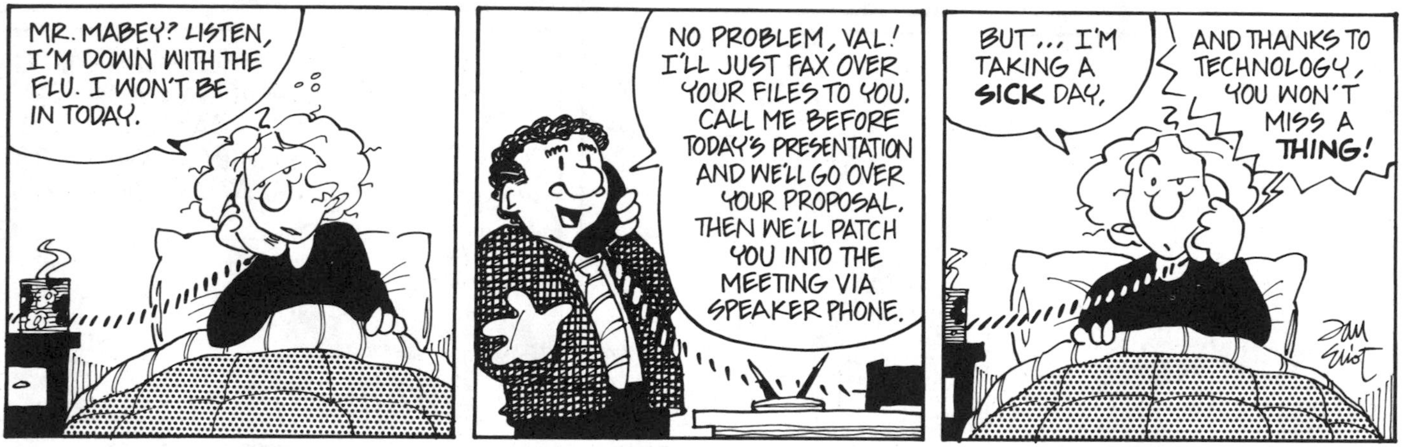
MR. MABEY? LISTEN, I'M DOWN WITH THE FLU. I WON'T BE IN TODAY.
NO PROBLEM, VAL! I'LL JUST FAX OVER YOUR FILES TO YOU. CALL ME BEFORE TODAY'S PRESENTATION AND WE'LL GO OVER YOUR PROPOSAL. THEN WE'LL PATCH YOU INTO THE MEETING VIA SPEAKER PHONE.
BUT... I'M TAKING A **SICK** DAY.
AND THANKS TO TECHNOLOGY, YOU WON'T MISS A **THING**!

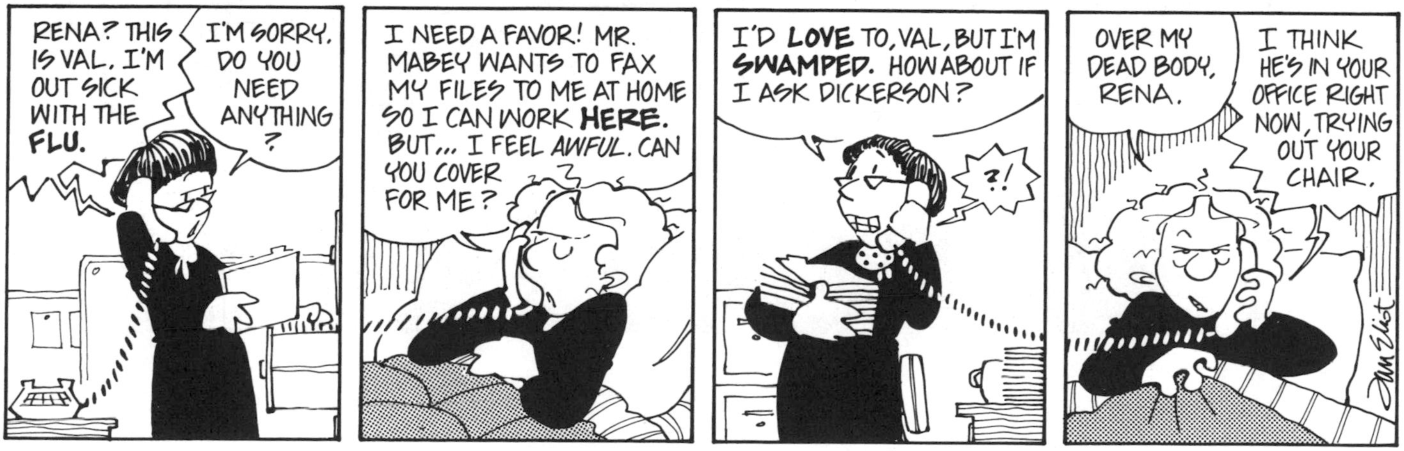
RENA? THIS IS VAL. I'M OUT SICK WITH THE **FLU**.
I'M SORRY. DO YOU NEED ANYTHING?
I NEED A FAVOR! MR. MABEY WANTS TO FAX MY FILES TO ME AT HOME SO I CAN WORK **HERE**. BUT... I FEEL *AWFUL*. CAN YOU COVER FOR ME?
I'D **LOVE** TO, VAL, BUT I'M **SWAMPED**. HOW ABOUT IF I ASK DICKERSON?
?!
OVER MY DEAD BODY, RENA.
I THINK HE'S IN YOUR OFFICE RIGHT NOW, TRYING OUT YOUR CHAIR.

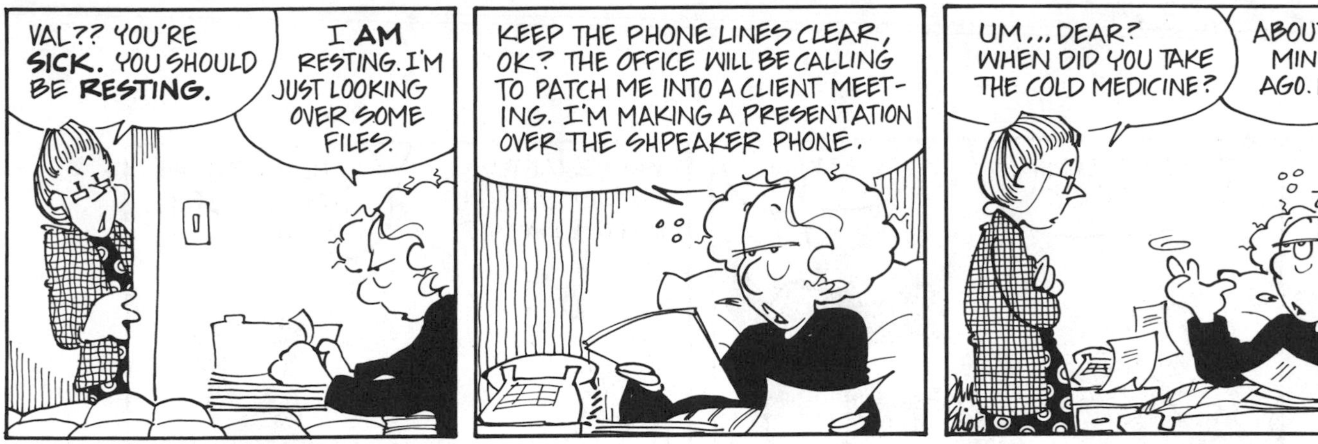
VAL?? YOU'RE **SICK.** YOU SHOULD BE **RESTING.**
I **AM** RESTING. I'M JUST LOOKING OVER SOME FILES.
KEEP THE PHONE LINES CLEAR, OK? THE OFFICE WILL BE CALLING TO PATCH ME INTO A CLIENT MEETING. I'M MAKING A PRESENTATION OVER THE SHPEAKER PHONE.
UM,... DEAR? WHEN DID YOU TAKE THE COLD MEDICINE?
ABOUT 20 MINITH AGO. WHYEE?

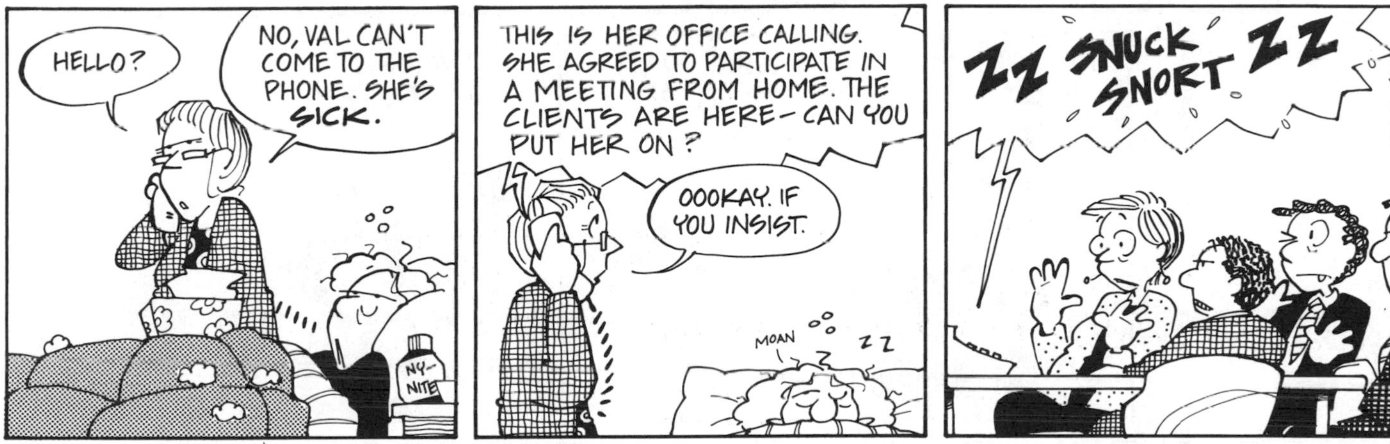
HELLO?
NO, VAL CAN'T COME TO THE PHONE. SHE'S **SICK.**
NY-NITE
THIS IS HER OFFICE CALLING. SHE AGREED TO PARTICIPATE IN A MEETING FROM HOME. THE CLIENTS ARE HERE — CAN YOU PUT HER ON?
OOOKAY. IF YOU INSIST.
MOAN
Z Z
ZZ SNUCK SNORT ZZ

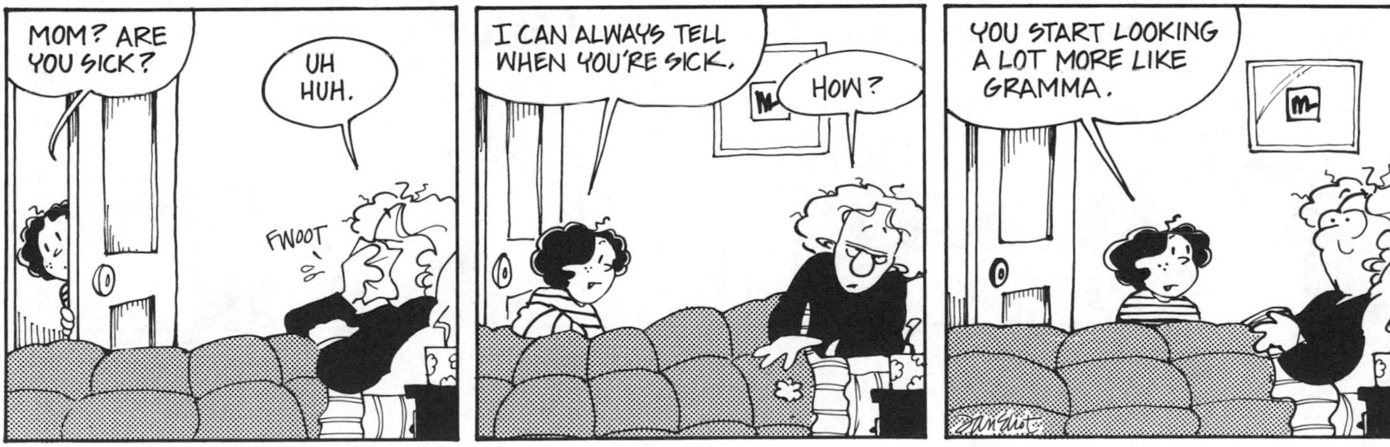
MOM? ARE YOU SICK?
UH HUH.
FWOOT
I CAN ALWAYS TELL WHEN YOU'RE SICK.
HOW?
YOU START LOOKING A LOT MORE LIKE GRAMMA.

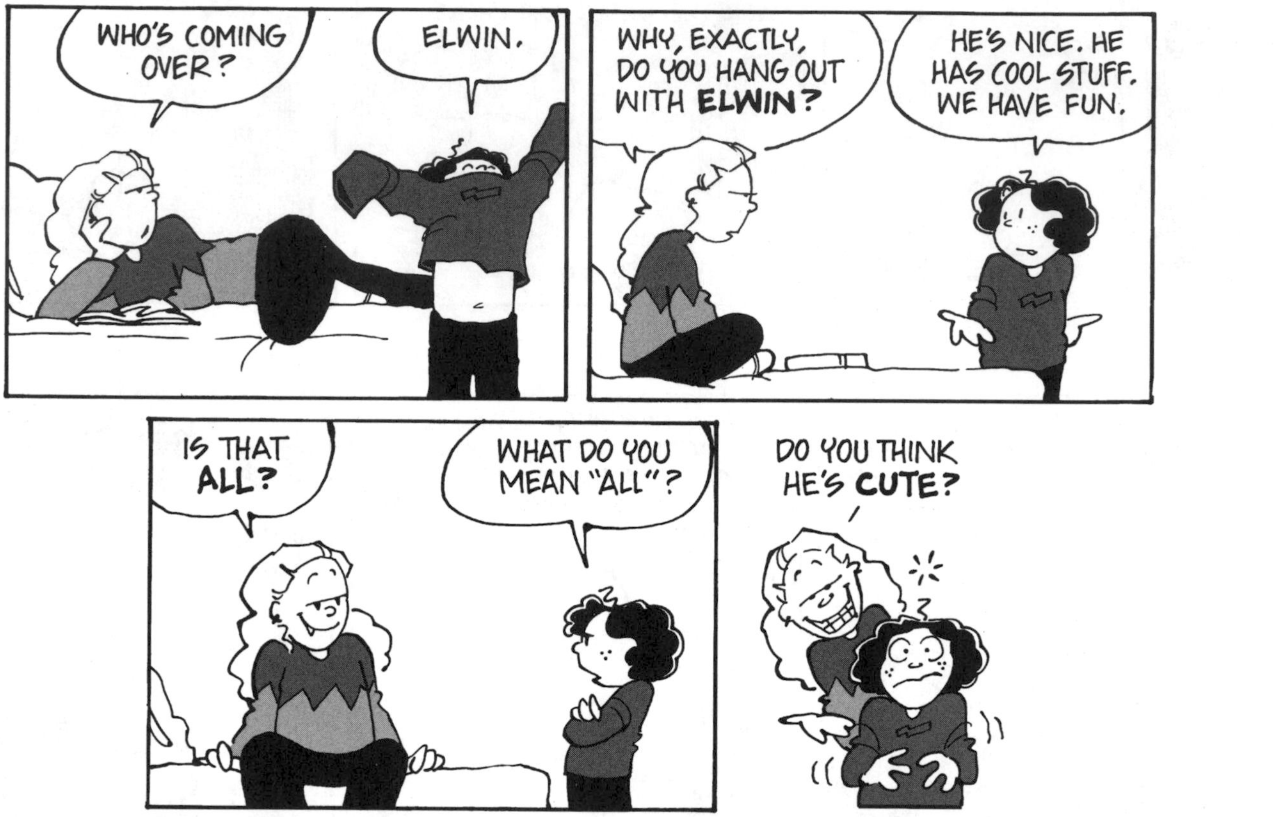
WHO'S COMING OVER?
ELWIN.
WHY, EXACTLY, DO YOU HANG OUT WITH **ELWIN**?
HE'S NICE. HE HAS COOL STUFF. WE HAVE FUN.
IS THAT **ALL**?
WHAT DO YOU MEAN "ALL"?
DO YOU THINK HE'S **CUTE**?

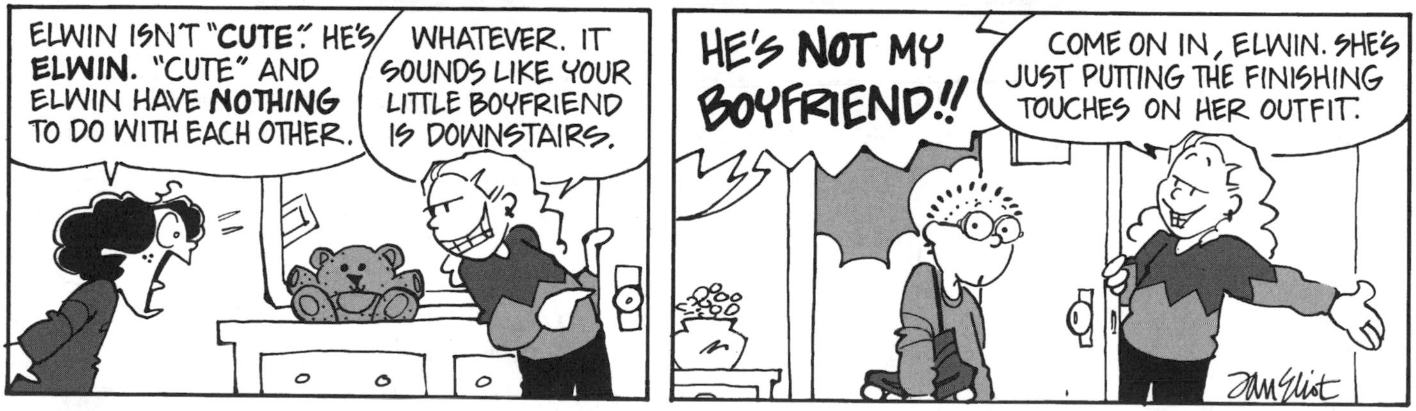
ELWIN ISN'T "**CUTE**." HE'S **ELWIN**. "CUTE" AND ELWIN HAVE **NOTHING** TO DO WITH EACH OTHER.
WHATEVER. IT SOUNDS LIKE YOUR LITTLE BOYFRIEND IS DOWNSTAIRS.
HE'S **NOT** MY BOYFRIEND!!
COME ON IN, ELWIN. SHE'S JUST PUTTING THE FINISHING TOUCHES ON HER OUTFIT.
Jan Eliot

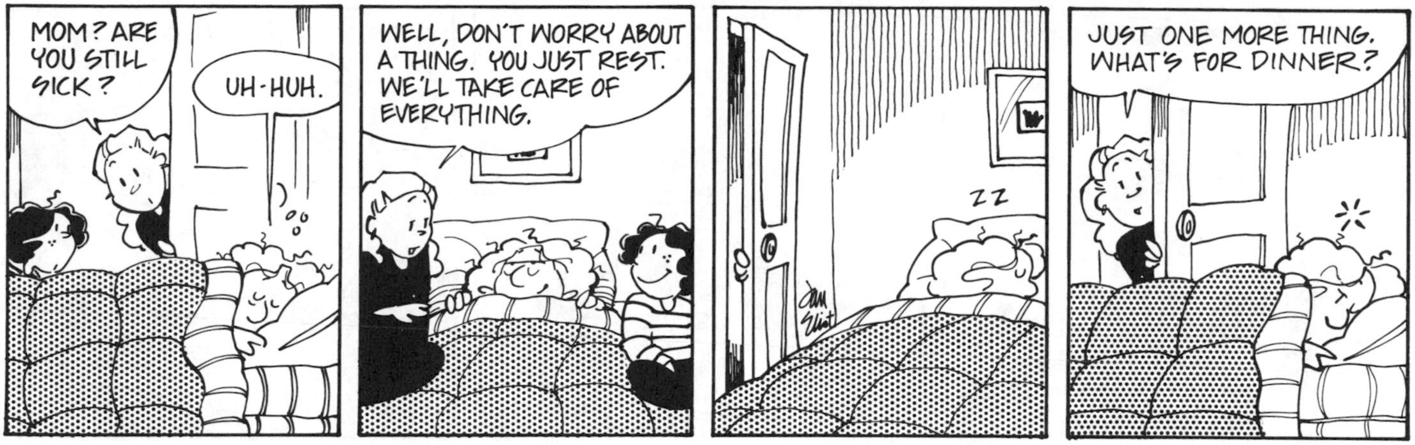
MOM? ARE YOU STILL SICK?
UH-HUH.
WELL, DON'T WORRY ABOUT A THING. YOU JUST REST. WE'LL TAKE CARE OF EVERYTHING.
ZZ
JUST ONE MORE THING. WHAT'S FOR DINNER?

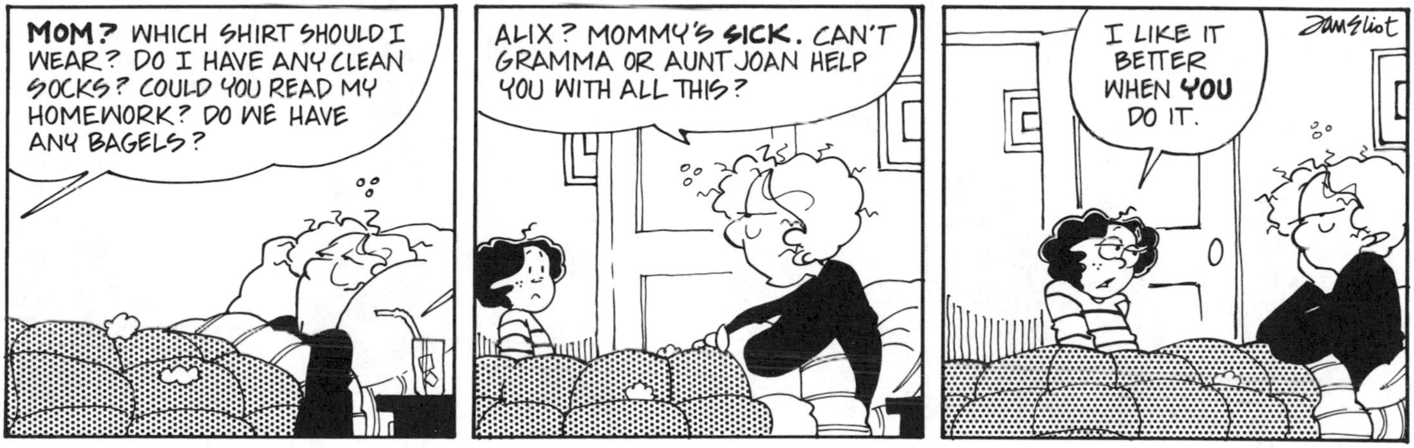
MOM? WHICH SHIRT SHOULD I WEAR? DO I HAVE ANY CLEAN SOCKS? COULD YOU READ MY HOMEWORK? DO WE HAVE ANY BAGELS?
ALIX? MOMMY'S SICK. CAN'T GRAMMA OR AUNT JOAN HELP YOU WITH ALL THIS?
I LIKE IT BETTER WHEN YOU DO IT.

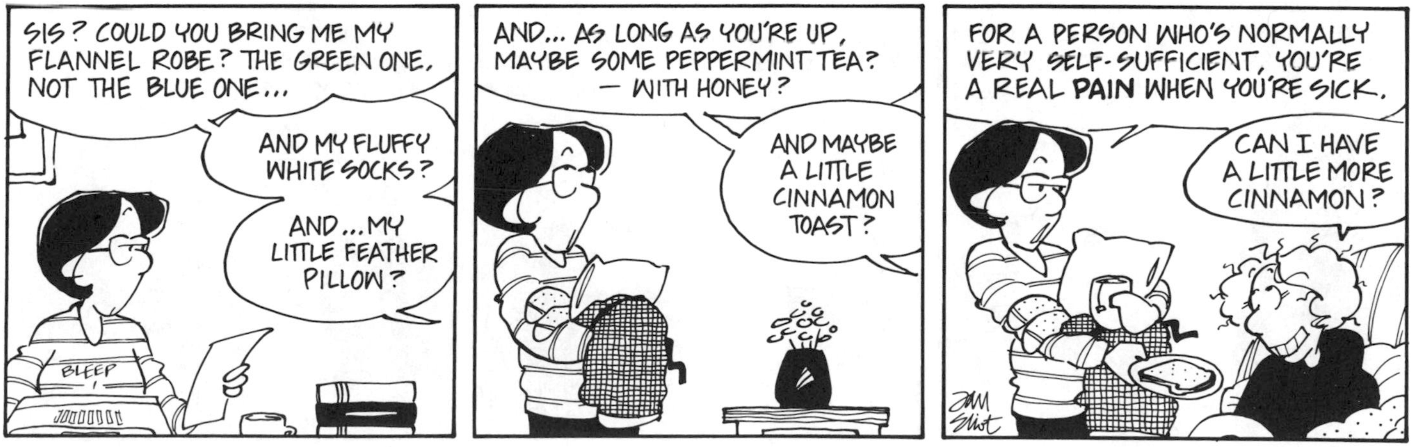
SIS? COULD YOU BRING ME MY FLANNEL ROBE? THE GREEN ONE, NOT THE BLUE ONE...
AND MY FLUFFY WHITE SOCKS?
AND...MY LITTLE FEATHER PILLOW?
BLEEP
AND... AS LONG AS YOU'RE UP, MAYBE SOME PEPPERMINT TEA? — WITH HONEY?
AND MAYBE A LITTLE CINNAMON TOAST?
FOR A PERSON WHO'S NORMALLY VERY SELF-SUFFICIENT, YOU'RE A REAL PAIN WHEN YOU'RE SICK.
CAN I HAVE A LITTLE MORE CINNAMON?

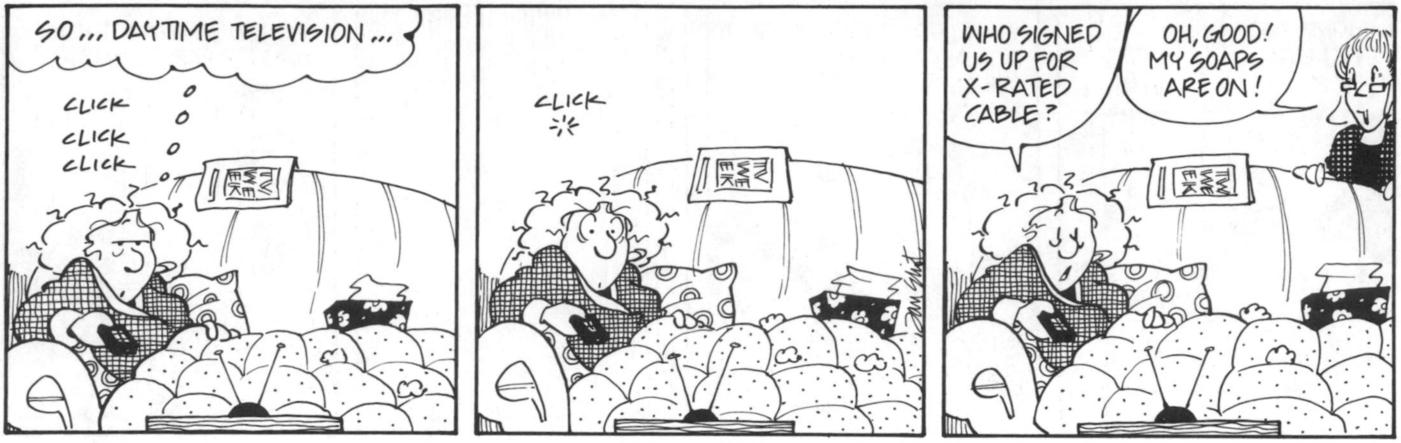
SO... DAYTIME TELEVISION...
CLICK
CLICK
CLICK
CLICK
WHO SIGNED US UP FOR X-RATED CABLE?
OH, GOOD! MY SOAPS ARE ON!

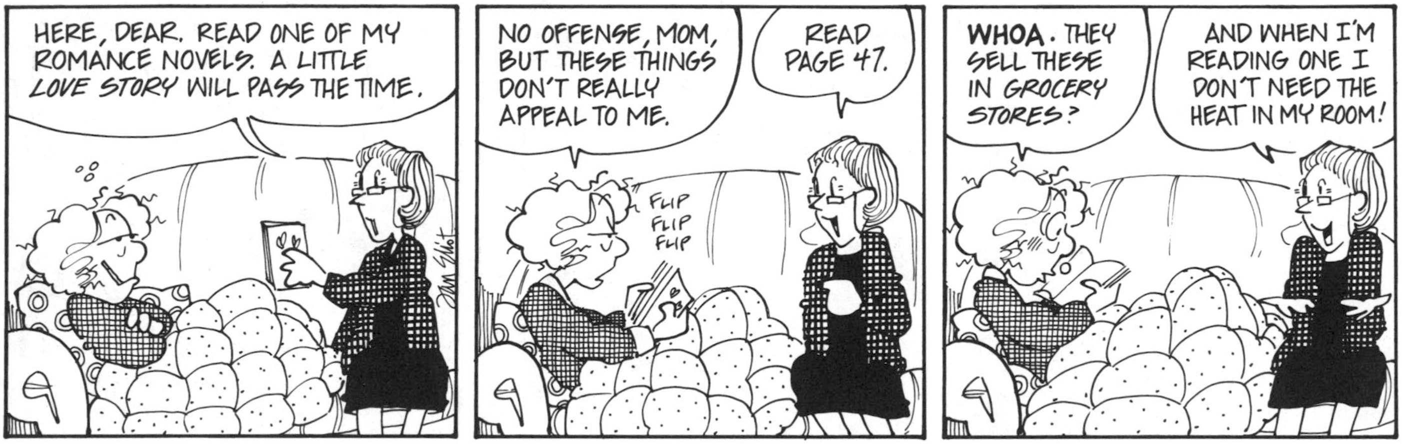
HERE, DEAR. READ ONE OF MY ROMANCE NOVELS. A LITTLE LOVE STORY WILL PASS THE TIME.
NO OFFENSE, MOM, BUT THESE THINGS DON'T REALLY APPEAL TO ME.
READ PAGE 47.
FLIP FLIP FLIP
WHOA. THEY SELL THESE IN GROCERY STORES?
AND WHEN I'M READING ONE I DON'T NEED THE HEAT IN MY ROOM!

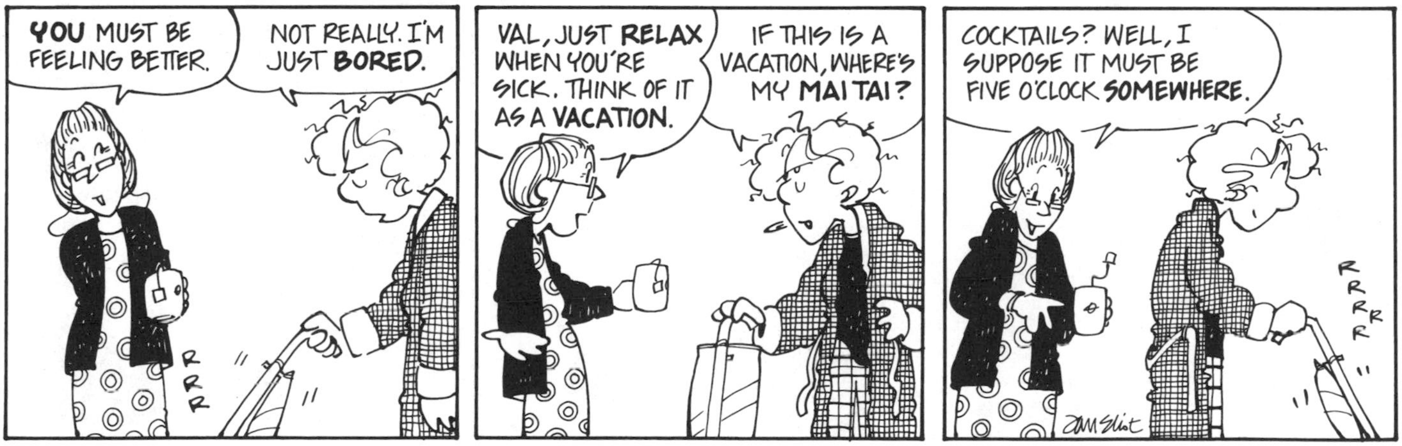
YOU MUST BE FEELING BETTER.
NOT REALLY. I'M JUST BORED.
RRR
VAL, JUST RELAX WHEN YOU'RE SICK. THINK OF IT AS A VACATION.
IF THIS IS A VACATION, WHERE'S MY MAI TAI?
COCKTAILS? WELL, I SUPPOSE IT MUST BE FIVE O'CLOCK SOMEWHERE.
RRRRR

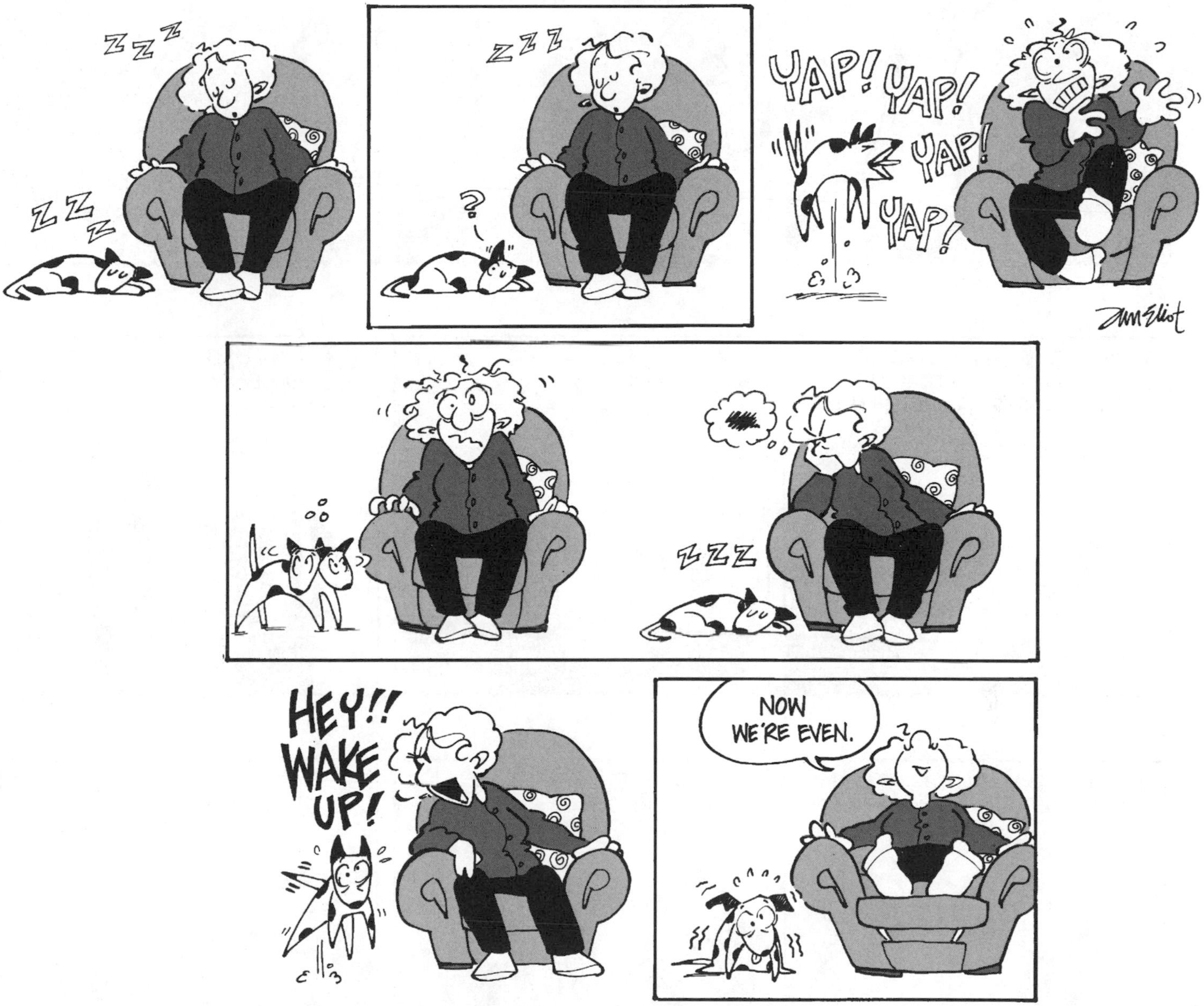
Z Z Z
Z Z Z
?
Z Z Z
YAP! YAP! YAP! YAP!
Jan Eliot
Z Z Z
HEY!! WAKE UP!
NOW WE'RE EVEN.

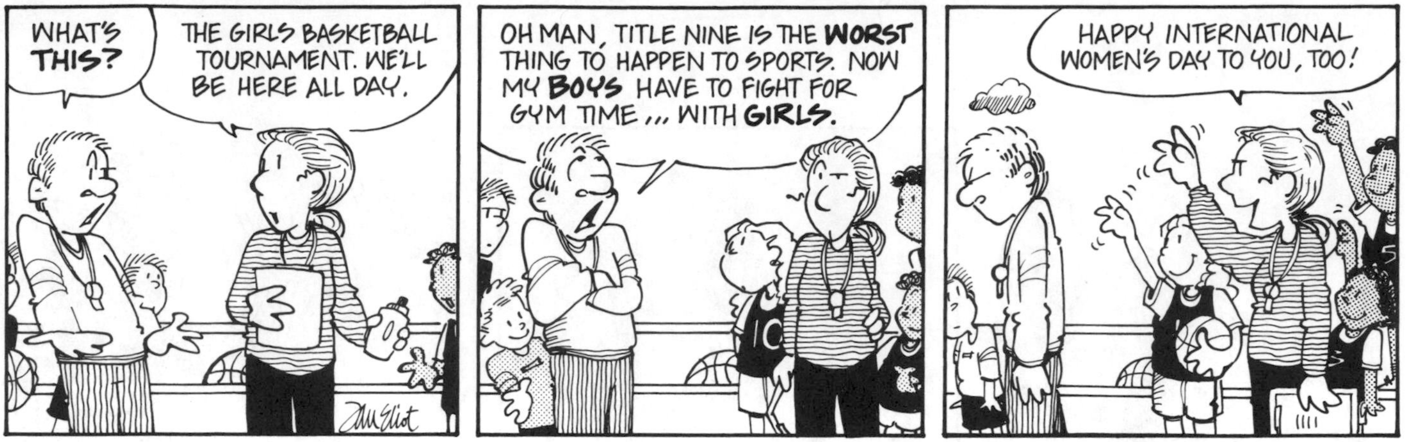
WHAT'S THIS?
THE GIRLS BASKETBALL TOURNAMENT. WE'LL BE HERE ALL DAY.
OH MAN, TITLE NINE IS THE WORST THING TO HAPPEN TO SPORTS. NOW MY BOYS HAVE TO FIGHT FOR GYM TIME ... WITH GIRLS.
HAPPY INTERNATIONAL WOMEN'S DAY TO YOU, TOO!

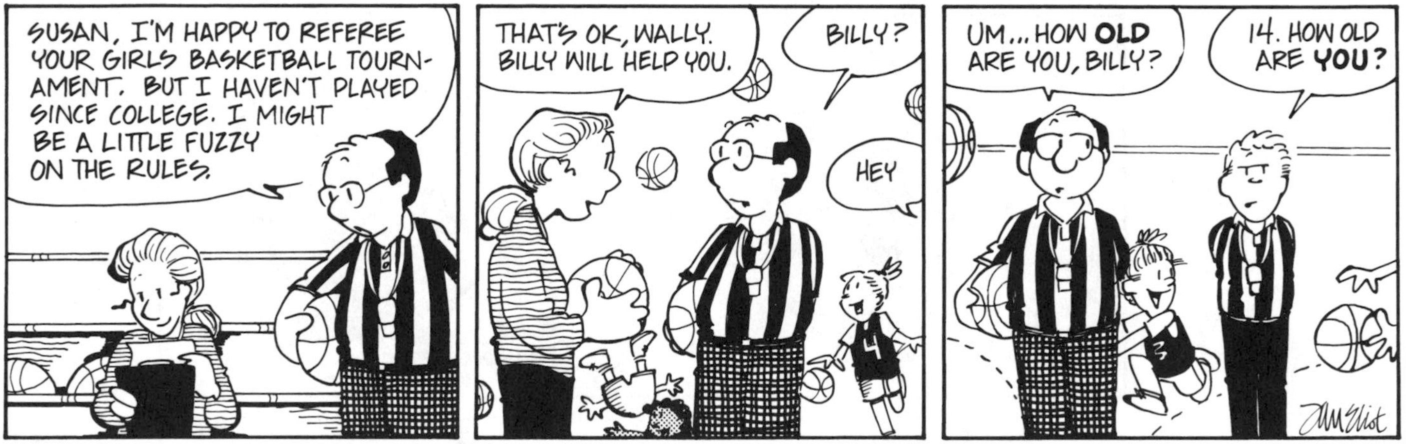
SUSAN, I'M HAPPY TO REFEREE YOUR GIRLS BASKETBALL TOURNAMENT. BUT I HAVEN'T PLAYED SINCE COLLEGE. I MIGHT BE A LITTLE FUZZY ON THE RULES.
THAT'S OK, WALLY. BILLY WILL HELP YOU.
BILLY?
HEY
UM... HOW OLD ARE YOU, BILLY?
14. HOW OLD ARE YOU?

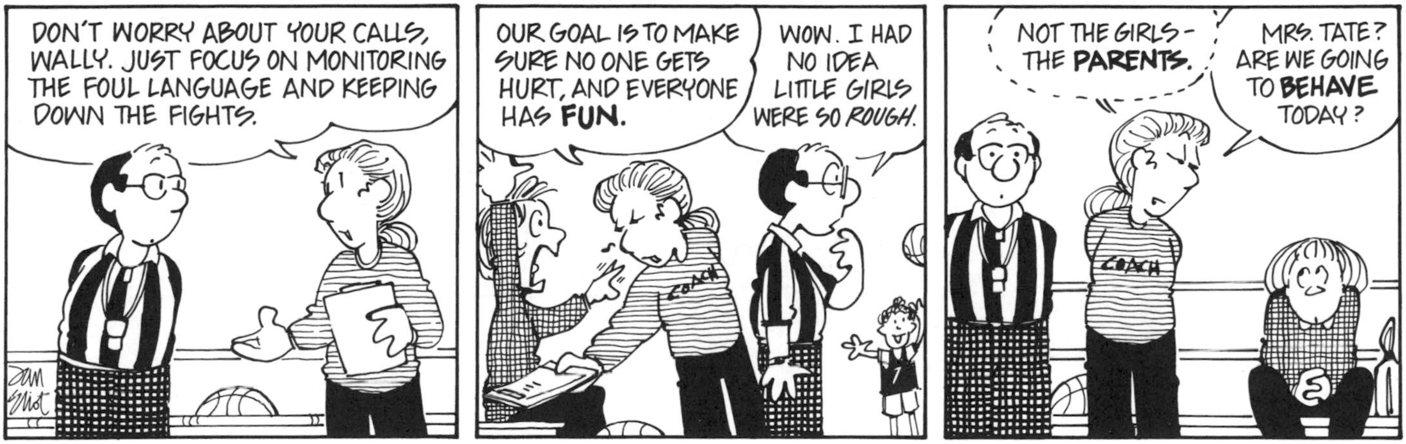
DON'T WORRY ABOUT YOUR CALLS, WALLY. JUST FOCUS ON MONITORING THE FOUL LANGUAGE AND KEEPING DOWN THE FIGHTS.
OUR GOAL IS TO MAKE SURE NO ONE GETS HURT, AND EVERYONE HAS FUN.
WOW. I HAD NO IDEA LITTLE GIRLS WERE SO ROUGH.
NOT THE GIRLS - THE PARENTS.
MRS. TATE? ARE WE GOING TO BEHAVE TODAY?

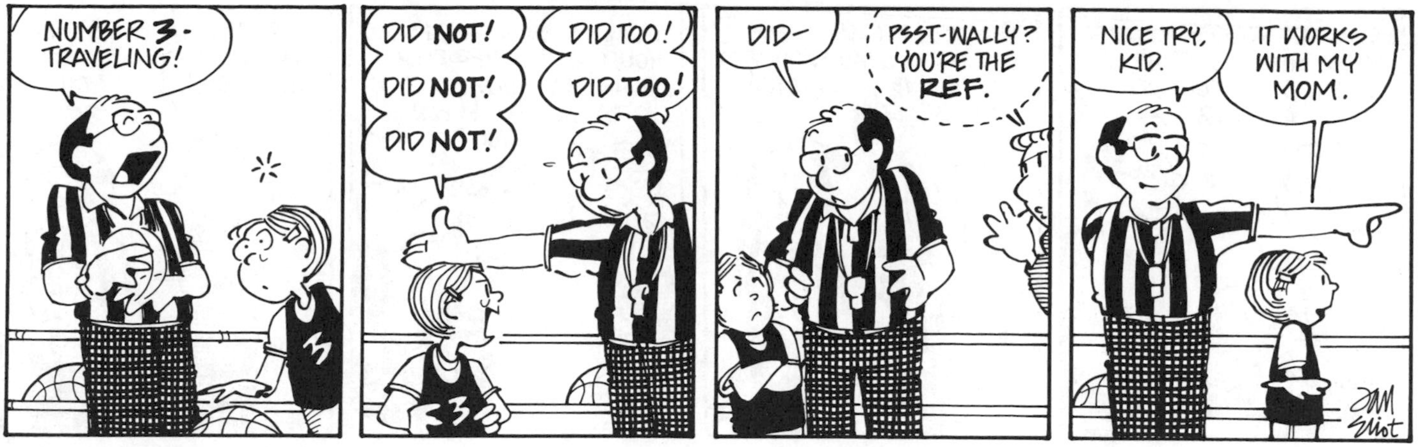
NUMBER 3 - TRAVELING!
DID NOT! DID NOT! DID NOT!
DID TOO! DID TOO!
DID-
PSST-WALLY? YOU'RE THE REF.
NICE TRY, KID.
IT WORKS WITH MY MOM.

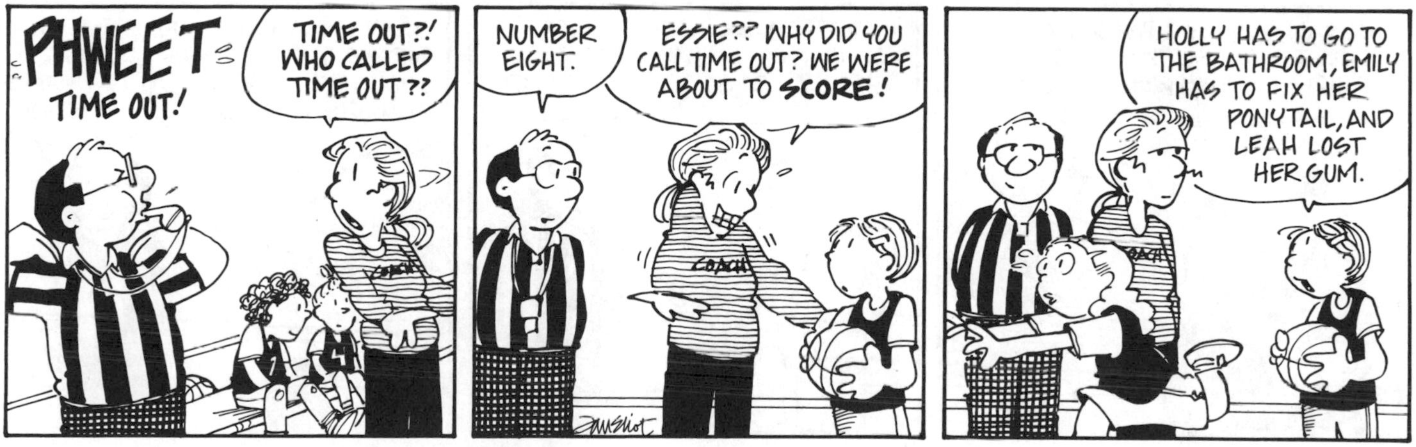
PHWEET
TIME OUT!
TIME OUT?! WHO CALLED TIME OUT??
NUMBER EIGHT.
ESSIE?? WHY DID YOU CALL TIME OUT? WE WERE ABOUT TO SCORE!
HOLLY HAS TO GO TO THE BATHROOM, EMILY HAS TO FIX HER PONYTAIL, AND LEAH LOST HER GUM.

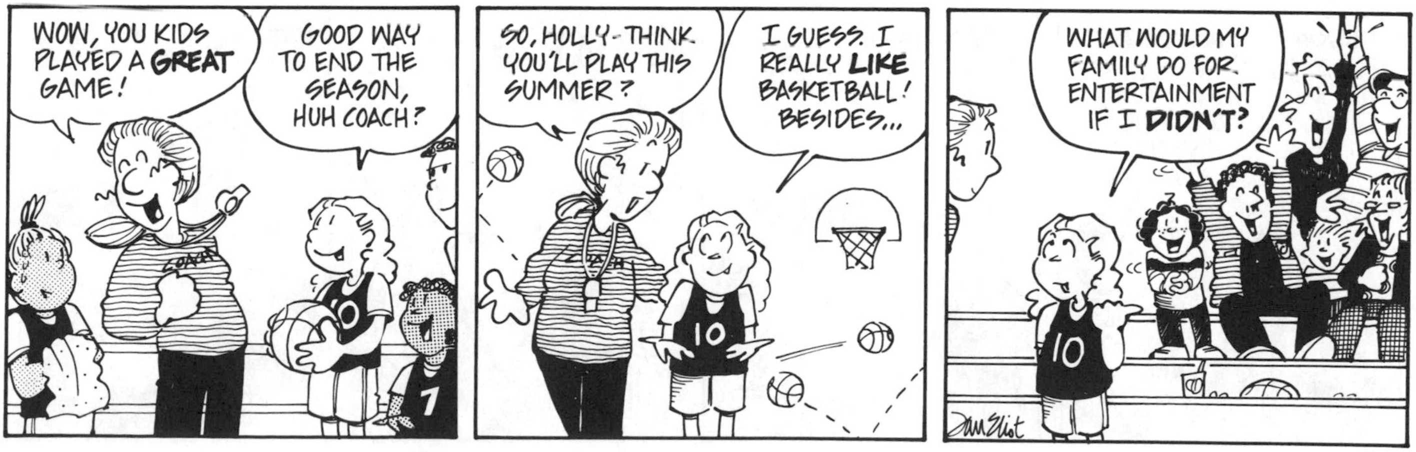
WOW, YOU KIDS PLAYED A GREAT GAME!
GOOD WAY TO END THE SEASON, HUH COACH?
SO, HOLLY- THINK YOU'LL PLAY THIS SUMMER?
I GUESS. I REALLY LIKE BASKETBALL! BESIDES...
WHAT WOULD MY FAMILY DO FOR ENTERTAINMENT IF I DIDN'T?

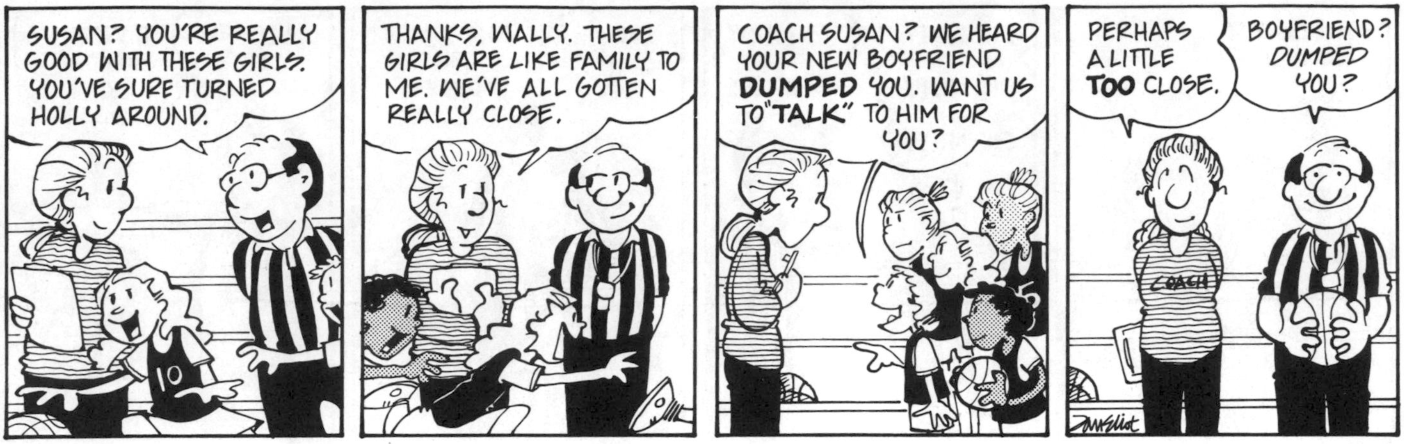
SUSAN? YOU'RE REALLY GOOD WITH THESE GIRLS. YOU'VE SURE TURNED HOLLY AROUND.
THANKS, WALLY. THESE GIRLS ARE LIKE FAMILY TO ME. WE'VE ALL GOTTEN REALLY CLOSE.
COACH SUSAN? WE HEARD YOUR NEW BOYFRIEND **DUMPED** YOU. WANT US TO "**TALK**" TO HIM FOR YOU?
PERHAPS A LITTLE **TOO** CLOSE.
BOYFRIEND? *DUMPED* YOU?
COACH

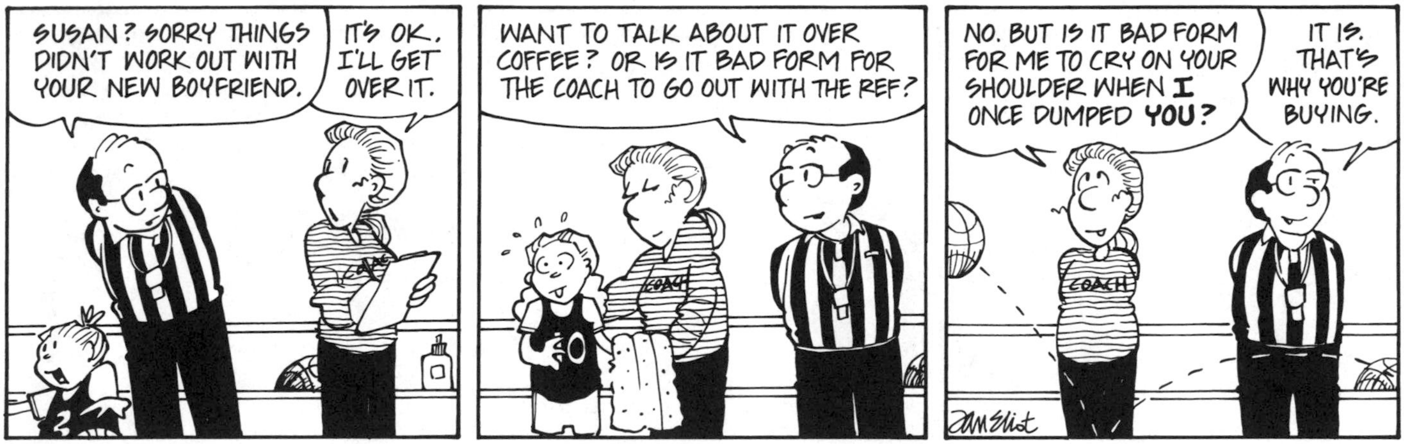
SUSAN? SORRY THINGS DIDN'T WORK OUT WITH YOUR NEW BOYFRIEND.
IT'S OK. I'LL GET OVER IT.
WANT TO TALK ABOUT IT OVER COFFEE? OR IS IT BAD FORM FOR THE COACH TO GO OUT WITH THE REF?
NO. BUT IS IT BAD FORM FOR ME TO CRY ON YOUR SHOULDER WHEN **I** ONCE DUMPED **YOU**?
IT IS. THAT'S WHY YOU'RE BUYING.
COACH

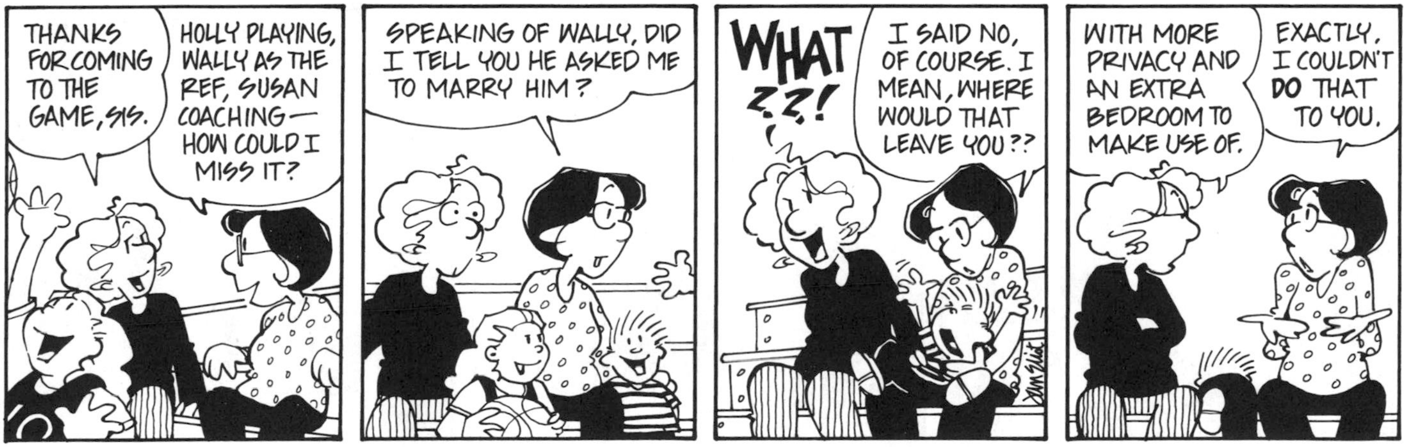
THANKS FOR COMING TO THE GAME, SIS.
HOLLY PLAYING, WALLY AS THE REF, SUSAN COACHING— HOW COULD I MISS IT?
SPEAKING OF WALLY, DID I TELL YOU HE ASKED ME TO MARRY HIM?
WHAT ??!
I SAID NO, OF COURSE. I MEAN, WHERE WOULD THAT LEAVE YOU??
WITH MORE PRIVACY AND AN EXTRA BEDROOM TO MAKE USE OF.
EXACTLY. I COULDN'T **DO** THAT TO YOU.

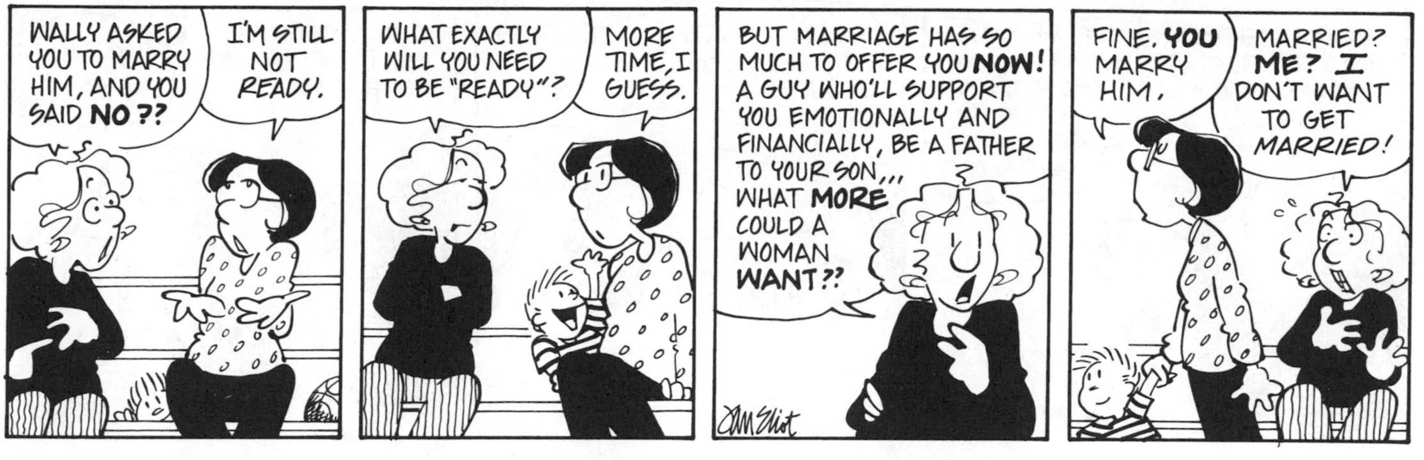
WALLY ASKED YOU TO MARRY HIM, AND YOU SAID **NO??**
I'M STILL NOT *READY.*
WHAT EXACTLY WILL YOU NEED TO BE "READY"?
MORE TIME, I GUESS.
BUT MARRIAGE HAS SO MUCH TO OFFER YOU **NOW!** A GUY WHO'LL SUPPORT YOU EMOTIONALLY AND FINANCIALLY, BE A FATHER TO YOUR SON,,, WHAT **MORE** COULD A WOMAN **WANT??**
FINE. **YOU** MARRY HIM.
MARRIED? **ME? I** DON'T WANT TO GET *MARRIED!*

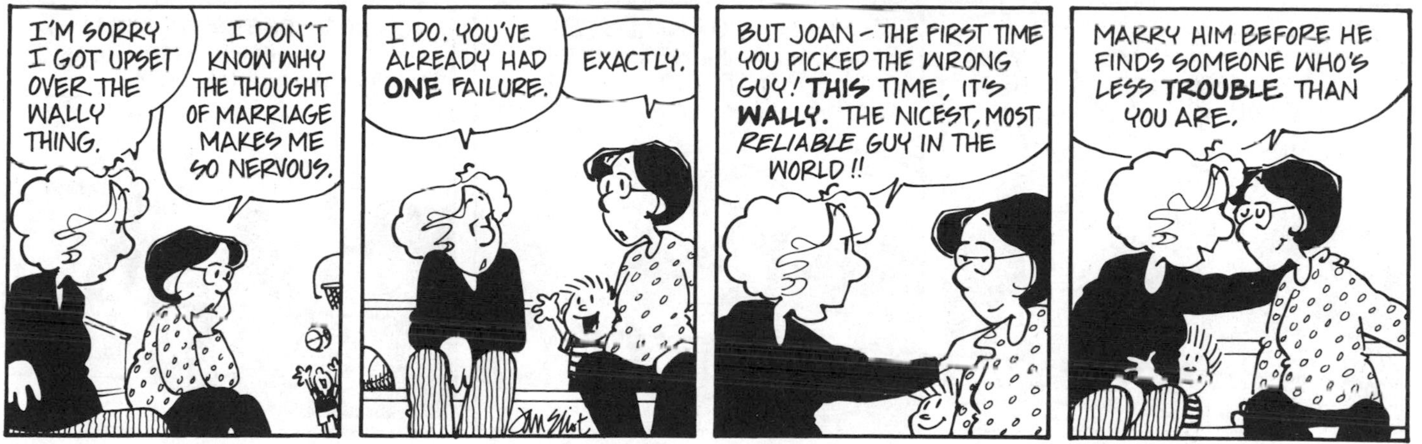
I'M SORRY I GOT UPSET OVER THE WALLY THING.
I DON'T KNOW WHY THE THOUGHT OF MARRIAGE MAKES ME SO NERVOUS.
I DO. YOU'VE ALREADY HAD **ONE** FAILURE.
EXACTLY.
BUT JOAN – THE FIRST TIME YOU PICKED THE WRONG GUY! **THIS** TIME, IT'S **WALLY.** THE NICEST, MOST *RELIABLE* GUY IN THE WORLD!!
MARRY HIM BEFORE HE FINDS SOMEONE WHO'S LESS **TROUBLE** THAN YOU ARE.

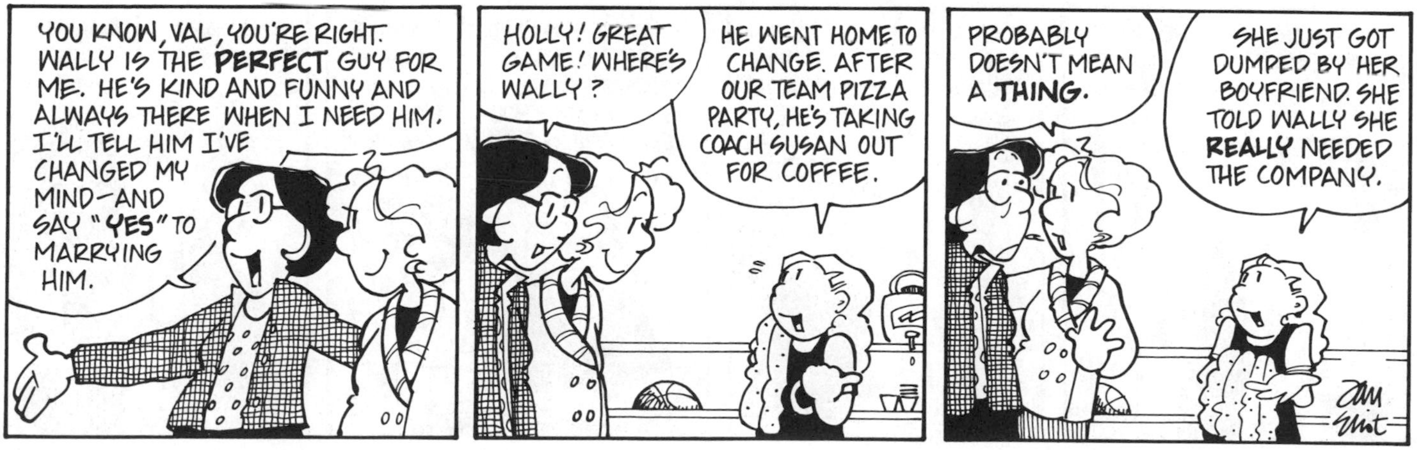
YOU KNOW, VAL, YOU'RE RIGHT. WALLY IS THE **PERFECT** GUY FOR ME. HE'S KIND AND FUNNY AND ALWAYS THERE WHEN I NEED HIM. I'LL TELL HIM I'VE CHANGED MY MIND–AND SAY "**YES**" TO MARRYING HIM.
HOLLY! GREAT GAME! WHERE'S WALLY?
HE WENT HOME TO CHANGE. AFTER OUR TEAM PIZZA PARTY, HE'S TAKING COACH SUSAN OUT FOR COFFEE.
PROBABLY DOESN'T MEAN A **THING.**
SHE JUST GOT DUMPED BY HER BOYFRIEND. SHE TOLD WALLY SHE **REALLY** NEEDED THE COMPANY.

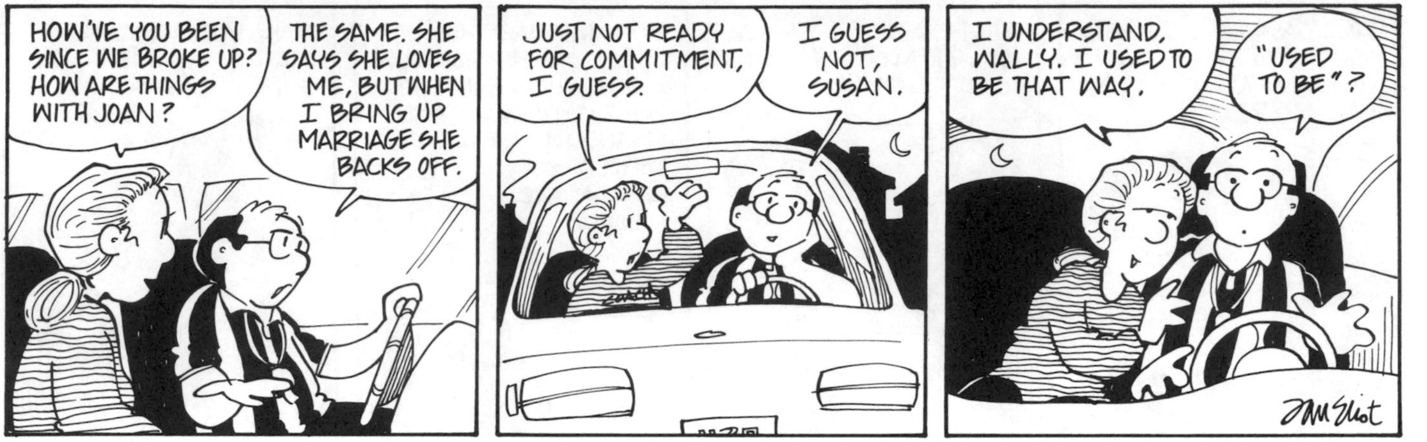
HOW'VE YOU BEEN SINCE WE BROKE UP? HOW ARE THINGS WITH JOAN?
THE SAME. SHE SAYS SHE LOVES ME, BUT WHEN I BRING UP MARRIAGE SHE BACKS OFF.
JUST NOT READY FOR COMMITMENT, I GUESS.
I GUESS NOT, SUSAN.
I UNDERSTAND, WALLY. I USED TO BE THAT WAY.
"USED TO BE"?

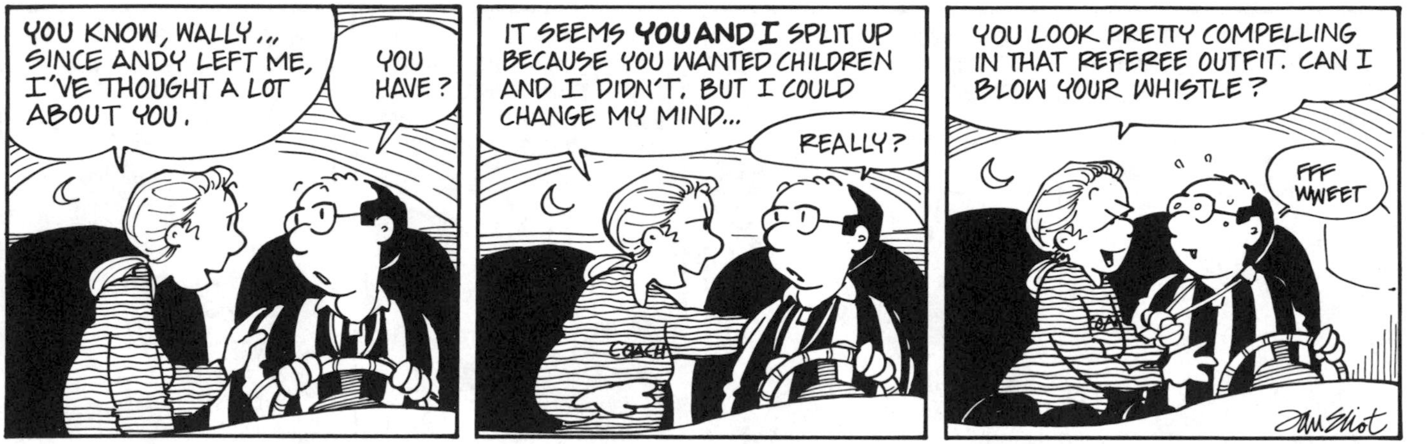
YOU KNOW, WALLY... SINCE ANDY LEFT ME, I'VE THOUGHT A LOT ABOUT YOU.
YOU HAVE?
IT SEEMS **YOU AND I** SPLIT UP BECAUSE YOU WANTED CHILDREN AND I DIDN'T. BUT I COULD CHANGE MY MIND...
REALLY?
YOU LOOK PRETTY COMPELLING IN THAT REFEREE OUTFIT. CAN I BLOW YOUR WHISTLE?
FFF WWEET

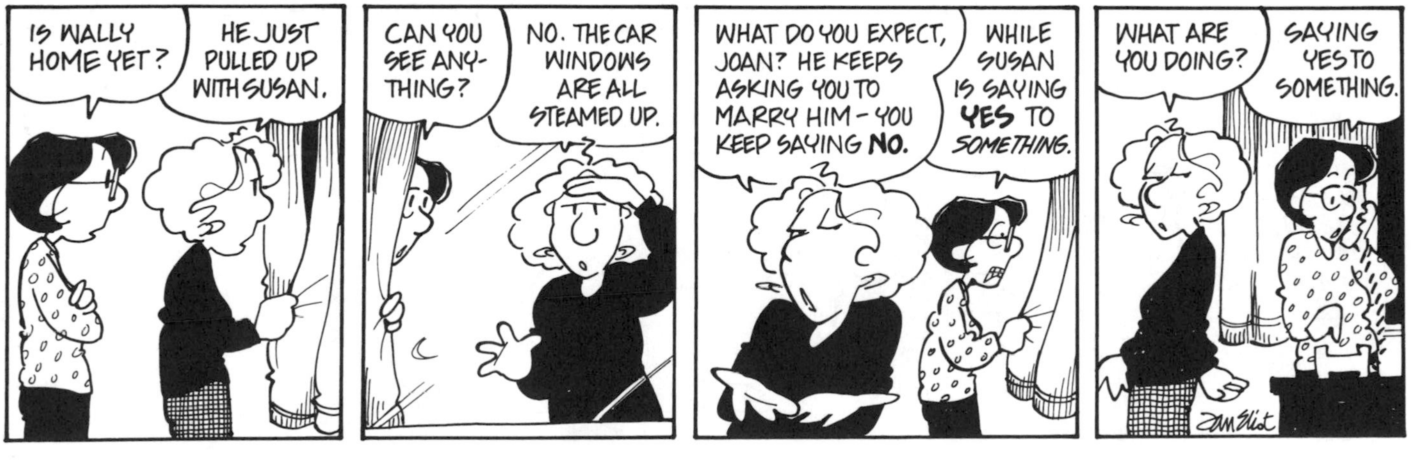
IS WALLY HOME YET?
HE JUST PULLED UP WITH SUSAN.
CAN YOU SEE ANY-THING?
NO. THE CAR WINDOWS ARE ALL STEAMED UP.
WHAT DO YOU EXPECT, JOAN? HE KEEPS ASKING YOU TO MARRY HIM - YOU KEEP SAYING **NO.**
WHILE SUSAN IS SAYING **YES** TO *SOMETHING.*
WHAT ARE YOU DOING?
SAYING YES TO SOMETHING.

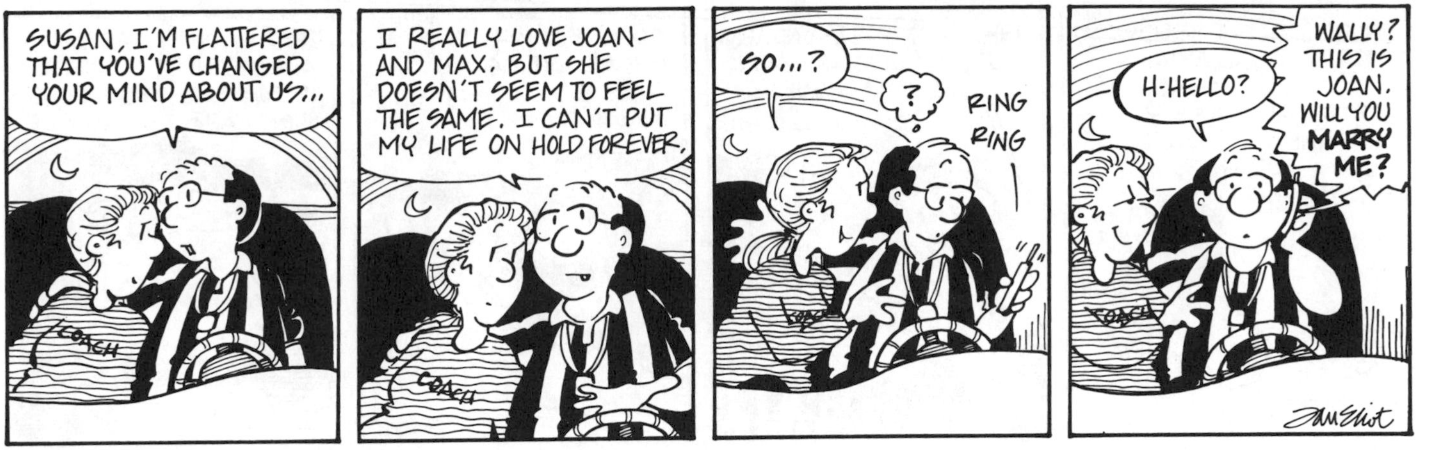
SUSAN, I'M FLATTERED THAT YOU'VE CHANGED YOUR MIND ABOUT US...
I REALLY LOVE JOAN - AND MAX. BUT SHE DOESN'T SEEM TO FEEL THE SAME. I CAN'T PUT MY LIFE ON HOLD FOREVER.
SO...?
?
RING RING
H-HELLO?
WALLY? THIS IS JOAN. WILL YOU MARRY ME?

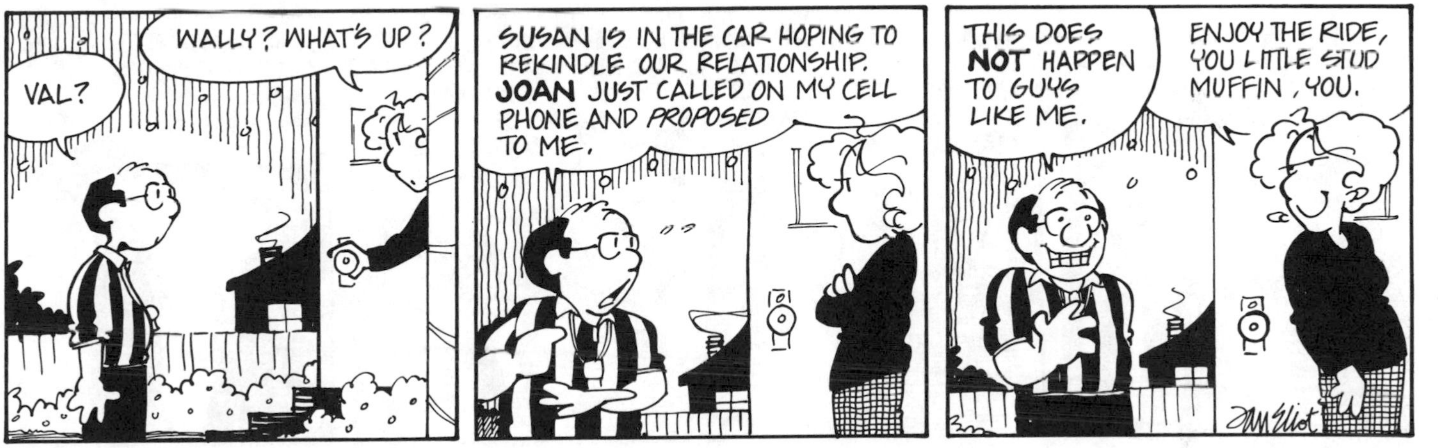
VAL?
WALLY? WHAT'S UP?
SUSAN IS IN THE CAR HOPING TO REKINDLE OUR RELATIONSHIP. JOAN JUST CALLED ON MY CELL PHONE AND PROPOSED TO ME.
THIS DOES NOT HAPPEN TO GUYS LIKE ME.
ENJOY THE RIDE, YOU LITTLE STUD MUFFIN, YOU.

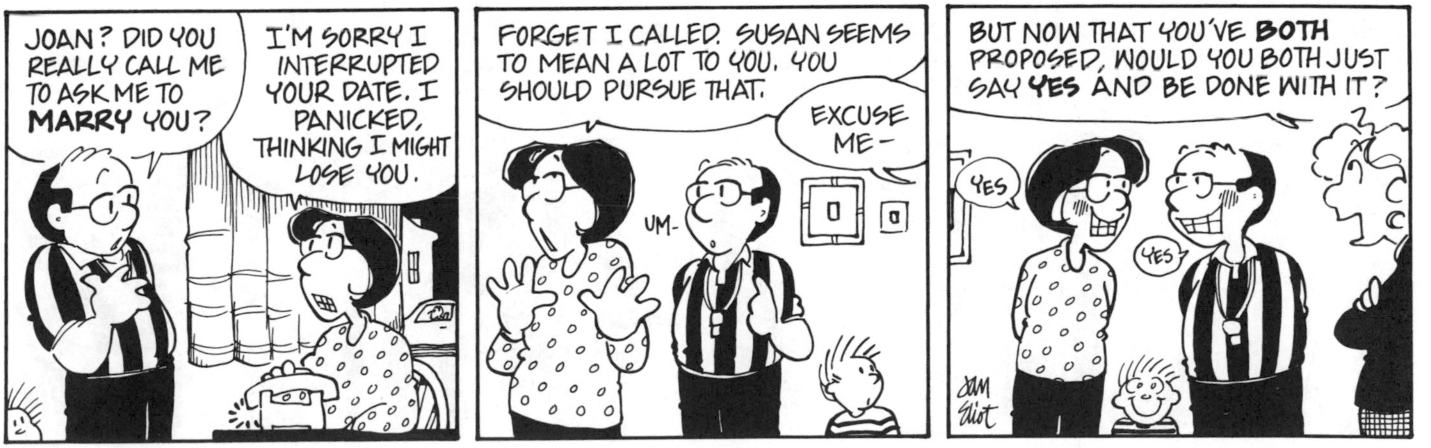
JOAN? DID YOU REALLY CALL ME TO ASK ME TO MARRY YOU?
I'M SORRY I INTERRUPTED YOUR DATE. I PANICKED, THINKING I MIGHT LOSE YOU.
FORGET I CALLED. SUSAN SEEMS TO MEAN A LOT TO YOU. YOU SHOULD PURSUE THAT.
UM-
EXCUSE ME-
BUT NOW THAT YOU'VE BOTH PROPOSED, WOULD YOU BOTH JUST SAY YES AND BE DONE WITH IT?
YES
YES

WOW. I CAN'T BELIEVE YOU TWO ARE FINALLY TAKING THE PLUNGE... AFTER ALL THESE YEARS OF WAFFLING BACK AND FORTH.

SIGH

WHAT'S UP?

WALLY AND AUNT JOAN ARE GETTING MARRIED!

COOL! BUT WHY IS SUSAN SITTING OUTSIDE IN WALLY'S CAR?

THERE YOU ARE! STILL UP FOR THAT NIGHTCAP?

ACTUALLY, UM..., SOMETHING'S COME UP.

WALLY, YOU DON'T HAVE TO EXPLAIN. I'VE ALWAYS KNOWN YOU WERE IN LOVE WITH JOAN...

YOUR EYES LIGHT UP EVERY TIME YOU SEE HER. AND HER SON MAX ADORES YOU.

THANKS FOR UNDERSTANDING, SUSAN.

WHEN'S THE BIG DAY?

SOON, I HOPE. IT MAKES SENSE ECONOMICALLY, AND I'M JUST RATTLING AROUND MY BIG HOUSE.

AND YOU WANT TO CATCH HER BEFORE SHE CHANGES HER MIND AGAIN.

THAT TOO.

SO YOU TOLD SUSAN?

YES. SHE'S HAPPY FOR US.

ANY LINGERING REGRETS ABOUT LEAVING THAT OPPORTUNITY BEHIND?

I MEAN, HER LIFE IS SO SIMPLE AND WELL-ORDERED COMPARED TO MINE...

BUT CHAOS AND CHANGE CAN MAKE LIFE INTERESTING!

YIP?

AND YOUR LIFE IS VERY INTERESTING!!

MA MA MA MAC

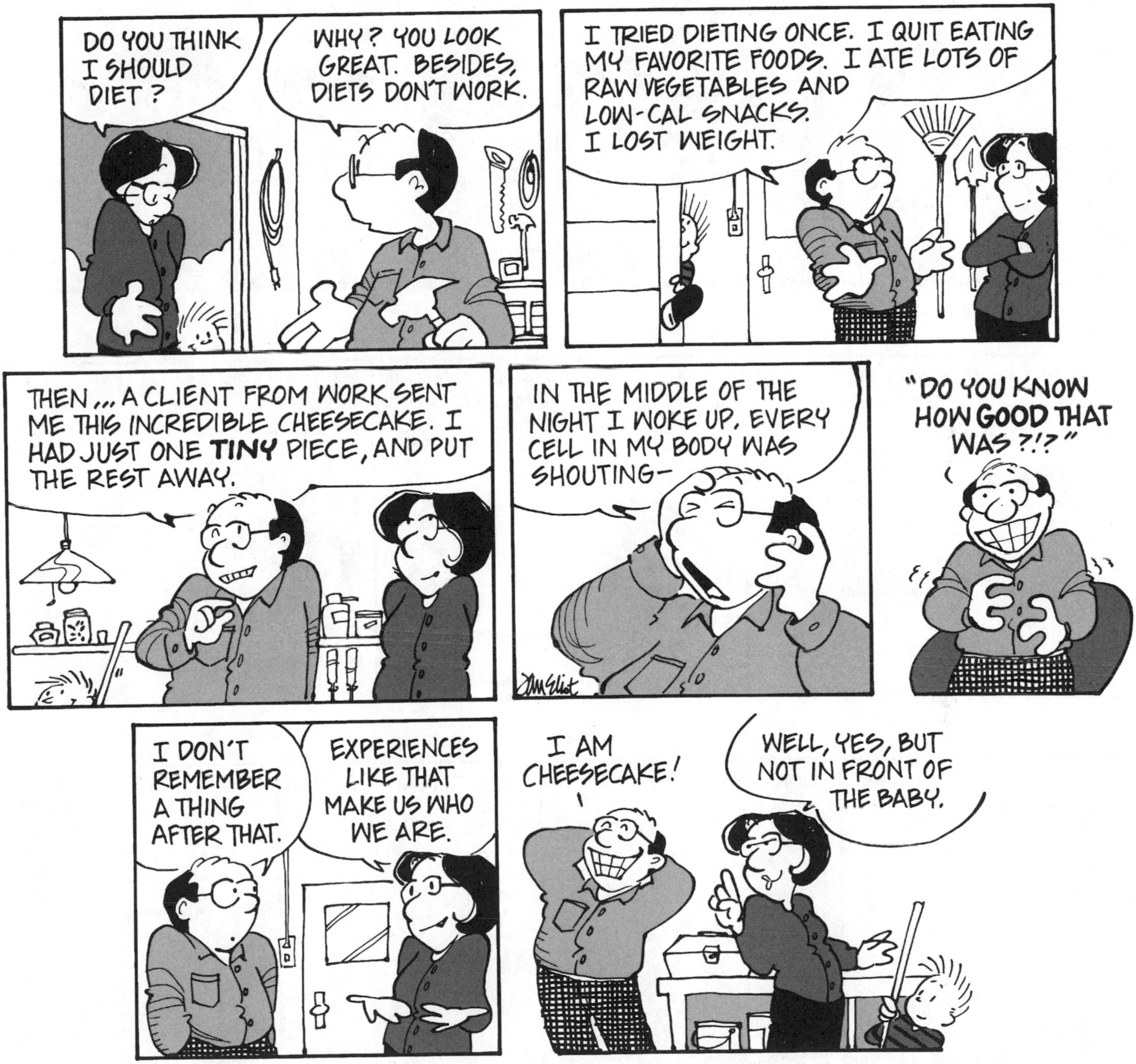

DO YOU THINK I SHOULD DIET ?
WHY ? YOU LOOK GREAT. BESIDES, DIETS DON'T WORK.
I TRIED DIETING ONCE. I QUIT EATING MY FAVORITE FOODS. I ATE LOTS OF RAW VEGETABLES AND LOW-CAL SNACKS. I LOST WEIGHT.
THEN ,,, A CLIENT FROM WORK SENT ME THIS INCREDIBLE CHEESECAKE. I HAD JUST ONE TINY PIECE, AND PUT THE REST AWAY.
IN THE MIDDLE OF THE NIGHT I WOKE UP. EVERY CELL IN MY BODY WAS SHOUTING–
"DO YOU KNOW HOW GOOD THAT WAS ?!?"
I DON'T REMEMBER A THING AFTER THAT.
EXPERIENCES LIKE THAT MAKE US WHO WE ARE.
I AM CHEESECAKE!
WELL, YES, BUT NOT IN FRONT OF THE BABY.

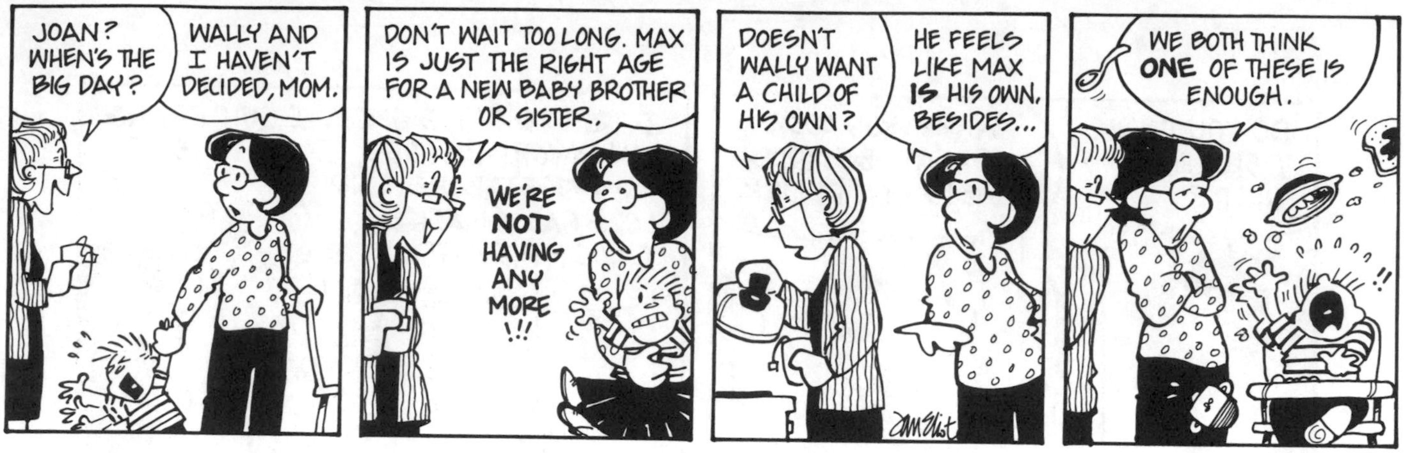
JOAN? WHEN'S THE BIG DAY?
WALLY AND I HAVEN'T DECIDED, MOM.
DON'T WAIT TOO LONG. MAX IS JUST THE RIGHT AGE FOR A NEW BABY BROTHER OR SISTER.
WE'RE NOT HAVING ANY MORE !!!
DOESN'T WALLY WANT A CHILD OF HIS OWN?
HE FEELS LIKE MAX IS HIS OWN. BESIDES...
WE BOTH THINK ONE OF THESE IS ENOUGH.

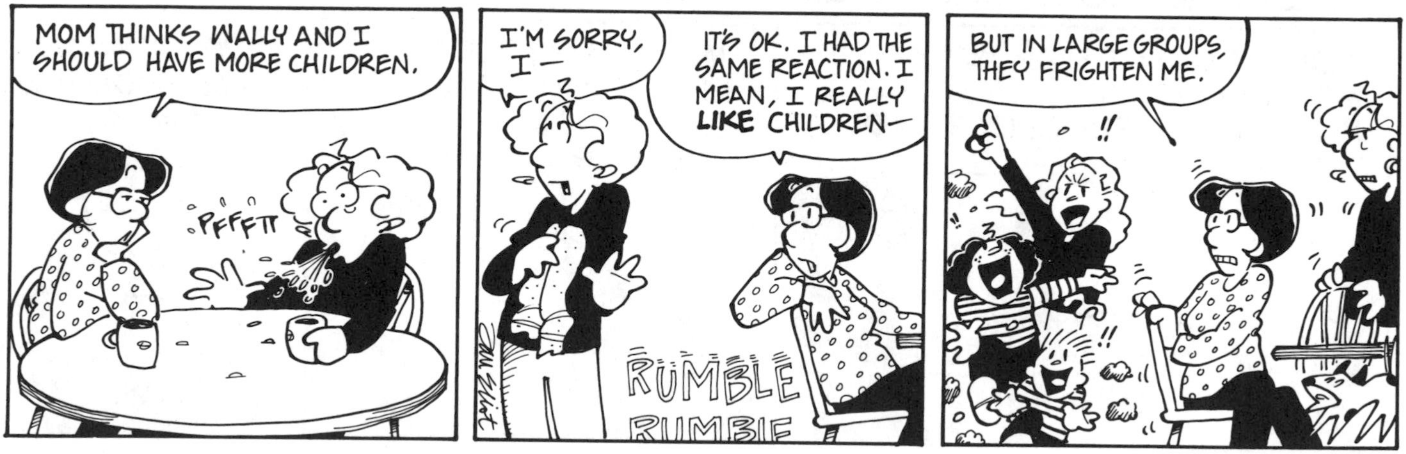
MOM THINKS WALLY AND I SHOULD HAVE MORE CHILDREN.
PFFFTT
I'M SORRY, I —
IT'S OK. I HAD THE SAME REACTION. I MEAN, I REALLY LIKE CHILDREN—
RUMBLE
BUT IN LARGE GROUPS, THEY FRIGHTEN ME.

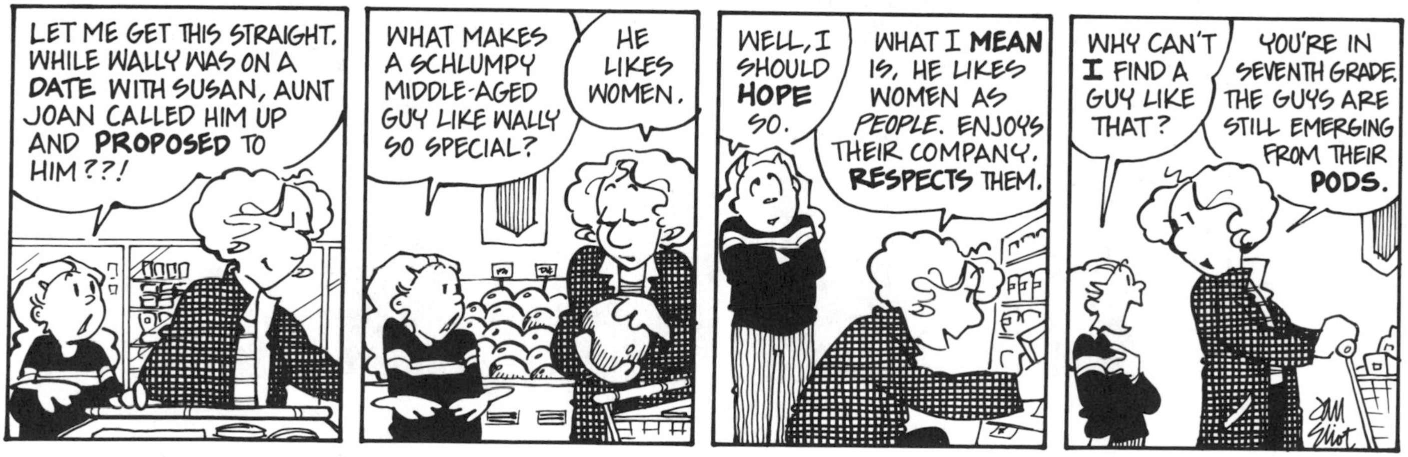
LET ME GET THIS STRAIGHT. WHILE WALLY WAS ON A DATE WITH SUSAN, AUNT JOAN CALLED HIM UP AND PROPOSED TO HIM??!
WHAT MAKES A SCHLUMPY MIDDLE-AGED GUY LIKE WALLY SO SPECIAL?
HE LIKES WOMEN.
WELL, I SHOULD HOPE SO.
WHAT I MEAN IS, HE LIKES WOMEN AS PEOPLE. ENJOYS THEIR COMPANY. RESPECTS THEM.
WHY CAN'T I FIND A GUY LIKE THAT?
YOU'RE IN SEVENTH GRADE. THE GUYS ARE STILL EMERGING FROM THEIR PODS.

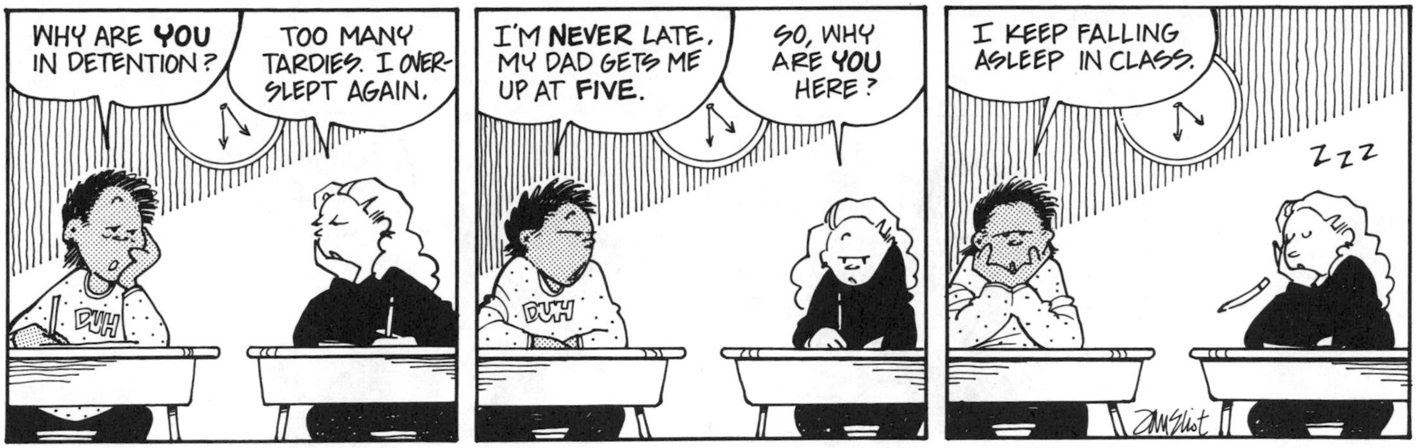
WHY ARE YOU IN DETENTION?
TOO MANY TARDIES. I OVER-SLEPT AGAIN.
I'M NEVER LATE. MY DAD GETS ME UP AT FIVE.
SO, WHY ARE YOU HERE?
I KEEP FALLING ASLEEP IN CLASS.
Z Z Z

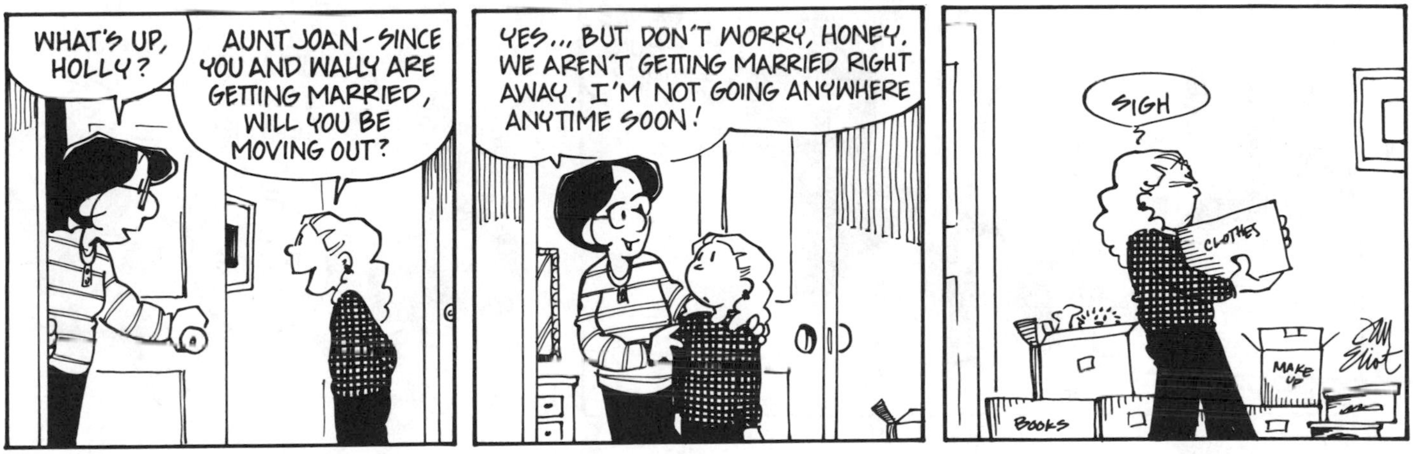
WHAT'S UP, HOLLY?
AUNT JOAN - SINCE YOU AND WALLY ARE GETTING MARRIED, WILL YOU BE MOVING OUT?
YES... BUT DON'T WORRY, HONEY. WE AREN'T GETTING MARRIED RIGHT AWAY. I'M NOT GOING ANYWHERE ANYTIME SOON!
SIGH
CLOTHES
MAKE UP
BOOKS

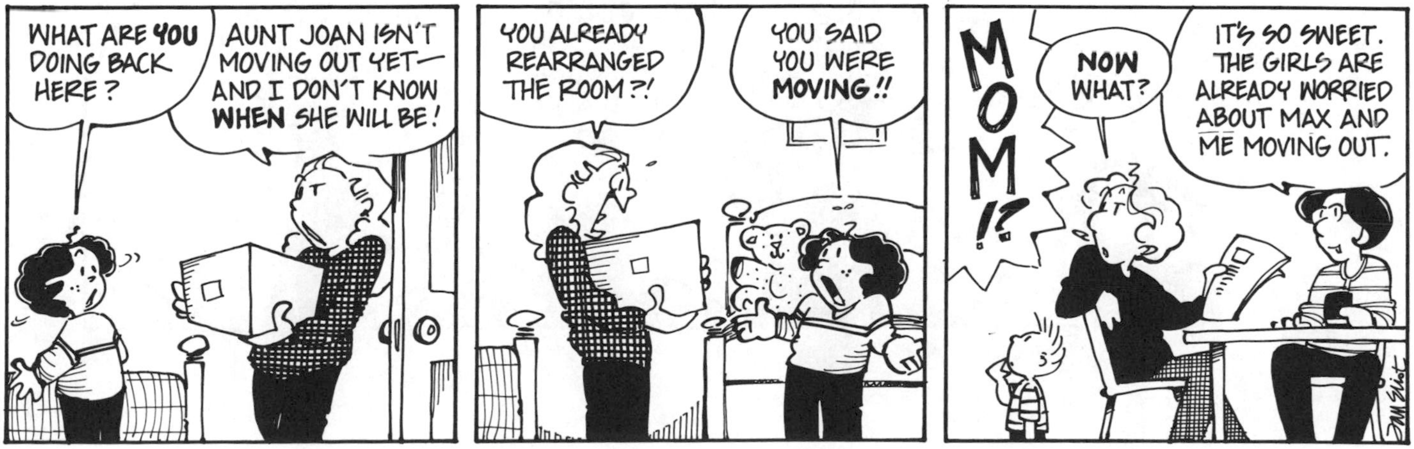
WHAT ARE YOU DOING BACK HERE?
AUNT JOAN ISN'T MOVING OUT YET— AND I DON'T KNOW WHEN SHE WILL BE!
YOU ALREADY REARRANGED THE ROOM?!
YOU SAID YOU WERE MOVING!!
MOM!?
NOW WHAT?
IT'S SO SWEET. THE GIRLS ARE ALREADY WORRIED ABOUT MAX AND ME MOVING OUT.

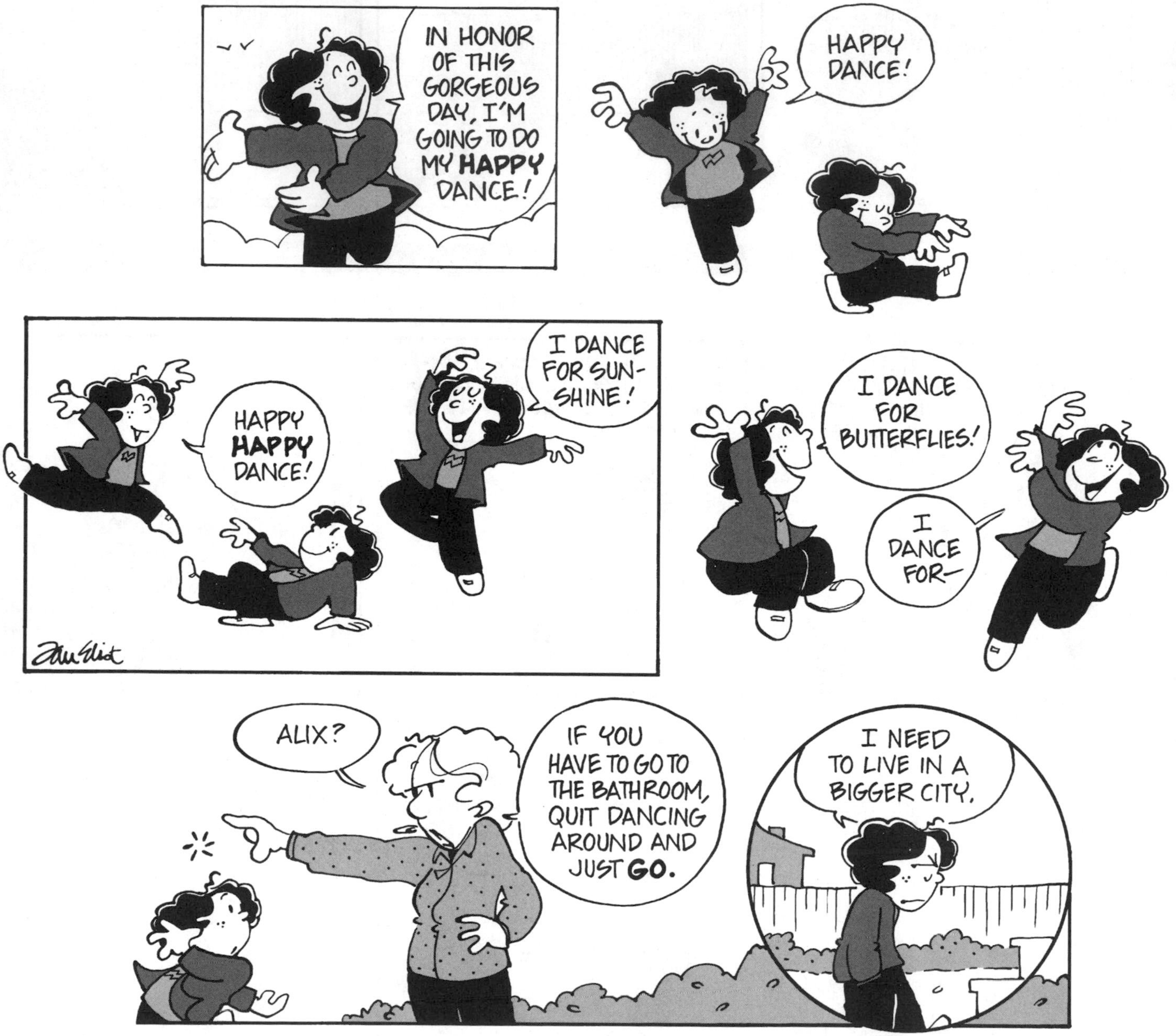

IN HONOR OF THIS GORGEOUS DAY, I'M GOING TO DO MY HAPPY DANCE!
HAPPY DANCE!
HAPPY HAPPY DANCE!
I DANCE FOR SUN-SHINE!
I DANCE FOR BUTTERFLIES!
I DANCE FOR—
ALIX?
IF YOU HAVE TO GO TO THE BATHROOM, QUIT DANCING AROUND AND JUST GO.
I NEED TO LIVE IN A BIGGER CITY.

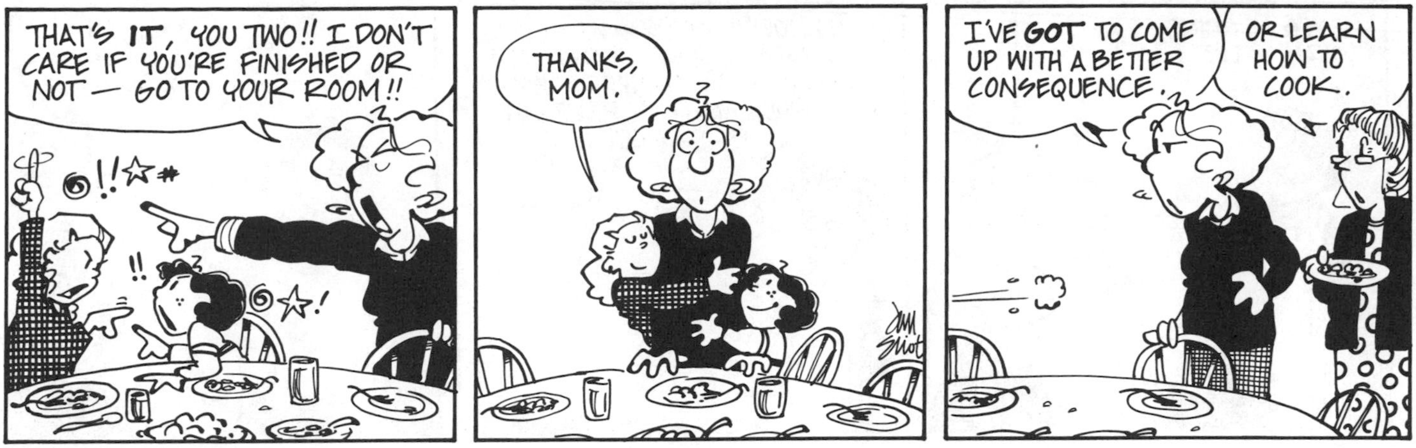
THAT'S IT, YOU TWO!! I DON'T CARE IF YOU'RE FINISHED OR NOT — GO TO YOUR ROOM!!
THANKS, MOM.
I'VE GOT TO COME UP WITH A BETTER CONSEQUENCE.
OR LEARN HOW TO COOK.

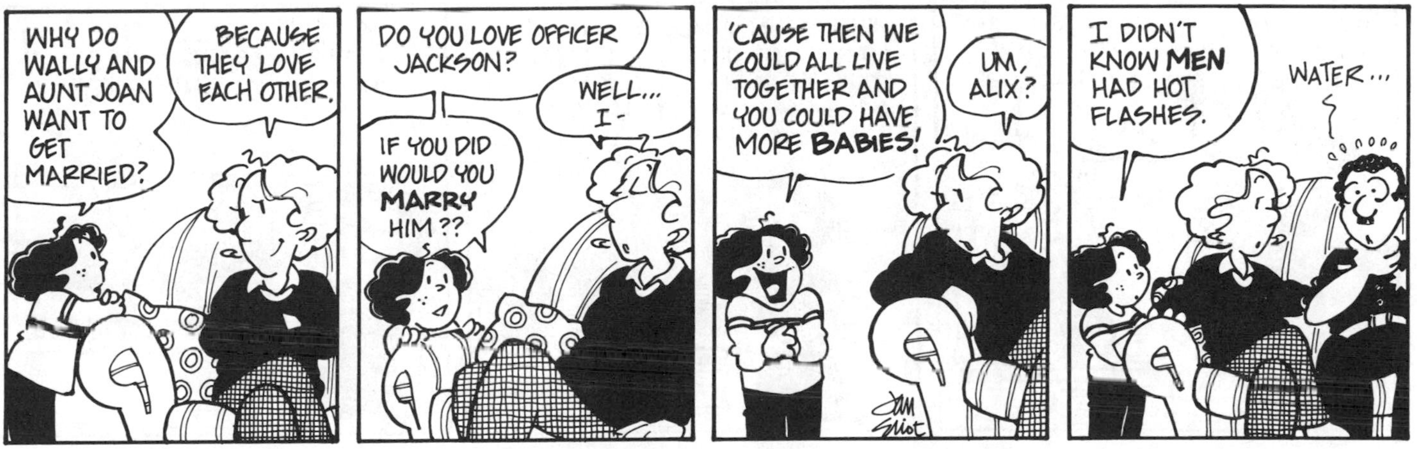
WHY DO WALLY AND AUNT JOAN WANT TO GET MARRIED?
BECAUSE THEY LOVE EACH OTHER.
DO YOU LOVE OFFICER JACKSON?
WELL... I-
IF YOU DID WOULD YOU MARRY HIM??
'CAUSE THEN WE COULD ALL LIVE TOGETHER AND YOU COULD HAVE MORE BABIES!
UM, ALIX?
I DIDN'T KNOW MEN HAD HOT FLASHES.
WATER...

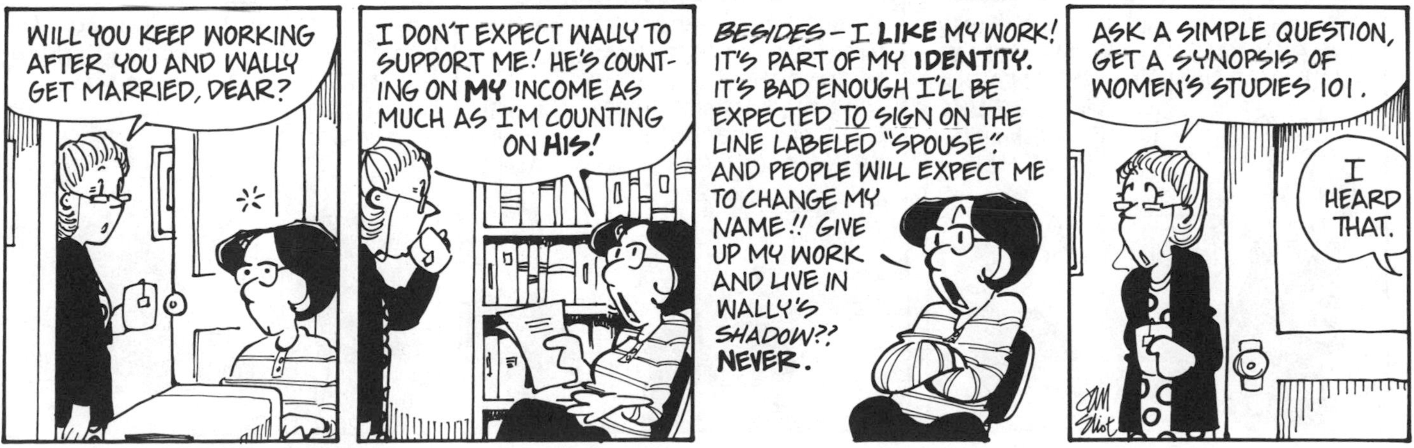
WILL YOU KEEP WORKING AFTER YOU AND WALLY GET MARRIED, DEAR?
I DON'T EXPECT WALLY TO SUPPORT ME! HE'S COUNTING ON MY INCOME AS MUCH AS I'M COUNTING ON HIS!
BESIDES – I LIKE MY WORK! IT'S PART OF MY IDENTITY. IT'S BAD ENOUGH I'LL BE EXPECTED TO SIGN ON THE LINE LABELED "SPOUSE". AND PEOPLE WILL EXPECT ME TO CHANGE MY NAME!! GIVE UP MY WORK AND LIVE IN WALLY'S SHADOW?? NEVER.
ASK A SIMPLE QUESTION, GET A SYNOPSIS OF WOMEN'S STUDIES 101.
I HEARD THAT.

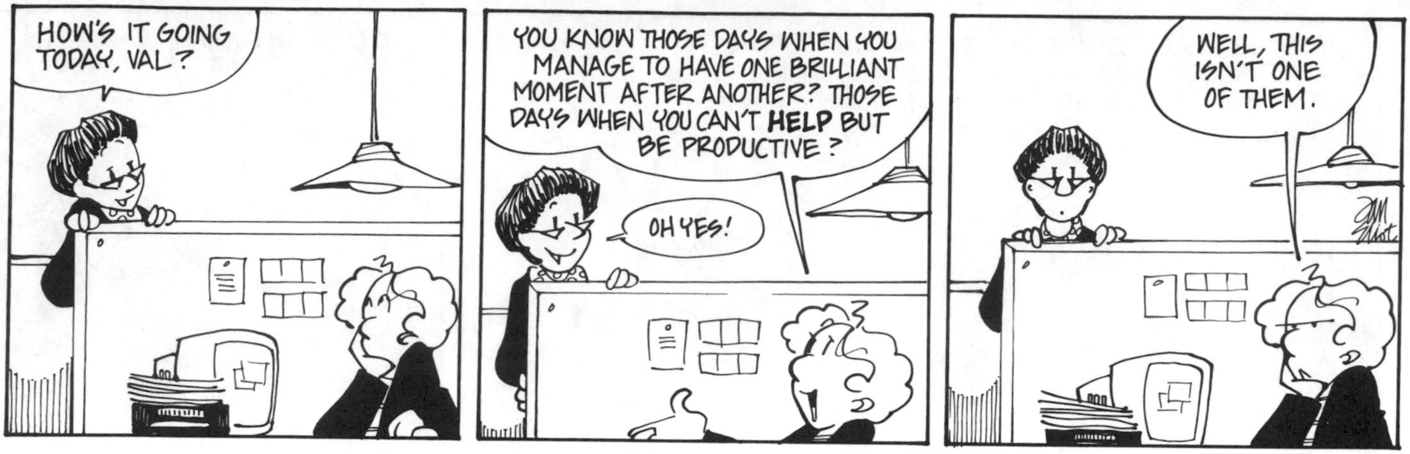
HOW'S IT GOING TODAY, VAL?
YOU KNOW THOSE DAYS WHEN YOU MANAGE TO HAVE ONE BRILLIANT MOMENT AFTER ANOTHER? THOSE DAYS WHEN YOU CAN'T **HELP** BUT BE PRODUCTIVE?
OH YES!
WELL, THIS ISN'T ONE OF THEM.

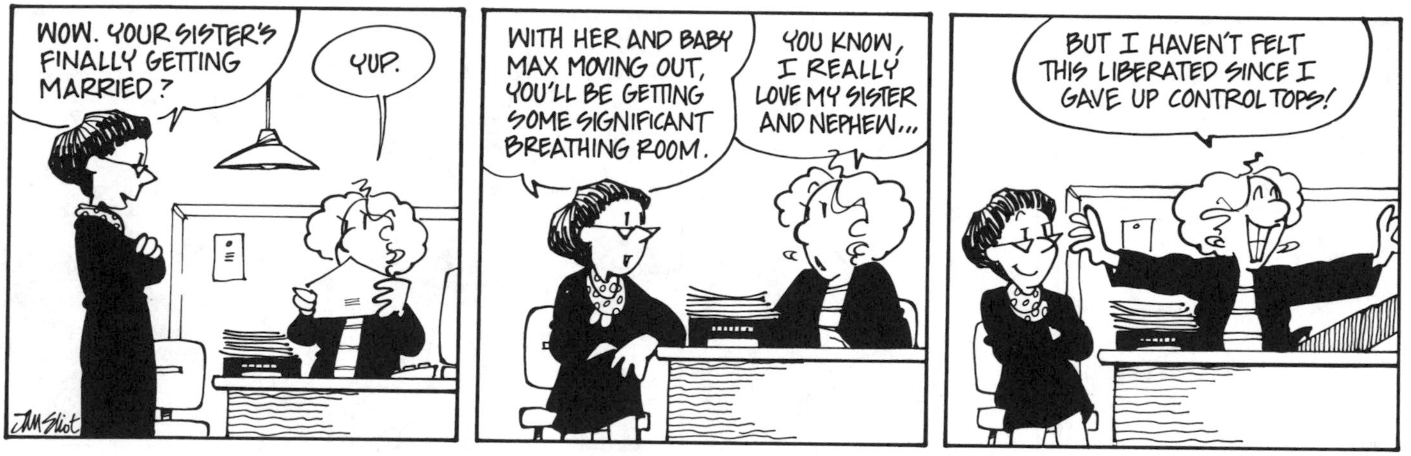
WOW. YOUR SISTER'S FINALLY GETTING MARRIED?
YUP.
WITH HER AND BABY MAX MOVING OUT, YOU'LL BE GETTING SOME SIGNIFICANT BREATHING ROOM.
YOU KNOW, I REALLY LOVE MY SISTER AND NEPHEW...
BUT I HAVEN'T FELT THIS LIBERATED SINCE I GAVE UP CONTROL TOPS!

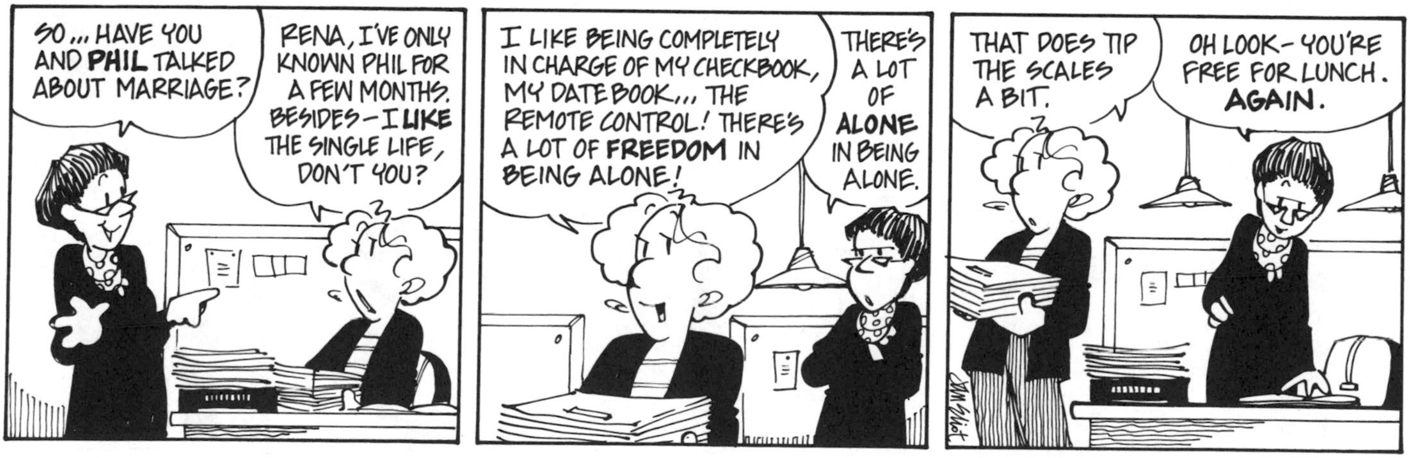
SO... HAVE YOU AND **PHIL** TALKED ABOUT MARRIAGE?
RENA, I'VE ONLY KNOWN PHIL FOR A FEW MONTHS. BESIDES — I **LIKE** THE SINGLE LIFE, DON'T YOU?
I LIKE BEING COMPLETELY IN CHARGE OF MY CHECKBOOK, MY DATE BOOK... THE REMOTE CONTROL! THERE'S A LOT OF **FREEDOM** IN BEING ALONE!
THERE'S A LOT OF **ALONE** IN BEING ALONE.
THAT DOES TIP THE SCALES A BIT.
OH LOOK — YOU'RE FREE FOR LUNCH. **AGAIN**.

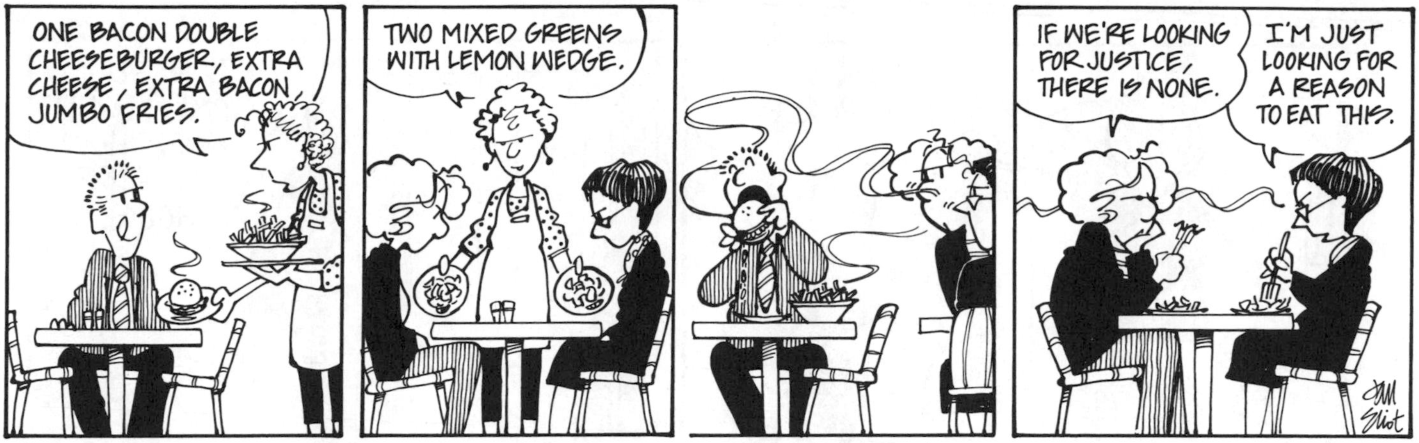
ONE BACON DOUBLE CHEESEBURGER, EXTRA CHEESE, EXTRA BACON, JUMBO FRIES.
TWO MIXED GREENS WITH LEMON WEDGE.
IF WE'RE LOOKING FOR JUSTICE, THERE IS NONE.
I'M JUST LOOKING FOR A REASON TO EAT THIS.

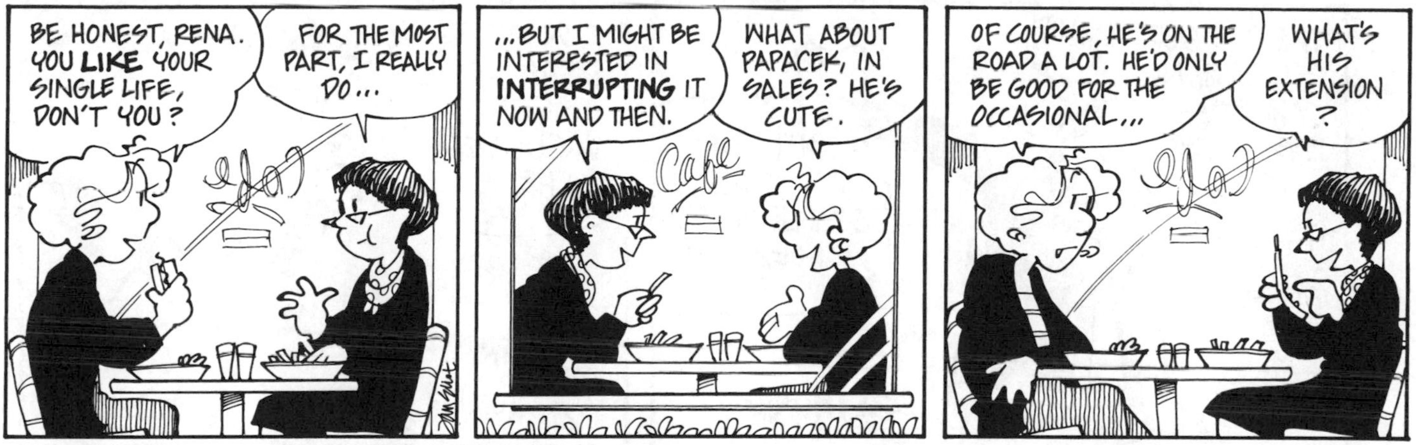
BE HONEST, RENA. YOU **LIKE** YOUR SINGLE LIFE, DON'T YOU?
FOR THE MOST PART, I REALLY DO...
...BUT I MIGHT BE INTERESTED IN **INTERRUPTING** IT NOW AND THEN.
WHAT ABOUT PAPACEK, IN SALES? HE'S CUTE.
Cafe
OF COURSE, HE'S ON THE ROAD A LOT. HE'D ONLY BE GOOD FOR THE OCCASIONAL...
WHAT'S HIS EXTENSION?

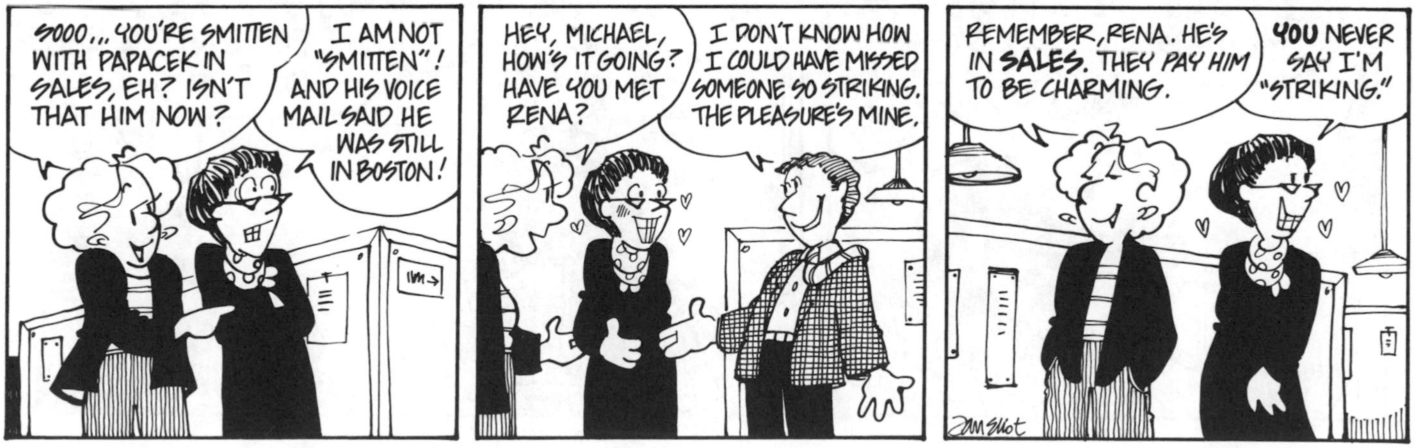
SOOO... YOU'RE SMITTEN WITH PAPACEK IN SALES, EH? ISN'T THAT HIM NOW?
I AM NOT "SMITTEN"! AND HIS VOICE MAIL SAID HE WAS STILL IN BOSTON!
HEY, MICHAEL, HOW'S IT GOING? HAVE YOU MET RENA?
I DON'T KNOW HOW I COULD HAVE MISSED SOMEONE SO STRIKING. THE PLEASURE'S MINE.
REMEMBER, RENA. HE'S IN **SALES**. THEY *PAY HIM* TO BE CHARMING.
YOU NEVER SAY I'M "STRIKING."

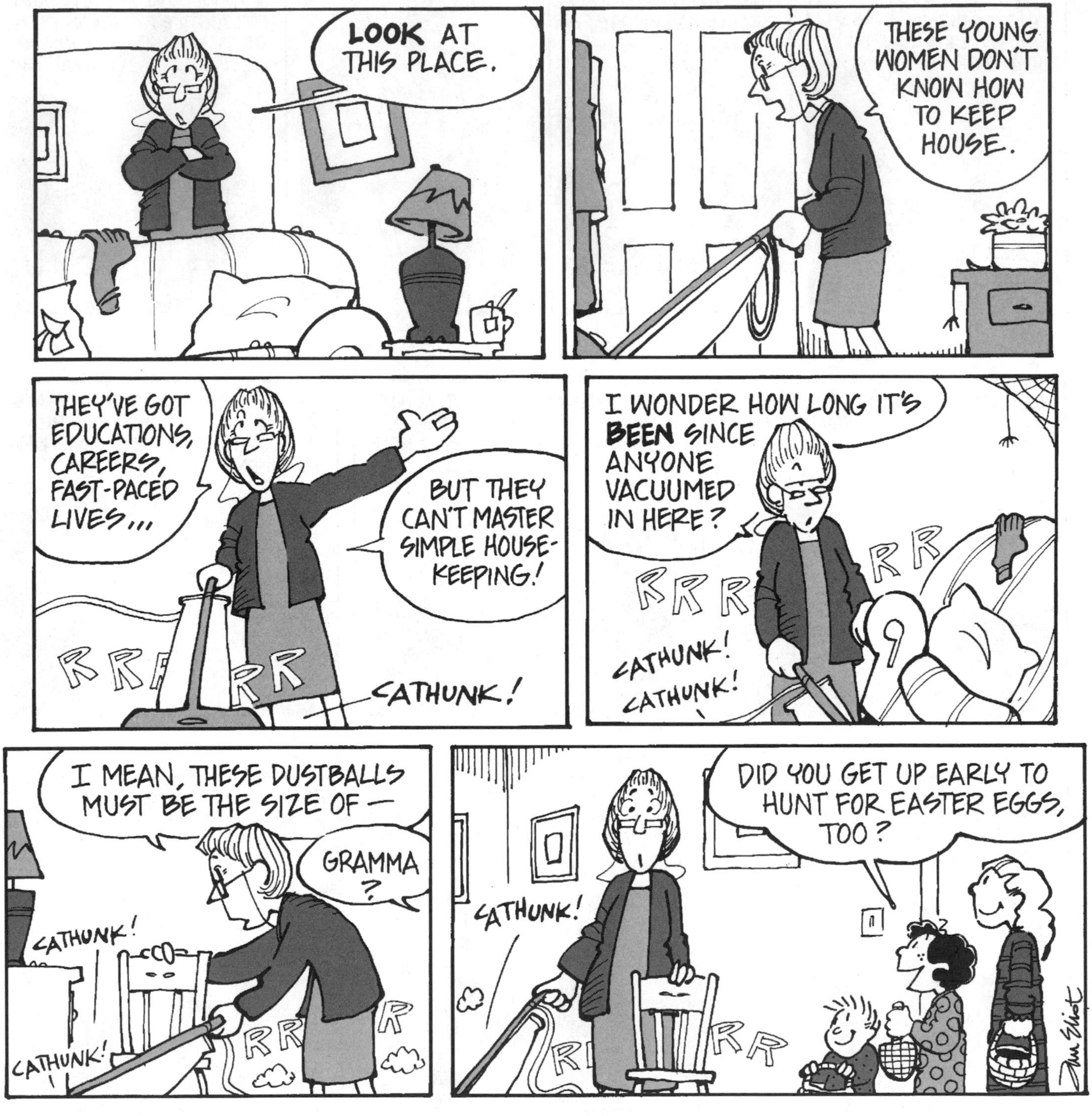

LOOK AT THIS PLACE.
THESE YOUNG WOMEN DON'T KNOW HOW TO KEEP HOUSE.
THEY'VE GOT EDUCATIONS, CAREERS, FAST-PACED LIVES...
BUT THEY CAN'T MASTER SIMPLE HOUSE-KEEPING!
RRRRR
CATHUNK!
I WONDER HOW LONG IT'S BEEN SINCE ANYONE VACUUMED IN HERE?
RRR RR
CATHUNK!
CATHUNK!
I MEAN, THESE DUSTBALLS MUST BE THE SIZE OF —
GRAMMA?
CATHUNK!
CATHUNK!
RR R
DID YOU GET UP EARLY TO HUNT FOR EASTER EGGS, TOO?
CATHUNK!
RR RR

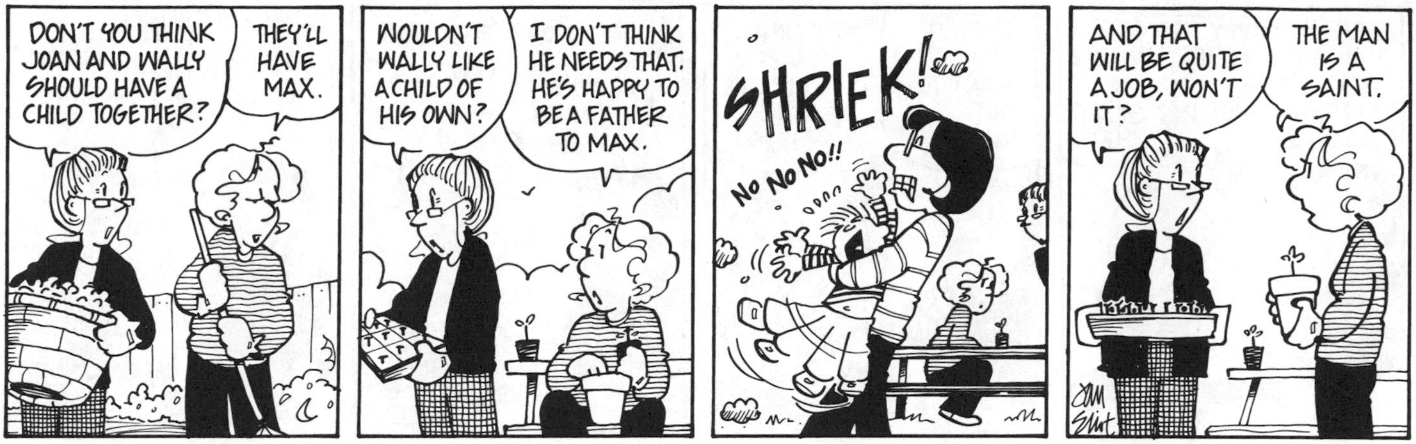
DON'T YOU THINK JOAN AND WALLY SHOULD HAVE A CHILD TOGETHER?
THEY'LL HAVE MAX.
WOULDN'T WALLY LIKE A CHILD OF HIS OWN?
I DON'T THINK HE NEEDS THAT. HE'S HAPPY TO BE A FATHER TO MAX.
SHRIEK!
No No No!!
AND THAT WILL BE QUITE A JOB, WON'T IT?
THE MAN IS A SAINT.

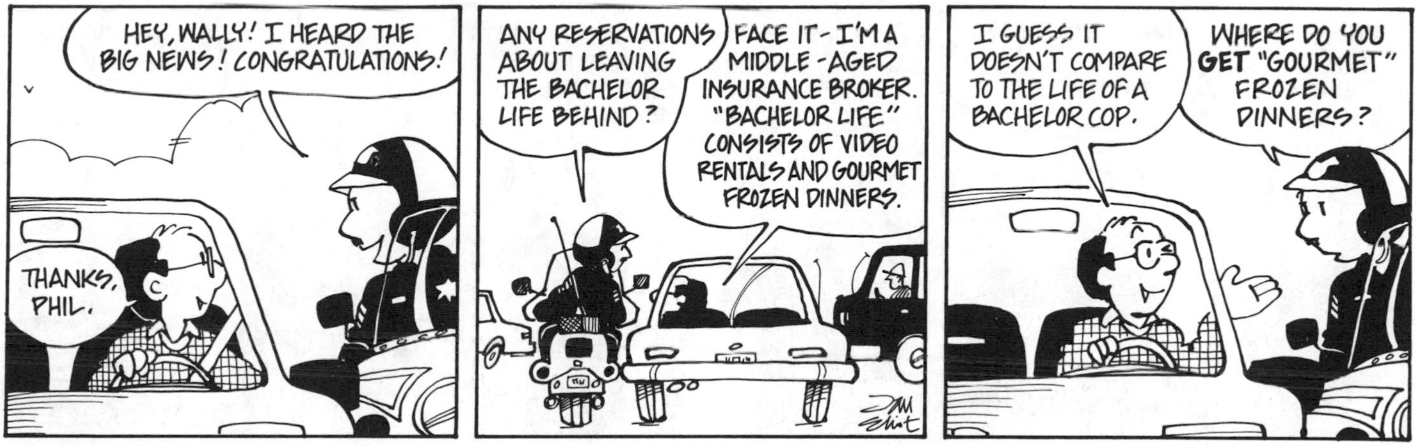
HEY, WALLY! I HEARD THE BIG NEWS! CONGRATULATIONS!
THANKS, PHIL.
ANY RESERVATIONS ABOUT LEAVING THE BACHELOR LIFE BEHIND?
FACE IT - I'M A MIDDLE-AGED INSURANCE BROKER. "BACHELOR LIFE" CONSISTS OF VIDEO RENTALS AND GOURMET FROZEN DINNERS.
I GUESS IT DOESN'T COMPARE TO THE LIFE OF A BACHELOR COP.
WHERE DO YOU GET "GOURMET" FROZEN DINNERS?

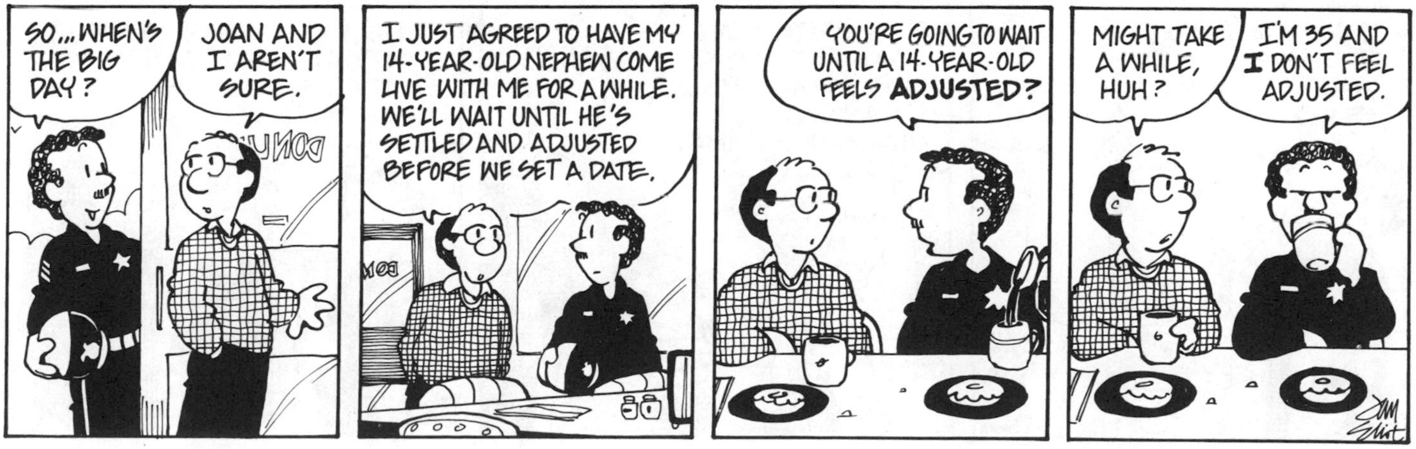
SO... WHEN'S THE BIG DAY?
JOAN AND I AREN'T SURE.
I JUST AGREED TO HAVE MY 14-YEAR-OLD NEPHEW COME LIVE WITH ME FOR A WHILE. WE'LL WAIT UNTIL HE'S SETTLED AND ADJUSTED BEFORE WE SET A DATE.
YOU'RE GOING TO WAIT UNTIL A 14-YEAR-OLD FEELS ADJUSTED?
MIGHT TAKE A WHILE, HUH?
I'M 35 AND I DON'T FEEL ADJUSTED.

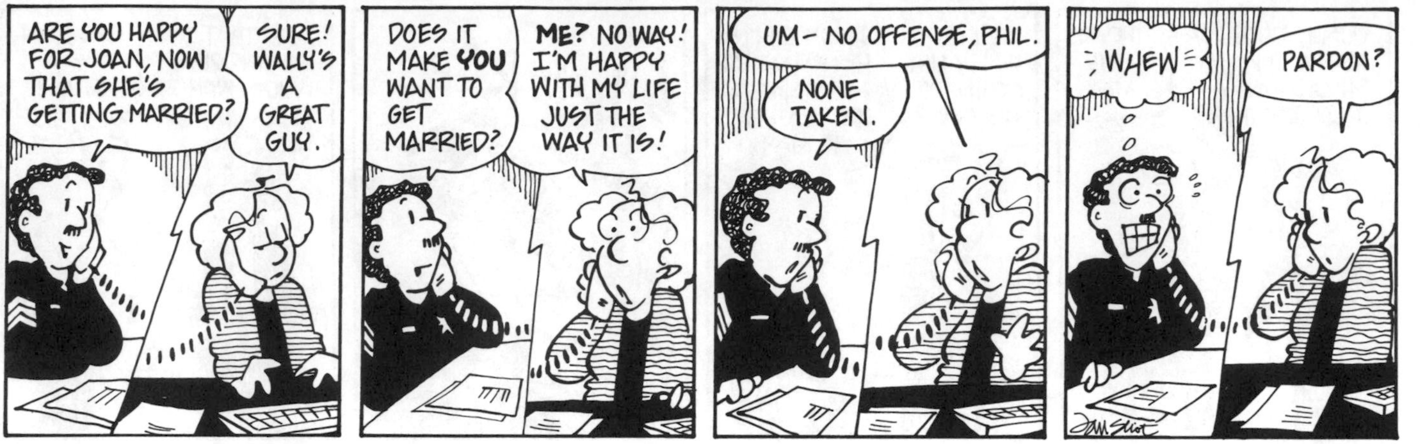
ARE YOU HAPPY FOR JOAN, NOW THAT SHE'S GETTING MARRIED?
SURE! WALLY'S A GREAT GUY.
DOES IT MAKE **YOU** WANT TO GET MARRIED?
ME? NO WAY! I'M HAPPY WITH MY LIFE JUST THE WAY IT IS!
UM– NO OFFENSE, PHIL.
NONE TAKEN.
WHEW
PARDON?

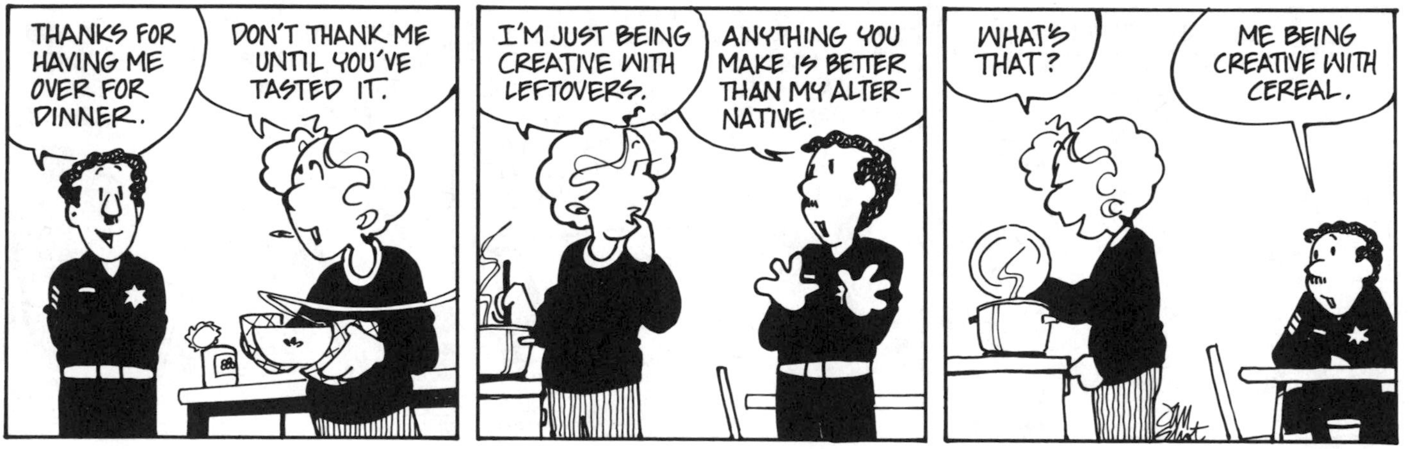
THANKS FOR HAVING ME OVER FOR DINNER.
DON'T THANK ME UNTIL YOU'VE TASTED IT.
I'M JUST BEING CREATIVE WITH LEFTOVERS.
ANYTHING YOU MAKE IS BETTER THAN MY ALTER-NATIVE.
WHAT'S THAT?
ME BEING CREATIVE WITH CEREAL.

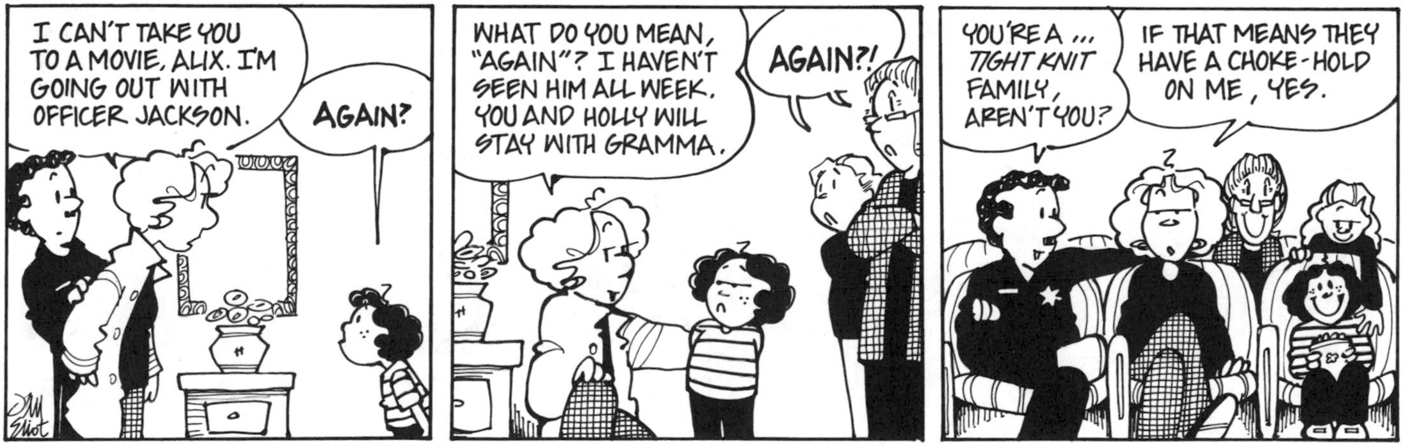
I CAN'T TAKE YOU TO A MOVIE, ALIX. I'M GOING OUT WITH OFFICER JACKSON.
AGAIN?
WHAT DO YOU MEAN, "AGAIN"? I HAVEN'T SEEN HIM ALL WEEK. YOU AND HOLLY WILL STAY WITH GRAMMA.
AGAIN?!
YOU'RE A ... *TIGHT KNIT* FAMILY, AREN'T YOU?
IF THAT MEANS THEY HAVE A CHOKE-HOLD ON ME, YES.

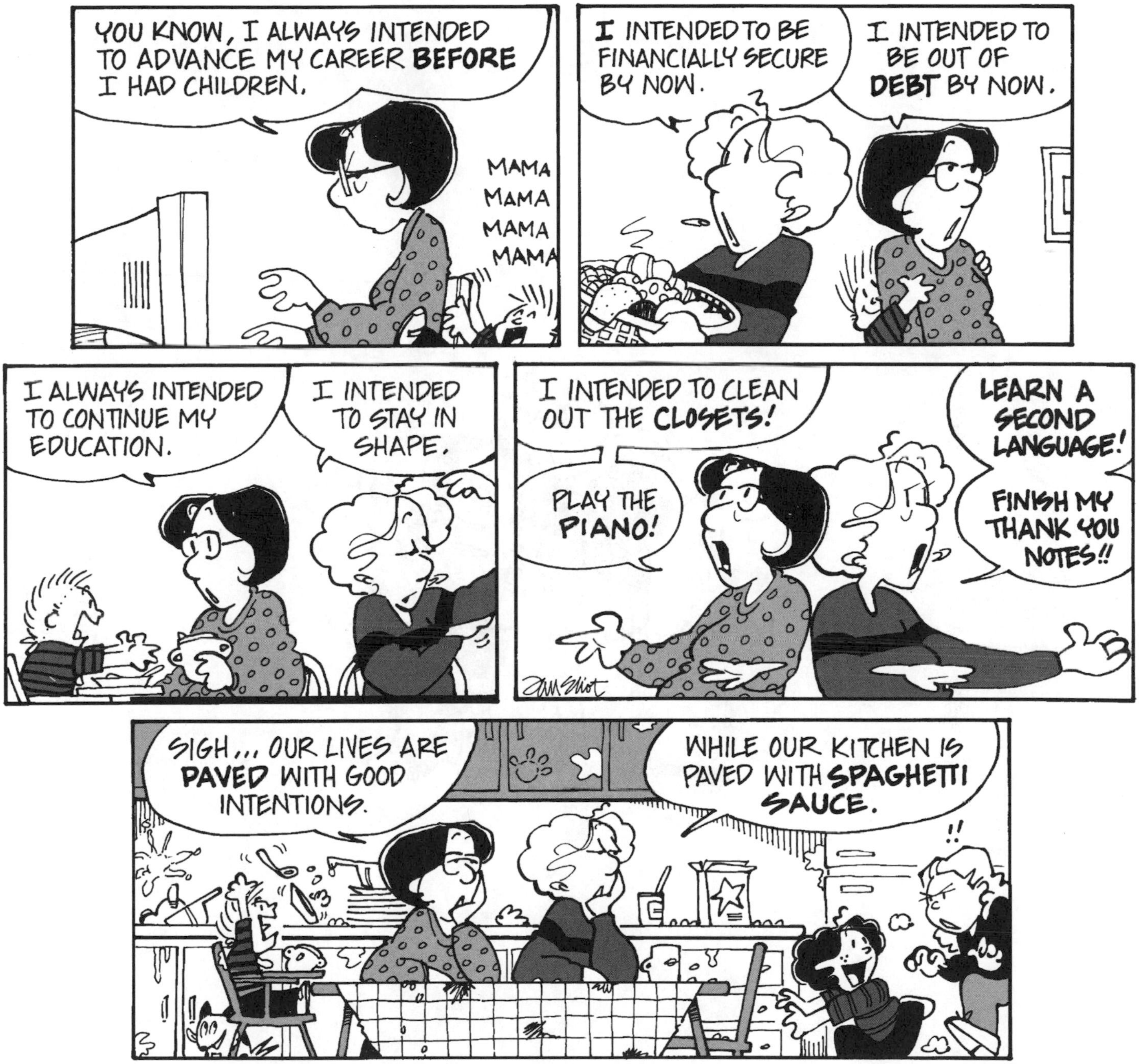
YOU KNOW, I ALWAYS INTENDED TO ADVANCE MY CAREER BEFORE I HAD CHILDREN.
MAMA MAMA MAMA MAMA
I INTENDED TO BE FINANCIALLY SECURE BY NOW.
I INTENDED TO BE OUT OF DEBT BY NOW.
I ALWAYS INTENDED TO CONTINUE MY EDUCATION.
I INTENDED TO STAY IN SHAPE.
I INTENDED TO CLEAN OUT THE CLOSETS!
LEARN A SECOND LANGUAGE!
PLAY THE PIANO!
FINISH MY THANK YOU NOTES!!
SIGH... OUR LIVES ARE PAVED WITH GOOD INTENTIONS.
WHILE OUR KITCHEN IS PAVED WITH SPAGHETTI SAUCE.
!!

Also by Jan Eliot:

Stone Soup *The First Collection of the Syndicated Cartoon*
from Andrews McMeel Publishing

You Can't Say Boobs On Sunday *The Second Collection of the Syndicated
Cartoon* from Four Panel Press

Stone Soup books are available through your local or online bookstore,
and at www.stonesoupcartoons.com.

To date, the comic strip *Stone Soup* has been syndicated by Universal Press
Syndicate to over 135 newspapers in the U.S., Canada, Europe and Asia. If your
local paper does not carry *Stone Soup*, you can contact the managing editor and
tell him or her that you'd like to be able to read *Stone Soup* every day.

Stone Soup can also be read daily online at **www.ucomics.com**, as well as at the
Web sites of subscribing newspapers.

Cartoonists love hearing from readers. If you have stories from your own family, or comments about *Stone Soup*, you can write Jan Eliot in care of Universal Press Syndicate, or through her Web site **www.stonesoupcartoons.com**.